Alex Young

△ φ

Volume Two

PROBLEMS IN ANCIENT HISTORY

The Roman World

VOLUME TWO PROBLEMS IN ANCIENT HISTORY

The Roman World

DONALD KAGAN

Cornell University

The Macmillan Company
Collier-Macmillan Limited, London

Sixth Printing, 1970

Library of Congress catalog card number: 66–16707

THE MACMILLAN COMPANY
COLLIER-MACMILLAN CANADA, LTD., TORONTO, ONTARIO

Printed in the United States of America

PREFACE

This anthology is an attempt to meet several problems facing the college student beginning the study of ancient history. It is meant to be used in conjunction with a narrative history or some suitable substitute. Together with such a narrative account it provides the material for instructive and, hopefully, exciting discussions. Each section is a self-contained unit that presents a problem of continuing interest to historians. In almost every case there is a selection of the pertinent sources in translation, with a number of modern viewpoints also presented. In this way the beginning student may experience immediately the nature of the historian's craft: the excitement of weighing and evaluating sources, the problem of posing meaningful and enlightening questions, the need to change hypotheses in the light of new evidence or new insights, the necessity in some cases of suspending judgment. This method aims at reproducing in some small measure the actual conditions of historical investigation and making the results available to the neophyte.

The problems have been selected on the basis of several criteria: first, they attempt to span the chronological period usually covered by courses in American colleges in a reasonably representative way; second, they are all real problems that continue to excite interest among scholars, and in almost every case they have been the subject of relatively recent study; finally, they are meant to be sufficiently varied in topic and approach to expose the student to a variety of historical methods and techniques. Each problem, along with an accompanying narrative text, is sufficient for a week's work, but teachers will be able to assign the material to meet their own needs. It is hoped that the sampling of the ancient authors offered here will provide an irresistible stimulus for the student to read them in their entirety.

D. K.

CONTENTS

VOLUME TWO   The Roman World

Volume Two

PROBLEMS IN ANCIENT HISTORY

The Roman World

SECTION I

Early Rome—Myth, Poetry, or History?

THE EARLY HISTORY of Rome, from its foundation to the beginning of the Punic Wars, has long been the subject of scholarly controversy turning on the question of the reliability of its sources. The stories of early Rome that have been handed down to us are filled with legendary, heroic, and poetic elements, and it is difficult to decide whether there is anything of historical value in them. The first Roman literature appeared after 240 B.C. in the epic poems of Naevius and Ennius and the first historical writing, by Quintus Fabius Pictor, came in the second century B.C. Even these are not available to us but are preserved in fragmentary quotations only. The crucial question is what were their sources and how reliable were they?

The first part of this section will present some Roman accounts of the Royal Period and the attempt of a modern scholar to combine traditional material with archaeological evidence. The second part will present modern opinions as to the reliability of the tradition.

1. THE FOUNDATION OF ROME*

Titus Livius (59 B.C.–A.D. 17) wrote a history of Rome from the beginnings to 9 B.C. in 142 books. Of these only books 1–10 and 21–45 are extant plus fragments and epitomes of the rest. Where it exists, Livy's history is our most important source for the history of the Roman Republic.

Now first of all it is sufficiently established that, Troy having been taken, the utmost severity was shown to all the other Trojans; but that towards two, Æneas and Antenor, the Greeks forbore all the rights of war, both in accordance with an ancient tie of hospitality, and because they had ever been the advisers of peace, and of the restoration of Helen—then that Antenor after various vicissitudes came into the innermost bay of the Adriatic Sea, with a body of the Heneti, who having been driven from Paphlagonia in consequence of civil commotion, were in quest both of a settlement and a leader, their king Pylæmenes having been lost at Troy; and that the Heneti and Trojans, having

* Livy, 1. 1–7, translated by D. Spillan, C. Edmonds, et al.

1

expelled the Euganei, who dwelt between the sea and the Alps, took possession of the country; and the place where they first landed is called Troy; from whence also the name of Trojan is given to the canton; but the nation in general is called Veneti: that Æneas was driven from home by a similar calamity, but the fates leading him to the founding of a greater empire, he came first to Macedonia: that he sailed from thence to Sicily in quest of a settlement: that from Sicily he made for the Laurentine territory; this place also has the name of Troy. When the Trojans, having disembarked there, were driving plunder from the lands,—as being persons to whom, after their almost immeasurable wandering, nothing was left but their arms and ships,—Latinus the king, and the Aborigines, who then occupied those places, assembled in arms from the city and country to repel the violence of the new-comers. On this point the tradition is two-fold: some say, that Latinus, after being overcome in battle, made first a peace, and then an alliance with Æneas: others, that when the armies were drawn out in battle-array, before the signals were sounded, Latinus advanced to the front of the troops and invited the leader of the adventurers to a conference. That he then inquired who they were, whence (they had come), or by what casualty they had left their home, and in quest of what they had landed on the Laurentine territory: after he heard that the host were Trojans, their chief Æneas, the son of Anchises and Venus, and that, driven from their own country and their homes, which had been destroyed by fire, they were seeking a settlement and a place for building a town, struck with admiration of the noble origin of the nation and of the hero, and their spirit, alike prepared for peace or war, he confirmed the assurance of future friendship by giving his right hand: that upon this a compact was struck between the chiefs, and mutual greetings passed between the armies: that Æneas was hospitably entertained by Latinus: that Latinus, in the presence of his household gods, added a family league to the public one, by giving Æneas his daughter in marriage. This event confirms the Trojans in the hope of at length terminating their wanderings by a fixed and permanent settlement. They build a town. Æneas calls it Lavinium, after the name of his wife. In a short time, too, a son was the issue of the new marriage, to whom his parents gave the name of Ascanius.

The Aborigines and Trojans were soon after attacked together in war. Turnus, king of the Rutulians, to whom Lavinia had been affianced before the coming of Æneas, enraged that a stranger had been preferred to himself, made war on Æneas and Latinus together. Neither side came off from that contest with cause for rejoicing. The Rutulians were vanquished; the victorious Aborigines and Trojans lost their leader Latinus. Upon this Turnus and the Rutulians, diffident of their strength, have recourse to the flourishing state of the Etruscans, and their king Mezentius; who holding his court at Cœre, at that time an opulent town, being by no means pleased, even from the commencement, at the founding of the new city, and then considering that the Trojan power was increasing much more than was altogether consistent with the safety of the neighbouring states, without reluctance joined his forces in alliance with the Rutulians. Æneas, in order to conciliate the minds of the Aborigines to meet the terror of so serious a war, called both nations Latins, so that they might all be not only under the same laws, but also the same name. Nor after that did the Aborigines yield to the Trojans in zeal and fidelity towards their king Æneas; relying therefore on this disposition of the two nations, who were now daily coalescing more and more, although Etruria was so powerful, that it filled with the fame of its prowess not only the land, but the sea also, through the whole length of Italy, from the Alps to the Sicilian Strait, though he might have repelled the war by means of fortifications, yet he led out his forces to the field. Upon this a battle ensued successful to the Latins, the last also of the mortal acts of Æneas. He was buried, by whatever name human and divine laws require him to be called, on the banks of the river Numicius. They call him Jupiter Indiges.

Ascanius, the son of Æneas, was not yet old enough to take the government upon him; that government, however, remained secure for him till the age of maturity. In the interim, the Latin state and the kingdom of his grandfather and father was secured for the boy under the regency of his mother (such capacity was there in Lavinia). I have some doubts (for who can state as certain a matter of such antiquity) whether this was the Ascanius, or one older than he, born of Creusa before the fall of Troy, and the companion of his father in his flight from thence, the same whom, being called Iulus, the Julian family call the author of their name. This Ascanius, wheresoever and of whatever mother born, (it is at least certain that he was the son of Æneas,) Lavinium being overstocked with inhabitants, left that flourishing and, considering these times, wealthy city to his mother or step-mother, and built for himself a new one at the foot of Mount Alba, which, being extended on the ridge of a hill, was, from its situation, called Longa Alba. Between the founding of Lavinium and the transplanting this colony to Longa Alba, about thirty years intervened. Yet its power had increased to such a degree, especially after the defeat of the Etrurians, that not even upon the death of Æneas, nor after that, during the regency of Lavinia, and the first essays of the young prince's reign, did Mezentius, the Etrurians, or any other of its neighbours dare to take up arms against it. A peace had been concluded between the two nations on these terms, that the river Albula, now called Tiber, should be the common boundary between the Etrurians and Latins. After him Sylvius, the son of Ascanius, born by some accident in a wood, ascends the throne. He was the father of Æneas Sylvius, who afterwards begot Latinus Sylvius. By him several colonies, called the ancient Latins, were transplanted. From this time, all the princes, who reigned at Alba, had the surname of Sylvius. From Latinus sprung Alba; from Alba, Atys; from Atys, Capys; from Capys, Capetus; from Capetus, Tiberinus, who, being drowned in crossing the river Albula, gave it a name famous with posterity. Then Agrippa, the son of Tiberinus; after Agrippa, Romulus Silvius ascends the throne, in succession to his father. The latter, having been killed by a thunderbolt, left the kingdom to Aventinus, who being buried on that hill, which is part of the city of Rome, gave his name to it. After him reigns Proca; he begets Numitor and Amulius. To Numitor, his eldest son, he bequeaths the ancient kingdom of the Sylvian family. But force prevailed more than the father's will or the respect due to seniority: for Amulius, having expelled his brother, seizes the kingdom; he adds crime to crime, murders his brother's male issue; and under pretence of doing his brother's daughter, Rhea Sylvia, honour, having made her a vestal virgin, by obliging her to perpetual virginity he deprives her of all hopes of issue.

But, in my opinion, the origin of so great a city, and the establishment of an empire next in power to that of the gods, was due to the Fates. The vestal Rhea, being deflowered by force, when she had brought forth twins, declares Mars to be the father of her illegitimate offspring, either because she believed it to be so, or because a god was a more creditable author of her offence. But neither gods nor men protect her or her children from the king's cruelty: the priestess is bound and thrown into prison; the children he commands to be thrown into the current of the river. By some interposition of providence, the Tiber having overflowed its banks in stagnant pools, did not admit of any access to the regular bed of the river; and the bearers supposed that the infants could be drowned in water however still; thus, as if they had effectually executed the king's orders, they expose the boys in the nearest land-flood, where now stands the ficus Ruminalis (they say that it was called Romularis). The country thereabout was then a vast wilderness. The tradition is, that when the water, subsiding, had left the floating trough, in which the children had been exposed, on dry ground, a thirsty she-wolf, coming from the neighbouring mountains, directed her course to the cries of the infants, and that she held down her dugs to them with so much gentleness, that the keeper of the king's flock found her licking the boys with her tongue. It is said his name was Faustulus; and that they were carried by him to his homestead to be nursed by his wife Laurentia. Some are of opinion that she was called Lupa among the shepherds, from her being a common prostitute, and that this gave rise to the surprising story. The children thus born and thus brought up, when arrived at the years of manhood, did not loiter away their time in tending the folds or following the flocks, but roamed and hunted in the forests. Having by this exercise improved their strength and courage, they not only encountered wild beasts, but even attacked robbers laden with plunder, and afterwards divided the spoil among the shepherds. And in company with these, the number of their young associates daily increasing, they carried on their business and their sports.

They say, that the festival of the lupercal, as now celebrated, was even at that time solemnized on the Palatine hill, which, from Palanteum, a city of Arcadia, was first called Palatium, and afterwards Mount Palatine. There they say that Evander, who belonged to the tribe of Arcadians, that for many years before had possessed that country, appointed the observance of a feast, introduced from Arcadia, in such manner, that young men ran about naked in sport and wantonness, doing honour to Pan Lycæus, whom the Romans afterwards called Inuus. That the robbers, through rage at the loss of their booty, having lain in wait for them whilst intent on this sport, as the festival was now well known, whilst Romulus vigorously defended himself, took Remus prisoner; that they delivered him up, when taken, to king Amulius, accusing him with the utmost effrontery. They principally alleged it as a charge against them, that they had made incursions upon Numitor's lands, and plundered them in a hostile manner, having assembled a band of young men for the purpose. Upon this Remus was delivered to Numitor to be punished. Now, from the very first, Faustulus had entertained hopes that the boys whom he was bringing up were of the blood royal; for he both knew that the children had been exposed by the king's orders, and that the time at which he had taken them up agreed exactly with that period: but he had been unwilling that the matter, as not being yet ripe for discovery, should be disclosed, till either a fit opportunity or necessity should arise. Necessity came first; accordingly, compelled by fear, he discovers the whole affair to Romulus. By accident also, whilst he had Remus in custody, and had heard that the brothers were twins, on comparing their age, and *observing* their turn of mind entirely free from servility, the recollection of his grand-children struck Numitor; and on making inquiries he arrived at the same conclusion, so that he was well nigh recognising Remus. Thus a plot is concerted for the king on all sides. Romulus, not accompanied by a body of young men, (for he was unequal to open force,) but having commanded the shepherds to come to the palace by different roads at a fixed time, forces his way to the king; and Remus, with another party from

Numitor's house, assists his brother, and so they kill the king.

Numitor, at the beginning of the fray, having given out that enemies had invaded the city, and assaulted the palace, after he had drawn off the Alban youth to secure the citadel with a garrison and arms, when he saw the young men, after they had killed the king, advancing to congratulate him, immediately called an assembly of the people, and represented to them the unnatural behavior of his brother towards him, the extraction of his grand-children, the manner of their birth and education, and how they came to be discovered; then he informed them of the king's death, and that he was killed by his orders. When the young princes, coming up with their band through the middle of the assembly, saluted their grandfather king, an approving shout, following from all the people present, ratified to him both that title and the sovereignty. Thus the government of Alba being committed to Numitor, a desire seized Romulus and Remus to build a city on the spot where they had been exposed and brought up. And there was an overflowing population of Albans and of Latins. The shepherds too had come into that design, and all these readily inspired hopes, that Alba and Lavinium would be but petty places in comparison with the city which they intended to build. But ambition of the sovereignty, the bane of their grandfather, interrupted these designs, and thence arose a shameful quarrel from a beginning sufficiently amicable. For as they were twins, and the respect due to seniority could not determine the point, they agreed to leave to the tutelary gods of the place to choose, by augury, which should give a name to the new city, which govern it when built.

Romulus chose the Palatine and Remus the Aventine hill as their stands to make their observations. It is said, that to Remus an omen came first, six vultures; and now, the omen having been declared, when double the number presented itself to Romulus, his own party saluted each king; the former claimed the kingdom on the ground of priority of time, the latter on account of the number of birds. Upon this, having met in an altercation, from the contest of angry feelings they turn to bloodshed; there Remus fell from a blow received in the crowd. A more common account is, that Remus, in derision of his brother, leaped over his new-built wall, and was, for that reason, slain by Romulus in a passion; who, after sharply chiding him, added words to this effect: "So shall every one fare, who shall dare to leap over my fortifications." Thus Romulus got the sovereignty to himself; the city, when built, was called after the name of its founder.

2. THE KINGS OF ROME AND THE EARLY REPUBLIC*

Eutropius lived in the reign of the Emperor Valens (A.D. 364–378) and wrote a compendium or epitome of Roman history. His brief and straightforward narrative is based on the accepted tradition of Roman history.

The Roman empire, than which the memory of man can recall scarcely any one smaller in its commencement, or greater in its progress throughout the world, had its origin from Romulus; who, being the son of a vestal virgin, and, as was supposed, of Mars, was brought at one birth with his brother Remus. While leading a predatory life among the shepherds, he founded, when he was eighteen years of age, a small city on the Palatine

* Eutropius, 1. 1–20, translated by John Selby Watson.

Hill, on the 21st day of April, in the third year of the sixth Olympiad, and the three hundred and ninety-fourth after the destruction of Troy.

After founding the city, which he called Rome, from his own name, he proceeded principally as follows. He took a great number of the neighbouring inhabitants into the city; he chose a hundred of the older men, by whose advice he might manage all his affairs, and whom, from their age, he named senators. Next, as both himself and his people were in want of wives, he invited the tribes contiguous to the city to an exhibition of games, and seized upon their young women. Wars having arisen in consequence of this outrage in capturing the females, he conquered the Cæninenses, the Antemnates, the Crustumini, the Sabines, the Fidenates, and the Vejentes; all whose towns lay around the city. And since, after a tempest that suddenly arose, in the thirty-seventh year of his reign, he was no longer to be seen, he was believed to have been translated to the gods, and was accordingly deified. The senators then ruled at Rome by periods of five days; and under their government a year was passed.

Afterwards Numa Pompelius was elected king, who engaged indeed in no wars, but was of no less service to the state than Romulus; for he established both laws and customs among the Romans, who, by the frequency of their wars, were now regarded as robbers and semi-barbarians. He divided the year, before unregulated by any computation, into ten months; and founded numerous sacred rites and temples at Rome. He died a natural death in the forty-third year of his reign.

To him succeeded Tullus Hostilius, who re-commenced war. He conquered the Albans, who lay twelve miles distant from Rome. He overcame also in battle the Vejentes and Fidenates, the one six, the other eighteen miles from Rome; and increased the dimensions of the city by the addition of the Cœlian hill. After

reigning thirty-two years, he was struck by lightning, and consumed together with his house.

After him, Ancus Martius, the grandson of Numa by a daughter, succeeded to the government. He fought against the Latins, added the Aventine and Janiculan hills to the city and founded Ostia, a city on the sea-coast, sixteen miles from Rome. He died a natural death in the twenty-fourth year of his reign.

Priscus Tarquinius was next invested with the government. He doubled the number of the senators, built a Circus at Rome, and instituted the Roman games, which continue even to our time. He also conquered the Sabines, and added a considerable extent of territory, which he took from that people, to the lands of Rome; he was also the first that entered the city in triumph. He built the walls and sewers, and commenced the Capitol. He was killed in the thirty-eighth year of his reign, by the sons of Ancus, the king whom he had succeeded.

After him Servius Tullius was placed on the throne, the son of a woman of noble origin, but who was, nevertheless, a captive and a slave. He also defeated the Sabines; annexed three hills, the Quirinal, Viminal, and Esquiline, to the city; and formed trenches round the city walls. He was the first to institute the census, which till that time was unknown throughout the world. The people being all subjected to a census during his reign, Rome was found to contain eighty-four thousand citizens, including those in the country. He was cut off in the forty-fifth year of his reign, by the criminal machinations of his son-in-law Tarquin the Proud, the son of the king to whom he had succeeded, and of his own daughter, whom Tarquin had married.

Lucius Tarquinius Superbus, the seventh and last of the kings, overcame the Volsci, a nation not far from Rome, on the road to Campania; reduced the towns of Gabii and Suessa Pometia; made peace with the Tuscans; and built a temple to

Jupiter in the Capitol. Afterwards, while he was besieging Ardea, a town that lay about eighteen miles from the city, he was deprived of his throne; for, as his younger son, who was also named Tarquin, offered violence to Lucretia, the wife of Collatinus, a most noble and chaste woman; and as she, after complaining to her husband, her father, and her friends, of the injury that she had suffered, slew herself in the sight of them all; Brutus, in consequence, who was a kinsman of Tarquinius, excited an insurrection among the people, and deprived Tarquin of his regal authority. The army, also, which was engaged with the king in besieging Ardea, soon after deserted him; and the king himself, on going to the city, found the gates closed against him; and, after having reigned five-and-twenty years, was forced to take flight with his wife and children.

Thus a regal form of government continued at Rome, under seven kings, for the space of two hundred and forty-three years, while as yet the dominion of the city, where its extent was greatest, hardly reached fifteen miles.

Henceforth, instead of one king, two consuls were chosen, with this view, that, if one should be disposed to act unjustly, the other, having equal authority, might exercise a control over him. It was determined also that they should not hold their office longer than a year; in order that they might not, by continued possession of power, grow too over-bearing; but, knowing that in a year they would return to the level of private persons, might constantly conduct themselves with moderation.

In the first year, then, after the expulsion of the king and his family, the consuls were Lucius Junius Brutus, who had been the chief agent in the banishment of Tarquin, and Tarquinius Collatinus, the husband of Lucretia. But that dignity was soon taken from Tarquinius Collatinus; for it was enacted that no one who bore the name of Tarquin should remain in the city. Having collected, therefore, all his private property, he removed from the city, and Valerius Publicola was made consul in his stead. King Tarquin, however, after his expulsion, stirred up war against Rome, and, having collected a large force from all quarters, in order that he might be reinstated on the throne, took the field.

In the first encounter, Brutus and Aruns, Tarquin's son, killed each other; but the Romans left the field conquerors. The Roman matrons mourned for Brutus, the guardian of their honour, as if he had been their common father, for the space of a year. Valerius Publicola fixed upon Spurius Lucretius Tricipitinus, the father of Lucretia, for his colleague; and he dying of some disease, he next chose Horatius Pilvillus for his fellow consul.

Thus the first year had five consuls; Tarquinius Collatinus having left the city on account of his name, Brutus having fallen in battle, and Spurius Lucretius having died a natural death.

In the second year also, Tarquin, with a view to being re-established on the throne, again made war on the Romans, and, as Porsena, king of Tuscany, afforded him aid, almost took Rome. But he was also defeated on that occasion.

In the third year after the expulsion of the royal family, Tarquin, as he could not get himself re-admitted into the kingdom, and as Porsena, who had made peace with the Romans, gave him no support, retired to Tusculum, a town which is not far from Rome; where he and his wife lived for fourteen years in a private station, and reached an advanced age.

In the fourth year after the abolition of the kingly power, the Sabines, having made war on the Romans, were conquered; and a triumph was celebrated over them.

In the fifth year, Lucius Valerius, the colleague of Brutus, and consul for the fourth time, died a natural death, and in such extreme poverty, that the expenses of his funeral were defrayed by a public subscription. The matrons mourned for him, as for Brutus, during a year.

In the ninth year after the overthrow of the kingly power, the son-in-law of Tarquin, having assembled a vast army, in order to avenge the wrongs of his father-in-law, a new office was introduced at Rome, which was called the dictatorship, and which was more absolute than the consulate. In the same year also a master of the horse was appointed to be an officer under the dictator. Nor can anything be named more like to the imperial authority, which your Serenity now enjoys, than the ancient dictatorship, especially since Cæsar Octavianus, also, of whom we shall speak hereafter, and Caius Cæsar before him, ruled with the title and rank of dictator. The first dictator at Rome was Lartius; the first master of the horse, Spurius Cassius.

In the sixteenth year after the termination of the regal power, the people at Rome, thinking themselves oppressed by the senate and consuls, broke out into a sedition. On this occasion they created for themselves tribunes of the people, as their own peculiar judges and defenders, by whom they might be protected against the senate and the consuls.

In the following year the Volsci recommenced hostilities against the Romans; and being overcome in the field, lost also Corioli, the best city that they had.

In the eighteenth year after the banishment of the royal family, Quintius Marcius, the Roman general who had taken Corioli, the city of the Volsci, being compelled to flee from Rome, directed his course, in resentment, to the Volsci themselves, and received from them support against the Romans. He obtained several victories over the Romans; he made his way even to the fifth mile-stone from the city; and, refusing to hear a deputation that came to sue for peace, would have laid siege even to the place of his birth, had not his mother Veturia and his wife Volumnia gone out from the city to meet him, by whose tears and supplications he was prevailed on to withdraw his army. He was the next after Tarquin that acted as general against his country.

In the consulate of Cæso Fabius and Titus Virginius, three hundred noblemen, members of the Fabian family, undertook alone a war against the Vejentes, assuring the senate and the people that the whole contest should be brought to an end by themselves. These illustrious men, therefore, each of whom was capable of commanding a large army, setting out on their expedition, all fell in battle. One only remained out of so numerous a family, who, from his extreme youth, could not be taken with them to the field. After these events a census was held in the city, in which the number of the citizens was found to be a hundred and nineteen thousand three hundred and nineteen.

In the following year, in consequence of the blockade of a Roman army on Mount Algidus, about twelve miles from the city, Lucius Quintius Cincinnatus was appointed dictator; a man who, possessing only four acres of land, cultivated it with his own hands. He, being found at his work, and engaged in ploughing, assumed, after wiping the sweat from his brow, the *toga prætexta*; and set free the army with great slaughter among the enemy.

In the three hundred and second year from the founding of the city, the consular government ceased; and, instead of two consuls, ten magistrates were appointed to hold the supreme authority, under the title of decemviri. These during the first year conducted themselves with honour; but in the second, one of them, Appius Claudius, proceeded to offer violence to the maiden daughter of a certain Virginius, who was at that time filling an honourable post on military service against the Latins on Mount Algidus; but the father slew her with his own hand, that she might not suffer violation from the decemvir, and, returning to the army, raised an insurrection among the soldiers. Their power was in consequence taken from the decemviri, and they themselves received sentences of condemnation.

In the three hundred and fifteenth year from the founding of the city, the Fidenates rebelled against the Romans. The Vejentes and their king Tolumnius gave them assistance. These two states are so near to Rome, that Fidenæ is only seven, Veii only eighteen miles distant. The Volsci also joined them; but they were defeated by Marcus Æmilius the dictator, and Lucius Quintius Cincinnatus the master of the horse, and lost also their king. Fidenæ was taken, and utterly destroyed.

Twenty years afterwards, the people of Veii resumed hostilities. Furius Camillus was sent as dictator against them, who first defeated them in battle, and then, after a long siege, took their city, the oldest and richest in Italy. He next took Falisci, a city of no less note. But popular odium was excited against him, on the ground that he had made an unfair division of the booty, and he was condemned on that charge and banished.

Soon after the Galli Senones marched towards Rome; and, pursuing the Romans, whom they defeated at the river Allia, eleven miles from the city, possessed themselves of the city itself, no part of which could be defended against them, except the Capitol. After they had besieged it a long time, and the Romans were suffering from famine, Camillus, who was in exile in a neighbouring city, attacked the Gauls unexpectedly, and gave them a severe defeat. Afterwards, on receiving a sum in gold, to desist from the siege of the Capitol, they retreated; Camillus, however, pursued them, and routed them with such a slaughter, that he recovered both the gold which had been given to them, and all the military standards which they had taken. Thus he entered the city for the third time in triumph, and received the appellation of a second Romulus, as if he also had been a founder of the city.

3. THE FALL OF THE MONARCHY*

The Rutulians, a nation very wealthy, considering the country and age they lived in, were at that time in possession of Ardea. Their riches gave occasion to the war; for the king of the Romans, being exhausted of money by the magnificence of his public works, was desirous both to enrich himself, and by a large booty to soothe the minds of his subjects, who, besides other instances of his tyranny, were incensed against his government, because they were indignant that they had been kept so long a time by the king in the employments of mechanics, and in labour fit for slaves. An attempt was made to take Ardea by storm; when that did not succeed, the enemy began to be distressed by a blockade, and by works raised around them. As it commonly happens in standing camps, the war being rather tedious than violent, furloughs were easily obtained, more so by the officers, however, than the common soldiers. The young princes sometimes spent their leisure hours in feasting and entertainments. One day as they were drinking in the tent of Sextus Tarquin, where Collatinus Tarquinius, the son of Egerius, was also at supper, mention was made of wives. Every one commended his own in an extravagant manner, till a dispute arising about it, Collatinus said, "There was no occasion for words, that it might be known in a few hours how far his Lucretia excelled all the rest. If then, added he, we have any share of the vigour of youth, let us mount our horses and examine the behaviour of

---

* Livy, 1. 57–60, translated by D. Spillan, C. Edmonds, *et al.*

our wives; that must be most satisfactory to every one, which shall meet his eyes on the unexpected arrival of the husband." They were heated with wine; "Come on, then," say all. They immediately galloped to Rome, where they arrived in the dusk of the evening. From thence they went to Collatia, where they find Lucretia, not like the king's daughters-in-law, whom they had seen spending their time in luxurious entertainments with their equals, but though at an advanced time of night, employed at her wool, sitting in the middle of the house amid her maids working around her. The merit of the contest regarding the ladies was assigned to Lucretia. Her husband on his arrival, and the Tarquinii, were kindly received; the husband, proud of his victory, gives the young princes a polite invitation. There the villanous passion for violating Lucretia by force seizes Sextus Tarquin; both her beauty, and her approved purity, act as incentives. And then, after this youthful frolic of the night, they return to the camp.

A few days after, without the knowledge of Collatinus, Sextus came to Collatia with one attendant only; where, being kindly received by them, as not being aware of his intention, after he had been conducted after supper into the guests' chamber, burning with passion, when every thing around seemed sufficiently secure, and all fast asleep, he comes to Lucretia, as she lay asleep, with a naked sword, and with his left hand pressing down the woman's breast, he says, "Be silent, Lucretia; I am Sextus Tarquin; I have a sword in my hand; you shall die, if you utter a word." When awaking terrified from sleep, the woman beheld no aid, impending death nigh at hand; then Tarquin acknowledged his passion, entreated, mixed threats with entreaties, tried the female's mind in every possible way. When he saw her inflexible, and that she was not moved even by the terror of death, he added to terror the threat of dishonour;

he says that he will lay a murdered slave naked by her side when dead, so that she may be said to have been slain in infamous adultery. When by the terror of this disgrace his lust, as it were victorious, had overcome her inflexible chastity, and Tarquin had departed, exulting in having triumphed over a lady's honour, Lucretia, in melancholy distress at so dreadful a misfortune, despatches the same messenger to Rome to her father, and to Ardea to her husband, that they would come each with one trusty friend; that it was necessary to do so, and that quickly. Sp. Lucretius comes with P. Valerius, the son of Volesus, Collatinus with L. Junius Brutus, with whom, as he was returning to Rome, he happened to be met by his wife's messenger. They find Lucretia sitting in her chamber in sorrowful dejection. On the arrival of her friends the tears burst from her eyes; and to her husband, on his inquiry "whether all was right," she says, "By no means, for what can be right with a woman who has lost her honour? The traces of another man are on your bed, Collatinus. But the body only has been violated, the mind is guiltless; death shall be my witness. But give me your right hands, and your honour, that the adulterer shall not come off unpunished. It is Sextus Tarquin, who, an enemy in the guise of a guest, has borne away hence a triumph fatal to me, and to himself, if you are men." They all pledge their honour; they attempt to console her, distracted as she was in mind, by turning away the guilt from her, constrained by force, on the perpetrator of the crime; that it is the mind sins, not the body; and that where intention was wanting guilt could not be. "It is for you to see," says she, "what is due to him. As for me, though I acquit myself of guilt, from punishment I do not discharge myself; nor shall any woman survive her dishonour pleading the example of Lucretia." The knife, which she kept concealed beneath her garment, she plunges into her heart, and falling forward on the wound, she dropped down expiring. The husband and father shriek aloud.

Brutus, while they were overpowered with grief, having drawn the knife out of the wound, and holding it up before him reeking with blood, said, "By this blood, most pure before the pollution of royal villany, I swear, and I call you, O gods, to witness my oath, that I shall pursue Lucius Tarquin the Proud, his wicked wife, and all their race, with fire, sword, and all other means in my power; nor shall I ever suffer them or any other to reign at Rome." Then he gave the knife to Collatinus, and after him to Lucretius and Valerius, who were surprised at such extraordinary mind in the breast of Brutus. However, they all take the oath as they were directed, and converting their sorrow into rage, follow Brutus as their leader, who from that time ceased not to solicit them to abolish the regal power. They carry Lucretia's body from her own house, and convey it into the forum; and assemble a number of persons by the strangeness and atrocity of the extraordinary occurrence, as usually happens. They complain, each for himself, of the royal villany and violence. Both the grief of the father moves them, as also Brutus, the reprover of their tears and unavailing complaints, and their adviser to take up arms against those who dared to treat them as enemies, as would become men and Romans. Each most spirited of the youth voluntarily presents himself in arms; the rest of the youth follow also. From thence, after leaving an adequate garrison at the gates at Collatia, and having appointed sentinels, so that no one might give intelligence of the disturbance to the king's party, the rest set out for Rome in arms under the conduct of Brutus. When they arrived there, the armed multitude cause panic and confusion wherever they go. Again, when they see the principal men of the state placing themselves at their head, they think that, whatever it may be, it was not without good reason. Nor does the heinousness of the circumstance excite less violent emotions at Rome than it had done at Collatia; accordingly they run from all parts of the city into the forum, whither, when they came, the public crier summoned them to attend the tribune of the celeres, with which office Brutus happened to be at that time vested. There an harangue was delivered by him, by no means of that feeling and capacity which had been counterfeited up to that day, concerning the violence and lust of Sextus Tarquin, the horrid violation of Lucretia and her lamentable death, the bereavement of Tricipitinus, to whom the cause of his daughter's death was more exasperating and deplorable than the death itself. To this was added the haughty insolence of the king himself, and the sufferings and toils of the people, buried in the earth in cleansing sinks and sewers; that the Romans, the conquerors of all the surrounding states, instead of warriors had become labourers and stone-cutters. The unnatural murder of king Servius Tullius was dwelt on, and his daughter's driving over the body of her father in her impious chariot, and the gods who avenge parents were invoked by him. By stating these and other, I suppose, more exasperating circumstances, which though by no means easily detailed by writers, the heinousness of the case suggested at the time, he persuaded the multitude, already incensed, to deprive the king of his authority, and to order the banishment of L. Tarquin with his wife and children. He himself, having selected and armed some of the young men, who readily gave in their names, set out for Ardea to the camp to excite the army against the king: the command in the city he leaves to Lucretius, who had been already appointed prefect of the city by the king. During this tumult Tullia fled from her house, both men and women cursing her wherever she went, and invoking on her the furies the avengers of parents.

News of these transactions having

reached the camp, when the king, alarmed at this sudden revolution, was going to Rome to quell the commotions, Brutus, for he had notice of his approach, turned out of the way, that he might not meet him; and much about the same time Brutus and Tarquin arrived by different routes, the one at Ardea, the other at Rome. The gates were shut against Tarquin, and an act of banishment passed against him; the deliverer of the state the camp received with great joy, and the king's sons were expelled. Two of them followed their father, and went into banishment to Cære, a city of Etruria. Sextus Tarquin, having gone to Gabii, as to his own kingdom, was slain by the avenger of the old feuds, which he had raised against himself by his rapines and murders. Lucius Tarquin the Proud reigned twenty-five years: the regal form of government continued from the building of the city to this period of its deliverance, two hundred and forty-four years. Two consuls, viz. Lucius Junius Brutus and Lucius Tarquinius Collatinus, were elected by the prefect of the city at the comitia by centuries, according to the commentaries of Servius Tullius.

4. ROME FROM ABOUT 700 TO THE BEGINNING OF THE FIFTH CENTURY B.C.: AN ARCHAEOLOGICAL SURVEY*

The following selection gives an excellent and up-to-date account of the light archaeological evidence sheds on the traditional account of early Rome.

By studying the archaeological discoveries in the different parts of archaic Rome along strictly topographical lines, it is possible to make out a slow but continuous progression in Roman culture from about 700 to 550 B.C. This time-division is justifiable, for after the first part of the sixth century the life of Rome takes on a different appearance and the collection of more or less united villages gives place to a prosperous town worthy of the name. But until this time the progress of Roman culture was far less rapid than the traditional story would have us believe.

As regards the first half of the seventh century, the localization of remains found indicates that the settlements were not very extensive. Although the Latin settlements continued an active existence, as can be seen from the archaeological layer corresponding with the period to which Italian prehistorians have given the name

* R. Bloch, *The Origins of Rome* (New York: F. A. Praeger, 1960), pp. 85–100. Reprinted by permission of Thames and Hudson Ltd., London.

of 'the Second Iron Age', it is surprising to find that there were fewer graves in the *sepolcreto* of the Forum. Not until the second half of the seventh century did burial-places increase again, though at that stage the dead were buried inside tree-trunks. On the other hand, recent important excavations in a region not far from the Forum, near the Arch of Augustus, have revealed three cremation graves for adults and five children's graves or *suggrundaria*.

Chronologically, the adult graves come midway between the two main series of *sepolcreto* graves and date from about the middle of the seventh century, filling-in a curious gap in the use of the Forum valley for funerary purposes. But the question of the settlements to which these new graves belonged remains open, for their culture, as illustrated by the material found, seems to differ slightly from that of the *sepolcreto* and shows affinities with an archaic Villanovan culture found in a group of graves on the La Tolfa hills. Does this indicate an influx of people from the

Allumiere-La Tolfa region? It is impossible to say. Often, as can be seen, new discoveries pose more problems than they solve; of necessity the progress of knowledge in a matter as complex as this is slow and difficult.

New excavations confirm that in the seventh century the Forum was not only used for burial but also inhabited in certain parts. They have revealed traces of hut-foundations with holes for post-supports between the temple of Julius and the Arch of Augustus. According to E. Gjerstad these date from the period following the years 670–660; floods destroyed the lowest inhabited zone shortly before 625 B.C. At first the settlement was restricted to its upper portion; then, after the installation of a drainage system foreshadowing the public works of the Etruscan kings, the whole of the zone was again occupied by huts from roughly 625 to 575 B.C. The drainage system allowed the settlement to extend as far as the lowest part of the Forum valley, as can be seen from the remains of huts of this period found during excavations on the site of the *Equus Domitiani*. In about 575 B.C., the age of huts came to an end, and soon rapid developments in all fields were to give a decisive impetus to the emergence of Rome proper.

During the seventh century the Esquiline cemetery continued to be used and even, it seems, to increase in size, so far as we can judge from the evidence of early excavations. The contents of the graves increase along parallel lines with that of the *sepolcreto* graves. First, there are painted urns with geometrical decoration, then Faliscan objects and the first appearance of the *bucchero*. In the second half of the seventh century, late proto-Corinthian urns appeared; they form part of the contents of a chamber-tomb which was probably used many times.

Outside these areas, finds dating back to the first half of the seventh century are sporadic, and insufficient for any firm conclusions. In the second half of the century the position changes. Traces of sanctuaries appear in the northern part of Rome, although there are no surviving architectural remains of the temples themselves. Their presence can, however, be inferred from the *favissae* or votive stores, originally situated alongside the sacred buildings themselves, whose contents have been found. A very productive *favissa* has been located at the northern extremity of the Quirinal, not far from the spot where the *fossa*-graves of the eighth century were found. The material seems to extend over the whole of the seventh century and the beginning of the next. There are several *bucchero* vases dating from the period 640–580, as well as painted Italo-Corinthian vases. Another *favissa* was discovered last century in front of the Palace of the Quirinal, but little is known about it. It is now almost impossible to date it.

The discoveries made on the Capitol are also important for this period. A pit surrounded by blocks of a tufa called *cappellaccio* was found between the temple of Jupiter on the Capitol and the church of Santa Maria dell' Aracoeli. Both its *bucchero* vases and those imitating the Corinthian style belong to about 600. The sanctuary indicated by this *favissa* must, therefore, have been older than the Etruscan temple of the Tarquins, and its disappearance was perhaps due to the work necessitated by the Etruscans' vast building projects. Shortly before the last war, remains of two temples, architectonic debris and many fragments of different vases were found at the foot of the Capitol, at the end of the small plain of the Forum Boarium, close by the church of Sant' Omobono. The pottery objects include embossed or undecorated *bucchero* ware, painted vases on Corinthian models and many Attic vases. Their dates range from the beginning to the end of the sixth century. It would seem, therefore, that the temples of Sant'Omobono were in use from about 600 to near the end of the Etruscan period.

In addition, various isolated, sporadic finds have revealed a body of material, mostly pottery, from different parts of the Forum and Palatine. As far as the first half of the seventh century is concerned, the number of objects of Faliscan origin or inspiration is striking. The material for the second half of the seventh century and the beginning of the sixth is considerably greater. Etruscan work is represented by a large number of *bucchero* vases in different forms, above all *oinochoai*, chalices and *kantharoi*. In various places fragments of painted Italo-Corinthian fragments have been found. Finally, Greek importations are evidenced by the presence of Ionic and Attic vases, the former dating from the end of the seventh, the latter from the first half of the sixth century.

What conclusions can be legitimately drawn from this necessary fragmentary and incomplete evidence which, nevertheless, in the aggregate, constitutes an impressive body of fact? Let us make a distinction between the topographical and cultural fields. Until about the middle of the seventh century there seems to have been little modification of the villages which had developed earlier; on the other hand, it is now realized that from about 670 the Forum, which had until then been used only as a burial ground, came to be used for dwellings, for a hut village, in fact. Then, from 650, both sacred and secular life developed considerably on the northern hills, the Quirinal, Viminal and Capitol, and also in the region of the Forum Boarium, bordering the Tiber. A yearly religious ceremony celebrated in the classical period in Rome and mentioned in many texts, the feast of the *Septimontium*, looked back, in fact, to a very early Roman federation which included only the villages that were by tradition Latin. On December 11 an archaic type of ceremony was celebrated by the peoples of the seven Latin hills: the three eminences of the

Palatine, Cermalus, Palatium and Velia; the three eminences of the Esquiline, Fagutal, Cispius and Oppius; and, lastly, Caelius (some texts add Subura, which was situated between Oppius and Cispius). They offered up seven separate sacrifices, recalling an ancient union between the different *montes*. The Quirinal, Viminal and Capitol in the north and the Aventine in the south were excluded from this first federation. So also were the valleys of the Forum and *Circus Maximus*.

It is difficult to give a precise date to the time when this federation was first formed. The absence of the Forum, which was inhabited from 670 to 660, suggests that it occurred very early, probably in the first quarter of the seventh century. Apart from archaeological evidence, the most conclusive proof of different stages of topographical development in Rome is provided by certain very ancient rites in the Roman religion.

By studying the archaeological evidence it is possible to reach a fairly exact idea of the level of culture reached by the city in the period under consideration. Until about 650 B.C. Rome presents the appearance of a small Latin town, very different from the wealthy towns of Etruria or Praeneste, but not completely self-contained. Like most of its neighbours in Latium it maintained constant commercial relations with the Falerians and Faliscan territory, as can be seen from the large quantity of Faliscan or Faliscan-inspired pottery found on its site. It was a town of merchants and workmen as well as of small farmers and stock-breeders.

In the next century Rome continued to grow and develop her intercourse with the countries north of the Tiber, the Faliscan area and southern Etruria. We have already remarked on the presence of many vases imported from the neighbouring lucumony of Caere. The Etruscan *bucchero* style reveals that the links between Rome and Etruscan territory were already close. But Rome was still a long way from the wealth and power of her Etruscan neighbours, such as Veii and Caere. The hut age continued until about 575, and shortly afterwards this long period of slow progression came to an end. Thus the conquests and foreign expansion attributed by classical historians to Rome in the seventh century are anachronisms; the inhabitants of the seven hills were certainly not in a position to destroy Alba or to found on the mouth of the Tiber a port which is, in any case, several centuries later in date. But now Rome's slow evolution was suddenly to speed up. The city leapt in one bound to greatness and prosperity.

ETRUSCAN ROME: FROM ABOUT 550 TO ABOUT 475 B.C.

This period is well documented by archaeological evidence. It is provided not by the cemeteries which have by now practically disappeared, but by numerous objects of different kinds, found mainly on the Forum and Palatine and including for the first time important traces of monuments, drains, walls and temples. Large quantities of Attic pottery with black-figure decoration have been found in Sant'Omobono and on the Forum and Palatine; the fragments are often of a very high quality and date from 550 to 500 B.C. This type of painted vase is followed in the first quarter of the fifth century by many fragments of Attic cups with red-figure decoration. Then, in about 480, the importation of Greek pottery to Rome seems almost to have ceased.

Beautiful polychrome terracottas, similar to original objects from other cities in Latium and Etruria, appear in various places, on the Capitol, the Palatine, the Esquiline, the Forum Romanum and the Forum Boarium. The terracottas in question are antefixes or fragments of friezes, proving the existence, on all the sites where they have been found, of richly decorated sacred buildings. According to tradition, it was Tarquin who completed the vast temple on the Capitol dedicated to Jupiter, Juno and Minerva. He devised a tripartite plan as appropriate to three divinities: Jupiter occupied the central *cella*, Juno and Minerva the two side *cellae*. The sanctuary thus had the appearance of an Etruscan temple, as in Vitruvius's detailed description (IV, 61); similar temples can be seen in many Etruscan cities. Only the base was of stone, the superstructure being of wood and the decoration and facings of terracotta. Now important traces of a powerful subfoundation have been found on the Capitol, along with fragments of antefixes dating from the end of the sixth century. These are without any doubt the remains of the famous Capitoline temple. Other vestiges of the building work of the Tarquins still exist. There are, for instance, the remains of the *Cloaca Maxima*, which drained the marshy land of the Forum. Of the walls built round Rome at different periods there remain a certain number of sections, about which there has been much scholarly disagreement; it is not easy to assign a definite date to these archaic walls, since the same types of construction often persisted for centuries. In my opinion, however, only one conclusion can be drawn from the ground-plans of protective walls built according to the technique of the *opera quadrata*, in which blocks of stone in the shape of parallelepipeds were juxtaposed and superimposed on one another without any mortar. The walls made of *cappellaccio*, a sort of grey tufa, date back to the Etruscan kings and represent the work attributed, by tradition, to King Servius. The wall in *grotta oscura*, a yellowish tufa quarried near Veii, is much later; it dates from after the capture of Rome by the Gauls in 390 and represents a defence reaction by the city, which had not yet recovered from the terrors of the barbarian invasion.

Thus Rome was a large city surrounded by a protective wall more than six miles long; the stranger entering Tarquins'

city would see a powerful line of fortifications and the rather massive, multi-
coloured bulk of the many sanctuaries on
the hills. So far, archaeology supports the
traditional story; the historian can, therefore, devote his attention to clarifying
important questions of chronology and
culture.

According to tradition, it will be remembered, Rome fell into the hands of the
Etruscan kings 138 years after its foundation by Romulus; in 616, according to
Varro's calculations. Etruscan domination
lasted a little more than a hundred years
and ended in 509 with the expulsion of the
hated tyrant. In fact, as we have seen,
though Etruscan influence was of very
early date, the actual presence of Etruscans
and the transformation of Rome into a
large city comparable with the lucumonies
of southern Tuscany, dates back only to
about 550. The Tuscan annexation of the
town on the banks of the Tiber must,
therefore, be post-dated by half a century.
In my opinion, archaeology does not
warrant an earlier date and, inversely, a
chronology which places the beginning
of the Tyrrhenian monarchy at the end
of the sixth century does not seem to me
to be acceptable. When did the Etruscans
finally leave Rome? According to the
same basic chronology, it could only have
been in about 450 B.C., more than fifty
years after the traditional date. This also
seems hard to believe. First of all, the later
the period, the more chance there is of the
traditional dates being correct. Nor does
archaeology seem to support this view. It is
true that Attic pottery continued to be
imported during the first quarter of the
fifth century, and the fragments of high-
quality vessels with red-figure decoration
date from the years between 500 and 480.
But imported Attic pottery became extremely rare in the following period, a sure
sign of impoverishment and a lower
economic level. The architectonic terracottas also disappeared. It is clear that
this very obvious change marks the

departure of the Etruscans and the return
of Rome to the status of a Latin city,
abandoned by its powerful invaders and
beset by all kinds of difficulties.

The period from 509 to about 475
remains doubtful. Even the traditional
account is rather confused and seems to be
intended mainly as a sop to Roman pride.
In outline it states that Tarquinius
Superbus left with his two sons for Caere
after his people had rebelled against him.
Seeking revenge, he raised two armies, one
at Veii, the other at Tarquinia, and
marched on Rome. But the Roman army,
led by the two consuls, Junius Brutus and
P. Valerius (Tarquinius Collatinus,
Brutus's one-time colleague had been
exiled in accordance with the decree of
banishment against the whole of the
Tarquin family), scattered the Etruscans.
The Tarquins then took refuge with
Porsenna in the great city of Clusium.
Porsenna, taking their part, marched on
Rome at the head of a large army. He took
possession of the Janiculum and was
making ready to penetrate into Rome itself
by means of a wooden bridge when he was
halted by the heroism of Horatius Cocles.
C. Mucius Scaevola attempted to kill the
Etruscan king, was stopped by his guards,
and to show his scorn of pain, placed his
right hand in the flames. Porsenna, moved
by this show of courage, agreed to conclude
a peace treaty with Rome.

He then led his expeditionary force
against the Latin town of Aricia to whose
aid came the surrounding Latin peoples
and the Greeks of Cumae. The soldiers of
Aricia were dispersed, but those of
Cumae surrounded the Tuscan army and
decimated it. So ended Porsenna's expedition.

But in another version he does not
retreat peaceably from before the walls of
Rome. The assault is made and the town
taken (Tacitus, *Histories*, III, 72). The
impression gained from these accounts is
that Rome, far from having taken the lead
in these dramatic events, was merely a

pawn in struggles between greater powers. From the third decade of the fifth century B.C., Etruria was beset by difficulties on all sides. On land her links with Campania were broken by the loss of Latium. On sea Cumae took the initiative and with the help of Syracusan ships, defeated her in 474—a defeat pregnant with consequences which marked the end of her supremacy in the Tyrrhenian sea. Thus, underneath the padding of the traditional story, a framework of fact can be perceived. It was, no doubt, the alliance between the Latin towns—all of which were hostile to the Etruscans—and the Greeks of Cumae, that drove them out of Rome and Latium as a whole. But beforehand, the Etruscan chiefs must have put up a stubborn resistance to their enemies. The Tarquins did not succumb to a mere internal revolt but to the combined forces of several enemies. And if Rome was, in fact, reconquered, even though only briefly, by the armies of the distant lucumony of Clusium, it shows the importance attached by the Tuscans to this key position on the Tiber. It was only lack of unity that prevented the various Etruscan towns from resisting the Greek-Latin alliance for a longer period.

The drama that was to decide the future of the Etruscan empire and, as a consequence, of Rome was played out in the last years of the sixth and the first quarter of the fifth century. This period saw the departure of the Tarquins from Rome, then the temporary reconquest of the city by allied Etruscan chiefs. Archaeology does not indicate cultural changes until about 475 B.C. Whatever the validity of the traditional date, 509, it was only after the first quarter of the fifth century that Rome became a small Latin city once again and Tyrrhenian luxury and splendour disappeared for good. Other records, to which we shall return later, confirm this first impression. In my opinion there is one kind of remembered fact—religious facts—which stands an unusually good

chance of having been preserved with accuracy and exactitude in the Roman memory. The weight of religious tradition and the temple archives allow almost no doubt as to the fidelity of such recollections. Partisan feelings and the distorting influence of the *gentes'* pride only contrived to modify the details of these accounts, not their substance. Now, the number and kind of cults which appeared in Rome between 509 and 475 B.C. are very revealing. The great temple of the Capitoline Triad was consecrated in 509, that of Saturn, an ancient Italic deity, in 496; that of Ceres, Liber and Libera in 493. Mercury, god of trade, was built a temple near the Porta Capena in 495 and in 484 the Dioscuri installed themselves in their temple on the Forum. This is an impressive series of buildings. During the whole of the rest of the century we know of the founding of only two temples, that of Dius Fidius in 466, and that of Apollo in 431. It is hard to imagine that so many sanctuaries would have been built in this short period and with such costly decorations, one at least executed under the direction of great Greek artists, at a time when Rome had just been abandoned and was entering on a period of difficulty and austerity.

The character of the newly instituted cults is no less significant. The triads of Jupiter, Juno and Minerva on the one hand and Ceres, Liber and Libera on the other have a Tyrrhenian appearance, while the god Saturn was of Italic origin. The cult of the Dioscuri came from the Etrusco-Latin town of Tusculum. Lastly the temples of the agrarian divinities and of Mercury, situated close to each other, were patronized by the plebs, who looked to these gods for protection and guidance. In fact, the sanctuary of Ceres, Liber and Libera on the Aventine became the religious centre of the plebeian community. All these important facts become explicable, it seems to me, if the Etruscan leaders had not yet left Rome and were left continuing to support the plebs against the landed proprietors of Latin stock. The latter reacted violently as soon as the Etruscans left, in about 475. This view also renders explicable a curious aspect of classical Rome: of the consuls at the beginning of the Republic, a certain number, among whom were Spurius Cassius and Junius Brutus, came from plebeian families. If at the beginning of the consular magistrature the Etruscans were still present, as I believe, they could have allowed the plebs to elect some of their most outstanding representatives into office.

In fact, Rome's history during the first quarter of the fifth century seems in every way similar to that of Latium as a whole and Etruria. Here again archaeology provides us with reliable data. Despite the inadequacy of the excavations undertaken in many Latin towns and the fact that some of them were carried out some time ago we possess, for this period, important fragments of cult-statues, many architec-tonic terracottas from Lanuvium, Satricum near Antium, and Civita Castellana. Thus the Latin and Faliscan towns also went through a period of great activity in religious building at the beginning of the fifth century, just as Rome did; as at Rome, the character of the decoration of the Latin sanctuaries is typically Etruscan, or sometimes, as at Satricum, Etrusco-Greek. It is hard to imagine that this architectural and religious boom, which stopped soon after in both the Latin cities and Rome, could have followed the Etruscans' departure. It is much more likely that it preceded it.

The conclusion suggested by all this seems clear. The evolution of a political system, in the sense of the Republic, at Rome must have begun towards the end of the sixth century; and, as aforesaid, the change from a royalty of a sacred character to a régime in which power was exercised, collegially or not, by magistrates nomi-nated for varying periods was a phen-omenon common to numerous Latin, Etruscan and Osco-Umbrian cities, far from being peculiar to Rome. Here and there the *rex* was replaced by a simple, supreme magistrate or a pair of magistrates in the form of praetors or consuls. There is therefore no reason to doubt that such a transformation did in fact take place in Rome at the end of the sixth century; the consuls had, moreover, a power which Livy calls the *regium imperium*. On the other hand, the final departure of the Etruscans did not take place until about thirty years later. Thus the Ancients, and after them the Moderns, fused together two separate sequences of events which, as I have tried to show elsewhere, took place at different times: the beginnings of a régime with republican tendencies on the one hand and the departure of the Etruscan tyrants on the other. This throws a new light on a crucial period for Rome which the classical historians, unable to understand close or distant relationships between cities and regions of ancient Italy, wrongly simplified.

5. The Value of the Tradition

Until the seventeenth century, the traditions of early Roman history were accepted without question, but then scholars began to look at them with a critical eye. Scepticism was carried to its extreme in the nineteenth century by the great German scholar Theodor Mommsen, who did not even trouble to recount the stories in his history of Rome. On the other hand, even in the seventeenth century some scholars suspected that there might be some foundation to the tradition in the form of folk epics and in the *Annales Maximi*, written records kept annually by the *pontifex maximus*. This view, that there is historical truth in the tradition, still has its champions, the most forceful of whom is Luigi Pareti.

THE CASE FOR BELIEF*

Whoever sets out to study the history of Rome for the archaic period cannot free himself from answering a preliminary and essential question on which every interpretive possibility depends. How and when did the information arise, and what value does it have? I mean the information from which the first annalists reconstructed the development of the life, institutions, and military fortunes of the city before the period in which they began their work, that is, before the Punic Wars. To answer such a fundamental question, it is necessary to investigate severally the origin and likely value of each of the possible categories of information which the first annalists used. These are: epic and epico-lyric songs that were utilized and retouched even by the first poets, such as Naevius and then Ennius; documents, official registrations, and compilations; genealogies, monumental records, epitaphs, and laudations of a private character; sparse references in the literary works of the Greek world, both metropolitan and colonial, especially in the historical and geographical epics; similar references in the literatures of other peoples of elevated culture, such as the Etruscans and Oscans; authentic oral tradition and learned pseudo-tradition (deduced by explaining linguistic, inconographic elements, etc.); anonymous legends that come together at Rome, and even, if they are not excluded *a priori*, some intentional falsifications.

Roman life with its successive wars of defense and of conquest was the material of heroism. With its unforeseen crises and its more fortunate successes it certainly constituted one of those experiences that is typically ambient, proud, and warlike, in love with glory and strife, in which the epic spontaneously manifests itself and

takes root, whether through the inclinations of the people or because of the subjects which the vicissitudes of the people themselves furnish. That a good part of the history of Rome in the first centuries has been collected and formulated chiefly by the popular epic is a truth already perceived by Perizonius (1685) and by Vico (1710), and then demonstrated especially in their historical treatises by Niebuhr and Gaetano de Sanctis. Cicero wrote in the *Brutus* (19.75): "Would that those songs still survived which Cato, in his *Origins*, records were sung at banquets many generations before his own time by individual diners in praise of illustrious men." Cicero, it is evident, did not mean to say that these songs existed *only* many centuries before Cato, because, in fact, still in the time of Dionysius of Halicarnassus "*Hymnoi patrioi*" [Patriotic hymns] were sung, for example, the tales of Romulus and Coriolanus. He laments that they have been lost because they were not transmitted in writing to posterity, especially the oldest, or edited in the original and genuine form that they had in the time of the first singers. How these songs were usually presented, at least in the more recent period, we are told by a passage in Varro, cited in a truncated form by Nonius (a grammarian to whom only its locution was of interest), but it is integrally reconstructible by using other quotations: "[the ancients were invited as table companions when] boys [were also present] at the banquets because there were sung aloud to the accompaniment of a flute the ancient songs containing the praises of their ancestors."

Themes, then, were handed down from generation to generation, normally orally. Therefore they had to undergo the fate of all popular epics: to collect, along with the parts that memory preserved, episodes and variants due to the extemporaneous imagination of successive singers and to the fusion with other poetic themes. But that their origin was very archaic, as Cato has

---

* Luigi Pareti, *Storia di Roma*, translated by Donald Kagan (Torino: Unione Tipografico—Editrice Torinese, 1952), Vol. 1, pp. 3-7; 56-57. Reprinted by permission of the publisher.

it, there is no reason to doubt, because we are told so much of the content of Rome's vicissitudes, worthy of an epic, and because in the seventh and sixth centuries the city was dominated by the Etruscans—who were already sufficiently developed in their artistic and literary evolution, by their own talent and through Greek influence—that they both knew the Greek epic and they themselves had productions of that type. If the use of epic songs which were more or less extemporaneous endured, even when the ancient traditions and sagas had been sung by poets like Naevius and Ennius and recounted in the *Annals* of the first writers of history, for centuries, it is easy to understand that they must have appeared all the more affecting when they still constituted the only fundamental glorification of the deeds of the past. Certainly, in a manner not different from what happens in all the analogous manifestations of popular epic poetry, we must imagine that the contents of these songs had to undergo a degree of deformation and amplification in the course of time. But in our judgment all contingencies acted in the opposite sense, in the direction of their preservation: the knowledge of writing at Rome *ab antiquo*, at least from the end of the eighth century, which would have permitted their fixing in writing from the earliest times, when the singers were at the same time the creators of these *carmina*, wholly or in epitome for the use of themselves or their families and friends; the not excessively imaginative Roman mind which had less need of bridling than that of the Greek poets; and the fact that these sagas, in distinction from what befell the Homeric epics and the later Carolingian ones, did not change their strictly epic character into epic-romance through fusion with other types of poetry and popular legend. With this we have implicitly said how great is the general historical credibility that we are disposed to attribute to the *primitive* Roman epic, even if, on the other hand, we

admit that it has idealized, magnified, or simplified reality, has inserted much that is ornamental and fantastic and beclouded chronological precision; and this popular genre, transmitted for centuries from person to person, has undergone retouching, additions and suppressions. But with all that, in general, it may have preserved a percentage of objective truth a good deal greater than poems, perhaps richer in art, such as the *Iliad* or *Orlando Furioso*, in which the elements of romance and fantasy have almost negated the concrete historical nucleus.

In any case, it remains for us a solid truth that at Rome through the centuries there developed a popular epic production and that in its contents were gathered in large part reports of the city, its life, and its most famous personages for the era before the emergence of a national historiography. If even to-day, reading the first books of the history of Livy in which the narrations of the *Annalists* are collected, we find ourselves confronted again and again with tales that are of poetical color and power, overflowing with patriotism and greatness of spirit of the youth of Romulus, of the rape of the Sabines, the punishment of Tarpeia, the conversations of Numa with the nymph Egeria, the duel of the Horatii and the Curiatii, the punishment of the traitor Mettius Fuffetius, the wisdom of Servius Tullius, the arrogance of Superbus, the undertaking of Porsenna from which derive the heroism of Horatius Cocles and Mucius Scaevola and Cloelius, the perilous battles of Regillus and Cremera, the glorious end of the Fabii and the long siege of Veii, of Cincinnatus and Coriolanus, of Virginia and the Decemvirs, of Brennus and Camillus . . . and of a hundred other episodes, the obvious explanation for this undeniable fact is that to the early annalists, as to the early poets of artificial epics [such as Naevius and Ennius and as opposed to the anonymous folk epics], coeval with them or a little earlier, there flowed the contents of old epic songs that formed the woof, for some of a native prose chronicle, for others, of the first poems of artistic pretension and national purpose.

[Analysis of other kinds of sources follows.]

* * *

Is it possible, after having said so much on the development of the Roman historiographic tradition, to try a reconstruction that is close to the truth of the historical development of the city and of its struggles for life and hegemony before the Punic Wars? We believe that it can be done methodically, avoiding at once the tendency to destroy the tradition at any cost, to the point of no longer being able to say anything concrete, and its opposite, the tendency supinely to repeat all the data of Livy and the other writers of antiquity without seeking to separate the true from the possible and from the absurd. One of our fundamental criteria will be, since it is logically impossible that the history of Rome has been *genuinely* transmitted in a more diffuse manner for the more remote periods and in a more succinct manner for the intermediate ones, that anomaly has its origins in a greater fantastic superstructure for the period of the beginnings. For this period, on the contrary, we must be content to be able to trace a very summary picture, separating in the traditional accounts how much is fundamental and more tenaciously transmittible and susceptible of proof from what is surely tenuous addition, whether by the poets, family glorifications, or priestly and learned inventions. But we are unable to deny that a basic nucleus of truth may be arrived at before the time of the first annalists because we believe in the existence of a popular Roman epic and in writing as far back as the eighth century, and therefore in precocious documents both authentic and preservable; because we also affirm that the first indigenous semi-historiographical publication was born at least a century and a half before Fabius Pictor with the reconstruction of the *Annales Maximi*; because, at last, we know that some weighty annalists like Cato profited not only from Greek historiography but also from the native type of the Etruscans.

We must, then, be content in principle with a history in broad outline. But it assumes greater detail at those points where authentic documents were at the base of the tradition, or where secure elements are furnished by archaeological or linguistic data, etc., scientifically validated.

6. THE CASE FOR SCEPTICISM*

The modern school of sceptical scholars is not so arbitrary as was Mommsen. It does not deny categorically the possibility that reliable information may be contained in the tradition. It is, however, very doubtful that much can be depended upon. One of the greatest of its adherents is Plinio Fraccaro, who responds to the optimism of Pareti by questioning the sources on which the tradition is based.

When we consider the information concerning the history of the earliest days of Rome which ancient authors have

---

* Plinio Fraccaro, "The History of Rome in the Regal Period," *Journal of Roman Studies*, 47 (London: Society for the Promotion of Roman Studies, 1957), pp. 59–65, translated by Ursula Erwins. Reprinted by permission of the publisher.

handed down to us, we have to ask ourselves: which parts of it are acceptable and which are not? What, after all, do we really know about early Roman history?

Modern scholars view these problems from very different psychological standpoints. Some of them ask why we should refuse credence to a venerable tradition which has been given an artistic form of great beauty by writers of genius, and which is full of lessons of political and moral importance. Others, however, seized with the full frenzy of the critic, and with uncompromising devotion to logic, discard all, or practically all, the tradition. Whatever the cost, they intend to reach the truth. These two conflicting tendencies prevail turn and turn about in accordance with the views dominating in different periods or with the different temperaments or ages of individual scholars. The situation becomes an almost painful one when a scholar has to take up a position in public, and in particular when he wishes to narrate, rather than to discuss, the early history of Rome. In these circumstances the better procedure is that of those historians who choose to recount the tradition first, to follow this with criticism of the tradition, and after such criticism, possibly ruthless, to build a reconstruction on the few elements which have been salvaged, as Ettore Pais did, especially in the first edition of his *Storia di Roma*. In this way the tradition does not disappear altogether; it is at least recounted before it is rejected. More difficult decisions have to be taken by one who intends to tell the story without first offering an exposition and critical analysis of the tradition. For example, in his *Römische Geschichte* Mommsen displays remarkable scepticism and takes no account at all of the traditional stories of the individual Roman kings, although he deals fully with the monarchy as an institution, attributes the Servian constitution to the regal period, and accepts the fact of the expulsion of the kings, which has been 'spun out into a legend' in our sources. The detailed accounts of the kings are for Mommsen all 'fables', 'die Sage, die für alles einen Ursprung weiss' (p. 47), 'quasi Historie.' In the first volume of his work the development and the civilization of early Rome and of the peoples who were in contact with her

have been reconstructed with the help of elements from other sources, differing from those derived from the historiographical tradition.

The distrust with which the Romans' own account of the earliest years of their city is viewed stems from the obviously legendary character of much of its contents and from the impression which other parts give of being explanations, worked up some time later, of rites, ceremonies, and monuments of which the origin had been forgotten. This distrust, however, comes also from a failure to see how detailed accounts of events which happened before the third century could have been handed down to the end of that century, when the Romans first began to write *annales*, began, that is, to arrange the information at their disposal year by year, with the help of the list of magistrates. To counter this second reason for scepticism, or to weaken its force, people have tried to think of some means or other by which information about the period of the monarchy or the early Republic could have reached the annalists of the end of the third century.

One possible vehicle was the subject of the well-known theory of Niebuhr, who thought of going back to the *carmina* which used to be sung to the accompaniment of flutes, in accordance with an ancient *mos epularum* recorded by Cato in the *Origines*, and which celebrated 'clarorum virorum laudes et virtutes'. This practice dated to a period some centuries before the time of Cato himself (Cic., *Br*. 75: 'multis saeculis ante suam aetatem') and therefore these *carmina* were not known to Cato, nor, it would seem, to the oldest annalists. Although Niebuhr's theory was not wellreceived, it was taken up by De Sanctis. For example, in discussing the story of Verginia he says: 'the pure strain of popular poetry is apparent in the story of Verginia' (*Storia dei Romani* II, 47). He is obviously using a very subjective standard of criticism. No one knows what these songs sung by Roman aristocrats at their banquets were like; but they were certainly in celebration of feats of war, not tragedies like that of Verginia, and they were based on simple themes that were easy to take up again. But recently this theory has been revived by the pupil of De Sanctis, Luigi Pareti.

Pareti, a student of ancient history who has won wide renown, has been publishing in the last few years (1952 and later) a full *Storia di Roma*, of which four volumes have already appeared, taking the account down to the accession of Vespasian. In *Athenaeum* xxx (1952), 142, I published a lengthy review of the first two volumes of the work. Pareti replied indirectly to the points I had made when, in a supplement to the Roman weekly, *Idea*, of 25th November, 1956, he discussed the paper entitled 'La storia romana arcaica' which I read at the inaugural meeting of the Istituto Lombardo di Scienze e Lettere in 1952.

There are two points of disagreement between Pareti and myself. One concerns the 'ancient heroic verse', which I did not mention in my paper, 'probably,' says Pareti, 'because he discounts it.' I do not either discount or value something about which nothing is known. Pareti thinks that 'the plots of such *carmina* could later have been handed down in writing, as well as orally'. Cicero says, however, *utinam extarent*, that is, he only knew of such songs from Cato. 'Even to-day,' writes Pareti, 'when we re-read the first books of Livy's History in which is collected the material of the annalists, we certainly find ourselves again and again in the presence of stories of poetical colour and power, overflowing with love of country and greatness of spirit. The obvious explanation of this undeniable fact is that the earliest serious epic poets, Naevius and Ennius, and the earliest annalists who were their contemporaries used material which was derived from the ancient popular heroic verse.'

I have quoted the words of Pareti in full, but I do not think that there is any point in discussing the matter further, since I believe that the vast majority of scholars are in agreement that this theory of Niebuhr, De Sanctis, and Pareti has no solid basis. A fuller examination, on the other hand, should be given to Pareti's other theory, concerning the *Annales Maximi*. According to Pareti the Roman annalistic tradition did not begin at the end of the third century. This, he maintains, is a false assumption, 'although it has been accepted as self-evident by those scholars to whom it should have appeared most awkward'. The tradition, he thinks, goes back to the *tabulae dealbatae* on which the Pontifices 'from the very beginning of the Republic noted everything of importance, whatever its nature, which happened in the course of the year, and which, after the destruction of the first set in the sack of Rome by the Gauls, were at once afterwards reconstructed by the Pontifices in their main outlines and were published in annalistic form, as *Annales Maximi*, with a preface concerning the regal period'.

The elder Cato does not seem to have had the same opinion as Pareti about the records made by the Pontifices; for he says that he does not wish to put into his *Origines* matters of no interest, like the price of corn or the changes in the heavenly bodies noted in the records of the Pontifices: 'Non lubet scribere, quod in tabula apud pontificem maximum est, quotient annona cara, quotiens lunae aut solis lumine caligo aut quid obstiterit' (Gellius 11, 28, 6). It is indeed probable that on the *tabula* there was recorded above all information of practical importance, for the benefit especially of Roman farmers, and this would include notes of the phases of the moon and eclipses.

We gain a somewhat different impression of the records of the Pontifices from the famous passage of Cicero, *De Or*, 11, 52. It appears that in the time of Cicero the *tabula dealbata* was no longer displayed. According to Cicero the Pontifex used to write on the boards *res omnes singulorum annorum* and used to expose these in public so that whoever wanted to might gain information from them. Servius Auctus on *Aen.* 1, 373, gives us a more detailed account: on the *tabula* there were put first the names of the consuls and of the other magistrates and afterwards 'digna memoratu ... domi militiaeque terra marique gesta', and these 'per singulos dies', that is, with a precise date.

It is difficult to explain why, if it contained all this, Cato spoke so slightingly of the *tabula* of the Pontifices and of its humdrum contents. Cicero continues by saying that the first Roman annalists followed the *similitudo scribendi* of the *tabulae pontificales*, recording 'sine ullis ornamentis monumenta solum temporum, hominum, locorum gestarumque rerum'; that is, the annals of the earliest historians were not very different from the *annales* of the Pontifices, about which Cicero himself says (*De Leg.* 1, 2, 5): 'nihil potest esse ieiunius' (considering them from the point of view of history as the work of the literary artist). There are two other pieces of information. Cicero, in the passage of the *De Oratore* already referred to, says that the record-keeping of the Pontifices ran 'ab initio rerum Romanarum usque ad P. Mucium pontificem maximum' (Pontifex from 130, Consul in 133 B.C.), and Servius, after the passage already referred to describing what the Pontifex Maximus did, continues 'cuius diligenitae annuos commentarios in octoginta libros veteres rettulerunt' and says that these were called *Annales Maximi*. This information is taken to mean that Scaevola stopped the publication of the *tabulae* and filled eighty books with a transcription of the *tabulae* down to that date.

Pareti, however, thinks that the publication did not take place on one single occasion, on the initiative of Scaevola, but at different periods. Ennius and Cato would therefore have known the work. But Cato speaks of the *tabula*, not of the *Annales Maximi*, and Cicero, *De re p.* 1, 16, 25, says that the eclipse which Ennius mentioned as happening 350 years *post Romam conditam* was recorded also in the *Annales Maximi*; which does not prove that Ennius himself took it from *tabulae* already published in book form.

The idea which we have been able to form of this publication of the *tabulae* is not in harmony with the statement of Servius that it comprised eighty books. Even allowing for considerable variation, one book must have had a certain length, and an enormous amount of material must have been needed to fill eighty books. (Livy reached the period of Scaevola, which is roughly that of the tribunate of Tiberius Gracchus, in fifty-nine books.) We cannot, therefore, have to deal with a simple collection of *tabulae*, even one of several hundred of yearly *tabulae*.

In this connection it would be interesting if we could discover how in practice these *tabulae* were used by the Pontifices. Originally their pronouncements must have been made orally, as we see from Varro (*De L. L.* v, 27) was the case with the proclamation of the Nones. When the change was made to written notification (we do not know the date of this change and it may have been a gradual one) a really large whitened board was certainly needed for an indication in legible characters of a considerable amount of material. I do not think it likely that at the end of a year a new whitened board was prepared for the following year while the old one was stored in the *Regia*. Some people seem to believe that at the time of Scaevola there were preserved hundreds of *tabulae*; even Pareti speaks of the 'first set of the *tabulae*' destroyed in the sack by the Gauls. But the *Regia* still exists, a tiny building which would never have contained such a mass of material. We may therefore suppose that from a certain date the Pontifices before rewhitening the *tabula* began to note on a *codex* such information from the record of the preceding year as they thought should be preserved. They did not, as we might think, do this primarily in order to store the information for historical purposes, but above all to preserve the memory of particular matters which had a bearing on the duties of the Pontifices, which were complicated and often obscure. This would explain why the few quotations which we have from the *Annales Maximi* refer to matters of religious or constitutional importance. For example, the story which Gellius IV, 5, obtained from Verrius Flaccus, and which came from the eleventh book of the *Annales Maximi* (of which it is the longest fragment preserved for us), deals with the expiation of a *prodigium*, for which Etruscan *aruspices* were summoned. As Beloch observed (*Röm. Gesch.* 103), this must have happened at a time when the Etruscan cities were, in general, under Roman control; that is, after 300 B.C. This would suggest that the books of the *Annales Maximi* later than the tenth contained material from about 300 B.C. This little story could not have appeared in the *tabula*, but must have been contained among the notes which the Pontifices added to particular incidents, notes which could have been extended without limit and go back to the most remote past. Vopiscus, *Vita Taciti* I, 1, tells us that the Pontifices 'penes quos scribendae historiae potestas fuit' had written that at the death of Romulus, the good king, the *interregnum* was instituted, in order to find another good king. If, as appears probable, we ought to read ἀρχιερεῦσι in the text of Dionysius I, 74, then in the records (πίναξ) of the Pontifices the foundation of Rome was placed in the second year of the seventh Olympiad, and naturally this had never been recorded on the *tabula dealbata*.

If the quotations in the *Origo gentis Romanae* are to be considered genuine, as Pareti seems to believe, the legends of Alba and the Alban kings were told in the fourth book of the *Annales Maximi*, and with particular attention to the miraculous.

We are dealing, therefore, with material of late date.

This also explains why the collection of pontifical records, chronologically arranged, came to grow beyond all measure, and reached eighty books by about 130 B.C. The story of the Etruscan *aruspices* allows us to see with what material it grew. We can also see why this history of histories, which modern writers so often invoke, was used so little by the ancient historians. Neither Livy nor Dionysius, if we except the passage already referred to where the text is not quite certain, mentions them; nor do the grammarians and antiquarians whose works survive, except for Verrius Flaccus; the one historian who does quote them, three times, is the author of the *Origo gentis Romanae*.

When did this record-keeping begin? We do not know. 'Ab initio rerum Romanarum,' says Cicero, and the *Origo* would confirm this in making the accounts in the *Annales Maximi* go back to the foundation of Alba.

The one piece of evidence with which a date is associated is the well-known passage of *De re p.* I, 16, 25, on eclipses. Ennius (*Ann.* fr. 163, Vahlen) recorded that:

anno quinquagesimo CCC fere post Romam conditam
Nonis Iunis soli luna obstitit et nox.

Atque hac in re tanta inest ratio atque sollertia, ut ex hoc die, quem apud Ennium et in maximis annalibus consignatum videmus, superiores solis defectiones reputatae sint usque ad illam, quae Nonis Quinctilibus fuit regnante Romulo.

According to the manuscript of the *De re p.*, Ennius dated the eclipse about 350 years *ab urbe condita*; that is, about 404 B.C. Beloch therefore suggested the reading CCCCL and the identification with the eclipse of 13th June (5th June in the Roman calendar) of 288, certainly visible from Rome (*Hermes* LVII, 1922, 123; *Röm. Gesch.* 92). Since this eclipse came to be used as a point of departure for the calculation of other eclipses, going back to the time of Romulus, Beloch thought it must have been the first recorded in the *Annales Maximi* (cf. Stuart Jones in *CAH* VII, 320). This is borne out by the fact that Livy only occasionally mentions prodigies in his first nine books, while in the tenth he records them in chapters 23 and 31 for 296 and 295 B.C.

The records of the Pontifices, therefore, had their beginning about 300 B.C., as a consequence, according to Beloch, of the reorganization of the college of Pontifices after the *Lex Ogulnia* of 300, which opened it and the college of augurs to the Plebs. Beloch reached the same result in investigating the reliability of the dates of triumphs (*Röm. Gesch.* 88), which are fixed from the end of the fourth century. The consular Fasti themselves are reliable from 300 B.C. The genuine records of the Pontifices must go back to this period.

Whatever value we wish to give to these acute observations of Beloch, it is certain in any case that we do not know when the *tabula dealbata* was first displayed.

When Pareti says that the *tabulae dealbatae* were destroyed in the sack of Rome by the Gauls but were at once afterwards reconstructed by the Pontifices in their main outlines, and so on, he is saying something for which there is not the slightest evidence. The unknown annalist Clodius, quoted by Plutarch, *Numa* I, said that the ancient ἀναγραφαί had disappeared in the Gallic sack and that their place had been taken by others containing falsifications in favour of individuals who were later of importance; Livy VI, 1, 9, thought that after the Gallic disaster an attempt was made to search out laws and treaties while the Pontifices, on the other hand, kept private even such prescriptions as had been preserved in order to conduct the rites as they pleased in the future. But no author mentions historical works.

Pareti accuses me of having too much confidence in a tradition which, in my view, was first put into writing from three to five centuries after the events it describes took place. This is not quite how things stand. Leaving aside the five-century interval and the events of the earlier part of the regal period, the events of the first years of the Republic would have been put into writing 300 years later. Now the first thing to bear in mind is that we are considering a trustworthiness which is admittedly only relative. For example, I accept as approximately right the Polybian dating of the first treaty between Rome and Carthage, but neither I nor others would stake a penny to back this opinion. A number of considerations makes us think that this dating is tenable and probable, but nothing more. Besides this, a number of facts have been associated with names in the list of eponymous magistrates and their dating is therefore almost certain: for example, the laws of the Twelve Tables, the capture of Veii, the sack of Rome by the Gauls. Several public and private documents which recorded events in the earliest period must have escaped destruction by the Gauls, and we have examples of these.

But these are only isolated facts, furnishing evidence of a very scanty nature. Now on the other hand, an attempt is being made to find in the *Annales Maximi* the historical basis of our accounts and this is not likely. At the centre of accretions of legend lie some historical facts of the fifth century B.C. of great importance, and the legends themselves are certainly often ancient and revealing, but the rest of the story was embroidered by the annalists in order to form a continuous and readable narrative. The earliest annals were, as Cicero says, *exiliter scripti*, and we are made aware of this whenever quotations are given with an indication of the book from which they come. This allows us to see the length to which the account ran. On this point Beloch's excellent discussion (*Röm. Gesch.* 95) should be consulted. The fuller treatment of the material of the annals is found for the first time in Cn. Gellius, who seems to have been writing about 100 B.C. The enrichment of material did not depend on the publication of the *Annales Maximi* but on the new tendency in historical writing to give a literary form and a richness of detail to the events narrated.

Anyone who wishes may believe with Pareti (I take my example from his *Storia*, p. 373) that Coriolanus was condemned by eleven tribes and acquitted by nine. I am convinced that Spurius Cassius fell for reasons of internal politics; it is very likely that, as Diodorus says, he was accused of aiming at tyranny, but we know nothing more about it. Livy himself, II, 41, 10, says so: 'ubi primum magistratu abiit, damnatum necatumque constat.' Everything else in Livy is obviously a later addition, and the opposing conjectures which he gives show that he knew nothing about the end of Spurius Cassius beyond the simple fact of his violent death.

Let us now turn to the period of the kings. Pareti, as we have seen, holds that, when the *tabulae* were reconstructed after the Gallic invasion, the Pontifices prefaced to them an account of the regal period, which had come to an end little more than a century earlier. If we are to accept the quotations in the *Origo*, we have to think of a preface of huge dimensions, since in the fourth book the subject was still the Alban kings.

It is a long time since Luigi Pareti and I read, in amazement, and, at least for my part, in admiration, in the first edition of Pais' historical work, that the kings were either the gods of the Roman hills or doubles one of another. (There are several cases in ancient history of local deities who have been made into kings; the difficulty consisted in giving proof of such transformations.) We have devoted many years to scholarship and now good sense finally gains the day, not over the critical spirit, but in it, for the moderation and detachment which grow stronger in us with

maturity and age bring restraint even into our critical activity as scholars.

It is certain that from very early times not a few legends about the Roman kings were in existence, and we can see this from the fragments of the oldest annalists. We can tell that there was quite a full treatment of the period of the kings compared with that of the early Republic. It is more than likely that the Pontifices elaborated considerably the accounts of the regal period, to trace there the origins of the religious, social, and political life of the city. But in doing this they were not contributing to history: if anything they were inventing it. For this reason I consider the view that the Pontifices of the period of the Gallic invasion wrote a preface, of a historical nature, on the period of the kings a mere fantasy (though one may adopt it in order to salvage information which one is sorry to have to abandon). It is hard to believe that in those days there existed at Rome a historical sense like that which developed in Greece, and in Rome later on, and in modern times. For the study of the earliest Roman history there are few books as instructive as Jacoby's *Atthis*, on the chronicles of early Athens. Jacoby has shown that the pre-literary chronicles of Ionia and of Athens and the chronicle of the *exegetai* imagined by Wilamowitz are modern fantasies; apart from a few documents there existed only an oral tradition, first put into written form by Herodotus.

The history of the kings of Rome has to be considered with a certain scepticism, but at the same time with a degree of optimism. We have the names of seven or eight kings. Are these all who reigned at Rome? We shall never know. Romulus is generally considered to be the eponym of the city; but *Romulii* existed at Rome from the very earliest times, and we are at liberty to believe that even Romulus may have been a historical personage. The other names I consider 'some at least of those who did in fact rule at Rome'. This is the way Pareti expresses my views, and it is substantially correct. But it must be understood in this sense: we have no means of proving (at least it has not so far been proved) that these kings were not real human kings, and that the Tarquins were one and not two. We should, therefore, allow these kings to keep their place in the history which we recount.

The same thing has to be said about the acts attributed to some of the kings by the tradition. We do not know how and why the name of Tullus Hostilius was associated with the destruction of Alba, but there is no reason for us to deny the association, and therefore, though we retain some doubts, we accept it. The archaeologists, who now and again refuse to accept the traditional account, have uncovered at Ostia the walls of the *oppidum* of the fourth century, but we cannot prove that these walls were those of the first Roman fortification placed to guard the port at the mouth of the Tiber, so that there is no reason to deny the connection between Ancus Martius and Ostia recorded in the tradition. The tradition does not tell us who, and at which point in the history of the Republic, gave to the Roman state its organization by classes and centuries, an organization which, on the other hand, seems to be presupposed in the Twelve Tables. It does not seem likely that such an important fact would have been lost from the tradition of the Republican age to be carried back into the period of the monarchy. Therefore, I have maintained that this organization could very well go back to one of the last kings, perhaps even to Servius Tullius, in some primitive form which we can no longer discern. Similarly, we may accept the statements about the building in the regal period of the Capitoline temple, the temple of Diana (marking the supremacy of Rome in Latium), of some stretches of the Cloaca Maxima, of a wall in tufa built around the enlarged city towards the end of the monarchical period, and so on. Also, since by the beginning of the Republican period the territory of Rome

was that of the sixteen rustic tribes, and much more extensive than it had been originally, it is evident that this land was acquired for Rome by the kings. When, however, I read in our sources that individual kings conquered, once or several times, the individual cities near Rome, then I do not place reliance on the individual statements, since I am not convinced that these statements had, even in antiquity, any foundation.

Similarly, as I have said, I accept the Polybian dating of the first treaty with Carthage, since it seems that the position of the Roman state in the first years of the Republic corresponds better with the clauses of the treaty. Polybius says that the Romans attributed it to the first consuls of the Republic, Brutus and M. Horatius. Was the name of Horatius in the treaty, as it was in documents relating to the Capitoline temple? The account by the Greeks of Campania of the struggles with the Etruscans in Campania and Latium helps us to envisage what happened at Rome in the transition from the regal to the Republican period, an event which is seriously obscured in the Roman tradition.

It is plain that in these cases we are dealing with state institutions or important historical facts, the memory of which, as I have said, could not have been erased from the tradition of the Republican period in order to carry it back to the regal period; or we are dealing with monuments of very great importance, with which the name of a king who built them could have remained permanently associated.

Pareti says that my confidence is excessive in a tradition which, if the chronicles of the Pontifices did not go back to the regal period, must have been put into writing from three to five hundred years after the events took place. If we were certain that from 600 to 200 B.C. no one ever wrote at all in Rome, the criticism would be serious: 400 years of oral tradition would be too many even for a relatively small city with a limited and traditionally-minded aristocracy, in which the remembrance of matters of state which were of direct importance to the families could have been long preserved. But we cannot be sure of this. Just as the name of the consul Horatius, the one historical personage among the legendary figures of the first year of the Republic, was preserved as it was connected with the dedication of the Capitoline temple, so the names of certain kings could have been preserved in very old inscriptions relating to certain events or buildings of which no trace has been preserved for us. Surely, for example, there stood in the Forum the column of bronze with the treaty of Spurius Cassius and the Latins inscribed upon it? (Cic., *Balb.* 23, 53). Very old documents and records, both public and private, could have been preserved by the families themselves, for it is one thing to feel a historian's interest and to write history, and another to preserve the memory of such deeds and events as are of personal interest. If, therefore, we cannot swear to the historicity of certain happenings of the regal period, neither can we deny it just because we cannot be sure how the record of them was preserved. Even for the fundamental facts we have only a greater or lesser probability, and never absolute certainty. These inquiries of ours into the very nature of the data we are forced to use cannot lead to more definite results.

I would therefore say that the most difficult virtue required by the historian of early Rome is that of being able to renounce the greater part of the information the ancients have handed down to us; next comes that of knowing how to interpret and illuminate the rest.

SECTION II

The Growth of the Roman Constitution:
The Institution of Consular Tribunes

THE DEVELOPMENT of the Roman republican constitution was a long and complicated process. No Roman imagined that it was designed by a single great lawgiver, such as Lycurgus or Solon. It was influenced by the native genius of the Roman people, of course, but two sets of circumstances were most influential in shaping it: the pressure of foreign affairs; and the domestic conflict between patricians and plebeians, which we call the struggle of the orders. An excellent example of the ways in which these forces molded the Roman constitution is provided by the institution in the mid-fifth century B.C. of the military tribunes with consular power. What were the conditions which led to the introduction of the new office? How trustworthy is our evidence? What were the true purposes of the reform? What were the results?

1. LIVY'S ACCOUNT*

The consuls who succeeded were M. Genucius and C. Curtius. The year was a troubled one both at home and abroad. In the beginning of the year C. Canuleius, a tribune of the plebs, introduced a law with regard to the intermarriage of patricians and plebeians. The patricians considered that their blood would be contaminated by it and the special rights of the houses thrown into confusion.

Then the tribunes began to throw out hints about one consul being elected from the plebs, and matters advanced so far that nine tribunes brought in a measure empowering the people to elect consuls from the plebeians or the patricians as they chose. The patricians believed that, if this were carried, the supreme power would not only be degraded by being shared with the lowest of the people, but would entirely pass away from the chief men in the State into the hands of the plebs.

The senate were not sorry, therefore, to hear that Ardea had revolted as a consequence of the unjust decision about the

* Livy, *History of Rome*, 4. 1–8, translated by Canon Roberts (New York: E. P. Dutton & Co. Inc.), pp. 222–232. Reprinted by permission of E. P. Dutton and J. M. Dent & Sons, London.

30

territory, that the Veientines had ravaged the districts on the Roman frontier, and that the Volscians and Ǣqui were protesting against the fortifying of Verrugo; so much did they prefer war, even when unsuccessful, to an ignominious peace.

On receiving these reports—which were somewhat exaggerated—the senate tried to drown the voice of the tribunes in the uproar of so many wars by ordering a levy to be made and all preparations for war pushed on with the utmost vigour, more so, if possible, than during the consulship of T. Quinctius. Thereupon C. Canuleius addressed the senate in a short and angry speech. It was, he said, useless for the consuls to hold out threats in the hope of distracting the attention of the plebs from the proposed law; as long as he was alive they should never hold a levy until the plebs had adopted the measures brought forward by himself and his colleagues. He at once convened an Assembly.

The consuls began to rouse the senate to take action against the tribunes, and at the same time the tribunes were getting up an agitation against the consuls. The consuls declared that the revolutionary proceedings of the tribunes could no longer be tolerated, matters had come to a crisis, there was a more bitter war going on at home than abroad. This was not the fault of the plebs so much as of the senate, nor of the tribunes more than of the consuls. Those things in a State which attain the highest development are those which are encouraged by rewards; it is thus that men become good citizens in times of peace, good soldiers in times of war. In Rome the greatest rewards are won by seditious agitations, these have always brought honour to men both individually and in the mass. Those present should reflect upon the greatness and dignity of the senate as they had received it from their fathers, and consider what they were going to hand on to their children, in order that they might be able to feel pride

in the extension and growth of its influence, as the plebs felt pride in theirs. There was no final settlement in sight, nor would there be as long as agitators were honoured in proportion to the success of their agitation. What enormous questions had C. Canuleius raised! He was advocating the breaking up of the houses, tampering with the auspices, both those of the State and those of individuals, so that nothing would be pure, nothing free from contamination, and in the effacing of all distinctions of rank, no one would know either himself or his kindred. What other result would mixed marriages have except to make unions between patricians and plebeians almost like the promiscuous association of animals? The offspring of such marriages would not know whose blood flowed in his veins, what sacred rites he might perform; half of him patrician, half plebeian, he would not even be in harmony with himself. And as though it were a small matter for all things human and divine to be thrown into confusion, the disturbers of the people were now making an onslaught on the consulship. At first the question of one consul being elected from the plebs was only mooted in private conversations, now a measure was brought forward giving the people power to elect consuls from either patricians or plebeians as they chose. And there was no shadow of doubt that they would elect all the most dangerous revolutionaries in the plebs; the Conuleii and the Icilii would be consuls. Might Jupiter Optimus Maximus never allow a power truly royal in its majesty to sink so low! They would rather die a thousand deaths than suffer such an ignominy to be perpetrated. Could their ancestors have divined that all their concessions only served to make the plebs more exacting, not more friendly, since their first success only emboldened them to make more and more urgent demands, it was quite certain that they would have gone any lengths in resistance sooner than allow these laws to be forced upon them.

Because a concession was once made in the matter of tribunes, it had been made again; there was no end to it. Tribunes of the plebs and the senate could not exist in the same State, either that office or this order (*i.e.* the nobility) must go. Their insolence and recklessness must be opposed, and better late than never. Were they to be allowed with impunity to stir up our neighbours to war by sowing the seeds of discord and then prevent the State from arming in its defence against those whom they had stirred up, and after all but summoning the enemy not allow armies to be enrolled against the enemy? Was Canuleius, forsooth, to have the audacity to give out before the senate that unless it was prepared to accept his conditions, like those of a conqueror, he would stop a levy being held? What else was that but threatening to betray his country and allowing it to be attacked and captured? What courage would his words inspire, not in the Roman plebs but in the Volscians and Æqui and Veientines! Would they not hope, with Canuleius as their leader, to be able to scale the Capitol and the Citadel, if the tribunes, after stripping the senate of its rights and its authority, deprived it also of its courage? The consuls were ready to be their leaders against criminal citizens before they led them against the enemy in arms.

At the very time when this was going on in the senate, Canuleius delivered the following speech in defence of his laws and in opposition to the consuls: "I fancy, Quirites, that I have often noticed in the past how greatly the patricians despise you, how unworthy they deem you to live in the same City, within the same walls, as they. Now, however, it is perfectly obvious, seeing how bitter an opposition they have raised to our proposed laws. For what is our purpose in framing them except to remind them that we are their fellow-citizens, and though we do not possess the same power, we still inhabit the same country? In one of these laws we demand the right of intermarriage, a right usually granted to neighbours and foreigners—indeed we have granted citizenship, which is more than intermarriage, even to a conquered enemy—in the other we are bringing forward nothing new, but simply demanding back what belongs to the people and claiming that the Roman people should confer its honours on whom it will. What possible reason is there why they should embroil heaven and earth, why recently in the Senate-house I was on the point of being subjected to personal violence, why they declare they will not keep their hands off, and threaten to attack our inviolable authority? Will this City be no longer able to stand, is our domination at an end, if a free vote is allowed to the Roman people so that they may entrust the consulship to whomsoever they will, and no plebeian may be shut out from the hope of attaining the highest honour if only he be worthy of the highest honour? Does the phrase 'Let no plebeian be made consul' mean just the same as 'No slave or freedman shall be consul'? Do you ever realise in what contempt you are living? They would rob you of your share in this daylight, if they could. They are indignant because you breathe and utter speech and wear the form of men. Why! Heaven forgive me, they actually say that it would be an act of impiety for a plebeian to be made consul! Though we are not allowed access to the 'Fasti' or the records of the pontiffs, do we not, pray, know what every stranger knows, that the consuls have simply taken the place of the kings, and possess no right or privilege which was not previously vested in the kings? I suppose you have never heard tell that Numa Pompilius, who was not only no patrician but not even a Roman citizen, was summoned from the land of the Sabines, and after being accepted by the people and confirmed by the senate, reigned as king of Rome? Or that, after him, L. Tarquinius, who belonged to no Roman house, not even to an Italian one, being the son of Demaratus of Corinth, who had settled in Tarquinii, was made king while the sons of Ancus were still alive? Or that, after him again, Servius Tullius, the illegitimate son of a female slave captured at Corniculum, gained the crown by sheer merit and ability? Why need I mention the Sabine Titus Tatius, with whom Romulus himself, the Father of the City, shared his throne? As long as no class of person in which conspicuous merit appeared was rejected, the Roman dominion grew. Are you then to regard a plebeian consul with disgust, when our ancestors showed no aversion to strangers as their kings? Not even after the expulsion of the kings was the City closed to foreign merit. The Claudian house, at all events, who migrated from the Sabines, was received by us not only into citizenship, but even into the ranks of the patricians. Shall a man who was an alien become a patrician and afterwards consul, and a Roman citizen, if he belongs to the plebs, be cut off from all hope of the consulship? Do we believe that it is impossible for a plebeian to be brave and energetic and capable both in peace and war, or if there be such a man, are we not to allow him to touch the helm of the State; are we to have, by preference, consuls like the decemvirs, those vilest of mortals—who, nevertheless, were all patricians—rather than men who resemble the best of the kings, new men though they were?

"But, I may be told, no consul, since the expulsion of the kings, has ever been elected from the plebs. What then? Ought no innovation ever to be introduced; and because a thing has not yet been done—and in a new community there are many things which have not yet been done—ought they not to be done, even when they are advantageous? In the reign of Romulus there were no pontiffs, no college of augurs; they were created by Numa Pompilius. There was no census in the State, no register of the centuries and classes; it was made by Servius Tullius. There were

never any consuls; when the kings had been expelled they were created. Neither the power nor the name of Dictator was in existence; it originated with the senate. There were no tribunes of the plebs, no ædiles, no quaestors; it was decided that these offices should be created. Within the last ten years we appointed decemvirs to commit the laws to writing and then we abolished their office. Who doubts that in a City built for all time and without any limits to its growth new authorities have to be established, new priesthoods, modifications in the rights and privileges of the houses as well as of individual citizens? Was not this very prohibition of intermarriage between patricians and plebeians, which inflicts such serious injury on the commonwealth and such a gross injustice on the plebs, made by the decemvirs within these last few years? Can there be a greater or more signal disgrace than for a part of the community to be held unworthy of intermarriage, as though contaminated? What is this but to suffer exile and banishment within the same walls? They are guarding against our becoming connected with them by affinity or relationship, against our blood being allied with theirs. Why, most of you are descended from Albans and Sabines, and that nobility of yours you hold not by birth or blood, but by co-optation into the patrician ranks, having been selected for that honour either by the kings, or after their expulsion by the mandate of the people. If your nobility is tainted by union with us, could you not have kept it pure by private regulations, by not seeking brides from the plebs, and not suffering your sisters or daughters to marry outside your order? No plebeian will offer violence to a patrician maiden, it is the patricians who indulge in those criminal practices. None of us would have compelled any one to enter into a marriage contract against his will. But, really, that this should be prohibited by law and the intermarriage of patricians and plebeians made impossible is indeed insulting to the plebs. Why do you not combine to forbid intermarriage between rich and poor? Everywhere and in all ages there has been an understanding that a woman might marry into any house in which she has been betrothed, and a man might marry from any house the woman to whom he has become engaged, and this understanding you are fettering by the manacles of a most insolent law, through which you may break up civil society and rend one State into two. Why do you not enact a law that no plebeian shall live in the neighbourhood of a patrician, or go along the same road, or take his place at the same banquet, or stand in the same Forum? For, as a matter of fact, what difference is there, if a patrician marries a plebeian woman or a plebeian marries a patrician? What rights are infringed, pray? Of course, the children follow the father. There is nothing that we are seeking in intermarriage with you, except that we may be reckoned amongst men and citizens; there is nothing for you to fight about, unless you delight in trying how far you can insult and degrade us.

"In a word, does the supreme power belong to you or to the Roman people? Did the expulsion of the kings mean absolute ascendancy for you or equal liberty for all? Is it right and proper for the Roman people to enact a law, if it wishes to do so, or are you going, whenever a measure is proposed, to order a levy by way of punishment? Am I to call the tribes up to vote, and as soon as I have begun, are you, the consuls, going to compel those who are liable for service to take the military oath, and then march them off to camp, threatening alike the plebs and the tribunes? Why, have you not on two occasions found out what your threats are worth against a united plebs? Was it, I wonder, in our interest that you abstained from an open conflict, or was it because the stronger party was also the more moderate one that there was no fighting? Nor will there be any conflict now,

Quirites; they will always try your courage, they will not test your strength.

"And so, consuls, the plebeians are ready to follow you to these wars, whether real or imaginary, on condition that by restoring the right of intermarriage you at last make this commonwealth a united one, that it be in their power to be allied with you by family ties, that the hope of attaining high office be granted to men of ability and energy, that it be open to them to be associated with you in taking their share of the government, and—which is the essence of equal liberty—to rule and obey in turn, in the annual succession of magistrates. If any one is going to obstruct these measures, you may talk about wars and exaggerate them by rumour, no one is going to give in his name, no one is going to take up arms, no one is going to fight for domineering masters with whom they have in public life no partnership in honours, and in private life no right of intermarriage."

After the two consuls had come forward into the Assembly, set speeches gave place to a personal altercation. The tribune asked why it was not right for a plebeian to be elected consul. The consuls gave a reply which, though perhaps true, was an unfortunate one in view of the present controversy. They said, "Because no plebeian could have the auspices, and the reason why the decemvirs had put an end to intermarriage was to prevent the auspices from being vitiated through the uncertainty of descent." This bitterly exasperated the plebeians, for they believed that they were held incompetent to take the auspices because they were hateful to the immortal gods. As they had got a most energetic leader in their tribune and were supporting him with the utmost determination, the controversy ended in the defeat of the patricians. They consented to the intermarriage law being passed, mainly in the belief that the tribunes would either abandon the struggle for plebeian consuls altogether, or would at least postpone it till after the war, and that the plebeians, contented with what they had gained, would be ready to enlist.

Owing to his victory over the patricians Canuleius was now immensely popular. Fired by his example, the other tribunes fought with the utmost energy to secure the passing of their measure, and though the rumours of war became more serious every day they obstructed the enlistment. As no business could be transacted in the senate owing to the intervention of the tribunes, the consuls held councils of the leaders at their own houses.

It was evident that they would have to yield the victory either to their foreign foes or to their own countrymen. Valerius and Horatius were the only men of consular rank who did not attend these councils. C. Claudius was in favour of empowering the consuls to use armed force against the tribunes; the Quinctii, Cincinnatus and Capitolinus, were averse from bloodshed or injury to those whom in their treaty with the plebs they had agreed to hold inviolable.

The result of their deliberations was that they allowed tribunes of the soldiers with consular powers to be elected from the patricians and plebeians indiscriminately; no change was made in the election of consuls. This arrangement satisfied the tribunes and it satisfied the plebs. Notice was published that an Assembly would be held for the election of three tribunes with consular powers. No sooner was this announcement made than everybody who had ever acted or spoken as a fomenter of sedition, especially those who had been tribunes, came forward as candidates, and began to bustle about the Forum, canvassing for votes. The patricians were at first deterred from seeking election, as in the exasperated mood of the plebeians they regarded their chances as hopeless, and were disgusted at the prospect of having to hold office with these men. At last, under compulsion from their leaders, lest they should appear to have withdrawn

from any share in the government, they consented to stand. The result of the election showed that when men are contending for liberty and the right to hold office their feelings are different from what they are when the contest is over and they can form an unbiassed judgement. The people were satisfied now that votes were allowed for plebeians, and they elected none but patricians. Where in these days will you find in a single individual the moderation, fairness, and loftiness of mind which then characterised the people as a whole?

The First Consular Tribunes. In the 310th year after the foundation of Rome (444 B.C.), military tribunes with consular powers for the first time took office. Their names were Aulus Sempronius Atratinus, L. Atilius, and T. Caecilius, and during their tenure of office concord at home procured peace abroad. Some writers omit all mention of the proposal to elect consuls from the plebs, and assert that the creation of three military tribunes invested with the insignia and authority of consuls was rendered necessary by the inability of two consuls to cope at the same time with the Veientine war in addition to the war with the Æqui and Volscians and the defection of Ardea. The jurisdiction of that office was not yet, however, firmly established, for in consequence of the decision of the augurs they resigned office after three months, owing to some irregularity in their election. C. Curtius, who had presided over their election, had not rightly selected his position for taking the auspices.

Ambassadors came from Ardea to complain of the injustice done them; they promised that if it were removed by the restoration of their territory they would abide by the treaty and remain good friends with Rome. The senate replied that they had no power to rescind a judgment of the people, there was no precedent or law to allow it, the necessity of preserving harmony between the two orders made it impossible. If the Ardeates were willing to wait their time and leave the redress of their wrongs in the hands of the senate, they would afterwards congratulate themselves on their moderation, and would discover that the senators were just as anxious that no injustice should be done them as that whatever had been done should speedily be repaired. The ambassadors said that they would bring the whole matter again before their senate, and were then courteously dismissed.

As the State was now without any curule magistrate, the patricians met together and appointed an interrex. Owing to a dispute whether consuls or military tribunes should be elected, the interregnum lasted several days. The interrex and the senate tried to secure the election of consuls; the plebs and their tribunes that of military tribunes. The senate conquered, for the plebeians were sure to confer either honour on the patricians and so refrained from an idle contest, whilst their leaders preferred an election in which no votes could be received for them to one in which they would be passed over as unworthy to hold office. The tribunes, too, gave up the fruitless contest out of complaisance to the leaders of the senate. T. Quinctius Barbatus, the interrex, elected as consuls Lucius Papirius Mugilanus and L. Sempronius Atratinus.

During their consulship the treaty with Ardea was renewed. This is the sole proof that they were the consuls for that year, for they are not found in the ancient annals nor in the official list of magistrates. The reason, I believe, was that since at the beginning of the year there were military tribunes, the names of the consuls who replaced them were omitted as though the tribunes had continued in office through the year. According to Licinius Macer, their names were found in the copy of the treaty with Ardea, as well as in the "Linen Rolls."

In spite of so many alarming symptoms of unrest amongst the neighbouring nations, things were quiet both abroad and at home.

The Institution of the Censorship. Whether there were tribunes this year, or whether they were replaced by consuls, there is no doubt that the following year the consuls were M. Geganius Macerinus and T. Quinctius Capitolinus; the former consul for the second time, the latter for the fifth time.

This year saw the beginning of the censorship, an office which, starting from small beginnings, grew to be of such importance that it had the regulation of the conduct and morals of Rome, the control of the senate and the equestrian order; the power of honouring and degrading was also in the hands of these magistrates; the legal rights connected with public places and private property, and the revenues of the Roman people, were under their absolute control. Its origin was due to the fact that no census had been taken of the people for many years, and it could no longer be postponed, whilst the consuls, with so many wars impending, did not feel at liberty to undertake the task. It was suggested in the senate that as the business would be a complicated and laborious one, not at all suitable for the consuls, a special magistrate was needed who should superintend the registrars and have the custody of the lists and assessment schedules and fix the valuation of property and the status of citizens at his discretion. Though the suggestion was not of great importance, the senate gladly adopted it, as it would add to the number of patrician magistrates in the State, and I think that they anticipated what actually happened, that the influence of those who held the office would soon enhance its authority and dignity. The tribunes, too, looking more at the need which certainly existed for such an office than at the lustre which would attend its administration, offered no opposition, lest they should appear to be raising troublesome difficulties even in small matters. The foremost men of the State declined the honour, so Papirius and Sempronius—about whose consulship doubts were entertained—were elected by the suffrages of the people to conduct the census. Their election to this magistracy made up for the incompleteness of their consulship. From the duties they had to discharge they were called Censors.

2. THE ACCOUNT OF DIONYSIUS OF HALICARNASSUS*

Dionysius was a rhetorician and historian of the first century B.C. Well known as a literary critic, he also wrote the *Roman Antiquities*, an account of Roman history from the foundation to the First Punic War in twenty books. Although its reliability is marred by the imposition of the author's theories, it is a valuable source of information for early Rome.

When Marcus Genucius and Gaius Quintius had assumed office, the political quarrels were renewed, the plebeians demanding that it be permitted to all Romans to hold the consulship; for hitherto the patricians alone had stood for that office and been chosen in the centuriate assembly. And a law concerning the consular elections was drawn up and introduced by the tribunes of that year, all the others but one, Gaius Furnius, having agreed upon that course; in this law they empowered the populace to decide each year whether they wished patricians or plebeians to stand for the consulship. At this the members of the senate were offended, seeing in it the overthrow of their own domination, and they thought they ought to endure anything rather than permit the law to pass; and outbursts of anger, recriminations and obstructions continually occurred both in private gatherings and in their general sessions, all the patricians having become hostile to all the plebeians. Many speeches also were made in the senate and many in the meetings of the popular assembly by the leading men of the aristocracy, the more moderate by men who believed that the plebeians were misled through ignorance of their true interest and the harsher by men who thought that the measure was concocted as the result of a plot and of envy toward themselves.

While the time was dragging along with no result, messengers from the allies arrived in the city reporting that both the Aequians and the Volscians were about to march against them with a large army and begging that assistance might be sent them promptly, as they lay in the path of the war. Those Tyrrhenians also who were called Veientes were said to be preparing for a revolt; and the Ardeates no longer gave allegiance to the Romans, being angry over the matter of the disputed territory which the Roman people, when chosen arbiters, had awarded to themselves the year before. The senate, upon being informed of all this, voted to enrol an army and that both consuls should take the field. But those who were trying to introduce the law kept opposing the execution of their decisions (tribunes have authority to oppose the consuls) by liberating such of the citizens as the consuls were leading off to make them take the military oath and by not permitting the consuls to inflict any punishment on the disobedient. And when the senate earnestly entreated them to put aside their contentiousness for the time being and only when the wars were at an end to propose the law concerning the

* Reprinted by permission of the publishers from Loeb Classical Library, Dionysius of Halicarnassus, *Roman Antiquities*, 11. 53–63, translated by E. Cary, Cambridge, Mass.: Harvard University Press, 1914–27, 1950.

consular elections, these men, far from yielding to the emergency, declared that they would oppose the decrees of the senate about other matters also and would not permit any decree on any subject to be satisfied unless the senate should approve by a preliminary decree the law they themselves were introducing. And they were so far carried away that they thus threatened the consuls not only in the senate, but also in the assembly of the people, swearing the oath which to them is the most binding, namely by their good faith, to the end that they might not be at liberty to revoke any of their decisions even if convinced of their error.

In view of these threats the oldest and most prominent of the leaders of the aristocracy were assembled by the consuls in a private meeting apart by themselves and there considered what they ought to do. Gaius Claudius, who by no means favoured the plebeians and had inherited this political creed from his ancestors, offered a rather arrogant motion not to yield to the people either the consulship or any other magistracy whatever, and, in the case of those who should attempt to do otherwise, to prevent them by force of arms, if they would not be convinced by arguments, giving no quarter to either private person or magistrate. For all who attempted to disturb the established customs and to corrupt their ancient form of government, he said, were aliens and enemies of the commonwealth. On the other hand, Titus Quintius opposed restraining their adversaries by violence or proceeding against the plebeians with arms and civil bloodshed, particularly since they would be opposed by the tribunes, "whose persons our fathers had decreed to be sacred and sacrosanct, making the gods and lesser divinities sureties for the performance of their compact and swearing the most solemn oaths in which they invoked utter destruction upon both themselves and their posterity if they transgressed a single article of that covenant."

This advice being approved of by all the others who had been invited to the meeting, Claudius resumed his remarks and said: "I am not unaware of how great calamities to us all a foundation will be laid if we permit the people to give their votes concerning this law. But being at a loss what to do and unable alone to oppose so many, I yield to your wishes. For it is right that every man should declare what he thinks will be of advantage to the commonwealth and then submit to the decision of the majority. However, this advice I have to give you, seeing that you are involved in a difficult and disagreeable business,—not to yield the consulship either now or hereafter to any but patricians, who alone are qualified for it by both religion and law. But whenever you are reduced, as at present, to the necessity of sharing the highest power and magistracy with the other citizens, appoint military tribunes instead of consuls, fixing their number as you shall think proper—in my opinion eight or six suffice—and of these men let the patricians not be fewer than the plebeians. For in doing this you will neither debase the consular office by conferring it upon mean and unworthy men nor will you appear to be devising for yourselves unjust positions of power by sharing no magistracy whatever with the plebeians." When all approved this opinion and none spoke in opposition, he said: "Hear now the advice I have for you consuls also. After you have appointed a day for passing the preliminary decree and the resolutions of the senate, give the floor to all who desire to say anything either in favour of the law or in opposition to it, and after they have spoken and it is time to ask for the expression of opinions, begin neither with me nor with Quintius here nor with anyone else of the older men, but rather with Lucius Valerius, who of all the senators is the greatest friend of the populace, and after him ask Horatius to speak, if he wishes to say anything. And when you have found out their opinions, then bid us older men to speak. For my part, I shall deliver an opinion contrary to that of the tribunes, using all possible frankness, since this tends to the advantage of the commonwealth. As for the measure concerning the military tribunes, if it is agreeable, let Titus Genucius here propose it; for this motion will be the most fitting and will create the least suspicion, Marcus Genucius, if introduced by your brother here." This suggestion was also approved, after which they departed from the meeting. But as for the tribunes, fear fell upon them because of the secret conference of these men; for they suspected that it was calculated to bring some great mischief upon the populace, since the men had met in a private house and not in public and had admitted none of the people's champions to share in their counsels. Thereupon they in turn held a meeting of such persons as were most friendly to the populace and they set about contriving defences and safeguards against the insidious designs which they suspected the patricians would employ against them.

When the time had come for the preliminary decree to be passed, the consuls assembled the senate and after many exhortations to harmony and good order they gave leave to the tribunes who had proposed the law to speak first. Then Gaius Canuleius, one of these, came forward and, without trying to show that the law was either just or advantageous or even mentioning that topic, said that he wondered at the consuls, who, after already consulting and deciding by themselves what should be done, had attempted to bring it before the senate as if it were a matter that had not been examined and required consideration, and had then given all who so chose leave to speak about it, thereby introducing a dissimulation unbecoming both to their age and to the greatness of their magistracy. He said that they were introducing the beginnings of evil policies by assembling secret councils in private houses and by summoning to them not even

all the senators, but only such as were most attached to themselves. He was not so greatly surprised, he said, that the other members had been excluded from this senatorial house party, but was astounded that Marcus Horatius and Lucius Valerius, who had overthrown the oligarchy, were ex-consuls and were as competent as anyone for deliberating about the public interests, had not been thought worthy to be invited to the meeting. He could not imagine on what just ground this had been done, but he could guess one reason, namely that, as they intended to introduce wicked measures prejudicial to the plebeians, they were unwilling to invite to these councils the greatest friends of the populace, who would be sure to express their indignation at such proposals and would not permit any unjust measure to be adopted against the interests of the people.

When Canuleius had spoken thus with great indignation and the senators who had not been summoned to the council resented their treatment, Genucius, one of the consuls, came forward and endeavoured to justify himself and his colleague and to appease the anger of the others by telling them that they had called in their friends, not in order to carry out any design against the populace, but in order to consult with their closest intimates by what course they might appear to do nothing prejudicial to either one of the parties, whether by referring the consideration of the law to the senate promptly or by doing so later. As for Valerius and Horatius, he said their only reason for not inviting them to the council had been to prevent the plebeians from entertaining any unwarranted suspicion of them as of men who had changed their political principles, in case they should embrace the other opinion, which called for putting off the consideration of the law to a more suitable occasion. But since all who had been invited to the meeting had felt that a speedy decision was preferable to a delayed one, the consuls were following the course thus favoured. Having spoken thus and sworn by the gods that he was indeed speaking the truth, and appealing for confirmation to the senators who had been invited to that meeting, he said that he would clear himself of every imputation, not by his words, but by his actions. For after all who desired to speak in opposition to the law or in favour of it had given their reasons, he would first call for questioning as to their opinions, not the oldest and the most honoured of the senators, to whom this privilege among others was accorded by established usage, nor those who were suspected by the plebeians of neither saying nor thinking anything that was to their advantage, but rather such of the younger senators as seemed to be most friendly to the populace.

After making these promises he gave leave to any who so desired to speak; and when no one came forward either to censure the law or to defend it, he came forward again, and beginning with Valerius, asked him what was to the interest of the public and what preliminary vote he advised the senators to pass. Valerius, rising up, made a long speech concerning both himself and his ancestors, who, he said, had always been champions of the plebeian party to the advantage of the commonwealth. He enumerated all the dangers from the beginning which had been brought upon it by those who pursued the contrary measures and showed that a hatred for the populace had been unprofitable to all those who had been actuated by it. He then said many things in praise of the people, alleging that they had been the principal cause not only of the liberty but also of the supremacy of the commonwealth. After enlarging upon this and similar themes, he ended by saying that no state could be free from which equality was banished; and he declared that to him the law, indeed, seemed just which gave a share in the consulship to all Romans,—to all, that is,

who had led irreproachable lives and had performed actions worthy of that honour, —but he thought the occasion was not suitable for the consideration of this law when the commonwealth was in the midst of war's disturbances. He advised the tribunes to permit the enrolling of the troops and not to hinder them when enrolled from taking the field; and he advised the consuls, when they had ended the war in the most successful manner, first of all things to lay before the people the preliminary decree concerning the law. These proposals, he urged, should be reduced to writing at once and agreed to by both parties. This opinion of Valerius, which was supported by Horatius (for the consuls gave him leave to speak next), had the same effect upon all who were present. For those who desired to do away with the law, though pleased to hear that its consideration was postponed, nevertheless accepted with anger the necessity of passing a preliminary decree concerning it after the war; while the others, who preferred to have the law approved by the senate, though glad to hear it acknowledged as just, were at the same time angry that the preliminary decree was put off to another time.

An uproar having broken out as the result of this opinion, as was to be expected, since neither side was pleased with all parts of it, the consul, coming forward, asked in the third place the opinion of Gaius Claudius, who had the reputation of being the most haughty and the most powerful of all the leaders of the other party, which opposed the plebeians. This man delivered a prepared speech against the plebeians in which he called to mind all the things the populace had ever done contrary, as he thought, to the excellent institutions of their ancestors. The climax with which he ended his speech was the motion that the consuls should not permit to the senate any consideration of the law at all, either at that time or later, since it was being introduced for the purpose of overthrowing the aristocracy and was bound to upset the whole order of their government. When even more of an uproar was caused by this motion, Titus Genucius, who was brother to one of the consuls, was called upon in the fourth place. He, rising up, spoke briefly about the emergencies confronting the city, how it was inevitable that one or the other of two most grievous evils should befall it, either through its civil strifes and rivalries to strengthen the cause of its enemies, or, from a desire to avert the attacks from outside, to settle ignominiously the domestic and civil war; and he declared that, there being two evils to one or the other of which they were bound to submit unwillingly, it seemed to him to be more expedient that the senate should permit the people to usurp a portion of the orderly constitution of the fathers rather than make the commonwealth a laughing-stock to other nations and to its enemies. Having said this, he offered the motion which had been approved by those who had been present at the meeting held in a private house, the motion made by Claudius, as I related, to the effect that, instead of consuls, military tribunes should be appointed, three from the patricians and three from the plebeians, these to have consular authority; that after they had completed the term of their magistracy and it was time to appoint new magistrates, the senate and people should again assemble and decide whether they wished consuls or military tribunes to assume the office, and that whichever course met with the approval of all the voters should prevail; moreover, that the preliminary decree should be passed each year.

This motion of Genucius was received with general applause, and almost all who rose up after him conceded that this was the best course. The preliminary decree was accordingly drawn up by order of the consuls; and the tribunes, receiving it with great joy, proceeded to the Forum. Then they called an assembly of the people, and after giving much praise to the senate, urged such of the plebeians as cared to do so to stand for this magistracy together with the patricians. But such a fickle thing, it seems, is desire apart from reason and so quickly does it veer the other way, particularly in the case of the masses, that those who hitherto had regarded it as a matter of supreme importance to have a share in the magistracy and, if this were not granted to them by the patricians, were ready either to abandon the city, as they had done before, or to seize the privilege by force of arms, now, when they had obtained the concession, promptly relinquished their desire for it and transferred their enthusiasm in the opposite direction. At any rate, though many plebeians stood for the military tribuneship and used the most earnest solicitations to obtain it, the people thought none of them worthy of this honour but, when they came to give their votes, chose the patrician candidates, men of distinction, namely Aulus Sempronius Atratinus, Lucius Atilius Luscus and Titus Cloelius Siculus.

These men were the first to assume the proconsular power, in the third year of the eighty-fourth Olympiad, when Diphilus was archon at Athens. But after holding it for only seventy-three days they voluntarily resigned it, in accordance with the ancient custom, when some heaven-sent omens occurred to prevent their continuing to conduct the public business. After these men had abdicated their power, the senate met and chose *interreges*, who, having appointed a day for the election of magistrates, left the decision to the people whether they desired to choose military tribunes or consuls; and the people having decided to abide by their original customs, they gave leave to such of the patricians as so desired to stand for the consulship. Two of the patricians were again elected consuls, Lucius Papirius Mugillanus and Lucius Sempronius Atratinus, brother to one of the men who had resigned the military tribuneship. These two magistracies, both invested with the supreme power, governed the Romans in the course of the same year. However, both are not recorded in all the Roman annals, but in some the military tribunes only, in others the consuls, and in a few both of them. I agree with the last group, not without reason, but relying on the testimony of the sacred and secret books. No event, either military or civil, worthy of the notice of history happened during their magistracy, except a treaty of friendship and alliance entered into with the Ardeates; for these, dropping their complaints about the disputed territory, had sent ambassadors, asking to be admitted among the friends and allies of the Romans. This treaty was ratified by the consuls.

The following year, the people having voted that consuls should again be appointed, Marcus Geganius Macerinus (for the second time) and Titus Quintius Capitolinus (for the fifth time) entered upon the consulship on the ides of December. These men pointed out to the senate that many things had been overlooked and neglected by reason of the continuous military expeditions of the consuls, and particularly the most essential matter of all, the custom relating to the census, by which the number of such as were of military age was ascertained, together with the amount of their fortunes, in proportion to which every man was to pay his contributions for war. There had been no census for seventeen years, since the [consulship] of Lucius Cornelius and Quintus Fabius.

3. Dio's Version*

Cassius Dio Cocceianus (ca. A.D. 155–230) was born in the Roman province of Bithynia, the son of a senator. He wrote a history of Rome from its origin to A.D. 229. Like Livy's *History*, only some books are preserved entire while others are available only in an epitomized form.

When the Romans thus fell into discord their adversaries took courage and came against them. It was in the following year, when Marcus Genucius and Gaius Curtius were consuls, that they turned against each other. The popular leaders desired to be consuls, since the patricians were in the habit of becoming tribunes by transference to their order, and the patricians clung tenaciously to the consular office. They indulged in many words and acts of violence against each other. But in order to prevent the populace from proceeding to greater extremities the nobles yielded to them the substance of authority though they would not relinquish the name; and in place of the consuls they named military tribunes in order that the honor

of the title might not be sullied by contact with the vulgar throng. It was agreed that three military tribunes be chosen from each of the classes in place of the two consuls. However, the name of consul was not lost entirely, but sometimes consuls were appointed and at other times military tribunes. This, at all events, is the tradition that has come down of what took place, with the additional detail that the consuls nominated dictators, though their own powers were far inferior to those appertaining to that office, and even that the military tribunes likewise did so sometimes. It is further said that none of the military tribunes, though many of them won many victories, ever celebrated a triumph.

It was in this way, then, that military tribunes came to be chosen at that time: censors were appointed in the following

---

* Dio Cassius, 7. 19, translated by H. B. Foster.

year, during the consulship of Barbatus and Marcus Macrinus. Those chosen were Lucius Papirius and Lucius Sempronius. The reason for their election was that the consuls were unable, on account of the number of the people, to supervise them all; the duties now assigned to the censors had until that time been performed by the consuls as a part of their prerogatives. Two was the original number of the censors and they were taken from the patricians. They held office at first and at the last for five-year periods, but during the intervening time for three half-years; and they came to be greater than the consuls, though they had taken over only a part of their functions. They had the right to let the public revenues, to supervise roads and public buildings, to make complete records of each man's wealth, and to note and investigate the lives of the citizens, enrolling those deserving of praise in the tribes, in the equestrian order, or in the senate (as seemed to fit the case of each one), and similarly erasing from any class the names of those who were not right livers: this power was greater than all those now left to the consuls. They made declarations attested by oath, in regard to every one of their acts, that no such act was prompted by favor or by enmity but that their considerations and performances were both the result of an unbiased opinion of what was advantageous for the commonwealth. They convened the people when

laws were to be introduced and for other purposes, and employed all the insignia of the greater offices save lictors. Such, at its inception, was the office of the censors. If any persons did not register their property and themselves in the census lists, the censors sold the property and the consuls the men. This arrangement held for a certain time, but later it was determined that a man once enrolled in the senate should be a senator for life and that his name should not be erased, unless one had been disgraced by being tried for the commission of a crime or was convicted of leading an evil life: the names of such persons were erased and others inscribed in their stead.

In the case of those who gave satisfaction in office principal honors were bestowed upon dictators, honors of the second rank upon censors, and third place was awarded to masters of horse. This system was followed without distinction, whether they were still in office or whether they had already laid it down. For if one descended from a greater office to an inferior one, he still kept the dignity of his former position intact. One particular man, whom they styled *principa* of the senate (he would be called *prokritos* by the Greeks) was preferred before all for the time that he was president (a person was not chosen for this position for life) and surpassed the rest in dignity, without wielding, however, any power.

4. A Statement of the Problem[*]

While Rome was winning notable victories over her neighbours, in her domestic politics she had failed to achieve a lasting peace. The *plebs* were not satisfied

* H. Stuart Jones, "The Making of a United State," *Cambridge Ancient History* (Cambridge, England: Cambridge University Press, 1928), Vol. 7, pp. 519–520. Reprinted by permission of the publisher.

with the concessions made to them by the settlement of 449 B.C. We now enter upon the period in which their efforts were concentrated upon obtaining access to the chief magistracy of the State. Our narratives of the years which follow bear the stamp of later politics and cannot be trusted in detail. The right to a triumph, claimed by Valerius and Horatius, was contested by the Senate which (according to the custom of the later Republic) reserved to itself the privilege of according this distinction; whereupon a tribune L. Icilius, is said to have 'brought the matter before the *populus*' and established a precedent for the granting of a triumph by the people. In 448 B.C., the patrician ex-consuls Aternius and Tarpeius are said to have been co-opted as tribunes, a violation of the constitution which provoked the passing of a law by a tribune named L. Trebonius providing that voting by the *plebs* should continue until the college of ten was at full strength.

The constitutional struggle became acute in 445 B.C., when a tribune named C. Canuleius proposed to abolish the prohibition of *conubium* between *patres* and *plebs* and at the same time to throw the consulship open to plebeians; and after a bitter dispute—in which Valerius and Horatius took the side of the *plebs*—the Senate allowed the first measure to go forward, presumably to the *concilium plebis*, but in order to defer a surrender on the second point, consented that in place of consuls, three officers (*tribuni militum*) enjoying the authority of consuls (*consulari potestate*) should be elected from either social order—whereupon the *plebs* showed unexampled magnanimity by electing three patricians. Dionysius (XI, 59 *sq.*) goes so far as to say that, by the terms of the law, three were to be patrician and three plebeian.

There seems no good reason for rejecting the tradition that the creation of this office was a political compromise; although Livy (IV, 7, 2) read in some of his authorities that these officers were set up because the military operations in prospect were on several fronts, and that they then assumed the authority and insignia of consuls. Hence it has been proposed to connect the number of *tribuni militum* with the growth of the military forces raised by Rome, each *tribunus* implying a levy (*legio*) of 1000 men. This was certainly not what the Romans meant when they spoke, like the Emperor Claudius, of 'the *imperium* put into commission' (*in plures distributum*, Dessau, 212).

In one point, however, the traditional version is open to criticism. If the object of the institution was to circumvent the admission of plebeians to the supreme magistracy, why do not the names of plebeians occur earlier and oftener in the recorded lists? According to Livy (V, 12) the first plebeian to obtain a place in the college was P. Licinius Calvus in 400 B.C. It is not, however, certain that Livy is right; since (whatever he and Dionysius may say) one of the three first elected, L. Atilius, bears a plebeian name, and so does Q. Antonius Merenda, who served the office in 422 B.C., and was evidently akin to the (supposed) plebeian decemvir of 450 B.C. An entirely different view is taken by Beloch, who thinks *all* plebeian names which appear in the Fasti of the period 444–367 B.C. interpolated, even those included in the four colleges in which plebeians are said to have obtained a majority (400, 399, 396, 379 B.C.), and by drastic manipulation of the lists arrives at the conclusion that the number of consuls (for this he considers to have been their title) was raised to four in 426 B.C. and to six in 405 B.C. In that case the whole story of the 'struggle of the orders' in this phase falls to the ground; and although the colouring is borrowed from the last century of the Republic, the main fact does not seem to be a pure invention.

5. MILITARY NECESSITY*

In the article from which the following excerpt is taken, Kurt von Fritz examines the entire constitutional struggle of the Roman Republic down to the Licinian-Sextian legislation in the fourth century. A major part of the problem is the evaluation of our sources for that period. Our selection begins with a summary of the author's views on their reliability.

In conclusion then it may be repeated that both the *fasti* and the *tabulae pontificum*, or whatever other year by year record existed of the period in question, clearly were not preserved in such a condition as to present no serious problems or no easy cause of errors to those who used or published them in later times. It may also be observed that the historians of Rome were certainly not so scrupulous as their modern colleagues and that many of the discrepancies between their quotations from the early lists or records may be simply a result of their carelessness. In some cases this is even quite obvious. But there can be hardly any doubt that there was a kernel of genuine tradition. While therefore it is hardly possible to attain any certainty concerning isolated facts, as for instance the accuracy of all the names of supreme magistrates in a given year or concerning the date or even historicity of individual military events, etc., it is very likely that conditions or developments which are reflected again and again in the sequence of events as they appear in the tradition are truly historical. This would apply to the changing numbers in the colleges of supreme magistrates and to the gradual intrusion of plebeians into the colleges of consular tribunes in the last decades before the restoration of the consulship.

It is then possible to return to the main question of the connection between the restoration of the consulate and the struggle between patricians and plebeians.

This problem is naturally closely connected with the question of the reason for the introduction of the consular tribuneship. . . . It is quite impossible to accept Livy's contention that the consular tribuneship was created in order to make the supreme office, in a somewhat diluted form, accessible to plebeians and that then, for forty-four years after its introduction, no plebeians were elected to that office. What then was the reason for the innovation? F. Cornelius has tried to show that this reason is to be found in military necessities, which made an increase in the number of military commanders imperative. He pointed out that the number of consular tribunes, which changes irregularly throughout this period, appears to be related to the extent and number of wars which the Romans had to wage at different times. At the same time he tried to relate the increasing numbers of the consular tribunes to increases in the Roman army and the Roman citizenry. On the basis of these considerations he came to the conclusion that the introduction of the consular tribuneship had no connection with the struggle between plebeians and patricians.

Cornelius's theory has been severely criticized by various reviewers of his book. It may however be sufficient to discuss the arguments set forth by W. Hoffmann, since his review, as far as I can see, is the most elaborate and incisive, that has appeared so far. Hoffmann tries to refute Cornelius's theory with three main arguments. He shows that Cornelius's assumptions concerning the size and the increase of the size of the Roman army are not supported by a careful interpretation of

* Kurt von Fritz, "The Reorganization of the Roman Government in 366 B.C.," *Historia*, 1 (Wiesbaden: Franz Steiner Verlag, 1950), pp. 37–41. Reprinted by permission of the publisher.

the tradition and quite improbable in themselves. In this respect Hoffmann is undoubtedly for the most part right. In fact, he might have added that the two parts of Cornelius's theory do not fit together very well. For the increase in the Roman army, according to Cornelius, was very rapid but steady. The increase of the number of the tribunes on the other hand, according to the *fasti* whose evidence Cornelius accepts, was not steady. The two increases therefore can hardly be quite so directly related to each other as Cornelius believes. Apart from this one may say that the tradition concerning the Roman army and the Roman census figures in the fifth century is so scanty and uncertain that no such conclusions can be drawn.

Hoffmann's second argument is much less convincing. He argues that the Romans could not know beforehand what wars they would have to wage in a given year and that therefore the number of consular tribunes to be elected cannot have been determined by the necessities arising from these wars. Now it is quite true that wars cannot always be predicted, except perhaps by those who plan them, and perhaps even not always by the latter. But this has not prevented nations and cities from preparing in advance for conflicts which they expected to break out or of which they at least suspected that they might break out. Perhaps one may argue that this general observation does not apply to the small scale world of Rome and its neighbors in the fifth century. But is this so certain? The steady expansion of the Roman territory since ca. 430 B.C., which became greatly accelerated in the first decade of the fourth century seems rather to indicate that the expansion—and perhaps then also the occasional pauses in the expansionist movement—were planned, and in this case the outbreaks of wars may have been to some extent, even if not altogether, predictable. It is true that here also Cornelius has tried to reconstruct the events

and their connection with one another in greater detail than the condition of the tradition permits. But basically his observation is not unsound. This will become clearer when Hoffmann's third argument is discussed.

In combatting Cornelius's contention that the introduction of the consular tribunate had nothing to do with the struggle between patricians and plebeians Hoffmann makes the following remark: "He is thereby confronted with the fact that the failure of the plebeians to share in the military tribunate in no way ended the previous situation. But it surely must signify something new if the new leaders of the state no longer must be descended from the old nobility, if they no longer saw the presuppositions of their power in the rank of their clans but in the levy of troops which the propertied classes included in the totality of the state."* What Hoffmann says here is essentially correct, but as an argument against Cornelius's theory it is only partly valid. Cornelius combatted above all Livy's contention that the consular tribuneship was introduced because the plebeians wanted it and that the plebeians wanted it because in this way they hoped to attain access to the highest office. But it makes a very great difference whether the innovation was made in order to make room for the plebeians, as Livy says, or whether it was introduced for other reasons but in consequence of a development which at the same time meant an increase of the power of the plebeians, as Hoffmann contends. Livy's explanation is clearly at variance with the evidence presented by the *fasti*. What Hoffmann says is quite acceptable. But it is not quite so far apart from Cornelius's theory as may appear at first sight. For when Hoffmann contends that the power of the consular tribunes was largely based on their command over

---

* Translated from the German by Donald Kagan.

the "Aufgebot", which included the propertied plebeians, and rested no longer exclusively on the position of their *gens* (and, one might add, their relation to their clients) he concedes that it was a change in the military setup which produced the consular tribuneship, which is exactly what Cornelius has affirmed, even if with some exaggerations. Even so, however, Hoffmann leaves the changing number of the consular tribunes unexplained.

Here then we come to the crucial point of the problem. The fact alone that the numbers of the tribunes varied either irregularly, as the *fasti* clearly indicate, or by a regular increase, as Beloch tried to show is sufficient to prove that the demand of the plebeians for a form of the highest office which would make it accessible to them, cannot have been the sole or even the main reason of the innovation. Or shall we assume that they first demanded the creation of a four man presidency in the hope of getting access to it, and then, when failing to succeed in this way, for the same reason had it increased to six but still for some time did not succeed in getting elected? Clearly the changing numbers must have had something to do with changing administrative needs. What is more, whether Cornelius's attempt to demonstrate the point by a year by year analysis of the tradition has been successful or not, these changing administrative needs must certainly for a large part have been of a military nature.

One of the most striking features of the Roman political or administrative setup is the lack of differentiation in the functions of what in modern terms would be called the members of the government. In the earliest times the consuls were actual, not like modern presidents, merely nominal commanders of the army or armies, judges, chief civil executives of the state, and heads of the city administration. Before the introduction of the censorship they probably even had to keep the citizen scrolls if something of this kind existed at that

period. When Rome was in its very beginning two men were sufficient for all these tasks. But it is clear that with the increasing expansion of Rome the task must have become more and more difficult. In regard to the fifth century another factor is probably still more important. Rome in this period, as both the tradition and Rome's expansion in all directions show, must often have waged war against more than one of its neighbors at the same time. Since, under the conditions prevailing at that time, it was not possible to direct the operations in different places, even when these were not so very far from one another, from one General Headquarters, there is nothing surprising in the fact that, at times, the Romans needed more than two commanders-in-chief, especially since their commanders-in-chief had also to attend to the distribution of justice and the civil administration. The Athenians of the fifth century, for similar reasons, had ten highest commanders. The difference is only that these generals were not at the same time official heads of the administration and that those, like Kimon, Perikles, etc. who acted at the same time as political leaders did so only incidentally and not because it was officially part of the functions of their office. But this is exactly what distinguishes the Roman system from those of most other republics.

If all this is taken into consideration it becomes crystal clear that Livy, or his authority, has confused cause and effect when he contends that the consular tribuneship was created on the demand of the plebeians because the latter wanted to attain access to the supreme office. The *fasti* show clearly that this story has no foundation in fact. But it is equally clear that the introduction of the consular tribuneship was connected with a change in the military organization which was partly the effect of the growth of a body of propertied and independent plebeians and partly the cause of a further increase of the power of this body. It was probably both in consequence of this growing power of the plebeians and of special military needs that the plebeians finally attained access to the supreme office in its diluted form.

6. POLITICAL PRESSURE*

Livy preserves two explanations of the Senatorial decision of 445 B.C. to suspend the election of consuls and to confer *imperium consulare* upon *tribuni militum*. One, which he himself accepts, is that it was a political compromise designed to appease agitation for plebeian representation in the consulship. The other is that the military situation demanded the appointment of at least three holders of *imperium*. Until some forty years ago the majority of scholars, even if ready to admit that the reform had military advantages, joined with Livy in laying the chief emphasis on the political motive. More recently, however, the tendency has been to disown the connection between the innovation and the struggle for office. The change is explained as necessitated wholly by growing military commitments or administrative needs. My purpose here is merely to defend once again the traditional account that the decision of 445 B.C. marked an important stage in the Struggle of the Orders and to remove the major difficulties which have discouraged its acceptance.

I would begin by stressing two considerations which may prove nothing of the motive for the change but at least indicate its positive effect. The first is that there coincided with the institution and abolition of the consular tribunate two measures which hold an important place in the history of the struggle for office— the law authorizing the election of censors, dated by tradition to 443 B.C., and the

Licinio-Sextian plebiscite of 367 B.C. which reserved at least one consulship for plebeians.

According to Livy the patriciate received the proposal for the institution of the censorship with great pleasure because it increased the number of patrician magistrates. A further explanation given by the tradition and accepted by Mommsen, that owing to pressure of work the ordinary magistrates had no leisure to discharge their censorial duties, is one which carries little weight, especially in view of the fact that the number of those who could in any one year hold the supreme magistracy had recently been increased. It was not indeed without reason that Schwegler argued that there was some vital connection between the establishment of the new office and the election of the first consular tribunes, and it may well be that the institution of the censorship was regarded by the patricians as a means of defence against a danger to which the substitution of consular tribunes for consuls had given rise, the danger of the all-important censorial powers including control over the composition of centuries and tribes being vested in a new man. With the creation of the censorship an office was formed as difficult for such a man to obtain as had been the consulship.

Similarly the terms of the Licinio-Sextian plebiscite which facilitated the permanent restoration of the consulship point to the conclusion that the office of consular tribune differed from that of consul in more than name, and that under the conditions prevailing before 366 B.C. it was more accessible to plebeians. Had the substitution of the consular tribunate for the consulship been demanded by the burden of external war, had the prospects

* E. S. Staveley, "The Significance of the Consular Tribunate," *Journal of Roman Studies*, 43 (London: Society for the Promotion of Roman Studies, 1953), pp. 30–36. Reprinted by permission of the publisher.

of plebeians who aspired to office been unaffected by the change, there would have been no opposition to the restoration of the consulship, when once the military situation had eased or when once a satisfactory alternative means had been found of meeting its demands. The condition imposed by Licinius and Sextius is indication enough that they regarded the existence of the consular tribunate as a temporary advantage not lightly to be foregone. Only on the assumption that in 445 B.C. the supreme magistracy was rendered easier of access to plebeians can these two measures be fully explained. If both were purely administrative in character, what account is to be given of the coincidence of the first appointment of censors with that of consular tribunes, or of the class-struggle culminating in the reforms of 367 B.C. which is both testified by the tradition and implicit in the text of the plebiscite?

A second matter which deserves serious thought is this. Remove the suggestion that the plebeian cause was favoured by the election of consular tribunes, and the entire structure of the annalistic account for the years 445–367 B.C. becomes unintelligible. The numerous conflicts between the Senate and the tribunes on the question whether consuls or consular tribunes should be elected, the fears felt by the patricians lest they should lose their monopoly, and the correspondingly increased expectancy of the plebeian tribunes which appears to date from the institution of the consular tribunate and which forms a nucleus around which Livy's account of this period is built—all must be regarded as fiction. It cannot be claimed that the evidence of Livy is even largely authentic or sufficient to enable us to explain all the variations in the form of government during this period. None the less it allows us to account for a great many and to form a more or less unbroken picture of the sequence of events which is both consistent and plausible. To maintain that the innovation of 445 B.C. was entirely

without political import not only involves the wholesale rejection of much of the material which Livy sets before us: it is to credit the historian—or his sources—with a gift for systematic and specious fabrication which he at least most surely did not possess.

Scholars seem to have been encouraged to take so bold a step by their inability to give what to them appeared a satisfactory answer to three leading questions which are raised by the traditional accounts. How except in terms of growing military requirements can the gradual progression in the number of consular tribunes annually elected be explained? In what respect was the change beneficial to the plebeians? Why, if beneficial it was, were so few plebeians successful at the *comitia*? In what follows it is hoped to show that these questions can be answered in a way which accords well with the tradition and with its beliefs concerning the purpose of the consular tribunate.

It cannot be denied that the increase in the number of *tribuni militum consulari potestate* elected annually from three to four and from four to six appears roughly to tally with the corresponding intensification of Rome's military activity and that the first year in which the Fasti record the names of six consular tribunes is the very year after that in which Rome declared war on Veii. It is not so obvious, however, that this increase bears any *direct* relation to military requirements. The theory that it was solely the need for a greater number of holders of *imperium* in times of crisis which regulated the numbers elected has already been severely criticized and is belied by a multitude of considerations— by Livy's references to the undesirability of a plurality of commanders, by the frequent appointment of dictators in time of serious war, by the fact that many of the years in which consular tribunes held office were years of peace, and by the continued election of six consular tribunes in all years but two from 405 to 367 B.C.

irrespective of the seriousness of the military situation. De Sanctis avoids these complications by assuming that all the *tribuni militum* elected in one year were necessarily invested with *imperium consulare* and by relating the number of *tribuni* elected to the number of thousands included in the annual levy. But neither can this solution be accepted. It is based on an arbitrary view of the development of the Roman army which has been thoroughly discounted by the arguments of Fraccaro. Even if Fraccaro's hypothesis that the double legionary army dates from 509 B.C. might be questioned, his attribution of a force of 6,000 legionaries to regal times can withstand all criticism. This being so, the number of *tribuni militum* appointed for ordinary duty at this time will have been at least six, and the decree of 445 B.C. may be supposed to have provided for the conferment of *imperium* not upon all of the *tribuni militum* but upon a number of them to be fixed annually by the Senate.

Such theories are conjectural and have little foundation in the tradition. If the unvarying progression is to be satisfactorily explained, we must discard the notion that the consular tribunate was a military convenience and accept Livy's own view that it was a political compromise. If there is any connection between the outbreak of hostilities against Veii and the increase in the number of consular tribunes to six, it is to be found in the fact that times of serious war, when the chief or sole aim of the government is to set up a united front against the enemy, provide the irresponsible agitator with an unrivalled opportunity to secure the satisfaction of his demands. Livy informs us that it was usual in Rome for internal dissension to subside through alarm for the general safety: he does not explicitly add, but certainly implies, that it was also usual for the settlement to be distinctly disadvantageous to the governing class. Although the plebeian tribunes depended to some extent on the support of

the electorate for advancement, they were no doubt frequently able to enforce their will upon the Senate. Their strength lay above all in the power to obstruct the levy which was frequently employed. The position, then, we may suppose, was this. Consular tribunes were elected only when the pressure brought to bear on the patrician State was sufficient to ensure that a decree was passed sanctioning their election. At first the tribunes were comparatively quiet and the Senate was able to hold its own: the desirability of experienced leadership and the solid undivided command prevailed in favour of the election of consuls. As time went on, however, the plebeian agitators became exasperated by failure and increasingly conscious of their powers: their efforts became more determined and with the growth of Rome's military responsibilities their position more formidable.

Objection has been raised that a mere increase in the number of places to be filled would have aided the plebeians little. This point has force only if it be assumed that the increase in the number of supreme magistrates constituted the full effect of the measure of 445 B.C. If, however, something was done in that year which considerably heightened the plebeian chances of election, such a demand for an increase would have been a natural one. It is the essential nature of the change, therefore, that must next be considered.

Livy interprets the plebeian victory quite simply. Until 367 B.C. none but a patrician was eligible for the consulship: plebeians were debarred from nomination *de iure*. The consular tribunate, on the other hand, was to be open to patricians and plebeians alike. This view has been generally accepted by modern scholars. A case against it, however, has been very forcibly argued by Bernardi. The most serious objection to it is presented by the Fasti which contain the names of many *gentes* not known in the later Republic to have contained patrician *stirpes*. Faced with this evidence, the exponents of the traditional view must adopt one of two equally unsatisfactory alternatives. They must either maintain that a patrician *stirps* in these *gentes* did exist in the fifth century B.C. and explain its disappearance by supposing that it became extinguished or passed over to the *plebs*, or, as did Beloch, they must reject all plebeian names on principle as interpolations.

If it be admitted, then, that plebeians were elected to the consulship before 367 B.C. the significance of the introduction of the consular tribunate could not have rested in the removal of a constitutional bar. Could it then be that the patricians undertook to stop imposing restrictions on the freedom of the electoral assembly to appoint candidates of its own choice? The withholding of the *patrum auctoritas* or of the *lex curiata de imperio*, the refusal of the presiding magistrate to accept plebeian candidates or to announce their success after the completion of the voting, the use of the *interregnum*, the falsification of the auspices—all have been cited as means by which the patriciate sought to establish its monopoly of political power. But not even Livy, who might be expected to retroject into the fifth century the political manœuvres of the late Republic, gives any indication that the patriciate commonly resorted to such tactics; and, even if there were reason to suppose that they did, it is hardly possible that by promising to abandon them in 445 B.C. they openly confessed to their previous misuse of prerogative.

There is, however, a further objection applicable to this and to the traditional view alike. Both rest on the assumption that the *comitia centuriata* were so constructed that, if left to their own devices, they would, or at least might, elect to the consulship those who were agitating for admission. Some years ago H. Last made the suggestion that a considerable number of immigrants, encouraged to Rome by the increased activity in trade and handicraft under the Etruscan domination, were admitted to the citizenship in regal times. Bernardi has recently enlarged on this possibility and has argued with good reason that wealthy members of this immigrant population were responsible in large measure for the agitation for a share in office in the fifth and fourth centuries. If he is right, such men could not have relied upon the support of other plebeians from the original landowning community; for these will have shared with the patriciate a feeling of disdain for the *nouveaux riches*. The immigrants were no doubt represented in the first class of the centuriate organization, but, in the face of the combined opposition of the patricians and those aristocratic plebeian families who had perhaps already been represented in the consulship in the pre-Decemviral period, they must have been powerless.

If, then, the measure of 445 B.C. did not constitute a change in a set of rules regulating the eligibility of candidates for the highest office, if it did not constitute a change of attitude among the patricians which displayed itself in a pledge not systematically to obstruct the election or candidature of plebeians, there remains but one possibility: it constituted a change in the nature of the electorate. The consular tribunes must have been elected in the *comitia populi tributa*. It is not possible to argue conclusively for or against this conclusion on the basis of the ancient tradition. Livy's evidence concerning the assembly employed is contradictory. He makes Camillus speak of 'comitia curiata quae rem militarem continent, comitia centuriata quibus consules tribunosque militum creatis'; and in his account of the elections of 400 B.C. appear the words 'plebeios alios tribunos militum consulari potestate omnes fere centuriae dixere'. But a little later he speaks of tribal elections: 'haud invitis patribus P. Licinium Calvum praerogativa tribunum militum non petentem creant...; omnesque deinceps ex collegio eiusdem anni refici apparebat,

L. Titinium P. Maenium Cn. Genucium
L. Atilium. qui priusquam renuntiarentur
iure vocatis tribubus, permissu interregis
P. Licinius Calvus ita verba fecit . . .' It is
not possible to confirm that Livy draws
on authentic material in any of these three
cases. The first passage clearly represents
only his own unthinking opinion. The
same can be said of the second, if only
because of the obvious exaggeration of the
statement in which the reference to the
assembly is made. It might, however, be
argued that the allusion to tribal voting is
based on reliable authority, if only because
it conflicts with his own opinion as expressed elsewhere and because he is here
describing an irregular election the details
of which may well have been preserved in
the pontifical records. Further, if it be
granted that the general picture of the
struggle during these years is basically
genuine, Livy may be thought to provide
surer support for our hypothesis. The men
against whom the tribunes railed and whom
they accounted responsible for their failure
at the *comitia* were those who sought
agrarian and debt relief, members of the
lower classes not concerned with attaining
office but imbued with the tradition of
patrician superiority, such people as one
would expect to be influential not in the
timocratic *comitia centuriata* but in the
democratic *comitia tributa*.

Finally in this connection the mode of
election of *tribuni militum* and quaestors in
the later Republic is not without interest.
In 362 B.C. the ordinary *tribuni militum*,
certainly elected in the *comitia tributa* in
the second century, were for the first time
chosen by popular vote. If, as Mommsen
urged, these *tribuni a populo* owed their
origin to the *tribuni pro consulibus*, they
may well have also inherited from them the
assembly in which they were appointed.
Quaestors, according to Tacitus, were first
popularly elected in 447 B.C., but in 421
B.C. the patricians are reported to have
conceded 'ut quemadmodum in tribunis
consulari potestate creandis usi sunt sic

in quaestoribus liberum esset arbitrium
populi'. Once again there is the tradition
that some change was brought about which
'opened' a magistracy to plebeians, and
from 421 B.C. onwards Livy fails to discern
any difference in the prospects of plebeians
for election to the quaestorship and the
consular tribunate. It may be suggested
that this year marked the beginning of the
practice, testified for the later Republic, of
electing quaestors by tribes.

We come now to the final question. If
the measure of 445 B.C. was a concession to
plebeian agitation, why were there only
two colleges of consular tribunes which
contained plebeian members before 400
B.C., and why were there only seven during
the period between the first major plebeian
success in this year and the passing of the
Licinio-Sextian legislation? Bernardi's recent attempt to answer this question
unfortunately constitutes the weakest and
most unsatisfactory part of his long article.
It rests basically on the false assumption
that the *comitia centuriata* were inclined to
elect plebeians. Until 426 B.C., Bernardi
believes, the three officers endowed with
imperium in certain years were not *tribuni
militum* but the *tribuni celerum*. These
were chosen by the *comitia curiata* in
which the immigrant population had no
part. Only in this year did the *comitia
centuriata* regain control, when as a result
of the increased prestige of the army the
tribuni celerum were replaced by four
tribuni militum. This account is extremely
speculative and runs counter to the commendable principle which Bernardi himself adopts, that the annalistic tradition
must serve as a basis for modern historical
construction. The *tribuni militum* are
regarded as a creation of the late fourth
century, the immigrants are without any
good reason excluded from the gentilician
state, and, perhaps what is most serious of
all, Livy's account under the year 445 B.C.
is so utterly reversed that the institution
of the consular tribunate is regarded not
as a compromise favouring the plebeians

but as a reactionary measure sponsored by the patricians.

A satisfactory solution to the question must accord to a greater extent with the tradition, and indeed Livy provides a very simple answer. Although the use of the tribal assembly may have increased the chances and raised the hopes of the plebeian tribunes, the common people who constituted the majority were not ready without very special reasons to cast their votes against their traditional rulers. Livy sums up the attitude of the voters when he writes of the quaestorian elections of 421 B.C.: 'nec ... valuit quin quorum patres avosque consules viderant eos nobilitate praeferrent.' They held the patriciate in a conservative and not altogether unwarranted respect, based, again in Livy's words, on 'omnia quibus patricii excellant, imperium atque honos, gloria belli, genus, nobilitas'. The ordinary citizen strove to better his condition and perhaps appointed members of the wealthier immigrant class to plead his cause, but in the further political advancement of his nominees he had little interest. The evidence of Livy is quite definite on this point. Throughout, the more ardent tribunes are represented as indulging in bitter recriminations against the electorate. So marked was the unconcern of the plebeian masses for the participation of leading members of their order in office that the change in the method of electing quaestors in 421 B.C., which was the outcome of a furious contest, had no effect. In 397 B.C. the tribunes saw fit to extort from the Senate a decree to the effect that at least half the consular tribunes elected in that year should be plebeian, so limiting the freedom of the assembly. In 367 B.C. the proposals for agrarian and debt reform were passed, we are told, while that which concerned the consulship was rejected. As Livy remarks: 'apparuit quae ex promulgatis plebi, quae lactoribus gratiora essent.'

The representation of the period as one of intense struggle between plebeian tribunes and Senate for the goodwill of the voter is one which there is no good reason to discredit. The refusal of Licinius and Sextius to allow two of their proposals to pass without the third provides the clue to one of the weapons of the tribunician agitators. Offers of help to the aggrieved classes were made with a view to a return in the form of election to the consular tribunate. Another weapon was adverse criticism of the ruling class. Every reverse in the field, every flaw in administration was seized upon and exaggerated beyond all recognition. The patriciate, on the other hand, started out with an advantage and they strove by every means in their power to preserve it. They attempted to consolidate a bond of tradition which already existed between them and the common people by laying frequent emphasis on their claims of birth and in time of war by playing upon their superior military renown. But they went further in an effort to drive a wedge between the two sections in the plebeian ranks. They tried on several occasions to regulate the composition of the college of plebeian tribunes and so to prevent their opponents from playing upon the feelings of the masses, they made concessions to economic agitation at opportune moments with a view to forestalling or outbidding the plebeian leaders, and it is probable that they also put up as rival candidates for the consular tribunate liberal-minded members of their own caste and plebeians of well-established families who would be preferred by the electorate.

The result of this rival activity was that the success of the plebeians was in general confined to years in which either the prestige of the patricians was damaged or their counter-activity proved ineffective to combat the propaganda of the tribunes. There is indeed in Livy's record of the late fifth century a remarkable association between the temporary eradication of patrician reputation for military competence resulting from tribunician prosecutions and plebeian victories in the *comitia*. In 423 B.C. the tribunes launched an attack upon two consular tribunes because of the unsuccessful battle which they had fought near Veii, and so worked on the feelings of the masses that a heavy fine was imposed. The result was the election of a plebeian among the consular tribunes of the following year. Owing largely to desperate patrician efforts the next plebeian success was not till 400 B.C. Once again it was preceded by a signal defeat incurred in the field which offered the tribunes the handle which they had been seeking. The guilty magistrates were accused of inefficiency and convicted. Thereafter plebeian successes were more frequent, but the patricians continued to keep their enemies at bay by making assignations of land and stressing the efficiency of Camillus.

Livy's own view, then, that the substitution of consular tribunes for consuls had a direct bearing on the Struggle of the Orders is not so absurd as has sometimes been supposed. In all likelihood the decision of 445 B.C. provided that in certain years to be determined by the Senate any number up to six *tribuni militum* should be elected by the *comitia tributa* and invested with *imperium consulare*. As with the advance of time Rome became further involved in warfare, the plebeian tribunes were able by threats to force an even more frequent decision to elect consular tribunes and to demand that the maximum number be appointed. They had scored a decided victory. Their own election was now a possibility. But possibilities are not realities. It was still necessary that the voters should be persuaded by propaganda or by offers of better conditions to abandon their support for their traditional rulers. Thanks to the astuteness and determined resistance of the patriciate this was not so easily accomplished as was perhaps at first anticipated.

7. A MIDDLE WAY*

The efforts of scholars have failed to find a generally accepted single reason for the institution of what it will be convenient to call Consular Tribunes, i.e. *Tribuni Militum consulari potestate* or *consulari imperio* or *pro consulibus*. The irregular oscillation between pairs of Consuls and three, and later four, Consular Tribunes which is attested for the first forty years of the institution (444–406 B.C.) appeared to Beloch, not without reason, to contain an element of irrationality and to be without parallel in ancient constitutional practice. But even those scholars who are least inclined to trust the consular Fasti would admit that, though they may contain interpolations or omissions or the misreading of names, the fact of this oscillation cannot be denied, and, moreover, that the names of magistrates of this period are, in the main, to be trusted.

What may be called the political explanation of the institution and continuance of the Consular Tribunes, viz. that it was due to a desire to preserve the Consulship for the patricians by having another form of magistracy open to plebeians can hardly survive the fact that in these forty years not more than two plebeian Consular Tribunes appear in the Fasti. The alternative explanation, also mentioned by Livy, that the Consular Tribunes were set up to meet the needs of wars on several fronts can hardly survive the fact that the decision to appoint Consular Tribunes rather than consuls must often have been taken before the

* F. E. Adcock, "Consular Tribunes and their Successors," *Journal of Roman Studies*, 47 (London: Society for the Promotion of Roman Studies, 1957), pp. 9–14. Reprinted by permission of the publisher.

need to meet enemies on several fronts could have been foreseen. And as regards both explanations we must admit that it is highly improbable that the Roman annalists were able to avail themselves, directly or indirectly, of any contemporary record of the motives that governed the Republic when the institution began. The literary tradition, preserved in Livy and Dionysius of Halicarnassus, may suit the political explanation, but it is generally admitted that this tradition, as regards internal affairs, was governed by an unhistorical retrojection of later conditions, of the political conflicts of the post-Gracchan period, so that, as Fraccaro has well said, it is the product of romance rather than of reconstruction. And if this annalistic literary tradition is fictitious, the following of it is more likely to lead to error than to truth.

When we come to the tradition about the external history of the Republic in this period we are on firmer ground. It shows, no doubt, the effects of family pride in the exaggeration, or even invention, of victories, but the general picture of the ups and downs of Roman power cannot be very far from the truth. That Rome's military strength increased is only to be expected and the modern theory that the institution of the Consular Tribunes, first three then four, within the period of forty years, reflects increases in her army is not, in itself, improbable. But the advance of Roman military establishment cannot be synchronized with the appearance of Consular Tribunes and with the increases in their numbers. Also we must suppose that the size of the military potential of Rome would be constant for fairly long periods of time, whereas the appointment of Consular Tribunes or that of Consuls shows a short-range variability. If the size of the military establishment calls for three or four commanders in this or that year, it is strange that two commanders suffice for the next. A variant of this theory is that it is not the total military potential, but the amount of it that is to be mobilized in any year, which is the governing factor in the appointment of Consular Tribunes. But this variant is open to the objection that the degree of mobilization, which must depend on military needs, cannot, as a rule, be foreseen when the decision is made whether to elect Consuls or Consular Tribunes.

A further modern explanation, that more magistrates than two Consuls were needed to provide for domestic administration as well as the conduct of war, has to meet the objection that the administrative needs of the Republic would be too constant to be met by a variation between two Consuls and three, or four, Consular Tribunes. If the Censorship was established in the year after the first Consular Tribunes, that would diminish the need for Consular Tribunes. It would not explain the continuance of Consular Tribunes; it would rather provide a partial substitute for them. It has also been suggested that the institution was required to satisfy the rival claims of the patricians for high office, but, if this is the reason, it is strange that the Republic did not have recourse to three, or later four, chief magistrates every year rather than to the attested variation. Also the decision to resort to Consular Tribunes would need to be taken before the elections, which might best reveal the competition for office. So far as my knowledge goes, this exhausts the suggestions that have been made. Thus, at least in so far as this first period is concerned, if we seek to find *one single* explanation which will be valid for the whole of this period, we are reduced to the *ars difficillima nesciendi*.

Before leaving the first period we may, however, find some consolation in the fact that the suggested reasons for the institution need not be mutually exclusive: and, what is more, the oscillation between the use of Consuls and of Consular Tribunes makes it possible to suppose that at different times different reasons were, in fact, operative. It will be observed that in this period there sometimes occur short runs, now of Consuls, now of Consular Tribunes, and this may mean that after what may be called Consular periods new considerations may induce resort to the Consular Tribunate; or the converse may happen. Suppose, for example, the very first set were appointed to meet administrative needs, the establishment of the censorship might be regarded as a more excellent way of relieving the Consuls of some of their duties. But after an interval of time, other needs may have appeared for which the Consular Tribunate might provide a possible provision. For example, it might be found that a series of Consuls had not sufficed to meet enemies on several fronts and so recourse to three Consular Tribunes might seem a promising alternative, even if that was not the reason for the original establishment of the office, and this might coincide with the need for more generals because of some increase in the military potential of Rome. The possibility that there was a political element in the election of the very first set of Consular Tribunes which contained a plebeian is not wholly removed by the fact that the motive did not prove strong enough to prevent a return to the Consulship or to secure the election of a plebeian when, for quite other than political reasons, a series of Consular Tribunes were appointed. If military considerations were at the moment predominant, we need only suppose that the Romans believed that for military purposes patricians were the most suitable candidates. And when in the literary tradition a reversion to Consular Tribunes is represented as political, this may only show that the later annalists invented political controversies where none existed. They had no means of knowing why on each occasion the Romans changed from Consuls to Consular Tribunes or vice versa and discerned changes politically because of their preoccupation with politics and because of their desire to dramatize any changes as part of a 'Struggle of the Orders' which they may have invented or exaggerated for literary effect.

The decision whether to hold elections for Consuls or Consular Tribunes would presumably rest with the Senate or with the presiding magistrate advised by the Senate. The doubt whether the Tribunes of the Plebs had access to the Senate in the fifth century only affects the credibility of the literary tradition. It has been argued that the Tribunes of the Plebs could obstruct the levy or threaten to do so and so put pressure on the Senate. This may be so, but it has to be remembered that the levy would happen after the elections had been held and that the tribunes in office before the election would only rarely be in office when the elections were held. It is not easy to believe that the *intercessio* of the tribunes would extend to the holding of elections for curule magistrates, and though an Assembly could refuse to elect candidates nominated by the presiding magistrate, it could do no more. In any event, the result of no elections being made would only induce an *interregnum*, in which the *interreges* were bound to be patricians. It is reasonable to suppose that the Senate was moved by a variety of considerations and in general acted according to its best judgment of the interests of the State at the moment.

Here the examination of the first forty years may end. As has been said, the possibility of different reasons at different times for a change from Consuls to Consular Tribunes and vice versa diminishes, almost removes, the apparent irrationality of what the Fasti disclose: what we are denied is confidence in any one sole reason for the establishment and continuation of the institution.

When we turn to the period from 405 to 367, after which year the Consular Tribunate disappears, we find a stretch of evidence which rewards observation from a different angle. The oscillation between Consuls and Consular Tribunes practically disappears from the Fasti in favour of a continuous series of groups of Consular Tribunes, almost all of them of six patricians. The exceptions to this general statement are few and will be considered later. The first characteristic of this second period of some forty years is that Rome was under increased military stress or showed increased military activity. First came operations against Veii and some of her neighbours or allies, which lasted, if not without some intermission, for a decade and led to an extension of Roman power north of the Tiber; then, a few years later, came the disaster of the Allia and the occupation of the City by the Gauls. The Roman army now needed to be revived, trained, and organized so as to restore Roman power and prestige, and recover her leadership of her allies, and this was bound to be a long and arduous process. Furthermore, within this period there were, beyond doubt, economic stresses induced by continuous campaigning (mitigated somewhat by the introduction of pay during the siege of Veii) and the effect of a harsh law of debt. Even if the literary tradition may give to the story a fictitious Gracchan colouring, there might well be discontent off and on throughout the whole period. This may in the end have led to something like a revolutionary movement. Both the military and the economic situation would naturally affect the appointment of the magistrates, the military situation most continuously, the economic situation more sporadically.

What first calls for comment is the vastly predominant appearance of patricians attested by the Fasti. By the beginning of this second period the legalized intermarriage of patricians and plebeians during the previous generation and more must have meant a progressive approach to social equality between the patrician and the plebeian gentry. It is, at first sight, strange that the visible creation of a new nobility of office embracing members of both Orders did not happen sooner than

it did, and also strange that the patricians could occupy so predominantly the office of Consular Tribune.

In the thirty years from 405 to 376 there were over 160 Consular Tribune places to be filled and it is a question how the patricians could fill so many of them. The answer is partly to be found in the fact that less than eighty men, between them, filled them all. This is due to a wider use of iteration, which is not surprising in view of the Roman respect for experience in difficult times. And the more the patricians had monopolized office the more they had monopolized military experience, and the less chance there had been for anyone else to show what he could do. The most approved generals were elected again and again at fairly short intervals.

Thus, the steady election of as many as six Consular Tribunes in each year reflected at once supply and demand. Apart from two consecutive years in the first decade of the fourth century there was no reversion to a pair of Consuls. It would seem that for nearly forty years the Romans believed that it was well to have plenty of generals assisted by colleagues whose activities might set them free to take the field, with the dictatorship always in reserve to give some unity of command if this proved necessary. And it is clear that the patrician body proved able, and indeed anxious, to produce a steady supply of officers and administrators who would naturally work together with a family tradition of co-operation. Such may be the explanation of the patrician predominance, which was the rule.

We may now consider the apparent exceptions to the rule. First, there is the brief reversion to the appointment of Consuls revealed by the Fasti for 393 and 392 B.C. It may be conjectured that this is due, in 393, to a desire to confer on the veteran general L. Valerius Potitus the more honorific office of Consul, and, in 392, to make good to him the loss of his Consulship as 'vitio factus' in the preceding year. Second, in the three years 400, 399, and 396 the Fasti show, in 400 four plebeian Consular Tribunes, in 399 five, in 396 five, and also in 379 (though some names are doubtful) almost certainly three. The first three of these years fall within the general period of the war with Veii, and Beloch is entitled to urge the improbability that the Romans would entrust their armies to men so inexperienced in command. Against this a robust faith in the soundness of the Fasti almost compels the assumption (which Beloch does not entirely rule out) that these three colleges reflect some serious discontent, perhaps economic in origin, which was revealed or placated by their election from among the most active of the plebeian notables of the day. The same may be true of 379. In 388 B.C. there appears what may be a plebeian name, L. Aquilius Corvus, but one swallow does not make a summer, and the same is true of M. Trebonius in 383.

If we review the whole course of the Consular Tribunate, the frequent changes in the first period from a pair of Consuls to a group of Consular Tribunes and, in the second period, the almost complete series of groups of six Consular Tribunes raise a minor matter which may be worth consideration, viz. that of the eponymous magistrate or magistrates of the year. In particular to have as many as six chief magistrates of equal status would seem to be inconvenient if their names were to rank as eponymous. It may be suggested that the way in which this difficulty was met was by counting as eponymous that magistrate to whom fell the duty of striking the *clavis annalis* in the temple of Capitoline Jupiter on the Ides of September. That magistrate, whether Consul or Consular Tribune, could bear the title *praetor maximus* to fulfil the ancient law about the striking of the nail. If a dictator or interrex was in office on the Ides of September the duty would devolve upon him and he would count as eponymous,

for, as Mommsen urged, *praetor maximus* in early days meant the magistrate who on that day ranked first. That the Consular Tribunes followed the Consular practice of presiding in the State according to terms reckoned in months, appears from the fact that there is no record of a college of Consular Tribunes that contained five members, who could not divide twelve months equally between them.

Finally, it is worth while to consider what happened when the Consular Tribunate was abandoned. The continuing practice for so many years of electing six Consular Tribunes makes it surprising that with 366 B.C. the Republic reverted to two Consuls (now reinforced by the new office of Praetor and two Curule Aediles) granted that, at need, there could be recourse to the dictatorship to meet any shortcomings. The military pressure on Rome may have seemed to be less, but even so, the change must have been dictated by a statesmanlike desire on the part of the Senate and the patricians to restore unity to the Republic after a decade marked, so it seems, by something approaching revolution led by strong and ambitious plebeian leaders whose programme included a change in the chief executive of the State. We are not here concerned by the way in which this result was attained, whether by plebeian legislation accepted or approved by the *patres* or by one of those practical compromises whereby patricians and plebeians succeeded in restoring the unity of the Commonwealth.

The Fasti reveal, after the disappearance of the Consular Tribunes, and for eleven years beginning with 366, the election of one plebeian to the consulship in each year. Whatever had happened in 367, the plebeian leaders had ensured that, whereas in the previous forty years ten plebeians at most had been Consular Tribunes, now they had an admitted claim to hold one of the two annual consulships. Experience had taught them to raise their sights and insist that for one place there should not be competition by the patricians. We may suppose, however, that, as was not unnatural after a long period of almost unbroken patrician control of the chief magistracy, there were not enough plebeians qualified by experience to justify themselves as Consuls. This practical consideration induced a short period marked by the occasional resort to pairs of patrician consuls; thereafter, the claim was in some way reaffirmed and became the regular practice of the Republic, hardly ever, if ever, broken again.

But it remains a question how the new order of things met the military needs of Rome. There is one thing that may have helped. We find not later than 362 B.C. the practice of electing by the People six military tribunes, who presumably occupied some intermediate position between the former Consular Tribunes and other military tribunes now appointed by the Consuls to be the lesser officers of the legions. This would help, and it is also possible that fewer generals were needed because of some closer organization of command within the legions as time went on.

We find, indeed, in the sixty years after 367 B.C. a variable recourse to iteration which modified the natural competition of the new nobility for the consulship, the hallmark of their rank. It is interesting to observe how the variation in degree of military stress affects the way in which the Republic accommodated itself to the new situation. In the years from 366 to 347 forty consular posts are filled by twenty men, twelve of them patricians, eight of them plebeians; one man held the consulship four times, two men three times, and six men twice. In the like years from 346 to 326 (omitting one 'dictator year') forty consular posts are filled by thirty men, sixteen patricians and fourteen plebeians; eight men hold the consulship twice, no one more than twice. In the years 325 to 305 (omitting two 'dictator years'), a period in which there is the main stress of the Samnite wars, thirty-eight consular posts are filled by twenty-six men, twelve of them patricians and fourteen plebeians. One man holds the consulship four times, two hold it three times, and five hold it twice. In the years from 304 to 284 (omitting one 'dictator year') forty consular posts are held by thirty-five men, sixteen of them patricians and nineteen plebeians. Within the whole period from 366 to 284 B.C. twenty-eight plebeian *gentes* have become what may be called consular, whereas fourteen patrician *gentes* continue to provide consuls. Meanwhile, in 311 B.C., the number of *tribuni militum* elected by the People was increased from six to sixteen, and what is far more important, the practice of employing magistrates after their term of office by *prorogatio* effectively added to the number of generals at the disposal of the Republic. Thus, it contrived to meet its military and administrative needs and, at the same time, to advance the new nobility of office without losing the services of the old patrician aristocracy. The same due balance of supply and demand which appears to be the most salient feature of the second period of Consular Tribunes is then to be detected in the time of their successors with modifications which attest the instinctive political sagacity, the positive realization of the brief 'salus populi suprema lex', of the Roman upper class at this stage of Republican history.

SECTION III

The Organization of Roman Italy

THE ANCIENT WORLD saw may conquerors and many empires. It was the unique achievement of the Romans to organize their empire in such a way as to make it enduring, acceptable, sometimes even desirable to the conquered. It brought peace, law, and order, usually without interfering unduly with the lives of the subjects of Rome. Like the Roman constitution, the Roman method of imperial government was not designed at one stroke but developed gradually. Rome adapted her methods to the exigencies of each occasion. Sometimes generosity was called for, at other times cruelty. Each defeated foe was treated differently, but even the most harshly treated was given hope of better treatment in return for future loyalty. The great test of the Roman system was to come with the invasions of Pyrrhus and Hannibal in the late third century, and that test was passed with flying colors. Most of the conquered Italians remained loyal to Rome in the most trying circumstances and enabled their conquerors to emerge victorious. What were the methods by which Rome accomplished this? What were the steps by which the system was achieved? What role was played by the extension of Roman citizenship to foreigners? Why did the development stop short of true representative government?

1. THE TREATMENT OF THE LATINS IN 338 B.C.*

One of the great turning points in the history of Rome's imperial organization came in the year 338. Taking advantage of Rome's struggle with the Samnites, the Latins revolted against Roman rule. Rome's treatment of the defeated Latins was characteristic of its approach.

When the other consul entered the Sabellian territory, he found that the

Samnites had no camp, no legions confronting him. Whilst he was laying waste their fields with fire and sword, envoys came to ask for peace and he referred them to the senate.

After permission had been given them to

* Livy, *History of Rome*, 8. 1–5; 11–14, translated by Canon Roberts (New York: E. P. Dutton), pp. 107–113; 120–126. Reprinted by permission of E. P. Dutton and J. M. Dent & Sons, London.

state their case, they laid aside their truculent manner and requested that peace might be granted them and also the right of making war against the Sidicines. They considered that they were the more justified in making this request because they had formed friendly relations with Rome when their affairs were prosperous, not as in the case of the Campanians when they were in adversity, and they were taking up arms against the Sidicines, who had always been their enemies and never friends of Rome, who had not, like the Samnites, sought its friendship in a time of peace, nor like the Campanians, asked for its help in a time of war, and who were not under the protection and suzerainty of Rome.

The praetor, T. Æmilius, put these demands to the senate, and they decided that the former treaty should be renewed with them. The reply given then by the praetor was to the effect that it was no fault of the Roman people that the friendship with them had not remained unbroken, and there was no objection to its being re-established since they themselves were weary of a war brought on them by their own fault. As to the Sidicines there was nothing to prevent the Samnites from being free to make either peace or war.

After the treaty was made the Roman army was at once withdrawn. The men had received a year's pay and three months' rations, for which the consul had stipulated, that he might allow time for an armistice until the envoys returned.

The Samnites advanced against the Sidicines with the same troops that they had employed in the war with Rome, and they were very hopeful of effecting an early capture of the city. Then at last the Sidicines took steps to make a surrender of themselves to Rome. The senate rejected it as being made too late and forced from them by extreme necessity. They then made it to the Latins who were already in arms on their own account. Even the Campanians did not refuse to take part in the hostile movement, so much keener was their sense of the injuries inflicted by the Samnites than of the kindness shown them by Rome.

One immense army, composed of these many nationalities and under Latin leadership, invaded the Samnite country and inflicted more disasters by ravages than by actual fighting. Although the Latins proved superior in the various encounters, they were not loath to retire from the enemy's territory lest they might have to fight too often. This allowed the Samnites time to send envoys to Rome. When they were admitted to an audience they complained to the senate that they were suffering more now that they were in treaty with them than they had before, when they were enemies; they very humbly requested them to be satisfied with having snatched from them the victory they had won over the Campanians and the Sidicines, and not permit them, in addition, to be conquered by these most cowardly people. If the Latins and Campanians were really under the suzerainty of Rome they should exert their authority to keep them off the Samnite land, if they renounced that suzerainty they should coerce them by force. They received an ambiguous reply, for the senate shrank from acknowledging that the Latins no longer recognised their authority, and on the other hand they were afraid, if they reprimanded them, that they might alienate them altogether. The circumstances of the Campanians were quite different; they were bound not by treaty but by the terms of surrender, and they must keep quiet whether they would or no. There was nothing in their treaty with the Latins which prevented them from making war with whom they pleased.

The Revolt of the Latins and Campanians. With this reply the Samnites were dismissed, quite uncertain as to what the Romans were going to do. But its effect was to completely estrange the Campanians, who now feared the worst, and it made the Latins more determined than ever, since the Romans refused any further concessions. Under the pretext of making preparations for a Samnite war, they held frequent meetings of their national council, and in all the consultations of their leaders they hatched plans in secret for war with Rome. The Campanians also took part in this movement against their preservers. But in spite of the careful secrecy with which everything was being conducted—for they wanted the Samnites to be dislodged from their rear before the Romans made any movement—some who had friends and relatives in Rome sent hints about the league which was being formed. The consuls were ordered to resign before the expiry of their year of office in order that the new consuls might be elected at an earlier date in view of such a formidable war. There were religious difficulties in the way of the elections being held by those whose tenure of office had been curtailed, and so an interregnum commenced. There were two interreges, M. Valerius and M. Fabius. The latter elected T. Manlius Torquatus (for the third time) and P. Decius Mus as consuls.

* * *

Although there could be no doubt as to the revolt of their allies—the Latin league—still, as though they were concerned for the Samnites and not for themselves, the Romans invited the ten chiefs of the league to Rome to give them instructions as to what they wanted. Latium at that time had two praetors, L. Annius of Setia and L. Numisius of Cerceii, both belonging to the Roman colonists. Through these men not only had Signia and Velitrae, themselves Roman colonies, but the Volsci also been instigated to take up arms. It was decided that they should be particularly invited by name. No one had the slightest doubt as to the reason for this invitation. A meeting of their council was accordingly held prior to their departure; they informed those present that they had been asked by the senate to go to Rome, and they requested them to decide as to what reply they should give with reference to the matters which they had reason to suppose would be discussed.

After various opinions had been expressed, Annius spoke as follows: "Although it was I who put the question to you as to what answer should be given, I still think that it is of more importance to the interests of the State to decide what must be done rather than what must be said. When our plans are developed it will be easy enough to fit words to facts. If even now we are capable of submitting to servitude under the shadowy pretext of a treaty on equal terms, what is to prevent us from deserting the Sidicines and receiving our orders not only from the Romans but even from the Samnites, and giving as our reply that we are ready to lay down our arms at the beck and call of the Romans? But if your hearts are at last touched by any yearning for independence; if a treaty, an alliance, an equality of rights really exists; if we are at liberty to boast of the fact that the Romans are of the same stock as ourselves, though once we were ashamed of it; if our army, which when united with theirs doubles their strength, and which the consuls will not dispense with when conducting wars which concern them alone—if, I say, that army is really an army of their allies, then why are we not on an equal footing in all respects? Why is not one consul elected from the Latins? Those who possess half the strength, do they possess half the government? This is not in itself too much honour for us, seeing that we acknowledge Rome to be the head of Latium, but we have made it appear so by our prolonged forbearance.

"But if ever you longed for an opportunity of taking your place in the government and of making use of your liberty, now is the time; this is the opportunity which has been given you by your own courage and the goodness of the gods. You tried their patience by refusing to supply troops. Who doubts that they were intensely irritated when we broke through a custom more than two centuries old? Still they put up with the annoyance. We waged war with the Paelignians on our own account; they who before did not allow us the right to defend our own frontiers did not intervene. They heard that the Sidicines were received into our protection, that the Campanians had revolted from them to us, that we were preparing an army to act against the Samnites with whom they had a treaty, they never moved out of their City. What was this extraordinary self-restraint due to but to a consciousness of our strength and of theirs? I have it on good authority that when the Samnites were laying their complaints about us they received a reply from the Roman senate, from which it was quite evident that they themselves do not now claim that Latium is under the authority of Rome. Make your rights effective by insisting on what they are tacitly conceding to you. If any one is afraid of saying this, I declare my readiness to say it not only in the ears of the Roman people and their senate but in the audience of Jupiter himself who dwells in the Capitol, and to tell them that if they wish us to remain in alliance with them they must accept one consul from us and half their senate."

His speech was followed by a universal shout of approval, and he was empowered to do and to say whatever he deemed to be furtherance of the interests of the State of Latium and of his own honour.

On their arrival in Rome, the senate assembled in the Capitol and granted them an audience. T. Manlius, the consul, acting on the instructions of the senate, recommended them not to make war upon the Samnites, with whom the Romans had a treaty, on which Annius, as though he were a conquerer who had captured the Capitol by arms instead of an ambassador protected by the law of nations, said:

"It is about time, Titus Manlius and senators, that you gave up treating us as though you were our suzerains, when you see the State of Latium raised by the bounty of the gods to a most flourishing position, both in population and in military power, the Samnites defeated, the Sidicines and Campanians in alliance with us, even the Volscians now making common cause with us, whilst your own colonies actually prefer the government of Latium to that of Rome. But since you cannot bring your minds to abandon your impudent claims to sovereignty, we will go so far, in recognising that we are kindred nations, as to offer peace upon the conditions of equal rights for both, since it has pleased the gods to grant equal strength to both; though we are quite able to assert the independence of Latium by force of arms. One consul must be elected from Rome, the other from Latium; the senate must contain an equal number of members from both nations; there must be one nation, one republic. And in order that there may be one seat of government and one name for all, since one side or the other must make some concession, let us, if this City really takes precedence, be all called Romans."

It so happened that the Romans had in their consul T. Manlius, a man who was quite as proud and passionate as Annius. He was so enraged as to declare that if the senate were visited by such madness as to accept these conditions from a man from Setia, he would come with his sword drawn into the Senate-house and kill every Latin he found there. Then turning to the image of Jupiter, he explained: "Hear, O Jupiter, these abominable words! Hear them, O Justice and Right! Thou, Jupiter, as though thou hadst been conquered and made captive, art to see in thy temple foreign consuls and a foreign senate! Were these the terms of the treaty, Latins, which Tullus, the King of Rome, made with your fathers of Alba, or which L. Tarquin made with you afterwards? Have you forgotten the battle at Lake Regillus? Are you so utterly oblivious of your defeats in the old days and of our kindness towards you?"

This outburst was followed by the indignant protest of the senate, and it is recorded that whilst on all hands appeals were being made to the gods, whom the consuls were continually invoking as the guardians of treaties, the voice of Annius was heard pouring contempt upon the divine majesty of the Jupiter of Rome. At all events when, in a storm of passion he was flinging himself out of the vestibule of the temple, he slipped down the steps and struck his head so heavily against the bottom step that he became unconscious. The authorities are not agreed as to whether he was actually killed, and I leave the question undecided, as also the statement that during the appeals to the gods to avenge the breach of treaties, a storm burst from the sky with a terrific roar; for they may either be true or simply invented as an appropriate representation of the wrath of the gods.

Torquatus was sent by the senate to conduct the envoys away, and when he saw Annius lying on the ground he exclaimed, loud enough to be heard by the senators and populace alike: "It is well. The gods have commenced a just and righteous war! There is a divine power at work; thou, O Great Jupiter, art here! Not in vain have we consecrated this to be thine abode, O Father of gods and men! Why do you hesitate, Quirites, and you, senators, to take up arms when the gods are your leaders? I will lay the legions of the Latins low, just as you see their envoy lying here."

The consul's words were received by the people with loud applause and raised them to such a pitch of excitement that when the envoys took their departure they owed their safety more to the care of the magistrates who, on the consul's order, accompanied them to protect them from the attacks of the angry people than to any respect felt for the law of nations.

*　*　*

In some authors I find it stated that it was only after the battle was over that the Samnites who had been waiting to see the result came to support the Romans. Assistance was also coming to the Latins from Lanuvium whilst time was being wasted in deliberation, but whilst they were starting and a part of their column was already on the march, news came of the defeat of the Latins. They faced about and re-entered their city, and it is stated that Milionius, their praetor, remarked that for that very short march they would have to pay a heavy price to Rome. Those of the Latins who survived the battle retreated by many different routes, and gradually assembled in the city of Vescia. Here the leaders met to discuss the situation, and Numisius assured them that both armies had really experienced the same fortune and an equal amount of bloodshed; the Romans enjoyed no more than the name of victory, in every other respect they were as good as defeated. The headquarters of both consuls were polluted with blood; the one had murdered his son, the other had devoted himself to death; their whole army was massacred, their hastati and principes killed; the companies both in front of and behind the standards had suffered enormous losses; the triarii in the end saved the situation. The Latin troops, it was true, were equally cut up, but Latium and the Volsci could supply reinforcements more quickly than Rome. If, therefore, they approved, he would at once call out the fighting men from the Latin and Volscian peoples and march back with an army to Capua, and would take the Romans unawares; a battle was the last thing they were expecting. He despatched misleading letters throughout Latium and the Volscian country, those who had not been engaged in the battle being the more ready to believe what he said, and a hastily-levied body of militia, drawn from all quarters, was got together. This army was met by the consul at Trifanum, a place between Sinuessa and Menturnae. Without waiting even to choose the sites for their camps, the two armies piled their baggage, fought and finished the war, for the Latins were so utterly worsted that when the consul with his victorious army was preparing to ravage their territory, they made a complete surrender and the Campanians followed their example.

Latium and Capua were deprived of their territory. The Latin territory, including that of Privernum, together with the Falernian, which had belonged to the Campanians as far as the Volturnus, was distributed amongst the Roman plebs. They received two *jugera* a head in the Latin territory, their allotment being made up by three-quarters of a *jugerum* in the Privernate district; in the Falerian district they received three entire *jugera*, the additional quarter being allowed owing to the distance. The Laurentes, amongst the Latins and the aristocracy of the Campanians, were not thus penalised because they had not revolted. An order was made for the treaty with the Laurentes to be renewed, and it has since been renewed annually on the tenth day after the Latin Festival. The Roman franchise was conferred on the aristocracy of Campania, and a brazen tablet recording the fact was fastened up in Rome in the temple of Castor, and the people of Campania were ordered to pay them each—they numbered 1600 in all—the sum of 450 *denarii* annually.

* * *

This year had been signalised by victories over many powerful nations, and still more by the noble death of one consul, and the stern, never-to-be-forgotten exercise of authority on the part of the other. It was followed by the consulship of Titus Æmilius Mamercinus and Q. Publilius Philo. They did not meet with similar materials out of which to build a reputation, nor did they study the interests of their country so much as their own or those of the political factions in the republic. The Latins resumed hostilities to recover the domain they had lost, but were routed in the Fenectane plains and driven out of their camp. There Publilius, who had achieved this success, received into surrender the Latin cities who had lost their men there, whilst Æmilius led his army to Pedum. This place was defended by a combined force from Tibur, Praeneste, and Velitrae, and help was also sent from Lanuvium and Antium. In the various battles the Romans had the advantage, but at the city itself, and at the camp of the allied forces which adjoined the city, their work had to be done all over again. The consul suddenly abandoned the war before it was brought to a close, because he heard that a triumph had been decreed to his colleague, and he actually returned to Rome to demand a triumph before he had won a victory. The senate were disgusted at this selfish conduct, and made him understand that he would have no triumph till Pedum had either been taken or surrendered. This produced a complete estrangement between Æmilius and the senate, and he thenceforth administered his consulship in the spirit and temper of a seditious tribune. As long as he was consul he perpetually traduced the senate to the people, without any opposition from his colleague, who himself also belonged to the plebs. Material for his charges was afforded by the dishonest allocation of the Latin and Falernian domain amongst the plebs, and after the senate, desirous of restricting the consuls' authority, had issued an order for the nomination of a Dictator to act against the Latins, Æmilius, whose turn it was then to have the *fasces*, nominated his own colleague, who named Junius Brutus as his Master of the Horse. He made his Dictatorship popular by delivering incriminatory harangues against the senate and also by carrying three measures which were directed against the nobility and were most advantageous to the plebs. One was that the decisions of the plebs should be binding on all the Quirites; the second, that measures which were brought before the Assembly of centuries should be sanctioned by the patricians before being finally put to the vote; the third, that since it had come about that both censors could legally be appointed from the plebs, one should in any case be always chosen from that order. The patricians considered that the consuls and the Dictator had done more to injure the State by their domestic policy than to strengthen its power by their successes in the field.

The consuls for the next year were L. Furius Camillus and C. Maenius. In order to bring more discredit upon Æmilius for his neglect of his military duties the previous year, the senate insisted that no expenditure of arms and men must be spared in order to reduce and destroy Pedum. The new consuls were peremptorily ordered to lay aside everything else and march at once. The state of affairs in Latium was such that they would neither maintain peace nor undertake war. For war their resources were utterly inadequate, and they were smarting too keenly under the loss of their territory to think of peace. They decided, therefore, on a middle course, namely, to confine themselves to their towns, and if they were informed of any town being attacked, to send assistance to it from the whole of Latium. The people of Tibur and Praeneste, who were the nearest, reached Pedum, but the troops from Aricium, Lanuvium, and Veliternae, in conjunction with the Volscians of Antium, were suddenly attacked and routed by Maenius at the river Astura. Camillus engaged the Tiburtines who were much the strongest force, and, though with greater difficulty, achieved a similar success. During the battle the townsmen made a sudden sortie, but Camillus, directing a part of his army against them, not only drove them back within their walls, but stormed and captured the town, after routing the troops sent to their assistance, all in one day. After this successful attack on one city, they decided to make a greater and bolder effort, and to lead their victor-ious army on to the complete subjugation of Latium. They did not rest until, by capturing or accepting the surrender of one city after another, they had effected their purpose. Garrisons were placed in the captured towns, after which they returned to Rome to enjoy a triumph which was by universal consent accorded to them. An additional honour was paid to the two consuls in the erection of their equestrian statues in the Forum, a rare incident in that age.

Before the consular elections for the following year were held, Camillus brought before the senate the question of the future settlement of Latium. "Senators," he said, "our military operations in Latium have by the gracious favour of the gods and the bravery of our troops been brought to a successful close. The hostile armies were cut down at Pedum and the Astura, all the Latin towns and the Volscian Antium have either been stormed or have surrendered and are now held by your garrisons. We are growing weary of their constant renewal of hostilities, it is for you to consult as to the best means of binding them to a perpetual peace. The immortal gods have made you so completely masters of the situation that they have put it into your hands to decide whether there shall be henceforth a Latium or not. So far, then, as the Latins are concerned, you can secure for yourselves a lasting peace by either cruelty or kindness. Do you wish to adopt ruthless measures against a people that have surrendered and been defeated? It is open to you to wipe out the whole Latin nation and create desolation and solitude in that country which has furnished you with a splendid army of allies which you have employed in many great wars. Or do you wish to follow the example of your ancestors and make Rome greater by conferring her citizenship on those whom she has defeated? The materials for her expansion to a glorious height are here at hand. That is assuredly the most firmly-based empire, whose subjects take a delight in rendering it their obedience. But whatever decision you come to, you must make haste about it. You are keeping so many peoples in suspense, with their minds distracted between hope and fear, that you are bound to relieve yourselves as soon as possible from your anxiety about them, and by exercising either punishment or kindness to pre-occupy minds which a state of strained expectancy has deprived of the power of thought. Our task has been to put you in a position to take the whole question into consultation, your task is to decree what is best for yourselves and for the republic."

The leaders of the senate applauded the way in which the consul had introduced the motion, but as the circumstances differed in different cases they thought that each case ought to be decided upon its merits, and with the view of facilitating discussion they requested the consul to put the name of each place separately.

Lanuvium received the full citizenship and the restitution of her sacred things, with the proviso that the temple and grove of Juno Sospita should belong in common to the Roman people and the citizens living at Lanuvium. Aricium, Nomentum, and Pedum obtained the same political rights as Lanuvium. Tusculum retained the citizenship which it had had before, and the responsibility for the part it took in the war was removed from the State as a whole and fastened on a few individuals. The Veliternians, who had been Roman citizens from old times, were in consequence of their numerous revolts severely dealt with; their walls were thrown down, their senate deported and ordered to live on the other side of the Tiber; if any of them were caught on this side of the river, he was to be fined 1000 *ases*, and the man who caught him was not to release him from confinement till the money was paid. Colonists were sent on to the land they had possessed, and their numbers made Velitrae look as populous as formerly.

Antium also was assigned to a fresh body of colonists, but the Antiates were permitted to enrol themselves as colonists if they chose; their warships were taken away, and they were forbidden to possess any more; they were admitted to citizenship. Tibur and Praeneste had their domains confiscated, not owing to the part which they, in common with the rest of Latium, had taken in the war, but because, jealous of the Roman power, they had joined arms with the barbarous nation of the Gauls. The rest of the Latin cities were deprived of the rights of intermarriage, free trade, and common councils with each other. Capua, as a reward for the refusal of its aristocracy to join the Latins, was allowed to enjoy the private rights of Roman citizens, as were also Fundi and Formiae, because they had always allowed a free passage through their territory. It was decided that Cumae and Suessula should enjoy the same rights as Capua. Some of the ships of Antium were taken into the Roman docks, others were burnt and their beaks (*rostra*) were fastened on the front of a raised gallery which was constructed at the end of the Forum, and which from this circumstance was called the Rostra.

2. COLONIZATION AND THE EXTENSION OF CITIZENSHIP*

Gaius Velleius Paterculus (*ca.* 19 B.C.– after A.D. 31) was a soldier who fought under Tiberius for eight years. His *Compendium of Roman History* is sketchy in its earlier part but grows fuller as it approaches his own time. The following is one of several valuable excursuses.

* Reprinted by permission of the publishers from Loeb Classical Library, Velleius Paterculus, *Compendium of Roman History*, 1. 14, translated by F. W. Shipley, Cambridge, Mass.: Harvard University Press, 1924.

Inasmuch as related facts make more impression upon the mind and eye when grouped together than when they are given separately in their chronological sequence, I have decided to separate the first part of this work from the second by a useful summary, and to insert in this place an account, with the date, of each colony founded by order of the senate since the capture of Rome by the Gauls; for, in the case of the military colonies, their very names reveal their origins and their founders. And it will perhaps not seem out of place, if, in this connexion, we weave into our history the various extensions of the citizenship and the growth of the Roman name through granting to others a share in its privileges.

Seven years after the capture of the city by the Gauls a colony was founded at Sutrium, another a year later at Setia, and another after an interval of nine years at Nepe. Thirty-two years later the Aricians were admitted to the citizenship. Three hundred and sixty years from the present date, in the consulship of Spurius Postumius and Veturius Calvinus, the citizenship without the right of voting was given to the Campanians and a portion of the Samnites, and in the same year a colony was established at Cales. Then, after an interval of three years, the people of Fundi and of Formiae were admitted to the citizenship, in the very year of the founding of Alexandria. In the following year the citizenship was granted to the inhabitants of Acerra by the censors Spurius Postumius and Philo Publilius. Three years later a colony was established at Tarracina, four years afterwards another at Luceria; others

three years later at Suessa Aurunca and Saticula, and another two years after these at Interamna. After that the work of colonization was suspended for ten years. Then the colonies of Sora and Alba were founded, and two years later that of Carseoli. But in the fifth consulship of Quintus Fabius, and the fourth of Decius Mus, the year in which King Pyrrhus began his reign, colonists were sent to Minturnae and Sinuessa, and four years afterwards to Venusia. After an interval of two years the citizenship without the right of suffrage was given to the Sabines in the consulship of Manius Curius and Rufinus Cornelius. This event took place three hundred and twenty years ago. In the consulship of Fabius Dorso and Claudius Canina, three hundred years before the present date, colonies were established at Cosa and Paestum. After an interval of five years, in the consulship of Sempronius Sophus and Appius, the son of Appius the Blind, colonists were sent to Ariminum and Beneventum and the right of suffrage was granted to the Sabines. At the outbreak of the First Punic War Firmum and Castrum were occupied by colonies, a year later Aesernia, Aefulum and Alsium seventeen years later, and Fregenae two years afterward. Brundisium was established in the next year in the consulship of Torquatus and Sempronius, Spoletium three years afterwards in the year in which the Floralia were instituted. Two years afterwards a colony was established at Valentia, and Cremona and Placentia were established just before Hannibal's arrival in Italy.

3. MUNICIPIA AND COLONIAE*

Two of the important devices of Roman rule were the *municipia* and the *coloniae*. By the second century of the Christian era, their meaning had become vague and it is our good fortune that Aulus Gellius, a writer of that period, took the trouble to clarify the issue.

* Reprinted by permission of the publishers from Loeb Classical Library, Aulus Gellius, *Attic Nights*, 16. 13, translated by J. C. Rolfe (Cambridge, Mass.: Harvard University Press, 1927).

Municipes and *municipia* are words which are readily spoken and in common use, and you would never find a man who uses them who does not think that he understands perfectly what he is saying. But in fact it is something different, and the meaning is different. For how rarely is one of us found who, coming from a colony of the Roman people, does not say what is far removed from reason and from truth, namely, that he is *municeps* and that his fellow citizens are *municipes*? So general is the ignorance of what *municipia* are and what rights they have, and how far they differ from a "colony," as well as the belief that *coloniae* are better off than *municipia*.

With regard to the errors in this opinion which is so general the deified Hadrian, in the speech which he delivered in the senate *In Behalf of the Italicenses*, from whom he himself came, discoursed most learnedly, showing his surprise that the Italicenses themselves and also some other ancient *municipia*, among whom he names the citizens of Utica, when they might enjoy their own customs and laws, desired instead to have the rights of colonies. Moreover, he asserts that the citizens of Praeneste earnestly begged and prayed the emperor Tiberius that they might be changed from a colony into the condition of a *municipium*, and that Tiberius granted their request by way of conferring a favour, because in their territory, and near their town itself, he had recovered from a dangerous illness.

Municipes, then, are Roman citizens from free towns, using their own laws and enjoying their own rights, merely sharing with the Roman people an honorary *munus*, or "privilege" (from the enjoyment of which privilege they appear to derive their name), and bounded by no other compulsion and no other law of the Roman people, except such as their own citizens have officially ratified. We learn besides that the people of Caere were the first *municipes* without the right of suffrage, and that it was allowed them to assume the honour of Roman citizenship, but yet to be free from service and burdens, in return for receiving and guarding sacred objects during the war with the Gauls. Hence by contraries those tablets were called *Caerites* on which the censors ordered those to be enrolled whom they deprived of their votes by way of disgrace.

But the relationship of the "colonies" is a different one; for they do not come into citizenship from without, nor grow from roots of their own, but they are as it were transplanted from the State and have all the laws and institutions of the Roman people, not those of their own choice. This condition, although it is more exposed to control and less free, is nevertheless thought preferable and superior because of the greatness and majesty of the Roman people, of which those colonies seem to be miniatures, as it were, and in a way copies; and at the same time because the rights of the municipal towns become obscure and invalid, and from ignorance of their existence the townsmen are no longer able to make use of them.

4. THE INTERNATIONAL RELATIONS OF ROME*

The peoples of Greece and Italy offer, amidst many general points of similarity, some striking differences in their conceptions of international relations. The

* A. H. J. Greenidge, *Roman Public Life* (London and New York: The Macmillan Company, 1901), pp. 289–310.

pan-Hellenic sentiment, which created a shadowy law of nations, has no pan-Italic counterpart. Outside the Greek city-state there was but the sentiment of nationality to create rules for human conduct; but, for this very reason, the rules, when created, were of pan-Hellenic validity.

In Italy we get narrower but closer groupings; its history is the history of leagues, and the inevitable result of this more concentrated life was a closeness of international ties between the federated members which stood in marked contrast to the vagueness of the relations between the isolated groups.

The ties of religion and of ethnic affinity, as expressed in an obvious similarity of institutions, were, in Italy as elsewhere, the strongest connecting forces between states; but in Italy they were but the first rude ligaments that gave place to a stronger political bond and that crumbled to pieces when the more enduring chain had been forged. The festival of the Alban Mount became to the Latins, as the sacred centre of Volsinii to the Etruscans, but the religious symbol of a lasting league. Beyond the limits of the league the national and religious sentiment was weak. There was no Delphi to direct the Italian peoples, and no Olympia at which they might meet.

This isolated grouping of the Italian peoples may have been partly due to the great mixture of the populations of Italy south of the Alps and south even of the Apennines; but the earliest Italian history reveals the fact that even the closely-related races of Latins, Umbrians, and Sabellians were not connected by much closer ties of an international character than those which bound each to the Etruscan, the Iapygian, the Gaul, and the Greek. It is true that with the progress of time something like an ethnic sentiment was created in the purely Italian group, with vast consequences to the history of the world. After the Umbrian power, which had once extended from sea to sea, had been weakened, on the left by the Etruscan, on the right by the Celt, Rome becomes the great frontier power, the bulwark of the group of blood-related nations against the foreign-speaking Tuscan and the Gaul whose kinship with herself she had forgotten; but the relation soon became political, and, therefore, more than international. That aggregation of vague human sentiments, which is called International Law, was not juristically stronger within the sphere of the blood-related than it was within the sphere of the Italian group of peoples.

Within this wider sphere of humanity, that was not yet "Italian," there are traces of the observance by Rome of customs relating to the conduct of war and to negotiations for procuring peace—customs which by their very existence show that, though the early Roman employed the same word to designate the stranger and the enemy, a state of war was not considered as the permanent relation even between *hostes*; which prove, by their elaboration, the antiquity of some sense of international obligation, and which exhibit, by the constancy with which they were applied, the existence of reciprocal forms and duties owed by the hostile state to Rome. The functions of the *Fetiales*, the priestly ambassadors (*oratores*) who demand reparation, declare war and ratify a peace, seem never to have been confined to those peoples with whom Rome had treaty relations, but to have been extended to any nation which had not by specific acts waged war on Rome. Four of the priestly guild of *Fetiales* were appointed to seek redress. These elected one of their number to become their representative, to be for the time the "ratifying father of the Roman people" (*pater patratus populi Romani*). At the borders of the offending tribe the *pater* with many imprecations called Jupiter to witness that the grievance was established, the demand reasonable. Three times did he make the same appeal— to the first sojourner he met in the stranger's territory, to the sentinel at the gate, and to the magistrate within the walls. Thirty days were allowed for the reply; on the first of these the standard was hoisted on the citadel of Rome, and the burgess army gathered for the threatening war. If an appeasing answer were not returned within these days of grace, the *pater* again set forth and launched a charred spear (the prehistoric weapon of hardened wood) into the territory of the offender, with words setting forth the menace of war. When the struggle was over it was he who struck the peace and the sacrificial victim with a flint-stone which symbolized the watchful Jupiter (*Jupiter lapis*). The sanctity of envoys, other than these priestly messengers, was as rigorously observed in the Italian as in the Greek world. A violent death on an embassy was a martyrdom deserving of immortality, and the ancient Rostra in the Comitium showed a group of statues erected to those who had met their fate in the cause of peace. The neutrality of ambassadors was exacted with equal care, and the disaster of the Allia might be looked on as a retribution for the impious precipitancy of the Fabii who, forgetting their sacred character, fought in the ranks of Clusium against the Celtic hordes.

In the agreements made by generals and envoys with a foreign people, the idea, common to most primitive minds, that it is the oath which makes the promise binding is strikingly present. We have already touched on the vast constitutional import of this conception in its connexion with the question posed but never completely answered by the too patriotic jurists: "Who could take the oath on behalf of the Roman people?" But the theory which on the whole prevailed, that it could not be taken by a general in the field, not only nullified the promise so made and rendered it a mere agreement (*sponsio*), valid between citizens but not between strangers, but exposed the rash swearer to the extremest penalties. With a strange inconsistency of judgment it was held that the oath, which was no oath, laid the guilt of perjury on the conscience of the people, unless the man who had caused the people unwittingly to sin was offered up as an atoning sacrifice. Naked and bound, like the sacrificial human victim of prehistoric times prepared for the altar, the *imperator* was surrendered to the offended people. It is not surprising that the latter—whether Samnites, Spaniards, or Numidians—refused to take the worthless gift from the hands of the *pater patratus*, and preferred to continue the conflict with a people still convicted of sin. The individual oath to return, made by a prisoner of war released on parole, though binding on his soul alone and, as a religious obligation, not punishable by the civil arm, was enforced by the public conscience. One—others said more than one—of the Roman captives sent by Hannibal after Cannae to negotiate an exchange of prisoners declined to return on the negotiations falling through. The pretext was that they had revisited the camp of the conqueror *after* the oath has been taken. Tradition varied as to the punishment imposed by Rome; some spoke of a summary arrest and enforced return to the Phoenician camp, others of a degradation by the censor and of a public detestation that drove the perjurer to suicide.

Such are some of the isolated specimens that have been handed down to us of rules of international right which Rome thought due to every nation. But, apart from such universal duties, the Roman mind, with its simple dichotomy of the world into enemies (*hostes*) and friends (*amici*), recognised varying degrees of obligation as due to either class. The *hostes* were all states or individuals with whom Rome had no treaty relations. With these there was no presupposition even of constant diplomatic relations, and their absence was symbolised by the manner in which envoys from such states were received. The tradition of "speaking with one's enemy in the gate" was rigorously preserved to the end of the Republic, and the Senate had to meet a messenger from the enemy outside the walls. The friends of Rome were those with whom she had any relations that approximated to a federative character. There might be no definite treaty, no specified interchange of obligations; but the vague term *amicitia* with kindred titles of affection was applied to the vaguest association as well as to the closest alliance with Rome; it was indifferently a symbol of the greatest independence or of the practical subjection of the contracting state. The members of the military symmachy in Italy could share this title with distant Carthage, and even the barbarous Aedui are "kinsmen and brothers" of the Roman people. Even in the case of these communities the perpetual representation of mutual interests by means of permanent ambassadors—an institution still in its infancy in the seventeenth century of our era—was naturally unknown; but their recognition as friends granted their envoys or representatives an entrance and an audience of the Senate within the walls.

Closer relations between Rome and her "friends" were generally conditioned by ethnic and their corresponding religious ties. But the foreign element in early Rome shows that this was not universally the case. The rape of the Sabine women in its least significance reveals the fact of the close tie of intermarriage between Rome and a non-Latin community; the first treaty with Carthage reveals commercial relations, which were accompanied by some form of international jurisdiction, with a Phoenician power.

The first, because the most universal, ties which attract our attention as based on treaty relations are those of commerce. Commercial treaties with the foreigner led, in the very infancy of Roman history, to the development both of common courts and of a common code.

In the later Republic and in the Empire we have frequent mention of a civil court which was believed to have had an international origin. Attempts have been made to assign to this court of *recuperatores* a purely Roman source; but its essential peculiarities—the large uneven number of jurors, three or five, when the ordinary civil courts knew but one; the rapidity and simplicity of the procedure; the *formula* framed by a magistrate and not taken from the *legis actiones* of the civil law—are best explained as survivals of a time when it was a mixed court of international jurisdiction. The two or four jurors probably represented the contracting states in equal proportions, the third or fifth may have been an arbitrator chosen from another community; the magistrate who gave the *formula* would have been an official of the town in which the mixed court sat.

But the *formula* implied a system of legal principles, and these could not easily be furnished by the civil law (*jus civile*) of each contracting state. It was not Roman pride that prevented the foreigner from participating in her native law; it was the unwillingness of the foreigner to be made subject to a code characterised by excessive cumbrousness, by danger and by delay, and the counter-objection of the Roman to be the victim of similar disadvantages in the contracting state. No merchant, to whom time meant money, would adopt the cumbrous form of conveyance known as the *mancipatio*, when ownership could be acquired by the simple transfer (*traditio*) known of all nations; none would care to repeat a *formula* (to be learnt only of the Roman pontiff), the least error in the utterance of which was sufficient to extinguish his claim; and the symbolic acts performed before the praetor, though possibly dear to the Roman mind, could not have been attractive to the foreigner. Convenience dictated a compromise, and this was found in the gradual collection of a body of rights (*jus*) from the customs of "the world" (*gentes*) as known to the Romans. This *jus gentium*, or body of rights possessed by man as a citizen of the world, was a code of private international law, and it cannot be regarded as being even purely Italian. A nation that borrowed its alphabet from a Chalcidian city, that imitated the military organisation of the Hellenes, that traded in the sixth century with Sicily, Sardinia, Libya and Carthage, must have been deeply imbued with the customs of the Greek and Phoenician world. Nor was this code a growth of Rome's supremacy, for her commercial preceded her political greatness. Its origin dates back to a time probably anterior to the Republic, certainly far earlier than the institution of the praetorship. We have already noticed how for more than a century the same civil judge administered both laws, that of the state and that of the *gentes*, and how the *jus civile* was insensibly modified by contact with its younger relative.

But closer relations than those of commerce might exist between Rome and states connected with her by neighbourhood or kindred. The interchange of the rights of private law, of ownership and of marriage, which the Greeks called ἰσοπολιτεία, was a natural out-growth of the Italian tendency to close political association. Such communion rendered each member of the contracting states in private law a *civis* of the other; the *conubium* carried with it the *patria potestas* and all the family rights that flowed from this power; the *commercium* allowed the citizen of the contracting state to own Roman land, to convey property by Roman forms, to make a contract by the ceremonial of the *sponsio*, to inherit from a Roman or to make a Roman his heir, while it gave the citizen of Rome corresponding rights in the alien city. There could be no question here of mixed tribunals or of private international law. The courts of each state were fully competent; if we may judge from the early relations of Rome with the Latin cities, the place in which the contract had been concluded, or, in other words, the forms of the contract, determined the competence of the court.

Still more definite bonds of union than these relations of private law (although often their primary condition) were certain political creations which made the ties between the states something more than international. It was a nucleus approaching a federal government which gave the first impulse to the extension of Roman power in Italy. Rome, as known to us in legend, is never quite a city-state. She is an offshoot of Alba Longa, the titular head of the Latin league. Tradition says that her conquest of her mother city led to her occupying a singular position with respect to the thirty cities of this league. She was one of the contracting parties, the cities were the other; she was the equal, not the member, of the group. The acceptance of this position by the confederate cities shows their eagerness for the protection of the frontier town; but the protectorate became burdensome, a war ensued, and Roman rule was shaken off only to be reimposed on firmer lines by the strong hand of the Etruscan dynasty represented by the Tarquins. Rome now became one at least of the religious centres of the league, and the Diana of the Aventine symbolised the lasting union of the Latin folk. The expulsion of the kings, while it stripped Rome of territory, shook for a time the allegiance of the league, and it was not until 493 B.C. that the old conditions were renewed; for the details that might in historical times be read in the treaty attributed to Sp. Cassius were doubtless but a replica of the old terms of the alliance. Eternal peace was enjoined, mutual support was to be given in war, and each contracting party was to share equally in the booty. The supreme command in war was to be held now by the Roman general, now by the commander of the confederate forces. But the closest bond was that of ἰσοπολιτεία, the mutual participation in *commercium* and doubtless also in *conubium*, which was accompanied by the proviso that the court of the state, in which the contract had been concluded and the case was therefore tried, should give speedy satisfaction to the claimant from each community. Reciprocity such as this was naturally accompanied by freedom in choice of domicile. The Roman settled in the Latin city and the Latin in the Roman retained the private rights of both communities. It is doubtful whether at this period the transference of residence was accompanied by a share in the voting rights of the state in which the immigrant sojourned.

To this association a third factor was soon added in the Hernican league. The extension of the confederation beyond its ethnic limits was a grand strategic move; for by the inclusion of the Hernici, Rome now presented a compact chain of fortresses against her enemies of the east and south, the Aequi and the Volsci. Their military importance explains why the newly admitted members were raised to the level of the older allies. They boasted the same reciprocity of private rights with Rome, they shared in a third part of the spoils of war, and they joined with Romans and Latins in the work of common colonisation.

This colonisation was at once a military and social measure, and the means by which the league extended its geographical and political limits. The custom of war, which permitted the Italian tribes to annex a third of all conquered land, had ever been used as a means of expansion by the powerful league. And this expansion was a very real one; for the Latin colonies (*coloniae Latinae*), as they were called, were full members of the society that gave them birth. Such towns as Suessa Pometia, Cora, and Velitrae had been military outposts in the territory of the Volsci; and now the Volscian, the Rutulian, and even the Etruscan were oppressed with the weight of new foundations by the three great powers. But the year 384 seems to mark a strange and unaccountable break in the history of this extension. Of all the Latin colonies founded after that date, but one is mentioned as a member of the confederacy—a circumstance which.has led to the conclusion that Rome (whether with or without the consent of the other members)

had cut off all future joint foundations from the religious and federal privileges of the league. Otherwise the consequences of this exclusion were not great; the new towns were military allies of the league, not of Rome, and their citizens still possessed those private rights which always remained of the essence of *latinitas*. Forty-seven cities—partly old Latin towns, partly Latin colonies earlier than 384—still participated in the Latin festival; that within this circle a distinction was drawn between thirty voting and seventeen non-voting members is an insecure conclusion based on the attempts of the annalists to reconstruct the traditional number of thirty Latin cities; there may still have been thirty votes, but these may well have been distributed in some way over the forty-seven cities of the league. That the closing of the Latin confederacy was due mainly to Roman pressure is perhaps shown by the series of dangerous revolts amongst its cities, which often sided with their ancient enemies the Volsci. The Hernicans were as eager to shake off the yoke; but Rome emerged from both crises with her power strengthened and her commonwealth enlarged. The latter result was due to a renewed employment of her old device of absorption. Tusculum in 381, and Satricum not long afterwards, had their commonwealths destroyed, and were forced, as a penal measure, to accept the full or partial Roman citizenship. At the close of the struggle in 358 the leagues were renewed and the relations of Rome with the two groups of states remodelled, probably on harder terms. In the Samnite war which followed, the Latin cities first clung to Rome, for they preferred a native to a Sabellian hegemony; but Rome's rapid conclusion of a treaty of peace and alliance with the Samnites, which the league was asked to accept and not to ratify, was taken as the final proof of actual subjection concealed under the name of a hegemony. The Latins made their last demands; they gave up their position as a military confederacy, but they did not wish to be absorbed into the body politic of Rome. They asked for the golden mean—a system of federal government, but one that should still preserve the fundamental distinction between Rome and the confederate cities. One of the consuls was to be a Roman, the other a Latin, and half the Senate was to be chosen from Latium. But the civic feeling was too strong at Rome; she would not herself surrender the communal constitution which she had so often wrested from others; she rejected the alternative which would have paralysed her power as a conquering state and made of her but a federal capital. Her "No!" to the Latins was one of the turning-points in the history of Italy and of the world.

The battles of Veseris and Trifanum gave her the victory, but she was sorely puzzled as to the use to be made of it. The league was to be broken up, its members isolated, and this work of disintegration was carried through with thoroughness; not only were the federal assemblies (*concilia*) abolished, but no right of inter-marriage or of commercial intercourse (*jus conubii et commercii*) was permitted between the cities. But how to deal with the individual communities was a far harder problem. The incorporation which had been the punishment of isolated revolt could not be applied to the *disjecta membra* of a whole league, for it would have changed the city-state into a nation. Hence the plan adopted was a compromise between the old policy of absorption and a new principle—that of alliance. Aricia, Pedum, and Lanuvium lost their independence and received the full Roman franchise; while Tibur, Praeneste, Lavinium were compelled to conclude separate treaties (*foedera*) with Rome, and formed the nucleus of the ever-growing class of *civitates foederatae*. Thirty years later (306 B.C.) a similar fate befell the remaining league of the Hernici. Their loyalty had not stood the test of the second Samnite war; but there were degrees of guilt

amongst the cities. Anagnia, the chief centre of the revolt, and other incriminated towns, were given merely the private rights of citizenship; the full citizenship was indeed offered to the three loyal towns of Aletrium, Ferentinum, and Verulae, but, on their expressing a preference for their own local constitutions and codes, they were permitted to retain an autonomy guaranteed by separate treaties. The break up of the Hernican league was only an incident in a triumphant career of conquest that was never followed by annexation. The Samnite wars and the struggle with Pyrrhus had ended in the acknowledgment of Rome's supremacy by every nation south of the Macra and the Rubicon. The three civilisations of Greece, Tuscany, and Italy furnished her in-differently with allies; the town and the tribal union were alike represented in her symmachy. Tibur and Praeneste in Latium, Aletrium and Ferentinum amongst the Hernici, Volaterrae and Clusium in Etruria, Iguvium in Umbria, the Pincentes, Marsi, and Peligni amongst the Sabellians, and Greek cities like Neapolis in Campania or Rhegium amongst the Bruttii, are types of the states and peoples that she numbered amongst her *socii*.

The effect of this unification, and of the tendencies which had preceded it, was to divide the inhabitants of Italy into two broad classes—those of citizens (*cives*) and those of allies (*socii*) of Rome. The first class (far the smaller numerically) represented the earlier effort at incorpora-tion; the second was the consequence of the later policy which founded a military league. Minuter distinctions of rights, which necessitate cross-divisions in the classification of the states, sometimes obscure this fundamental analysis; but it was never lost sight of and was the guiding light to the Roman lawyer, as it is to us, in his path through the labyrinth of the complex organisation of Italy.

The *cives* of Rome bear this name either in a full or a partial sense; they may be citizens with voting rights or citizens in private law alone (*cives sine suffragio*). If we fix our attention on the first of these classes, we find that historically there were two modes in which the *civitas* was gained by a commune outside the city. It might be due to the incorporation of an already existing state, or it might be the consequence of the planting of a Roman colony. The merging of some of the Latin communities in Rome has already furnished instances of the former mode of conferment; the Roman colonies which illustrate the second (*coloniae civium Romanorum*) were outlying fragments of the Populus, planted as a defensive garrison on the third of the conquered land, which was the legitimate spoil of the invader. A social was from the first combined with the military object; but the enforced exodus of portions of the burgess body on some occasions proves that, in this form of colonisation, the interest of the state came before that of the individual. It was, in fact, a military levy ordained by law, although voluntary profession usually took the place of the compulsory summons of the regular *dilectus*. In military array, with standards flying, the squadron marched to the appointed place under the leadership of the commissioners appointed by the people. When a new town was to be founded, or an old one reconstituted, it was done with the imposing ceremonies that marked the birth and enlargement of Rome. After the will of the gods had been tested and happy omens gained, the commissioners, with veiled heads and loins girt up, guided a plough, to which were yoked an ox and a cow. They thus drew the *pomerium* of the state, only staying the furrow where the gates of the city were to be. The greater number of these settlements of Roman citizens were for the protection of the Italian coasts, and the members of the maritime colonies (*coloniae maritimae*) were allowed exemption from active military service. Few in numbers (often but a handful of 300 men), and

settled in an already existing political society, the colonists formed a privileged patriciate amongst its older members. The town-council, and such subordinate magistrates as Rome allowed them to possess, were probably chosen from the new settlers alone; but, as the autonomy which they enjoyed was not great, as they possessed no high judicial magistrates of their own, and as their voting power at Rome was more a potential than an actual right, they differed little from the native inhabitants, who as *cives sine suffragio* came equally under the jurisdiction of the Roman courts and their representatives.

Whether the commune of Roman citizens had had a natural or artificial growth, it was never in early times a true state (*civitas*). Roman law knew of ἰσοπολιτεία, but not of the close bond of συμπολιτεία; and the principle that no Roman citizen could be a full member of another state, although in the later Republic it had given place to the theory of the municipal independence of the *civis*, was always maintained in international relations with states of the outer world. As the negation of state life implied the negation of communal independence, we are not surprised to find that none of these communities of Roman citizens possessed a true civic organisation of its own. We cannot define the rights of their town-councils, we cannot assert the absolute non-existence of popular gatherings for certain purposes; but the absence of the *imperium* and of a true judicial magistracy is clearly discerned. These communes fell under the immediate civil jurisdiction, originally of the consuls, later of the *praetor urbanus*. Originally it may have been necessary for every case not settled by voluntary arbitration to be brought to Rome, but the distance of some of these towns from the capital would have soon rendered this principle of jurisdiction impossible. The modern solution, that the judge should go on circuit, could not be thought of in a state where the bench consisted of a single man, and where this individual was prohibited by law from leaving the city for more than ten days during his year of office. The only alternative was furnished by the favorite Roman device of delegation. The praetor nominated praefects for jurisdiction (*praefecti juri dicundo*), and these were sent, sometimes as standing magistrates, sometimes perhaps as mere circuit judges, through the Roman towns, which were thence known as *praefecturae*. Delegation implies either a division of competence or, in the case of the lower court possessing full jurisdiction, an appeal to the delegating authority. There is no trace of the latter practice at Rome, and a systematic division of authority, although motives of convenience may sometimes have led the praetor to permit it, is inconsistent with the Roman idea of jurisdiction flowing direct from the *imperium*. Possibly the praetor permitted the praefect to regulate almost every kind of contentious jurisdiction, subject to his own right of summoning any case he pleased from the delegate to Rome. By a legal fiction the courts of the *praefecturae* were held to be within the praetor's sphere of competence, i.e. within a single milestone of the city; they were, to use the technical Roman expression, *judicia legitima*. No trace whatever has been preserved of the criminal procedure applied to such communities. The fact that the praefect was the delegate of a civil magistrate would not prove that he was incapable of exercising criminal jurisdiction, for *jurisdictio* of every kind is latent in the praetor's *imperium*. All higher jurisdiction was reserved for the people; but there was only one *populus Romanus*, that of the city of Rome. Hence when the citizen of Ostia or Tusculum was accused of an offence, the penalty for which demanded a popular sanction, we may assume that he could either make the appeal, through a fiction like that underlying the civil jurisdiction, in spite of his

local separation from Rome, or that he stepped, or was brought within, the first milestone of the city, the limit inside which the *provocatio* could legally be made.

The second type of *cives* are those without the right of suffrage (*sine suffragio*). There can be little question that the idea of this *status* was derived from Rome's relations with the cities of the Latin league; in her process of absorption, however, she conferred it on towns to which she did not grant the other typically Latin rights; in this way she made of it an independent *status*. The Etruscan town of Caere is said to have won this right in 353 as a gift for good service to Rome. After the dissolution of the Latin league in 338 B.C. a group of Campanian townships, Capua, Cumae, Atella, and Calatia, were with (the then Latin) Fundi and Formiae brought into this relation with the now dominant city of Latium; others nearer home, such as Arpinum of the Volsci, were similarly rewarded or absorbed (303 B.C.), while the *status* was imposed as a means of degrading and reducing to impotence rebellious townships such as Anagnia, the leading city of the Hernici. The motives of the conferment, although it might make a difference to the rights of the towns, produced none in the relations of their respective *cives* to Rome.

The *civis sine suffragio* was known as a *municeps*, and the state, all of whose full members enjoyed this *status*, derived from its occupants the name of *municipium*. The name of this type of citizen—the "taker up of burdens"—aptly expresses his subjection to the chief duties (*munera*) of Roman citizenship, such as service in the Roman legions, forced labour in raising defences, the payment of the war-tax (*tributum*), and his exclusion from the usually corresponding rights of suffrage and of office; it emphasises the fact, strange to the early Roman mind, of public duties not balanced by public rights, but it contains no implication of the strangest characteristic of the *municeps*—one almost unknown in ancient legal systems—the possession of a personality in private which is not the result of a personality in public law. The *municeps* possesses *commercium* with all its consequences; he possesses *conubium* with Rome; he is, from the point of view of private law, in every sense a citizen.

This possession of citizenship carried with it as a necessary consequence his subjection to the praetor's court. His home, the *municipium*, is therefore, equally with the community of full Roman citizens, a *praefectura*, and the rules of jurisdiction were the same in both classes of states. To the praefects nominated by the praetor were in course of time added others elected by the *comitia tributa*, and reckoned amongst the minor magistrates known as the *viginti-sex-viri*. These latter were the four praefects of Capua, Cumae, and the Campanian coast; but, in regard to the mode of election, there is no difference discernible between the judicial magistrates of the *municipia* and those of the communities of Roman citizens. Elected praefects visited the *municipium* of Capua and the Roman colony of Puteoli, while nominated praefects held their court in the colony of Saturnia and the municipal town of Anagnia.

But the praefect was far from representing the higher functions of government in every *municipium*. These towns fall into two broad divisions, not according to the rights which they receive, but according to the rights which they retain. The *civitas sine suffragio* might be granted *honoris causa* to a state which maintained its complete independence or its communal autonomy. It was thus conferred on Capua, Cumae, Formiae, and Fundi, and the gift of the partial citizenship under these conditions was a valued privilege. It enabled a Capuan to own Roman land, to settle on the *ager publicus*, to marry into the noble houses of Rome, and to serve, not in the auxiliary cohort, but in her army or in the legion raised from the *municipes*.

But meanwhile his own magistrate, the *meddix tuticus*, administers in the Campanian courts the native Sabellian law, his senate deliberates, and his popular assembly decides. Sometimes, as in the case of Capua, the state is still bound by treaty relations to Rome, and the two conflicting principles of armed alliance and of absorption are for once commingled.

Yet, in spite of their independence, there is every reason to believe that the inevitable praefects visited these states. We must assume, at least in the cases where autonomy reached the grade which is visible in Capua, that a dual system of law prevailed in these communities; the court and the procedure would follow the form of contract, whether Sabellian or Roman, and the parties might appear indifferently before the Capuan *meddix* or the Roman praefect. In other cases, where a large measure of administrative autonomy is visible, but where no magistrate with a rank than that of aedile is found within the state, it is possible that Roman law alone prevailed and that the Roman praefect was the only judge.

The lower class of *municipia* was represented by states "whose whole commonwealth had been merged in that of Rome." Of this class Anagnia, the degraded town of the Hernici, was a type. Stripped of all the active rights of citizenship, and under the direct government of a Roman praefect, the members of such towns possessed no personality in public law at all. Their position was that of the free Plebeians previous to their admission to the *suffragium* and the *honores*.

The second principle in Rome's Italian policy, first projected after the close of the Latin war and carried to its completion after the struggle with Pyrrhus, resulted in a great military hegemony over states, whose treaty relations enabled them to call themselves the "allies" (*socii*) of Rome. Collective names were soon devised to indicate the closeness of the union thus formed; at first the confederates were "wearers of the toga" (*togati*), a name that applied equally to the Latin, Sabellian, and Etruscan. But the introduction of the Greek *pallium* into the league destroyed this basis of classification; and the later term *Italici* was evolved, a word whose geographical signification emphasises the idea of a territorial limit to certain rights—one which, as we shall see, was not rigorously preserved, but which marks the distinction, valid alike for the Republic and the Principate, between Italy as the privileged and the provinces as the unprivileged world.

The condition of a conquered town, whether in Italy or the provinces, before its alliance with Rome, is described by the word *deditio*, a term which implies absolute surrender to the power (*ditio, potestas*) or to the honour (*fides*) of the Roman people, the two latter expressions being to the Roman mind legally equivalent. Such a *dediticia civitas* is in the negative condition of an absolute suspension of rights, and remains in this case until some are given back to Rome with a guarantee of their permanence. *Deditio* is, therefore, a temporary *status*, although it might be occasionally prolonged as a penal measure, as it was in the case of the revolted Bruttii after the Hannibalic war. In Italy, as a rule, the terms that Rome dictated were those of a military alliance, the conditions for membership of this being, firstly, external sovereignty (*libertas*), as conditioned by the terms and objects of the league; secondly, internal independence—a condition which the Greek cities called αὐτονομία, and which, in a Latin charter to a provincial town, appears in the form of the permit *suis legibus uti*; thirdly, a basis for these rights, as also for the obligations which these states owed to Rome. In dealings with the extra-Italian world this basis was either a charter (*lex data*), given by the Roman people and revocable by them, or a treaty (*foedus*), equally sanctioned by the people but irrevocable, as being sworn to by the two

contracting parties; its revocation could only be the consequence of a genuine *casus belli*. In the first case the state is a *libera civitas*, in the second a *libera et foederata civitas*, or, in its more general and briefer designation, a *foederata civitas*. In Italy positive evidence furnishes us only with the *foederatae*, but the existence of the *liberae civitates* must be assumed, since, immediately on the beginning of provincial organisation in Sicily, this *status* is adopted.

In Italy also there was doubtless the distinction between the higher and the lower kind of *foedus*—the *foedus aequum* and the *foedus iniquum*. In all treaties concluded between Rome and cities in her symmachy there was a recognition of partial dependence in the latter; but some of these treaties contained a "suzerainty" clause to the effect that the state in question should "in a friendly spirit respect the majesty of the Roman people." This clause did not diminish the *libertas* of the state accepting it, but merely strengthened the position of Rome. It was a characteristic of the *iniquum foedus*.

The duties of the federate cities expressed in their name (*socii*, σύμμαχοι) were primarily the furnishing of requisitions whether in men or ships. The latter were demanded from the Greek cities of the coast, but Italy as a whole furnished the auxiliary land armies of Rome, the *togati* liable to the levy. Every state had to keep a register of its effective strength in accordance with a principle of assessment (*formula*). The general demands of Rome were specified in the treaties; the special levies required at any given time were dictated by the Senate and consuls.

Military requisitions necessarily involve pecuniary burdens. But these were all indirect. Each city had complete control of its own finances; no tribute was imposed by Rome, and the antithesis to the *socius* is the *stipendiarius*. This immunity was originally based on the theory of treaty relations; later, when the view had grown up that the tribune paid by the stipendiary states was the result of their precarious tenure as *possessores*, the Italians were held to be owners of their land. The *jus Italicum* of the Principate confers on any state to which it is granted quiritarian ownership, and, therefore, immunity from taxation on land.

Enjoyment of their own laws and control of their own courts were other symbols of the autonomy of the allies. Rome could not legislate for the Italian *socii*, and they were beyond the judicial authority of the Roman magistrate in Italy.

But the necessities of social and commercial intercourse rendered it advisable that the Italian allies—more especially the Latins—should be brought into close legal relations with Rome, and the acceptance by the latter of innumerable civil laws of the central state is attested by Cicero. The Italians are known to have been bound by a *plebiscitum* concerning loans—this, however, only made contracts of a certain kind between them and Romans invalid, and may not have demanded their consent; but their formal acceptance must have been required for the Didian law, which extended the sumptuary regulations of the *lex Fannia* to all the *Italici*. The "free" as well as the "federate" city has the right to accept or decline a legislate proposal put before it by the Roman government.

Closest of all to Rome were the Latins. As members of federate cities they were amongst the *socii*, and it is only as a class with special privileges that they are distinguished from the latter. *Latinitas* had, through the efforts of colonisation, long lost its geographical and ethnic significance. It was the name for a *status* often accepted by Roman citizens, which combined the anomalies of sovereignty and a partial Roman citizenship. The sovereign rights are those possessed by the *socii*, the civic privileges were originally those held by the *municipia*; but it is possible that on and after the foundation of Ari-

minum and the last twelve Latin colonies *commercium* alone was granted, *conubium* refused. The most distinctive privilege of the Latin had been the concession of facilities for acquiring Roman political rights. A Latin who migrated from his town and became a domiciled immigrant (*incola*) of Rome had retained his civic rights in private law, and gained a limited power of suffrage. He could even by complete expatriation (*exilium*) surrender his own *civitas* and attain the full Roman citizenship. But the conditions subsequently imposed on this right were evaded, immigration continued unchecked, and there was a danger of the depopulation of the districts from which the exiles came. This evil suggested the later method, which gave the Latins admission to the *civitas*. The holder of a magistracy in his native town was, by the mere fact of his position, to become a full citizen of Rome. It is improbable that this right replaced the right of exile possessed by already existing Latin towns, and the date of its origin is unknown; but it possibly accompanied the remodelling of Latin rights in 268 B.C., and is henceforth the typical privilege of the Latin colony. Another mode in which the individual Latin could acquire the Roman *civitas* was by conducting a successful prosecution under the Acilian and Servilian laws of extortion.

The freedom of the cities, whether Latin or Italian, seems to have won rigid respect from Rome and her magistrates. The burdens of military service were, indeed, unevenly distributed between the central city and her allies, while the spoils of war were mainly for the Roman. But it was a shock and a surprise when in 173 B.C. a consul made personal requisitions on the federate city of Praeneste. The lesson once learnt was only too faithfully followed, and the illegal demands of Roman officials were accompanied by acts of capricious violence. But the burden of service and the misuse of power were not the only motives urging the allies to seek the *civitas* of Rome; nor was it merely a sentimental desire to be invested with the Roman name. The citizenship had a positive value both as a protection and a source of gain. The protection against capital or corporal penalties tacitly accorded to Romans by provincial governors could not be claimed by the allies, and, although there is no evidence that Rome, in her final organisation of the Italian confederacy, continued her early policy of inhibiting *commercium* between the towns,

yet citizenship had a commercial value. Ownership of land in the provinces was protected by the praetor and the proconsul, but only when it was held by a Roman. To the Roman trade with the barbarian was secure, to the Italian precarious; and everywhere he had to face the competition of the commercial companies of Roman knights. The grounds of interest coincided with those of sentiment in producing a demand which the progressive party amongst the Romans strove to meet.

5. The Organization of Italy*

It is not our purpose, in this study, to trace the development of Rome from a small township to the leading power in Italy. At the starting-point of our main investigation, this process is practically complete, and Italy, except for the Gauls and Ligurians, united under Roman leadership. But since we shall be concerned with the changes in the relative positions of Rome and the rest of Italy which accompanied and followed the further expansion of Roman power, and with the development of Roman ideas on imperial organization, we must briefly survey the organization of Italy in the late third century and the various ways in which Roman statecraft had attached the many cities and nations of ancient Italy to the leading state. For purposes of convenience, we shall consider the situation before the outbreak of the Second Punic War and discuss the various forms of association in turn.

(i) *Ciues Romani.* The most direct form was incorporation in the Roman state, the mark of which was the conferment of citizenship. This was an old and unsophisticated way, which was bound to reach its natural limits soon, under the

influence of increasing difficulties presented by distance and national differences. Originally it implied the transfer of the conquered population to Rome and the destruction of the town concerned: the new Roman citizen had to come to the city of Rome. It is not certain when this primitive method was outgrown. The discovery that alliance could also be used for subordination certainly did not put an end to it where it was still practicable. Probably the compulsory transfer of the population was soon abandoned: it was only the city as a body politic that had to be destroyed. The inhabitants were no doubt received into the new tribes that were formed for Roman emigrants to the newly-conquered territories. But the next major step was taken some time in the fourth century: it was the invention (or, more probably, re-application) of *ciuitas sine suffragio*. The origins of this concept, as of that of *municipium* (related to it), are wrapped in obscurity, which it is not our task to pierce. The first part of Festus' confused note on 'municipium' makes it probable that the concept had always existed: 'The term *municipium* is applied to that class of men who, when they came to Rome, were not Roman citizens but shared in all the privileges along with the Roman citizens except for voting and holding magistracies; ... after a number of

* E. Badian, *Foreign Clientelae 264–70 B.C.* (Clarendon, 1958), pp. 15–24. Reprinted by permission of The Clarendon Press, Oxford.

years they became Roman citizens.'* The category is probably that of aliens who had settled in Rome (under the *ius migrationis*) and were waiting for the censors to complete their enfranchisement. Their status was ambiguous, but temporary; and there is no reason why the institution should not, like the *ius migrationis* itself, date back to the beginning. At some time in the fourth century this concept was applied in a new sense. The city of Caere had been more closely linked with Rome than any other city in Etruria. By its assistance in the Gallic crisis it earned the special thanks of the Romans. Later, Caere joined Tarquinii in a war against Rome and was defeated. On this occasion, according to Livy, the memory of their old friendship earned the Caerites lenient treatment: they were given *indutiae* for 100 years and (apparently) not further punished. Bernardi rejects the Livian account and thinks that Caere was incorporated *sine suffragio* at this time; and there is much to be said for such a view. Livy, or his source, may simply be applying to Caere the scheme of limited truces which was Rome's normal method of dealing with Etruscan states; and the Horatian scholiast actually informs us (on what authority, he neglects to say) that Caere got its *ciuitas sine suffragio* after a defeat. The Etruscan War had made clear to the Romans the desirability of firmly controlling the territory north of the city, as far as the 'natural boundary' of the Ciminian Forest. An independent Caere might be a dangerous neighbour in the case of a *coniuratio Etruriae*. It is, as Fraccaro points out, at least likely that the Romans saw this need for protecting their northern flank—and if not immediately, then certainly as soon as they were engaged in the major wars in the south that followed a decade later. It was necessary to eliminate Caere as a potential enemy; and a truce (or even a *foedus*) would fail to give the necessary

security. The only alternative, on accepted policy, was the destruction of the city. But this is where the *uetus meritum* of the Caerites—and the close ties that bound the city to Rome—may have moved the Romans: they could not simply be sold into slavery, like the Veientines. On the other hand, they could not—even if incorporation *optimo iure* had already been invented, or was then considered—simply receive the franchise: Rome's problem was that of dealing, for the first time, with a largely non-Latin city that yet had sentimental claims. The solution was *ciuitas sine suffragio*: the city remained in existence, but the inhabitants were made Roman citizens—except for the two main privileges of citizens (that of voting and that of holding office). Their status, in fact, was assimilated to that of resident aliens waiting for enfranchisement—but there was no promise that enfranchisement was ever to follow. The censors were bidden to enrol the new citizens in a special list, the *Caerites tabulae* (the resident aliens—the original *municipes*—had, of course, not been on any census list: for when they *were* enrolled, it was on the list of citizens and completed their enfranchisement). In return for this inferiority, Caere was probably granted a certain degree of local autonomy. This case, then, provided the pattern that Rome was to follow extensively during the next half-century, in particular in the case of Campanian and Volscian communities, where the situation was very similar to that of Caere—Rome wanted direct control, but the cities, though non-Latin, had strong claims to consideration.

Thus the principle of receiving whole communities into the citizenship (or a form of it) was established. Its application was soon extended. The non-Latin city could not be given full citizenship immediately (and it is idle to inquire whether the *ciuitas sine suffragio* was meant to be 'permanent'—it was certainly not meant to be a short-term status); but when

---

* Translated from the Latin by Donald Kagan.

Rome decided to annex the territory of some Latin cities, for strategic reasons, after the great Latin War, the communities were received into the full citizenship. The difference—though important—was one of degree; the Latin was related to the Roman: he spoke the same language and could make an intelligent voter. This is probably the simple explanation of the difference in treatment between the Latin and the non-Latin *municipium*. But both were communities of citizens, with autonomous organization, within the Roman state. The principle of Caere, when applied to Latium, led to the *municipium ciuium Romanorum optimo iure*. And many of the *municipia ciuium sine suffragio* attained this full status in due course—though unfortunately we often do not know the precise date and circumstances.

By the end of the fourth century, then, Rome was much more than a city-state: she had recognized the principle of autonomous local organizations of her citizens within the state, even to the extent of making treaties with them. The possibility of the 'Roman world' had been created. But the body of Roman citizens was—and for centuries remained—only a small part of the population of Italy, and *ager Romanus* a small part of its area. We must therefore go on to consider the relation of Rome to those communities not incorporated in her state.

(ii) *Latini*. The nearest to Rome, in every way, were the Latins. Rome herself had once been no more than one of the numerous Latin *populi*, and both ancient and modern scholarship has been much concerned with her rise to hegemony and rule. It is generally accepted, nowadays, that about 500 B.C. Rome was already in control of a considerable part of the Latin coast. In the first treaty with Carthage, several 'peoples' in that area are described as ὑπήκοοι of Rome; and, what is perhaps even more interesting, Rome claims, by implication, a protectorate even over the independent cities of Latium. As Polybius

notices, there is as yet no mention of any states outside Latium. How the protectorate over the ὑπήκοοι was obtained and exercised, is not clear. Most probably we may assume treaties that in some way assured Roman superiority. In any case, the 'peoples' concerned were still regarded as politically independent: they could still, it appears, be members of the council of Ferentina. This was the political body corresponding to the League of Aricia, in which Rome (according to tradition) obtained the leading place under the last of the kings: it was probably this position that gave Rome the right to regard the Latin cities which were not ὑπήκοοι as also under her protection, and Latium as her sphere of influence.

With the Etruscan domination removed, this claim was contested by the Latins, who in a large measure regained their full independence. But with the appearance of invading hill-tribes in the fifth century, the need for coalition became plain: in some form, Roman hegemony was recognized in what is traditionally known as the treaty of Sp. Cassius. This was followed by a treaty with the Hernici—Rome's first extension of her hegemony beyond Latium. To supplement these treaties, which gave her a general position of pre-eminence in her small world, Rome probably again began to make special treaties with various smaller Latin states, perhaps making them ὑπήκοοι again. At any rate, by the middle of the fourth century, these 'subjects' again appear, and again do not include all Latium. Unfortunately, we know little of developments in Latium between these two dates. We do know that other states—notably Tibur and Praeneste—built up their own leagues of ὑπήκοοι, and consequently sometimes clashed with Rome. And we know that the Latins and Hernicans became restive as they saw federal armies used to increase the Roman *Hausmacht* in the north, while they themselves were insufficiently protected against the hill-tribes. But the threat of a new

Gallic invasion again united the Latins: the treaty of Cassius was renewed and, whatever it was before, it now became a treaty on equal terms between Rome and the rest of the Latins. In the second treaty with Carthage, Latium is again a Roman sphere of influence.

With the Volsci and Aequi warded off, the Latin League faced the Samnite Confederacy. The clash was bound to come, and it was precipitated by the Roman alliance with Capua. The Latins had probably again become restive under what was becoming the Roman yoke: even the Volsci could now be regarded as friends. It seemed advisable to the Roman leaders to confront their luke-warm allies with the Samnite danger, before the Latin League was too disunited to be able to deal with it—especially as this danger would strike the allies first and not approach Roman territory immediately. However, this time Rome miscalculated. The citizen army thought the war unnecessary; the Volsci attacked, and the Latin allies, as Rome's reverses proved her weakness, prepared to revolt. But the Samnites too were facing difficulties, especially in the south, where Archidamus might be dangerous. The result, after much diplomatic intrigue, was the Latin War: Rome had been unable to protect her allies in Latium and Campania against the Samnite danger, which moreover (in the case of Latium) she had wantonly brought upon them; thus the reason for acknowledging the hegemony of Rome had disappeared, and with it the fear of her. The Latins and Campanians, in their elation, thought they could both attack their fallen leader and continue the war against the Samnites. This was their fatal mistake. They were defeated by the combined force of Rome and Samnium, and the settlement of 338 saw the end of the Latin League and of the independent political importance of the Latin states. Rome had begun, perhaps, by protecting her Latin neighbours against the Etruscans

(though we cannot safely build on the quicksands of the prehistory of Rome and Latium), and certainly by representing and safeguarding them, after freeing herself from Etruscan domination, against the Etruscans' great Punic ally. She had borne the brunt of the Gallic invasion, and organized the Latin defence against the Gauls in the north and the hill-tribes in the east. In times of peace and apparent security the Latins had been restive at the growth of Rome's private power; but in times of danger the allies, on the whole, had held together and had looked to Rome for leadership. Rome, on the other hand, might claim (until 343) to have played her part fairly. If she had expanded her power in Etruria, she did thereby help to keep the threat of an Etruscan return from the Latins—and that might seem more important than the prevention of a Volscian raid. She had successfully led the Latins in their wars of defence and brought them rich booty. She had turned over parts of the conquered territory to their citizens in the form of Latin colonies; and she had not unwarrantably interfered with their freedom. She had not confiscated any of their territory as a result of their revolts, nor destroyed (or annexed) any of their cities. But her very success both increased her power and made her protection seem unnecessary to the Latins; and their consequent restiveness seemed faithless to Rome and helped to drive her to the unwise decision that was meant to show her allies the need for continued unity. The settlement of 338 marks the failure of Rome's first protectorate—the first of such failures that turned out to be the steps to her greatness.

Fortunately, as we have seen, by 338 Rome had worked out the principle of incorporation that enabled her to deal with her late allies. The whole of Latium was annexed, except for the larger states of Tibur and Praeneste, Ardea (which must have remained faithful), and probably Lavinium. Roman citizens were sent to occupy positions in Latium and Campania, and the key city of Antium received a Roman colony. And for the first time, as we have noticed, *ager Romanus* and *ciuitas Romana* were extended over large areas and important cities outside Latium.

The effect of the settlement on the concept of *Latinitas* was before long to dissociate it from the geographical concept of Latium and, in a different sphere, to begin the assimilation of 'Roman' and 'Latin' in meaning. Sherwin-White has traced and illustrated the development of this 'intangible bond', and we shall return to it in so far as it falls within the limits of our inquiry. Mean while we need only notice that by the beginning of the second century A. Albinus could call himself 'homo Romanus natus in Latio' and Ennius could talk about 'rem Romanam Latium-que augescere'. This (given, of course, the initial kinship) was due to the fact that the geographical unit called Latium was now mainly *ager Romanus* and, with the swift extension of the latter, came to be regarded as its 'home territory'. On the other hand, *Latini* were, on the whole, members of Latin colonies (which continued to be sent out on an increasing scale to safeguard new conquests), many—or most—of them of Roman stock, and none of them (except accidentally) born or living in Latium. Thus *Latinitas* came to be regarded as a status independent of residence and beyond treaties: though based on the Cassian treaty, which does not appear to have been formally abrogated it was derived in fact from the unilateral declaration of the Roman government by which a Latin colony was established, or (in the case of the few states in Latium) that by which, in 338, they had had *res suae redditae*. This status could be conferred on anyone not born into it, if it so pleased the Roman People: at some time it was conferred on the Hernici, and in due course on other men who were legally *peregrini*, but of partly Roman stock. As Sherwin-White remarks, the effect of the settlement of 338 resembles the punishment inflicted on the Campanians in that a group of people were attached to (but not incorporated in) the Roman state by mere decision of the latter; though, as we have seen, a vague contractual basis seems to have remained. As we shall see when discussing the second century, Rome thus came to acquire a new idea of her position as 'protecting' state: the settlement of 338 led to the 'freedom of Greece' and to the *ciuitas libera*, the 'client state' proper. At the same time, the peculiar precedent of a (now) unimportant treaty serving as the foundation of a complex moral and sentimental superstructure was to shape Rome's position in Italy in the second century.

6. THE ROMAN CONFEDERACY AFTER THE PYRRHIC WAR*

From Ariminum and Pisa to Rhegium and Brundisium, the whole of Italy was now bound together in the Roman federation. The main lines of policy which wrought this crowning achievement of the early Republic have already been described, but it is well to consider the completed organization which endured nearly two hundred years until all the inhabitants of Italy received full franchise after the Social War. The two guiding principles of Roman policy were Incorporation and Alliance. Peoples covered by the former principle became in some sense citizens of Rome; communities grouped in alliance remained in theory independent states, whose members were politically allies (*socii*) and legally aliens (*peregrini*). But both classes alike were subject to military service under the Roman government.

* H. H. Scullard, *A History of the Roman World from 753 to 146 B.C.*, 3rd ed. (London: Methuen & Co., 1961), pp. 126–132. Reprinted by permission of the publisher.

First then the Citizens who fall into two clearly defined classes: full-citizens and half-citizens. The full-citizens constitute three groups, two originating direct from Rome, the third formed by incorporation. (*a*) Those who lived in Rome itself or who had been granted individually (*viritim*) allotments of 3–7 *iugera* of public land annexed during the conquest of Italy. All these were enrolled in the four urban or thirty-one rustic tribes. (*b*) The Roman colonies, which comprised about 300 Roman citizens and their families and were founded on *ager publicus*. The colonists formed a garrison and this duty excused them military service in the Roman army. At first they constituted a strong contrast to the older inhabitants who were generally made half-citizens; but they gradually mingled. In early days they must have been subject to some local military authority and control, but its precise nature is uncertain, while the civil competence of magistrates must have been small. Later, however, when after 183 B.C. the size of new colonies was increased, municipal authority was vested in praetors or *duoviri*. The early citizen colonies were all on the coast (Ostia; Antium 338; Tarracina 329; Minturnae and Sinuessa, 296; Sena Gallica and Castrum Novum Picenti, *c.* 290; and possibly Castrum Novum Etrurii, 264); and they were few in number, because the colonists found it difficult in practice to exercise their rights as Roman citizens, so that Romans preferred to share in Latin colonies which formed autonomous states. (*c*) Communities incorporated into the Roman state: *oppida civium Romanorum*, as Tusculum and cities like Lanuvium, Aricia and Nomentum, which were incorporated when the Latin League was dissolved. Called municipalities, in imitation of the proper municipalities of half-citizens, they retained their local magistrates, who had however limited judicial and financial power. Their proximity to Rome involved supervision by the Roman praetors, while they were not allowed to mint money. But they exercised full political rights in Rome and were registered in the tribes. Occasionally a new tribe would be established to include newly-incorporated communities (e.g. the tribes Quirina and Velina for Sabines and Picentes in 241), but generally these were enrolled in neighbouring tribes and new ones were formed only for Roman citizens who received viritane allotments.

Secondly there were the incorporated *cives sine suffragio*, who enjoyed only the private rights of *provocatio*, *commercium* and *conubium*; they could not vote in the Roman assemblies or stand for office and were not enrolled in the Thirty-five Tribes. The earliest *municipia* had been willing allies with full local autonomy, but gradually the status of *municeps* came to be regarded as an inferior limited franchise which was given to conquered peoples (e.g. Sabines and Picentes) before they were considered ripe for full citizenship. Thus their conditions varied considerably. Some were allowed no local government (e.g. Anagnia, which was taken in 306, and Capua after 211); but the majority were allowed to keep their magistrates, local municipal councils and popular assemblies. Roman law was encouraged but perhaps was not enforced. Jurisdiction was divided between the local magistrates and the Roman praetor, who exercised it in Rome itself or else locally through deputies (*praefecti*); it is uncertain whether such prefects or circuit judges were sent to all municipalities. The local magistrates had fairly extensive powers and their variety was maintained (e.g. meddix at Cumae, dictator at Caere, aedile at Fundi); the local authorities were not adapted to the Roman model as quickly as those of the allies. Local languages persisted and local cults survived, though under supervision by the Roman pontiffs. With certain exceptions, the municipalities were not allowed to mint money, but they enjoyed the civil rights of *conubium* and *commercium* with other Roman citizens. By this training in citizenship they were gradually raised to the privileges of full citizenship, which the Sabines, for instance, received in 268; by about 150 they disappeared as a class. Thus full or half citizenship was granted to a large part of central Italy from Latium to Picenum, from sea to sea, including the south of Etruria and the north of Campania.

The rest of Italy was associated with Rome by Alliance, and consisted of Treaty States (*civitates foederatae*), whose inhabitants were aliens and allies (*peregrini* and *socii*) and not Roman citizens. Each city or state was bound to Rome by a separate treaty, but while many had only the *ius peregrinum*, others formed a special class of allies with peculiar privileges called the *ius Latinum*. It will be well to consider these allies of the Latin name before those who were merely *foederati*. These Latins, who represent the creation of a new Latium after the destruction of the old Latin League, fall into three classes: (*a*) a few original federal colonies of the Latin League, namely, Signia, Norba, Ardea, Circeii, Nepete, Sutrium and Setia; (*b*) Latin colonies founded after the Latin War between 338 and 268 and formed partly by Roman colonists who surrendered their citizenship; (*c*) Latin colonies planted after 268 with restricted *ius migrandi*, such as Firmum, Aesernia or Brundisium. All these Latin colonies had complete internal government. They were bound to Rome, not to one another, but this early mutual segregation must gradually have broken down. With Rome they had rights of *conubium* and *commercium* and any of their citizens on migrating to Rome could obtain Roman citizenship, although after 266 he had to leave a son behind in the colony; further, a Latin visiting Rome could vote in an especially allotted tribe. Though Latin colonies had to raise and pay their quota of troops, they did this on their own authority. The number of colonists, which varied in different colonies, was large, varying from 2,500 to 6,000. It was these fortresses, linked closely with the road-system, that held Italy together. They guarded southern Etruria and the Adriatic coast and formed an iron ring around the Samnites.

The remainder of Rome's allies (*civitates liberae*) were bound to her by treaties, which contained varying conditions; many were bilateral (*foedera aequa*) but some were unilateral. Like the Latin colonies, these allies had to supply military or naval contingents, which were kept distinct from the citizen troops. The number to be supplied by each state was fixed, but normally it would not be necessary to call up the whole contingent. The majority of the allies were free from direct Roman supervision, although Tarentum had to maintain a Roman garrison. They had full independence in civil and ordinary internal affairs, though they tended to adapt their institutions to the Roman model and to refer their disputes to Roman arbitration. Perhaps they had the right to coin money, but apart from purely local coinage, they soon ceased to use this right. Their citizens were probably limited in the exercise of the rights of *commercium* and *conubium* both with Roman citizens and with other allies. In this respect their status may have varied individually in accordance with their previous history: voluntary alliance and alliance imposed by conquest would produce different privileges. Indeed, the units with which the Romans made treaties varied. Their policy was to choose the smallest existing group, either the city as in Etruria and Magna Graecia, or the tribe as among the hills of central Italy. Where an ethnic group, as the Samnites, appeared dangerous, it was cut down to the minimum by separate alliances with the outlying members; further, it was watched by Latin colonies. Rome ever followed the policy of 'divide and rule,' and when she had made her divisions she tended to treat each section according to its degree of civilization. Etruria, which was alien alike in language and religion, was not assimilated till after the Social War, while the more cognate Sabines were soon welcomed into Roman citizenship. But 'divide and rule' is only a half-truth. By this policy Rome had won the hegemony of Italy; she retained her position only because she welded the divisions into a higher unity.

Such, in brief, was the Roman confederation, ranging from Roman colonies and municipalities of full citizens through municipalities of half citizens to the allies of the Latin name and other allies of varying privilege. The claims that Rome made on Italy were small compared with the advantages she bestowed, but she did demand some surrender of independent sovereignty and the offering of men and money. Those who received the Roman franchise merely merged their interests with a wider loyalty; of the allies some officially retained their independence, though others surrendered all individual foreign policy. In fact, however, as Rome was so much more powerful than her separate allies, her will was paramount and she even interfered on occasion with the internal affairs of cities. The main burden imposed by Rome was military service. Both citizens and allies had to supply troops; the former provided a little under half the total force. The allied troops were kept distinct from the Roman citizens, but came under Roman command. As in military service, so in taxation the citizens and allies were organized separately. All Roman citizens had to pay a direct capital tax according to their capacity; at first this was levied on real property alone, but after 312 the whole personal estate of the taxpayer was included. This tax (*tributum*), however, was not permanent. It was only levied for military purposes in time of need, and taxpayers might later be reimbursed by the Treasury if it could afford it. The allies, on the other hand, were free from all direct taxation, although any who had settled on Roman state land naturally paid a regular rent (*vectigal*). Finally, citizens and allies alike were subject to a tariff in the form of customs-duties (*portoria*).

But Rome's gifts to Italy easily outweighed her impositions. The greatest of these was the *pax Romana*. Peace was substituted for war as the normal condition. Foreign invaders, save only Hannibal, were held at arm's length, the coasts were protected by a line of Roman colonies, neighbouring cities could no longer fly at each other's throats, and party strife within each city was quelled. Rome, who had won her hegemony at the point of the sword, now assumed the rôles of judge and policeman. By skilfully grading the status of the various members of the body politic, she avoided the risk that the Italians might develop a sense of unity among themselves as a subject people under the heel of a common mistress. Instead she trained them all to look to her away from one another, and thus she obtained law and order throughout the peninsula as well as the loyal co-operation of its peoples. Rome was the head of a confederacy, not primarily a dominating military power. The *pax Romana* also fostered the growth of economic life. Except under the Etruscans and among the Greek towns of the south, commerce had been somewhat restricted. Now, protected by Roman law, it could spread throughout Italy along the Roman roads which, like the railways of to-day, began to link up the peninsula. The Viae Appia, Latina, Salaria, Flaminia, Clodia and Aurelia were the real arteries of the economic life of Italy, which was further united when Roman coinage began to oust local currencies. Other public works beside roads, such as bridges, aqueducts and drains, benefited Italy. The roads also helped to diffuse Roman culture. The Romans did not impose their civilization on Italy, but just as they themselves succumbed to Greek cultural influences from southern Italy, so their own civilization penetrated slowly throughout Italy. Local languages, customs and cults gradually gave place to a common culture based on the Latin tongue and Roman law, and very slowly but surely the various races of Italy became a nation.

The creation of a confederacy which gave the whole of Italy some kind of political, economic and social unity was a landmark in the political history of the ancient world. It was not an enlarged commonwealth like Sparta with her Perioikoi, nor a confederation of separate sovereign states such as the Panhellenic League of Corinth founded by Philip II and upheld by Alexander; it was not a federal state of the type created by a king, as Thessaly, or a League that grew out of a cantonal commune, as the Aetolian League, or a League of Cities, as the Achaean; nor was it the imperial rule of a city state over subject communities, as the Athenian land-empire of Pericles. It was a new creation which blended many of these principles into a unique confederacy. By about 260 B.C. it extended for some 52,000 square miles, of which about 10,000 consisted of Roman territory; of the remaining 42,000 square miles of allied territory the Latins occupied nearly 5,000. It thus exceeded the empires of Macedonia, Carthage and the Ptolemies; it was inferior in size only to the Seleucid kingdom. The adult male Roman citizens numbered 292,000 in 264 B.C. The allies, excluding the southern Greeks and Bruttians, could supply 375,000 regular troops in 225 B.C.; perhaps this figure should be doubled to represent the total number of adult male allies. That is, the Roman and allied adult males numbered over one million, although not all would be fit for active military service. The Roman citizens and their families numbered nearly one million, the allies double that figure; perhaps nearly a quarter of the allies enjoyed Latin rights. This total of some three million was small compared to the thirty millions of the Seleucids, the ten millions of the Ptolemies, the five millions of the Carthaginian Empire; it approximated to the population of Macedonia. But though the numbers were small, the military experience and the moral qualities of the old Roman character easily counter-balanced the hordes of Syria. Rome had become a world power and when once the Carthaginian Empire had been broken there was no other military power in the whole Mediterranean basin that could meet her on equal terms.

7. THE NATURE OF ROME'S FEDERATION*

The Roman federation now extended the whole length of Italy through Ariminum and bore the character which it retained until the Social War secured citizenship to all the inhabitants of the peninsula. At this time the territory of full citizenship included Latium, a small portion of Etruria from below Caere and Mt. Soracte, then a wide corridor across the peninsula including the Sabines and Praetuttians and a few maritime colonies.

The inhabitants of this region could doubtless all speak Latin, since the Sabine dialect had been latinized, and the bulk of the population of Veientane Etruria were of Italic stock like the Latins and had not been under Etruscan domination much longer than the Romans. The territory of citizenship without franchise included Caere on the north, the coastland on the south as far as Neapolis and inland with an irregular boundary line extending about as far as Sora and Arpinum. These peoples were doubtless learning the Latin language especially in camp and in trade and were considered to be candidates for full

* Tenney Frank, "Pyrrhus," *Cambridge Ancient History* (Cambridge, England: Cambridge University Press, 1928), Vol. 7, pp. 658–662. Reprinted by permission of the publisher.

citizenship at an early date. Intermarriage with Romans was legal, property rights were under Roman law and Roman judicial prefects held court in these regions, though their municipal governments were otherwise undisturbed. There should be included under Roman territory some strips of land which the Romans had taken as public property but not yet colonized, apparently for want of settlers, a large part of the Ager Gallicus, a part of Picenum, of Umbria, and of lower Etruria between Caere and Vulci.

The so-called Latin colony continued to be the chief device for garrisoning strategic points; including the original colonies of the Latin league there were some twenty-eight of these. The method adopted was to confiscate a portion of arable territory which was fertile enough to attract settlers at points which needed protection and possessed a strong site readily fortified. The colonists would serve as a garrison in time of need and were also liable to army service in the league forces at times when they could safely be called from home. The official language of such colonists was Latin, but the presence of foreign inscriptions in many of them proves that the settlers, drawn as they were from several of the allied states, might to some extent at least be more at home in Oscan, Greek, or Etruscan. These colonists seem to have had the rights of intermarriage and of property-holding with Romans and, at least up to the time of the foundation of Ariminum, they were readily accorded citizenship in Rome by residence in the city. But restrictions were later imposed upon them chiefly because the colonial governments complained that it was difficult for them to provide their military contingents when their citizens were permitted to take up residence at Rome and change their citizenship. Their magistrates, however, *ipso facto* received Roman citizenship and this privilege was never questioned. A

glance at the map will show that by 264 these settlements had been founded mainly in order to surround Samnium and to protect lower Etruria and the Adriatic coast with cities friendly to Rome: about Samnium are found Interamna, Suessa, Cales, Saticula, Beneventum, Venusia, and Luceria; in lower Etruria, Nepete, Sutrium, and Cosa; on the upper Adriatic, Ariminum, Castrum Novum, Firmum and Hadria.

The rest of the Italian tribes and cities were allied to Rome by a great diversity of treaties similar only in the fact that, while such allies had local autonomy and were not subject to tribute to Rome or the league, they were under contract to contribute a contingent to the army which was under the command of a Roman consul. Although these treaties were in the form of alliances of mutual defence and Rome was always quick to respond if the allied territory was invaded—on the Gallic border for instance—the federation now was bounded by sea and mountains so that few wars were apt to arise because of disturbances on the boundary of an ally. Furthermore, all neighbours recognized Rome's supremacy in the league so that, when disputes arose, the discussion was carried on at Rome and not in some allied city. Hence, from the time of Pyrrhus onwards it was seldom, except in theory, a question of mutual defence.

The diversity in the status of the allies was due to several causes: partly to the circumstances attending their entry, whether by voluntary adhesion as in the case of Neapolis, or by subjection after a war as in the case of Samnium; partly to the cultural status of the ally—Rome had always admired the Greek cities of Italy, and was apt to invite their goodwill; partly to the nature of the allied government. It has been noticed, for instance, that in Etruria and Umbria Rome preferred to see the larger tribes broken up into smaller units. This was doubtless in part due to the product principle of *divide et impera*, for Gallic raids would be far less dangerous if Etruria were not inflammable as a whole. But this is not the sole reason. In both Etruria and Umbria strong cities had long existed with separatist loyalties so that responsible united action was difficult to secure. In neither was any treaty of the whole league very dependable. Fractions would secede in times of danger. It was therefore essential that the treaties be signed with the fractions. Hence, while Rome did not disturb religious associations and leagues in Etruria and Umbria, she did insist upon having her treaties signed by the individual cities. Among the Sabellian tribes, however, which had not yet developed strong urban units and where the tribes of villagers presented responsible governments, there was far less segregating. Only in Samnium, where the Frentani, Hispini and Pentri readily fell into separate groups, did Rome apply the device of severing. The Samnite tribe thus trimmed down was accepted as a unit, and so were also the mountain tribes that went under the names of Marsi, Marrucini, Paeligni, Vestini, Frentani, and Lucani. Finally, it is to be noticed that religion, language, and custom counted for something in determining the status of allies. The Sabines, whose customs and language most resembled the Roman, were among the first to attain the franchise, while the strange Etruscans, whose language has not yet yielded interpretation, and who, even when they adopted Italic gods, Tuscanized their names, were not hurried into close union. After the first experiments citizenship was not extended in Etruria till the Social War, and no colonies were planted in the heart of their country. Indeed, in the early days, though it was Rome's custom to make her alliances for all time, her treaties in this region had always been made for a limited term of years. The Romans apparently felt that this people would not readily be assimilated.

The question has often been raised why, now that Rome's imaginary walls extended to the Adriatic, the representative principle of government was not adopted in order to facilitate the effective participation of people who lived so far away. We may assume that the possibility was discussed from time to time, for at the very beginning of Rome's expansion the Latins had asked to be represented in the Roman Senate, and again during the Punic war a similar proposal was made by Carvilius, a Roman senator. It is doubtful whether the people of Rome would have had much patience with this proposal. The town-meeting was an old Latin institution, one of the most sacred; direct participation of every citizen in the meeting which decided whether there should be war or peace seemed an unquestionable right. History seemed also to have proved the adequacy of this government. When hordes had poured in from the north, tribes within had quarrelled and ambitious tyrants had invaded from the south, other tribes and cities had proved ineffective, but the Roman assembly advised by the Senate had alone followed the prudent course, taken up arms for any sacrifice, and organized their neighbours for steadfast defence. The federation of the whole of Italy seemed a miraculous feat. Why change a government which had accomplished that? Again, it seemed well that those nearest the city, who spoke the language, who worshipped and thought as the Romans did, should for the sake of united action control the government. Sabines of the Adriatic coast, Etruscans of Caere, Ausonians and the rest might in time bring into a representative parliament a predominant number which would destroy unity of purpose and create an ineffective government when, to control the vast federation, decision and speed were necessary. We may also suppose that the recent victory of the principle of popular sovereignty debarred the acceptance of the representative idea. It was naturally assumed that a representative group would form a body like the Senate, and it was the

Senate which the assemblies had had to curb for over two hundred years. It was only in 287 that the complete victory had finally been won by which the people could, if they desired, override the Senate on any question of legislation and administration and make their own decisions. A representative Senate would become as conservative as the old one had been, for in the society of that day the landed nobility with their broad estates and many clients would win the seats in the Senate as surely as they now won the elections to the magistracy. And if such a parliament displaced the primary assembly, the struggle of centuries would apparently be lost. Such must have been the feelings of the Romans when the question was raised. It must be admitted that the primary assembly still deserved the confidence it expected and that a change would have been unwise until the federation was far more unified in language and custom than it was in the third century.

SECTION IV

The Causes of the Second Punic War

THE SECOND PUNIC WAR was the climactic struggle between Rome and Carthage to decide who should rule the western Mediterranean and the lands along its coasts. It put an end to the burgeoning power of Carthage and launched Rome upon a career of imperial conquest. It marked a great turning point in both the domestic and foreign policy of the Roman Republic; some would say it was the beginning of the end of that republic. How did it come about? Who was responsible? Was it inevitable? Since this problem is better documented than most in ancient history, it is particularly rewarding to ponder these questions.

1. LIVY ON THE ORIGINS OF THE WAR*

I may be permitted to premise at this division of my work, what most historians have professed at the beginning of their whole undertaking; that I am about to relate the most memorable of all wars that were ever waged: the war which the Carthaginians, under the conduct of Hannibal, maintained with the Roman people. For never did any states and nations more efficient in their resources engage in contest; nor had they themselves at any other period so great a degree of power and energy. They brought into action too no arts of war unknown to each other, but those which had been tried in the first Punic war; and so various was the fortune of the conflict, and so doubtful

the victory, that they who conquered were more exposed to danger. The hatred with which they fought also was almost greater than their resources; the Romans being indignant that the conquered aggressively took up arms against their victors; the Carthaginians, because they considered that in their subjection it had been lorded over them with haughtiness and avarice. There is besides a story, that Hannibal, when about nine years old, while he boyishly coaxed his father Hamilcar that he might be taken to Spain, (at the time when the African war was completed, and he was employed in sacrificing previously to transporting his army thither,) was conducted to the altar; and, having laid his hand on the offerings, was bound by an oath to prove himself, as soon as he could, an enemy to the Roman

* Livy, 21. 1–18, translated by D. Spiller and C. Edmonds.

93

people. The loss of Sicily and Sardinia grieved the high spirit of Hamilcar: for he deemed that Sicily had been given up through a premature despair of their affairs; and that Sardinia, during the disturbances in Africa, had been treacherously taken by the Romans, while, in addition, the payment of a tribute had been imposed.

Being disturbed with these anxieties, he so conducted himself for five years in the African war, which commenced shortly after the peace with Rome, and then through nine years employed in augmenting the Carthaginian empire in Spain, that it was obvious that he was revolving in his mind a greater war than he was then engaged in; and that if he had lived longer, the Carthaginians under Hamilcar would have carried the war into Italy, which, under the command of Hannibal, they afterwards did. The timely death of Hamilcar and the youth of Hannibal occasioned its delay. Hasdrubal, intervening between the father and the son, held the command for about eight years. He was first endeared to Hamilcar, as they say, on account of his youthful beauty, and then adopted by him, when advanced in age, as his son-in-law, on account of his eminent abilities; and, because he was his son-in-law, he obtained the supreme authority, against the wishes of the nobles, by the influence of the Barcine faction, which was very powerful with the military and the populace. Prosecuting his designs rather by stratagem than force, by entertaining the princes, and by means of the friendship of their leaders, gaining the favour of unknown nations, he aggrandized the Carthaginian power, more than by arms and battles. Yet peace proved no greater security to himself. A barbarian, in resentment of his master's having been put to death by him, publicly murdered him; and, having been seized by the bystanders, he exhibited the same countenance as if he had escaped; nay, even when he was lacerated by tortures, he preserved such an expression of face, that

he presented the appearance of one who smiled, his joy getting the better of his pains. With this Hasdrubal, because he possessed such wonderful skill in gaining over the nations and adding them to his empire, the Roman people had renewed the treaty, on the terms, that the river Iberus should be the boundary of both empires; and that to the Saguntines, who lay between the territories of the two states, their liberty should be preserved.

There was no doubt that in appointing a successor to Hasdrubal, the approbation of the commons would follow the military prerogative, by which the young Hannibal had been immediately carried to the prætorium, and hailed as general, amid the loud shouts and acquiescence of all. Hasdrubal had sent for him by letter, when scarce yet arrived at manhood; and the matter had even been discussed in the senate, the Barcine faction using all their efforts, that Hannibal might be trained to military service and succeed to his father's command. Hanno, the leader of the opposite faction, said, "Hasdrubal seems indeed to ask what is reasonable, but I, nevertheless, do not think his request ought to be granted." When he had attracted to himself the attention of all, through surprise at this ambiguous opinion, he proceeded: "Hasdrubal thinks that the flower of youth which he gave to the enjoyment of Hannibal's father, may justly be expected by himself in return from the son: but it would little become us to accustom our youth, in place of a military education, to the lustful ambition of the generals. Are we afraid that the son of Hamilcar should be too late in seeing the immoderate power and splendour of his father's sovereignty? or that we shall not soon enough become slaves to the son of him, to whose son-in-law our armies were bequeathed as an hereditary right? I am of opinion, that this youth should be kept at home, and taught, under the restraint of the laws and the authority of magistrates, to live on an equal footing with the rest of the citizens, lest at some time or other this small fire should kindle a vast conflagration."

A few, and nearly every one of the highest merit, concurred with Hanno; but, as usually happens, the more numerous party prevailed over the better. Hannibal, having been sent into Spain, from his very first arrival drew the eyes of the whole army upon him. The veteran soldiers imagined that Hamilcar, in his youth, was restored to them; they remarked the same vigour in his looks and animation in his eye, the same features and expression of countenance; and then, in a short time, he took care that his father should be of the least powerful consideration in conciliating their esteem. There never was a genius more fitted for the two most opposite duties of obeying and commanding; so that you could not easily decide whether he were dearer to the general or the army; and neither did Hasdrubal prefer giving the command to any other, when any thing was to be done with courage and activity; nor did the soldiers feel more confidence and boldness under any other leader. His fearlessness in encountering dangers, and his prudence when in the midst of them, were extreme. His body could not be exhausted, nor his mind subdued, by any toil. He could alike endure either heat or cold. The quantity of his food and drink was determined by the wants of nature, and not by pleasure. The seasons of his sleeping and waking were distinguished neither by day nor night. The time that remained after the transaction of business was given to repose; but that repose was neither invited by a soft bed nor by quiet. Many have seen him wrapped in a military cloak, lying on the ground amid the watches and outposts of the soldiers. His dress was not at all superior to that of his equals: his arms and his horses were conspicuous. He was at once by far the first of the cavalry and infantry; and, foremost to advance to the charge, was last to leave the engagement. Excessive vices counter-balanced these

high virtues of the hero; inhuman cruelty, more than Punic perfidy, no truth, no reverence for things sacred, no fear of the gods, no respect for oaths, no sense of religion. With a character thus made up of virtues and vices, he served for three years under the command of Hasdrubal, without neglecting any thing which ought to be done or seen by one who was to become a great general.

But from the day on which he was declared general, as if Italy had been decreed to him as his province, and the war with Rome committed to him, thinking there should be no delay, lest, while he procrastinated, some unexpected accident might defeat him, as had happened to his father, Hamilcar, and afterwards to Hasdrubal, he resolved to make war on the Saguntines. As there could be no doubt that by attacking them the Romans would be excited to arms, he first led his army into the territory of the Olcades, a people beyond the Iberus, rather within the boundaries than under the domination of the Carthaginians, so that he might not seem to have had the Saguntines for his object, but to have been drawn on to the war by the course of events; after the adjoining nations had been subdued, and by the progressive annexation of conquered territory. He storms and plunders Carteia, a wealthy city, the capital of that nation; at which the smaller states being dismayed, submitted to his commands and to the imposition of a tribute. His army, triumphant and enriched with booty, was led into winter-quarters to New Carthage. Having there confirmed the attachment of all his countrymen and allies by a liberal division of the plunder, and by faithfully discharging the arrears of pay, the war was extended, in the beginning of spring, to the Vaccæi. The cities Hermandica and Arbocala were taken by storm. Arbocala was defended for a long time by the valour and number of its inhabitants. Those who escaped from Hermandica joining themselves to the exiles of the Olcades, a nation subdued the preceding summer, excite the Carpetani to arms; and having attacked Hannibal near the river Tagus, on his return from the Vaccæi, they threw into disorder his army encumbered with spoil. Hannibal avoided an engagement, and having pitched his camp on the bank, as soon as quiet and silence prevailed among the enemy, forded the river; and having removed his rampart so far that the enemy might have room to pass over, resolved to attack them in their passage. He commanded the cavalry to charge as soon as they should see them advanced into the water. He drew up the line of his infantry on the bank with forty elephants in front. The Carpetani, with the addition of the Olcades and Vaccæi, amounted to a hundred thousand, an invincible army, were the fight to take place in the open plain. Being therefore both naturally ferocious and confiding in their numbers; and since they believed that the enemy had retired through fear, thinking that victory was only delayed by the intervention of the river, they raise a shout, and in every direction, without the command of any one, dash into the stream, each where it was nearest to him. At the same time, a heavy force of cavalry poured into the river from its opposite bank, and the engagement commenced in the middle of the channel on very unequal terms; for there the foot-soldier, having no secure footing, and scarcely trusting to the ford, could be borne down even by an unarmed horseman, by the mere shock of his horse urged at random; while the horseman, with the command of his body and his weapons, his horse moving steadily even through the middle of the eddies, could maintain the fight either at close quarters or at a distance. A great number were swallowed up by the current; some being carried by the whirlpools of the stream to the side of the enemy, were trodden down by the elephants; and whilst the last, for whom it was more safe to

retreat to their own bank, were collecting together after their various alarms, Hannibal, before they could regain courage after such excessive consternation, having entered the river with his army in a close square, forced them to fly from the bank. Having then laid waste their territory, he received the submission of the Carpetani also within a few days. And now all the country beyond the Iberus, excepting that of the Saguntines, was under the power of the Carthaginians.

As yet there was no war with the Saguntines, but already, in order to bring on a war, the seeds of dissension were sown between them and their neighbours, particularly the Turdetani, with whom when the same person sided who had originated the quarrel, and it was evident, not that a trial of the question of right, but violence, was his object, ambassadors were sent by the Saguntines to Rome to implore assistance in the war which now evidently threatened them. The consuls then at Rome were Publius Cornelius Scipio and Tiberius Sempronius Longus, who, after the ambassadors were introduced into the senate, having made a motion on the state of public affairs, it was resolved that envoys should be sent into Spain to inspect the circumstances of the allies; and if they saw good reason, both to warn Hannibal that he should refrain from the Saguntines, the allies of the Roman people, and to pass over into Africa to Carthage, and report the complaints of the allies of the Roman people. This embassy having been decreed but not yet despatched, the news arrived, more quickly than any one expected, that Saguntum was besieged. The business was then referred anew to the senate. And some, decreeing Spain and Africa as provinces for the consuls, thought the war should be maintained both by sea and land, while others wished to direct the whole hostilities against Spain and Hannibal. There were others again, who thought that an affair of such importance should not be entered on rashly;

and that the return of the ambassadors from Spain ought to be awaited. This opinion, which seemed the safest, prevailed; and Publius Valerius Flaccus, and Quintus Bæbius Tamphilus, were, on that account, the more quickly despatched as ambassadors to Hannibal at Saguntum, and from thence to Carthage, if he did desist from the war, to demand the general himself in atonement for the violation of the treaty.

While the Romans thus prepare and deliberate, Saguntum was already besieged with the utmost vigour. That city, situated about a mile from the sea, was by far the most opulent beyond the Iberus. Its inhabitants are said to have been sprung from the island Zacynthus, and some of the Rutulian race from Ardea to have been also mixed with them; but they had risen in a short time to great wealth, either by their gains from the sea or the land, or by the increase of their numbers, or the integrity of their principles, by which they maintained their faith with their allies, even to their own destruction. Hannibal having entered their territory with a hostile army, and laid waste the country in every direction, attacks the city in three different quarters. There was an angle of the wall sloping down into a more level and open valley than the other space around; against this he resolved to move the vineæ, by means of which the battering-ram might be brought up to the wall. But though the ground at a distance from the wall was sufficiently level for working the vineæ, yet their undertakings by no means favourably succeeded, when they came to effect their object. Both a huge tower overlooked it, and the wall, as in a suspected place, was raised higher than in any other part; and a chosen band of youths presented a more vigorous resistance, where the greatest danger and labour were indicated. At first they repelled the enemy with missile weapons, and suffered no place to be sufficiently secure for those engaged in the works; afterwards, not only did

they brandish their weapons in defence of the walls and tower, but they had courage to make sallies on the posts and works of the enemy; in which tumultuary engagements, scarcely more Saguntines than Carthaginians were slain. But when Hannibal himself, while he too incautiously approached the wall, fell severely wounded in the thigh by a javelin, such flight and dismay spread around, that the works and vineæ had nearly been abandoned.

For a few days after, while the general's wound was being cured, there was rather a blockade than a siege: during which time, though there was a respite from fighting, yet there was no intermission in the preparation of works and fortifications. Hostilities, therefore, broke out afresh with greater fury, and in more places, in some even where the ground scarcely admitted of the works, the vineæ began to be moved forward, and the battering-ram to be advanced to the walls. The Carthaginian abounded in the numbers of his troops; for there is sufficient reason to believe that he had as many as a hundred and fifty thousand in arms. The townsmen began to be embarrassed, by having their attention multifariously divided, in order to maintain their several defences, and look to every thing; nor were they equal to the task, for the walls were now battered by the rams, and many parts of them were shattered. One part by continuous ruins left the city exposed; three successive towers and all the wall between them had fallen down with an immense crash, and the Carthaginians believed the town taken by that breach; through which, as if the wall had alike protected both, there was a rush from each side to the battle. There was nothing resembling the disorderly fighting which, in the storming of towns, is wont to be engaged in, on the opportunities of either party; but regular lines, as in an open plain, stood arrayed between the ruins of the walls and the buildings of the city, which lay but a slight distance from the walls. On the one side hope, on the other despair, inflamed their courage; the Carthaginian believing that, if a little additional effort were used, the city was his; the Saguntines opposing their bodies in defence of their native city deprived of its walls, and not a man retiring a step, lest he might admit the enemy into the place he deserted. The more keenly and closely, therefore, they fought on both sides, the more, on that account, were wounded, no weapon falling without effect amidst their arms and persons. There was used by the Saguntines a missile weapon, called falarica, with the shaft of fir, and round in other parts except towards the point, whence the iron projected: this part, which was square, as in the pilum, they bound around with tow, and besmeared with pitch. It had an iron head three feet in length, so that it could pierce through the body with the armour. But what caused the greatest fear was, that this weapon, even though it stuck in the shield and did not penetrate into the body, when it was discharged with the middle part on fire, and bore along a much greater flame, produced by the mere motion, obliged the armour to be thrown down, and exposed the soldier to succeeding blows.

When the contest had for a long time continued doubtful, and the courage of the Saguntines had increased, because they had succeeded in their resistance beyond their hopes, while the Carthaginian, because he had not conquered, felt as vanquished, the townsmen suddenly set up a shout, and drive their enemies to the ruins of the wall; thence they force them, while embarrassed and disordered; and lastly, drove them back, routed and put to flight, to their camp. In the mean time it was announced that ambassadors had arrived from Rome; to meet whom messengers were sent to the sea-side by Hannibal, to tell them that they could not safely come to him through so many armed bands of savage tribes, and that Hannibal at such an important conjunc-

ture had not leisure to listen to embassies. It was obvious that, if not admitted, they would immediately repair to Carthage: he therefore sends letters and messengers beforehand to the leaders of the Barcine faction, to prepare the minds of their partisans, so that the other party might not be able in any thing to give an advantage to the Romans.

That embassy, therefore, excepting that the ambassadors were admitted and heard, proved likewise vain and fruitless. Hanno alone, in opposition to the rest of the senate, pleaded the cause of the treaty, amidst deep silence on account of his authority, and not from the approbation of the audience. He said: that he had admonished and forewarned them by the gods, the arbiters and witnesses of treaties, that they should not send the son of Hamilcar to the army; that the manes, that the off-spring of that man could not rest in peace, nor ever, while any one of the Barcine name and blood survived, would the Roman treaties continue undisturbed. "You, supplying as it were fuel to the flame, have sent to your armies a youth burning with the desire of sovereign power, and seeing but one road to his object, if by exciting war after war, he may live surrounded by arms and legions. You have therefore fostered this fire, in which you now burn. Your armies invest Saguntum, whence they are forbidden by the treaty: ere long the Roman legions will invest Carthage, under the guidance of those gods through whose aid they revenged in the former war the infraction of the treaty. Are you unacquainted with the enemy, or with yourselves, or with the fortune of either nation? Your good general refused to admit into his camp ambassadors coming from allies and in behalf of allies, and set at nought the law of nations. They, however, after being there repulsed, where not even the ambassadors of enemies are prohibited admittance, come to you: they require restitution according to the treaty: let not guilt attach to the state, they demand to have delivered up to them the author of the transgression, the person who is chargeable with this offence. The more gently they proceed,—the slower they are to begin, the more unrelentingly, I fear, when they have once commenced, will they indulge resentment. Set before your eyes the islands Ægates and Eryx, all that for twenty-four years ye have suffered by land and sea. Nor was this boy the leader, but his father Hamilcar himself, a second Mars, as these people would have it: but we had not refrained from Tarentum, that is, from Italy, according to the treaty; as now we do not refrain from Saguntum. The gods and men have, therefore, prevailed over us; and as to that about which there was a dispute in words, whether of the two nations had infringed the treaty, the issue of the war, like an equitable judge, hath awarded the victory to the party on whose side justice stood. It is against Carthage that Hannibal is now moving his vineæ and towers: it is the wall of Carthage that he is shaking with his battering-ram. The ruins of Saguntum (oh that I may prove a false prophet!) will fall on our heads; and the war commenced against the Saguntines must be continued against the Romans. Shall we, therefore, some one will say, deliver up Hannibal? In what relates to him I am aware that my authority is of little weight, on account of my enmity with his father. But I both rejoice that Hamilcar perished, for this reason, that, had he lived, we should have now been engaged in a war with the Romans; and this youth, as the fury and firebrand of this war, I hate and detest. Nor ought he only to be given up in atonement for the violated treaty; but even though no one demanded him, he ought to be transported to the extremest shores of earth or sea, and banished to a distance, whence neither his name nor any tidings of him can reach us, and he be unable to disturb the peace of a tranquil state. I therefore give my opinion, that ambassadors be sent immediately to Rome to satisfy the senate; others to tell Hannibal to lead away his army from Saguntum, and to deliver up Hannibal himself, according to the treaty to the Romans; and I propose a third embassy, to make restitution to the Saguntines."

When Hanno had concluded, there was no occasion for anyone to contend with him in debate, to such a degree were almost all the senators devoted to Hannibal; and they accused Hanno of having spoken with more malignity than Flaccus Valerius, the Roman ambassador. It was then said, in answer to the Roman ambassadors, "that the war had been commenced by the Saguntines, not by Hannibal; and that the Roman people acted unjustly if they preferred the Saguntines to the most ancient alliance of the Carthaginians." Whilst the Romans waste time in sending embassies, Hannibal, because his soldiers were fatigued with the battles and the works, allowed them rest for a few days, parties being stationed to guard the vineæ and other works. In the meantime he inflames their minds, now by inciting their anger against the enemy, now with the hope of reward. But when he declared before the assembled army, that the plunder of the captured city should be given to the soldiers, to such a degree were they all excited, that if the signal had been immediately given, it appeared that they could not have been resisted by any force. The Saguntines, as they had a respite from fighting, neither for some days attacking nor attacked, so they had not, by night or day, ever ceased from toiling, that they might repair anew the wall in the quarter where the town had been exposed by the breach. A still more desperate storming than the former then assailed them; nor whilst all quarters resounded with various clamours, could they satisfactorily know where first or principally they should lend assistance. Hannibal, as an encouragement, was present in person, where a movable tower, exceeding in height all the fortifications of the city, was urged forward. When being brought up it had cleared the walls of their defenders by means of the catapultæ and ballistæ ranged through all its stories, then Hannibal, thinking it a favourable opportunity, sends about five hundred Africans with pickaxes to undermine the wall: nor was the work difficult, since the unhewn stones were not fastened with lime, but filled in their interstices with clay, after the manner of ancient building. It fell, therefore, more extensively than it was struck, and through the open spaces of the ruins troops of armed men rushed into the city. They also obtain possession of a rising ground; and having collected thither catapultæ and ballistæ, so that they might have a fort in the city itself, commanding it like a citadel, they surround it with a wall: and the Saguntines raise an inner wall before the part of the city which was not yet taken. On both sides they exert the utmost vigour in fortifying and fighting: but the Saguntines, by erecting these inner defences, diminish daily the size of their city. At the same time, the want of all supplies increased through the length of the siege, and the expectation of foreign aid diminished, since the Romans, their only hope, were at such a distance, and all the country round was in the power of the enemy. The sudden departure of Hannibal against the Oretani and Carpetani revived for a little their drooping spirits; which two nations, though, exasperated by the severity of the levy, they had occasioned, by detaining the commissaries, the fear of a revolt, having been suddenly checked by the quickness of Hannibal, laid down the arms they had taken up.

Nor was the siege of Saguntum, in the mean time, less vigorously maintained; Maharbal, the son of Himilco, whom Hannibal had set over the army, carrying on operations so actively that neither the townsmen nor their enemies perceived that the general was away. He both engaged in several successful battles, and

with three battering-rams overthrew a portion of the wall; and showed to Hannibal, on his arrival, the ground all covered with fresh ruins. The army was therefore immediately led against the citadel itself, and a desperate combat was commenced with much slaughter on both sides, and part of the citadel was taken. The slight chance of a peace was then tried by two persons; Alcon a Saguntine, and Alorcus a Spaniard. Alcon, thinking he could effect something by entreaties, having passed over, without the knowledge of the Saguntines, to Hannibal by night, when his tears produced no effect, and harsh conditions were offered as from an exasperated conqueror, becoming a deserter instead of an advocate, remained with the enemy; affirming that the man would be put to death who should treat for peace on such terms. For it was required that they should make restitution to the Turdetani; and after delivering up all their gold and silver, departing from the city each with a single garment, should take up their dwelling where the Carthaginian should direct. Alcon having denied that the Saguntines would accept such terms of peace, Alorcus, asserting that when all else is subdued, the mind becomes subdued, offers himself as the proposer of that peace. Now at that time he was a soldier of Hannibal's but publicly the friend and host of the Saguntines. Having openly delivered his weapon to the guards of the enemy and passed the fortifications, he was conducted, as he had himself requested, to the Saguntine prætor; whither when there was immediately a general rush of every description of people, the rest of the multitude being removed, an audience of the senate is given to Alorcus; whose speech was to the following effect:

"If your citizen Alcon, as he came to implore a peace from Hannibal, had in like manner brought back to you the terms of peace proposed by Hannibal, this journey of mine would have been unnecessary; by which circumstance I should not have had to come to you as the legate of Hannibal, nor as a deserter. Since he has remained with your enemies, either through your fault or his own, (through his own, if he counterfeited fear; through yours, if among you there be danger to those who tell the truth,) that you may not be ignorant that there are some terms of safety and peace for you, I have come to you in consideration of the ancient ties of hospitality which subsist between us. But that I speak what I address to you for your sake and that of no other, let even this be the proof: that neither while you resisted with your own strength, nor while you expected assistance from the Romans, did I ever make any mention of peace to you. But now, after you have neither any hope from the Romans, nor your own arms nor walls sufficiently defend you, I bring to you a peace rather necessary than just: of effecting which there is thus some hope, if, as Hannibal offers it in the spirit of a conqueror, you listen to it as vanquished; if you will consider not what is taken from you as loss, (since all belongs to the conqueror,) but whatever is left as a gift. He takes away from you your city, which, already for the greater part in ruins, he has almost wholly in his possession; he leaves you your territory, intending to mark out a place in which you may build a new town; he commands that all the gold and silver, both public and private, shall be brought to him; he preserves inviolate your persons and those of your wives and children, provided you are willing to depart from Saguntum, unarmed, each with two garments. These terms a victorious enemy dictates. These, though harsh and grievous, your condition commends to you. Indeed I do not despair, when the power of every thing is given him, that he will remit something from these terms. But even these I think you ought rather to endure, than suffer, by the rights of war, yourselves to be slaughtered, your wives and children to be

ravished and dragged into captivity before your faces."

When an assembly of the people, by the gradual crowding round of the multitude, had mingled with the senate to hear these proposals, the chief men suddenly withdrawing before an answer was returned, and throwing all the gold and silver collected, both from public and private stores, into a fire hastily kindled for that purpose, the greater part flung themselves also into it. When the dismay and agitation produced by this deed had pervaded the whole city, another noise was heard in addition from the citadel. A tower, long battered, had fallen down; and when a Carthaginian cohort, rushing through the breach, had made a signal to the general that the city was destitute of the usual outposts and guards, Hannibal, thinking that there ought to be no delay at such an opportunity, having attacked the city with his whole forces, took it in a moment, command being given that all the adults should be put to death; which command, through cruel, was proved in the issue to have been almost necessary. For to whom of those men could mercy have been shown, who, either shut up with their wives and children, burned their houses over their own heads, or abroad in arms made no end of fighting, except in death.

The town was taken, with immense spoil. Though the greater part of the goods had been purposely damaged by their owners, and resentment had made scarce any distinction of age in the massacre, and the captives were the booty of the soldiers; still it appears that some money was raised from the price of the effects that were sold, and that much costly furniture and garments were sent to Carthage. Some have written that Saguntum was taken in the eighth month after it began to be besieged; that Hannibal then retired to New Carthage, into winter quarters; and that in the fifth month after he had set out from Carthage he arrived in Italy. If this be so, it was impossible that Publius Cornelius and Tiberius Sempronius could have been consuls, to whom both at the beginning of the siege the Saguntine ambassadors were despatched, and who, during their office, fought with Hannibal; the one at the river Ticinus, and both some time after at the Trebia. Either all these events took place in a somewhat shorter period, or Saguntum was not begun to be besieged, but taken at the beginning of the year in which Publius Cornelius and Tiberius Sempronius were consuls. For the battle at Trebia could not have been so late as the year of Cneius Servilius and Caius Flaminius, since Flaminius entered on the office at Ariminum, having been created by the consul Tiberius Sempronius; who, having repaired to Rome after the battle at Trebia for the purpose of creating consuls, returned when the election was finished to the army into winter quarters.

Nearly about the same time, both the ambassadors who had returned from Carthage brought intelligence to Rome that all appearances were hostile, and the destruction of Saguntum was announced. Then such grief, and pity for allies so undeservingly destroyed, and shame that aid was withheld, and rage against the Carthaginians, and fear for the issue of events, as if the enemy were already at the gates, took at once possession of the senators, that their minds, disturbed by so many simultaneous emotions, trembled with fear rather than deliberated. For they considered that neither had a more spirited or warlike enemy ever encountered them nor had the Roman state been ever so sunk in sloth, and unfit for war: that the Sardinians, the Corsicans, the Istrians, and the Illyrians, had rather kept in a state of excitement than exercised the Roman arms; and with the Gauls it had been more properly a tumult than a war. That the Carthaginian, a veteran enemy, ever victorious during the hardest service for twenty-three years among the tribes of Spain, first trained to war under Hamilcar, then Hasdrubal, now Hannibal, a most

active leader, and fresh from the destruction of a most opulent city, was passing the Iberus; that along with them he was bringing the numerous tribes of Spain, already aroused, and was about to excite the nations of Gaul, ever desirous of war; and that a war against the world was to be maintained in Italy and before the walls of Rome.

The provinces had already been previously named for the consuls; and having been now ordered to cast lots for them, Spain fell to Cornelius, and Africa with Sicily to Sempronius. Six legions were decreed for that year, and as many of the allies as should seem good to the consuls, and as great a fleet as could be equipped. Twenty-four thousand Roman infantry were levied, and one thousand eight hundred horse: forty thousand infantry of the allies, and four thousand four hundred horse: two hundred and twenty ships of five banks of oars, and twenty light galleys, were launched. It was then proposed to the people, "whether they willed and commanded that war should be declared against the people of Carthage;" and for the sake of that war a supplication was made through the city, and the gods were implored that the war which the Roman people had decreed might have a prosperous and fortunate issue. The forces were thus divided between the consuls. To Sempronius two legions were given, (each of these consisted of four thousand infantry and three hundred horse,) and sixteen thousand of the infantry of the allies, and one thousand eight hundred horse: one hundred and sixty ships of war, and twelve light galleys. With these land and sea forces Tiberius Sempronius was despatched to Sicily, in order to transport his army to Africa if the other consul should be able to prevent the Carthaginian from invading Italy. Fewer troops were given to Cornelius, because Lucius Manlius, the prætor, also had been sent with no weak force into Gaul. The number of ships in particular was reduced to Cornelius. Sixty of five banks of oars were assigned to him, (for they did not believe that the enemy would come by sea, or would fight after that mode of warfare,) and two Roman legions with their regular cavalry, and fourteen thousand of the infantry of the allies, with one thousand six hundred horse. The province of Gaul being not as yet exposed to the Carthaginian invasion, had, in the same year, two Roman legions, ten thousand allied infantry, one thousand allied cavalry, and six hundred Roman.

These preparations having been thus made, in order that every thing that was proper might be done before they commenced war, they send Quintus Fabius, Marcus Livius, Lucius Æmilius, Caius Licinius, and Quintus Bæbius, men of advanced years, as ambassadors into Africa, to inquire of the Carthaginians if Hannibal had laid siege to Saguntum by public authority; and if they should confess it, as it seemed probable they would, and defend it as done by public authority, to declare war against the people of Carthage. After the Romans arrived at Carthage, when an audience of the senate was given them, and Quintus Fabius had addressed no further inquiry than the one with which they had been charged, then one of the Carthaginians replied: "Even your former embassy, O Romans, was precipitate, when you demanded Hannibal to be given up, as attacking Saguntum on his own authority: but your present embassy, though so far milder in words, is in fact more severe. For then Hannibal was both accused, and required to be delivered up: now both a confession of wrong is exacted from us, and, as though we had confessed, restitution is immediately demanded. But I think that the question is not, whether Saguntum was attacked by private or public authority, but whether it was with right or wrong. For in the case of our citizen, the right of inquiry, whether he has acted by his own pleasure or ours, and the punishment also, belongs to us. The only dispute with you is, whether it was allowed to be done by the treaty. Since, therefore, it pleases you that a distinction should be made between what commanders do by public authority, and what on their own suggestion, there was a treaty between us made by the consul Lutatius; in which, though provision was made for the allies of both, there is no provision made for the Saguntines, for they were not as yet your allies. But in that treaty which was made with Hasdrubal, the Saguntines are excepted; against which I am going to say nothing but what I have learned from you. For you denied that you were bound by the treaty which Caius Lutatius the consul first made with us, because that it had neither been made by the authority of the senate nor the command of the People; and another treaty was therefore concluded anew by public authority. If your treaties do not bind you unless they are made by your authority and your commands, neither can the treaty of Hasdrubal, which he made without our knowledge, be binding on us. Cease, therefore, to make mention of Saguntum and the Iberus, and let your mind at length bring forth that with which it has long been in labour." Then the Roman, having formed a fold in his robe, said, "Here we bring to you peace and war; take which you please." On this speech they exclaimed no less fiercely in reply: "he might give which he chose;" and when he again, unfolding his robe, said "he gave war," they all answered that "they accepted it, and would maintain it with the same spirit with which they accepted it."

2. Polybius on the Causes of the War*

Polybius (ca. 203–120 B.C.) was a citizen of Magalopolis, a major city in the Achaean League. The son of Lycortas, an important leader of the faction which advocated an independent policy for the League, he was taken to Rome as a political hostage after the Third Macedonian War. In Rome he became a member of the famous Scipionic circle and a personal friend of Scipio Aemilianus. He wrote a *Universal History* for the period 264–144 B.C. in forty books, of which only some are preserved.

Some historians of the Hannibalian war, when they wish to point out to us the causes of this contest between Rome and Carthage, allege first the siege of Saguntum by the Carthaginians, and, secondly, their breach of treaty by crossing the river called by the natives the Iber. But though I should call these the first actions in the war, I cannot admit them to be its causes. One might just as well say that the crossing of Alexander the Great into Asia was the *cause* of the Persian war, and the descent of Antiochus upon Demetrias the *cause* of his war with Rome. In neither would it be a probable or true statement. In the first case, this action of Alexander's could not be called the cause of a war, for which both he and his father Philip in his lifetime had made elaborate preparations: and in the second case, we know that the Aetolian league had done the same, with a view to a war with Rome, before Antiochus came upon the scene. Such definitions are only worthy of men who cannot distinguish between a first overt act and a cause or pretext; and who do not perceive that a *cause* is the first in a series of events of which such an overt act is the last. I shall therefore regard the first attempt to put into execution what had already been determined as a "beginning," but I shall look for "causes" in the motives which suggested such action and the policy which dictated it; for it is by these, and the calculations to which they give rise, that men are led to decide upon a particular line of conduct. The soundness of this

method will be proved by the following considerations. The true causes and origin of the invasion of Persia by Alexander are patent to everybody. They were, first, the return march of the Greeks under Xenophon through the country from the upper Satrapies; in the course of which, though throughout Asia all the populations were hostile, not a single barbarian ventured to face them: secondly, the invasion of Asia by the Spartan king Agesilaus, in which, though he was obliged by troubles in Greece to return in the middle of his expedition without effecting his object, he yet found no resistance of any importance or adequacy. It was these circumstances which convinced Philip of the cowardice and inefficiency of the Persians; and comparing them with his own high state of efficiency for war, and that of his Macedonian subjects, and placing before his eyes the splendour of the rewards to be gained by such a war, and the popularity which it would bring him in Greece, he seized on the pretext of avenging the injuries done by Persia to Greece, and determined with great eagerness to undertake this war; and was in fact at the time of his death engaged in making every kind of preparation for it.

Here we have the *cause* and the *pretext* of the Persian war. Alexander's expedition into Asia was the *first action* in it.

So too of the war of Antiochus with Rome. The *cause* was evidently the exasperation of the Aetolians, who, thinking that they had been slighted in a number of instances at the end of the war with Philip, not only called in the aid of Antiochus, but resolved to go to every

---

* Polybius, 3. 6–10; 14–15; 20–21; 27–30, translated by D. Shuckburgh.

extremity in satisfying the anger which the events of that time had aroused in them. This was the *cause*. As for the *pretext*, it was the liberation of Greece, which they went from city to city with Antiochus proclaiming, without regard to reason or truth; while the *first act* in the war was the descent of Antiochus upon Demetrias.

My object in enlarging upon this distinction is not to attack the historians in question, but to rectify the ideas of the studious. A physician can do no good to the sick who does not know the causes of their ailments; nor can a statesman do any good who is unable to conceive the manner, cause, and source of the events with which he has from time to time to deal. Surely the former could not be expected to institute a suitable system of treatment for the body; nor the latter to grapple with the exigencies of the situation, without possessing this knowledge of its elements. There is nothing, therefore, which we ought to be more alive to, and to seek for, than the causes of every event which occurs. For the most important results are often produced by trifles; and it is invariably easier to apply remedial measures at the beginning, before things have got beyond the stage of conception and intention.

Now the Roman annalist Fabius asserts that the cause of the Hannibalian war, besides the injury inflicted upon Saguntum, was the encroaching and ambitious spirit of Hasdrubal. "Having secured great power in Iberia, he returned to Libya with the design of destroying the constitution and reducing Carthage to a despotism. But the leading statesmen, getting timely warning of his intention, banded themselves together and successfully opposed him. Suspecting this Hasdrubal retired from Libya, and thenceforth governed Iberia entirely at his own will without taking any account whatever of the Carthaginian Senate. This policy had had in Hannibal from his earliest youth a zealous supporter and imitator; and when he succeeded to the command in Iberia he continued it: and accordingly, even in the case of this war with Rome, was acting on his own authority and contrary to the wish of the Carthaginians; for none of the men of note in Carthage approved of his attack upon Saguntum." This is the statement of Fabius, who goes on to say, that "after the capture of that city an embassy arrived in Carthage from Rome demanding that Hannibal should be given up on pain of a declaration of war."

Now what answer could Fabius have given if we had put the following question to him? "What better chance or opportunity could the Carthaginians have had of combining justice and interest? According to your own account they disliked the proceeding of Hannibal: why did they not submit to the demands of Rome by surrendering the author of the injury; and thus get rid of the common enemy of the state without the odium of doing it themselves, and secure the safety of their territory by ridding themselves of the threatened war—all of which they could have effected by merely passing a decree?" If this question were put, I say, it would admit of no answer. The fact is that, so far from doing anything of the sort, they maintained the war in accordance with Hannibal's policy for seventeen years; and refused to make terms until, at the end of a most determined struggle, they found their own city and persons in imminent danger of destruction.

I do not allude to Fabius and his annals from any fear of their wearing such an air of probability in themselves as to gain any credit,—for the fact is that his assertions are so contrary to reason, that it does not need any argument of mine to help his readers to perceive it,—but I wished to warn those who take up his books not to be misled by the authority of his name, but to be guided by facts. For there is a certain class of readers in whose eyes the personality of the writer is of more account than what he says. They look to the fact that Fabius was a contemporary and a member of the Senate, and assume without more ado that everything he says may be trusted. My view, however, is that we ought not to hold the authority of this writer lightly: yet at the same time that we should not regard it as all-sufficient; but in reading his writings should test them by a reference to the facts themselves.

This is a digression from my immediate subject, which is the war between Carthage and Rome. The cause of this war we must reckon to be the exasperation of Hamilcar, surnamed Barcas, the father of Hannibal. The result of the war in Sicily had not broken the spirit of that commander. He regarded himself as unconquered; for the troops at Eryx which he commanded were still sound and undismayed: and though he yielded so far as to make a treaty, it was a concession to the exigencies of the times brought on by the defeat of the Carthaginians at sea. But he never relaxed in his determined purpose of revenge; and, had it not been for the mutiny of the mercenaries at Carthage, he would at once have sought and made another occasion for bringing about a war, as far as he was able to do so: as it was, he was preoccupied by the domestic war, and had to give his attention entirely to that.

When the Romans, at the conclusion of this mercenary war, proclaimed war with Carthage, the latter at first was inclined to resist at all hazards, because the goodness of her cause gave her hopes of victory,—as I have shown in my former book, without which it would be impossible to understand adequately either this or what is to follow. The Romans, however, would not listen to anything: and the Carthaginians therefore yielded to the force of circumstances; and though feeling bitterly aggrieved, yet being quite unable to do anything, evacuated Sardinia, and consented to pay a sum of twelve hundred talents, in addition to the former indemnity paid them, on condition of avoiding the

war at that time. This is the second and the most important cause of the subsequent war. For Hamilcar, having this public grievance in addition to his private feelings of anger, as soon as he had secured his country's safety by reducing the rebellious mercenaries, set at once about securing the Carthaginian power in Iberia with the intention of using it as a base of operations against Rome. So that I record as a third cause of the war the Carthaginian success in Iberia: for it was the confidence inspired by their forces there which encouraged them to embark upon it.

[Polybius describes Hannibal's pacification of Spain south of the Ebro River.]

* * *

After the defeat of this host, no one south of the Iber rashly ventured to face him except the people of Saguntum. From that town Hannibal tried his best to keep aloof; because, acting on the suggestions and advice of his father Hamilcar, he did not wish to give the Romans an avowed pretext for war until he had thoroughly secured the rest of the country.

But the people of Saguntum kept sending ambassadors to Rome, partly because they foresaw what was coming, and trembled for their own existence, and partly that the Romans might be kept fully aware of the growing power of the Carthaginians in Iberia. For a long time the Romans disregarded their words: but now they sent out some commissioners to see what was going on. Just at that time Hannibal had finished the conquests which he intended for that season, and was going into winter quarters at the New Town again, which was in a way the chief glory and capital town of the Carthaginians in Iberia. He found there the embassy from Rome, granted them an interview, and listened to the message with which they were charged. It was a strong injunction to him to leave Saguntum alone, as being under the protection of Rome;

and not to cross the Iber, in accordance with the agreement come to in the time of Hasdrubal. To this Hannibal answered with all the heat of youth, inflamed by martial ardour, recent success, and his long-standing hatred of Rome. He charged the Romans with having a short time before, when on some political disturbances arising in the town they had been chosen to act as arbitrators, seized the opportunity to put some of the leading citizens to death; and he declared that the Carthaginians would not allow the Saguntines to be thus treacherously dealt with, for it was the traditional policy of Carthage to protect all persons so wronged. At the same time he sent home for instructions as to what he was to do "in view of the fact that the Saguntines were injuring certain of their subject allies." And altogether he was in a state of unreasoning anger and violent exasperation, which prevented him from availing himself of the real causes for war, and made him take refuge in pretexts which would not admit of justification, after the manner of men whose passions master all considerations of equity. How much better it would have been to demand of Rome the restoration of Sardinia, and the remission of the tribute, which she had taken an unfair opportunity to impose on pain of a declaration of war. As it was, he said not a word of the real cause, but alleged the fictitious one of the matter of Saguntum; and so got the credit of beginning the war, not only in defiance of reason, but still more in defiance of justice. The Roman ambassadors, finding that there must undoubtedly be a war, sailed to Carthage to enter the same protest before the people there. They expected, however, that they would have to fight not in Italy, but in Iberia, and that they would have Saguntum as a base of operations.

[Saguntum is besieged and taken by Hannibal.]

* * *

But when news came to Rome of the fall of Saguntum, there was indeed no debate on the question of war, as some historians assert; who even add the speeches delivered on either side. But nothing could be more ridiculous. For is it conceivable that the Romans should have a year before proclaimed war with the Carthaginians in the event of their entering the territory of Saguntum, and yet, when the city itself had been taken, should have debated whether they should go to war or no? Just as absurd are the wonderful statements that the senators put on mourning, and that the fathers introduced their sons above twelve years old into the Senate House, who, being admitted to the debate, refrained from divulging any of its secrets even to their nearest relations. All this is as improbable as it is untrue; unless we are to believe that Fortune, among its other bounties, granted the Romans the privilege of being men of the world from their cradles. I need not waste any more words upon such compositions as those of Chaereas and Sosilus; which, in my judgment, are more like the gossip of the barber's shop and the pavement than history.

The truth is that, when the Romans heard of the disaster at Saguntum, they at once elected envoys, whom they despatched in all haste to Carthage with the offer of two alternatives, one of which appeared to the Carthaginians to involve disgrace as well as injury if they accepted it, while the other was the beginning of a great struggle and of great dangers. For one of these alternatives was the surrender of Hannibal and his staff to Rome, the other was war. When the Roman envoys arrived and declared their message to the Senate, the choice proposed to them between these alternatives was listened to by the Carthaginians with indignation. Still they selected the most capable of their number to state their case, which was grounded on the following pleas.

Passing over the treaty made with

Hasdrubal, as not having ever been made, and, if it had, as not being binding on them because made without their consent (and on this point they quoted the precedent of the Romans themselves, who in the Sicilian war repudiated the terms agreed upon and accepted by Lutatius, as having been made without their consent)—passing over this, they pressed with all the vehemence they could, throughout the discussion, the last treaty made in the Sicilian war; in which they affirmed that there was no clause relating to Iberia, but one expressly providing security for the allies of both parties to the treaty. Now, they pointed out that the Saguntines at that time were not allies of Rome, and therefore were not protected by the clause. to prove their point, they read the treaty more than once aloud. On this occasion the Roman envoys contented themselves with the reply that, while Saguntum was intact, the matter in dispute admitted of pleadings and of a discussion on its merits; but that, that city having been treacherously seized, they had only two alternatives,—either to deliver the persons guilty of the act, and thereby make it clear that they had no share in their crime, and that it was done without their consent; or, if they were not willing to do that, and avowed their complicity in it, to take the consequences.

[Polybius records all the treaties between Rome and Carthage in the period 509–241 B.C.]

* * *

At the end of the first Punic war another treaty was made, of which the chief provisions were these: "The Carthaginians shall evacuate Sicily and all islands lying between Italy and Sicily.

"The allies of neither of the parties to the treaty shall be attacked by the other.

"Neither party shall impose any contribution, nor erect any public building, nor enlist soldiers in the dominions of the other, nor make any compact of friendship with the allies of the other.

"The Carthaginians shall within ten years pay to the Romans two-thousand two-hundred talents, and a thousand on the spot; and shall restore all prisoners, without ransom, to the Romans."

Afterwards, at the end of the Mercenary war in Africa, the Romans went so far as to pass a decree for war with Carthage, but eventually made a treaty to the following effect: "The Carthaginians shall evacuate Sardinia, and pay an additional twelve hundred talents."

Finally, in addition to these treaties, came that negotiated with Hasdrubal in Iberia, in which it was stipulated that "the Carthaginians should not cross the Iber with arms."

Such were the mutual obligations established between Rome and Carthage from the earliest times to that of Hannibal.

As we find then that the Roman invasion of Sicily was not in contravention of their oaths, so we must acknowledge in the case of the second proclamation of war, in consequence of which the treaty for the evacuation of Sardinia was made, that it is impossible to find any reasonable pretext or ground for the Roman action. The Carthaginians were beyond question compelled by the necessities of their position, contrary to all justice, to evacuate Sardinia, and to pay this enormous sum of money. For as to the allegation of the Romans, that they had during the Mercenary war been guilty of acts of hostility to ships sailing from Rome,—that was barred by their own act in restoring, without ransom, the Carthaginian prisoners, in gratitude for similar conduct on the part of Carthage to Romans who had landed on their shores; a transaction which I have spoken of at length in my previous book.

These facts established, it remains to decide by a thorough investigation to which of the two nations the origin of the Hannibalian war is to be imputed.

I have explained the pleas advanced by the Carthaginians; I must now state what is alleged on the contrary by the Romans.

For though it is true that in this particular interview, owing to their anger at the fall of Saguntum, they did not use these arguments, yet they were appealed to on many occasions, and by many of their citizens. First, they argued that the treaty of Hasdrubal could not be ignored, as the Carthaginians had the assurance to do: for it did not contain the clause, which that of Lutatius did, making its validity conditional on its ratification by the people of Rome; but Hasdrubal made the agreement absolutely and authoritatively that "the Carthaginians should not cross the Iber in arms."

Next they alleged that the clause in the treaty respecting Sicily, which by their own admission stipulated that "the allies of neither party should be attacked by the other," did not refer to then existing allies only, as the Carthaginians interpreted it; for in that case a clause would have been added, disabling either from making new alliances in addition to those already existing, or excluding allies, taken subsequently to the making of the treaty, from its benefits. But since neither of these provisions was made, it was plain that both the then existing allies, and all those taken subsequently on either side, were entitled to reciprocal security. And this was only reasonable. For it was not likely that they would have made a treaty depriving them of the power, when opportunity offered, of taking on such friends or allies as seemed to their interest; nor, again, if they had taken any such under their protection, was it to be supposed that they would allow them to be injured by any persons whatever. But, in fact, the main thing present in the minds of both parties to the treaty was, that they should mutually agree to abstain from attacking each other's allies, and on no account admit into alliance with themselves the allies of the other: and it was to subsequent allies that this particular clause applied, "Neither shall enlist soldiers, or impose contributions on the provinces or allies of the other; and all shall be alike secure of attack from the other side."

These things being so, they argued that it was beyond controversy that Saguntum had accepted the protection of Rome, several years before the time of Hannibal. The strongest proof of this, and one which would not be contested by the Carthaginians themselves, was that, when political disturbances broke out at Saguntum, the people chose the Romans, and not the Carthaginians, as arbitrators to settle the dispute and restore their constitution, although the latter were close at hand and were already established in Iberia.

I conclude, then, that if the destruction of Saguntum is to be regarded as the cause of this war, the Carthaginians must be acknowledged to be in the wrong, both in view of the treaty of Lutatius, which secured immunity from attack for the allies of both parties, and in view of the treaty of Hasdrubal, which disabled the Carthaginians from passing the Iber with arms. If on the other hand the taking Sardinia from them, and imposing the heavy money fine which accompanied it, are to be regarded as the causes, we must certainly acknowledge that the Carthaginians had good reason for undertaking the Hannibalian war: for as they had only yielded to the pressure of circumstances, so they seized a favourable turn in those circumstances to revenge themselves on their injurers.

3. THE ACCOUNT OF DIO CASSIUS*

In the succeeding year the Romans became openly hostile to the Carthaginians, and the war, though of far shorter duration than the previous one, proved to be both greater and more baneful in its exploits and effects. It was brought on chiefly by Hannibal, general of the Carthaginians. This Hannibal was a child of Hamilcar Barca, and from his earliest boyhood had been trained to fight against the Romans. Hamilcar said he was raising all his sons like so many whelps to fight against them, but as he saw that this one's nature was far superior to that of the rest, he made him take an oath that he would wage war upon them, and for this reason he instructed the boy in warfare above all else when only fifteen years old. On account of this youthfulness Hannibal was not able, when his father died, to succeed to the generalship. But when Hasdrubal was dead, he delayed no longer, being now twenty-six years of age, but at once took possession of the army in Spain and after being acclaimed as leader by the soldiers brought it about that his right to lead was confirmed also by those in authority at home. After effecting this he needed a plausible excuse for his enterprise against the Romans, and this he found in the Saguntines of Spain. These people, dwelling not far from the river Iber and a short distance above the sea, were dependents of the Romans, and the latter held them in honor and in the treaty with the Carthaginians had made an exception of them. For these reasons, then, Hannibal began a war with them, knowing that the Romans would either assist the Saguntines or avenge them if they suffered injury. Hence for these reasons as well as because he knew that they possessed great wealth, which he particularly needed, and for various other causes that promised him

advantages against the Romans he made an attack upon the Saguntines.

Spain, in which the Saguntines dwell, and all the adjoining land is in the western part of Europe. It extends for a considerable distance along the inner sea, beside the Pillars of Hercules, and along the ocean; furthermore it occupies the upper part of the mainland for a very great distance, as far as the Pyrenees. THIS RANGE, BEGINNING AT THE SEA CALLED ANCIENTLY THE SEA OF THE BEBRYCES BUT LATER THE SEA OF THE NARBONENSES, REACHES TO THE GREAT OUTER SEA, AND CONFINES MANY DIVERSE NATIONALITIES; IT ALSO SEPARATES SPAIN FROM THE NEIGHBORING LAND OF GAUL. The tribes did not employ the same language nor carry on a common government. This resulted in their not having a single name. The Romans called them Hispanii, but the Greeks Iberians, from the river Iber.

These Saguntines, then, being besieged sent to those near them and to the Romans asking for aid. But Hannibal checked any local movement, and the Romans sent ambassadors to him bidding him not come near the Saguntines, and threatening in case he should not obey to sail to Carthage at once and lay accusations against him. When the envoys were now close at hand, Hannibal sent some of the natives who were to pretend that they were kindly disposed to them and were instructed to say that the general was not there but had gone some distance away into parts unknown; they advised the enemy, therefore (they were to say), to depart as quickly as possible and before their presence should be reported lest in the disorder prevailing because of the absence of the general they should lose their lives. The envoys accordingly believed them and set off for Carthage. An assembly being called some of the Carthaginians counseled maintaining peace with the Romans, but the party attached to Hannibal affirmed that the Saguntines

---

* Dio Cassius, 8. 21–22, translated by H. B. Foster.

were guilty of wrong-doing and the Romans were meddling with what did not concern them. Finally those who urged them to make war won the day.

Meanwhile Hannibal in the course of his siege was conducting vigorous assaults. Many kept falling and many more were being wounded on Hannibal's side. One day the Carthaginians succeeded in shaking down a portion of the outer circuit and had been daring enough to enter through the breach, when the Saguntines made a sortie and scared them away. This gave the besieged strength and the Carthaginians fell back in dejection. They did not leave the spot, however, till they had captured the city, though the siege dragged on to the eighth month. Many unusual events happened in that time, one of which was Hannibal's being dangerously wounded. The place was taken in this manner. They brought to bear against the wall an engine much higher than the fortification and carrying heavy-armed soldiers, some visible, some concealed. While the Saguntines, therefore, were quite strenuously fighting against the men they saw, thinking them the only ones, those hidden had dug through the wall from below and found their way inside. The Saguntines overwhelmed by the unexpectedness of the event ran up to the citadel and held a conference to see whether by any reasonable concessions they might be preserved. But as Hannibal held out no moderate terms and no assistance came to them from the Romans, they begged for a cessation of the assaults until they should deliberate a little about their position. During this respite they gathered together the most highly prized of their treasures and cast them into the fire; then such as were incapable of fighting committed suicide, and those who were in their prime advanced in a body against their opponents and in a desperate struggle were cut down.

For their sakes the Romans and the Carthaginians embarked upon war. Hannibal after gaining numerous allies was hastening toward Italy. The Romans on ascertaining this assembled in their senate-hall, and many speeches were delivered. Lucius Cornelius Lentulus addressed the people and said they must not delay but vote for war against the Carthaginians and separate consuls and armies into two detachments, and send the one to Spain and the other to Libya, in order that at one and the same time the land of the enemy might be desolated and his allies injured; thus neither would he be able to assist Spain nor could he himself receive assistance from there. To this Quintus Fabius Maximus rejoined that it was not so absolutely and inevitably necessary to vote for war, but they could first employ an embassy, and then if the Carthaginians persuaded them that they were guilty of no wrong, they should remain quiet, but if the same people were convicted of wrong-doing, they might thereupon wage war against them, "in order," he said, "that we may cast the responsibility for the war upon them." THE OPINIONS OF THE TWO MEN WERE SUBSTANTIALLY THESE. THE SENATE DECIDED TO MAKE PREPARATIONS, TO BE SURE, FOR CONFLICT, BUT TO DESPATCH ENVOYS TO CARTHAGE AND DENOUNCE HANNIBAL; AND IF THE CARTHAGINIANS REFRAINED FROM APPROVING THE EXPLOITS, THEY WOULD ARBITRATE THE MATTER, OR IF ALL RESPONSIBILITY WERE LAID UPON HIS SHOULDERS, THEY WOULD DEMAND HIS EXTRADITION, AND IF HE WERE NOT GIVEN UP, THEY WOULD DECLARE WAR UPON THE NATION.

The envoys set out and the Carthaginians considered what must be done. And a certain Hasdrubal, one of those who had been primed by Hannibal, counseled them that they ought to get back their ancient freedom and shake off by means of money and troops and allies, all welded together, the slavery imposed by peace, adding: "If you only permit Hannibal to act as he wishes, the proper thing will be done and you will have no trouble." After such words on his part the great Hanno, opposing Hasdrubal's argument, gave it as his opinion that they ought not to draw war upon themselves lightly nor for small complaints concerning foreigners, when it was in their power to settle a part of the difficulty and divert the rest of it upon the heads of those who had been active in the matter. With these remarks he ceased, and the elder Carthaginians who remembered the former war sided with him, but those in robust manhood and especially all the partisans of Hannibal violently gainsaid him. INASMUCH, THEN, AS THEY MADE NO DEFINITE ANSWER AND SHOWED CONTEMPT FOR THE ENVOYS, MARCUS FABIUS THRUSTING HIS HANDS BENEATH HIS TOGA AND HOLDING THEM WITH PALMS UPWARD SAID: "HERE I BRING TO YOU, CARTHAGINIANS, BOTH WAR AND PEACE: DO YOU CHOOSE WHICHEVER OF THEM YOU WISH." UPON THEIR REPLYING THAT THEY CHOSE NEITHER, BUT WOULD READILY ACCEPT EITHER THAT THE ROMANS SHOULD LEAVE, HE IMMEDIATELY DECLARED WAR UPON THEM.

In this way, then, and for these reasons the Romans and the Carthaginians became involved in war for the second time. And

the Divinity beforehand indicated what was to come to pass. For in Rome an ox talked with a human voice, and another at the Ludi Romani threw himself out of a house into the Tiber and was lost, many thunderbolts fell, and blood in one case was seen coming from sacred statues whereas in another it dripped from the shield of a soldier, and the sword of another soldier was snatched by a wolf from the very midst of the camp. Many unknown wild beasts went before Hannibal leading the way, as he was crossing the Iber, and a vision appeared to him in a dream. He thought that the gods once, sitting in assembly, sent for him and bade him march with all speed into Italy and receive from them a guide for the way, and that by this guide he was commanded to follow without turning around. He did turn around, however, and saw a great tempest moving and an immense serpent accompanying it. In surprise he asked his conductor what these creatures were; and the guide said: "Hannibal, they are on their way to help you in the sack of Italy."

4. THE ACCOUNT OF APPIAN*

Appian of Alexandria was probably born in the reign of Trajan, held office in his native city, became a Roman citizen, and then moved to Rome. Under Antoninus Pius he wrote an account of Rome's conquests in chronological order and arranged according to the peoples conquered. It is most valuable in the section on the *Civil Wars*, where it is often the only consecutive narrative we have.

The Carthaginians, enjoying the gains they had received from Spain, sent another army thither and appointed Hasdrubal, the son-in-law of Hamilcar, who was still in Spain, commander of all their forces there. He had with him in Spain Hannibal, the son of Hamilcar and brother of his own wife, a young man zealous in war, beloved

by the army, and who soon after became famous for his military exploits. Him he appointed lieutenant-general. Hasdrubal brought many Spanish tribes to his support by persuasion, for he was attractive in personal intercourse, and where force was needed he made use of the young man. In this way he pushed forward from the Western ocean to the interior as far as the river Iberus (Ebro), which divides Spain about in the centre, and at a distance of

* Appian, *The Spanish Wars*, 6. 6–13, translated by Horace White. Reprinted by permission of the Loeb Classical Library.

about five days' journey from the Pyrenees flows down to the Northern ocean.

The Saguntines, a colony of the island of Zacynthus, who lived about midway between the Pyrenees and the river Iberus, and other Greeks who dwelt in the neighborhood of Emporia and other Spanish towns, having apprehensions for their safety, sent ambassadors to Rome. The Senate, who were unwilling to see the Carthaginian power augmented, sent an embassy to Carthage. It was agreed between them that the limit of the Carthaginian power in Spain should be the river Iberus; that beyond that river the Romans should not carry war against the subjects of Carthage, nor should the Carthaginians cross it for a similar purpose; and that the Saguntines and the other Greeks in Spain should remain free and autonomous. So these agreements were added to the treaties between Rome and Carthage.

Some time later, while Hasdrubal was governing that part of Spain belonging to Carthage, a slave whose master he had cruelly put to death killed him secretly in a hunting expedition. Hannibal convicted him of this crime and put him to death with dreadful tortures. Now the army proclaimed Hannibal, although still very young, yet greatly beloved by the soldiers, their general, and the Carthaginian Senate confirmed the appointment. Those of the opposite faction, who had feared the power of Hamilcar and Hasdrubal, when they learned of their death, despised Hannibal on account of his youth and prosecuted their friends and partisans with the old charges. The people took sides with the accusers, bearing a grudge against those now prosecuted, because they remembered the old severities of the times of Hamilcar and Hasdrubal, and ordered them to turn into the public treasury the large gifts that Hamilcar and Hasdrubal had bestowed upon them, as being enemy's spoils. The prosecuted parties sent messengers to Hannibal asking him to assist them, and admonished him that, if he should neglect

those who were able to assist him at home, he would be thoroughly despised by his father's enemies.

He had foreseen all this and he knew that the persecution of his friends was the beginning of a plot against himself. He determined that he would not endure this enmity as a perpetual menace, as his father and brother-in-law had done, nor put up forever with the fickleness of the Carthaginians, who usually repaid benefits with ingratitude. It was said also that when he was a boy he had taken an oath upon the altar, at his father's instance, that when he should arrive at man's estate he would be the implacable enemy of Rome. For these reasons he thought that, if he could involve his country in arduous and protracted undertakings and plunge it into doubts and fears, he would place his own affairs and those of his friends in a secure position. He beheld Africa, however, and the subject parts of Spain in peace. But if he could stir up a war with Rome, which he strongly desired, he thought that the Carthaginians would have enough to think about and to be afraid of, and that if he should be successful, he would reap immortal glory by gaining for his country the government of the habitable world (for when the Romans were conquered there would be no other rivals), and if he should fail, the attempt itself would bring him great renown.

Conceiving that if he should cross the Iberus that would constitute a brilliant beginning, he suborned the Turbuletes, neighbors of the Saguntines, that they should complain to him that the latter were overrunning their country and doing them many other wrongs. They made this complaint. Then Hannibal sent their ambassadors to Carthage, and wrote private letters saying that the Romans were inciting Carthaginian Spain to revolt, and that the Saguntines were coöperating with the Romans for this purpose. Nor did he desist from this deception, but kept sending messages of this kind until the

Carthaginian Senate authorized him to deal with the Saguntines as he saw fit. Since he had a pretext, he arranged that the Turbuletes should come again to make complaints against the Saguntines, and that the latter should send legates also. When Hannibal commanded them to explain their differences to him, they replied that they should refer the matter to Rome. Hannibal thereupon ordered them out of his camp, and the next night crossed the Iberus with his whole army, laid waste the Saguntine territory, and planted engines against their city. Not being able to take it, he surrounded it with a wall and ditch, stationed plenty of guards, and pushed the siege at intervals.

The Saguntines, oppressed by this sudden and unheralded attack, sent an embassy to Rome. The Senate commissioned its own ambassadors to go with them. They were instructed first to remind Hannibal of the agreement, and if he should not obey to proceed to Carthage and complain against him. When they arrived in Spain and were approaching his camp from the sea, Hannibal forbade their coming. Accordingly they sailed for Carthage with the Saguntine ambassadors, and reminded the Carthaginians of the agreement. The latter accused the Saguntines of committing many wrongs on their subjects. When the Saguntines offered to submit the whole question to the Romans as arbitrators, the Carthaginians replied that there was no use of an arbitration because they were able to avenge themselves. When this reply was brought to Rome some advised sending aid to the Saguntines. Others favored delay, saying that the Saguntines were not inscribed as allies in the agreement with them, but merely as free and autonomous, and that they were still free although besieged. The latter opinion prevailed.

The Saguntines, when they despaired of help from Rome, and when famine weighed heavily upon them, and Hannibal kept up the siege without intermission (for he had heard that the city was very prosperous and wealthy, and for this reason relaxed not the siege), issued an edict to bring all the silver and gold, public and private, to the forum, where they melted it with lead and brass, so that it should be useless to Hannibal. Then, thinking that it was better to die fighting than starve to death, they made a sally by night upon the besiegers while they were asleep and not expecting an attack, and killed some as they were getting out of bed, others as they were clumsily arming themselves, and still others who were actually fighting. The battle continued until many of the Africans and all the Saguntines were slain. When the women witnessed the slaughter of their husbands from the walls, some of them threw themselves from the housetops, others hanged themselves, and others slew their children and then themselves. Such was the end of Saguntum, once a great and powerful city. When Hannibal learned what had been done with the gold he was angry, and put all the surviving adults to death with torture. Observing that the city was not far from Carthage and with good land about it situated on the sea, he rebuilt it and made it a Carthaginian colony, and I think it is now called Spartarian Carthage.

The Romans now sent ambassadors to Carthage to demand that Hannibal should be delivered up to them as a violator of the treaty unless they wished to assume the responsibility. If they would not give him up, war was to be declared forthwith. The ambassadors obeyed their instructions, and when the Carthaginians refused to give up Hannibal they declared war. It is said that it was done in the following manner. The chief of the embassy, pointing to the fold of his toga and smiling, said: "Here, Carthaginians, I bring you peace or war, you may take which ever you choose." The latter replied: "You may give us whichever you like." When the Romans offered war they all cried out: "We accept it."

5. THE CASE FOR ROME*

We now reach the Second Punic War, the importance of which could not readily be overstated. Who has not at his finger tips a list of the "remote and immediate causes" of this struggle? Because of the supreme importance of the event, it is desirable in this instance to examine the validity of the general belief that the two nations involved could not brook rivalry and that the subjection of one or the other of them was an *a priori* necessity. Such a view takes for granted that both nations were bent upon conquest at all costs. This misconception will best be refuted by a full statement of the causes, but it may be worth while to point out that it has its origin, not in a study of Roman history, but in a misapplication of Oriental, as well as of more modern ideals, to Roman methods. Before the history of the eastern states— Babylonia, Egypt, and Persia—was as thoroughly studied as it now is, the possibility existed of loosely grouping their political ideals with those of Greece and Rome and arriving at the popular generalization that the "ancient" state was imperialistic in a sense that, since the creation of the modern "concert of powers," no longer exists. Now it is true that the eastern monarchies were generally imperialistic. The empire of the East was seldom a nation of one tongue, one race, one worship; it was held together artificially by its ruler and his effective instrument, a mercenary army. Conquests which brought tribute—the sinews of the ruler's wars—were absolutely essential to the life of the dynasty. How different was the Greco-Roman city-state whose very origin lay in the homogeneous small group which constituted its own army, paid its own expenses, and chose its own magistrates from its own body! Even in such a state, of course, greed for conquest might

arise, but it would manifestly go against the grain, for the citizen himself must shoulder the danger and the cost, and the conviction is ever present that expansion is suicidal, for the city-state constitution must go under with the acquisition of dependencies. The monarchical form, on the other hand, was adapted to and lived by conquest and the monarch compelled his subjects to fight for it. Obviously a general comparison between ancient monarchies and republics in this respect is wholly misleading.

Certain modern parallels have also led to a misunderstanding of Greco-Roman ideals. Imperialism has acquired a momentum in medieval and modern times which it did not have in the third century B.C., and we must guard against projecting present-day convictions into that period. The factors in the development of modern imperialism are several—none of which ever influenced Rome. In the first place, the church, representing a religion that demanded world-wide recognition, must of necessity, so soon as it claimed temporal power at all, set up the demand for universal empire. Secondly, the awe-inspiring ideal of the Roman empire inherited through Charlemagne, not only by the central "Holy Roman Empire," but more locally by France, was for centuries an example, comparable to which nothing existed for the Roman republic. And thirdly, modern empires have been built up by monarchical dynasties directed by the same driving force which vitalized the old Oriental monarchies. But the Romans of the third century had no such imperialistic background. To them the history of the great Oriental monarchies was a closed book. The one great conquest of which they knew anything had proved unsuccessful, for Macedonia was then weaker than before Alexander's day. Even the Diadochian powers which professed to follow Alexander had reached a *modus*

* Tenney Frank, *Roman Imperialism* (New York: The Macmillan Co., 1914), pp. 119–126. Reprinted by permission of the publisher.

vivendi which much resembles our "concert of powers." It is safe to say that the idea of universal power never occurred to any Roman before the Punic war. He was accustomed to a world of petty city-states which owned a few square miles outside their walls and did not ask for more. If, therefore, we hope to understand the groping, stumbling, accidental expansion of Rome, we must rid ourselves of anachronistic generalizations and "remote causes" and look instead for the specific accidents that led the nation unwittingly from one contest to another until, to her own surprise, Rome was mistress of the Mediterranean world.

In order to weigh these causes correctly it will be necessary to review the western policy of the two states interested in Spain at this time, Massilia and Carthage. In the early sixth century a Greek colony from Phocæa, in Asia Minor, settled Massilia, a town not far from the mouth of the Rhone. This city quickly grew wealthy in bartering with neighboring tribes and established numerous trading stations along the coast from Nice to Spain. It showed no desire for empire, wishing only to have the privilege of trading in peace. Presently, its traders established posts in Spain for the interchange of goods with the Iberians, among them Emporiæ and Rhodæ in the north,—two flourishing towns in the third century. Other stations for the same purpose were established much farther south, in the region where New Carthage later stood. With the arrival of Carthaginian merchants, however, came the new principle of trade monopoly. Southern Spain became a part of the Punic empire, and Punic ships patrolled the waters, sinking any trader of a foreign nation that dared appear. Naturally, there was trouble between the shippers of the two peoples, and in the end the Massiliots lost their ports in the south. Now the significance of this struggle is due to the fact that Massilia was one of Rome's closest friends and most loyal allies. It is said that

Massilia stored Roman gifts in her treasure house at Delphi as early as 396 B.C., and that she helped Rome to pay the ransom exacted by the Gauls in 387. The old statue of Diana on the Aventine was a copy of the Massilian Artemis. Throughout the Punic war the Massilian fleet appears to have been the mainstay of Rome's navy and, in fact, it won the severest naval battle of the war, if we may believe a recently discovered fragment of Sosylos. It was apparently Massilia that introduced Rome to the Ilian alliance in Asia Minor, which, as it turned out, served to open a way to participation in Asiatic politics. Finally, in payment for many favors, when Massilia was attacked by barbarians in 154, Rome sent an army which liberated the city, and won for it an extension of territory, and special trading privileges among the Gauls.

Carthage was all the while pursuing her own purposes in Spain. An early trading treaty with Rome (dating about 348) had forbidden Roman vessels to trade beyond Mastia in southern Spain, and, as we have seen, about the same time Carthage blocked the Massiliots from their posts somewhat north of this point. For a century, the Punic conquests in Spain progressed slowly. But immediately after the great war with Rome, Hamilcar Barcas, filled with bitterness at the loss of Sicily and Sardinia, set out to establish a Punic power in Spain. There can be little doubt that his intention was to secure control of a sturdy population for the Punic army rather than revenue for the treasury, and that his prime motive was to bring a war of revenge against Rome in return for the defeats he had suffered. He met with striking success, for his generalship was superb and his rule was firm, though not oppressive. When in 229 he fell in battle, Hasdrubal, a member of the same family, succeeded to his command and carried on the work of winning over the Iberian tribes even more rapidly than before. The Massiliots realized, of course, that these

Carthaginian victories would soon deprive them of all their Spanish trade—for no other nation could trade where the Punic standard was planted. There can be little doubt that it was Massilia that drew Rome's attention to Spanish affairs. She had gradually lost a large part of her Iberian trade and in a year or two her flourishing colonies of Emporiæ and Rhodæ would doubtless go under. If Rome cared little for the question of open ports in Spain, the Massilians had other ways of arousing her interest. They could urge that a Punic attack upon Emporiæ would be a declaration of war against Massilia, which, in turn, must involve Rome because of their alliance; and she could din into the ears of Roman senators the reports that were current in Spain that the ultimate purpose of the Barcids was a war of revenge upon Rome. Her diplomacy was effective, at any rate. Rome became thoroughly concerned about Punic advances in Spain, and sent envoys to Hasdrubal in 226 with requests for a treaty defining that "the Carthaginians should not cross the river Iber in arms." Rome obtained what she desired and presently, in pursuit of the same policy of anticipating Carthaginian success, she entered into a defensive alliance with Saguntum, an independent Iberian city of considerable strength, a hundred miles south of the Iber.

Thus matters stood when, in 221, Hannibal, the young son of Hamilcar, succeeded to the command of Spain. He at once subdued the whole peninsula as far as the Iber, with the exception of Saguntum, and then, at the head of a splendidly trained army, in accordance with the plan and purpose that his father had taught him from youth, he made ready to bring on a war with Rome. Saguntum, as it happened, offered a plausible excuse, for it had committed some hostile act against a Spanish tribe that was allied to Carthage. By picking up this quarrel, Hannibal hoped to force a declaration of war from Rome and throw the onus of the ensuing conflict upon his enemy. If the declaration came from Rome, Carthage would be forced to support him, which it certainly would not do if he invaded Italy on his own initiative, for the Punic aristocracy which lived by trade strongly favored peace. The capture of Saguntum would, furthermore, wipe out the last unfriendly people in his rear, would enable him to close the harbor to the Roman navy, and would secure him the booty with which—according to Polybius—he hoped to mollify the home government and equip his army for the long march. He accordingly attacked Saguntum in 219 when the Roman consuls were busy in Illyricum, and, after a siege of eight months, captured it. The Romans sent envoys to Carthage, demanding the punishment of Hannibal and, upon the refusal of their request, declared war.

What then were the causes of this war? Livy and Appian, who wish to exculpate Rome, recklessly state that Hannibal broke the treaty of 226 by crossing the Iber to attack Saguntum, not knowing that the city lay a hundred miles south of that river. Polybius belittles Hannibal's provocation to attack Saguntum and holds that Carthage should have based her grievance upon the seizure of Sardinia twenty years before. This seems to be a very peculiar argument from a statesman of Polybius' experience, for ancient states did not assume the privilege of annulling old treaties on the ground of severity any more than modern states do. Most modern historians assert that Rome's alliance with Saguntum was an infraction of the spirit at least of the Iber treaty; for they assume that the treaty defined the Iber River as the boundary of the Punic and Roman "spheres of influence" in Spain. This, I think, is a grave misconception of third-century international politics. Rome had made the Saguntine alliance several years before the war, and yet not a word of protest had been raised against it. Hannibal attacked Saguntum, not on the ground that the Saguntine alliance encroached upon the Punic sphere, but on the ground of the wrongs committed by Saguntum against Spanish allies. In no ancient source is there the slightest indication that Carthage considered her rights in Spain to have been infringed by the Saguntine treaty. Polybius, in his very full discussion, does not hint at such a theory. In fact he definitely assumes that Rome had full power to make any alliances she chose with free states in Spain, and asserts that all such allies were entitled to security by the terms of former treaties. Nor did Rome know anything of the modern doctrine of "spheres of influence," although it may have had some meaning for the ancient monarchies of the eastern Mediterranean. Rome's alliances showed in general an abhorrence of loose ends, and always insisted upon clear definitions of boundaries. A penumbra of undefined influence over a hinterland of unexplored territory would have been entirely beyond her understanding at that time. She had hitherto dealt with a patchwork of innumerable city-states and tribes whose petty areas in every case were precisely defined. She had signed at least a hundred alliances with such states, and the jurisdiction of each of these hundred treaties was clearly and definitely known. Not one of them assumed any kind of influence or interest beyond the precise boundaries of the signatories. Accordingly, although an affair like the Saguntine alliance would call for immediate protest in a day of Monroe Doctrines and African protectorates, there is no reason to suppose that in the third century, when it occurred, it involved any infraction of rights or that it could, in any way, have offended Hasdrubal and Hannibal, except in so far as it revealed Rome's success in gaining an ally coveted by them.

The cause of the war, therefore, was neither desire for world conquest on the part of either power, nor a dispute over predominant influence in Spain. The nations came to blows because the Barcid family—whose war policy had met with defeat in 242 and 238—were able to keep alive the bitter feelings aroused by former defeats and to discover a situation at the right moment whereby they could force their government to support a raid of vengeance upon Italy. If a brilliant son of Hamilcar Barcas had not survived to carry on the policy of his father till the favorable moment arrived, there is not the slightest reason for assuming that Rome and Carthage would not have found a *modus vivendi* in the same way that the neighboring powers of the eastern Mediterranean had.

The purposes of the two contestants are fairly well revealed by subsequent events. Rome, upon whom an unwelcome war had been thrust, made no move to acquire territory in Spain. She simply tried to end matters by a quick thrust. Knowing that the Carthaginian government had been inveigled into the contest against its wishes, she ordered her whole army and navy against Africa, wisely reasoning that Carthage would quickly recall Hannibal if hard pressed. Rome doubtless intended if successful to demand an indemnity and end the affair. Against Hannibal's veteran army of 50,000 she sent only a mere 10,000 new recruits, whose object it was to worry the enemy and hold the mountain passes until the main army in Africa should accomplish its mission.

Hannibal's designs are also made clear by his early maneuvers. Not daring to rely on the home government for transports, he chose the hazardous land route through Gaul and the Alps. When once in Italy, he hoped to double and treble his army with the Gallic tribes of the Po which had recently been at war with Rome. He did not intend to destroy Rome and make Italy a dependency of Carthage, for the terms of his alliance with Philip of Macedonia, made in the heyday of his greatest successes, prove that he assumed Rome would continue a strong power. But he did hope to humiliate her and to cut off her northern and southern allies in such a way that her power would be definitely limited. He did not even hope to gain tributary empire in Italy, for he knew, of course, that Rome's allies would not leave the Italian federation except upon better terms than they were already enjoying. What he actually promised the south Italian allies was absolute autonomy under Punic protection, a form of alliance that would have brought little benefit to the Carthaginians, who already enjoyed the ordinary rights of commerce in southern Italy and who would scarcely have dared to propose the establishment of a commercial monopoly there. It was, therefore, not a war of extermination nor of conquest. Its purpose was simply to administer a thorough humiliation that would wipe out the disgrace of former defeats.

6. THE CASE FOR CARTHAGE*

The Second Punic War has rightly been regarded by ancient and modern writers alike as the greatest in the history of Rome. The deep insight of Polybius, who lived to see Rome undisputed mistress of the Mediterranean, has noted and recorded how the issue of the struggle inaugurated a new era in Europe. A unity of ancient history begins, with Rome as the focus, which ends only when the Roman Empire split into two halves. The military history of the war down to Cannae and the outstanding personality of Hannibal are illuminated by the concise and orderly account of the Greek historian and by the literary skill of Livy.

It is true that Livy's patriotic bias, moral purpose and rhetorical colour, added to a lack of any real understanding of how wars are waged and battles fought, are immediately perceptible where the crystal stream of Polybius can be used for comparison. Consequently, when Polybius is lacking and Livy becomes almost the only source, extreme caution is needed if we would endeavour to reproduce a narrative of what happened rather than a mirror of the garbled Roman tradition. But Polybius and Livy alike reflect the grandeur of the theme which so captured the imagination of the Romans that even under the Empire 'Should Hannibal have crossed the Alps?' or 'Should Hannibal have marched on Rome after Cannae?' were debated by boys in the schools and by mature rhetoricians. And lastly, apart from the intrinsic military interest of the battles and sieges, apart from the dramatic vividness of the personalities of Hannibal and Scipio Africanus, the war reveals the Roman character and the Roman constitution tested in the supreme ordeal by fire.

Though the course of the war testifies to the high qualities of the Romans, its causes and occasions are part of a different picture. The differences extend to the sources: even Polybius was dominated by the Roman literature of justification, and at Carthage a *défaitiste* government towards the close of the war sought not so much to justify the action of Carthage as to shift the responsibility wholly on to the broad shoulders of Hannibal. It is, therefore, no wonder that the meagre and distorted tradition or confusion of traditions about the antecedents of the war has left historians in perplexity about both the events and their true interpretation. The general course of Roman policy in the two decades that followed the close of the First Punic War has been described elsewhere (vol. VII, chap. XXV). It remains to examine more closely the causes of the war, and the manner in which it came about.

* B. L. Hallward, "Hannibal's Invasion of Italy," *Cambridge Ancient History* (Cambridge, England: Cambridge University Press, 1930), Vol. 8, pp. 25–32. Reprinted by permission of the publisher.

In 237 B.C. the Romans, with no shadow of right, had forced Carthage to surrender Sardinia and to pay an additional indemnity of 1200 talents. Six years later, when the successes of Hamilcar were extending Punic power in Spain, Roman envoys, probably sent at the instance of Massilia to protest, accepted his assurances that he was seeking the means to pay the indemnity imposed by Rome. Two years later, Hasdrubal succeeded Hamilcar and by diplomacy as much as by arms continued the Carthaginian advance, until, in 226 or 225, the Romans, faced by a war with the Gauls of the Po valley, wished to set some limits to the Carthaginian Empire in Spain. Accordingly, Roman envoys came to an agreement with Hasdrubal which pledged the Carthaginians not to carry their arms north of the Ebro. We may assume that the Ebro instead of the Pyrenees was made the dividing line in order to give protection to the Massiliote colonies of Emporium and Rhode and greater protection to Massilia itself, the ally of Rome. It is to be presumed that Hasdrubal, as Hannibal after him, had with him assessors from the home government, and that the agreement was as binding as that made by Hannibal and his assessors later with Philip of Macedon (p. 119), that it was, in fact, a valid treaty. As the Romans were not in a position to impose this limit on Hasdrubal by their simple *fiat*, it must be assumed further that they undertook in return not to carry their arms south of the Ebro, or to interfere in the Carthaginian dominion. Saguntum, however, a smallish Iberian town of slight strategical and no great commercial importance a hundred miles south of the river, was already under Roman protection, probably brought under it through the agency of Massilia, with which city Saguntum, as her coinage testifies, had close trade relations. It is even possible that Rome had made something like an alliance with Saguntum as early as 231 (vol. VII, p. 809). This alliance

was not invalidated by the Ebro treaty, which, however, carried with it the implied obligation on Rome not to use the town as an instrument to hinder Carthaginian expansion within the sphere recognized as open to her.

So long as the war with the Gauls hung in the balance, Rome was careful to respect the treaty and its implications. It is admitted that Carthage in turn had done nothing to injure Saguntum, and, if this was of deliberate policy, it points to the fact that the alliance of the town with Rome was taken account of both after and before the treaty. By 221 B.C. the Romans had proved victorious against the Gauls, and they now intervened at Saguntum to bring into power, not without bloodshed, a party hostile to Carthage and to promote friction with the neighbouring tribe of the Torboletae, who were subjects of the Carthaginians. In fact, after enjoying the benefits of the Ebro treaty, Rome began to use Saguntum as a tool to undermine Punic power south of the river and to loosen the hold of Carthage on the enviable wealth of Spain.

This does not mean that the Senate contemplated bringing about an immediate war. For with the threat of Gallic invasion removed, it probably reckoned on repeating, if need be, in Spain the successful bullying by which Rome had secured Sardinia. And so, late in 220 B.C., envoys were sent to warn Hannibal, who had succeeded Hasdrubal as governor of Carthaginian Spain, not to attack Saguntum, because the town was under the protection of Rome. But neither from Hannibal nor at Carthage, whither they then went, did they receive the submissive assurances which they probably expected. Finally, in the spring of 219 when Saguntum, relying on Rome, remained intransigent, Hannibal attacked the town, which he took after an eight months' siege. All this time the Romans sent no force to assist the defenders. Both consuls were engaged in Illyria, and the Senate was probably undecided how far their protection of Saguntum should go. When about November 219 news came that the town had fallen, the *patres* took long to decide whether or not to regard it as a *casus belli*. Saguntum was unimportant and distant, and the material interests of Rome, and of Massilia, were protected by the Ebro treaty, which Hannibal showed no sign of violating. Many senators, no doubt, were opposed to embarking on a serious war in the West, particularly at a time when Rome might find herself involved in a conflict with Macedon. On the other hand, Roman prestige was concerned, above all in Spain, and, if Rome took no action, she would find it difficult afterwards to hinder the consolidation of Carthaginian power south of the Ebro.

Finally the plea of prestige, which really meant the claim to interfere effectively in Carthaginian Spain, prevailed, and late in March 218 envoys were sent to Carthage to demand the surrender of Hannibal and of his Carthaginian assessors who had concurred in the attack on Saguntum. The demand was the *rerum repetitio* which, if not complied with, led to formal declaration of war, and the Romans envoys were no doubt authorized to state definitely what would be the result of refusal. The Carthaginian Senate denied—and with justice—that they were under any formal obligation not to attack Saguntum, which was not in the list of Roman allies whom Carthage had pledged herself to respect in the peace of 241 B.C. Since that date Carthage had made no engagement with Rome which could affect her dealings with Saguntum. The purely juridical case was irrefutable. Indeed, Roman apologists were later driven to the expedient of declaring that Saguntum was expressly safeguarded by the Ebro treaty, or even that it lay north of the river. This latter fiction seems to find an echo even in Polybius, and both were served by the assertion that the Carthaginian Senate denied the validity of the Ebro treaty. This assertion is probably the perversion of what may be true, that the Carthaginians limited the discussion to the precise legal point at issue. Carthage then refused the Roman demand, and the Roman envoys declared that Carthage was choosing war. Strong as was the legal and indeed moral case for Carthage, because Rome was using Saguntum to undermine her power in Spain, the fact remained that Hannibal had attacked and taken—with the approval of his government—a town which Rome had declared to be under her protection. This is the core of truth in the Roman tradition which sought to convince the legally-minded citizens that the cause of Rome was the cause of justice.

It cannot be said that the war which followed was from the beginning inevitable. The first conflict between Rome and Carthage had not entailed the destruction or subjection of either. The two states could continue to exist side by side in the Western Mediterranean, but only if each was willing to respect the other's sphere of influence. The treaty of 241 B.C. might have formed the basis of some such balance of power as Hellenistic statecraft had reached east of the Adriatic. The foreign policy of Carthage in the previous three centuries is evidence of the paramount importance in her counsels of commercial interests and motives, and it is extremely probable that she would have wished to keep the peace in order to exploit the immense resources of her newly re-acquired and extended province in Spain. Rome, in effective possession of Sicily, might well be content to leave to her the Eldorado of the Spanish mines and Spanish markets. Indeed, had the Roman Senate's policy been sincerely pacific, there is small reason to think that the nobles of the house of Barca, great as was their influence due to the services of Hamilcar in crushing the Mercenaries' revolt and to the political adroitness of Hasdrubal, would have been able to lead her into a war of revenge against Rome. The picture of the Barcids as viceroys in Spain independent of the home government is itself false. Neither Hamilcar, Hasdrubal nor Hannibal was a Wallenstein. They knew themselves to be the generals of a Republic, and their policy had to take account of the views of the Carthaginian ring of aristocrats whose hand was upon the machine of government. Many of these nobles doubtless cared more for their estates in Africa than for the old tradition of commercial and naval supremacy in the Western Mediterranean. In fact, the Carthaginian navy had been allowed to decline, partly, it may be, to avoid the semblance of a challenge to Rome, her successful rival by sea. Yet the home government, which knew well that it was the Spanish mines that had made easy the punctual payment of the indemnity and that opened to Carthage a new hope of commercial prosperity, were not likely to risk Spain for the sake of a war, though they might be ready to risk war for the sake of Spain. Finally, had it been the set purpose of the house of Barca to attack Rome, Hasdrubal would not have made the Ebro treaty, but would have urged Carthage to seize at once an opportunity more favourable than any which was likely to offer itself later.

The 'wrath of the house of Barca' and 'the revenge of Hannibal' belong mainly to a Roman tradition which obscures, and was meant to obscure, the extent to which the Roman seizure of Sardinia and her interference in Spain drove Carthage to war. Nor does the tradition sufficiently emphasize the effect of Massiliote diplomacy in urging Rome to challenge the eastward expansion of Carthage in Spain which, it is true, menaced the trade, if not the security, of Massilia. The Roman claim to forbid Hannibal to attack Saguntum showed that the Senate had no intention of binding itself by the implications of the Ebro treaty, and Carthage might well feel that Roman aggression which had advanced by way of Sardinia

might pass by way of Saguntum to Nova Carthago and even to Africa itself. The process might be slow. Rome's policy at this time was not consistently imperialistic: it was often vacillating, timid, inert, but her malignity, in which now fear, now jealousy, now arrogant self-confidence, now greed of wealth and power was dominant, must have seemed beyond question. It is true that it was Hannibal's attack on Saguntum, undertaken in full knowledge of the almost inevitable consequences, that precipitated the war, but the historian must decide that, so far as attack and defence have a meaning in the clash between states, the balance of aggression must incline against Rome.

The legend that the war sprang from the ambition or revengefulness of Hannibal is one with the legend that Carthage was not behind him when in 220/19 he refused to be turned aside by the menaces of the Senate. Fabius Pictor declared that none of the substantial citizens of Carthage approved of Hannibal's action at Saguntum, but this is contradicted by the whole course of events and must be regarded as the self-deception of a Roman at war, turned to the purposes of propaganda. That at Carthage, despite a just resentment of Rome's actions, there were nobles jealous of the house of Barca, or men who believed that Carthage should seek to placate where she could not perhaps hope to conquer, is doubtless true. But Hannibal had acted with the full knowledge and approval of the home government, he was the chosen general of the finest army and the governor of the richest province of Carthage, and to disown him and his assessors was to divide the State in the face of an enemy whose forbearance could not be trusted. Hannibal himself could not be lightly surrendered to Roman vengeance, even though the full meaure of his greatness in the field had not as yet revealed itself to Carthage, much less to Rome. At the age of twenty-six he had succeeded his kinsman Hasdrubal in

Spain (221 B.C.). To the diplomatic skill of his predecessor he added his father Hamilcar's unbending spirit and a double portion of his father's energy and generalship. Schooled in arms from boyhood, he had behind him the fruits of long experience in the handling of the mercenaries and levies that made up the mass of the Carthaginian armies. The siege of Saguntum showed him a worthy namesake of the conqueror of Selinus and Himera, and two lightning campaigns in Eastern Spain had confirmed his innate consciousness of a genius for command. We may well believe that the Carthaginian government had already recognized that this was the moment and the man. If Carthage was to remain secure and untroubled in the enjoyment of her commerce and of Spain

she must defend herself resolutely, and to Hannibal the best defence was attack.

Herein lay the responsibility of Hannibal, not for the fact that the war happened —granted that Rome would one day set before Carthage the choice of war or the steady undermining of its power—but for the moment of its happening. Rome's intrigues from Saguntum could be permitted for a time without serious loss; Hannibal decided to force the issue at once, and this he did on the basis of a military calculation which was probably his alone, for the essence of it was secrecy. It was enough that the Carthaginian Senate should be convinced of the need of an immediate defensive war and assured that its young general could make it not entirely hopeless.

7. THE CASE FOR INEVITABILITY*

The proximate cause of the Second Punic War was the Saguntine affair, which Polybius prefers to regard as the first incident in, rather than a cause of, the war. The question at issue was whether by attacking Saguntum Hannibal violated any treaty with Rome. Patriotic Roman annalists hastened to invent fictions to show that he had: for instance, they said that he broke the Ebro treaty by crossing the river to attack Saguntum, whereas the town lies a hundred miles south of the Ebro; or they suggest that a special clause was inserted in the Ebro treaty to the effect that Rome and Carthage should respect the neutrality of Saguntum. But it is not by such means that the blame can be assigned to Carthage.

There were two treaties which Hannibal's action might have infringed: that of Lutatius in 241 and the Ebro convention of 226. Rome's alliance with Saguntum was later than the treaty of Lutatius, so

that the town was not included in the list of Rome's allies whom the Carthaginians had promised to respect. The latter therefore were quite correct in insisting that Hannibal had not violated this treaty. But what of the Ebro agreement? Unfortunately, it cannot be related chronologically to Rome's alliance with Saguntum with any degree of certainty; nor are its terms altogether clear. Even its validity has been questioned; but unnecessarily. Rome regarded it as legally binding on both parties, for the Carthaginians did not disavow their general who made it or his successor who, according to the Roman claim, transgressed it. By its terms Hasdrubal renounced all hostile action north of the Ebro; his *quid pro quo* is not stated. Some suggest that he received little, others much. For instance, it is alleged the treaty was unilateral and that as a member of a conquered nation Hasdrubal had to acquiesce in Rome's wish; or on the other hand, it is believed that the Ebro treaty defined the spheres of influence of the two nations and that it

* H. H. Scullard, *A History of the Roman World from 752 to 146* B.C., 3rd ed. (London: Methuen & Co., 1961), pp. 181–185. Reprinted by permission of the publisher.

imposed on the Romans, either explicitly or implicitly, the obligation not to interfere south of the river. Probably, however, the concession made by Rome in face of the Gallic peril was to leave Hasdrubal free to extend his Spanish Empire up to the river. How this affected Rome's Saguntine alliance depends on the date assigned to the latter, which Polybius places 'several years before the time of Hannibal.' If, as seems more probable, the alliance was prior to the treaty, it was then virtually annulled by the spirit or perhaps the letter of the new covenant; or at any rate, it could not in equity be used by the Romans as a handle to check Punic expansion in the south. If Rome accepted the alliance after 226, she automatically infringed the Ebro treaty. Whichever date then is correct, Rome had no legal ground to restrain Hannibal from attacking Saguntum; indeed she made no military attempt to do this. However unwise the Carthaginian general may have been, he was within his legal rights and was no treaty-breaker.

But if Hannibal's conscience was clear on the legal score, if he was merely returning the compliment for Rome's interference with the Torboletae, he could not turn a blind eye to the political aspect. He was attacking a town which was under the declared protection of Rome, and he had been warned that its capture would be regarded as a *casus belli*. Yet he persisted —and from no military necessity. The frontier quarrel between the Saguntines and Torboletae need not involve hostilities, unless Hannibal wished. True, the acquisition of Saguntum would remove an awkward thorn from his side, in the event of war with Rome; but its military value was not sufficient to warrant the risk of war. Nor had the Romans thrown a protective garrison into the town, as they had into Messana in 264; such an act would have violated treaty rights, which they were unwilling to disregard till the fall of the town made action imperative. Hannibal therefore persisted for other reasons; because he judged war with Rome was inevitable and because by manoeuvring the Romans into a false position he had forced on them the onus of declaring war, so that he could expect the continued support of his home government. His capture of Saguntum may not have been the cause of the war, but it undoubtedly caused the outbreak of war at that moment.

The proximate cause of war was thus the action of Hannibal and his government, but what were the underlying causes? Polybius finds three. First, the hatred of Hamilcar towards Rome; after his forced surrender in Sicily he lived for revenge and his spirit survived him. Secondly, the bitterness felt at Carthage when Rome seized Sardinia and renewed the threat of war. Thirdly, resulting from this, Hamilcar's activity and the Carthaginian success in Spain. Did then the Second Punic War owe its origin to the hatred of the house of Barca; was it a war of revenge? The answer must depend on the interpretation given to the motives of the Barcids in Spain. Were they building up resources and an army with which to hurl themselves against Rome or were they merely trying to compensate their country for its loss of Sicily and Sardinia; was the object of their empire-building offensive or defensive?

Hamilcar had gone to Spain immediately after his country had been humiliated by Rome in 237; he cannot have forgotten his enforced capitulation in Sicily; and he made his son swear eternal hatred to Rome. These facts establish beyond doubt his hatred of Rome, but they do not prove that he contemplated revenge or that he went to Spain to plan it. Rather, he went with the intention of re-establishing his country's lost empire. He must have foreseen the possibility of renewed rivalry and he wanted to equip Carthage for the future, whatever that might hold. The fact that he did not rebuild a large Punic navy probably means that in the event of war he planned to fight by land as Hannibal did when the day came. He wished to be prepared rather than to reopen the question. Hasdrubal pursued still more clearly a defensive policy. When Rome was seriously engaged with the Gauls, so far from joining hands with them, he deliberately concluded a treaty with Rome, which confined his activity to Spain. Hannibal, however, had to face somewhat different circumstances, for the Romans began to interfere in Saguntum. It is not likely that they acted with the desire of bringing a hornets' nest about their ears. But when they were freed from the Gallic peril, they began to look askance at the growing Punic power in Spain which they themselves had sanctioned; doubtless Massilia brought the situation to their notice. Their action at Saguntum was little more than a gentle hint to Hannibal to walk warily, but it was enough to fan his smouldering wrath to a blaze. He determined to make it a test case to see whether Rome would abide by her treaty; but he must have foreseen the result. The Barcids had remained true to a defensive policy till they feared, whether with good cause or not, a repetition of the Sardinian question. And this time the Carthaginians refused to bow their necks.

Hannibal had cleverly precipitated a crisis in which the Romans were technically at fault, but from which they could not retreat without loss of prestige. He was thus immediately responsible for a war which neither Rome nor Carthage had deliberately engineered. Yet it was improbable that the two Republics could have lived at peace indefinitely. A balance of powers, such as existed in the Hellenistic East, might have been maintained for a time, yet causes of friction would inevitably occur, now that Rome had been forced to become a world power. But throughout the years between the first two Punic wars, Rome had not followed a deliberately aggressive policy. It has been suggested that there was strong disagreement in the state between an agrarian party under Flaminius, which limited its outlook to Italy, and a capitalistic party which favoured a *Weltpolitik*. While admitting a real clash of interests, it is unlikely that the latter party formed any deliberate imperialistic policy. The Senate rather met practical solutions than followed a consistent and carefully conceived scheme. The seizure of Sardinia, which was the aggressive act of a nervous bully, represented a passing mood. The Gallic wars were defensive in spirit, though they caused Rome to safeguard her northern frontier. Her early action in Spain was due more to the apprehension of her ally, Massilia, than to a studied western policy. The intervention in Illyria was a necessary piece of police work. True, all these acts involved future responsibility. Once she had set her hand to the plough there could be no turning back. But Rome could hardly be expected to anticipate the ultimate result of each action. She dealt with each situation as it arose and if Hannibal chose to challenge her interference in Spain, she was willing to face the consequences and to determine the lordship of the western Mediterranean.

SECTION V

The Crisis of the Hellenistic World

THE HELLENISTIC WORLD into which Rome moved after the Hannibalic War was quite different from the world of Pericles or even Demosthenes. The city-state had given way to the nation-state, and the center of the Greek world had moved eastward. Egypt and Syria were ruled by Graeco-Macedonian dynasties, and Greek soldiers and settlers could be found in central Asia. Initially, great wealth had poured into Greek coffers after the victories of Alexander, but by the third century B.C. poverty already presented a vital problem to the cities of Greece. In the third and second centuries, Greece suffered from depopulation and social revolution. The Hellenistic Kingdoms that confronted Rome were empty shells. Their vitality had been sapped by a social and economic crisis which they could not survive. What was the nature of the crisis? What were its roots? Because of the scattered nature of the evidence, no ancient sources are included in this section; instead, three modern accounts are given which present the evidence and try to answer the questions.

1. POVERTY AND SOCIAL REVOLUTION*

No prosperity among the upper classes could alter the fundamental fact of life in Greece: the country had only a limited amount of arable land, and could not of itself support one man beyond a fixed number, long since reached. Imported food had to be paid for; and as there was no mineral wealth except Laurium, now fast failing, and as every city round the Mediterranean could do its own sea-carriage, food could only be paid for by exporting manufactures or by transit duties. Corinth grew wealthy on its transit trade; but the primitive Greek system of manufacture, though it might enrich a few individuals, was of little account to states as a whole. Consequently the whole of old Greece lived always under the shadow of the fear of too many mouths to feed. In late fourth and early third centuries this was met by mercenary service and emigration to Asia. Fourth-century writers were still concerned with over-population, and about 300 there was still a considerable surplus; but the surplus gradually vanished. Polybius says that Greeks in the middle of the second century were refusing to rear

* W. W. Tarn and G. T. Griffith, *Hellenistic Civilization* (London: Edward Arnold, 1952), pp. 100–125. Reprinted by permission of the publisher.

more than one, or at most two, children; and there is plenty of evidence to bear him out.

The prevalence of infanticide in Greece has been strenuously asserted from the literary texts, and as strenuously denied; but for the late third and the second centuries the inscriptions are conclusive. The evidence, so far as I have collected it, can only be summarised briefly here. Of some thousand families from Greece who received Milesian citizenship c. 228–220, details of 79, with their children, remain; these brought 118 sons and 28 daughters, many being minors; no natural causes can account for those proportions. Similarly Epicteta's relatives, c. 200, numbered 25 males to 7 females. Of the Miletus families, 32 had one child and 31 two; and they show a certain striving after two *sons*. The inscriptions at large bear this out. Two sons are fairly common, with a sprinkling of three; at Eretria, third century, certainly two families in 19 had more than one son, which is lower than the Miletus immigrants, but agrees with the evidence from Delphi; at Pharsalus possibly one in seven; and one must allow for some sons having emigrated. But more than one daughter was practically never reared, bearing out Posidippus' statement that 'even a rich man always exposes a daughter'. Of 600 families from Delphic inscriptions, second century, just 1 per cent. reared 2 daughters; the Miletus evidence agrees, and throughout the whole mass of inscriptions cases of sisters can almost be numbered on one's fingers, with *one strange* local exception: a second-century list of women subscribers from Paros *perhaps* shows 20 sisters (8 families) out of 62 names, but the islands were prosperous and untouched by war, and in population questions must be classed with Asia, not Greece. Some allowance must be made for loss of fertility; thus at Rhodes adoptions were so common that we get (c. 100) seven adopted sons in a list of 40 magistrates, and on her deme Telos a case of three in four,

while adoption, even of daughters, was not uncommon elsewhere; people do not kill their own children to adopt others. Telos too boasts a family of seven, perhaps the only known Hellenistic family over five, except the eight children of Cleopatra Thea by three marriages; but the prevalence of artificial restriction is shown by revival of families of four and five at Athens during her after-bloom of prosperity in the late second century.

The general conclusion from c. 230 onwards seems certain: the one child family was commonest, but there was a certain desire for two sons (to allow for a death in war); families of four or five were very rare; more than one daughter was very seldom reared; and infanticide on a considerable scale, particularly of girls, is not in doubt. Now it takes an average of three children per fertile marriage to keep a population stationary; the home-born Greek population *must* therefore have declined considerably by 100 B.C. Greece had overdone the precautions against her secular fear; yet, except among Jews, no voice was raised against infanticide on moral grounds till under the Empire the Stoics Musonius and Epictetus spoke their minds. Philip V after Cynoscephalae, for military reasons, took steps to check it in Macedonia and encourage large families, and raised Macedonia's armed strength nearly 50 per cent. in a generation; and under the Antonines Thebes made the practice illegal, perhaps the only people except the Jews who ever did till Christianity intervened.

Certainly there was no actual depopulation in Greece till the Roman civil wars. Single cities, of course, might fail for many reasons; Larisa under Philip V was half depopulated by war and the exile of Aetolian partisans, and Heraclea-Latmos and Thyrreion in Acarnania contracted their ring-walls; but then Thyrrheion, a little city, had been holding a ring-wall larger than the Theban. These things mean nothing; Aristotle quotes temporary cases of the sort as common enough; and in the third century cities who wanted new citizens—Larisa, Dyme, Miletus (to settle Myus)—had no difficulty in getting enough Greeks from other places. But by 100 enfranchisement or incorporation of aliens must have been taking place on a considerable scale in Greece, as it did in Asia (p. 156); no other explanation of the facts seems possible, for the decline of the true Greek population is certain. Evidence is not easy to get, as aliens took Greek names; but Italians were now commonly accepted as ephebes, and if one foreign people was accepted, others were not excluded. It is notable that Pergamum in 133 and Ephesus *c*. 85 gave metic status to the slaves then liberated; and Philip V's idea that the solution of the future might lie in enfranchising freedmen may be correct, for the Greek cities became full of freedmen. Certainly in the first century Greece contained a large alien population, enfranchised or not, and what was happening in Asia and Egypt was happening on a smaller scale in Greece; the Orontes flowed into the Ilissus before it flowed into the Tiber, and Juvenal's esurient Greekling had often little that was Greek about him but his name and speech. This change in the nature of the population can be detected fairly early at Corinth, which in the third century could only muster one quarter the hoplite force of the fifth, though the city had grown; at Delos from 166 onwards it is self-evident. The process can also be seen at work in the breaking down of class and race distinctions. By the first century, when a wealthy man gave a feast to his fellow-citizens, he often invited the metics, the freedmen, and even the slaves; sacrifices were sometimes now offered for the health, not of the citizens, but of all the inhabitants of the city; and clubs occur like that of (?) Sidectas in Laconia, whose members were the men and women of his family, some city magistrates, many artisans both free and freedmen, and a slave-girl.

One form of slavery in Hellenism stood apart from others, the mines (p. 254); they were a hell on earth which neither Stoicism nor Delphi could touch, and kings and cities were equally guilty. But ordinary domestic slavery was often not unkindly; the slave might be better born and educated than the master, and more than one philosopher who shook the world was, or had been, a slave. Athens, which tolerated the horrors of Laurium, had for long—another strange contradiction—strictly limited the punishments allowable in the case of other slaves, and the Public Health law of Pergamum followed her example. Stoicism worked for a better treatment of slaves, and gradually changed the atmosphere; slaves were to be pitied rather than punished, and all through the third century manumission of slaves by will, especially in philosophic circles, became increasingly common. Some manumission there had always been, but about 200 a great innovation began; under the influence of Delphi, always ready during the Aetolian domination to champion the cause of humanity, it became possible for the slave to *purchase* his freedom through the machinery of a fictitious sale to some god; the movement was aided by the mundane consideration that cheap free labour was rendering industrial slavery unprofitable. Some slaves earned money at their craft, and manumission soon became very common—at Larisa 36 slaves were freed in one year, at Halos, a small town, over 40 in two—and freedmen came to constitute a definite class in the cities, differing slightly in status from metics. But even manumission had its shadow side. That the freed slave-woman was often bound to stay on with her mistress during the latter's life, to work off her purchase-money, was not in itself unfair, but she really stayed on under servile conditions; she could be fettered and flogged and even sold, and any children she bore were still slaves—a horrible thing unless the act of manumission had freed them (sometimes conditionally) in advance. She was sometimes even obliged to provide and even rear one or more children as slaves for her mistress. She might occasionally commute this obligation for a money payment; but her usual course was obvious, and the clause was a compulsion to immorality.

Of the number of slaves in Greece, or their proportion to the free population, nothing is known; but in other respects the manumissions at Delphi and Naupactus have thrown some light on the slave population of Northern Greece. Among purchased slaves the proportions of men and women were equal; but among house-born, judging by those liberated, women so preponderated that seemingly the girl baby born of a slave-mother had a better chance of life than if her mother were free. Purchased slaves were far more numerous than house-born; the commonest nationalities were Greek, Thracian, and Syrian, though every people is represented, from the Bastarnae to Arabia. The standard price of a slave was 3 to 4 minae for either sex; but among purchased slaves some nationalities fetched more. Macedonia easily heads the list with an average of $5\frac{3}{4}$ minae for men and $5\frac{1}{4}$ for women, bearing out what Polybius says of the qualities of that great race. Among men, Thracians with $5\frac{2}{5}$ and Romans and Italians (some of Hannibal's prisoners) with $5\frac{1}{4}$ shew up well, but their women only fetched the standard price; Galatian men with $4\frac{1}{2}$ also stand out, but among women the Greeks with $4\frac{2}{5}$ come next to the Macedonians. There is a curious difference in sex price as well as in sex proportions between house-born and purchased slaves; among purchased, 96 men whose nationalities are known average $3\frac{1}{3}$ minae and 98 women just under 4, but among house-born, while 101 women average just over 4, 47 men average $5\frac{1}{3}$; taken as a whole, the house-born slave, trained from infancy, was the more valuable. The highest recorded price is 25 minae for a Phrygian woman; the few high prices known generally resulted from some special skill.

The most urgent question in Greece was the corn supply. The price of imported wheat at Athens in Demosthenes' time had normally averaged 5 drachmae the *medimnos* (bushel). As Alexander's circulation of the Persian treasure drove down the value of the drachma, wheat naturally rose in price; about 300, with the drachma (6 obols) worth 3 obols, wheat, neglecting the seasonal variation, must have averaged some 10 dr. the bushel; it fell gradually as money rose, but was still $5\frac{1}{3}$ dr. about 200. There was plenty of wheat in the world; export of corn was well organised by the Ptolemies, and Athens, Corinth, Delos, many islands, Ionia, and perhaps other cities, relied primarily on imported corn; but usually a city depended on its own harvest, though it might sometimes have to supplement it. A failure of a city's crop meant, therefore, anything from short rations to famine; local famines throughout the period are common, land communication being very bad. Normally some magistracy, the *agoranomos* or *sitophylaces*, looked after the corn dealers and saw that the city was fed at a reasonable price. But when prices rose in a shortage this system regularly broke down, unless the *agoranomos* bought corn himself or could persuade some wealthy merchant to sell it under cost price; the great number of men who thus paid the difference themselves furnishes a remarkable testimony to the sound public spirit in the cities. But this was only a palliative; and in the great famine of 329–325, which extended to all Greece and Epirus and was aggravated by the corner in Egyptian wheat engineered by Cleomenes, Alexander's governor in Egypt, the State at Athens stepped in, raised a subscription, and appointed a commission, which bought corn as best it could and retailed it at the normal price, the people also being rationed; bread tickets are not a modern discovery. These special commissions, and the 'measuring out' of corn, became thenceforth a regular system in shortages. But it was an imperfect system; subscription was voluntary, and might be inadequate; and the poor could not always pay for their ration.

It was perhaps Samos—alarmed by her series of famines about 246, when the money raised was twice lost by the merchants employed and the city was only saved by a private citizen, Bulagoras—who took the final step and formed a permanent corn-fund; enough was raised somehow from the rich and invested for the yearly interest to suffice to supply the city with corn. Samos' example was largely followed; a system of state supply obtained at Priene and perhaps elsewhere, and permanent corn-funds are known at Miletus, Teos, Demetrias, Delos, Aegina, and Thuria; possibly they became almost universal. Even under rationing these funds meant that the rich (who provided the original capital) were feeding the poor, as the rich at Rhodes were voluntarily doing by their food liturgies, under which each wealthy man looked after a certain number of poor. But Samos and Thuria went beyond this; at Samos the corn was distributed free every year to all citizens, at Thuria (c. 100) to the poor only, the rich apparently paying increased prices. As kings and wealthy men often also gave a largesse in corn, and as at Arcesine and Minoa in the second century (and this was hardly unique) wealthy men also began to distribute free tickets of admission to the local festivals, we see that the demoralising *panem et circenses*, free food and free games, were merely copied by Rome from later Hellenism.

In an age full of contradictions, none is more startling than the contrast between the miserable state of wages and the amazing liberality of the wealthy. They would not pay; but they would give. What they gave was, however, invariably given to the State, the citizens (or the inhabitants) treated as a whole. Many a city seemed able to call on some wealthy man to rescue it whenever it chose: to

give, or lend without interest, large sums to meet some special expenditure; to go on embassies without pay and champion the city against kings or Roman tax-gatherers; to build the bridge, the gymnasium, the temple, if funds ran short; to supply war material, endow a new festival or a new school, fill the burdensome liturgies, provide oil for the athletes, prizes for the school-boys, banquets for the citizens and their wives; finally to be honoured with a statue, for which he himself sometimes paid. Men like Protogenes at Olbia, Menas at Sestos, Moschion at Priene, Polycritus at Erythrae, almost seem to carry the city on their shoulders. This constant reliance on some rich man stepping into the breach seems to indicate that the cities were not on a sound economic basis; but few ages can have shown more public spirit, even if sometimes it was perhaps the equivalent of purchasing a title. 'He impaired his own livelihood for the public good' was Epidaurus' testimony to one Aristobulus, while Pergamum said of Diodorus, 'His care for the common weal prevented him taking thought for his own'. And such public spirit was not confined to the wealthy. Nothing leaves a more pleasing impression than the numerous decrees of thanks passed to physicians. The municipal doctors were not a wealthy class—the one salary known is £40 a year; but often they forwent their salaries during epidemics, and nevertheless, like Damiades of Sparta, 'made no difference between rich and poor, free and slaves'. When all the Coan doctors were down with an epidemic Xenotimus came voluntarily to the city's aid, and Apollonius of Miletus fought the plague in the islands without reward; there was a high standard of devotion in the profession. Philosophers, too, sometimes remitted the fees for their lectures to those unable to pay. There really seem to have been quite a number of people who thought other things more important than money.

Yet, amid all the philanthropic feeling and public spirit of the time, philanthropy in our sense—the organised aid of the poor by the rich—was almost unknown. Broadly speaking, pity for the poor had little place in the normal Greek character, and consequently for the poor, as such, no provision usually existed; the idea of democracy and equality was so strong that anything done must be done for all alike; there was nothing corresponding to our mass of privately organised charities and hospitals. When we have mentioned the food liturgies at Rhodes, Athens' dole to men crippled, the well-to-do sharing with the poor at Tarentum, Polybius' statement that Opheltas in Boeotia helped the poor from State funds, and Heracleides' that the prosperous people of Tanagra were good to their poor,—'it is easy', he adds drily, 'to be good when you have enough to eat' —we have about exhausted the list, unless we include the cases where organised bodies like demesmen supported the daughter of a deceased member. Distributions of meat from the sacrifices, on which stress has been laid, cannot have been common, unless conceivably at Athens; the priests generally kept their perquisites, for which after all they had often paid, and anyhow meat scarcely came within the purview at all. The Myconos catalogue of *c*. 200, supplementary to one lost, mentions one distribution in four months, a dinner to wives of citizens and women initiated only. A Coan list, covering a few days, twice mentions meat which went 'to the city', but it does not follow it was distributed; St. Paul seems clear that much normally found its way into the shops. It might have been expected that the Stoics and Cynics, with their sense of human brotherhood, would have taken up philanthropy; but neither did. To Stoics, poverty, like slavery, affected only the body, and what affected only the body was a matter of indifference; the poorest slave could be a king in his own soul, so they concentrated on the soul and let the body be—the reason

why they never advocated abolition. The Cynics glorified the poverty they themselves practised; if absence of possessions did not actually constitute virtue, it was the indispensable condition of acquiring virtue; apparently they did not distinguish between the involuntary poverty of the labourer and the voluntary renunciation of the philosopher. The one expression of philanthropy in literature—Cercidas' poem —was apparently evoked by Cleomenes' revolution.

The prosperity of the Hellenistic age has often been alluded to in this chapter; the matter must now be looked at more closely. Prior to Sulla, and with local fluctuations, it was without question a prosperous time for the upper classes: the enormous expansion of trade (Chap. VII) tells its own story, as does the growth of clubs, of new festivals, of table luxury with its accompanying literature, of luxury in women's dress, especially silk and gold woven cloth, of better-planned cities, improved private houses, and more elaborate furniture. A distinction must however be drawn between Greece itself and Asia (with the islands). Not all of Greece felt the rising tide; Corinth and Aetolia, Ambracia and Pagasae grew richer but Athens, as regards wealth, fell back till the late second-century revival, as did Sparta for other reasons. Northern Greece was generally prosperous, as is shown by the number of slaves and the manner in which cities hardly heard of before now come into prominence; and the state of things at Messene *c*. 100–91 has been rather a revelation, for Messenia was an agricultural country, unimportant and out of the trade streams. The average fortune of Messenian citizens at the time, according to Professor Wilhelm's calculation, was about one-fifth of a talent, as against one-fourth at Athens in Demosthenes' time, and the 2 per cent. land-tax produced about 2.5 drachmae a head, as against 2.75 fr. in France in 1908, the purchasing power of the drachma being of course far greater than that of the franc; the women often spent over 100 dr. on a dress, and affected the expensive transparent silks; silver plate was common, and fines ran up to 2,000 dr. Another point, easy to follow, is the growth in the scale of penalties for breach of arbitration awards; in the fifth century the highest known is 5 talents, but in the second we get 20 (Cyclades), 30 and 50 (Asia Minor), and 60 (Locris). As to individuals, the richest man in Demosthenes' Greece, the Athenian Diphilos, perhaps possessed 160 talents: the richest c. 200, Alexander the Isian in Aetolia, had 200. We are justified in saying that, while Greece did not grow in prosperity like Asia, it enjoyed a very tolerable measure of it down to Sulla.

For Asia and the islands the evidence, quite apart from the growth of the cities and the expansion of trade, is overwhelming. Athens had drawn 15 talents a year tribute from Byzantium and 1 to 2 talents apiece from her Carian cities; c. 200 Byzantium paid 80 talents a year to the Gauls, and subsequently Rhodes drew 120 talents a year from her Carian possessions, chiefly Caunos and Stratonicea. The scale of girls' dowries at Myconos compared to those in fourth-century Athens, the size of the subscriptions raised at Cos c. 200, the scale of fines in Epicteta's club at Thera compared to Athenian practice, the new custom, originating in the clubs of Cos and Thera, of honouring members with crowns of gold instead of leaves, all tell an unmistakable story. In Asia Minor, whatever happened politically, prosperity and wealth grew steadily down to 88, perhaps down to the Civil Wars. That kings' ministers should make great fortunes was natural, but by the first century private citizens too were sometimes wealthy out of all proportion to anything known in Greece; one Hieron at Laodicea on the Lycus possessed over 2,000 talents, and at one time Pompey's friend Pythodorus of Tralles was worth over 4,000 talents, including his land. But the best evidence is the amount Rome found to plunder in Asia. In 63 the publican Falcidius, having bought the taxes of Tralles for 900,000 sesterces (say 39 talents), offered a bribe of 50 talents to get them for a second year at the same figure, i.e. he had made at least 100 talents in one year out of one second-class city— and the whole Macedonian land-tax had only produced some 200 talents annually. This is more eloquent than the vast fortunes extracted from Asia by Pompey and Crassus. In 86 Mithridates took 2,000 talents from Chios; in 70 the Senate demanded 4,000 talents from Crete. Cassius took 500 talents from Rhodes and 8,090 more from individual Rhodians. Sulla in 84 took 20,000 talents from the province of Asia, called 5 years' arrears of taxes; Brutus took 16,000 as a year's tax; and finally Antony demanded 200,000, called nine years' taxes in advance, a greater sum than the treasure amassed by the Persian kings over two centuries from half the continent. One need not elaborate the story; the days when the Hellenistic world was called 'poverty stricken' are, or should be, long past.

This wealth was reflected in people's amusements; not merely the multiplication of games, but the increased cost of celebration, the performers being now professionals. A complete list of the new Hellenistic festivals would fill a page. Between Alexander's death and 189 a great number, with games and sacrifices, entailing corresponding expense, were founded by the cities everywhere, while five annual festivals, at Thespiae, Cos, Delphi, Magnesia, and Miletus, were turned into 'crowned' games, great quadrennial celebrations. Beside these were the mass of festivals founded by various kings, hardly inferior in number; the greatest of these was the Ptolemaieia at Alexandria, the only festival whose honours ranked equal to those of the Olympia, though several were reckoned equal to the Pythia. In the second century several cities founded festivals called Romaia in honour of Rome—at least 13 are known, that at Delphi in 189 being the first; while even after 146 the Boeotian Ptoia became quadrennial, and Tanagra founded her Serapieia. Then came Sulla; and there were no more foundations till Augustus' peace. Naturally the performers at these festivals, the Dionysiac artists, grew enormously in importance. Their oldest association, the Athenian, dates from soon after Alexander; its privileges were secured to it by the Amphictyons soon after 279. The Isthmian association, with its centre at Corinth and special relations with Thespiae, formed soon afterwards; by the second century it embraced the whole of old Greece except Athens, and had sections in many cities. The destruction of Corinth in 146 hit it hard; internal strife among the sections followed, some joined the Athenian association, and the Isthmian body never recovered. A third association early formed in Asia, with its centre at Teos; it subsequently amalgamated with the players of the Pergamene court theatre, the association of Dionysus Kathegemon, and the whole body became dependent on the Attalids. In their palmy days the Dionysiac artists were almost an independent state, sending and receiving ambassadors; on them were lavished honours, privileges, immunity, safe-conducts; they were subsidised by kings and cities, and the Athenian association had the right to wear the purple; it would seem that it was better to amuse people than to govern them.

The rate of interest is some guide to the capital wealth of a country; but in Greece it is not a certain guide, for there were few of the modern facilities for the circulation of capital. Private banks were normally small, and the chief sources of capital available for traders or farmers to borrow were either some endowment, the capital of which was lent out at interest to obtain an annual revenue for the object of the endowment, or temple funds; but the *liquid* funds of a temple were generally small, and the temple at Delos for centuries lent at 10 per cent. regardless of changes in the value of money. However, the interest curve may be given so far as known. In Alexander's reign the usual rate was 12 per cent., omitting the risky maritime loans, which ran much higher. By about 300 the rate had fallen to 10 per cent., reflecting the fall in the value of the drachma consequent upon the circulation of the Persian treasure, and 10 per cent. remained usual throughout the third century, though $8\frac{1}{3}$ and 6 (this last apparently a political favour) also occur; in the first half of the second century we meet 7 and $6\frac{2}{3}$, both business transactions. After the middle of the century the rate rises again and by Sulla's time it has got back to the old 12 per cent. After Sulla, interest is an index of nothing but Roman rapacity; Lucullus stemmed the rise in Asia for a time by fixing 12 per cent. as a maximum, but in the Civil Wars extraordinary rates, up to 48 per cent., were extorted by Romans. So far as it goes, interest indicates continuous prosperity down to 146 anyhow, with money (as the world went) plentiful and cheap. The drachma had become stable again before 200, for the farm tenants at Thespiae have apparently the option then of renewing at the same rent, while at Delos *c*. 300 they could only renew at a rent 10 per cent. higher; but whether it ever quite got back to the value of Alexander's time—wheat at 5 drachmae—is uncertain; there are indications that down to *c*. 100 wheat remained at somewhat over 5 drachmae.

A certain development in banking took place, but too much must not be made of Greek banking, which never attained the importance of the Roman. Private banks, beside money-changing, took money on deposit and made loans. The so-called 'state' banks in some Greek cities, were not a mere monopoly of money-changing farmed out to some individual, were really an adjunct of the Treasury; they received and paid out the revenue, kept the city accounts, and might advance money for an unforeseen disbursement, recouping themselves later; they did thus save the city the trouble of borrowing abroad, which otherwise it often had to do.

For most of the city borrowing met with was mere machinery; it had no more to do with poverty than municipal borrowing today. The reason was simple. A city had no budget; certain receipts were merely earmarked to certain expenses; an unforeseen expense, however small, meant a new tax or a subscription, which took time, and the city borrowed the amount for convenience and repaid at leisure. There was sometimes deliberate procrastination over repayment, but again this had nothing to do with poverty. One instance may be given. About 220–200, says Polybius, there was plenty of money in Boeotia; but Heracleides says debts were almost irrecoverable. Now during this period Orchomenus borrowed twice; over Nicareta's loan the city procrastinated to the utmost, while Eubulus' was paid off before the appointed day; obviously the governing considerations were personal or political, not economic. The city of Delos understood systematic borrowing, and was regularly financed from the temple funds, perpetually borrowing and repaying. Officially, of course, almost every city was poor, for the city Treasury rarely had any reserves; but that did not mean that the citizens were poor—Cambridge men are not necessarily poor because the University is. It meant however that one city could seldom lend to another; but its *citizens* could and did, by a subscription in the city's name. The cities really lived from hand to mouth. For this reason Ephesus once raised money to arm some friends by selling a dozen citizenships as a favour; Thasos *c.* 285 sold four or five at a great price, 2,000 drachmae apiece; in the Social War Tritaea sold some to raise mercenaries; these things had no more to do with poverty than the sale of memberships by the Marylebone Cricket Club to build its present pavilion. A particular city of course might lose credit; Oropus once had to entice lenders by the promise of civic honours. And the wealthiest might be thrown out of gear by war; thus in 201 the actions of Philip V in Caria prevented Miletus getting in her revenue, and she had to borrow from her citizens in order to carry on, repaying by means of life annuities. But cities thus damaged soon recovered, as simple economic forms do.

The worst trouble of this immature financial system was the difficulty of carrying out public works. Co-operative works—even decent roads—were almost impossible unless kings took the lead, as they did when the world co-operated to restore Thebes in 316 and Rhodes after the earthquake of 225; and even city works were difficult unless a city had some special resource. Eretria did get a marsh drained by giving the contractor substantial privileges; but Delos paid for her new harbour from the new trade Rome presented to her, and Miletus' superb market-places, where not built for her by the Seleucids, must have been made possible by the fact that the city itself owned wool factories, like a king.

It was not that the cities did not tax themselves. Direct taxes were repugnant to Greeks; the traditional 10 per cent. of the harvest was Asiatic. Still, necessity sometimes compelled them to overcome their repugnance: Athens had long had a tax, the *eisphora*, on the sum total of a man's property, and in the Hellenistic period this was adopted by some cities, notably Miletus. Others, as Crannon and Delos, did take 10 per cent. of the harvest, or, as Delos and Cos, 10 per cent. of house rents. But generally money was raised indirectly, and very many indirect taxes are known. A tax of 2 per cent. on all exports and imports, a pasture tax on the number of animals reared, harbour dues, and taxes on stalls in the market, were general; Cos had a special export duty on its wine, and taxed bread, flour, vegetables, salt fish, and many other things; Teos in the third century taxed ploughing oxen, timber mules, timber cutting, sheep and pigs, garments woven from Milesian wool (possibly the raw material also), purple dyeing, gardens, and bees. In some cases such taxation was perhaps partly due to the city having to raise taxes (tribute) for some king; the city did not get the whole benefit. But, even if it did, there was, throughout the whole vexatious system, no proper means of making private wealth available to the state except where the *eisphora* obtained, and even the *eisphora* was imperfect, for men were taxed on a simple declaration of their property, and often under-declared. Farming-out of taxes was known, but was unimportant till the coming of the Roman tax-farmer, the hated publican.

We have sketched the prosperity of the Greek world; we must now turn to the reverse side, the condition of the small man and the working class. Apart from some Asiatic cities like Miletus, industry in Greece had not kept pace with trade; and the little man who employed a dozen hands could not compete with the great serf and slave factories of Alexandria and Pergamum. As to farming, it has been thought that the real fall in farm rents at Delos after 250 means that agriculture was failing; but it only means that *on Delos* men found transit trade more lucrative, for the perpetual desire of men throughout the third and second centuries for a division of land suggests that farming was much as usual, though in several countries— Laconia, Aetolia, Thessaly—land at different times became over-burdened with debt. The great cities naturally tended to form a proletariat class, but of *consumers*; the few industries of Hellenism were small and scattered, and there was no class-conscious proletariat of *producers*. But evidence on the whole subject is lamentably defective, except in one quarter; we do know the condition of the working man on Delos *c*. 300–250, and where a particular trade like cutting inscriptions can be traced later, conditions do not improve; and as men came to Delos from other islands, one must suppose the outlook in the other islands, prosperous as they were, was worse.

The depreciation of money about 300 led to a corresponding rise in prices; wheat about doubled, oil rose $3\frac{1}{2}$ times, common wine $2\frac{1}{2}$ times. The average rent of a house at Delos, under 20 drachmae in the fourth century, was 100 dr. by the second, though here local overcrowding played a part; but food prices everywhere had not got back to the level of Demosthenes' time by 250, and possibly not by 200. Against this, wages at Delos had actually fallen compared with Demosthenes' Athens, probably the result of untempered competition. The line of bare subsistence, the pauper and slave rate, with wheat at 5 drachmae, was 2 obols a day per year for one man and a drachma (6 obols) for a family; but at Delos a skilled artisan was only making, *at best*, 4 obols a day per year, and the unskilled 2 obols, sometimes less, even while wheat might be anything up to 10 dr.; that is, unskilled free labour, which could be replaced by slaves, could not rise above the slave rate and occasionally fell below it. Consequently, as compared with the fourth century, the gap between rich and poor grew wider; and that was the most unhealthy phenomenon in Hellenism. The bearing of this on the population question is obvious; for the poor, rearing children was most difficult. That the year included many non-working (festival) days is immaterial; men must eat on Sundays. These wages may explain why some cities were driven to free corn, *i.e.* pauperisation.

Of course there was social unrest. There were no trade organisations, and in a slave society strikes were almost impossible. The bakers at Paros once came out because their wages were withheld—

apparently no uncommon event; the *agoranomos* promptly intervened, saw that they were paid, and got them back. No other strike is recorded till those in Roman Asia in the second century A.D., when trade guilds were beginning to form, while the first recorded strike for better conditions was not till the fifth century A.D. If things became quite unbearable, the only known resource was a rising or a revolution.

The fourth century was already obsessed by the fear of social revolution—one reason why the well-to-do turned to Macedonia as champion of the existing order. In the treaties between Alexander and the cities of the League of Corinth it was provided that Macedonia and the League should repress, in any League city, any movement for abolition of debt, division of land, confiscation of personal property, or liberation of slaves to assist the revolution; the constitution of Demetrius' revived League of 303 contained similar provisions. The revolution therefore had now a general programme under four heads. The poor desired the land, but with the small men of every type the driving force was debt; simple communities may be patient of rude conditions of life, but they always hate the creditor. The temple accounts of Delos, which show many very small loans and many bad debts, throw some light on the debt question.

From quite another angle, philosophy made its contribution to the subject; the Stoic insistence on equality and brotherhood sank into men's souls, and inspired visions of something better than the existing order. Some took refuge from civilisation in drawing fancy pictures of virtuous barbarians living according to Nature, prototypes of Tacitus' *Germania*; and Utopias began to appear. Plato and Aristotle had indeed drawn Ideal States, but not states of much use to working men; and the first Utopia, Zeno's, was too splendid and too remote for human nature to grasp. But Euhemerus (*c.* 300)

and Iambulus (third century) created true modern Utopias, located on islands in the Indian Ocean; and in Iambulus' great Sun-state Communism appears full-grown. The people were equal in all respects, even in wisdom; they lived in social bodies or 'systems' in which all worked equally and equally shared the produce; they escaped 'slavery to the means of production' because the island fortunately bore crops, partly by itself, all the year round; each in turn filled every duty from servant to governor, the governor of each system being the oldest member, who had to die at a certain age (a provision taken from a tradition at Ceos); there was thus no place for wealth, ambition, or learning, the foes of equality, or for class war, because there were no classes; above all things the people prized Homonoia and were united in concord and love. What Iambulus and his fellows really aimed at was the abolition of that class war whose horrors many Greeks had seen; and indeed, even while revolutionary philosophers and conservative governments were alike honouring Concord, some practical devotees of that goddess were always ready to massacre their fellows in her name.

Except possibly for a slave rising in Chios, the first outbreak recorded in the third century was a proletarian revolt at Cassandreia in 279, engineered by one Apollodorus, who made himself tyrant, tortured the wealthy, and gave part of their property to his followers; he showed that a mercenary force made this easy of accomplishment, and had a powerful career till Antigonus Gonatas suppressed him. Four disturbances in the islands followed, one certainly between rich and poor, which the kings got settled without open revolt. But the great revolutions of the third century were the two at Sparta, which was in an unhealthy state because a few had monopolised all the land. Agis IV (*acc.* 244) attempted to cancel debts and divide up the land by peaceful reform, and failed; his stronger successor Cleomenes

III, aided by the Stoic Sphaerus, Zeno's pupil, carried the reform through by force, abolished debts, and nationalised the land, which he divided into 4,000 lots for Spartiates and 15,000 for Perioeci, filling up the Spartiate body from Perioeci and metics. Neither king touched the Helot question, for both believed that, far from being revolutionaries, they were restoring the old Sparta of Lycurgus; but Greece thought that Cleomenes was carrying out the programme of the revolution, and in his ensuing war with the Achaean League he had the poor in every city on his side; at one city, Cynaetha, the revolution went through and the land was divided. Had he for gone his military ambitions, which aimed at the headship of the Peloponnese, he could have made his reform at Sparta a permanent success; but the well-to-do rulers of the League in desperation called on Macedonia for help, and Antigonus Doson took Sparta (222) and restored the old state of things. Revolution broke out again at Sparta in 207 under the lead of Nabis; he carried out all the four points of the revolutionary programme, freeing many Helots, though he too never dealt radically with the Helot question; every Greek revolution, except perhaps the Pergamene, conveys a sense of unreality, as it never included slaves. Nabis plundered the wealthy, but—so he said—solely for the State; perhaps the State now paid for the common meals (this, if many Helots were freed, would have been unavoidable), and there are indications that Nabis was not as cruel as his enemies have drawn him. Rome, having overthrown Macedonia, ultimately intervened in Macedonia's stead and clipped Nabis' wings; and though she did not interfere with the revolution in Sparta itself, the wealthy in Greece were henceforth ready to welcome her as their champion.

About 200 there was trouble between debtors and creditors in the Aetolian League; the successful general Scopas tried to cancel debts, failed before the opposition of the wealthy, and went into exile to Egypt, the trouble continuing for years. There was also chronic trouble in Thessaly, and in Boeotia in the last quarter of the third century and later; and Eumenes II accused Perseus before the Senate of intending to use the Thessalian debtors to murder Rome's wealthy friends —in fact of favouring social revolution—a changed rôle indeed for a Macedonian king. But no great outbreak is known between 200 and 132, whether from lack of information or because prices had reached a better relation to wages. Certainly in 146, in the last struggle with Rome, the Achaean League decreed a moratorium and the freeing and arming of 12,000 slaves (though the number of men the League put into the field, 14,700, shows that this was not carried out); but this was hardly revolution, though the debtors' rising in Dyme after the Roman conquest, when the town archives were burnt, may have been. Mithridates however did attempt later to use social revolution as a weapon against Rome, while Ephesus employed much the same weapon to counter him. The great slave rising in Sicily affected the Aegean; the slaves rose on Delos (130), but were suppressed; they rose in the mines of Macedonia; they rose at Laurium, captured Sunium, and for some time ravaged Attica; they apparently rose at Pergamum. Professor Kahrstedt has argued that there was a sort of Red International c. 130–63, and that Sulla and Pompey delivered the world from Bolshevism; but Bolshevism was a very strict social-economic theory, and these slave-risings, as I see them, were a blind product of the misery of mass slavery in mines or royal factories or (in Italy) on the great estates. Slaves rose to get liberty, debtors to get property; as to Mithridates, he would have utilised anything that promised vengeance on Rome. There was only one movement, apart from those at Sparta, which was working on a theory or which can be called socialistic; and the Pergamene, if we had details, might be more interesting than the Spartan, since for the first time a new constructive idea emerged. When Aristonicus in 132 raised the banner of revolt against Rome he threw in his lot with the slave rising, and was joined by the Stoic Blossius of Cumae, the outspoken friend of Tiberius Gracchus, who played the part of Sphaerus at Sparta; and the two proposed to set up something re-sembling Iambulus' Sun-State upon earth. The effect on their mixed following—Asiatic mercenaries, city volunteers, Mysian highlanders, broken men and slaves—was such that they destroyed a Roman consul and a consular army, which even Macedonia had never done. It was indeed a great dream. But Rome finally conquered Aristonicus and shattered the hope of a Sun-State; and under Roman rule there was no further place for dreams.

2. THE ROLE OF THE BOURGEOISIE*

The *bourgeois* class in the Greek cities was both a social and economic, and a political phenomenon. It was an important and often a decisive element in Greek politics during the vicissitudes of the Hellenistic period. It is not, however, the political but the social aspect of the *bourgeoisie* that I wish to emphasize, and the part that it played in the formation of a new Greek mode of thought.

I may begin by stating what I mean precisely by the somewhat ill-defined modern term *bourgeoisie*. I understand by it—in the Hellenistic period and especially in respect of the Greek cities of that time—a class of men who had achieved by their efforts or inherited from their parents a certain degree of prosperity, and lived not on the income derived from their manual labour but from the investment of their accumulated capital in some branch of economic activity. In the field of agriculture the *bourgeois* of the Greek cities were landowners whose land was tilled by tenants, hired hands, and slaves, or who were themselves tenants employing labour of the latter classes. In the field of industry they were owners of workshops, supervising and directing their employees, slaves or free men. In the field of commerce they were owners or tenants of shops in the retail trade, or of ships and storehouses for trade between cities or States. Many of them were money-lenders of one kind or another, who lent their accumulated capital mostly on mortgage to those who needed it. Some may have been professional *trapezitai* (bankers), though this vocation, was classed as a τέχνη and the bankers as *technitai*. Many were slave-owners and derived their income from their slaves, hiring them out to owners of mines, shops, or ships, or permitting them to conduct a business of their own on condition of paying a regular fee. In many cases their investments were diversified and they were interested in a variety of enterprises.

The main and most characteristic feature of the *bourgeoisie* from an economic stand-point was, however, not their manner of investing their capital, but the fact that they were not professionals, craftsmen of one kind or another, salaried employees, or the like, but investors of accumulated capital and employers of labour.

It was this class which formed the respectable society of the Greek cities and which is prominent in the literary and epigraphical evidence relating to the life of those cities in the Hellenistic period. As

* M. Rostovtzeff, *The Social and Economic History of the Hellenistic World* (Clarendon, 1941), Vol. 2, pp. 1115-1126. Reprinted by permission of The Clarendon Press, Oxford.

a rule its members were citizens of their respective cities. But some of them may have been metics. The sharp dividing line between these two groups, typical in the pre-Hellenistic period, was gradually vanishing in Hellenistic times. The *bourgeois* were not necessarily aristocrats or descendants of aristocratic families of the past, though some may have claimed such a standing. In fact they were in the mass the middle class, probably of mixed origin, though the majority of them belonged to the old stock of citizens of their city. Nor can we say that they were a kind of plutocracy, a small group of very rich men. Most of them were well-to-do, judged by ancient standard, which does not mean that they were wealthy. There were some rich persons among them, but these were exceptions. The exceedingly rich man who towers high above his class and exerts an overwhelming influence on city life was not a typical figure in the third or even in the second century. Such men became common in the times of general misery and ruin, that is to say, in the late second and the first centuries B.C.

From the modern point of view we should be inclined to class with the above the members of the so-called liberal professions, specialists in some branch or other of the technical, intellectual, or artistic crafts. This group of men became more and more numerous and played an increasingly important part in the cities of the Hellenistic period. The growth of professionalism was not confined to the eastern Hellenistic monarchies. By such specialists (*technitai*) I mean officials in the service of the cities, some of them public slaves (δημόσιοι), mercenary soldiers and officers, teachers, either salaried employees in public schools or independent tutors receiving fees from their pupils, doctors either in the city service or free practitioners, engineers and architects, sculptors and painters, artists of various kinds, and lawyers. But I must emphasize the fact that from the Greek point of view,

i.e. the point of view of the Greek cities, which was not entirely adopted by the Greeks of the Hellenistic monarchies, these were *technitai*, not differing in kind from the various artisans. Most of them lived, like other artisans, on wages paid them by their employers or on fees which they received from their clients. Their salaries—including those of the mercenaries—were very modest, a little more than the wages of hired hands in the various professions, and their fees—with rare exceptions—were not very high. Most of them were foreign residents in the Greek cities and some of them even slaves. They were of no interest to the dramatists of the New Comedy, and they were not members of the respectable city society.

The leading traits of the *bourgeoisie* of the Hellenistic cities, their moral tone and the characteristic features of their political, social, and economic activities are comparatively well known to us from various sources. As regards Athens in the late fourth century, I have referred to the extant comedies and the many fragments of the lost comedies of Menander, and the similar comedies of the 'new' style by other authors (in Greek and in the Latin versions). I have also cited the *Characters* of Theophrastus in the same connexion. And I have pointed out the importance of the mimes of Herondas and Theocritus as throwing light on the conditions that prevailed in Cos in the early third century B.C.

The materials relating to this subject to be drawn from the works of these professional painters of human life are rich, varied, and highly instructive. But they have their limitations. Their evidence is confined to two places and to two comparatively short periods. Moreover, the pictures drawn by these authors, detailed and fascinating as they are, are not, and were not intended by them to be, complete representations of the life of the *bourgeois* class as a whole, or even of individual members of it. Menander, Theophrastus, Herondas, and Theocritus had in view quite other ends, chiefly of a literary character. They were creators of new *genres* of literature, and they endeavoured to produce the best possible specimens of these.

To achieve their literary aims, which are well known and cannot be discussed here, they naturally chose as subjects of their observation and analysis the people whom they knew best, with whom they lived, whom they met every day—typical representatives, that is to say, of the city *bourgeoisie* and its dependants. In dealing with these, in producing them on the stage, they naturally confined themselves to such traits in their characters as best revealed them, and in analysing these traits they were careful that their public, their judges, men and women of the class which was the object of their psychological study, should not be too deeply offended. Their object was to stimulate their audiences by amusing and delighting them, not by lashing them with bitter sarcasm. This accounts for the elimination from their pictures of many salient features of the life of the time, which are of much interest to us, but were irrelevant to them. Instead, they present the predominance of purely personal motives, such as love, jealousy, and avarice. And even in these fields the pictures are not realistic and individualized, they are typical, and represent typical situations and typical actions. If in forming our estimate of the city *bourgeoisie* in its social aspect and role we were restricted to the authors indicated above, our information would be hopelessly incomplete and misleading.

Fortunately we are able to supplement these by knowledge derived from other sources of a documentary or literary character. I allude to those occasional passages in other texts which illuminate one side or another of *bourgeois* life, especially some highly instructive pages in the work of Polybius, and to the hundreds of inscriptions scattered all over the Hellenistic world and belonging to all periods of its history. It is on these sources mainly that I have drawn when referring to the city *bourgeoisie* in the preceding chapters, and on them are based the rapid outlines here presented.

It is impossible to estimate the numbers of this class in the various cities of the Hellenistic period and at various times. As regards most of the cities, we have not the slightest idea of the proportion that it bore to the working classes (including the *technitai*) and the slaves. There are no statistics at our disposal, apart from some figures relating to Athens, which are susceptible of more than one interpretation.

The *bourgeoisie*, however, whatever its numerical strength, formed the backbone of the Hellenistic cities. The cumulative evidence that we possess is decisive on this point, and cannot be interpreted otherwise. The most salient trait of their behaviour and mental attitude is their fervent devotion to their respective cities, to the traditional features of urban life, political, religious, and social.

Some modern scholars are wont to speak of the political death of the Greek cities after the days of Philip and Alexander, and to regard the Greek *homo politicus*, the main support of these, as consequently dead also, or confined to a very modest role in contemporary affairs. This conception of the political condition of the Hellenistic world is not, I think, supported by the facts, which, as set forth above, rather point to the contrary. No Hellenistic monarch would have admitted it, still less the Greek cities themselves. Every Hellenistic king looked upon the Greek cities as a factor in politics not less powerful than his rivals, the other Hellenistic monarchs. Such was also the opinion of the Romans when they first appeared on the political horizon of Hellenism. Every reader of the preceding chapters will realize, I hope, the importance of the part played by almost all the Greek cities, whether politically independent or not, in the political evolution of the Hellenistic world and of each of the Hellenistic monarchies. If the city-state was still an important factor in Hellenistic history, it was certainly because the Greek was still pre-eminently a *homo politicus*, especially in the mother country.

That the heroes of Menander and of his fellow-dramatists, the characters of Theophrastus, the personages of Herondas and Theocritus hardly ever mention politics and show apparently no great interest in them, is not to be interpreted as suggesting their complete indifference to the subject. Nor does it indicate such indifference on the part of Menander and Theophrastus, or even of Herondas and Theocritus. It merely signifies that the reactions of their characters to political events and problems were, from an artistic standpoint, of no interest to any of them, and that their public preferred not to be reminded of this grave and melancholy topic when they sought recreation, aesthetic impressions, and amusement.

Nor does it appear possible to invoke the philosophers of this period in aid of the thesis that the city-state and the *homo politicus* had died a premature death in Hellenistic Greece. No doubt all the philosophies in question had their interest centred in the individual. They all were dogmatic philosophies of conduct, semi-religious doctrines intended to guide the individual in his life, in his relations with God, the Universe, the State, the family and himself, all this in accordance with the general structure of the world as the various schools of thought conceived it. This trend in philosophical thought may be explained in part by the political and social conditions of the time, by the growing demand of the intellectual citizen for guidance and help in his doubts and difficulties, but it must be remembered on the other hand that the general development of philosophy had been in this direction since the time of the Sophists,

and that the new Hellenistic schools were not in this respect innovators or revolutionaries. This is not the place for a full discussion of the subject, but I may point out that none of the Hellenistic philosophies ignored the existence of the State, of the *polis*, and its importance in the life of the individual. Each school treated the problem of the relation of the individual to the State differently, but none neglected it or regarded it as irrelevant. The Epicureans and the Cynics repudiated any such relation and recommended complete retirement from political life. The most influential of the new schools, the Stoa, at the outset ignored the State as it existed and substituted its own ideal, the universal State, in which the unity of the world found expression; but it very soon changed its attitude. In view of the important part which the actual State played in the lives of its pupils, of whom many were statesmen in Rome and Greece, the Middle Stoa made strenuous efforts to reconcile its individualism and 'cosmopolitism' with the State as it existed, which to them again was the city-state. They did not pay so much attention now to βασιλεία, but concentrated their efforts on the guidance of statesmen and citizens of the city-state. In this direction the activity of Panaetius was decisive, and in framing his 'political' philosophy he had in mind not his influential Roman friends alone.

It may perhaps be suggested that the upper, intellectual class in general lost its interest in politics, which survived only among a few politicians and in the mob. This I regard again as unsupported by the facts. If the *homo politicus* was dead and politics a matter of complete indifference to so large and influential a group of the urban population as the *bourgeoisie*, including the intellectuals, how can we account for the political struggle of the Greek cities, which never abated until the last days of the Hellenistic period? It was not under the compulsion of a few politicians and of the proletariat alone that the middle class built ships and organized armies to defend the political liberty of their cities, or to extend their territories and their sphere of influence. They preferred to employ mercenaries to wage their wars. Was this exclusively because they were cowardly and unwilling to risk their lives, or was it partly because the military and technical superiority of mercenaries over citizens was universally recognized in the Hellenistic world? In my opinion it was the city *bourgeoisie* that was chiefly responsible for the great struggle for liberty carried on by the cities, an often disappointing and, as it proved, a hopeless struggle.

Devoted to his city as a body politic, the *bourgeois* was no less devoted to its traditional gods and ancestral religion. It was members of his class who built new temples and repaired old ones, who adorned them with statues and pictures by the best artists, and filled them with votive offerings, sometimes of a costly character. It was the *bourgeoisie* again that maintained the old festivals and inaugurated new ones, where professionals and the young men of the cities competed in games and contests, and that organized the gorgeous processions, so typical of the religious life of the period. It was members of the same class who made pilgrimages to the great Panhellenic shrines (all of them highly prosperous at this time), who sent sacred embassies (θεωροί) to represent their cities at important celebrations in these and other notable sanctuaries, and who filled their treasuries with gifts and instituted foundations for the support of certain religious ceremonies in them. The hundreds of inscriptions at Delphi, Delos, Olympia, Epidaurus, which record honours conferred on foreigners, and the lists of *proxenoi* of these sanctuaries, are eloquent of the religious zeal of the *bourgeois*.

It is customary with modern historians of Greek religion to attribute these practices to the vainglory of the *bourgeoisie*, not to their real religious feelings. The city-states, they say, were dying, and with them the devotion to the great Olympians and to the gods of the city; the splendour of their cults was an empty mummery. Most of the educated Greeks of the Hellenistic period, they assert, were sceptics or agnostics, some of them atheists; if some were religious, their devotion was to new gods and new religious conceptions. It is no doubt true that Greek religion was not static in Hellenistic times: religious conceptions were certainly changing; new cults were being organized, new forms of religious thought were growing, new gods and among them many foreign gods were being worshipped. But this does not mean that the old religion was dead. We have no means of penetrating into the souls of those who worshipped their ancestral gods in the manner above described and we are not warranted in decrying their religious practices as demonstrations of mere traditionalism and ostentatious vanity. Such outbursts of religious feeling as that which swept over the Hellenistic world when the Gauls almost captured Delphi were certainly genuine. Later phenomena of the same kind in Asia Minor connected with catastrophic events, the belief in the epiphany of the ancestral gods in critical moments of the city's life, the registration of such manifestations in special historical works (of which there is evidence in Lindus, in Chersonesus in the Crimea, and elsewhere), were likewise unmistakable displays of religious feeling. This was understood by the philosophy of the day. Epicurus, in spite of his materialistic conception of life, never discarded the gods completely. The Stoics made the greatest efforts to reconcile their philosophical conceptions with the traditional piety. Without discussing the subject in detail, I may say that, everything considered, I regard the devotion of the Greek *bourgeoisie* to the Panhellenic and city gods as a genuine reflection of their religious sentiment, not less genuine than the worship of the Τύχη, of the great men of the time, and of certain foreign gods.

Besides supporting the traditional religion, the *bourgeois* of the cities did their best to make these beautiful and comfortable. As in modern America, they liked, in the measure of their means, to present to them beautiful new buildings of various kinds. If they were not sufficiently wealthy to do this individually, they contributed what they could to the subscriptions organized by the cities for these and similar purposes.

They showed great enthusiasm in maintaining and extending the traditional education of the young, such as they had themselves received in their youth. Several donations and foundations of this kind are known. The office of the gymnasiarch was one of the most important in the city. They endeavoured to secure the most meritorious and trustworthy teachers for their schools, laying stress on their moral, as distinguished from their technical, qualifications. Being themselves well educated, they took a lively interest in philosophy, literature, and art. They demanded the best companies of actors for their theatres regardless of cost; they were ready to pay high fees to travelling lecturers, reciters of their own poems, and musicians; they spent lavishly on the adornment of their temples and public buildings with the finest statues, bas-reliefs, and paintings; they liked to ornament their own houses in the same way, and they buried with their dead exquisite products of the minor arts. They were not indifferent to public health, witness the spread of public medical attendance, of which I have spoken. And they strove hard to avert the spectre of famine from their cities, a vital problem for them all, which I have already discussed. The offices of *agoranomoi* (market managers) and σιτῶναι and ἐλαιῶναι (buyers of corn and of olive-oil) had an importance in the life of the cities equal to that of the gymnasiarch.

It is true that in many cases the *bourgeoisie*, as I have explained, was acting wholly or to some extent under compulsion in these matters. The attention that they paid to supplies and to displays, their frequent distributions of foodstuffs and oil, must be attributed in part to their desire to keep the proletariat quiet, to preserve concord (ὁμόνοια) between the classes, to avoid social and political revolutions. Again, it might often happen that a liturgy was undertaken by some member of the *bourgeoisie* under pressure from the government. But this does not mean that all such things were done under compulsion, and that other, and especially patriotic, motives were not the most potent factors in evoking the zeal of the *bourgeoisie* on behalf of their native or adoptive cities.

To sum up this brief sketch of the urban *bourgeoisie*, which might be made much longer and more impressive and convincing, I may say that it was owing chiefly to their conservatism and patriotism, to their sincere devotion to their civic institutions and traditions, that the Greek cities experienced no radical changes in their political, social, economic, and cultural structure, such as might have been imposed either by pressure from above, from the autocratic rulers of the Hellenistic States, or from below, from the proletariat. It is idle to speculate what course of action the kings would have followed had they not met with such staunch fidelity to the traditional features of their mode of life on the part of the population of the cities, and especially of their leaders, the *bourgeoisie*. The kings no doubt showed great respect for the Greek city-state and of course the *bourgeoisie* was often prepared to make far-reaching concessions to the kings, especially when faced with social revolution from within. But the kings apparently knew very well that extreme measures would lead to endless conflicts, and on the other hand they understood that Greek civilization, which was their own civilization, would die out if the foundations of the traditional Greek city-state were undermined. This is the main reason why they accepted the Greek city as such, never tried to make any fundamental change in its constitution, and preferred endless negotiations and sometimes great political inconvenience to any radical reform. What would have happened to the city-state if the proletariat had been successful in its attempts to modify profoundly its social and economic structure, it is difficult to say. Social revolution was always in the air in the Greek cities of the Hellenistic period. But it never met with any enduring success, at least on a large scale. The joint efforts of the *bourgeoisie* and of the kings, and later of the Romans, always averted this danger, sometimes at the last moment.

Some of my readers may feel that the description that I have given of the urban *bourgeoisie* is too glowing and too flattering, and does not accord with the rather sombre picture to be found in most of our literary sources. The Athenian *bourgeois* depicted by Menander or Theophrastus and the respectable citizens of Cos as drawn by Herondas are not very attractive figures. The *Graeculi* of the Romans were in many respects their lineal descendants and reveal to a large extent the same character. They certainly were selfish, their conception of life was materialistic, their

ideals somewhat distasteful, and their morality low. What they wanted was a quiet and easy life of pleasure, with the minimum of work and worry. They showed very little interest in the State or in religion. Their main endeavour was to increase their material possessions and to bequeath them to their posterity. Love plays an important part in their lives, but it was not the basis of marriage: the latter was simply a business transaction. They showed some tenderness for their infant children, but were ready, in case of necessity, to expose those that were not wanted, especially the girls.

This picture is certainly a true one, though a little exaggerated. But its fundamental elements apply, to a certain extent, to the *bourgeoisie* of all times and of all countries. It does not contradict and is not irreconcilable with that which I have drawn above. No human beings are perfect, and the *bourgeoisie* of Hellenistic times was no exception to the rule. Moreover, as time went on, it deteriorated even further in respect of its failings. And yet what I have said of its ultimate role in the destinies of Greece is exact. It was in the main the Hellenistic *bourgeoisie* which preserved— for good or for evil—the leading traits of Greek city life and bequeathed them, with the sanction of their own support, to posterity.

3. The Causes of Decline*

I have traced in the preceding chapters the economic and social development of the Hellenistic world during the three centuries that followed Alexander's death. I may now, for the convenience of the reader, briefly summarize what I have written. The conquest of the Near East by Alexander relieved the Greek city-states

of continental Greece and of the islands from an acute political, economic, and social sphere in a growing overpopulation of Greece, in the reduction of the masses to indigence and the concentration of wealth in the hands of a small class; while a diminishing demand for the products of Greek industry on both the home and foreign markets brought about a gradual decrease in industrial production and a corresponding decline of commercial activity.

* M. Rostovtzeff, *The Social and Economic History of the Hellenistic World* (Clarendon, 1941), Vol. 2, pp. 1026–1032. Reprinted by permission of The Clarendon Press, Oxford.

Alexander's Eastern conquests provided the Greeks with new markets for their wares and offered them excellent opportunities for emigration and the recovery of economic status. They helped to set Greece on her feet again and led to a period of great commercial activity and prosperity. But this revival was of short duration. It was impeded fom the outset not only by the incessant wars of Alexander's successors, which especially affected Greece, but also by the buoyant economic development of the Near East on Greek lines, which slowly but continuously reduced the demand for Greek products in the Asiatic and African parts of the former empire of Alexander.

The years that followed, known as the period of the political balance of power, witnessed a certain stabilization of economic and social conditions in the Hellenistic world. The three leading monarchies that emerged from the turmoil of the time of the Successors were actively occupied in consolidating their position and remodelling their economic and social life. In the East this was done with the help of an ever-increasing host of Macedonian and Greek immigrants distributed throughout the former Oriental monarchies in larger and smaller groups. The same process was begun in certain minor monarchical States and in some of the leading Greek city-states which had succeeded in retaining their political independence.

The leading role, both politically and in other respects, was played by the two largest and wealthiest regions of the Hellenistic world—Egypt under the Ptolemies and Syria under the Seleucids. Both the Ptolemies and the Seleucids had a great task before them in the organization of their States on new administrative, financial, social, and economic lines, with a view to their strength, wealth, and contentment, and in their political consolidation. The main problem before them was to establish a reasonable *modus vivendi* between the two constituent parts

of the population of their kingdoms, the two foundations on which their dominion rested—on the one hand the new settlers, for the most part associates of the king and instruments in his hands, chiefly Macedonians and Greeks; on the other the natives, the economic backbone of the two countries. These two groups had at first very little in common: their mentality was utterly different and so was the structure of their relations, social, commercial, and industrial. A new economic organization that would produce the harmonious co-operation of the two parts was indispensable in each kingdom, but to achieve it was a matter of extreme difficulty. Without this co-operation the Ptolemies and the Seleucids could not attain their principal objects, the fusion of their kingdoms into solid political units and their strengthening and enrichment by the development and more rational exploitation of their natural resources.

The efforts of the first Ptolemies, of whom we know much, and of the early Seleucids, of whom we know much less, appear to have met with fair success. Egypt and the Asiatic empire of the Seleucids became, if not solid and enduring political, economic, and social units (for the problem of the amalgamation of the Greeks and the natives was not satisfactorily solved either by the first Ptolemies or by the Seleucids), at least strong and wealthy States; these enabled their rulers to play in the Hellenistic world the part not only of political but also of economic leaders, at the expense of, but without crushing detriment to, the other constituent parts of it, especially the Greek cities of the mainland and the islands. The result of this hegemony was a certain stabilization and political and economic balance of power, which seemed likely to endure.

But the stabilization and balance of power thus established were never firmly founded and never remained undisturbed for long. They were undermined from the very start by certain elements in the situation: by the political rivalry between the three leading monarchies, entailing recurrent wars in which the minor States took an active part; by the fierce struggle of the Greek cities for political independence and their conflicts among themselves, aggravated and complicated by internal discords and social revolutions in some of the leading cities; by the gradual but steady disintegration of the Seleucid monarchy under the pressure of foreign wars, of the Galatian invasion of Asia Minor, and of the revival of national spirit in India and Iran. The consequences of the instability of the balance of power were most acutely felt in Greece, the weakest and least consolidated part of the Hellenistic world. A gradual impoverishment, connected with the steadily growing economic emancipation of the East from the Greek motherland, became the leading feature of its life, and this impoverishment was responsible for the revival of acute social and economic unrest.

A strong effort to give greater political and economic stability to the Hellenistic world, on the basis of the political hegemony of the leading Powers, was made at the end of the third century B.C. by Antiochus III of Syria and Philip V of Macedonia, to the detriment of Egypt, which had hitherto been the strongest Hellenistic State and the pivot of Hellenistic equilibrium. Under the combined military pressure of Macedonia and Syria Egypt lost its control of the Aegean and its leading position in the commercial life of the Hellenistic world. These it was unable to recover, for it was involved in a difficult internal struggle, due to the inability of the Ptolemies to find a satisfactory solution of the main problem that confronted them—how to develop friendly relations between the Greeks and the natives and secure their harmonious co-operation in the economic life of the country, which they were organizing on the basis of a strict State control. The result was a gradual decline in the prosperity of Egypt and its growing isolation.

Meanwhile the efforts of Antiochus and Philip, successful at the outset, were disconcerted by a new development. The minor States, whose very existence was threatened by these endeavours to unite the Hellenistic world, called into the political arena a new force, which proved unexpectedly decisive. They appealed to Rome, the new predominant Power of the West.

The intervention of Rome had two important consequences. The protagonists in the attempt at stabilization—Macedonia and Syria—were eliminated by Rome in a series of effective strokes. Rome herself assumed the task of pacifying and stabilizing the Hellenistic world under her benevolent hegemony, and carried it out successfully for a time. After a period during which the Greek city-states, in particular, of the mainland, the islands, and Asia Minor, experienced great sufferings and suffered severe losses as a result of the wars of liberation and enslavement, the Hellenistic territories were at last granted a breathing-space. For about fifty years they lived in a condition of peace and unity enforced upon them by the heavy hand of Rome and only temporarily interrupted by short periods of local wars. This enforced peace had its beneficial results. Greece and Asia Minor enjoyed a phase of prosperity, more conspicuous in the latter, less so in Greece. But this prosperity was not shared by Egypt and Syria; for Egypt was still helplessly struggling with its internal problems and was rapidly decaying, while Syria, in its Oriental seclusion, was prevented from quietly enjoying its natural wealth and its economic opportunities by the forces of disintegration, supported and intensified by the political action of Rome.

Still more important than the partial and compulsory peace was another factor in the economic development of the Hellenistic States, which also was a consequence of Roman intervention and protectorate. I allude to the closer political, social, and economic connexion of the two parts of the civilized world of that time: the Western, centred around Italy and Rome, and the Eastern, more or less re-united under the pressure of the Roman protectorate. For the Eastern region the increasingly intimate interpenetration of the two worlds meant not only a new market for its goods, a market con-tinuously increasing in size and purchasing capacity, and perhaps a new field for emigration (mostly through slavery), but also an influx of new capital and new energies from the West. These made their way into the East with the steady flow of enterprising and well-to-do new settlers, the 'Roman' *negotiatores*. What the *nego-tiatores* brought with them was not only a brisk business spirit but also capital ready for investment. This was no doubt capital that had formerly been accumulated by the East and had been transferred to the West in the form of loot, booty, and indemnities. Nevertheless, it was some compensation to the East that at least in part it was not invested in the West, but returned to its original home to revivify and reorganize the anaemic and disorganized economy of the East.

The recovery of the Hellenistic world brought about by the Roman protectorate was, however, partial and local. It did not affect the richest parts of it—Syria and Egypt—and therefore never restored in full the prosperity that had prevailed under the Successors and under the creators of the Hellenistic balance of power. This blessed age never returned. Moreover, the recovery was short-lived. It was inter-rupted and shaken to its very foundations by the revolt, led by Mithridates, of Asia Minor and Greece against Roman domina-tion; and was completely reversed during the civil wars that followed, when the East was ruthlessly exploited and utterly humiliated by its masters, who were fighting their own fierce battles for power

on Greek soil and with the help of the resources of the East. Even in the short intervals between the successive stages of the Roman civil war the East had no rest. Roman domination and the Roman system of provincial administration weighed heavily and unremittingly upon it.

Such in brief were the successive phases of the economic and social development of the Hellenistic world. It had failed to find solutions for its principal problems: the establishment of political unity or at least of a more or less peaceful political co-operation, that is to say, of a durable balance of power. This was made im-possible by the ceaseless struggles for political hegemony, which had a disastrous effect not only in the political but also in the economic and social spheres. No doubt these struggles stimulated the energies of the rivals, compelling them to efforts whereby the productivity and trade of their respective territories might be in-creased. But, on the other hand, the wars absorbed or destroyed an enormous volume of human energy which otherwise would have been active in the economic field, and large quantities of actual or prospective goods; they encouraged and developed the destructive spirit of indi-viduals and groups (for example, piracy); and they created in the masses of the population an ever-increasing sense of uncertainty, which gradually and in-evitably induced depression and apathy.

Within the great monarchical States (other than Macedonia) the rulers never succeeded in attaining stabilization and consolidation. They never found a way of escape from the great antinomy in the political, social, and economic life of their dominions, to which the conquest of Alexander had given rise: the conflict between the two leading forms of civilized life, the Eastern and the Western, between Greek city-states and Oriental monarchies —between Greek 'politai' and Oriental subjects; between the Greek economic system, based on freedom and private initiative, and the State economy of the East, supervised, guided, and controlled. And finally they were faced with the great eternal problem of human society, as acute in the ancient world as it is in the modern: the antinomy between the rulers and the ruled, the 'haves' and the 'have-nots,' the *bourgeoisie* and the working classes, the city and the country.

It was in the main the inability of the Hellenistic world to find, if not the solution of these problems, at least an acceptable compromise, which was respon- sible for its easy defeat by Rome and its incorporation in the fabric of the Roman Empire. The destinies of the old Hellenistic States as parts of the Roman Empire have been dealt with by me in another work and do not concern us here. I may, however, observe that although the problem of political unity was solved by the Romans, at least for a certain time, the other problems were not; and it was this inability to solve them that was the under- lying cause of the political dissolution of the Roman Empire.

4. THE CAUSES OF DECLINE*

In one of the most popular anthology passages in Latin, Servius Sulpicius, writing to console Cicero for his daughter's death, describes how, as he reached Greek waters, sailing from Asia, he began to look about him at the ruins of Greece. 'Behind me was Aegina, in front of me Megara, on the right the Piraeus, on the left Corinth, cities which had once been prosperous, but now lay shattered ruins before my sight.' *Oppidum cadavera* he goes on to call them—corpses of cities! The picture, it will probably be objected, is overdrawn; certainly the ruin of Greece was, by Cicero's time, already a rhetorical commonplace, to be echoed by Horace, Ovid and Seneca in turn. But it was based upon an essential truth. The Saronic Gulf, once the centre of the world, was now, for all that Greece meant, a dead lake lapping about the foundations of dead cities. In that tragic decay—which was not confined to mainland Greece—we are confronted with one of the most urgent problems of ancient history, and one with a special significance for our generation, who were already living in an age of economic, political and spiritual upheaval, even before the bombs began to turn our own cities into shattered ruins.

This, then, is my reason for reopening a subject on which there is scope for such diverse opinion: *adeo maxima quaeque ambigua sunt.* If any further justification is required, then I will only add that the recent publication of Professor Michael Rostovtzeff's classic study of the social and economic life of the Hellenistic Age is at once an invitation and a challenge.

With this work Rostovtzeff completes an historical survey reaching from Alex- ander to Constantine; and, throughout, he lays stress very emphatically upon the word 'history.' His four volumes are designed not simply as a compilation of factual material, but as an interpretation of the historical development of six hundred years of ancient civilisation. Both histories, the Hellenistic and the Roman, are pessimistic in outlook, for both recount a failure; in the one case that of Greek and Hellenistic civilisation, in the other the collapse of the ancient world itself. Yet there is a difference of tone. In 1926 the author had ended on a now famous query. 'Is it possible,' he asked, 'to extend a higher civilisation to the lower classes without debasing its standard and diluting its quality to the vanishing point? Is not every civilisation bound to decay as soon as it penetrates the mass?' These questions, with their echoes of Plato, go far beyond the scope of the particular problem of the decay of classical culture, and were undoubtedly prompted by the writer's own personal experience as an *émigré* from Soviet Russia. And in the formulation of certain other problems—Why was the victorious advance of capitalism stopped? Why was machinery not invented? Why were the business systems not perfected? Why were the primal forces of primitive economy not overcome (*RE*, 484)—and especially in his interpretation of the chaos of the third century A.D. as a proletarian revolution carried out through the army, his view of ancient history appears to have been influenced by his own vivid apprehension of certain contemporary events in Europe. The comparison between Bolshevik Russia and the ancient world in decay is constantly implicit in his narrative, and frequently he pauses to draw a direct analogy.

Many of these questions are fundamental to the problem of the collapse of ancient civilisation; yet, having raised them, Rostovtzeff left them unanswered. Meanwhile his links with Russia were broken, and in any case events there took a turn which falsified his earlier comparison; and so, for a variety of reasons, when in 1941 he published his study of the earlier period, he apparently no longer felt it so urgent a matter even to ask these questions, though, as Prof. Gordon Childe points out, they are equally pertinent to the problem of why Greece and the Hellenistic World went so far and no farther. For in fact the Greek and the Roman failures are in essence one. No one can read through Rostovtzeff's work without being struck by the way in which the earlier forms of decay foreshadow the later, and how, *mutatis mutandis*, the end of Augustus's empire is in its general features an echo

of the end of Alexander's. Both failures, in fact, sprang from something deep in the very character of classical civilisation.

The problem of Greek decline may be approached from two sides. First, in the social-political sphere there is the failure of the Greeks to achieve the unity which alone might have enabled them to preserve their freedom from outside conquest. In this respect the conflicts between Alexander's successors are a repetition on a larger scale of the old wars of the city-states; there was the same fatal disunity, the same squandering of material and cultural capital, the same ultimate betrayal to the outside enemy.

This failure was one of which many Greeks were themselves conscious. Persia, Macedon and Rome are three stages in a tragic descent, three notes which find a constant echo in the propaganda and ideology of the third and second centuries B.C. It is no coincidence that the last struggle of mainland Greece was constantly interpreted in terms of the fourth-century struggle against Macedon, that the Arcadian Polybius launched into a passionate defence of his pro-Macedonian countrymen whom Demosthenes had dubbed traitors, that Philip V of Macedon sought to recall the deeds of Philip II and Alexander, claiming them as ancestors, that Flamininus, going back yet a century earlier, had himself hailed as the new Xerxes, come not to enslave, but to liberate. This sequence is no matter of chance; it is the measure of Greek concern for a superb triumph followed by failure and catastrophe.

Secondly, there is the cultural failure of the Hellenistic age. At an early date, the Greek intellect had gained unrivalled success in its clarity and breadth of thought. The observational science of the Ionians (albeit still wedded to the remnants of pre-rational thinking), the splendid objectivity of Thucydides, the unity of theory and practice in the works of the Hippocratic school, had all pointed forward to further intellectual triumphs; while in the Attic tragedians the moral problems of man's relations with the forces inside himself and inside society had been cast into an artistic form which made its direct appeal to the whole population of Athens. Yet the dawn was false. At the highest moment of the Athenian achievement, in Plato himself, notwithstanding his many magnificent contributions to human thought, the gates were opened to the enemy. The *Laws*, Plato's last attempt to construct the just city, is concerned with the implanting of beliefs and attitudes convenient to authority through the medium of suggestion, and not with the stimulation of man's native curiosity to seek and enquire. A strict and ruthless censorship, the substitution of myths and emotional ceremonies for factual knowledge, the isolation of the citizen from contact with the outside world, the creation of types with standardised reactions, the invoking of the sanctions of a police-state against all kinds of nonconformity—this is Plato's final disastrous contribution to Greek political thought.

Even so, it is as much a symptom as a cause. It represents Plato's reaction to the catastrophe of Aegospotami and to his personal experience of democracy, as he saw it in action at Athens and Syracuse. And though the day was passing when the separate city-state could still be the vehicle of man's intellectual and political progress, he closed his eyes to history and sacrificed the substance of Greek achievement to preserve the husk. In this he was not alone. Aristotle too, for all his mastery in the sphere of scientific observational method, remained politically identified with an obsolescent environment. His *Politics* pre-suppose the city-state throughout; and Dr. Ehrenberg has recently emphasised the complete and astounding lack of contact between him and his great pupil, Alexander. In all the Hellenistic philosophies, likewise, though their field of contemplation had expanded beyond

the walls of the city, there is nevertheless a common note of defeat, a drawing-in of the scope of human thought and endeavour. To the disintegration of society the Cynic reply was to 'deface the currency,' a sharp criticism of all ideals and all standards, the indulging of moral indignation, in short no constructive answer at all. The Stoics turned their thoughts inwards, and sought to proof the individual soul against the raging storms of Fortune; and the Epicureans, though drawing on the materialist speculations of Democritus, also laid their emphasis on the separate moral problem, and tried to live unnoticed in their Garden.

No one, examining the evidence of Greek failure, cultural and social-political, can fail to perceive how closely the two aspects are interwoven. Yet neither is the cause of the other: both reflect something deeper and more fundamental, something which had begun to operate before the end of the fifth century. For the decline of the Greek world, though worked out to its bitter end under the Hellenistic kings and leagues, goes back to cultures already active within the body of the city-state. This more fundamental cause is rooted in the social relation of the classes. It reveals itself most clearly in the failure of the middle class inside the Greek cities to maintain and extend democracy.

At Athens, of which we know most, the rise of the middle class followed the revolutionary changes of the sixth century, when the aristocracy finally capitulated before the successive blows of Solon, Peisistratus and Cleisthenes. The fruit of this victory was Athenian democracy and the defeat of the Persian armada. But success brought new ambitions and new opportunities; and very soon the Athenian fleet, the democratic instrument of Salamis, was being employed as the police force of the Athenian empire. Democracy had become imperialism, forms of society ultimately inconsistent. And though the Athenian defeat at Aegospotami meant the end of the empire, the vice of exclusiveness persisted. The democrats fought with courage and idealism to suppress the oligarchy of Plato's friend Critias, and the rest of the Thirty; but it was the restored democracy which rejected Thrasybulus' proposal to bestow citizenship on all who had fought for Athenian freedom at the Piraeus.

One could hardly find a more significant illustration of the limitations of Greek democracy, and of what Prof. Toynbee calls 'the poisonous ingredients with which it had been contaminated from the outset.' After 400 B.C., in one city after another, democracy gradually faded out. It had failed because it was inconsistent with the exclusiveness and parochialism of the middle-class citizen, who clung tightly to the privileges which his citizenship brought him, whether in money or prestige. Throughout the fifth century the Athenian middle class had concentrated its energies in agriculture, usury and the paid posts provided by the civil service and the empire. Citizenship was a door which was kept tightly barred against the stranger and the foreigner, who might settle and make money in banking, trade and manufacture, but could not aspire to the full fruits enjoyed by the citizen class. In this exclusiveness the middle class had support of the workers, who saw in the various forms of state subsidy the one perquisite which divided the poor but free citizen from the slave. Thus, whether rich or poor, the citizen of fifth century Athens felt himself to be the member of a compact, brilliant, exclusive and highly conscious community, which was, in fact, living largely at the expense of the resident alien, the slave and the subject ally.

Sooner, or later, however, this exclusiveness was bound to break down. It was a struggle against the tide. And from the fourth century onwards there are clear signs that the division made by the possession of citizenship was growing less distinct. The wealthy on both sides of the line began to coalesce to form a single social group, the bourgeoisie, to whom the old parochial exclusiveness had little meaning; and under Alexander and his successors it was this class which became the driving force throughout the Greek world. To Prof Rostovtzeff we owe a fascinating description of its achievements during the Hellenistic Age. The bourgeoisie he defines as that section of the population which lived off the proceeds of capital invested in some branch of economic activity. It included landowners and tenant farmers; owners of industrial workshops; owners or tenants of shops, ships and warehouses; moneylenders; and slave-owners, who hired out their slaves for work in ships, mines and workshops, or who let them conduct business directly on their master's own behalf. It was this class that controlled the wealth and the culture of the Greek cities and the monarchies of the Hellenistic Age, having crystallised into a recognisable group in the course of the fourth century.

Since city-state hegemonies no longer existed, it was easy now to treat on terms of friendly equality with the city that would formerly have seemed a potential subject or mistress. Moreover, the new foundations in Asia were free from the old traditions of exclusiveness which had historical roots in the cities of Greece proper. Hence this form of particularism had to and did give way. But vertically the bourgeoisie remained as rigidly exclusive as ever their predecessors were. Indeed, certain new developments of the Hellenistic age tended to accentuate class differentiation. With the increase in the number of slaves throughout the Greek world as a result of the wars of Alexander's successors, society was drawn out towards greater extremes of wealth and poverty. Having annexed the older lands of the Nile and the Euphrates, the Greeks became acquainted with a more rigid, oriental, caste-system, which had all the authority of antiquity, and seemed more impervious to social change than the forms of society they had known at home. The old antinomy between the town-dweller and the peasant within the ancient agrarian empires of Asia, was now inherited by the successor states of Alexander; and in Egypt, where a unique system of royal monopoly was adapted and perfected by the Ptolemies, a peasant population of legally free *fellahin* filled the role elsewhere assigned to slaves. Barring a few faint notes, which swelled loudest in Judaea, this subject class remained voiceless and unheard; the stream of history passed it by.

Nevertheless the growing polarisation of society eventually made itself felt in a series of class struggles of a new type. Struggles to throw off an effete aristocracy or oligarchy the Greeks had known; the bitterness and resentment of the vanquished can still be read in the pages of Theognis. But now the Hellenistic Age saw fierce conflicts provoked by the basic classes of society, slave revolts like those of Sicily and Pergamum, the Carthaginian mercenary war, and such proletarian movements as that which gave its misguided support to the Spartan revolution of Cleomenes, and prompted the setting-up of the counter-revolutionary Symmachy of Antigonus Doson, an important function of which was to protect the Achaean bourgeoisie from the spread of Spartan 'communism' among the masses in their own cities. This increase of class-war coincided with a decline in the prosperity of the bourgeoisie themselves. 'The rapid growth of wealth in the hands of a few members of the class,' comments Rostovtzeff, 'did not compensate for its impoverishment as a whole' (*HW*, 1204). This was especially true in Greece proper, where an acute problem of depopulation from the end of the third century onwards offers perhaps the clearest indication of general decay. Indeed, just as four centuries later the decline of Italy prefigures the decay and break-up of the Roman Empire, so now mainland Greece

offers the first, warning sign of the decline of the Hellenistic World.

This failure of the Greek middle class to preserve and enlarge the democracy it had established, and the gradual accentuation of class-differences and class-conflicts, is an underlying factor easily traceable beneath the general features of social-political and cultural decline. 'Greece and poverty,' wrote Herodotus, 'have always been foster-sisters'; and as a corollary to this Aristotle characterised poverty as the parent of revolution and crime. Continued exclusiveness in a world of poverty could only lead to an explosion and to the chronic *stasis* endemic in ancient Greece; its effects on the quality of social and cultural life had already been catalogued in the sombre pages of the third book of Thucydides. In a community based on the exploitation of slave and neighbour, where the distinction between the 'city-state of the sponge' and the 'vast military empire of the shark' was to be measured solely by the lack or presence of power and opportunity, where the artistic achievement of the Athenian Acropolis was made possible only by a tyrannous imposition exacted from unwilling subjects, what hope was there of unity? And what meaning was there in freedom? The Persian and the Macedonian could always find his allies in Greece itself; and later, in the Hellenistic period, the bourgeoisie, in fear of those classes from whose labours its wealth was drawn, would always make common cause with the kings under the slogan of *Homonoia*. In the long run they were prepared to surrender all. To save the Achaean bourgeoisie from Cleomenes, Aratus was ready to nullify his life's work, and readmit the Macedonians to the Acrocorinth; a generation later his successors in the Achaean League obediently went over to Rome, still bent on safeguarding their own special interests. All over Greece the upper classes came to terms with the barbarian, and the Greek wars of the second century were all more or less wars of class against class—*externa ac plerumque permixta*; after the swift Roman victory of 146, Polybius informs us, there was a proverbial saying commonly heard on the lips of his defeated compatriots: 'If we had not perished so quickly, we should never have been saved!'

In the cultural life of Hellenic society the poison was also at work, and the havoc it wrought could not long be concealed. Here a single example must suffice. Discussing the collapse of the Roman Empire, Rostovtzeff points to the significance of the wave of superstitions and oriental cults which swept over the lower classes from the east, until ultimately the bourgeoisie and the cultured classes were also submerged and the light of Greek rationalism finally put out (*RE*, 479). A similar phenomenon accompanied the decline of the Hellenistic world in the third and second centuries; Professor G. Murray once summed it up as a 'failure of nerve.' What caused it? Did it correspond to a spontaneous revulsion from rational thinking on the part of the masses? Or did the trustees of Greek culture deliberately 'Medise,' if we may borrow a metaphor from the parallel sphere of politics? There is no simple answer. Times of stress are always rich in superstition. But the question may also be answered in part, if we consider once more the tragic role of Plato, who, in the *Laws*, deliberately welcomes and inculcates superstition as a mental pabulum not only for the lower classes, but even for the wardens of his ideal state. For the former the old Olympian cults, for the latter the new astral deities are to be an object of faith which may not be challenged. Whether Plato himself believed in either is extremely dubious; despite temperamental differences, his attitude here is fundamentally, if less frankly, that of Polybius, who, two hundred years later, expressed his admiration for the use to which the Roman State put religion, keeping the lower classes in subjection by a judicious compound of terrors and pageantry. Yet to the impartial observer such a renunciation of honest thinking can surely appear only as the blackest treason to that flowering of the human spirit which we call Hellenism, treason, too, in its most gifted exponent, and explicable only as the outcome of a motive of irresistible compulsion. That motive was unquestionably the maintenance of privilege, the preservation of an oligarchic and paternal form of society with power and responsibility concentrated at the top. In the interest of such a social order and its perpetuation Plato is prepared to purge and censor most of the finest products of Greek genius. He had set out with the purest motives; he followed the light as he saw it. But what he did not see was that obscurantism cannot be confined to the lower orders; like a plague arising among city slums, it sweeps outwards and upwards until it has infected every rank of society. When that happens, society must either root it out or perish.

Two issues the generations after Plato never faced: one was the unfettered application of the observational method to the problems of nature, the other the questioning of the basic organisation of society. It is not easy to over-estimate the importance of the teaching of the Academy in turning men's minds away from observation, and inspiring what Glanvill, many centuries later, described as 'thinking in the national way,' deduction, that is to say, of the particular from the general, this having first been arrived at on *a priori* principles. Not even Aristotle could shake himself wholly free from this legacy. Correspondingly, in the social sphere, there was no serious challenge to slavery, or to such other concomitant abuses as the inferior position of women. As Rostovtzeff points out, the various utopias of Zeno, Hecataeus of Abdera, Euhemerus and Iambulus were 'mere products of theoretical speculation .... and had no relation to or influence on practical politics' (*HW*, 1132). The Stoics began by asserting the equality of slaves and free men; but they never drew the obvious conclusion that slavery should therefore be abolished, and later, in the Middle Stoa, they reverted to the Aristotelian view that slavery was a natural institution. In short, Hellenistic thought remained closely bound up with the patterns of behaviour of the Hellenistic bourgeoisie. The renunciation which Plato was driven to make deliberately and consciously his successors made unconsciously and without effort.

It seems clear, then, that the increasing economic cleavage of Greek society into rich and poor, privileged and exploited, was a basic factor in both the social-political and the cultural decline which became apparent from the fifth and fourth centuries respectively. This cleavage necessarily raised the problems which were occupying Rostovtzeff's attention in 1926. Why, we must ask, did Greek middle-class democracy stop short? Why was the economic system never expanded to enable wealth, and with it culture, to spread downwards throughout society? Why was the accumulation of wealth in the Hellenistic world never used as a basis for capitalist and industrial expansion, instead of going (as it so often did) into unproductive channels, such as temples, festivals and public luxury? In fine, why did ancient society, having reached a certain point, stop short in its tracks, and then begin to decay instead of advancing towards a fuller democracy based on an increasing mastery over the forces of nature?

Stated in these terms, the problem identifies itself—as ultimately it must—with what is perhaps *the* question of ancient history, namely: What caused the decline and fall of the Roman Empire? The more important contributions to the discussion of this topic have been reviewed in a recent paper by Prof. N. Baynes, and they need not detain us here. There is, however, one point I would make in connection with Rostovtzeff's approach to the problem in his *Social and Economic*

History of the Roman Empire. Towards the end of this work the author deals with the theories of certain of his predecessors, dismissing some as untenable, and characterising others as only partial answers; and in the end his conclusion is *non liquet*, accompanied by a hint that all approaches have made a definite contribution to our understanding of the problem (*RE*, 486–7). In a sense this is true. But what he perhaps does not make clear is that many of these 'explanations' are, in fact, symptoms; and though symptoms are essential in a diagnosis, the cause of the disease is usually something quite independent of their sum total.

In particular, Rostovtzeff's approach is handicapped by his unwillingness to admit the priority of any one field or category of human activity—social, political, economic or religious—over the rest. This view, which is implicit in all his work, is clearly stated in his introduction to the volumes on the Hellenistic Age. 'I have kept before me as a guiding principle,' he writes, 'in this as in the other historical works which I have written, the maxim that the complexity of life should never be forgotten and that no single feature should ever be regarded as basic or decisive' (*HW*, viii). This view (with its significant echoes from Tolstoy) postulates a series of parallel, partial causes for any historical event, sometimes linked together mechanically, but never organically; history becomes something amorphous, eclectic; and in view of the 'complexity of life' the historian renounces the function which he has claimed from the days of Thucydides, that of explaining not only *how*, but also *why* things happen.

Now admittedly one result of this principle has been that Prof. Rostovtzeff has admirably resisted the temptation which besets the 'economic historian' to see an economic cause for every incident, and so to over-simplify the process of history. Indeed, he will command general support in his rejection of Salvioli's theory that the ancient world failed because it never advanced beyond the stage of household economy, or the rival theory of Simkhovitch which puts the root of the trouble in soil-exhaustion. On the other hand, having made these points, he is inclined to assume that he has disposed of the mode of production as a basic factor in the situation. And this is far from being so.

Rostovtzeff's own work makes it clear that classical civilisation was at all times based on a technique that was backward not merely relatively to that of modern times, but absolutely; that is to say, the exploitation of nature and the development of natural wealth was at so low a level that the leisure and culture of the few had to be balanced by the toil and want of the many, whether their status was that of poor workman or peasant, serf or slave. The difference between slave and free proletarian was important psychologically; but in Hellenistic times the 'hireling for life,' as Chrysippus called him, differed in terms of real welfare from the slave only in his 'personal freedom and more precarious situation as regards work and food' (*HW*, 1149). Thus the intensive exploitation of man replaced, and indeed excluded its alternative—the intensive exploitation of nature. Once slavery has spread from the home to the mine and the workshop, it appears to rule out the development of an advanced industrial technique. For the kind of slaves employed in the big productive processes such as agriculture or mining are not capable of operating complicated machinery or advanced methods of natural exploitation, still less of improving them. Hence slavery militates against the development of mechanical power; and at the same time it brings few advantages in the concentration of industry, and therefore offers little opposition to the tendency of production to fly outwards to the periphery of the economic area. Furthermore, when slaves are there as an alternative, the producer has no incentive to economise labour; and

the bargaining power of the poor, free, worker is automatically reduced where the two classes are in competition (as they frequently were in the Hellenistic Age), and consequently there arises what is today termed the problem of the 'poor white.'

But equally important is the psychological effect of this social cleavage between those who possess the power and the wealth, and those who actually do the work. More than once Rostovtzeff mentions the 'conservative spirit of the Hellenistic period in regard to technical innovations in the field of industry' (*HW*, 1219). To speak of a 'conservative spirit' is, of course, to define, not to explain; and there can be little doubt that the search for an explanation brings one back immediately to the fact of a well-differentiated class system, which produced an atmosphere wholly unsympathetic to invention and technical progress. Certainly it was the new spirit of the early Greek trading cities, where the power of land was already broken, but wealth was not yet unduly concentrated, which transformed the scientific traditions of the east to create the amazing results of the Ionian Renaissance. Again, the general flux of the early Hellenistic Age, the new cities with their go-ahead 'middle-west' outlook, the stimulus of new trade and new ideas, released a fresh burst of creative activity in the late fourth and early third centuries. But as the world settled down in its new shape, classes rigidified again, retardation once more set in: it forms a constant refrain in the work of Rostovtzeff, who indeed emphasises the slow rate of technical progress and the failure to achieve mass production. For this he offers a threefold reason: (1) the local production of manufactured goods, (2) the arrested development of large industrial centres, (3) the low buying capacity and restricted number of consumers (*HW*, 1230). It will be observed that none of these is a primary cause; but the last and most important raises the fundamental problem with which we are concerned here —the bourgeois monopoly of wealth, and so of purchasing power.

If we attempt to analyse further the failure to make progress in technique, we shall find that it links up with the contempt felt by the Greek middle class for manual work of all kinds. That this attitude grew stronger during the Hellenistic Age seems indicated by an interesting fact to which Rostovtzeff draws attention, namely, the disappearance of representations of working craftsmen from the pottery of this period, and instead the depicting of mythological and abstract themes (*HW*, 1201). This pottery is, of course, produced by craftsmen; but the themes the craftsman introduces reflect the interests of his public. Hence it appears that the Hellenistic bourgeoisie, unlike their predecessors, found pictures of craftsmen working either vulgar or tedious. Moreover, there is plenty of other evidence for this widespread attitude. Hasebroek has assembled a number of instances from the fifth and fourth centuries; and Rostovtzeff has himself stressed the significant fact that the Greek bourgeoisie never accepted the *technites*, or member of what we should today term the liberal professions (*i.e.*, civil servants, professional soldiers, teachers, doctors, engineers, architects, sculptors, painters, artists and lawyers), as a social equal. Because these *technitai earned* their living, by practising a skill and for wages, they were regarded as being socially on the level of the artisan. Their incomes were low and they were frequently outside the citizen body, as metics or slaves; their absence from among the solid characters of the New Comedy supports the view that they were not considered respectable (*HW*, 1117).

This distinction, which clearly reflects the bisection of society into two classes with antithetical interests, had disastrous effects in every sphere of life. Prof. B.

Farrington has described these effects, at a later stage, on the practice of medicine, perhaps the most realistic and progressive of all the crafts; and at an early date one result was the diversion of scientific thought away from practical observation and experiment, into notional and metaphysical channels, and the consequent check on technical progress.

However, it would be misleading to suggest that there were no exceptions to this rule. In building and engineering the Hellenistic world, like the Roman Empire afterwards, made certain notable advances. Particularly inside the monarchies there was a considerable programme of building, including the construction of roads and aqueducts, and this in turn stimulated various allied crafts (*HW*, 1231–2). Even more, in the science of engineering, in its relation to warfare, there was constant technical innovation. Vitruvius' account (x. 16. 3ff.) of the rivalry during the siege of Rhodes between the two engineers Callias and Diognetus is an interesting example of the way in which ancient inventiveness could forge ahead where a pressing situation overrode any prejudice against linking up theory and tradition with experimentation and practice. As a result, the architect and the engineer were exceptional, not only in the attitude with which they approached their tasks, but also in the prestige which their professions seem to have enjoyed (*HW*, 1234–5). Such figures as Ctesibius of Alexandria, Philo of Byzantium and Archimedes of Syracuse, theoretical writers and practical inventors alike, enjoyed a position in society well above that ordinarily accorded to the *technites*. Yet their exceptional status did not mean that such of their inventions as had no direct application to warfare—for instance, Ctesibius's pump or the many ingenious devices recorded in Hero of Alexandria—were rationally employed otherwise. Indeed, it it perhaps symbolic of the position of ancient applied science that Hero's inventions, far from being used for the benefit of mankind, were employed by the priests of Egypt to simulate miracles, and so, by facilitating a pious fraud on the faithful, to assist in the secular struggle of superstition against reason.

Why were the architect and the engineer in a special category? Why in this case was it experience modified by scientific experiment, and in the other crafts experience alone that set its seal upon practice? Rostovtzeff points to the steady demand for the work of engineers and architects (*HW*, 1237). But one must go farther, and ask why that demand existed here and not elsewhere. The answer seems to be that the demand was created by the pressing needs of the Hellenistic monarchs to expand their realms and to defeat their rivals in warfare. The reason they sought expansion and military success, though knit up with such questions as prestige and personal power, lies fundamentally in the nature of ancient society, which equated expansion with greater revenues and a wider field of exploitation. The progress made in building and engineering is thus in part at least a by-product of a process which in the long run was inimical to the interests of society; the modern parallel is the stimulus given by warfare to the progress of the aeroplane, wireless telegraphy and atomic research.

The other branches of technique were far from enjoying similar conditions. Here there was no growing demand because there was no large market for the products of industry; and there was no such market because the form of exploitation kept the masses at the level of poverty, and the price of labour cheap, whether free or slave. The modern world has solved a similar dilemma up to a point by exporting its surplus overseas; but this method was not open to a civilisation which was still geographically circumscribed, after absorbing as much territory as it could digest. Moreover, the structure of society *outside* the areas of Hellenism (and later

of the Roman Empire) was not such as to provide markets for goods for mass consumption. Accordingly one is here driven to ask: Why then did antiquity never attempt a radical solution to this *impasse*? In short, why was the bourgeoisie not superseded as the governing class in society by a revolt of the oppressed masses? From the Hellenistic Age onwards there were frequent proletarian and slave risings. The part played by social revolution and its threat in the wars of Sparta against the Achaean League has already been mentioned; and later on there are the revolts of Aristonicus at Pergamum, the Mithridatic War, the Sicilian slave revolts, slave risings in Attica, Macedonia and Delos, and the rising of Spartacus in Italy. But a significant feature of these movements is that 'in the few cases where social revolution was successful,' as Rostovtzeff observes, 'this was the result of political conjunctures which prompted the leaders of the day to lend their support to the aspirations of the proletariat' (*HW*, 1128). Perhaps the most notable example of this is to be seen in the careers of the Roman *populares* and the use they made of the urban mass at Rome. This constant diversion of the revolutionary movement to serve the interests of someone outside it is only to be explained as a measure of weakness in the movement itself; it is the mark of immaturity and inadequate internal organisation and drive. Hence it never appeared likely that the proletariat would succeed not merely in overthrowing the middle classes, but also in setting up in the place of the existing state a wider social order, capable of conserving classical culture and extending it to a broader section of society.

Indeed it is very questionable whether such a thing was economically possible, without a radical change in the level of production. Technique in the ancient world had never supported more than a minority culture; and though it can be argued, with justice, that this minority culture had always been very wasteful, investing its resources in luxuries and non-productive forms of wealth, this is not to say that with the most careful planning and management the resources and technique actually available would have been sufficient to keep the whole community at a level bearing any relation to classical civilisation as we know it. In any case, if the purely economic problem is most safely left open, there are other factors which wholly rule out the possibility of such a revolution. Even the most effective of the slave-revolts, for instance the Sicilian risings of Eunus in 135 and Athenion in 104 (both of whom made some attempt to plan their resources with an eye on the future), did not reveal a sufficient unity of idea and purpose among the rebels to give any prospect of lasting success. For the general effect of slavery was to split the proletariat, not to strengthen it. There is every reason to think that a proletarian victory, if by some miracle it could have been achieved, would have meant nothing more than a change of masters. In fact, looking back from the vantage-point of the present, we can see that an organised proletariat capable of displacing the bourgeoisie, and both maintaining and expanding civilisation, first came into existence with the industrial revolution, which provided both the improved technique and increased wealth essential to mass civilisation, and also the concentration of the proletariat in factories and mines under conditions which enabled it to attain a community of purpose and a realisation of its own strength.

These conditions never existed in the ancient world; and the Hellenistic bourgeoisie, conscious that it was a question of themselves or nothing, constantly set their faces against any movement designed to secure social readjustment. In this respect their propaganda was consistent with their practice. Plato had spoken of cities as divided as if between two armies watching each other; and his contemporary, Aeneas

Tacticus, awake to the dangers inherent in the use of mercenaries, urges the setting up of a citizen militia from among the 'reliable' citizens, who have most to lose from social revolution. For the same reason the Hellenistic philosophers were united in ignoring the issues raised by the antagonism between rich and poor; realising that their own existence was bound up with the predominance of the wealthier class, they were, in Rostovtzeff's words, agreed in treating 'the problem of πενία and πλοῦτς not as an important social and economic issue, but as a question of individual morals' (*HW*, 1129). It is unlikely that this interpretation was reached solely on philosophical grounds; more probably, as Rostovtzeff points out, in discussing the Stoics and Epicureans, 'the attitude of both schools towards wealth was in part dictated to them by their regard for their pupils and followers, who mostly belonged to the circle of intellectuals and the bourgeoisie' (*HW*, 1130). At the same time the city governments were mostly too timid or too poor to set up what Dr. Tarn has called 'shock-absorbers in the social system,' food doles and benefactions such as the Romans leant to use with such effect.

Thus the ancient world seems to have been caught in a dilemma. The economy both of the Hellenistic world and, later, of the Roman Empire, was based on a low level of technique and a form of exploitation which neither encouraged nor engendered technical progress. Moreover, the mental attitude inspired by this system was one which, among the bourgeoisie, turned men's interests away from the creation of wealth to its consumption, which accentuated exclusiveness and class hatred and fear, which on the one hand encouraged contempt for physical work and, ultimately, even for such intellectual work as rested upon it, and on the other hand set up an exaggerated respect for notional thinking—an attitude which led up to and beyond the intellectual treason of Plato; meanwhile, among the workers themselves it induced the slave mentality, the frame of mind which was satisfied perforce with little and fell back on a pattern of behaviour which could only reinforce the contempt in which the middle classes already held those upon whose backs they lived.

Was there any available way out? In this question, as in others, speculation will always busy itself with 'ifs'; but the fact that history must face is that throughout the whole of classical civilisation no radical solution was devised for the problems outlined above. Of course the decline was not along a regular downward slope. The expansion of Alexander and his successors, and the consolidation effected by Augustus and Hadrian, each for a time put a brake upon the process of decay and even facilitated a partial recovery. But the real causes were never eradicated, and after a while the decline always set in again. Ultimately the supply of slaves dried up, and the western empire stabilised itself at a low level, its production in the hands of serfs and tied craftsmen, and its government a rigid bureaucracy.

Yet all was not lost. As Prof. Baynes has recently reminded us, the eastern empire went on after the western half had foundered; and even in the west there was never a clear and complete break. Consequently, when the barbarian invasions were themselves events of the distant past, and new towns began to spring up in Europe, inhabited by neither serfs nor slaves, the techniques of the ancient world were there for men to build on. Unobtrusively the craftsmen grouped around manor or monastery had passed their knowledge down from father to son. And so once more, in an atmosphere free from the deadening effect of the ever more rigid class-system of late antiquity, men could go forward to the mastery of nature. With them they bore the full cultural legacy of the ancient world, adapted now to a task from which antiquity itself had necessarily drawn back, but which gave promise of easy accomplishment to the new and fruitful partnership between mind and hand.

SECTION VI

Rome's Conquest of the Mediterranean in the Second Century B.C.

ROME'S LONG STRUGGLE with Hannibal came to an end in 201 B.C. Worn out with years of fighting, the masters of more land than they could farm, the Romans seemed to need nothing so much as a good rest. Yet within a year they were plunged into another war and launched on a series of campaigns which by 133 would find them the unchallenged rulers of the entire Mediterranean. It is plain that the Roman decision to fight Philip V of Macedon in 200 B.C. was a vital turning point in Rome's history, and the central problem of this section is to ascertain what were Rome's motives in entering that war. It will be interesting, too, to see whether Rome's motives remained the same throughout the course of her conquests. It will also be possible to catch some glimpses of the effects of Roman imperialism on the internal character of the state and its citizens.

1. THE RULES OF ROMAN WARFARE—THE FETIAL LAW*

The Roman religion enjoined the Roman to fight only just wars in which they were the injured party. According to Livy the ritual formula for going to war was prescribed by King Numa and faithfully followed ever after.

The ambassador, when he comes to the frontiers of the people from whom satisfaction is demanded, having his head covered with a fillet, (the fillet is of wool,) says, "Hear, O Jupiter, hear, ye confines, (naming the nation they belong to,) let Justice hear. I am a public messenger of the Roman people; I come justly and religiously deputed, and let my words gain credit." He then makes his demands; afterwards he makes a solemn appeal to Jupiter, "If I unjustly or impiously demand those persons and those goods to be given up to me, the messenger of the Roman people, then never permit me to enjoy my native country." These words he repeats when he passes over the frontiers; the same to the first man he meets; the same on entering the gate; the same on entering the forum, some few words in the form of the declaration and oath being

* Livy, 1. 32, translated by D. Spillan, C. Edmonds, et al.

160

changed. If the persons whom he demands are not delivered up, on the expiration of thirty-three days, for so many are enjoined by the rule, he declares war, thus: "Hear, Jupiter, and thou, Juno, Romulus, and all ye celestial, terrestrial, and infernal gods, give ear! I call you to witness, that this nation (naming it) is unjust, and does not act with equity; but we will consult the fathers in our own country concerning these matters, and by what means we may obtain our right." After that the messenger returns to Rome to consult: the king immediately used to consult the fathers almost in the following words: "Concerning such matters, differences, and quarrels, as the pater patratus of the Roman people, the Quirites, has conferred with the pater patratus of the ancient Latins, and with the ancient Latin people, which matters ought to be given up, performed, discharged, which matters they have neither given up, performed, nor discharged, declare," says he to him, whose opinion he first asked, "what think you?" Then he said, "I think that they should be demanded by a just and regularly declared war, therefore I consent, and vote for it." Then the others were asked in order, and when the majority of those present agreed in the same opinion, the war was resolved on. It was customary for the fecialis to carry in his hand a javelin pointed with steel, or burnt at the end and dipped in blood, to the confines of the enemy's country, and in presence of at least three grown-up persons, to say, "Forasmuch as the states of the ancient Latins, and the ancient Latin people, have offended against the Roman people, the Quirites, forasmuch as the Roman people, the Quirites, have ordered that there should be war with the ancient Latins, and the senate of the Roman people, the Quirites, have given their opinion, consented, and voted that war should be made with the ancient Latins, on this account I and the Roman people declare and make war on the states of the ancient Latins, and on the ancient Latin people." After he had said that, he threw the spear within their confines. After this manner restitution was demanded from the Latins at that time, and war proclaimed: and that usage posterity have adopted.

2. APPIAN ON THE ORIGINS OF THE SECOND MACEDONIAN WAR*

The origins of the Second Macedonian War go back to Philip V's treaty with Hannibal in 215 and the so-called First Macedonian War (214–205 B.C.) that ensued. Appian of Alexandria, a historian of the second century A.D., gives a brief summary of the events leading to the war.

The Romans paid no attention to Philip, the Macedonian, when he began war against them. They were so busy about other things that they did not even think of him, for Italy was still scourged by Hannibal, the Carthaginian general, and they were at war in Africa, Carthage, and Spain, and were restoring order in Sicily.

Philip himself, moved by a desire of enlarging his dominions, although he had suffered nothing whatever at the hands of the Romans, sent an embassy, the chief of which was Xenophanes, to Hannibal in Italy, proposing to aid him in Italy if he would promise to assist him in the subjugation of Greece. Hannibal agreed to this arrangement and took an oath to support it, and sent an embassy in return to receive the oath of Philip. A Roman trireme intercepted the ambassadors of both on their

* Appian, *Macedonian Affairs*, 1, 2, 3, translated by Horace White. Reprinted by permission of the Loeb Classical Library.

return and carried them to Rome. Thereupon Philip in his anger attacked Corcyra, which was in alliance with Rome.

* * *

Ambassadors from Ptolemy, king of Egypt, and with them others from Chios and Mitylene, and from Amynander, king of the Athamanes, assembled at two different times at the place where the Ætolians were accustomed to call their citires together for consultation, to compose the differences between the Romans, the Ætolians, and Philip. But as Sulpicius said that it was not in his power to conclude peace, and wrote privately to the Senate that it was for the advantage of the Romans that the Ætolians should continue the war against Philip, the Senate forbade the treaty and sent 10,000 foot and 1000 horse to assist the Ætolians. With their help the Ætolians took Ambracia, which Philip recovered, not long afterward, on their departure. Again the ambassadors assembled and said that it was very evident that Philip and the Ætolians, by their differences, were subjecting the Greeks to servitude to the Romans, because they were accustoming the latter to make frequent attempts upon Greece. When Sulpicius rose to reply to them the crowd would not hear him, but shouted that the ambassadors had told the truth.

Finally the Ætolians took the initiative and made peace with Philip by themselves without the Romans, and messengers were sent to Rome by Philip himself and by the commander of the Roman forces in order to come to an agreement. Peace was made between them on the condition that neither party should do any injury to the friends of the other. This was the result of the first trial of strength between them, and neither of them believed that the treaty would be lasting, since it was not based on goodwill.

Not long afterward Philip, having ordered a fleet to be prepared by his maritime subjects, took Samos and Chios and devastated a part of the territory of King Attalus. He even attempted Pergamus itself, not sparing temples or sepulchres. He also ravaged Peræa, which belonged to the Rhodians, who had been promoters of the treaty of peace. With another part of his army he ravaged Attica and laid siege to Athens, as though none of these countries concerned the Romans. It was reported also that a league had been made between Philip and Antiochus, king of Syria, to the effect that Philip should help Antiochus to conquer Egypt and Cyprus, of which Ptolemy IV., surnamed Philopator, who was still a boy, was the ruler; and that Antiochus should help Philip to gain Cyrene, the Cyclades islands, and Ionia. This rumor, so disquieting to all, the Rhodians communicated to Rome. After the Rhodians, ambassadors of Athens came complaining of the siege instituted by Philip. The Ætolians also had repented of their treaty, and they complained of Philip's bad faith toward them and asked to be inscribed again as allies. The Romans reproached the Ætolians for their recent defection, but they sent ambassadors to the kings ordering Antiochus not to invade Egypt, and Philip not to molest the Rhodians, or the Athenians, or Attalus, or any other ally of theirs. To them Philip made answer that it would be well if the Romans would abide by the treaty of peace they had entered into with him. Thus was the treaty dissolved and a Roman army hastened to Greece, Publius commanding the land forces and Lucius the fleet.

3. Polybius on the Origins of the War*

In the first of these selections, Polybius describes and comments upon the treaty between Philip and Antiochus the Great, one of the major causes of the war according to some scholars. In the second, he describes the roles of King Attalus of Pergamum, the Rhodians, and the Athenians in bringing Rome into the war against Philip.

Is it not astonishing that while Ptolemy Philopator was alive and did not need such assistance, these two kings were ready with offers of aid, but that as soon as he was dead, leaving his heir a mere child, whose kingdom they were bound by the ties of nature to have defended, they then egged each other on to adopt the policy of partitioning the boy's kingdom between themselves, and getting rid entirely of the heir; and that too without putting forward any decent pretext to cover their iniquity, but acting so shamelessly, and so like beasts of prey, that one can only compare their habits to those ascribed to fishes, among which, though they may be of the same species, the destruction of the smaller is the food and sustenance of the larger. This treaty of theirs shows, as though in a mirror, the impiety to heaven and cruelty to man of these two kings, as well as their unbounded ambition. However, if a man were disposed to find fault with Fortune for her administration of human affairs, he might fairly become reconciled to her in this case; for she brought upon those monarchs the punishment they so well deserved, and by the signal example she made of them taught posterity a lesson in righteousness. For while they were engaged in acts of treachery against each other, and in dismembering the child's kingdom in their own interests, she brought the Romans upon them, and the very measures which they had lawlessly designed against another, she justly and properly carried out against them. For both of them, being promptly beaten in the field, were not only

prevented from gratifying their desire for the dominions of another, but were themselves made tributary and forced to obey orders from Rome. Finally, within a very short time Fortune restored the kingdom of Ptolemy to prosperity; while as to the dynasties and successors of these two monarchs, she either utterly abolished and destroyed them, or involved them in misfortunes which were little short of that. . . .

* * *

The Athenian people sent envoys to king Attalus, both to thank him for the past, and to urge him to come to Athens to consult with them on the dangers that still threatened them. The king was informed a few days afterwards that Roman ambassadors had arrived at the Peiraeus; and, believing that it was necessary to have an interview with them, he put to sea in haste. The Athenian people, being informed of his coming, passed very liberal votes as to the reception and general entertainment of the king. Arrived at the Peiraeus, Attalus spent the first day in transacting business with the Roman ambassadors, and was extremely delighted to find that they were fully mindful of their ancient alliance with him, and quite prepared for the war with Philip. Next morning, in company with the Romans and the Athenian magistrates, he began his progress to the city in great state. For he was met, not only by all the magistrates and the knights, but by all the citizens with their children and wives. And when the two processions met, the warmth of the welcome given by the populace to the Romans, and still more to Attalus, could not have been exceeded. At his entrance into the city by the gate Dipylum the

---

* Polybius, 15. 20; 16. 25–27, translated by E. S. Shuckburgh.

priests and priestesses lined the street on both sides: all the temples were then thrown open; victims were placed ready at all the altars; and the king was requested to offer sacrifice. Finally they voted him such high honours as they had never without great hesitation voted to any of their former benefactors: for, in addition to other compliments, they named a tribe after Attalus, and classed him among their eponymous heroes.

They next summoned an ecclesia and invited the king to address them. But upon his excusing himself, on the plea that it would be ill-bred for him to appear before the people and recount his own good services in the presence of those on whom they had been bestowed, they gave up asking for his personal appearance; but begged him to give them a written statement as to what he thought was the best thing to do in view of the existing circumstances. On his consenting to do this, and writing the document, the magistrates produced the despatch to the ecclesia. The contents of this written communication were briefly these: he recalled the good services he had done the people in the past; enumerated the things he had accomplished in the existing war against Philip; and lastly exhorted them to activity in this war, and protested that, if they did not determine resolutely to adopt the policy of hostility to Philip in common with the Rhodians, Romans, and himself, and yet afterwards wished to share in the benefits which had been secured by others, they would miss securing the true interests of their country. As soon as this despatch had been read, the people, influenced both by its contents and by their

warm feeling towards Attalus, were prepared to vote the war: and when the Rhodians also entered and argued at great length to the same effect, the Athenians at once decreed the war against Philip. They gave the Rhodians also a magnificent reception, honoured their state with a crown of valour, and voted all Rhodians equal rights of citizenship at Athens, on the ground of their having, besides other things, restored the Athenian ships which had been captured with the men on board them. After concluding this arrangement, the Rhodian ambassadors sailed to Ceos with their fleet to visit the islands. . . .

While the Roman ambassadors were still at Athens, Nicanor, by the command of Philip, made a raid upon Attica, and came as far as the Academy. Thereupon the Romans sent a herald to him, and bade him announce to his master Philip that "The Romans admonished him to make no war upon any Greek State, and to submit to an arbitration before a fair tribunal as to the injuries he had inflicted upon Attalus: that, if he did this, he might have peace with Rome, but, if he refused to obey, the opposite would immediately follow." On the receipt of this message Nicanor retired. Then the Romans sailed along the coast of Epirus and delivered a similar announcement in regard to Philip in the town of Phoenice; also to Amynandrus in the district of Athamania; also to the Aetolians in Naupactus, and the Achaeans in Aegium. And having thus by the mouth of Nicanor given Philip this clear warning, the Roman envoys themselves sailed away to visit Antiochus and Ptolemy with a view to settle their controversies. . . .

4. LIVY'S ACCOUNT OF THE ORIGINS OF THE WAR*

The peace with Carthage was quickly followed by a war with Macedonia: a war,

* Livy, 31. 1–2; 5–8, translated by D. Spillan, C. Edmonds, *et al*.

not to be compared to the former, indeed, either in danger, or in the abilities of the commander, or the valour of the soldiers; but almost more remarkable with regard to the renown of their former kings, the ancient fame of that nation, and the vast extent of their empire, in which they had formerly comprehended a large part of Europe, and the greater part of Asia. The contest with Philip, which had begun about ten years before, had been intermitted for the three last years; the Ætolians having been the occasion both of the war and the peace. The entreaties of the Athenians whom, having ravaged their lands, Philip had driven into their city, excited the Romans to a renewal of the war, left, as they were, disengaged by the Carthaginian peace, and incensed against him as well for his treacherous negotiation of peace with the Ætolians and the other allies in that region, as on account of the auxiliaries sent by him with money into Africa to Hannibal and the Carthaginians.

About the same time, ambassadors arrived both from king Attalus, and from the Rhodians, with information that the Macedonian was tampering with the states of Asia. To these embassies an answer was given, that the senate would give attention to the affairs of Asia. The determination with regard to the making war on him, was left open to the consuls, who were then in their provinces. In the mean time, three ambassadors were sent to Ptolemy, king of Egypt, namely, Caius Claudius Nero, Marcus Æmilius Lepidus, and Publius Sempronius Tuditanus, to announce their conquest of Hannibal and the Carthaginians; to give thanks to the king for his faithful adherence to his engagements in the time of their distress, when even the nearest allies of the Romans abandoned them; and to request that if, compelled by ill treatment, they should undertake a war with Philip, he would preserve his former disposition towards the Roman people.

*　*　*

In the year five hundred and fifty-two from the building of the city, Publius Sulpicius Galba and Caius Aurelius being consuls, within a few months after the con-clusion of the peace with the Carthaginians, the war was entered upon against king Philip. This was the first business intro-duced by the consul, Publius Sulpicius, on the ides of March, the day on which, in those times, the consulship commenced; and the senate decreed, that the consul should perform sacrifices with the greater victims, to such gods as they should judge proper, with prayers to this purpose,—that "the business which the senate and people of Rome had then under delibera-tion, concerning the state, and the entering on a new war, might issue prosperously and happily to the Roman people, the allies, and the Latin confederacy;" and that, after the sacrifices and prayers, they should consult the senate on the state of public affairs, and the provinces. At this time, very opportunely for exciting their minds to war, the letters were brought from Marcus Aurelius, the ambassador, and Marcus Valerius Lævinus, proprætor. A fresh embassy, likewise, arrived from the Athenians, to acquaint them that the king was approaching their frontiers, and that in a short time, not only their lands, but their city also, must fall into his hands, unless they received aid from the Romans. When the consuls had made their report, that the sacrifices had been duly performed, and that the gods had accepted their prayers; that the aruspices had declared that the entrails showed good omens, and that enlargement of territory, victory, and triumph were portended; the letters of Valerius and Aurelius were read, and audience given to the ambassadors of the Athenians. After which, a decree of the senate was passed, that thanks should be given to their allies, because, though long solicited, they had not, even when in fear of a siege, renounced their fidelity. With regard to sending assistance to them, they resolved, that an answer should be given as soon as the consuls should have cast lots for the provinces; and when the consul to whose lot Macedonia fell should have pro-posed to the people, that war should be declared against Philip, king of the Macedonians.

The province of Macedonia fell by lot to Publius Sulpicius; and he proposed to the people to declare, "that they chose and ordered, that on account of the injuries and hostilities committed against the allies of the Roman people, war should be proclaimed against king Philip, and the Macedonians under his government." . . . At the first meeting of the people, the proposal concerning the Macedonian war was rejected by almost all the tribes. This was done partly spontaneously, as the people were wearied by the length and severity of the late war, and disgusted with toils and dangers; and partly by Quintus Bæbius, tribune of the people, who, pursuing the old practice of criminating the patricians, charged them with multiplying wars one after another, so that the people could never enjoy peace. This proceeding the patricians with difficulty brooked, and the tribune was severely reprehended in the senate; where each severally urged the consul to call a new assembly, for passing the proposal; to rebuke the backwardness of the people; and to prove to them how much loss and disgrace the delay of this war would occasion.

The consul, having assembled the people in the field of Mars, before he dismissed the centuries to the vote, required their attention, and addressed them thus: "Citizens, you seem to me not to understand that the question before you is not whether you choose to have peace or war: for Philip, having already commenced hostilities with a formidable force, both on land and sea, allows you not that option. The question is, Whether you must transport your legions to Macedonia, or admit the enemy into Italy? How important the difference is, if you never experienced it before, you certainly did in the late Punic war. For who entertains a doubt, but if, when the Saguntines were besieged, and implored our protection, we had assisted them with vigour, as our fathers did the

Mamertines, we should have averted the whole weight of the war upon Spain; which, by our dilatory proceedings, we suffered to our extreme loss to fall upon Italy? Nor does it admit a doubt, that we confined this same Philip in Macedonia, (after he had entered into an engagement with Hannibal, by ambassadors and letters, to cross over into Italy,) by sending Lævinus with a fleet to make war aggressively upon him. And what we did at that time, when we had Hannibal to contend with in Italy, do we hesitate to do now, after Hannibal has been expelled Italy, and the Carthaginians subdued? Suppose that we allow the king to experience the same inactivity on our part, while he is taking Athens, as we suffered Hannibal to experience while he was taking Saguntum: it will not be in the fifth month, as Hannibal came from Saguntum, but on the fifth day after he sets sail from Corinth, that he will arrive in Italy. Perhaps you may not consider Philip as equal to Hannibal; or the Macedonians to the Carthaginians: certainly, however, you will allow him equal to Pyrrhus. Equal, do I say? what a vast superiority has the one man over the other, the one nation over the other! Epirus ever was, and is at this day, deemed but an inconsiderable accession to the kingdom of Macedonia. Philip has the entire Peloponnesus under his dominion; even Argos itself, not more celebrated for its ancient glory than for the death of Pyrrhus. Now compare our situation. How much more flourishing was Italy, how much greater its strength, with so many commanders, so many armies unimpaired, which the Punic war afterwards consumed, when Pyrrhus attacked and shook it, and advanced victorious almost to the Roman capital! and not the Tarentines only, and the inhabitants of that tract of Italy which they call the greater Greece, whom you may suppose to have been led by the similarity of language and name, but the Lucanian, the Bruttian, and the Samnite revolted from us. Do you believe that these would continue quiet and faithful, if Philip should come over to Italy? They subsequently continued faithful, forsooth, during the Punic war! Be assured those states will never fail to revolt from us, except when there is no one to whom they can go over. If you had been annoyed at passing into Africa, you would this day have had Hannibal and the Carthaginians to contend with in Italy. Let Macedonia, rather than Italy, be the seat of war. Let the cities and lands of the enemy be wasted with fire and sword. We have already found by experience, that our arms are more powerful and more successful abroad than at home. Go to the vote with the blessing of the gods; and what the senate have voted, do you ratify by your order. This resolution is recommended to you, not only by your consul, but even by the immortal gods themselves; who, when I offered sacrifice, and prayed that the issue of this war might be happy and prosperous to me and to the senate, to you and the allies and Latin confederates, to our fleets and armies, portended all joyful and prosperous results."

After this speech of Sulpicius, being sent to give their votes, they declared for the war as he had proposed. On which, in pursuance of a decree of the senate, a supplication for three days was proclaimed by the consuls; and prayers were offered to the gods at all the shrines, that the war which the people had ordered against Philip might turn out well and happily. The consul Sulpicius inquiring of the heralds, whether they would direct the declaration of the war against king Philip to be made to himself in person, or whether it would be sufficient to publish it in the nearest garrison, within the frontiers of his kingdom, they answered, that they would do rightly whichever course they should adopt. The consul received authority from the senate to send any person whom he thought proper, not being a senator, as ambassador, to denounce war against the king. Then they arranged for the armies of the consuls and prætors. The consuls were ordered to levy two legions, and to disband the veteran troops. Sulpicius, to whom the management of this new and highly important war had been decreed, was allowed permission to carry with him as many volunteers as he could procure out of the army which Publius Scipio had brought home from Africa; but he was not empowered to take with him any veteran soldier against his will. . . .

5. The Treaty of Peace and Rome's Settlement of Greece*

In 197 B.C., at Cynocephalae, the Roman general Flamininus defeated Philip and put an effective end to hostilities. Livy gives the terms of the peace and the reaction of Rome's allies to it. In the following year, Flamininus made his dramatic announcement at the Isthmian games near Corinth in which he made clear the limited nature of Roman war aims and Rome's plans for the future of Greece.

A few days after this, the ten ambassadors arrived from Rome, in pursuance of whose counsel, peace was granted to Philip on the following conditions: "That all the Grecian states, as well those in Asia as those in Europe, should enjoy liberty, and their own laws: That from such of them as had been in the possession of Philip, he should withdraw his garrisons, particularly from the following places in Asia; Euromus, Pedasi, Bargylii, Iassus, Myrina, Abydus; and from Thasus and Perinthus, for it was determined that these likewise

* Livy, 33, 30–33, translated by D. Spillan, C. Edmonds, *et al.*

should be free: That with respect to the freedom of Cius, Quinctius should write to Prusias, king of Bithynia, the resolutions of the senate, and of the ten ambassadors: That Philip should return to the Romans the prisoners and deserters, and deliver up all his decked ships, excepting five and the royal galley,—of a size almost unmanageable, being moved by sixteen banks of oars: That he should not keep more than five hundred soldiers, nor any elephant: That he should not wage war beyond the bounds of Macedonia without permission from the senate: That he should pay to the Roman people one thousand talents: one half at present, the other by instalments, within ten years." Valerius Antias writes, that there was imposed on him an annual tribute of four thousand pounds' weight of silver, for ten years, and an immediate payment of twenty thousand pounds' weight. The same author says, that an article was expressly inserted, that he should not make war on Eumenes, Attalus's son, who had lately come to the throne. For the performance of these conditions hostages were received, among whom was Demetrius, Philip's son. Valerius Antias adds, that the island of Ægina, and the elephants, were given as a present to Attalus, who was absent; to the Rhodians, Stratonice, and other cities of Caria which had been in the possession of Philip; and to the Athenians, the islands of Paris, Imbros, Delos, and Scyros.

While all the other states of Greece expressed their approbation of these terms of peace, the Ætolians alone, in private murmurs, made severe strictures on the determination of the ten ambassadors. They said, "it consisted merely of an empty piece of writing varnished over with a fallacious appearance of liberty. For why should some cities be put into the hands of the Romans without being named, while others were particularized, and ordered to be enfranchised without such consignment; unless the intent was, that those in Asia, which, from their distant situation, were more secure from danger, should be free;

but those in Greece, not being even mentioned by name, should be made their property: Corinth, Chalcis, and Oreum; with Eretria, and Demetrias." Nor was this charge entirely without foundation: for there was some hesitation with respect to Corinth, Chalcis, and Demetrias; because, in the decree of the senate in pursuance of which the ten ambassadors had been sent from Rome, all Greece and Asia, except these three, were expressly ordered to be set at liberty; but, with regard to these, ambassadors were instructed, that, whatever measures the exigencies of the state might render expedient, they should determine to pursue in conformity to the public good and their own honour. King Antiochus was one of whom they did not doubt that, so soon as he was satisfied that his forces were adequate, he would cross over into Europe; and they were unwilling to let these cities, the possession of which would be so advantageous to him, lie open to his occupation. Quinctius, with the ten ambassadors, sailed from Elatia to Anticyra, and thence to Corinth. Here the plans they had laid down respecting the liberation of Greece were discussed for about three days in a council of the ten ambassadors. Quinctius frequently urged, that "every part of Greece ought to be set at liberty, if they wished to refute the cavils of the Ætolians; if they wished, that sincere affection and respect for the Roman nation should be universally entertained; or if they wished to convince the world that they had crossed the sea with the design of liberating Greece, and not of transferring the sovereignty of it from Philip to themselves." The Macedonians alleged nothing in opposition to the arguments made use of in favour of the freedom of the cities; but "they thought it safer for those cities themselves that they should remain, for a time, under the protection of Roman garrisons, than be obliged to receive Antiochus for a master in the room of Philip." Their final determination was, that "Corinth be restored to the Achæans, but that a Roman garrison should continue in the citadel; and that Chalcis and Demetrias be retained, until their apprehensions respecting Antiochus should cease."

The stated solemnity of the Isthmian games was at hand. These have ever been attended by very numerous meetings, as well on account of the universal fondness entertained by this nation for exhibitions of skill in arts of every kind, as well as of contests in strength and swiftness of foot; as also, because of the convenience of the locality, which furnishes commercial advantages of all kinds by its two opposite seas, and by which it had obtained the character of a rendezvous for all the population of Asia and Greece. But on this occasion, all were led thither not only for their ordinary purposes, but by an eager curiosity to learn what was thenceforward to be the state of Greece, and what their own condition; while many at the same time not only formed opinions within themselves, but uttered their conjectures in conversation. Scarcely any supposed that the Romans, victorious as they were, would withdraw from the whole of Greece. They took their seats, as spectators; and a herald, preceded by a trumpeter, according to custom, advanced into the centre of the theatre, where notice of the commencement of the games is usually made, in a solemn form of words. Silence being commanded by sound of trumpet, he uttered aloud the following proclamation: THE SENATE AND PEOPLE OF ROME, AND TITUS QUINCTIUS, THEIR GENERAL, HAVING SUBDUED KING PHILIP AND THE MACEDONIANS, DO HEREBY ORDER, THAT THE FOLLOWING STATES BE FREE, INDEPENDENT, AND RULED BY THEIR OWN LAWS: THE CORINTHIANS, PHOCIANS, AND ALL THE LOCRIANS; THE ISLAND OF EUBŒA, AND THE MAGNESIANS; THE THESSALIANS, PERRHÆBIANS, AND THE ACHÆANS OF PHTHIOTIS. He then read a list of all the states which had been under subjection to king Philip. The joy occasioned by hearing these words of the herald was so great, that the people's minds

were unable to conceive the matter at once. Scarcely could they believe that they had heard them; and they looked at each other, marvelling as at the empty illusion of a dream. Each inquired of his neighbours about what immediately concerned himself, altogether distrusting the evidence of his own ears. As every one desired not only to hear, but to see the messenger of liberty, the herald was called out again; and he again repeated the proclamation. When they were thus assured of the reality of the joyful tidings, they raised such a shout, and clapping of hands, and repeated them so often, as clearly to show that of all blessings none is more grateful to the multitude than liberty. The games were then proceeded through with hurry; for neither the thoughts nor eyes of any attended to the exhibitions, so entirely had the single passion of joy pre-occupied their minds, as to exclude the sense of all other pleasures.

But, when the games were finished, every one eagerly pressed towards the Roman general; so that by the crowd rushing to one spot, all wishing to come near him, and to touch his right hand, and throwing garlands and ribands, he was in some degree of danger. He was then about thirty-three years of age; and besides the vigour of youth, the grateful sensations excited by so eminent a harvest of glory, increased his strength. Nor was the general exultation exhausted in the presence of all the assembly, but, through the space of many days, was continually revived by sentiments and expressions of gratitude. "There was a nation in the world," they said, "which, at its own expense, with its own labour, and at its own risk, waged wars for the liberty of others. And this was performed, not merely for contiguous states, or near neighbours, or for countries that made parts of the same continent; but they even crossed the seas for the purpose, that no unlawful power should subsist on the face of the whole earth; but that justice, right, and law should every where have sovereign sway. By one sentence, pronounced by a herald, all the cities of Greece and Asia had been set at liberty. To have conceived hopes of this, argued a daring spirit; to have carried it into effect, was a proof of the most consummate bravery and good fortune."

6. THE PEACE WITH ANTIOCHUS—188 B.C.*

One reason for the relative leniency of the peace Rome offered Philip was fear of Antiochus the Great. As Polybius (18. 39) put it, "The principal motive of Flamininus in being thus forward in coming to terms was the information he had received that Antiochus had started from Syria with an army, with the intention of crossing over into Europe." After Flamininus' dramatic announcement at Isthmia in 196 B.C. he received an embassy from Antiochus. The Roman attitude toward the ambitions of Antiochus was made very clear:

The king was required in express terms to evacuate the cities of Asia, which had been in possession of either Philip or Ptolemy; not to meddle with the free cities, or ever take arms against them, and to be in a state of peace and equality with all the cities of Greece wherever they might be. Above all it was insisted on that he should neither come himself into Europe, nor transport any army thither. (Livy 33. 34)

After a period of diplomatic maneuvering, Antiochus accepted an Aetolian invitation to come to Greece and embark on a war in which both sides claimed to be fighting for "Greek freedom." In 189 B.C. the Romans inflicted a crushing defeat on Antiochus. The terms of peace they imposed indicate that "Greek freedom" was not the only benefit they derived from the war.

"There shall be perpetual peace between Antiochus and the Romans if he fulfils the provisions of the treaty.

"Neither Antiochus nor any subject to him shall allow any to pass through their territories to attack the Romans or their allies, nor supply then with aught. Neither shall the Romans or their allies do the like for those attacking Antiochus or those subject to him.

"Antiochus shall not wage war upon the Islanders or the dwellers in Europe.

"He shall evacuate all cities and territory (this side Taurus). His soldiers shall take nothing out with them except the arms they are carrying. If they chance to have taken anything away they shall restore it to the same cities.

"He shall receive neither soldiers nor other men from the territory of king Eumenes.

"If there be any men in the army of Antiochus coming from any of the cities taken over by the Romans, he shall deliver them up at Apameia.

"If there be any from the kingdom of Antiochus with the Romans or their allies, they may remain or depart as they choose.

"Antiochus and those subject to him shall give back the slaves, captives, and deserters of the Romans or their allies and any captive received from any quarter. Antiochus shall give up, if it be within his power so to do, Hannibal, son of Hamilcar, the Carthaginian, Mnesilochus the Acarnaian, Thoas the Aetolian, Euboulidas and Philo the Chalcidians, and such of the Aetolians as have held national offices.

"Antiochus shall give up all his elephants, and shall have none henceforth.

"Antiochus shall surrender his ships of

---

* Polybius, 24. 11–12, translated by E. S. Shuckburgh.

war, their tackle, and fittings, and henceforth have only ten decked ships. He shall not have a vessel rowed by thirty oars, [or by less] for purposes of war begun by himself.

"He shall not sail west of the river Calycadnus and the promontory of Sarpedon, except to convey tribute or ambassadors or hostages.

"It shall not be lawful for Antiochus to enlist soldiers or receive exiles from the territory subject to Rome.

"Such houses as belonged to the Rhodians or their allies, in the territory subject to Antiochus, shall continue to belong to the Rhodians as before the war: any money owed to them shall still be recoverable: and any property left behind by them, if sought for, shall be restored.

"The Rhodians shall, as before the war, be free from tribute.

"If Antiochus has given any of the towns to others which he is bound to restore, he shall remove from them also his garrisons and men. And if any shall wish hereafter to desert to him, he shall not receive them.

"Antiochus shall pay to the Romans ten thousand talents, in ten yearly instalments, of the best Attic silver, each talent to weigh not less than eighty Roman pounds, and ninety thousand medemni of corn.

"Antiochus shall pay to king Eumenes three hundred and fifty talents in the five years next following, in yearly instalments of seventy talents; and in lieu of the corn, according to the valuation of Antiochus himself, one hundred and twenty-seven talents, two hundred and eight drachmae, which sum Eumenes has consented to accept 'as satisfying his claims.'

"Antiochus shall give twenty hostages, not less than eighteen nor more than forty-five years old, and change them every three years.

"If there be in any year a deficit in the instalment paid, Antiochus shall make it good in the next year.

"If any of the cities or nations, against whom it has been hereby provided that Antiochus should not make war, should commence war against him, it shall be lawful for Antiochus to war with them; but of such nations and cities he shall not have sovereignty nor attach them as friends to himself.

"Such complaints as arise between the parties to this treaty shall be referred to arbitration.

"If both parties agree in wishing anything to be added to or taken from this treaty, it shall be lawful so to do."

7. Greece as a Roman Protectorate*

In 194 B.C., Flamininus carried out his promised evacuation of Greece, but Rome's involvement did not cease. Having destroyed the Macedonian hegemony and created a power vacuum, the Romans were compelled to intervene in Hellenic quarrels. Under the leadership of Philopoemen, the Achaean League tried to unite the entire Peloponnese under its leadership, a policy that led to war with Sparta. At first the Romans, occupied with Antiochus, remained aloof, but at last they were forced to intervene. After the death of Philopoemen, there was a struggle for leadership of the Achaean League. One faction, led by Lycortas, the father of the historian Polybius, took the concept of freedom seriously and advocated a policy of free negotiation with Rome. Its opponents, led by Callicrates, argued for complete submission to the wishes of Rome, a program which was practical, if not admirable. The faction of Callicrates won out. His arguments and the Roman response are reported by Polybius.

* Polybius, 24. 11-12, translated by E. S. Shuckburgh.

For he said that "The Romans were themselves responsible for the Greeks neglecting their letters and orders instead of obeying them. For in all the democratic states of the day there were two parties,— one recommending obedience to the Roman rescripts, and holding neither law nor tablet nor anything else to be superior to the will of Rome; the other always quoting oaths and tablets, and exhorting the people to be careful about breaking them. Now the latter policy was by far the most popular in Achaia, and the most influential with the multitude; consequently the Romanisers were discredited and denounced among the populace— their opponents glorified. If then the Senate would give some sign of their interest in the matter, the leaders, in the first place, would quickly change to the Romanising party, and, in the next place, would be followed by the populace from fear. But if this were neglected by the Senate, the tendency towards the latter of the two parties would be universal, as the more creditable and honourable in the eyes of the populace. Thus it came about that at that very time certain statesmen, without any other claims whatever, had obtained the highest offices in their own cities, merely from coming forward to speak against the rescripts of the Senate, with the view of maintaining the validity of the laws and decrees made in the country. If then the Senate was indifferent about having their rescripts obeyed by the Greeks, by all means let it go on as it is now doing. But if the Senate wished that its orders should be carried out, and its rescripts be despised by no one, it must give serious attention to that subject. If it did not do so, he knew only too well that the exact opposite of the Senate's wishes would come about, as in fact had already been the case. For but lately, in the Messenian disturbance, though Quintus Marcius had taken many precautions to prevent the Achaeans adopting any measures with regard to the Messenians without the consent of the Romans,

they had disobeyed that order; had voted the war on their own authority; had not only wasted the whole country in defiance of justice, but had in some cases driven its noblest citizens into exile, and in others put them to death with every extremity of torture, though they had surrendered, and were guilty of no crime but that of appealing to Rome on the points in dispute. Again, too, though the Senate had repeatedly written to order the restoration of the Lacedaemonian exiles, the Achaeans were so far from obeying, that they had actually set up an engraved tablet, and made a sworn agreement with the men actually in possession of the city that these exiles should never return. With these instances before their eyes, the Romans should take measures of precaution for the future."

After delivering a speech in these words, or to this effect, Callicrates left the Senate-house. He was followed by the envoys of the exiles, who retired after delivering a short address, stating their case, and containing some of the ordinary appeals to pity. The Senate was persuaded that much of what Callicrates had said touched the interests of Rome, and that it was incumbent upon it to exalt those who supported its own decrees, and to humble those who resisted them. It was with this conviction, therefore, and at this time that it first adopted the policy of depressing those who in their several states took the patriotic and honourable side, and promoting those who were for appealing to its authority on every occasion, right or wrong. The result of which was that gradually, as time went on, the Senate had abundance of flatterers, but a great scarcity of genuine friends. However, on this occasion the Senate did not write about the restoration of the exiles to the Achaeans only, but also to the Aetolians, Epirotes, Athenians, Boeotians, and Acarnanians, calling them all as it were to witness, in order to break down the power of the Achaeans. Moreover, they added to their answer, without saying a word to his colleagues, a remark confined entirely to Callicrates himself, that "everybody in the various states should be as Callicrates." This man accordingly arrived in Greece with his answer, in a great state of exultation, little thinking that he had become the initiator of great miseries to all the Greeks, but especially to the Achaeans.

8. THE THIRD MACEDONIAN WAR*

The terms of the peace of 197 B.C. had been very lenient to Philip V. Far from destroying Macedonian power, they left it free to grow. As Macedon recovered its prestige and influence the Romans once more became alarmed. At the same time the policy of the Scipios and Flamininus was suffering from a reaction at Rome and the emergence of a new policy advocated chiefly by Cato, who disliked things Greek and their corrupting influence on the Roman character. When Philip died in 179 B.C. he was succeeded by his older son Perseus, who lacked some of his father's prudence. Not only did he continue to build Macedonian policy in Europe, he contracted marriage alliances with Seleucus IV of Syria and the king of Bithnia in Asia Minor. No less alarming to the Romans was his support of democratic and revolutionary elements in the Greek cities. Spurred on by Eumunes of Pergamum, the Romans finally declared war in 171 B.C.

In this consulate of Publius Licinius and Caius Cassius, not only the city of Rome, but the whole of Italy, with all the kings and states both in Europe and in Asia, had their attention fixed on the approaching war between Rome and Macedon. Not only old hatred, but also recent anger, because by the villainy of Perseus he had been almost slaughtered like a victim at Delphi, urged Eumenes against him. Prusias, king of Bithynia, resolved to keep clear of hostilities, and to wait the event; for as he did not think it proper to carry arms on the side of the Romans against his wife's brother, so he trusted that, in case of Perseus proving victorious, his favour might be secured through the means of his sister. Ariarathes, king of Cappadocia, besides having, in his own name, promised aid to the Romans, had, ever since he was allied by affinity to Eumenes, united with him in all his plans, whether of war or peace. Antiochus indeed entertained designs on the kingdom of Egypt, since he despised the unripe age of Ptolemy, and the inactive disposition of his guardians,

and thought that he might, by raising a dispute about Cœlesyria, find sufficient pretext for proceeding to extremities, and carry on a war there without any impediment, while the Roman arms were employed against Macedon: yet, by his ambassadors to the senate, and to their ambassadors sent to him, he made the fairest promises. Ptolemy, on account of his age, was then influenced by the will of others; and his guardians, at the same time while they were preparing for war with Antiochus, to secure possession of Cœlesyria, promised the Romans every support in the war against Macedon. Masinissa both assisted the Romans with supplies of corn, and prepared to send into the field, to their assistance, a body of troops and a number of elephants, with his son Misagenes. He so arranged his plans as to answer every event that might take place; for if success should attend the Romans, he judged that his own affairs would rest in their present state, and that he ought to seek for nothing further, as the Romans would not suffer violence to be offered to the Carthaginians; and if the power of the Romans, which at that time protected the Carthaginians, should be reduced, then all

---

* Livy, 42. 29–30, translated by D. Spillan, C. Edmonds, *et al.*

Africa would be his own. Gentius, king of Illyria, had indeed given cause of suspicion to the Romans; but he had not yet determined which party to espouse, and it was believed that he would join either one or the other through some sudden impulse of passion, rather than from any rational motive. Cotys, the Thracian king of the Odrysians, was openly in favour of the Macedonians.

Such were the inclinations of the several kings, while in the free nations and states the plebeians, favouring as usual the weaker cause, were almost universally inclined to the Macedonians and their king; but among the nobles might be observed different views. One party was so warmly devoted to the Romans, that, by the excess of their zeal, they diminished their own influence. Of these a few were actuated by their admiration of the justice of the Roman government; but by far the greater number supposed that they would become powerful in their state, if they displayed remarkable exertions. A second party wished to court the king's favour, as debt, and despair of their affairs, while the same constitution remained, urged them hastily to complete revolution; and others, through a fickleness of temper, followed Perseus as the more popular character. A third party, the wisest and the best, wished, in case of being allowed the choice of a master, to live under the Romans rather than under the king. Yet, could they have had the free disposal of events, they wished that neither party should become more powerful by the destruction of the other, but rather that, the strength of both being uninjured, peace should continue on that account; for thus the condition of their states would be the happiest, as one party would always protect a weak state from any

ill treatment intended by the other. Judging thus, they viewed in silence from their safe position the contest between the partisans of the two contending powers. The consuls, having on the day of their entering on office, in compliance with the order of the senate, sacrificed victims of the larger kinds in all the temples where the lectisternium was usually celebrated for the greater part of the year, and having from them collected omens that their prayers were accepted by the immortal gods, reported to the senate that the sacrifices had been duly performed, and prayers offered respecting the war. The aruspices declared, that "if any new undertaking was intended, it ought to be proceeded in without delay; that victory, triumphs, and extension of empire were portended." The senate then resolved, that "the consuls should, on the first proper day, propose to the people assembled by centuries,—that whereas Perseus, son of Philip, and king of Macedon, contrary to the league struck with his father, and after Philip's death renewed with himself, had committed hostilities on the allies of Rome, had wasted their lands, and seized their towns, and also had formed a design of making war on the Roman people, and had for that purpose prepared arms, troops, and a fleet; unless he gave satisfaction concerning those matters, that war should be proclaimed against him." The question was carried among the commons. Then a decree of the senate was passed, that "the consuls should settle between themselves, or cast lots, for the provinces of Italy and Macedon; that the one to whose lot Macedon fell should seek redress by force of arms from king Perseus, and all who concurred in his designs, unless they made amends to the Roman people."

9. The Sack of Epirus*

In 168 B.C. L. Aemilius Paullus defeated Perseus at Pydna, bringing the war to a close. The Roman policy continued to be the same: freedom for Greece and Macedonia and no annexations. A tribute was imposed in lieu of a war indemnity and the Macedonian kingdom was broken up into four independent republics. Such measures may well have been justified by considerations of security, and it is likely that each faction at Rome approved the peace. There is, however, clear evidence of an increasingly selfish, even brutal, behavior on the part of the Romans. In Aetolia, members of the anti-Roman party were put to death. In Achaea, one thousand hostages, Polybius among them, were sent to Rome. Surely the worst example of Roman brutality is provided by the events in Epirus. After settling affairs in Illyria, Paullus encamped at Passaro.

Not far from this was the camp of Anicius, to whom he sent a letter, desiring him not to be alarmed at any thing that should happen, for "the senate had granted to his soldiers the plunder of those cities in Epirus which had revolted to Perseus." Having despatched centurions, who were to give out that they came to bring away the garrisons, in order that the Epirotes might be free, as well as the Macedonians; he summoned before him ten of the principal men of each city, and after giving them strict injunctions that all their gold and silver should be brought into the public street, he then sent cohorts to the several states. Those that were destined for the more remote states set out earlier than those who were sent to the nearer, that they might all arrive on the same day. The tribunes and centurions were instructed how to act. Early in the morning all the treasure was collected; at the fourth hour the signal was given to the soldiers to plunder, and so ample was the booty acquired, that the shares distributed were four hundred denariuses to a horseman, and two hundred to a footman. One hundred and fifty thousand persons were led away captive. Then the walls of the plundered cities, they were about seventy in number, were razed; the effects sold, and the soldiers' shares paid out of the price. Paullus then marched down to the sea to Oricum, having by no means satisfied the wishes of his men as he had imagined, for they were enraged at being excluded from sharing in the spoil of the king, as if they had not waged any war in Macedon.

* Livy 45. 34, translated by D. Spillan, C. Edmonds, et al.

10. A Roman Triumph*

Plutarch's account of the triumph given the hero of Pydna provides a vivid picture of the rewards offered by Roman imperialism.

The people erected scaffolds in the forum, in the circuses, as they call their buildings for horse-races, and in all other parts of the city where they could best behold the show. The spectators were clad in white garments; all the temples were open, and full of garlands and perfumes; the ways were cleared and kept open by numerous officers, who drove back all who crowded into or ran across the main avenue. This triumph lasted three days.

* Plutarch, *Aemilius Paullus*, 32–34, translated by John Dryden.

On the first, which was scarcely long enough for the sight, were to be seen the statues, pictures, and colossal images which were taken from the enemy, drawn upon two hundred and fifty chariots. On the second was carried in a great many waggons the finest and richest armour of the Macedonians, both of brass and steel, all newly polished and glittering; the pieces of which were piled up and arranged purposely with the greatest art, so as to seem to be tumbled in heaps carelessly and by chance: helmets were thrown upon shields, coats of mail upon greaves; Cretan targets, and Thracian bucklers and quivers of arrows, lay huddled amongst horses' bits, and through these there appeared the points of naked swords, intermixed with long Macedonian sarissas. All these arms were fastened together with just so much looseness that they struck against one another as they were drawn along, and made a harsh and alarming noise, so that, even as spoils of a conquered enemy, they could not be beheld without dread. After these waggons loaded with armour there followed three thousand men who carried the silver that was coined, in seven hundred and fifty vessels, each of which weighed three talents, and was carried by four men. Others brought silver bowls and goblets and cups, all disposed in such order as to make the best show, and all curious as well for their size as the solidity of their embossed work.

On the third day, early in the morning, first came the trumpeters, who did not sound as they were wont in a procession or solemn entry, but such a charge as the Romans use when they encourage the soldiers to fight. Next followed young men wearing frocks with ornamented borders, who led to the sacrifice a hundred and twenty stalled oxen, with their horns gilded, and their heads adorned with ribbons and garlands; and with these were boys that carried basins for libation, of silver and gold. After this was brought the gold coin, which was divided into vessels

that weighed three talents, like those that contained the silver; they were in number seventy-seven. These were followed by those that brought the consecrated bowl which Æmilius had caused to be made, that weighed ten talents, and was set with precious stones. Then were exposed to view the cups of Antigonus and Seleucus, and those of the Thericlean make, and all the gold plate that was used at Perseus's table. Next to these came Perseus's chariot, in which his armour was placed, and on that his diadem. And, after a little intermission, the king's children were led captives, and with them a train of their attendants, masters, and teachers, all shedding tears, and stretching out hands to the spectators, and making the children themselves also beg and entreat their compassion. There were two sons and a daughter, whose tender age made them but little sensible of the greatness of their misery, which very insensibility of their condition rendered it the more deplorable; insomuch that Perseus himself was scarcely regarded as he went along, whilst pity fixed the eyes of the Romans upon the infants; and many of them could not forbear tears, and all beheld the sight with a mixture of sorrow and pleasure, until the children were passed.

After his children and their attendants came Perseus himself, clad all in black, and wearing the boots of his country, and looking like one altogether stunned and deprived of reason, through the greatness of his misfortunes. Next followed a great company of his friends and familiars, whose countenances were disfigured with grief, and who let the spectators see, by their tears and their continual looking upon Perseus, that it was his fortune they so much lamented, and that they were regardless of their own. Perseus sent to Æmilius to entreat that he might not be led in pomp, but be left out of the triumph; who, deriding, as was but just, his cowardice and fondness of life, sent him this answer, that as for that, it had been before, and was now, in his own power; giving him to understand that the disgrace could be avoided by death; which the faint-hearted man not having the spirit for, and made effeminate by I know not what hopes, allowed himself to appear as a part of his own spoils. After these were carried four hundred crowns, all made of gold, sent from the cities by their respective deputations to Æmilius, in honour of his victory. Then he himself came, seated on a chariot magnificently adorned (a man well worthy to be looked at, even without these ensigns of power), dressed in a robe of purple, interwoven with gold, and holding a laurel branch in his right hand. All the army, in like manner, with boughs of laurel in their hands, divided into their bands and companies, followed the chariot of their commander; some singing verses, according to the usual custom, mingled with raillery; others, songs of triumph and the praise of Æmilius's deeds; who, indeed, was admired and accounted happy by all men, and unenvied by every one that was good; except so far as it seems the province of some god to lessen that happiness which is too great and inordinate, and so to mingle the affairs of human life that no one should be entirely free and exempt from calamities; but, as we read in Homer, that those should think themselves truly blessed whom fortune has given an equal share of good and evil.

11. The Destruction of Corinth*

The Roman policy of no annexations in Greece finally was abandoned when Andriscus, a pretender to the Macedonian throne, stirred up a rebellion in 149 B.C. In the following year, a Roman army defeated him and Rome now created the province of Macedonia to be governed by a Roman magistrate. In the same year, Roman senators were attacked by a mob in Corinth, and war broke out in the Peloponnese. When quiet was restored, the Romans determined to make an example of Corinth and in 146 B.C. sent an army under Mummius to destroy the city.

Mummius did not enter Corinth at first, though the gates were open, as he thought some ambush lay in wait for him within the walls, not till the third day did he take Corinth in full force and set it on fire. And most of those that were left in the city were slain by the Romans, and the women and children were sold by Mummius, as also were the slaves who had been manumitted and had fought on the side of the Achæans, and had not been killed in action. And the most wonderful of the votive offerings and other ornaments he carried off *to Rome*, and those of less value he gave to Philopœmen, the general of Attalus' troops, and these spoils from Corinth were in my time at Pergamus. And Mummius razed the walls of all the cities which had fought against the Romans, and took away their arms, before any advisers what to do were sent from Rome. And when they arrived, then he put down all democracies, and appointed chief-magistrates according to property qualifications. And taxes were laid upon Greece, and those that had money were forbidden to have land over the borders, and all the general meetings were put down altogether, as those in Achaia, or Phocis, or Bœotia, or any other part of Greece.

---

* Pausanius, *Description of Greece*, 7. 16, translated by A. R. Shilleto.

12a. The Destruction of Carthage*

Carthage, although rendered impotent by the terms of the treaty that ended the Hannibalic War, continued to be an object of fear, hatred, and suspicion to many Romans. Cato was the most implacable enemy of Carthage.

Some will have the overthrow of Carthage to have been one of his last acts of state; when, indeed, Scipio the younger did by his valour give it the last blow, but the war, chiefly by the counsel and advice of Cato, was undertaken on the following occasion. Cato was sent to the Carthaginians and Masinissa, King of Numidia, who were at war with one another, to know the cause of their difference. He, it seems, had been a friend of the Romans from the beginning; and they, too, since they were conquered by Scipio, were of the Roman confederacy, having been shorn of their power by loss of territory and a heavy tax. Finding Carthage, not (as the Romans thought) low and in an ill condition, but well manned, full of riches and all sort of arms and ammunition, and perceiving the Carthaginians carry it high, he conceived that it was not a time for the Romans to adjust affairs between them and Masinissa; but rather that they themselves would fall into danger, unless they should find means to check this rapid new growth of Rome's ancient irreconcilable enemy. Therefore, returning quickly to Rome, he acquainted the senate that the former defeats and blows given to the Carthaginians had not so much diminished their strength, as it had abated their imprudence and folly; that they were not become weaker, but more experienced in war, and did only skirmish with the Numidians to exercise themselves the better to cope with the Romans: that the peace and league they

had made was but a kind of suspension of war which awaited a fairer opportunity to break out again.

Moreover, they say that, shaking his gown, he took occasion to let drop some African figs before the senate. And on their admiring the size and beauty of them, he presently added, that the place that bore them was but three days' sail from Rome. Nay, he never after this gave his opinion, but at the end he would be sure to come out with this sentence, "Also, Carthage, methinks, ought utterly to be destroyed." But Publius Scipio Nasica would always declare his opinion to the contrary, in these words, "It seems requisite to me that Carthage should still stand." For seeing his countrymen to be grown wanton and insolent, and the people made, by their prosperity, obstinate and disobedient to the senate, and drawing the whole city, whither they would, after them, he would have had the fear of Carthage to serve as a bit to hold the contumacy of the multitude; and he looked upon the Carthaginians as too weak to overcome the Romans, and too great to be despised by them. On the other side, it seemed a perilous thing to Cato that a city which had been always great, and was now grown sober and wise, by reason of its former calamities, should still lie, as it were, in wait for the follies and dangerous excesses of the over-powerful Roman people; so that he thought it the wisest course to have all outward dangers removed, when they had so many inward ones among themselves.

Thus Cato, they say, stirred up the third and last war against the Carthaginians.

---

* Plutarch, *Cato the Elder*, 25–26, translated by John Dryden.

12b. The Destruction of Carthage*

In 146 B.C., the same year as the razing of Corinth, Scipio Aemilianus took Carthage.

Scipio, beholding this city, which had flourished 700 years from its foundation and had ruled over so many lands, islands, and seas, rich with arms and fleets, elephants and money, equal to the mightiest monarchies but far surpassing them in bravery and high spirit (since without ships or arms, and in the face of famine, it had sustained continuous war for three years), now come to its end in total destruction—Scipio, beholding this spectacle, is said to have shed tears and publicly lamented the fortune of the enemy. After meditating by himself a long time and reflecting on the rise and fall of cities, nations, and empires, as well as of individuals, upon the fate of Troy, that once proud city, upon that of the Assyrians, the Medes, and the Persians, greatest of all, and later the splendid Macedonian empire, either voluntarily or otherwise the words of the poet escaped his lips:

"The day shall come in which our sacred Troy
And Priam, and the people over whom
Spear-bearing Priam rules, shall perish all."
(*Iliad*, vi, 448, 449; Bryant's translation.)

Being asked by Polybius in familiar conversation (for Polybius had been his tutor) what he meant by using these words, he said that he did not hesitate frankly to name his own country, for whose fate he feared when he considered the mutability of human affairs. And Polybius wrote this down just as he heard it.

Carthage being destroyed, Scipio gave the soldiers a certain number of days for plunder, reserving the gold, silver, and temple gifts. He also gave prizes to all who had distinguished themselves for bravery, except those who had violated the shrine of Apollo. He sent a swift ship, embellished with spoils, to Rome to announce the victory. He also sent word to Sicily that whatever temple gifts they could identify as taken from them by the Carthaginians in former wars they might come and take away. Thus he endeared himself to the people as one who united clemency with power. He sold the rest of the spoils, and, in sacrificial cincture, burned the arms, engines, and useless ships as an offering to Mars and Minerva, according to the Roman custom.

When the people of Rome saw the ship and heard of the victory early in the evening, they poured into the streets and spent the whole night congratulating and embracing each other like people just now delivered from some great fear, just now confirmed in their world-wide supremacy, just now assured of the permanence of their own city, and winners of such a victory as never before. Many brilliant deeds of their own, many more of their ancestors, in Macedonia and Spain and lately against Antiochus the Great, and in Italy itself, had they celebrated; but no other war had so terrified them at their own gates as the Punic wars, which ever brought peril to them by reason of the perseverance, skill, and courage, as well as the bad faith, of those enemies. They recalled what they had suffered from the Carthaginians in Sicily and Spain, and in Italy itself for sixteen years, during which Hannibal destroyed 400 towns and killed 300,000 of their men in battles alone, more than once marching up to the city and putting it in extreme peril. Pondering on these things, they were so excited over this victory that they could hardly believe it,

* Appian, *Punic Wars*, 8. 19. 132–135, translated by Horace White (London and New York: The Macmillan Company, 1899), pp. 231–234. Reprinted by permission of the publisher.

and they asked each other over and over again whether it was really true that Carthage was destroyed. And so they gabbled the whole night, telling how the arms of the Carthaginians were got away from them and how, contrary to expectation, they supplied themselves with others; how they lost their ships and built a great fleet out of old material; how the mouth of their harbor was closed, yet they managed to open another in a few days. They talked about the height of the walls, and the size of the stones, and the fires that so often destroyed the engines. They pictured to each other the whole war, as though it were just taking place under their own eyes, suiting the action to the word; and they seemed to see Scipio on the ladders, on shipboard, at the gates, in the battles, and darting hither and thither. In this way the people of Rome passed the night.

The next day there were sacrifices and solemn processions to the gods by tribes, also games and spectacles of various kinds. The Senate sent ten of the noblest of their own number as deputies to arrange the affairs of Africa in conjunction with Scipio, to the advantage of Rome. They decreed that if anything was still left of Carthage,

Scipio should obliterate it and that nobody should be allowed to live there. Direful threats were levelled against any who should disobey and chiefly against the rebuilding of Byrsa or Megara, but it was not forbidden to go upon the ground. The towns that had allied themselves with the enemy it was decided to destroy, to the last one. To those who had aided the Romans there was an allotment of lands won by the sword, and first of all to the Uticans was given the territory of Carthage itself, extending as far as Hippo. Upon all the rest a tribute was imposed, both a land tax and a personal tax, upon men and women alike. It was decreed that a prætor should be sent from Rome yearly to govern the country. After these arrangements had been carried out by the deputies, they returned to Rome. Scipio did all that they directed, and he instituted sacrifices and games to the gods for the victory. When all was finished, he sailed for home and was awarded the most glorious triumph that had ever been known, splendid with gold and gorged with statues and votive offerings that the Carthaginians had gathered from all parts of the world through all time, the fruit of their countless victories.

13. ROMAN ATROCITIES IN SPAIN*

The Romans were engaged in the difficult task of pacifying Spain from the end of the Hannibalic War until the fall of Numantia in 133 B.C. The difficulties of the terrain and the toughness of the natives drove the Romans to excesses of brutality in their attempts to reduce the territory. Appian describes some of the shocking methods employed by the Romans.

Lucullus being greedy of fame and needing money, because he was in straitened circumstances, invaded the territory of the Vaccæi, another Celtiberian tribe, neighbors of the Arevaci, against whom war had not been declared by the Senate, nor had

they ever attacked the Romans, or offended Lucullus himself. Crossing the river Tagus he came to the city of Cauca, and pitched his camp near it. The citizens asked him what he had come for and what occasion there was for war, and when he replied that he had come to aid the Carpetani whom the Vaccæi had maltreated they retired inside their walls, from which they sallied out and fell upon his wood-cutters

* Appian, *Punic Wars*, 6. 9. 51–52; 59–60, translated by Horace White. Reprinted by permission of the Loeb Classical Library, Harvard University Press.

and foragers, killing many and pursuing the remainder to the camp. When battle was joined the Caucæi, who resembled light-armed troops, had the advantage at first, but when they had expended all their darts they were obliged to fly, not being accustomed to a standing fight, and while forcing their way through the gates about 3000 of them were slain.

The next day the elders of the city came out wearing crowns on their heads and bearing olive-branches, and asked Lucullus what they should do to establish friendly relations. He replied that they must give hostages and 100 talents of silver, and furnish a contingent of horse to the Roman army. When all these demands had been complied with he asked that a Roman garrison should be admitted to the city. When the Caucæi assented to this he brought in 2000 soldiers carefully chosen, to whom he gave orders that when they were admitted they should occupy the walls. When this was done Lucullus introduced the rest of his army and ordered them at the sound of the trumpet to kill all the adult males of the Caucæi. The latter, invoking the gods who preside over promises and oaths, and upbraiding the perfidy of the Romans, were cruelly slain, only a few out of 20,000 escaped by leaping down the sheer walls at the gates. Lucullus sacked the city and brought infamy upon the Roman name.

* * *

Lucullus, who had made war on the Vaccæi without authority, was wintering in Turditania. When he discovered that the Lusitanians were making incursions in his neighborhood he sent out some of his best lieutenants and slew about 4000 of them. He killed 1500 others while they were crossing the straits near Gades. The remainder took refuge on a hill and he drew a line of circumvallation around it and captured an immense number of them. Then he invaded Lusitania and gradually depopulated it. Galba did the same on the

other side. When some of their ambassadors came to him desiring to renew the treaty made with Atilius, his predecessor in the command, though they had transgressed this treaty, he received them favorably, and made a truce and pretended to sympathize with them because they had been compelled by poverty to rob, make war, and break their engagements. "For, of course," said he, "poorness of soil and penury forced you to do these things. If you wish to be friendly, I will give you a good land for your poor people and settle them in three divisions, in a fertile country."

Beguiled by these promises they left their own habitations and came together at the place where Galba directed. He divided them into three parts, and showing to each division a certain plain, he commanded them to remain in this open country until he should assign them their places. Then he came to the first division and told them as friends to lay down their arms. When they had done so he surrounded them with a ditch and sent in soldiers with swords who slew them all, they, meanwhile, crying aloud and invoking the names and faith of the gods. In like manner he hastened to the second and third divisions and destroyed them while they were still ignorant of the fate of the first. Thus he avenged treachery with treachery in a manner unworthy of a Roman, but imitating barbarians. A few escaped, among them Viriathus, who not long afterward became the leader of the Lusitanians and killed many Romans and performed the greatest exploits, which I shall relate hereafter. Galba, being even more greedy than Lucullus, distributed a little of the plunder to the army and a little to his friends and kept the rest himself, although he was already one of the richest of the Romans. Not even in time of peace, they say, did he abstain from lying and perjury in order to get gain. Although generally hated, and called to account for his rascalities, he escaped punishment by means of his wealth.

MODERN OPINIONS

14. BRUTAL IMPERIALISM*

The following selection is from the introduction to a collection of essays in which Carcopino offers his interpretation of Roman imperialism in general.

In my opinion the imperialism of the Romans was born in the minds of their leaders when, during the hard years of the struggle against Hannibal, it awoke to the idea of an irresistible pre-eminence. Scipio Africanus, the proconsul fortunate enough to defeat Carthage on its own territory, proud enough of his perpetually successful actions to feel a vocation to indefinite victory born in him, had meditated on the history of Alexander, and composed for himself an attitude of the soldier inspired by the gods who already called forth a comparison with the Macedonian hero. His fellow citizens still thought only of fighting to defend themselves against Philip V and against the Seleucids. Deep within them, however, he and his peers nursed the conviction, developed by years of unlimited authority and of campaigns without a reverse, that the people by whom they had been elected would no longer be willing to tolerate in their vicinity nations which were fully equal to their state. They were still in the process of subduing Spain when they began to impose themselves everywhere. In my first essay . . . I have tried to seize upon the moment, toward the end of the third century B.C., when the Romans, apparently disinterested, by means of the arrogance of their generals, became imperialists without wishing to do so.

During the thirty-five years that followed, we witness repeated manifestations

of this negative ambition. Under the pretext of defending their security, the Romans did not cease to affirm, with sword in hand, the latent primacy that they arrogated to themselves in its name. Successively they fought and defeated Philip V at Cynoscephalae (197 B.C.), Antiochus III the Great at Magnesia (190 B.C.), Perseus at Pydna (168 B.C.). Satisfied to destroy the forces capable of resisting them, they distributed to their allies the territories which they had taken from the vanquished and pretended to take nothing for themselves. From all those campaigns in which their legions accumulated laurels, they carried off only tiny acquisitions: Zante and Cephalonia. In the same way, England in 1715 and 1815 appropriated only the rock of Gibraltar and the island of Malta. But like the British Empire after the fall of Napoleon, the Roman Empire, which after the humiliation of the Hellenistic monarchies controlled by itself the destinies of the Oecumene, was virtually realized. We must not be deceived by the apparent renunciations of senatorial Rome. I have shown elsewhere, and I will return to them here, the crimes of its sterile and reticent megalomania, the ruin that it piled up everywhere without profit for anyone, and also the temptations which it could not completely repel and which, from the implications of a universal protectorate, must, in later generations, lead to systematic and brutal conquests.

So long as hostilities lasted, the generals plundered without shame. When they signed the peace they did not ask for land, but they required heavy and lasting indemnities. Then, in the triumphs that suc-

* Jérôme Carcopino, Points de vue sur l'impérialisme romain, Collection Saint-Germain-des Prés No. 12, pp. 10–13, Le Divan, 37 Rue Bonaparte, Paris, 1934, translated by Donald Kagan. Reprinted by permission of the publisher.

ceeded one another in the second century B.C., enormous quantities of gold and silver, carried on litters before the wondering throng in the form of coins, jewels, and bullion, played a conspicuous part in the procession that climbed up the Capitoline. And after 167 B.C., the Roman people stopped paying a tax rendered superfluous by payments coming from Macedonia. The booty and the tribute had begun to be levied only to mark the subjugation of the vanquished and to perpetuate it. They concluded by pleasing in themselves because they enriched the leaders and raised the level of the lives of all citizens. The same year that the Carthaginians completed the last of the fifty annual payments required of them by the treaty of 201 B.C., Rome decided to declare a war of extermination against them that would end with the creation of the province of Africa, several months after the creation of the province of Macedonia (146 B.C.). Certainly, among the number of feelings that drove her to

these atrocious resolutions, we must include fear; but the existence of powerful metropolises did not so much mar her tranquility as her unavowed dream of uncontestable leadership. But the method with which Mummius proceeded at the sack of Corinth and the distribution of the spoils will suffice to prove that Rome was already obedient to the desire to increase her riches and her pleasures by force of arms, a desire impossible to contain much longer.

Henceforth she was engaged in the terrible toils of conquest to the limit. Each country drawn up as a province, and as such subjected to her eminent domain, opened a new field of exploitation for Rome. The Roman people received revenues from each. The governors reconstituted or increased their patrimony. The tax collectors, entrepreneurs, bankers, traffickers of every kind, swooped down one by one . . . like crows on the bloody battlefield, after the battle.

15. PHILHELLENISM*

In fact a storm was gathering against Philip in the west, which did not permit him to continue the plundering of defenceless Egypt. The Romans, who had at length in this year concluded peace on their own terms with Carthage, began to give serious attention to these complications in the east. It has often been affirmed, that after the conquest of the west they forthwith proceeded to the subjugation of the east; a serious consideration will lead to a juster judgment. It is only dull prejudice which fails to see that Rome at this period by no means grasped at the sovereignty of the Mediterranean states, but, on the contrary, desired nothing

further than to have neighbours that should not be dangerous in Africa and in Greece; and Macedonia was not really dangerous to Rome. Its power certainly was far from small, and it is evident that the Roman senate only consented with reluctance to the peace of 548–9, which left it in all its integrity; but how little any serious apprehension of Macedonia were or could be entertained in Rome, is best shown by the small number of troops—who yet were never compelled to fight against a superior force—with which Rome carried on the next war. The senate doutbless would have gladly seen Macedonia humbled; but that humiliation would be too dearly purchased at the cost of a land war carried on in Macedonia with Roman troops; and accordingly, after the withdrawal of the Aetolians, the senate voluntarily concluded peace at once on the basis of the

* Theodor Mommsen, *The History of Rome*, translated by William Purdie Dickson (New York: Charles Scribner's Sons, 1911), Vol. 2, pp. 413–415; 442–443. Reprinted by permission of the publisher.

status quo. It is therefore far from made out, that the Roman government concluded this peace with the definite design of beginning the war at a more convenient season; and it is very certain that, at the moment, from the thorough exhaustion of the state and the extreme unwillingness of the citizens to enter into a second transmarine struggle, the Macedonian war was in a high degree unwelcome to the Romans. But now it was inevitable. They might have acquiesced in the Macedonian state as a neighbour, such as it stood in 549; but it was impossible that they could permit it to acquire the best part of Asiatic Greece and the important Cyrene, to crush the neutral commercial states, and thereby to double its power. Further, the fall of Egypt and the humiliation, perhaps the subjugation, of Rhodes would have inflicted deep wounds on the trade of Sicily and Italy; and could Rome remain a quiet spectator, while Italian commerce with the east was made dependent on the two great continental powers? Rome had, moreover, an obligation of honour to fulfil towards Attalus her faithful ally since the first Macedonian war, and had to prevent Philip, who had already besieged him in his capital, from expelling him from his dominions. Lastly, the claim of Rome to extend her protecting arm over all the Hellenes was by no means an empty phrase: the citizens of Neapolis, Rhegium, Massilia, and Emporiae could testify that that protection was meant in earnest, and there is no question at all that at this time the Romans stood in a closer relation to the Greeks than any other nation—one little more remote than that of the Hellenized Macedonians. It is strange that any should dispute the right of the Romans to feel their human, as well as their Hellenic, sympathies revolted at the outrageous treatment of the Cians and Thasians.

Thus in reality all political, commercial, and moral motives concurred in inducing Rome to undertake the second war against Philip—one of the most righteous, which the city ever waged. It greatly redounds to the honour of the senate, that it immediately resolved on its course and did not allow itself to be deterred from making the necessary preparations either by the exhaustion of the state or by the unpopularity of such a declaration of war.

* * *

It is only contemptible disingenuousness or weakly sentimentality, which can fail to perceive that the Romans were entirely in earnest with the liberation of Greece; and the reason why the plan so nobly projected resulted in so sorry a structure, is to be sought only in the complete moral and political disorganization of the Hellenic nation. It was no small matter, that a mighty nation should have suddenly with its powerful arm brought the land, which it had been accustomed to regard as its primitive home and as the shrine of its intellectual and higher interests, into the possession of full freedom, and should have conferred on every community in it deliverance from foreign taxation and foreign garrisons and the unlimited right of self-government; it is mere paltriness that sees in this nothing save political calculation. Political calculation made the liberation of Greece a possibility for the Romans; it was converted into a reality by the Hellenic sympathies that were at that time indescribably powerful in Rome, and above all in Flamininus himself. If the Romans are liable to any reproach, it is that all of them, and in particular Flamininus who overcame the well-founded scruples of the senate, were hindered by the magic charm of the Hellenic name from perceiving in all its extent the wretched character of the Greek states of that period, and so allowed yet further freedom for the doings of communities which, owing to the impotent antipathies that prevailed alike in their internal and their mutual relations, knew neither how to act nor how to keep quiet. As things stood, it was really necessary at once to put an end to such a freedom, equally pitiful and pernicious, by means of a superior power permanently present on the spot; the feeble policy of sentiment, with all its apparent humanity, was far more cruel than the sternest occupation would have been. In Boeotia for instance Rome had, if not to instigate, at least to permit, a political murder, because the Romans had resolved to withdraw their troops from Greece and, consequently, could not prevent the Greeks friendly to Rome from seeking their remedy in the usual manner of the country. But Rome herself also suffered from the effects of this indecision. The war with Antiochus would not have arisen but for the political blunder of liberating Greece, and it would not have been dangerous but for the military blunder of withdrawing the garrisons from the principal fortresses on the European frontier. History has a Nemesis for every sin—for an impotent craving after freedom, as well as for an injudicious generosity.

16. Sentimental Politics*

Finally, Athens became involved in a quarrel with Philip's ally, Acarnania, and being unable to protect herself against the attacks of the Macedonian army, she too sent envoys to Rome. Apparently all Greece felt that Rome had such cause to hate Philip that the appeal would not be in vain.

Could Rome heed the appeal? Even apart from the question of expedience, there were two very serious objections against aligning herself with the enemies of Philip: the strong disinclination of the people to undertake a new war, and the illegality of such a war from the point of view of the *ius fetiale*. The people would at first not hear of it, and voted down the motion. They had suffered too severely in the war just ended to desire a new one. The toll of dead and wounded had been appalling. Their fields were wasted. Taxes were high because of the interest on the public debt, and a part of the principal on that debt was already overdue. Experience had taught them that the state could no longer turn war into a profitable undertaking, since even the indemnity imposed upon Carthage would come in such small installments that they would hardly support one Roman legion. The populace yielded only when the leaders who favored the motion called the assembly together a second time and convinced them that Philip would invade Italy and devastate their fields as Hannibal had done, unless they forestalled him.

The second objection, that of legality, was also serious, for the people were not in a mood to invite the wrath of heaven by breaking the sacred injunctions of the *ius fetiale*. The difficulty lay in the fact that the rules of the sacred college did not permit of any except defensive wars—that is, wars in defense of the state and her oath-bound *socii* of good standing; and the appealing nations in this case were not *socii*, they were only *amici*. The importance of this distinction may be brought out by a brief review of Rome's international policy. Since the old fetial rules had recognized only defensive wars, the state had built up its federation hitherto on defensive alliances, and had always been averse to treaties of mere neutrality or friendship. The *foedera* varied somewhat in content, granting privileges according to the deserts of the ally, but, wherever Rome had her own way, they were invariably based upon the central stipulation of mutual defense in case of an enemy's incursion. This form of treaty she had been able to impose upon every one of her hundred allies in Italy, and these alliances held "for all time." The *ius fetiale* was accordingly the dominant

* Tenney Frank, *Roman Imperialism* (New York: The Macmillan Company, 1914), pp. 145–151. Reprinted by permission of the publisher.

factor in the Italian federation. When, however, Rome met strong foreign nations which had for centuries employed other forms of treaties, she found that these nations were far from willing to make alliances with her at her own very exacting terms. If now Rome insisted upon her old practices, she would obviously be excluded from political association with the older nations. At first she was ready to accept an inferior advantage for the sake of retaining the old form, and thus in the case of the south Italian Greeks and Naples, she bound herself to protective duty, although requiring none from her ally. But with nations farther off, this was out of the question. Hence, during her distressing contest with Philip of Macedonia, she had signed alliances of *amicitia* and short-term *foedera* with the Greek states according to the Greek customs. But now the question came up as to the standing of these *amici* in fetial law. The Greek practice, whereby *amici* made free to form temporary coalitions against a common danger, seemed much more reasonable than Rome's; and several Roman admirals who had campaigned in the First Macedonian war with King Attalus and various Greek admirals had had every occasion to learn the advantages of these coalitions. They knew that Rome could never assume a dignified place among the time-honored nations unless she were willing to participate in the Hellenic coalitions. Doubtless the senators who were experienced in diplomacy wished to break away from the old restrictions. But the fact remained that for a thousand years the Romans had acted on the belief that an infraction of the *ius fetiale* would bring a curse upon the state. Nevertheless, the Macedonian problem was referred to the fetial priests, and they were apparently influenced by the new school. They decided to disregard the vital distinction between *societas* and *amicitia* and to extend, for the present occasion, the provisions of the *ius fetiale* over the *amici*. It is characteristic of Roman legal-mindedness that the Romans

then began to substitute the delusive phrase *socius et amicus*—which had hitherto had no legal standing—for the simple word *amicus*. They would stretch the fetial law to new needs, but they dared not disregard it.

Having thus convinced the populace of the necessity of the war and allayed their fears regarding the sacrilege it might incur, the Roman senate sent three envoys to investigate conditions and to consult with the appealing powers at Athens. It is apparent that the senate gave the envoys general instructions to work for peace in the Ægean and to demand reparation for injuries done, but left the exact wording of the stipulations to the judgment of the envoys after they should have consulted with the injured states. At the Piræus the Roman legates spent a day with Attalus, who, together with the Rhodian envoys, then persuaded the Athenians to declare war. The advice of Attalus was apparently based upon instructions, or at least promises, given by the Romans. Philip answered the declaration by sending a force to attack Athens, whereupon the Roman envoys delivered their decision in the name of the senate that Philip must not wage war with any Greek state and must submit the claims of Attalus to arbitration (Pol. XVI, 27). The phrasing of this deliverance shows clearly the results of the day's interview with Attalus. His claims alone are mentioned, and the particularistic doctrine that he advocated is adopted outright. Thus it was Attalus upon whom the responsibility for the phrasing of the proclamation rested. To the senate, which had determined upon war with Philip in any case if he continued to play his reckless game, the exact wording was not important, provided it accomplished its purpose, satisfied the appellants, and secured the greatest possible support for the common cause.

The envoys, following the old Roman custom of proclaiming international demands to all concerned, sailed the length of the coast of Greece, announcing their ultimatum—doubtless to the amusement of the more sophisticated Greeks—and then proceeded to Rhodes. A conference with the Rhodians resulted in the addition of two items suggested by the interests of that republic, and from this it is apparent that a full understanding with Rhodes had not been reached at the Athenian conference. The new demands were that the Rhodian claims, like those of Attalus, be submitted to arbitration, and that Philip cease interfering with the possessions of Ptolemy. These combined demands Æmilius Lepidus presented to Philip in the spring of 200 when the king was besieging the free city of Abydos. As the ultimatum was greeted with scorn, Rome declared war and sent her consul with an army to Illyricum, even before Philip had returned home from his sack of Abydos.

But what after all induced the senate to entangle itself in a new war when the state had just barely escaped destruction by Hannibal? This is a question upon which our sources are far from satisfactory. Livy holds that Rome was bound by her treaties to aid Greek states, but we now know that her treaties of *amicitia* with them entailed no such obligations. The senate, according to the same author, told the populace that Philip was on the point of invading Italy, but the senate could hardly have thought such an invasion imminent. Polybius, the Greek, to whom a coalition of friendly states seems wholly natural, does not even pause to set himself the question. Modern historians are, therefore, left to their own conjectures. We are told, on the one hand, that the senate's decision was due to an outburst of sentimental philhellenism, and, on the other hand, that the real motive power was greed for empire hidden under a veil of hypocrisy. One distinguished historian affirms that Rome was forced by her position to accept the appeals of the Greeks, another that Rome's interference was as criminal as the brigandage of Philip which she undertook to suppress. What shall we believe?

That the senate desired mere territorial expansion we cannot assume, since Rome took no land after the war, not even claiming Illyricum, which Philip had won from her in 205. There was, besides, more devastated land in Italy awaiting development than the capitalistic investments of Rome could hope to care for within a generation.

The impulse eastward came from other considerations. Rome had no love for Philip, and the desire to punish him for his treacherous attack at a time when she was defenseless must have been strong. The acknowledgment of defeat in 205 and the cession of the Illyrian mainland still rankled. Of course a treaty of peace had been made in 205, so that the preceding events could hardly be openly avowed as cause for hostility; but if both ancient and modern historians have excused the Barcids for keeping in mind the seizure of Sardinia, we must grant that Rome had even greater cause for resentment against Philip.

Mingled with this hatred of Philip was Rome's fear that his aggression might soon have to be met. Of course, we need not believe that an invasion of Italy was imminent. But Philip was a man of singular daring and force, and the Greeks had found him a lawless neighbor. In the year 201 he had a long series of victories to his credit: he had reëstablished the Macedonian power throughout the extent of Greece; he had gained control of the northern Ægean, the entrance to the Black Sea, Thrace, and several strongholds of Asia Minor. The Eastern world was, it seemed, about to be divided between him and Antiochus. That he had inherited the ambitions of Alexander was a matter of everyday talk. The question for the senate to decide was not whether Rome might weaken a possible rival,—as yet Rome thought only of becoming a member of the Mediterranean concert of powers,—but whether Philip, her neighbor, was a man who observed the laws of neutrality and respected the ordinary rights of his neighbors. This Philip did not do. And Rome knew from her own experience with him and from the tales of the Greek envoys that Philip would honor his treaty with her only so long as she was in a position to defend herself.

But Rome had another reason besides fear and hatred of Philip for greeting this opportunity of entering the East. The Romans felt bitterly the slur conveyed in the term *barbari* which the Greeks still applied to them. They counted for nothing in the civilized world. In the voluminous world histories that Greek writers published year after year, every petty incident of effete Greek villages was recorded in detail, whereas Rome's epoch-making transactions were relegated to parentheses and explanatory notes. Her heroes still remained unsung *carent quia vate sacro*. Entrance into the Ægean concert of powers would change all this, adding immeasurably to the dignified position of the state, gaining it prestige among the old-world civilizations, and, incidentally, ministering to the pride of Roman senators. We need not assume that the nobles whom such considerations influenced were aiming at any definite material advantages. Men like the Scipios, Flamininus, the Fabii, and Paulus did not have palms itching for gold, but they were to some degree touched by "that last infirmity" of all Romans; such men it was who stamped the Roman character on the words *gloria, fama*, and *dignitas*. They now saw the door open to a more dignified position. Who shall say that such enticements do not often outweigh economic considerations in world politics?

Finally, the great historian was doubtless right who pointed out the importance of philhellenism as a factor in the decision. Never at Rome was the enthusiasm for things Greek so outspoken as during this time. The performance of Greek tragedies and comedies in translations good, bad, and indifferent promised to become the national form of festival entertainment. The fountain of native literature was well-nigh choked by the wholesale importation of Greek products, and the entire nation was assimilating the form and substance of a transmarine art with an avidity that can hardly be paralleled. Even Roman senators began to write their nation's history in Greek. And the Hellenic culture was being woven into the very fabric of Roman institutions. The Roman gods had been identified with those of Greece, and the priests conducted many of the sacred rites *Graeco ritu*. The oracle at Delphi was resorted to as a final court of appeal in times of danger, and the Greek legends were being grafted into the main stock of Rome's national tradition. Later, to be sure, a day came when familiarity with the *Graeculus* bred contempt, and the discovery was made that Roman character was surrendering some of its best elements in exchange for an ill-fitting culture which carried corruption within. But that was later. In the year 200 men felt only the magic of Greece, and the appeal of the Greek states for aid in preserving their liberty struck a chord of response full of genuine good will for the imperiled people. Nor did this feeling subside during the war: within two years the senate enlarged its demands upon Philip by requiring not only that he desist from his attacks upon Greeks, but also that he liberate those whom he held in subjection.

These, then, were the motives that led the senate to abandon its ancient fetial practices, to adopt the Greek methods of international association, and to enter the Hellenic concert. And it must be borne in mind that this was not a war between Philip and Rome, but—in the beginning, at least—a war conducted by an Hellenic coalition of which Rome was but a modest member, participating with only a small part of her forces.

17. DEFENSIVE WAR*

In the late summer 201 Pergamene and Rhodian envoys appeared before the Senate.

Careful of their dignity, the *patres* deferred giving any promise, but their decision was taken at once. About November Sulpicius Galba was re-elected consul; this meant that he would be commander in a new Macedonian war. 'Macedonia' was indeed one of the consular provinces and fell to him.

The decision of the Senate, on the morrow of the struggle against Carthage, with people and army war-weary and longing for peace, the treasury empty, the state-creditors restive, is most astonishing—the more so since Rome had certainly no grievance against Philip. The force he is said to have sent to Hannibal before Zama, and his aggressions against certain unnamed 'Greek allies of Rome,' are merely clumsy fabrications of later times, invented to justify the hostile behaviour of the Roman government. In reality, fearing Rome greatly, Philip kept peace with her most correctly. As for his conflict with Attalus and Rhodes, that obviously could not justify the armed intervention of the Romans. Rhodes had naturally no title to their assistance; Attalus, included in the recent peace, might claim it in principle, but, in fact, he—like the Rhodians—in attacking Philip had been the aggressor. This war, decided upon so quickly, was thus without legitimate cause; it was simply willed by the Senate. A year earlier, they had apparently no thought of it: otherwise they would have forgotten for the moment their grievances against Aetolia (as later in 200), and would have listened to her complaints against Philip. Thus their conversion to a warlike policy was sudden indeed.

_____

* Maurice Holleaux, *Cambridge Ancient History* (Cambridge, England: Cambridge University Press, 1930), Vol. 8, pp. 156–160; 237–240. Reprinted by permission of the publisher.

The reason for this change—evidently a strong one—is not directly known, for the explanations given by our sources are quite untrustworthy; it can only be inferred from an examination of the circumstances. The present writer would therefore indicate what seems to him the most probable.

Attalus, a warm friend of Rome, the Rhodians, serious, sensible, trusted and esteemed, inspired confidence in the Senate. Knowing little of eastern affairs, the *patres* must have listened attentively to their representatives; doubtless their arguments greatly influenced the Roman decision, and we can conjecture, with some probability, what they were. Apparently the envoys laid little stress on the grievances of Attalus and Rhodes against Philip, since these were unlikely to move the Senate, which would care little about the seizure by Philip of some Hellespontine or Asiatic town whose very name was unknown in Rome. Wishing to persuade them to fight Philip immediately, they must have reviewed the matter from the standpoint of Roman interests, showing how dangerous inaction would be to Rome, and how easy it was to act at once. Rhodes and Attalus had got wind of the compact between Antiochus and Philip; they had good reasons for doubting its stability, but their envoys could use it to frighten the Senate. According to them, Antiochus was a conqueror from whom anything might be feared; his understanding with Philip constituted a certain danger for Rome. At the moment, the two kings aspired to make Egypt their prey, but, once strengthened by its spoils, what might they not do? Would not Philip, ever the enemy of Rome, bring in Antiochus against her? She must break this threatening alliance by crushing the ally within reach. Antiochus was just then occupied in Syria, Philip, much weakened, blockaded in Caria—it was a fine opportunity to invade Macedonia. If

Philip succeeded in returning home, his defeat would nevertheless be swiftly achieved. Rome would have with her, besides the Pergamene and Rhodian fleets, the Aetolians thirsting for vengeance, Amynander who had recently quarrelled with Philip, and, of course, the barbarian enemies of Macedonia. Moreover, Philip's Greek allies now hated him; his crimes at Cius and Thasos aroused their common horror; all Greece, doubtless, would join Rome.

The ambassadors could not fail to move the senators by talking of Antiochus. Rome had no relations with him, but his resounding fame had long made them uneasy. Laevinus and Sulpicius had many times in Greece heard first the Aetolians, then Attalus, relate his exploits; Laevinus was in Pergamum when Antiochus returned from the Far East; and the Alexandrians had recently asked for protection against him. The Romans were very ready to see an enemy in every monarch, and Antiochus, so powerful, fortunate, and undoubtedly of unbounded ambitions, seemed especially disquieting. They pictured him lord of the fabulous treasures, the unnumbered hosts of Asia; he reminded them at once of Xerxes and of Alexander; above all, he was for them the unknown that is terrible. When they heard that he was secretly in league with Philip, his hostility to them seemed beyond doubt. Conqueror of the East, he would assuredly dispute the West with Rome, thus helping Philip to his revenge.

Therefore it was necessary to take prompt measures to counteract this danger, profit by Antiochus' momentary absence to act against Philip—not to destroy him (a too difficult and lengthy undertaking), but cripple him and, further, drive him from Greece. Greece which had hitherto meant little to the Senate, since they did not fear Philip alone, suddenly assumed peculiar importance: it was the natural point of concentration for the two kings, their common base against Italy.

They must, accordingly, be prevented from using it, and it must at the same time be brought under Roman control. Not that there was any question of subjugating it— that would have been to provide Philip and Antiochus with the profitable rôle of 'liberator.' This rôle Rome would assume herself; she would restore Greek freedom, destroyed or restricted by Philip, thereby securing the enthusiastic gratitude of the Greeks, and then constitute herself their permanent protectress. Liberated and shielded by Rome, Greece would be closed to the kings, Rome's enemies, closed to Antiochus if, after Philip's defeat, he should pursue alone the aggressive designs concerted with him.

Such, it seems, were the fears and calculations which gave rise to the warlike policy of the Senate, hitherto so little inclined to entangle itself in Eastern affairs. Apparently aggressive, but really preventive, its object was to checkmate the dangerous purposes attributed to Antiochus and Philip, and, with this aim, make Greece the outwork of Italy's defences to the East. It is, however, quite possible that these leading motives were reinforced by subsidiary considerations of sentiment: the longing to cancel an inglorious peace and punish Philip for his alliance with Carthage, a proud desire in some Romans to conquer the unconquerable Macedonians, and also accomplish something spectacular in extending Roman primacy over the illustrious peoples of Greece. Of an over-romantic ardent sympathy for the Greeks, Philip's victims, such as is often attributed to the Senate, the present writer can find no clear evidence. The Roman nobility had steeped itself in Hellenic culture, but had no tenderness for Greeks, as the late war had shown plainly enough Their philhellenism confined itself to things of the spirit, and was not allowed to be a factor in their public actions. They were, it is true, going to use against Philip a 'philhellenic' policy, but only as Hannibal, for instance, had used a 'philitalian' policy against Rome—because it suited their purpose, not through love of Greece.

However urgent may have been Attalus and the Rhodians, Rome could not begin the war before 200 B.C. The Senate had first to make ready for it. Military preparation was easy: Macedonia was known to be drained of men, and if Philip returned before the Romans arrived, he would only dispose of a very limited field-army, the more as he would have to garrison his many strongholds in Greece. It would be long enough to pit against him a normal consular army of two legions, especially as Rome counted upon numerous allies; and this army would partly be raised by the enlistment, nominally voluntary, of veterans returning from Africa. As for the fleet, Pergamene and Rhodian assistance would allow of its reduction to some 50 warships. Under such conditions the war would cost little. However, as the treasury was depleted, the repayment of loans contracted during the Hannibalic War had to be suspended, and to disarm the opposition of creditors the Senate decided to indemnify them by large concessions of public land.

There remained the main achievement of statecraft, the political preparation for the war, that is the creation in peace time of a clash between Rome and Philip which would inevitably result in war. This seemed a difficult problem; for, as we have noticed, Rome had no grievance against Philip, and if the Senate desired war, it stood alone in desiring it. Philip would do anything to avoid war if he were allowed to negotiate, and would not shrink from even considerable concessions provided they were not dishonouring. As for the Roman people, upon whose vote everything ultimately depended, its feelings were entirely peaceful. In this apparently embarrassing situation the Senate, despite what has often been asserted, experienced no difficulty; supreme in matters of foreign policy and unhampered by scruples, it manœuvred so that Philip and the Roman citizens were driven into a war which neither desired. It had only to present to Philip, without previous negotiation, an offensive ultimatum based on an imaginary *casus belli*, then use his refusal to comply with it to secure the people's vote for war.

* * *

According to a generally accepted opinion, the decisive struggle in which Rome engaged, first against Macedonia, then against Syria, was, in essence, not indeed a struggle for territorial aggrandizement, but a struggle for wealth and even more for power, initiated by the imperialistic ambition of the Senate. And the results of the Macedonian and Syrian Wars would, at first sight, seem to justify this opinion. That the Romans, in waging these wars, did not yield to a desire for territorial expansion, is unquestionably true. Beyond the Adriatic they limited themselves to the recovery of Lower Illyria, of which they had become masters in 228, adding to it only the two island dependencies of Zacynthus and Cephallenia—modest acquisitions indeed: in Greece, Macedonia, Asia, where they might have seized land at their pleasure, they took nothing; this is conclusive. On the other hand, these wars were highly lucrative. The indemnities and booty of their defeated enemies caused vast wealth to pour into Rome. In ten years alone (197 to 187) the minted and unminted gold and silver paid into the treasury exceeded 90 million *denarii*, and to this must be added the multitude of works of art and precious objects of incalculable value, which lent such unexampled brilliance to the triumphs of Flamininus, L. Scipio 'Asiagenus', Manlius and Fulvius. And above all, these wars had political consequences infinitely more important than any pecuniary benefits. Following upon the defeat of Carthage, they brought about the supreme control of the Roman people over the civilized world. The supremacy of Rome by land and sea

γῆς καὶ θαλάσσης σκῆπτρα καὶ μοναρχίαν

already sung by the poet Lycophron on the morrow of Cynoscephalae was an established fact after Magnesia.

The Romans were certainly not indifferent to money (as is proved by the example of Manlius and Fulvius) or to power: their victory over Antiochus, the thought that they had no longer a rival, filled them with pride. Yet it does not follow nor does it seem probable to the present writer that it was greed of wealth and empire which determined their course of action. Indeed it is most noteworthy that they never thought of turning their victories to economic advantage: the treaties which they made contained no commercial stipulation in their own favour (though the treaty of Apamea contained one in favour of Rhodes), and they did not impose tribute on any of the peoples whom they conquered—a sufficiently clear proof that in deciding on their policy they were little if at all obsessed by thoughts of gain. And, as we have seen, not one of their political acts from 200 to 188 bears the clear stamp of imperialism or cannot be explained except by a passion for domination. The attribution to the Senate of 'Eastern plans' or of a 'Mediterranean programme' which it was only waiting for a favourable opportunity to carry out, is no more than arbitrary conjecture, unsupported by the facts. There is nothing to show that in 200 the *patres* were more attracted than before to Greek lands or that their eastern policy, hitherto entirely dictated by the needs of the moment, changed its character at that date. Everything leads us to believe that then, as before, their intervention was merely the result of external circumstances which seemed to impose action upon them. As in 229 they would not have crossed the Adriatic but for the provocation offered them by Teuta, and in 214 would not have gone into Greece but for the necessity of countering the alliance of Philip with Hannibal, so, in all likelihood, they would not have turned eastward again but for

their discovery of the alliance between Philip and Antiochus and the threat which they saw in it.

The truth is that they imagined themselves to be threatened when they were not. The insincere alliance of the two kings was in no way aimed at them; and, moreover, when they did allow it to alarm them, it was already breaking down. If their intervention had been less prompt, they would probably have seen the erstwhile allies open enemies: a war would have broken out between them, which would have freed Rome from all anxiety from that quarter. In any event, as is shown by his prompt seizure of Lysimacheia, Philip would have prevented Antiochus from setting foot in Europe, and so would have vanished even the phantom of that 'Seleucid peril' which, from the first, was the constant preoccupation of the Romans. Indeed it was their act, when they crippled Philip thinking thereby to weaken Antiochus, that allowed the latter a free road westwards and enabled him to cross the Hellespont. But, even then, there was, as we have seen, no real Seleucid peril. If it ever existed, it was in 192, when the Great King marched down into Greece with Hannibal in his train, and it was again the Romans who created it by their errors of policy, the fruit of their vain alarms. To guard against an imaginary threat of aggression they were unconscionably persistent in urging Antiochus to withdraw from Europe and their offensive insistence only succeeded in exhausting his patience. By an ironic paradox, the two enterprises which brought them so much glory and laid the foundation of their world-supremacy had their origin in a groundless fear. Had they been more keensighted and less easily alarmed, they would not have come to dominate the Hellenic world. More probably they would have concentrated their efforts in the neighbouring barbarian countries west of Italy —and that with more reason and more advantage to themselves.

If they were thus misled by unfounded

fears it was due partly to the suspicious temper of the Senate which inclined them to detect only too readily dangerous neighbours plotting the ruin of Rome, partly to their profound ignorance of eastern affairs. The *patres* had omitted to inform themselves about these matters, and strangely neglected for a long time to do so—one is surprised to find, for example, that in 196 they had not got wind of the treaty about to be concluded between Antiochus and Egypt. Lacking the knowledge necessary for forming an opinion of their own, they believed what they were told and were curiously swayed by foreign influences. This was no new thing: it has been maintained, and with much probability, that the quarrel between Rome and Carthage over Spain was largely due to the reports and intrigues of the Massiliotes in

Rome. It is even more certain that the real authors of the Second Macedonian War were Attalus and Rhodes, and that the war against Antiochus was mainly the work of Eumenes—the same Eumenes who was to have so large a hand in bringing about the war against Perseus. So far as the East is concerned, the Senate, so jealous of its authority and reputed so clear-sighted, only saw through the eyes of others and only acted upon the impulse of others—of others who had an interest in impelling it to act. After 200 B.C. in their eastern policy the Romans, little as they knew it, followed where others led: while they thought they were only providing for the safety of Rome, they were, in reality, serving the cause and furthering the interests of Pergamum and Rhodes.

18. FEAR AND HATRED*

We now come to the outbreak of the Second Macedonian War; and the events that led up to it are surpassed in obscurity only by its causes. The former—fortunately—do not concern us as such; at the latter we must glance before proceeding.

We have seen that the Peace of Phoenice did not, as Holleaux thought, mark the end of Roman interest in Greece and the East. He has, indeed, only one main argument in support of his view: the treatment of the Aetolian embassy that came to ask for Roman support, probably in 202. But, even if this embassy is historical—which is far from certain—, we know nothing about its outcome except that Rome did not help the Aetolians, probably on the grounds that the alliance no longer existed. This, however, is not surprising, especially considering that Roman attention must have been concentrated on North Africa, where (before Zama) the war was not by any

means decided. To involve herself, at this critical time, in a war with Philip, by the side of allies who (apart from all else) had already shown themselves unable to stand up to him, would be inexcusable folly and might well endanger the situation in Illyria which Rome was so carefully maintaining; for the Hannibalic War had strained Italian manpower to the utmost and, until the war was finished, there was no certainty that the strain would not again increase. The historian knows that there was no danger: the Senate knew only the past.

Roman interest in the East was limited to securing Illyria and merely watching Greece. The Senate had wanted peace with Philip. But now Philip had shown that peace with him was dangerous: if he were allowed to continue his activities, the whole of Illyria might change its allegiance. This was the state of affairs when Rhodes and Attalus sent envoys in 201, reporting Philip's aggression in the East and his 'pact' with Antiochus. Action was quick

* E. Badian, *Foreign Clientelae* (*264–70* B.C.) (Clarendon, 1958), pp. 62–69. Reprinted by permission of The Clarendon Press, Oxford.

and bellicose. Galba, a 'Macedonian expert', was elected consul, and in the spring of next year a Roman embassy crossed to Greece and visited Philip's most important Greek allies, proclaiming the new Roman policy, a statement of which they finally handed to the King's general, Nicanor. They met Attalus at Athens and seem to have given him some assurances; but they had to be careful, especially as the Roman Assembly had not yet voted for war. They then stayed in Rhodes, where they were informed that this vote had at last been passed; thereupon they sent Lepidus (one of their members) to deliver the formal declaration of war to Philip, and proceeded to Syria and Egypt—for what purpose and with what results is uncertain, but certainly in connexion with the war about to begin. This quick decision to attack Philip need not surprise us as much as it surprises those who attribute to the Fathers a complete lack of interest in the East between 205 and 201. But it is, in any case, a change and needs explaining. No one line of explanation, though, is enough. Holleaux attributes it to fear of the pact between Philip and Antiochus, which the Rhodian and Pergamene envoys announced in Rome; Rome, he thinks, tended to believe that all kings were the natural enemies of the Republic. Though there is little evidence for such a belief—only of anti-Roman propaganda attributing it to Rome—and it is indeed absurd to imagine anything of the sort at a time when Rome was about to wage war in defence of Attalus, it is no doubt true that rumour of the pact with the remote and famed Antiochus must have made Philip seem a potential threat. But we must not overstress this: for Philip had not fared too well in his Eastern campaign, and there had been little trace of any help for him from the Seleucid. Attalus and Rhodes knew this, and the Romans must have heard of it before their army crossed the Adriatic. Yet they decided to prosecute the war. Nor did they at any time fear an invasion

of Italy: for no preparations (such as we shall later meet before the war with Antiochus) were made to counter such a threat. Griffith, recognizing the insufficiency of this motive, has added to it Roman fear of Philip's renewed naval power. This can hardly have been very important: in 201 Rome had no interests in the Aegean, and a fleet operating there was not the sort of thing to frighten the Senate into war—especially as that fleet had shown its inability to master those of Rhodes and Pergamum, and as it had, in any case, contained only fifty-three cataphracts even before the battle of Chios and ceased to be a danger after it.

These and other reasons may in varying degrees have influenced the Senate—but none of them seems sufficient to justify a major war at a time when Roman manpower and economic resources needed nothing more than recovery. And we are driven to recognizing that the Illyrian situation contains a main part of the answer to our question: the Senate had tried a policy of peace with Philip and failed, and now war seemed inevitable. Besides, more irrational motives must (as so often) have played an important part. Philip had tried to stab Rome in the back when she was, he thought, on the point of defeat by Hannibal. And the Romans did not forgive their enemies, especially those whom they thought treacherous. We shall see, in the case of the Third Punic War, how the spirit of stark hatred could intervene in Roman politics, even against political interest. In the same way, we may well believe, many senators in 201 may have felt that the time for their revenge had come: Philip was in trouble in the East and had made powerful enemies; Rome had defeated her only great antagonist—it was time to pay the King back in his own coin. Who were the propounders of this policy, we cannot tell with certainty. It has been suggested that Scipio was opposed to it. But there is no evidence for this, and indeed it is not certain that he, with experience only of war and diplomacy in the West, had any set Eastern policy on his return. Galba and Tuditanus, the principal Eastern experts, supported it: Galba was made consul and sent to Greece; Tuditanus was on the mission which presented the ultimatum and visited Syria and Egypt. Cotta, the other consul, was related to M. Cotta, whom we found in Illyria: the aggressive policy, it seems, had the support of the 'Eastern lobby'. It was these men, no doubt, who knew Philip's weakness and who had discovered how the Greeks could be turned against him, especially at a time when his treachery and cruelty had already made a strong impression upon them. It was they, moreover, who knew that Illyria would only be safe when Macedon had been humbled.

The method chosen to achieve this appears in the ultimatum which the Roman mission proclaimed to the principal leagues of Greece and finally handed to Nicanor. Philip was not to wage war on any Greeks and was to submit his dispute with Attalus to arbitration; only on these conditions could he live in peace with Rome. The subtlety of these conditions is greater than has sometimes been seen: for some historians have thought them brutal demands, running counter to all justice to such an extent as to ensure rejection and war. But it is clear that Rome did not want war, if the same result could be achieved peacefully: it was perhaps unlikely that the terms would be accepted—for Rome had no legal *locus standi*, and Philip would see their long-range implications; but if they were, so much the better. The caution of the Roman embassy at Athens is not due *entirely* to the fact that they 'had to drive two unwilling parties into conflict, the Roman people and Philip': it may have been partly due to hopes of a peace with honour and advantage. For the real aim, as is seen in the peace made after the war, was to make Philip into a client prince and (as an inevitable consequence) Greece into a protectorate.

There is nothing harsh in the request that Philip's differences with Attalus should be discussed ἐν ἴσῳ κριτηρίῳ: Holleaux, and those who follow him, must not be allowed to usurp the function of the court that never sat and—without evidence—persuade us of Philip's innocence. Much—even the respective chronology of the battles of Lade and Chios—has been made to hinge on this assertion; yet, on investigation, we must suspend judgement. For all we know is that Attalus' fleet was present at Chios, but not at Lade; that Philip invaded Pergamene territory; and that Theophiliscus of Rhodes persuaded Attalus to take strong action. We do not know the order of these events, and we do not know what action is referred to. We have only Philip's word against the Senate's (i.e. that of Attalus' envoys). And in any case, it is more than likely that Rhodes and Attalus could make out a *prima facie* case. The Senate's proposal, whatever the true facts, was not 'in plain contradiction' to what facts it was likely to know. Nor does the other demand go as far as has been suggested; for it only means that Philip should cease attacking Greek states. It is wildly extravagant to claim that this simple demand 'by implication . . . declared unjustified all former wars waged by himself or his predecessors against Greeks, and thus denied validity to the result of their victories'. It might as easily be claimed that present-day demands that certain powers should stop their policy of aggression seek to confine the powers concerned to their frontiers of several hundred years ago. In fact there is not even the more moderate claim of the 'freedom of the Hellenes': Rome had not yet moved quite as far as that.

In fact the Roman ultimatum is only a further extension of an old Roman political idea, which we have seen at work quite often: just as, originally, Rome had invented a method of evading the requirements of fetial law—that wars must be waged only in defence of one's own or of allied territory—by making alliances with, and thereby assuming 'legitimate' protection over, states actually facing attack, so now states were unilaterally taken under Roman protection without even the formality of a treaty. This is a natural consequence of the greater elasticity that Roman diplomatic categories had acquired since 264, though its practical effect was, of course, to do away with the last restrictions (except purely formal ones) which fetial law imposed upon policy. In the two generations since Roman armies first crossed the sea, the system of the Confederacy, already made less rigid by the ambiguous status of the Latins after 338, had—as we have seen—been practically abandoned as far as further expansion was concerned. Instead, there had grown up a system of informal connexion with free states, beginning in Sicily and further tested in Illyria, the elastic obligations of which fitted into the Roman habits of social thought which we know as 'clientela' and, while thus acquiring moral sanction, also fitted in well with the practical requirements of power politics. As this system was extended and became firmly established, it even transformed by its influence the earlier concept of *amicitia*—which Rome knew well, e.g. in the case of Massilia or Egypt—until the Romans could no longer imagine the co-existence of genuinely equal states: her *amici* could only be her clients.

But this was still in the future. In the meantime, Rome presented her ultimatum on behalf of her new friends, the Greeks. If Philip rejected it—as was likely—, it meant war; and Rome was prepared and had a fair cause and good allies. If he accepted it—and, as we have seen, it was not so intolerably harsh as to preclude this —and withdrew from his new conquests, he would cease to be a danger and become dependent on Rome, though to all appearances still a powerful monarch. For his schemes of expansion in the East would have gone the way of those in the West; and to the Greeks he would be the humbled aggressor and Rome the champion—a reversal of roles which his influence even among his old Greek allies could not long survive. However, despite all this it might have been better for him to accept humiliation and wait for his chance—Rome's clash with Antiochus, and the reversal of Greek feeling, both of which he might have promoted. But he was outraged by Roman arrogance and faithlessness and decided on war.

The war thus arose from a complex of causes; principally Roman fear and Roman hatred, but also Philip's decision not to submit. Rome, though she had no legal justification for it, created a pretext by an extension of traditional practice—an extension which, though legally perhaps unwarranted, is historically quite comprehensible in the light of the development of Roman diplomatic categories since 264. And this, in the course of war, led to that important event, the 'liberation' of the Greeks.

SECTION VII

The Roman Revolution—Phase One:
The Gracchi

THE CHANGES that the second century had brought Rome both at home and in foreign affairs produced problems—economic, social, political, and constitutional—which demanded attention. The senatorial government was slow to move toward their solution, and the first major attempt at reform was not undertaken until 133 B.C. under the leadership of Tiberius Gracchus. Events soon made it clear that the alternative to reform was revolution, and the collapse of the Republic had begun. What were the true causes of the crisis? Who was responsible for the violence that ensued? Were the Gracchi reformers or revolutionaries?

1. APPIAN ON THE GRACCHAN CRISIS*

The Romans, as they subdued the Italian nations successively in war, seized a part of their lands and built towns there, or established their own colonies in those already existing, and used them in place of garrisons. Of the land acquired by war they assigned the cultivated part forthwith to settlers, or leased or sold it. Since they had no leisure as yet to allot the part which then lay desolated by war (this was generally the greater part), they made proclamation that in the meantime those who were willing to work it might do so for a share of the yearly crops—a tenth of the grain and a fifth of the fruit. From those who kept flocks was required a share of the animals, both oxen and small cattle. They did these things in order to multiply the Italian race, which they considered the most laborious of peoples, so that they might have plenty of allies at home. But the very opposite thing happened; for the rich, getting possession of the greater part of the undistributed lands, and being emboldened by the lapse of time to believe that they would never be dispossessed, and adding to their holdings the small farms of their poor neighbors, partly by purchase and partly by force, came to cultivate vast tracts instead of single estates, using for this purpose slaves as laborers and herdsmen, lest free laborers should be drawn from agriculture into the army. The ownership of slaves itself brought them great gain from the multitude of their

* Appian, *Civil War*, 1. 7–27, translated by Horace White (London and New York: The Macmillan Company, 1899), pp. 5–22.

197

progeny, who increased because they were exempt from military service. Thus the powerful ones became enormously rich and the race of slaves multiplied throughout the country, while the Italian people dwindled in numbers and strength, being oppressed by penury, taxes, and military service. If they had any respite from these evils they passed their time in idleness, because the land was held by the rich, who employed slaves instead of freemen as cultivators.

For these reasons the people became troubled lest they should no longer have sufficient allies of the Italian stock, and lest the government itself should be endangered by such a vast number of slaves. Not perceiving any remedy, as it was not easy, nor exactly just, to deprive men of so many possessions they had held so long, including their own trees, buildings, and fixtures, a law was once passed with difficulty at the instance of the tribunes, that nobody should hold more than 500 jugera of this land, or pasture on it more than 100 cattle or 500 sheep. To ensure the observance of this law it was provided also that there should be a certain number of freemen employed on the farms, whose business it should be to watch and report what was going on. Those who held possession of lands under the law were required to take an oath to obey the law, and penalties were fixed for violating it, and it was supposed that the remaining land would soon be divided among the poor in small parcels. But there was not the smallest consideration shown for the law or the oaths. The few who seemed to pay some respect to them conveyed their lands to their relations fraudulently, but the greater part disregarded it altogether.

At length Tiberius Sempronius Gracchus, an illustrious man, eager for glory, a most powerful speaker, and for these reasons well known to all, delivered an eloquent discourse, while serving as tribune, concerning the Italian race,

lamenting that a people so valiant in war, and blood relations to the Romans, were declining little by little in pauperism and paucity of numbers without any hope of remedy. He inveighed against the multitude of slaves as useless in war and never faithful to their masters, and adduced the recent calamity brought upon the masters by their slaves in Sicily, where the demands of agriculture had greatly increased the number of the latter; recalling also the war waged against them by the Romans, which was neither easy nor short, but long-protracted and full of vicissitudes and dangers. After speaking thus he again brought forward the law, providing that nobody should hold more than 500 jugera of the public domain. But he added a provision to the former law, that the sons of the present occupiers might each hold one-half of that amount, and that the remainder should be divided among the poor by triumvirs, who should be changed annually.

This was extremely disturbing to the rich because, on account of the triumvirs, they could no longer disregard the law as they had done before; nor could they buy the allotments of others, because Gracchus had provided against this by forbidding sales. They collected together in groups, and made lamentation, and accused the poor of appropriating the results of their tillage, their vineyards, and their dwellings. Some said that they had paid the price of the land to their neighbors. Were they to lose the money with the land? Others said that the graves of their ancestors were in the ground, which had been allotted to them in the division of their fathers' estates. Others said that their wives' dowries had been expended on the estates, or that the land had been given to their own daughters as dowry. Moneylenders could show loans made on this security. All kinds of wailing and expressions of indignation were heard at once. On the other side were heard the lamentations of the poor—that they had been reduced from competence to extreme penury, and from that to childlessness, because they were unable to rear their offspring. They recounted the military services they had rendered, by which this very land had been acquired, and were angry that they should be robbed of their share of the common property. They reproached the rich for employing slaves, who were always faithless and ill-tempered and for that reason unserviceable in war, instead of freemen, citizens, and soldiers. While these classes were lamenting and indulging in mutual accusations, a great number of others, composed of colonists, or inhabitants of the free towns, or persons otherwise interested in the lands and who were under like apprehensions, flocked in and took sides with their respective factions. Emboldened by numbers and exasperated against each other they attached themselves to turbulent crowds, and waited for the voting on the new law, some trying to prevent its enactment by all means, and others supporting it in every possible way. In addition to personal interest the spirit of rivalry spurred both sides in the preparations they were making against each other for the day of the comitia.

What Gracchus had in his mind in proposing the measure was not wealth, but an increase of efficient population. Inspired greatly by the usefulness of the work, and believing that nothing more advantageous or admirable could ever happen to Italy, he took no account of the difficulties surrounding it. When the time for voting came he advanced many other arguments at considerable length and also asked them whether it was not just to divide among the common people what belonged to them in common; whether a citizen was not worthy of more consideration at all times than a slave; whether a man who served in the army was not more useful than one who did not; and whether one who had a share in the country was not more likely to be devoted to the public

interests. He did not dwell long on this comparison between freemen and slaves, which he considered degrading, but proceeded at once to a review of their hopes and fears for the country, saying that the Romans had acquired most of their territory by conquest, and that they had hopes of occupying the rest of the habitable world, but now the question of greatest hazard was, whether they should gain the rest by having plenty of brave men, or whether, through their weakness and mutual jealousy, their enemies should take away what they already possessed. After exaggerating the glory and riches on the one side and the danger and fear on the other, he admonished the rich to take heed, and said that for the realization of these hopes they ought to bestow this very land as a free gift, if necessary, on men who would rear children, and not, by contending about small things, overlook larger ones; especially since they were receiving an ample compensation for labor expended in the undisputed title to 500 jugera each of free land, in a high state of cultivation, without cost, and half as much more for each son of those who had sons. After saying much more to the same purport and exciting the poor, as well as others who were moved by reason rather than by the desire for gain, he ordered the scribe to read the proposed law.

Marcus Octavius, another tribune, who had been induced by those in possession of the lands to interpose his veto (for among the Romans the tribune's veto always prevailed), ordered the scribe to keep silence. Thereupon Gracchus reproached him severely and adjourned the comitia to the following day. Then he stationed a sufficient guard, as if to force Octavius against his will, and ordered the scribe with threats to read the proposed law to the multitude. He began to read, but when Octavius again vetoed he stopped. Then the tribunes fell to wrangling with each other, and a considerable tumult arose among the people. The leading citizens besought the tribunes to submit their controversy to the Senate for decision. Gracchus seized on the suggestion, believing that the law was acceptable to all well-disposed persons, and hastened to the senate-house. There, as he had only a few followers and was upbraided by the rich, he ran back to the forum and said that he would take the vote at the comitia of the following day, both on the law and on the magistracy of Octavius, to determine whether a tribune who was acting contrary to the people's interest could continue to hold his office. And so he did, for when Octavius, nothing daunted, again interposed, Gracchus distributed the pebbles to take a vote on him first. When the first tribe voted to abrogate the magistracy of Octavius, Gracchus turned to him and begged him to desist from this veto. As he would not yield, the votes of the other tribes were taken. There were thirty-five tribes at that time. The seventeen that voted first angrily sustained this motion. If the eighteenth should do the same it would make a majority. Again did Gracchus, in the sight of the people, urgently importune Octavius in his present extreme danger not to prevent this most pious work, so useful to all Italy, and not to frustrate the wishes so earnestly entertained by the people, whose desires he ought rather to share in his character of tribune, and not to risk the loss of his office by public condemnation. After speaking thus he called the gods to witness that he did not willingly do any despite to his colleague. As Octavius was still unyielding he went on taking the vote. Octavius was forthwith reduced to the rank of a private citizen and slunk away unobserved.

Quintus Mummius was chosen tribune in his place, and the agrarian law was enacted. The first triumvirs appointed to divide the land were Gracchus himself, the proposer of the law, his brother of the same name, and his father-in-law, Appius Claudius, since the people still feared that

the law might fail of execution unless Gracchus should be put in the lead with his whole family. Gracchus became immensely popular by reason of the law and was escorted home by the multitude as though he were the founder, not of a single city or race, but of all the nations of Italy. After this the victorious party returned to the fields from which they had come to attend to this business. The defeated ones remained in the city and talked the matter over, feeling bitterly, and saying that as soon as Gracchus should become a private citizen he would be sorry that he had done despite to the sacred and inviolable office of tribune, and had opened such a fountain of discord in Italy.

At the advent of summer the notices for the election of tribunes were given, and as the day for voting approached it was very evident that the rich were earnestly promoting the election of those most inimical to Gracchus. The latter, fearing that evil would befall if he should not be re-elected for the following year, summoned his friends from the fields to attend the comitia, but as they were occupied with their harvest he was obliged, when the day fixed for the voting drew near, to have recourse to the plebeians of the city. So he went around asking each one separately to elect him tribune for the ensuing year, on account of the danger he had incurred for them. When the voting took place the first two tribes pronounced for Gracchus. The rich objected that it was not lawful for the same man to hold the office twice in succession. The tribune Rubrius, who had been chosen by lot to preside over the comitia, was in doubt about it, and Mummius, who had been chosen in place of Octavius, urged him to turn over the comitia to his charge. This he did, but the remaining tribunes contended that the presidency should be decided by lot, saying that when Rubrius, who had been chosen in that way, resigned, the casting of lots ought to be done over again for all. As there was much strife over this question, Gracchus, who was getting the worst of it, adjourned the voting to the following day. In utter despair he clothed himself in black, while still in office, and led his son around the forum and introduced him to each man and committed him to their charge, as if he were about to perish at the hands of his enemies.

The poor were moved with deep sorrow, and rightly so, both on their own account (for they believed that they were no longer to live in a free state under equal laws, but were reduced to servitude by the rich), and on account of Gracchus himself, who had incurred such danger and suffering in their behalf. So they all accompanied him with tears to his house in the evening, and bade him be of good courage for the morrow. Gracchus cheered up, assembled his partisans before daybreak, and communicated to them a signal to be displayed in case of a fight. He then took possession of the temple on the Capitoline hill, where the voting was to take place, and occupied the middle of the assembly. As he was obstructed by the other tribunes and by the rich, who would not allow the votes to be taken on this question, he gave the signal. There was sudden shout from those who saw it, and a resort to violence in consequence. Some of the partisans of Gracchus took position around him like body-guards. Others, having girded themselves, seized the fasces and staves in the hands of the lictors and broke them in pieces. They drove the rich out of the assembly with such disorder and wounds that the tribunes fled from their places in terror, and the priests closed the doors of the temple. Many ran away pell-mell and scattered wild rumors. Some said that Gracchus had deposed all the other tribunes, and this was believed because none of them could be seen. Others said that he had declared himself tribune for the year without an election.

Under these circumstances the Senate assembled at the temple of Fides. It is astonishing to me that they never thought of appointing a dictator in this emergency, although they had often been protected by the government of a single ruler in such times of peril. Although this resource had been found most useful in former times few people remembered it, either then or later. After reaching the decision that they did reach, they marched up to the Capitol, Cornelius Scopio Nasica, the pontifex maximus, leading the way and calling out with a loud voice, "Let those who would save the country follow me." He wound the border of his toga about his head either to induce a greater number to go with him by the singularity of his appearance, or to make for himself, as it were, a helmet as a sign of battle for those who looked on, or in order to conceal from the gods what he was about to do. When he arrived at the temple and advanced against the partisans of Gracchus they yielded to the reputation of a foremost citizen, for they saw the Senate following with him. The latter wrested clubs out of the hands of the Gracchans themselves, or with fragments of broken benches or other apparatus that had been brought for the use of the assembly, began beating them, and pursued them, and drove them over the precipice. In the tumult many of the Gracchans perished, and Gracchus himself was caught near the temple, and was slain at the door close by the statues of the kings. All the bodies were thrown by night into the Tiber.

So perished on the Capitol, and while still tribune, Gracchus, the son of the Gracchus who was twice consul, and of Cornelia, daughter of that Scipio who subjugated Carthage. He lost his life in consequence of a most excellent design, which, however, he pursued in too violent a manner. This shocking affair, the first that was perpetrated in the public assembly, was seldom without parallels thereafter from time to time. On the subject of the murder of Gracchus the city was divided between sorrow and joy. Some mourned for themselves and for him, and deplored the present condition of things, believing that the commonwealth no longer existed, but had been supplanted by force and violence. Others considered that everything had turned out for them exactly as they wished. These things took place at the time when Aristonicus was contending with the Romans for the government of Asia.

After Gracchus was slain Appius Claudius died, and Fulvius Flaccus and Papirius Carbo were appointed, in conjunction with the younger Gracchus, to divide the lands. As the persons in possion neglected to hand in lists of their holdings, a proclamation was issued that informers should furnish testimony against them. Immediately a great number of embarrassing lawsuits sprang up. Wherever a division of land had been made with allies, the whole district had to be carefully inquired into on account of the measurement of this one field, to discover how it had been sold and how divided. Not all owners had preserved their contracts, or their allotment titles, and even those that were found were often ambiguous. When the land was resurveyed some owners were obliged to give up their fruit-trees and farm-buildings in exchange for naked ground. Others were transferred from cultivated to uncultivated lands, or to swamps, or pools. In fact, the measuring had not been carefully done when the land was first taken from the enemy. As the original proclamation authorized anybody to work the undistributed land who wished to do so, many had been prompted to cultivate the parts immediately adjoining their own, till the line of demarkation between them had faded from view. The progress of time also made many changes. Thus the injustice done by the rich, although great, was not easy of ascertainment. So there was nothing but a general turn-about, all parties being moved out of their own places and settled down in other people's.

The Italian allies who complained of these disturbances, and especially of the lawsuits hastily brought against them, chose Cornelius Scipio, the destroyer of Carthage, to defend them against these grievances. As he had availed himself of their valiant services in war he was reluctant to disregard their request. So he came into the Senate, and although, out of regard for the plebeians, he did not openly find fault with the law of Gracchus, he expatiated on its difficulties and held that these causes ought not to be decided by the triumvirs, because they did not possess the confidence of the litigants, but should be turned over to others. As his view seemed reasonable, they yielded to his persuasion, and the consul Tuditanus was appointed to give judgement in these cases. But when he took hold of the work he saw the difficulties of it, and marched against the Illyrians as a pretext for not acting as judge, and since nobody brought cases for trial before the triumvirs they relapsed into idleness. From this cause hatred and indignation arose among the people against Scipio because they saw him, in whose favor they had often opposed the aristocracy and incurred their enmity, electing him consul twice contrary to law, now taking the side of the Italian allies against them. When Scipio's enemies observed this, they cried out that he was determined to abolish the law of Gracchus utterly and was about to inaugurate armed strife and bloodshed for that purpose.

When the people heard these charges they were in a state of alarm until Scipio, after placing near his couch at home one evening a tablet on which he intended to write during the night the speech he intended to deliver before the people, was found dead in his bed without a wound. Whether this was done by Cornelia, the mother of the Gracchi (aided by her daughter, Sempronia, who was married to Scipio, and was unloved and unloving because she was deformed and childless), lest the law of Gracchus should be abolished, or whether, as some think, he committed suicide because he saw plainly that he could not accomplish what he had promised, is not known. Some say that slaves, who were subjected to torture, testified that unknown persons were introduced through the rear of the house by night who suffocated him, and that those who knew about it hesitated to tell because the people were angry with him still and rejoiced at his death. So died Scipio, and although he had been of immense service to the Roman power he was not honored with a public funeral; so much does the anger of the present moment outweigh gratitude for the past. And this event, sufficiently important in itself, took place as an incident of the sedition of Gracchus.

Those who were in possession of the lands even after these events postponed the division on various pretexts for a very long time. Some thought that the Italian allies, who made the greatest resistance to it, ought to be admitted to Roman citizenship so that, out of gratitude for the greater favor, they should no longer quarrel about the land. The Italians were glad to accept this, because they preferred Roman citizenship to possession of the fields. Fulvius Flaccus, who was then both consul and triumvir, exerted himself to the utmost to bring it about, but the Senate was angry at the proposal to make their subjects equal citizens with themselves. For this reason the attempt was abandoned and the people, who had been so long in the hope of acquiring land, became disheartened. While they were in this mood Gaius Gracchus, who had made himself agreeable to them as a triumvir, offered himself for the tribuneship. He was the younger brother of Tiberius Gracchus, the promoter of the law, and had been silent for some time on the subject of the fate of his brother, but since many of the senators treated him scornfully he announced himself as a candidate for the office of tribune. As soon as he was elected

to this distinguished position he began to lay plots against the Senate, and proposed that a monthly distribution of corn should be made to each citizen at the public expense, which had not been customary before. Thus he got the leadership of the people quickly by one measure of policy, in which he had the coöperation of Fulvius Flaccus. Directly after that he was chosen tribune for the following year, for in cases where there was not a sufficient number of candidates the law authorized the people to choose from the whole number then in office.

Thus Gaius Gracchus became tribune a second time. Having bought the plebeians, as it were, he began, by another like political manœuvre, to court the equestrian order, who hold the middle place between the Senate and the plebeians. He transferred the courts of justice, which had become discredited by reason of bribery, from the senators to the knights, reproaching the former especially with the recent examples of Aurelius Cotta, Salinator, and, third in the list, Manius Aquilius (the one who subdued Asia), all notorious bribetakers, who had been acquitted by the judges, although ambassadors sent to complain against them were still present, going around uttering hateful accusations against them. The Senate was extremely ashamed of these things and yielded to the law, and the people ratified it. In this way were the courts of justice transferred from the Senate to the knights. It is said that soon after the passage of this law Gracchus remarked that he had broken the power of the Senate once for all. This saying of Gracchus has been even more confirmed by experience in the course of events. This power of sitting in judgment on all Romans and Italians, including the senators themselves, in all matters as to property, civil rights, and banishment, exalted the knights like rulers over them and put senators on the same level with subjects. Moreover, as the knights voted in the election to sustain the power of the tribunes, and obtained from them whatever they wanted in return, they became more and more formidable to the senators. So it shortly came about that the political mastery was turned upside down, the power being in the hands of the knights, and the honor only remaining with the Senate. The knights went so far that they not only held power over the senators, but they openly flouted them beyond their right. They also became addicted to bribe-taking, and having once tasted these enormous gains, they indulged in them even more basely and immoderately than the senators had done. They suborned accusers against the rich and did away with prosecutions for bribe-taking alto-gether, partly by concert of action and partly by force and violence, so that the practice of this kind of investigation became entirely obsolete. Thus the judiciary law gave rise to another struggle of factions, which lasted a long time and was not less baneful than the former ones.

Gracchus made long roads throughout Italy and thus put a multitude of con-tractors and artisans under obligations to him and made them ready to do whatever he wished. He proposed the founding of numerous colonies. He also called on the Latin allies to demand the full rights of Roman citizenship, since the Senate could not with decency refuse this privilege to their blood relations. To the other allies, who were not allowed to vote in Roman elections, he sought to give the right of suffrage, in order to have their help in the enactment of laws which he had in contemplation. The Senate was very much alarmed at this, and it ordered the consuls to give the following public notice, "Nobody who does not possess the right of suffrage shall stay in the city or approach within forty stades of it while voting is going on concerning these laws." The Senate also persuaded Livius Drusus, another tribune, to interpose his veto against the laws proposed by Gracchus, but not to tell the people his reasons for

doing so; for a tribune was not required to give reasons for his veto. In order to conciliate the people they gave Drusus the privilege of founding twelve colonies, and the plebeians were so much pleased with this that they began to scoff at the laws proposed by Gracchus.

Having lost the favor of the rabble, Gracchus sailed for Africa in company with Fulvius Flaccus, who, after his consulship, had been chosen tribune for the same reasons as Gracchus himself. A colony had been voted to Africa on account of its reputed fertility, and these men had been expressly chosen the founders of it in order to get them out of the way for a while, so that the Senate might have a respite from demagogism. They marked out a town for the colony on the place where Carthage had formerly stood, disregarding the fact that Scipio, when he destroyed it, had devoted it with curses to sheep-pasturage forever. They assigned 6000 colonists to this place, instead of the smaller number fixed by law, in order further to curry favor with the people thereby. When they returned to Rome they invited the 6000 from the whole of Italy. The functionaries who were still in Africa laying out the city wrote home that wolves had pulled up and scattered the boundary marks made by Gracchus and Fulvius, and the soothsayers con-sidered this an ill omen for the colony. So the Senate summoned the comitia, in which it was proposed to repeal the law concerning his colony. When Gracchus and Fulvius saw their failure in this matter they were furious, and declared that the Senate had lied about the wolves. The boldest of the plebeians joined them, carrying daggers, and proceeded to the where the assembly was to be held in reference to the colony.

Now the people were assembled, and Fulvius had begun speaking about the business in hand, when Gracchus arrived at the Capitol attended by a body-guard of his partisans. Disturbed by what he knew about the extraordinary plans on foot he turned aside from the meeting-place of the assembly, passed into the portico, and walked about waiting to see what would happen. Just then a plebeian named Antyllus, who was sacrificing in the portico, saw him in this disturbed state, seized him by the hand, either because he had heard something or suspected something, or was moved to speak to him for some other reason, and asked him to spare his country. Gracchus, still more disturbed, and startled like one detected in a crime, gave the man a piercing look. Then one of his party, although no signal had been displayed or order given, inferred merely from the very sharp glance that Gracchus cast upon Antyllus that the time for action had come, and thought that he should do a favor to Gracchus by striking the first blow. So he drew his dagger and slew Antyllus. A cry was raised, the dead body was seen in the midst of the crowd, and all who were outside fled from the temple in fear of a like fate. Gracchus went into the assembly desiring to exculpate himself of the deed. Nobody would so much as listen to him. All turned away from him as from one stained with blood. Gracchus and Flaccus were nonplussed and, having lost the chance of accomplishing what they wished, they hastened home, and their partisans with them. The rest of the crowd occupied the forum throughout the night as though some calamity were impending. Opimius, one of the consuls, who was staying in the city, ordered an armed force to be stationed at the Capitol at daybreak, and sent heralds to convoke the Senate. He took his own station in the temple of Castor and Pollux in the centre of the city and there awaited events.

When these arrangements had been made the Senate summoned Gracchus and Flaccus from their homes to the senate-house to defend themselves. But they ran out armed toward the Aventine hill, hoping that if they could seize it first the Senate would agree to some terms with them.

They ran through the city offering freedom to the slaves, but none listened to them. With such forces as they had, however, they occupied and fortified the temple of Diana, and sent Quintus, the son of Flaccus, to the Senate seeking to come to an arrangement and to live in peace. The Senate replied that they should lay down their arms, come to the senate-house, tell what they wanted, or else send no more messengers. When they sent Quintus a second time the consul Opimius arrested him, as being no longer an ambassador after he had been warned, and at the same time sent an armed force against the Gracchans. Gracchus fled across the river by the Sublician bridge, with one slave, to a grove where he presented his throat to the slave, as he was on the point of being arrested. Flaccus took refuge in the workshop of an acquaintance. As his pursuers did not know which house he was in they threatened to burn the whole row. The man who had given shelter to the suppliant hesitated to point him out, but directed another man to do so. Flaccus was seized and put to death. The heads of Gracchus and Flaccus were carried to Opimius, and he gave their weight in gold to those who brought them. The people plundered their houses. Opimius arrested their fellow-conspirators, cast them into prison, and ordered that they should be strangled. He allowed Quintus, the son of Flaccus, to choose his own mode of death. After this a lustration was performed in behalf of the city for the bloodshed, and the Senate ordered the building of a temple to Concord in the forum.

So the sedition of the younger Gracchus came to an end. Not long afterward a law was enacted to permit the holders to sell the land about which they had quarrelled; for even this had been forbidden by the law of the elder Gracchus. Presently the rich bought the allotments of the poor, or found pretexts for seizing them by force. So the condition of the poor became even worse than it was before, until Spurius Borius, a tribune of the people, brought in a law providing that the work of distributing the public domain should no longer be continued, but that the land should belong to those in possession of it, who should pay rent for it to the people, and that the money so received should be distributed. This distribution was a kind of solace to the poor, but it did not serve to increase the population. By these devices the law of Gracchus (most excellent and useful if it could have been carried out) was once for all frustrated, and a little later the rent itself was abolished at the instance of another tribune. So the plebeians lost everything. Whence resulted a still further decline in the numbers of both citizens and soldiers, and in the revenue from the land and the distribution thereof; and about fifteen years after the enactment of the law of Gracchus, the laws themselves fell into abeyance by reason of the slackness of the judicial proceedings.

2. Plutarch on the Gracchi*

Of the land which the Romans gained by conquest from their neighbours, part they sold publicly, and turned the remainder into common; this common land they assigned to such of the citizens as were poor and indigent, for which they were to pay only a small acknowledgment into the public treasury. But when the wealthy men began to offer larger rents, and drive the poorer people out, it was enacted by law that no person whatever should enjoy more than five hundred acres of ground. This act for some time checked the avarice of the richer, and was of great assistance to the poorer people, who retained under it their respective proportions of ground, as they had been formerly rented by them. Afterwards the rich men of the neighbourhood contrived to get these lands again into their possession, under other people's names, and at last would not stick to claim most of them publicly in their own. The poor, who were thus deprived of their farms, were no longer either ready, as they had formerly been, to serve in war or careful in the education of their children; insomuch that in a short time there were comparatively few freemen remaining in all Italy, which swarmed with workhouses full of foreign-born slaves. These the rich men employed in cultivating their ground of which they dispossessed the citizens. Caius Lælius, the intimate friend of Scipio, undertook to reform this abuse; but meeting with opposition from men of authority, and fearing a disturbance, he soon desisted, and received the name of the Wise or the Prudent, both which meanings belong to the Latin word *Sapiens.*

But Tiberius, being elected tribune of the people, entered upon that design without delay, at the instigation, as is most commonly stated, of Diophanes, the rhetorician, and Blossius, the philosopher. Diophanes was a refugee from Mitylene, the other was an Italian, of the city of Cuma, and was educated there under Antipater of Tarsus, who afterwards did him the honour to dedicate some of his philosophical lectures to him.

Some have also charged Cornelia, the mother of Tiberius, with contributing towards it, because she frequently upbraided her sons, that the Romans as yet rather called her the daughter of Scipio, than the mother of the Gracchi. Others again say that Spurius Postumius was the chief occasion. He was a man of the same age with Tiberius, and his rival for reputation as a public speaker; and when Tiberius, at his return from the campaign,

---

* Plutarch, *Tiberius Gracchus* and *Gaius Gracchus* (abridged), translated by John Dryden.

found him to have got far beyond him in fame and influence, and to be much looked up to, he thought to outdo him, by attempting a popular enterprise of this difficulty and of such great consequence. But his brother Caius has left it us in writing, that when Tiberius went through Tuscany to Numantia, and found the country almost depopulated, there being hardly any free husbandmen or shepherds, but for the most part only barbarian, imported slaves, he then first conceived the course of policy which in the sequel proved so fatal to his family. Though it is also most certain that the people themselves chiefly excited his zeal and determination in the prosecution of it, by setting up writings upon the porches, walls, and monuments, calling upon him to reinstate the poor citizens in their former possessions.

However, he did not draw up his law without the advice and assistance of those citizens that were then most eminent for their virtue and authority; amongst whom were Crassus, the high-priest, Mucius Scævola, the lawyer, who at that time was consul, and Claudius Appius, his father-in-law. Never did any law appear more moderate and gentle, especially being enacted against such great oppression and avarice. For they who ought to have been severely punished for transgressing the former laws, and should at least have lost all their titles to such lands which they had unjustly usurped, were notwithstanding to receive a price for quitting their unlawful claims, and giving up their lands to those fit owners who stood in need of help. But though this reformation was managed with so much tenderness that, all the former transactions being passed over, the people were only thankful to prevent abuses of the like nature for the future, yet, on the other hand, the moneyed men, and those of great estates, were exasperated, through their covetous feelings against the law itself, and against the lawgiver, through anger and party-spirit. They therefore endeavoured to seduce the people, declaring that Tiberius was designing a general redivision of lands, to overthrow the government, and put all things into confusion.

But they had no success. For Tiberius, maintaining an honourable and just cause, and possessed of eloquence sufficient to have made a less creditable action appear plausible, was no safe or easy antagonist, when, with the people crowding around the hustings, he took his place, and spoke in behalf of the poor. "The savage beasts," said he, "in Italy, have their particular dens, they have their places of repose and refuge; but the men who bear arms, and expose their lives for the safety of their country, enjoy in the meantime nothing more in it but the air and light; and, having no houses or settlements of their own, are constrained to wander from place to place with their wives and children." He told them that the commanders were guilty of a ridiculous error, when, at the head of their armies, they exhorted the common soldiers to fight for their sepulchres and altars; when not any amongst so many Romans is possessed of either altar or monument, neither have they any houses of their own, or hearths of their ancestors to defend. They fought indeed and were slain, but it was to maintain the luxury and the wealth of other men. They were styled the masters of the world, but in the meantime had not one foot of ground which they could call their own. An harangue of this nature, spoken to an enthusiastic and sympathising audience, by a person of commanding spirit and genuine feelings, no adversaries at that time were competent to oppose. Forbearing, therefore, all discussion and debate, they addressed themselves to Marcus Octavius, his fellow-tribune, who being a young man of a steady, orderly character, and an intimate friend of Tiberius, upon this account declined at first the task of opposing him; but at length, over-persuaded with the repeated importunities of numerous considerable persons, he was prevailed upon to do so, and hindered the passing of the law; it being the rule that any tribune has a power to hinder an act, and that all the rest can effect nothing, if only one of them dissents. Tiberius, irritated at these proceedings, presently laid aside this milder bill, but at the same time preferred another; which, as it was more grateful to the common people, so it was much more severe against the wrongdoers, commanding them to make an immediate surrender of all lands which, contrary to former laws, had come into their possession. Hence there arose daily contentions between him and Octavius in their orations. However, though they expressed themselves with the utmost heat and determination, they yet were never known to descend to any personal reproaches, or in their passion to let slip any indecent expressions, so as to derogate from one another.

For not alone—

"In revellings and Bacchic play,"

but also in contentions and political animosities, a noble nature and a temperate education stay and compose the mind. Observing that Octavius himself was an offender against this law, and detained a great quantity of ground from the commonalty, Tiberius desired him to forbear opposing him any further, and proffered, for the public good, though he himself had but an indifferent estate, to pay a price for Octavius's share at his own cost and charges. But upon the refusal of this proffer by Octavius, he then interposed an edict, prohibiting all magistrates to exercise their respective functions, till such time as the law was either ratified or rejected by public votes. He further sealed up the gates of Saturn's temple, so that the treasurers could neither take any money out from thence, nor put any in. He threatened to impose a severe fine upon those of the prætors who presumed to disobey his

commands, insomuch that all the officers, for fear of this penalty, intermitted the exercise of their several jurisdictions.

* * *

When the people were met together again, Tiberius placed himself in the rostra, and endeavoured a second time to persuade Octavius. But all being to no purpose, he referred the whole matter to the people, calling on them to vote at once, whether Octavius should be deposed or not; and when seventeen of the thirty-five tribes had already voted against him, and there wanted only the votes of one tribe more for his final deprivation, Tiberius put a short stop to the proceedings, and once more renewed his importunities; he embraced and kissed him before all the assembly, begging with all the earnestness imaginable, that he would neither suffer himself to incur the dishonour, nor him to be reputed the author and promoter of so odious a measure. Octavius, we are told, did seem a little softened and moved with these entreaties; his eyes filled with tears, and he continued silent for a considerable time. But presently looking towards the rich men and proprietors of estates, who stood gathered in a body together, partly for shame, and partly for fear of disgracing himself with them, he boldly bade Tiberius use any severity he pleased. The law for his deprivation being thus voted, Tiberius ordered one of his servants, whom he had made a freeman, to remove Octavius from the rostra, employing his own domestic freed servants in the stead of the public officers.

* * *

This being done, the law concerning the lands was ratified and confirmed, and three commissioners were appointed, to make a survey of the grounds, and see the the same equally divided. These were Tiberius himself, Claudius Appius, his father-in-law, and his brother, Caius Gracchus, who at this time was not at

Rome, but in the army under the command of Scipio Africanus before Numantia. These things were transacted by Tiberius without any disturbance, none daring to offer any resistance to him; besides which, he gave the appointment as tribune in Octavius's place, not to any person of distinction, but to a certain Mucius, one of his own clients. The great men of the city were therefore utterly offended, and, fearing lest he grew yet more popular, they took all opportunities of affronting him publicly in the senate house. For when he requested, as was usual, to have a tent provided at the public charge for his use, while dividing the lands, though it was a favour commonly granted to persons employed in business of much less importance, it was peremptorily refused to him; and the allowance made him for his daily expenses was fixed to nine obols only. The chief promoter of these affronts was Publius Nasica, who openly abandoned himself to his feelings of hatred against Tiberius, being a large holder of the public lands, and not a little resenting now to be turned out of them by force.

* * *

About this time king Attalus, surnamed Philometor, died, and Eudemus, a Pergamenian, brought his last will to Rome, by which he had made the Roman people his heirs. Tiberius, to please the people, immediately proposed making a law, that all the money which Attalus left should be distributed amongst such poor citizens as were to be sharers of the public lands, for the better enabling them to proceed in stocking and cultivating their ground; and as for the cities that were in the territories of Attalus, he declared that the disposal of them did not at all belong to the senate, but to the people, and that he himself would ask their pleasure herein. By this he offended the senate more than ever he had done before, and Pompeius stood up and acquainted them that he was the next neighbour to Tiberius, and so had the opportunity of knowing that Eudemus, the Pergamenian, had presented Tiberius with a royal diadem and a purple robe, as before long he was to be king of Rome.

* * *

His friends, apprehending the dangers which seemed to threaten him, and the conspiracy that was gathering head against him, were of opinion that the safest way would be for him to petition that he might be continued tribune for the year ensuing. Upon this consideration he again endeavoured to secure the people's good-will with fresh laws, making the years of serving in the war fewer than formerly, granting liberty of appeal from the judges to the people, and joining to the senators, who were judges at that time, an equal number of citizens of the horsemen's degree, endeavouring as much as in him lay to lessen the power of the senate, rather from passion and partisanship than from any rational regard to equity and the public good. And when it came to the question whether these laws should be passed, and they perceived that the opposite party were strongest, the people as yet being not got together in a full body, they began first of all to gain time by speeches in accusation of some of their fellow-magistrates and at length adjourned the assembly till the day following.

Tiberius then went down into the market-place amongst the people, and made his addresses to them humbly and with tears in his eyes; and told them he had just reason to suspect that his adversaries would attempt in the night-time to break open his house and murder him. This worked so strongly with the multitude, that several of them pitched tents round about his house, and kept guard all night for the security of his person. . . .

* * *

At the same time several messengers came also from his friends, to desire his presence at the capitol, saying that all things went there according to expectation. And indeed Tiberius's first entrance there was in every way successful; as soon as ever he appeared, the people welcomed him with loud acclamations, and as he went up to his place, they repeated their expressions of joy, and gathered in a body around him, so that no one who was not well known to be his friend might approach. Mucius then began to put the business again to the vote; but nothing could be performed in the usual course and order, because of the disturbance caused by those who were on the outside of the crowd, where there was a struggle going on with those of the opposite party, who were pushing on and trying to force their way in and establish themselves among them.

Whilst things were in this confusion, Flavius Flaccus, a senator, standing in a place where he could be seen, but at such a distance from Tiberius that he could not make him hear, signified to him by motions of his hand, that he wished to impart something of consequence to him in private. Tiberius ordered the multitude to make way for him, by which means, though not without some difficulty, Flavius got to him, and informed him that the rich men, in a sitting of the senate, seeing they could not prevail upon the consul to espouse their quarrel, had come to a final determination amongst themselves that he should be assassinated, and to that purpose had a great number of their friends and servants ready armed to accomplish it. Tiberius no sooner communicated this confederacy to those about him, but they immediately tucked up their gowns, broke the halberts which the officers used to keep the crowd off into pieces, and distributed them among themselves, resolving to resist the attack with these. Those who stood at a distance wondered, and asked what was the occasion; Tiberius, knowing that they could not hear him at that distance, lifted his hand to his head wishing to intimate the great danger which

he apprehended himself to be in. His adversaries, taking notice of that action, ran off at once to the senate house, and declared that Tiberius desired the people to bestow a crown upon him, as if this were the meaning of his touching his head. This news created general confusion in the senators, and Nasica at once called upon the consul to punish this tyrant, and defend the government. The consul mildly replied, that he would not be the first to do any violence; and as he would not suffer any freeman to be put to death, before sentence had lawfully passed upon him, so neither would he allow any measure to be carried into effect, if by persuasion or compulsion on the part of Tiberius the people had been induced to pass an unlawful vote. But Nasica, rising from his seat, "Since the consul," said he, "regards not the safety of the commonwealth, let every one who will defend the laws, follow me." He then, casting the skirt of his gown over his head, hastened to the capitol; those who bore him company, wrapped their gowns also about their arms, and forced their way after him. And as they were persons of the greatest authority in the city, the common people did not venture to obstruct their passing, but were rather so eager to clear the way for them, that they tumbled over one another in haste. The attendants they brought with them had furnished themselves with clubs and staves from their houses, and they themselves picked up the feet and other fragments of stools and chairs, which were broken by the hasty flight of the common people. Thus armed, they made towards Tiberius, knocking down those whom they found in front of him, and those were soon wholly dispersed and many of them slain. Tiberius tried to save himself by flight. As he was running, he was stopped by one who caught hold of him by the gown; but he threw it off, and fled in his under-garment only. And stumbling over those who before had been knocked down, as he was endeavouring to get up again, Publius Satureius, a tribune, one of his colleagues, was observed to give him the first fatal stroke, by hitting him upon the head with the foot of a stool. The second blow was claimed, as though it had been a deed to be proud of, by Lucius Rufus. And of the rest there fell above three hundred killed by clubs and staves only, none by an iron weapon.

This, we are told, was the first sedition amongst the Romans, since the abrogation of kingly government, that ended in the effusion of blood. All former quarrels which were neither small nor about trivial matters, were always amicably composed, by mutual concessions on either side, the senate yielding for fear of the commons, and the commons out of respect to the senate. And it is probable indeed that Tiberius himself might then have been easily induced, by mere persuasion, to give way, and certainly, if attacked at all, must have yielded without any recourse to violence and bloodshed, as he had not at that time above three thousand men to support him. But it is evident, that this conspiracy was fomented against him, more out of the hatred and malice which the rich men had to his person, than for the reasons which they commonly pretended against him. In testimony of which, we may adduce the cruelty and unnatural insults which they used to his dead body. For they would not suffer his own brother, though he earnestly begged the favour, to bury him in the night, but threw him, together with the other corpses, into the river. Neither did their animosity stop here; for they banished some of his friends without legal process, and slew as many of the others as they could lay their hands on.

* * *

[Plutarch begins the account of Caius by describing his early career and the hostility felt toward him by the Senate. Caius rose in the people's estimation because of his rhetorical skill, and at last was elected to the tribuneship.]

CAIUS GRACCHUS

Of the laws which he now proposed, with the object of gratifying the people and abridging the power of the senate, the first was concerning the public lands, which were to be divided amongst the poor citizens; another was concerning the common soldiers, that they should be clothed at the public charge, without any diminution of their pay, and that none should be obliged to serve in the army who was not full seventeen years old; another gave the same right to all the Italians in general, of voting at elections, as was enjoyed by the citizens of Rome; a fourth related to the price of corn, which was to be sold at a lower rate than formerly to the poor; and a fifth regulated the courts of justice, greatly reducing the power of the senators. For hitherto, in all cases, senators only sat as judges, and were therefore much dreaded by the Roman knights and the people. But Caius joined three hundred ordinary citizens of equestrian rank with the senators, who were three hundred likewise in number, and ordained that the judicial authority should be equally invested in the six hundred. While he was arguing for the ratification of this law, his behaviour was observed to show in many respects unusual earnestness, and whereas other popular leaders had always hitherto, when speaking, turned their faces towards the senate house, and the place called the comitium, he, on the contrary, was the first man that in his harangue to the people turned himself the other way, towards them, and continued after that time to do so. An insignificant movement and change of posture, yet it marked no small revolution in state affairs, the conversion, in a manner, of the whole government from an aristocracy to a democracy, his action intimating that public speakers should address themselves to the people, not the senate.

When the commonalty ratified this law, and gave him power to select those of the knights whom he approved of, to be judges, he was invested with a sort of a kingly power, and the senate itself submitted to receive his advice in matters of difficulty; nor did he advise anything that might derogate from the honour of that body. As, for example, his resolution about the corn which Fabius the proprætor sent from Spain, was very just and honourable; for he persuaded the senate to sell the corn, and return the money to the same provinces which had furnished them with it; and also that Fabius should be censured for rendering the Roman government odious and insupportable. This got him extraordinary respect and favour among the provinces. Besides all this, he proposed measures for the colonisation of several cities, for making roads, and for building public granaries; of all which works he himself undertook the management and superintendence, and was never wanting to give necessary orders for the despatch of all these different and great undertakings; and that with such wonderful expedition and diligence, as if he had been but engaged upon one of them; insomuch that all persons, even those who hated or feared him, stood amazed to see what a capacity he had for effecting and completing all he undertook. As for the people themselves, they were transported at the very sight, when they saw him surrounded with a crowd of contractors, artificers, public deputies, military officers, soldiers, and scholars. All these he treated with an easy familiarity, yet without abandoning his dignity in his gentleness; and so accommodated his nature to the wants and occasions of every one who addressed him, that those were looked upon as no better than envious detractors, who had represented him as a terrible, assuming, and violent character. He was even a greater master of the popular leader's art in his common talk and his actions, than he was in his public addresses.

* * *

When the day for election of consuls was at hand, and all in great expectation, he appeared in the Field with Caius Fannius, canvassing together with his friends for his election. This was of great effect in Fannius's favour. He was chosen consul, and Caius elected tribune the second time, without his own seeking or petitioning for it, but at the voluntary motion of the people. But when he understood that the senators were his declared enemies, and that Fannius himself was none of the most zealous of friends, he began again to rouse the people with other new laws. He proposed that a colony of Roman citizens might be sent to re-people Tarentum and Capua, and that the Latins should enjoy the same privileges with the citizens of Rome. But the senate, apprehending that he would at last grow too powerful and dangerous, took a new and unusual course to alienate the people's affections from him, by playing the demagogue in opposition to him, and offering favours contrary to all good policy. Livius Drusus was fellow-tribune with Caius, a person of as good a family and as well educated as any amongst the Romans, and noways inferior to those who for their eloquence and riches were the most honoured and most powerful men of that time. To him, therefore, the chief senators made their application, exhorting him to attack Caius, and join in their confederacy against him; which they designed to carry on, not by using any force, or opposing the common people, but by gratifying and obliging them with such unreasonable things as otherwise they would have felt it honourable for them to incur the greatest unpopularity in resisting.

Livius offered to serve the senate with his authority in this business; and proceeded accordingly to bring forward such laws as were in reality neither honourable nor advantageous for the public; his whole design being to outdo Caius in pleasing and cajoling the populace (as if it had been in some comedy), with obsequious flattery and every kind of gratifications; the senate thus letting it be seen plainly that they were not angry with Caius's public measures, but only desirous to ruin him utterly, or at least to lessen his reputation. For when Caius proposed the settlement of only two colonies, and mentioned the better class of citizens for that purpose, they accused him of abusing the people; and yet, on the contrary, were pleased with Drusus, when he proposed the sending out of twelve colonies, each to consist of three thousand persons, and those, too, the most needy that he could find. When Caius divided the public land amongst the poor citizens, and charged them with a small rent, annually to be paid into the exchequer, they were angry at him, as one who sought to gratify the people only for his own interest; yet afterwards they commended Livius, though he exempted them from paying even that little acknowledgment. They were displeased with Caius for offering the Latins an equal right with the Romans of voting at the election of magistrates; but when Livius proposed that it might not be lawful for a Roman captain to scourge a Latin soldier, they promoted the passing of that law. And Livius, in all his speeches to the people, always told them that he proposed no laws but such as were agreeable to the senate, who had a particular regard to the people's advantage. And this truly was the only point in all his proceedings which was of any real service, as it created more kindly feelings towards the senate in the people; and whereas they formerly suspected and hated the principal senators, Livius appeased and mitigated this perverseness and animosity, by his profession that he had done nothing in favour and for the benefit of the commons without their advice and approbation.

* * *

[In accordance with his program, Gaius went to Africa, to the former site of Carthage, where he presided over the foundation of the colony called Junonia.]

After his return to Rome, he quitted his house on the Palatine Mount, and went to live near the market-place, endeavouring to make himself more popular in those parts, where most of the humble and poorer citizens lived. He then brought forward the remainder of his proposed laws, as intending to have them ratified by the popular vote; to support which a vast number of people collected from all quarters. But the senate persuaded Fannius, the consul, to command all persons who were not born Romans to depart the city. A new and unusual proclamation was thereupon made, prohibiting any of the allies or Confederates to appear at Rome during that time. Caius, on the contrary, published an edict, accusing the consul for what he had done, and setting forth to the Confederates, that if they would continue upon the place, they might be assured of his assistance and protection. However, he was not so good as his word; for though he saw one of his own familiar friends and companions dragged to prison by Fannius's officers, he, notwithstanding, passed by without assisting him; either because he was afraid to stand the test of his power, which was already decreased, or because, as he himself reported, he was unwilling to give his enemies an opportunity, which they very much desired, of coming to actual violence and fighting.

* * *

As soon as Opimius also was chosen consul, they presently cancelled several of Caius's laws, and especially called in question his proceedings at Carthage, omitting nothing that was likely to irritate him, that from some effect of his passion they might find out a tolerable pretence to put him to death. Caius at first bore these things very patiently; but afterwards, at the instigation of his friends, especially Fulvius, he resolved to put himself at the head of a body of supporters, to oppose the consul by force.

* * *

When the day came in which Opimius designed to abrogate the laws of Caius, both parties met very early at the capitol; and the consul having performed all the rites usual in their sacrifices, one Quintus Antyllius, an attendant on the consul, carrying out the entrails of the victim, spoke to Fulvius, and his friends who stood about him, "Ye factious citizens, make way for honest men." Some report that, besides this provoking language, he extended his naked arm towards them, as a piece of scorn and contempt. Upon this he was presently killed with the strong stiles which are commonly used in writing, though some say that on this occasion they had been manufactured for this purpose only. This murder caused a sudden consternation in the whole assembly, and the heads of each faction had their different sentiments about it. As for Caius, he was much grieved, and severely reprimanded his own party, because they had given their adversaries a reasonable pretence to proceed against them, which they had so long hoped for. Opimius, immediately seizing the occasion thus offered, was in great delight, and urged the people to revenge; but there happening a great shower of rain on a sudden, it put an end to the business of that day.

Early the next morning, the consul summoned the senate, and whilst he advised with the senators in the senate-house, the corpse of Antyllius was laid upon a bier, and brought through the market-place there exposed to open view, just before the senate-house, with a great deal of crying and lamentation.

* * *

The senators, after some time, withdrew, and presently ordered that Opimius, the consul, should be invested with extra-ordinary power to protect the common-wealth and suppress all tyrants. This being decreed, he presently commanded the senators to arm themselves, and the Roman knights to be in readiness very early the next morning, and every one of them to be attended with two servants well armed. Fulvius, on the other side, made his preparations and collected the populace.

* * *

Fulvius, when the people were gathered together in a full body, by the advice of Caius sent his youngest son into the market-place, with a herald's rod in his hand. He, being a very handsome youth, and modestly addressing himself, with tears in his eyes and a becoming bashful-ness, offered proposals of agreement to the consul and the whole senate. The greatest part of the assembly were inclinable to accept of the proposals; but Opimius said, that it did not become them to send messengers and capitulate with the senate, but to surrender at discretion to the laws, like loyal citizens, and endeavour to merit their pardon by submission. He com-manded the youth not to return, unless they would comply with these conditions. Caius, as it is reported, was very forward to go and clear himself before the senate; but none of his friends consenting to it, Fulvius sent his son a second time to intercede for them, as before. But Opimius, who was resolved that a battle should ensue, caused the youth to be apprehended and committed into custody; and then with a company of his foot-soldiers and some Cretan archers set upon the party under Fulvius. These archers did such execution, and inflicted so many wounds, that a rout and flight quickly ensued. Fulvius fled into an obscure bathing-house; but shortly after being discovered, he and his eldest son were slain together. Caius was not observed to use any violence against any one; but extremely disliking all these outrages, retired to Diana's temple. There he attempted to kill himself, but was hindered by his faithful friends, Pomponius and Licinius; they took his sword away from him, and were very urgent that he would endeavour to make his escape. It is reported that, falling upon his knee and lifting up his hands, he prayed the goddess that the Roman people, as a punishment for their ingratitude and treachery, might always remain in slavery. For as soon as a proclamation was made of a pardon, the greater part openly deserted him.

Caius, therefore, endeavoured now to make his escape, but was pursued so close by his enemies, as far as the wooden bridge, that from thence he narrowly escaped.

* * *

As he ran along, everybody encouraged him, and wished him success, as standers-by may do to those who are engaged in a race, but nobody either lent him any assistance, or would furnish him with a horse, though he asked for one; for his enemies had gained ground, and got very near him. However, he had still time enough to hide himself in a little grove, consecrated to the Furies. In that place, his servant Philocrates having first slain him, presently afterwards killed himself also, and fell dead upon his master.

* * *

That which angered the common people most was, that at this time, in memory of his success, Opimius built the Temple of Concord, as if he gloried and triumphed in the slaughter of so many citizens. Somebody in the night time, under the inscription of the temple added this verse:

"Folly and Discord Concord's temple built,"

Yet this Opimius, the first who, being consul, presumed to usurp the power of a dictator, condemning, without any trial, with three thousand other citizens, Caius Gracchus and Fulvius Flaccus, one of whom had triumphed and been consul, the other far excelled all his contemporaries in virtue and honour, afterwards was found incapable of keeping his hands from thieving: and when he was sent ambassador to Jugurtha, King of Numidia, he was there corrupted by presents, and at his return, being shamefully convicted of it, lost all his honours, and grew old amidst the hatred and the insults of the people; who, though humble, and affrighted at the time, did not fail before long to let everybody see what respect and veneration they had for the memory of the Gracchi. They ordered their statues to be made and set up in public view; they consecrated the places where they were slain, and thither brought the first-fruits of everything, according to the season of the year, to make their offerings. Many came likewise thither to their devotions, and daily worshipped there, as at the temple of the gods.

3. THE ACHIEVEMENT OF THE GRACCHI*

The significance of the Gracchi in Roman history has been described in the most divergent terms. Champions of Socialism in its extremest forms have found in them the heralds of doctrines which even now are thought advanced,

* Hugh Last, "Gaius Gracchus," *Cambridge Ancient History* (Cambridge, England: Cambridge University Press, 1932), Vol. 9, pp. 89–93. Reprinted by permission of the publisher.

and by others they have been dismissed as demagogues of the most commonplace type, not even distinguished from the rest of their kind by any serious contribution to the political ideas of the age in which they lived. Both estimates are wide of the mark. The Gracchi were children of their time, and it was with the special problems of Rome in the latter half of the second century B.C. that they were concerned.

The business of Tiberius was to relieve the widespread unemployment of the urban population, and the plan he adopted to achieve this end was a scheme for the partial redistribution of the public land— a scheme so sane in its conception and so successful in its results that it is futile to charge its author either with reckless vote-catching or with the Utopian aspirations of unpractical ignorance. This work it was one of the tasks of Gaius to continue, though in his continuation a slight change of method appears. Probably because most of the scattered land, only suitable for distribution among individual settlers, had already been assigned, Gaius had recourse to the foundation of colonies, some at least of which were intended to provide opportunities for commercial employment. But the *lex agraria* of Tiberius Gracchus had provoked open expression of a grievance which for long had riddled the peoples of Italy with discontent: the time had come when a re-organization of the Roman confederacy could no longer with safety be delayed. This was the final goal towards which Gaius set his course, and on its attainment he staked not only his political future but his life. If he failed, his failure was inevitable: all the appeals and arguments of one young man could never break down the incorrigible selfishness of the Roman 'democracy,' from which nothing less than the menace of the Social War was enough to wring concessions.

For the rest, his achievements consist of minor changes in the administrative system; and they were changes which were salutary in themselves and free from the taint of political corruption. Even in the final phase of his career, when Gaius had undoubtedly ceased to respect the feelings of his oligarchical opponents, it is impossible to find a measure which can be said with assurance to have been framed as nothing but a bribe to some section of the people. It is not to be denied that by several of his proposals he must have gained friends for himself, as the author of any true reform is bound to do: but even the transference of the *quaestio repetundarum* to the wealthiest class outside the senatorial ring was an act which not only may well have seemed expedient at the time but also was by no means condemned by its effect. Of Gaius Gracchus it may be said that, however much some of his reforms may have served to strengthen his own position, he never helped himself by a measure which did not help the State as well. And the figures in Roman history to whom a higher tribute can honestly be paid are few indeed.

But the programmes of the Gracchi were of far less importance than the issues which they raised unwittingly. Tiberius had called attention to the problem of the unemployed: Gaius had put the gravity of the Italian question beyond dispute. But more serious even than these was the challenge which they flung down to the whole practice of the constitution and the prevailing domination of the Senate. That they were prepared to approach the Concilium Plebis with proposals for legislation which had not received senatorial approval was a trifling breach of custom, and not without parallel. If the Senate could not stop the promulgation of a bill, it had every reason to believe that a tribune would easily be found to use his veto against it. The first danger came with the deposition of Octavius. If tribunes distasteful to the People's passing mood were to be deprived of office, the way to demagogic control was barred by nothing but the Senate's claim to pro-bouleutic powers—a claim which had no statutory sanction and which had been regularly flouted in the Gracchan age— and the flimsy obstacle of *obnuntiatio*. Barriers such as these were useless. If the right to unseat an obstructive tribune were admitted, the senatorial position was lost. Tiberius Gracchus, in his dealings with Octavius, took a long step towards constitutional revolution. Still more drastic was the doctrine—adumbrated by Tiberius and made effective by Gaius—that a tribune should be capable of immediate re-election, and for an indefinite number of years. The supremacy of the first citizen, unhampered by the veto, was to be limited by nothing but the endurance of popular support; and, as can be seen from Tiberius' handling of the Asiatic bequest, no branch of government was to be immune from direct interference by the People and their chosen leader.

Such were the gravest implications of these famous tribunates. It was not the professed objects of the Gracchan programmes which mattered most, nor was it the violence which marked their authors' ends. The true cause for justifiable alarm lay in the tendency towards democracy of the most reckless type. The insignificant and unworthy fraction of the Roman People which formed the Concilium Plebis on all but exceptional occasions was to be freed of every trammel in the exercise of its legislative powers. From day to day, as bills were introduced, nothing was to prevent the enactment of those proposals which appealed most strongly to the taste of the urban mob. That way disaster clearly lay. Not even the most zealous democrat could seriously maintain that the *plebs urbana* was well equipped for the task of governing an empire, nor was it probable that the proletariate of Rome would for ever refrain from a selfish use of its authority to the detriment of the interests of the Populus Romanus as a whole.

Yet it is easy to misjudge the Gracchi. The issue, raised most acutely by the problem of Appian's value as an authority for the career of the elder brother and associated in recent times particularly with the names of Schwartz and von Pöhlmann, between those who would call them revolutionaries and those who regard them as mere reformers cannot be decided outright. A distinction must be drawn between the content of the programmes and the implications of the methods adopted to secure their passage into law. The legislative proposals contained nothing to which constitutional objection could be raised, and on this score their authors could claim to be reformers of the most legitimate type. But on the other hand it cannot be denied that some of the expedients employed in carrying the reforms could not be reconciled with the existing constitution. They implied the destruction of that equilibrium between the magistrates, the Senate and the People to which Polybius rightly ascribed much of Rome's past success, and the development in its place of an unfettered democracy wherein effective sovranty would lie with that section of the citizen body which chanced to live at Rome. But, though their behaviour reveals a familiarity with the practices of Greece which is intelligible in pupils of Blossius and Diophanes, there is no reason to believe that either of the brothers set out from the beginning to create a democracy of the Hellenic type. So far as can be seen, if no attempt, like that of M. Octavius, had been made to block the *lex agraria* by veto, Tiberius would have left the constitution unimpaired. He was honestly convinced of the value of his agrarian scheme; and, if so excellent a measure had been accepted without protest, the weapon of obstruction would have been left intact for use against less worthy proposals. But when resistance came, Tiberius, convinced of the justice of his cause and declining to see his programme burked, secured its passage by recourse to means which boded ill. The dormant sovranty of the People was stirred to a new and sinister activity. There was, indeed, no cause for alarm so long as the popular hero, whose plans it would be the business of the assembly to enact, was a man with the honesty and patriotism of a Gracchus. But the peril of a democracy swayed by its first citizen is the shortness of the step from Pericles to Cleophon; and the error of the Gracchi was their failure to reflect that not all tribunes could boast a rectitude and public spirit such as theirs. Undoubtedly the system which they adumbrated was one which differed widely from the existing practice, and to that extent the Gracchi may justly be branded as revolutionary. But constitutional change found no place in their programmes as originally conceived. The measures wherein it was latent were hurriedly framed at a later stage to counter the irrational opposition of the conservatives, and the worst that can be said of the ill-considered replies is that their authors, in the enthusiasm of youth for a noble cause, did not pause adequately to consider the dangers which the State might run in days when there were tribunes less honest than themselves.

Whatever judgment may be passed on the characters and motives of the Gracchi, the wider significance of their careers, as a milestone in the course of Roman history, is clear. An elaborate attempt to remove some crying abuses of the day had been thwarted by the forces of conservatism. The mainspring of the opposition was the Senate, and to the Senate a challenge had been flung down. The Assemblies had been used by both sides, and they were to remain pawns in the struggle henceforward. Issue had been joined about the future of the Roman constitution, and the revolutionary age had begun. When it ended with the principate of Augustus the tribunate and the Assemblies alike had sunk into insignificance, and the Senate itself only survived because its independence was henceforward to be curbed by monarchical control.

4. The Urban Side of the Gracchan Economic Crisis[*]

The critical period for the Roman Republic, it is often recognized, began in 133 B.C., the year of the tribuneship of Tiberius Gracchus. The measures which he and after him his brother Gaius (tribune in 123 and 122 B.C.) forced, over the opposition of most of the reluctant senatorial aristocracy, exposed the weaknesses of the Roman constitution with its dual development and divided responsibility and created new, irreconcilable factions whose strife eventually overthrew the Republic. The modern, who is likely to think of the English example of progress toward democracy through a series of concessions by the ruling classes, will perhaps conclude that the Gracchi only

checked what might have been a similar evolution in Roman government. On the other hand, it is quite possible that Gaius Gracchus intended to foster development toward democracy, but along Greek lines, that is, by setting himself up as a tyrant, a popular champion, who would ally himself with the merchant class to destroy the power of the aristocratic families. Uncompromising nobles like Scipio Nasica and Lucius Opimius, who did not hesitate to use violence against the Gracchi and their followers, must certainly be held chiefly accountable for the vicious nature of the subsequent factional strife which racked the state until Augustus. In any case, the Gracchan period was the beginning of the end for the Republic and is consequently worth careful study.

It is the thesis of the paper that the most pressing problems, those which precipitated the disastrous political tug of war, were economic and that they were of a peculiarly urban nature not before fully recognized by historians of Rome.

[*] Henry C. Boren, "The Urban Side of the Gracchan Economic Crisis," *American Historical Review* (Washington, D.C.: American Historical Association, 1957–58), Vol. 63, pp. 890–902. Reprinted by permission of the author and publisher.

This study was made possible, in part, through a research grant from Southern Illinois University.

These conclusions are based partly on new evidence but depend primarily upon heretofore overlooked negative evidence and a fresh look at the traditional sources.

In their discussions of the economic crisis of this period, the historians, following Appian, Plutarch, and Tiberius Gracchus himself, have emphasized the rise of the slave-operated *latifundia*, the decline of the small farmer, and the failure to enforce the centuries-old Licinian-Sextian laws limiting individual holdings of public land. This is quite proper, up to a point, for there is no doubt that there was a serious agrarian social and economic crisis from which stemmed many serious problems. But it will be seen that for Rome the most troublesome problems were urban, though these were related, certainly, to agrarian conditions; further, the urban economic situation was the most important factor in the immediate crisis.

Evidence is presented in this paper to show that the city of Rome was generally prosperous during the middle of the second century, that spending on construction and luxuries was especially heavy in the years before the Gracchi, that there was a sharp decline in building and government spending generally just before 133, and that this decline, along with other economic factors, precipitated an especially acute crisis affecting particularly the city itself in 135–134, just as Tiberius Gracchus stood for office. It is inferred that the economy of the city had become geared closely to state expenditure, though, of course, it was also dependent upon heavy private spending in the area. The tremendous income and expenditure in the 140's and the sharp curtailment in succeeding years therefore reacted directly in every phase of the city's economy.

A survey of some widely used general works will show the extent to which this study modifies the customary views of the period. A. H. J. Greenidge, after giving some attention to economic life of the city

of Rome, says "Italian agriculture was still the basis of the brilliant life of Rome. Had it not been so, the epoch of revolution could not have been ushered in by an agrarian law."[1] But the agrarian law did not "usher in" the epoch; Tiberius' measures were not seriously opposed as revolutionary until constitutional issues were injected into the struggle, when he challenged senatorial control of the provinces and of the public purse and threatened to make the tribuneship completely independent of senatorial authority by "recall" of unpopular tribunes and successive reelection of popular ones.[2]

Hugh Last writes of a general economic crisis in this period but refers primarily to the agricultural situation. He mentions the influx of large quantities of booty but notes the results only as they affected the rapid growth of the *latifundia*. He says: "Since there was no longer a livelihood to be got in the countryside, there was a movement to the towns. . . . An export trade was the only hope of employment for the fresh arrivals." Though undeniable in part, each of these views requires reexamination. Last recognizes that Tiberius' main problem was to reduce the number of "paupers" in Rome.[3]

William E. Heitland discusses the subject in a conventional manner, remarking that "Gracchus . . . was right in recognizing the land-question as the fundamental problem of the state."[4] Tenney

---

[1] *A History of Rome from the Tribunate of Tiberius Gracchus to the End of the Jugurthine War*, B.C. *133–104* (London, 1904), p. 59.

[2] It is worth noting that in its initial stages Tiberius' program was little more than an episode in the struggle between the Claudian and Scipionic factions. See Ronald Syme, *Journal of Roman Studies*, XXIV (1934), 104; K. Bilz, "Die Politik des P. Cornelius Scipio Aemilianus," *Würzburger Studien zur Altertumswissenschaft*, VII (1936), 66; also my article, "Livius Drusus, t. p. 122, and His Anti-Gracchan Program," *Classical Journal*, LII (1956), 27 f.

[3] In the *Cambridge Ancient History*, IX, 2–10.

[4] *The Roman Republic* (3 vols., Cambridge, Eng., 1923), II, 268.

Frank also treats the period in the usual fashion,[5] and so, too, does H. H. Scullard, in his recent revision of Frank B. Marsh's survey of the later republic.[6] A few writers recognize to some degree that the city of Rome had its own problems, that the influx of booty in the middle of the century had its effect on the economy, and even that the wars of the 130's seriously drained the treasury.[7] The present writer, however, knows of no one who has sufficiently emphasized the impact of the influx of wealth on the economy of the city of Rome nor anyone who has closely considered the specifically urban side of the crisis with which Tiberius Gracchus tried to deal. Tiberius, of course, did make an agrarian law the core of his program, but the immediate crisis was less agrarian than urban, less concerned with land than with people. The land distribution law was merely his answer to the really pressing problem of what to do with the growing masses of the underprivileged in Rome.

Why had so many Latin and Italian small-holders streamed into the capital? It is not necessary to accept wholly the reasoning of Tiberius, who regarded the slave-operated *litifundia* as the chief factor in the migration. It would be equally logical to insist that the chief reason for the growing urban population in the United States today is the extensive adoption of modern farm machinery. The new and more profitable and efficient capitalistic farm operation in each instance certainly accounts for the dispossession of some farmers, but there are many reasons for such a migration. Early in the second century large numbers of men from the cities of the Italian allies already were

flocking to Rome,[8] and there is no real evidence that the movement was not for the most part voluntary. The average Roman or Italian peasant living on his tiny hereditary acreage scrabbled desperately for a bare existence. Surely he longed for something better. The ex-centurion who about 171 B.C. helped put down opposition to the military levy for the war against Perseus illustrates the bleak prospect the veterans faced.[9] This man, after twenty-two years of service in the army, had been willing to return to his inheritance—a single *iugerum* of land (about three fifths of an acre) and a small hut—but how many such veterans could endure the old family farm after service in Greece or Asia? Soldiers who became acquainted with city life often preferred its numerous opportunities and varied activities to the farm. Moreover, those who held no land were exempt from military service.

During most of the first two thirds of the second century Rome was a busy place, requiring large numbers of laborers and artisans. There was much construction, financed by indemnities, booty, tribute, and the income from mines. The armies were supplied, and ships were built; numerous shops supplied the needs of the city's growing population.[10] The extensive colonization programs of the 180's and 170's may indicate that during this period not all emigrating peasants could be assimilated into the urban population. Conversely, the cessation of colonization at mid-century (no Latin colonies were established after 181 and no Roman colonies between 157 and 122[11]) indicates that for many years before the Gracchi the

---

[5] *An Economic History of Rome* (2d ed., Baltimore, Md., 1927), pp. 127 ff.

[6] *A History of the Roman World from 146 to 30* B.C. (2d ed., London, 1953), pp. 32 ff.

[7] See, for example, Guglielmo Ferrero, *The Greatness and Decline of Rome*, tr. Alfred E. Zimmern (5 vols., New York, 1907–1909), I, 50 ff.

[8] Livy 41.8. For a carefully written account of agricultural change in this period, see Tenney Frank, *Aspects of Social Behavior in Ancient Rome* (Cambridge, Mass., 1932), pp. 64 ff. Frank points out the possibility of overemphasizing the role of the *latifundia* in this period.

[9] Livy, 42–34.

[10] Greenidge speaks of the growth of the various trades in his *History*, p. 56.

[11] Velleius, 1.15; Livy 11.34.

migrating Romans and Italians were readily absorbed into the swelling, bustling metropolis.

A survey of economic activity affecting Rome in the first half of the second century and a more detailed study of the decade prior to 133 B.C. will both suggest what opportunities were available to immigrants in this period and help to show, as the result of an obvious interconnection between income and spending and economic well-being, what were the fluctuations in the city's economy in these years.

The first third of the century saw an influx of money to the city from indemnities (chiefly from Carthage, Macedonia, and Syria) and bullion from the Spanish mines that amounted to an estimated 300,000,000 *denarii*.[12] Much of the metal was quickly coined. It has been estimated that during a forty-three-year period 250,000,000 silver *denarii* were struck.[13] There was even an issue of gold coinage in 167 due to the "enormous quantities of gold staters . . . imported to Rome, partly as spoils of war and partly as payments of tribute."[14] Sale of slaves was a source of additional income. Individual soldiers brought back booty. Macedonian mines were reopened in 158[15] and yielded some precious metals. By 157, a considerable surplus was reported in the treasury.[16] Despite a possible short deflationary period in the late 180's and 170's, the period generally was one of inflation—"inflation of a better kind, the issue of ever-increasing amounts of good money."[17] This new

wealth of silver brought a change in the proportionate value of silver and copper, resulting in a gradual reduction of the weight of the bronze *as* from one ounce in 200 B.C. to half that amount at the end of the century (this may show merely that the *as* had become fiduciary coinage).

Money flowed rather freely in Rome in the decade of the 140's. Although the treasury was reported "in straits" from about 150 to about 146,[18] booty from Carthage, Corinth, and Macedonia soon bolstered public and private purses. Unfortunately, the available information is not very exact. According to Pliny, Carthage yielded 4,370 pounds of silver and "much" gold.[19] Frank estimates that Rome gained at least 45,000,000 *denarii* from both Carthage and Corinth.[20] Officers and soldiers brought back large amounts of private loot, especially from Corinth, and there were large numbers of slaves whose sale brought considerable sums. Rome, of course, had other sources of income. The productive mines in Spain, for example, increased in yield in this period.[21] Newly acquired gold mines in the Piedmont operated by Roman companies about this time produced so much metal that there was a considerable although short-lived drop in the value of gold.[22]

The extraordinary quantity of money moving into public and private coffers was not permitted to gather dust in the vaults. The years following 146 B.C. saw unusual spending in the city. Several important public buildings were put up in these years. Q. Caecilius Metellus, the conqueror of Macedonia, after his triumph built temples to Jupiter Stator and to Juno Regina, apparently within a magnificent portico erected shortly before.[23] Greek

---

12 Frank, *An Economic Survey of Ancient Rome*, Vol. I, *Rome and Italy of the Republic* (Baltimore, Md., 1933), p. 146.
13 *Ibid.*
14 Edward A. Sydenham, *The Coinage of the Roman Republic* (London, 1952), p. xxvi.
15 Frank, *Economic Survey*, I, 256.
16 Pliny, *Natural History* 33.3.55. See the estimated balance sheet for the period 200–257 in Frank, *Economic Survey*, I, 145.
17 Harold Mattingly, *Roman Coins from the Earliest Times to the Fall of the Western Empire* (London, 1928), p. 94.

18 Frank, *Economic Survey*, I, 266.
19 *Natural History* 33.141.
20 *Economic Survey*, I, 230.
21 Francis J. Wiseman, *Roman Spain* (London, 1956), p. 17; Frank, *Economic Survey*, I, 138.
22 Strabo 4.6.12.
23 See Samuel B. Platner and Thomas Ashby, *A Topographical Dictionary of Ancient Rome*

architects and sculptors were called in to design these buildings, which were reported to be the first temples in Rome of all-marble construction. "Liberated" Greek art works graced their interiors; in the central area before the temples were set Lysippus' famous statues of Alexander's generals. L. Mummius, the spoiler of Corinth, vowed a temple to Hercules Victor, which seems to have been dedicated by himself as censor in 142.[24] Pliny says Mummius filled Rome with statuary.[25] He furnished works of art, including statues by Praxiteles, for the embellishment of a temple dedicated to Felicitas, which was erected soon after 146 by L. Licinius Lucillus from booty taken in a Spanish campaign of 150–151.[26]

A major expenditure during the 140's was the construction of the Marcian aqueduct by Q. Marcius Rex at a cost of 180,000,000 *sesterces*.[27] At the same time (144–140 B.C.) Marcius repaired the Aqua Appia and the Aqua Anio Vetus. These additions to the water supply system testify to the almost explosive population growth of the city. Other major construction projects of the 140's included the rebuilding of the Pons Aemilius and the fortification of the Janiculum in 142.[28] Typical of the lavish expenditure of the times was the decision to gild the ceiling of the Capitoline temple, the first such ceiling in Rome.[29] Another large temple was undertaken in 138 B.C. by D. Junius Brutus Callaicus. Placed in the Circus

Flaminius and dedicated to Mars, it contained statuary by Scopas.[30]

Significantly corroborative of heavy government spending in this period is the present author's statistical study of coin hoards of the time, which shows a relatively heavy volume of coinage for the 140's.[31] Since the Roman *tresviri monetales* ordinarily struck coins only as they were needed to met expenses of state, coinage volume is a reliable reflection of public expenditure. Issues of *denarii* (to which the study was confined) during these years were consistently large—as one would expect on the basis of evidence presented in the paragraphs above.

It can be surmised that the years which saw such an extensive public building program also witnessed heavy spending by private persons. Much booty from the profitable wars of the 140's fell into private purses. Pliny associates the fall and looting of Corinth and Carthage with the introduction of new standards of luxury into the state.[32] In addition, contractors, artisans, and merchants would have prospered as a result of the heavy disbursements in and near Rome by the government. It must again be emphasized, however, that despite large private outlays which affected the prosperity level, it was inevitable that the general economy of the city should become intricately linked with the level of state expenditure and that any curtailment of that spending should immediately and disastrously react upon the economic fortunes of the masses of laborers and artisans at Rome.

In contrast with the prosperous 140's, the evidence—mostly negative—indicates a sharp reduction of public spending in the years after 138 B.C. Following construction of the temple to Mars in that year, there is no trace of further important public

---

(London, 1929), pp. 424, 304 f.; also Marian Elizabeth Blake, *Ancient Roman Construction in Italy from the Prehistoric Period to Augustine* (Washington, D.C., 1947), p. 131, with the references there cited, especially Velleius 1.11.3–5 and 2.1.1; Ferrero, I, 44, with references; Gaetano de Sanctis, *Storia dei Romani*, IV, 2 (Florence, 1953), pp. 76 ff., with his excellent notes.

[24] Platner and Ashby, p. 256 (based on *Corpus Inscriptionum Latinarum*, I² 626).

[25] *Natural History* 34.36.

[26] Platner and Ashby, p. 207.

[27] Frank, *Economic Survey*, I, 227.

[28] Platner and Ashby, pp. 397 f.

[29] Pliny *Natural History* 33.57.

[30] See references in Platner and Ashby, p. 328.

[31] "Numismatic Light on the Gracchan Crisis," *American Journal of Philology*, LXXIX (Apr., 1958), 140–155.

[32] *Natural History* 33.148–50.

construction for thirteen years, until 125 B.C., when there was built the Tepulan aqueduct, less than a fifth as long as the Marcian, delivering less than a tenth the volume of water.[33] This sudden drop in the scale of public spending is corroborated by the statistical coin study mentioned above. Although the issues of coins cannot be dated with sufficient accuracy to permit a year-by-year analysis, the statistics show with high probability that the pattern of consistently large issues of *denarii* in the 140's was not repeated in the 130's. The total volume of coins struck in these years was decidedly lower.[34]

Additional evidence for the changed economic pattern of the 130's may be deduced from the nature of the wars Rome waged in this decade. These military operations, relatively minor, included wars against the Numantines in Spain, against the Scordisci in Macedonia, and against a slave revolt in Sicily. None of these conflicts could have produced much booty and no doubt, in fact, represented a net loss—which means that there was proportionally less available money to use for outlays in Rome. In the later stages of the Numantine War, Scipio Aemilianus used about sixty thousand troops;[35] the city provided little spoil, and in his triumph Scipio distributed only seven *denarii* each to his soldiers[36]—hardly enough for an extended spending spree in the big city! Probably the normal tribute from Spain was reduced by the disturbed conditions, and the flow of bullion from the mines may also have been lowered,[37] although the most productive mines, near New Carthage, probably were not affected. The repulsion of the Scordisci in Macedonia in 135 was no doubt a small

task,[38] but for a time the tribute may have been lessened and income from the mines reduced.[39] The most significant of these three military operations was the Sicilian Slave War, which worsened about 135 when Eunus organized the revolt into a war of serious proportions. Wide areas were devastated.[40] The grain tithe, on which Rome had come to depend not only for income but also for food, was in large part uncollectible. This cut in grain imports did much to precipitate the immediate crisis in Rome—which must now be scrutinized more closely.

The multitude of immigrants into Rome during the years before the Gracchi could not have relished their existence in the city, even though they came, for the most part, with a wave of prosperity. Housing was inadequate, and the newcomers were crowded into large, many-storied apartment houses called *insulae*. The long, gradual inflation which characterized most decades of the century brought with it gradually rising prices and no doubt tended to benefit the commercial classes. But in an age when there were no labor unions or cost-of-living wage increases to compensate, the economic condition of the lowest classes could not have been satisfactory even during the prosperity of the 140's. "The rise in prices was more automatic and inevitable than the rise in pay."[41] Moreover, the wars which brought huge booty to Rome had brought also large numbers of slaves. While many of these were used in farm operations, no doubt there was also a tendency in the city to replace free labor with slave labor, which during the 140's and for some years following was in such excellent supply.

---

33 Platner and Ashby, pp. 27 f.
34 "Numismatic Light," pp. 144 f., 149 f.
35 Wiseman, p. 25; cf. Frank, *Economic Survey*, I, 222 f.
36 Florus 1.39; Pliny *Natural History* 33.141.
37 Oliver Davies, *Roman Mines in Europe* (Oxford, 1935), p. 94.

38 M. I. Rostovtzeff in *Social and Economic History of the Hellenistic World* (3 vols., Oxford, 1941), II, 758 f.
39 These mines were almost worked out, however, and did not yield much ore. See Frank, *Economic Survey*, I, 256.
40 Diodorus 36.1; Florus 2.7.
41 Mattingly, *Roman Coins*, p. 94.

M. I. Rostovtzeff, noting that in Gracchan times there was unrest generally throughout the Mediterranean (and suggesting that this unrest was more important than the meager evidence indicates), attributes it in part to the abundance of cheap slave labor, which displaced free workers.[42] Fritz M. Heichelheim attributes these uprisings to a general drastic rise in grain prices, which reduced many of the proletarians to starvation levels.[43] The reported remarks to the Roman mob of Scipio Aemilianus, who called its members "step-children" of Italy and declared that he had brought most of them to Rome in chains,[44] indicate that there were numerous freedmen or others of foreign birth in the jeering crowd. If the lower-class wage earner lagged behind financially in times of relative prosperity, the years of depression in the 130's must have brought widespread unemployment and unrelieved misery.

The factor in the situation which was most critical, which aroused the leaderless mob, which cried out for action, which led to the election of Tiberius Gracchus, and which influenced the direction his reform program would take was a shortage of grain and the consequent high price for bread, both chiefly the result of the Sicilian Slave War. This seems certain, even in the absence of literary evidence. Grain prices were already extremely high.[45] The city of Rome had long depended on Sicily for grain. Cicero

quotes old Cato as saying that Sicily was "the nation's storehouse, the nurse at whose breast the Roman people is fed."[46] Rome was accustomed not only to receive the grain tithe in tribute from Sicily but also to purchase additional quantities of Sicilian grain on the open market. Perhaps as much as 25 or 30 per cent of the Sicilian crop thus furnished bread for Rome's thousands.[47] Frank says that Rome, even before this period, was dependent for about half of all her grain on overseas imports, most, no doubt, from Sicily.[48] The substantial diminution of the Sicilian tenth and of regular, additional imports from Sicily therefore meant a shortage of tremendous proportions in Rome. Speculation surely followed, as was usual at Rome.[49] It appears also that grain prices in the Mediterranean area, already abnormally high, were further inflated by unusual pirate activity in this period.[50] The result was that at a time of economic distress for many wage earners, the price of bread, the staple of their diet, shot up to prohibitive levels. In Rome there must have been danger of actual starvation. Perhaps it was at this time that Lucilius wrote

> Deficit alma ceres,
> Nec plebes pane potitur.[51]

To Tiberius Gracchus, it seemed that in one stroke all the social and economic changes of recent decades showed their dire-

---

[42] Op. cit., II, 756 f., 807 f. See also Greenidge, History, pp. 57 f., 203.

[43] See "On Ancient Price Trends from the Early First Millennium B.C. to Heraclius I," Finanzarchiv, XV (1954/55), 507.

[44] Valerius Maximus 6.2.3; Velleius 2.4.4.

[45] Fritz M. Heichelheim, in the Finanzarchiv article, also "Römische Sozial- und Wirtschaftsgeschichte," in Historia Mundi (Bern, 1956), IV, 412, estimates a rise of grain prices in the Mediterranean area of 500 per cent between 140 and 138 B.C. and 1200 per cent between 140 and 127 B.C. (A personal letter from Heichelheim informs me the date 124 B.C. in Historia Mundi is a misprint.) These rather precise figures are based on a study of recent papyrus finds bearing on wheat prices, especially in Egypt. The same author, in Wirtschaft-

liche Schwankungen der Zeit von Alexander bis Augustus (Jena, 1930), p. 77, has noted the possible effect of the Sicilian Slave War on western Mediterranean markets.

[46] In Verrem 2.2.5.

[47] Vincent M. Scramuzza, Roman Sicily (Vol. III of Economic Survey), pp. 240–263.

[48] Economic History, p. 92.

[49] Theodor Mommsen, The History of Rome, tr. W. P. Dickson (4 vols., New York, 1887), IV, 597.

[50] See Heichelheim, Wirtschaftliche Schwankungen, p. 77; also Henry A. Ormerod, Piraty in the Ancient World (London, 1924), pp. 184 f.

[51] 5.fr.214; collected by W. H. Warmington for the Loeb Classical Library, Remains of Old Latin (Cambridge, Mass., 1938), III, 66.

ful consequences: the new *latifundia*, using slave labor, had drastically lowered the numbers of the old peasant stock; the immigration to Rome had given the city a numerous, noisy, and economically stricken human substratum; the new agriculture had concentrated on crops such as the olive and the grape, so that the agricultural area no longer could supply the city with grain and Rome was forced to depend on importation. Whatever proportion of this latter development was caused by the inability of Roman grain to compete with state and other imports was probably overlooked by Tiberius. Faced with the starveling proletariat and convinced that the problems were all of a piece, Tiberius saw an easy solution. He would relieve the overcrowded city and the unemployed by putting the latter on small farms. This would partially eliminate the extreme dependence on imports of overseas grain and at the same time inhibit the further development of the *latifundia*, or even reduce their numbers.

From a broader view, with longer perspective, it can now be seen that Tiberius oversimplified the problem, that the agricultural approach could not possibly have been extensive enough or popular enough with the lower-class Romans to solve the crisis, even if enough land had been available for distribution. Tiberius was not, in short, attempting to solve the most immediate, emphatically urban, problem. He was trying to turn back the clock. It must be admitted that Tiberius was actuated by other motives, of course. Appian reports, for example, his concern for the declining numbers of citizens eligible for army duty.[52]

The economic program begun by Gaius Gracchus ten years after the death of his brother is itself eloquent testimony that the problems with which he tried to deal were essentially urban. This has been rather generally recognized, though there has been a tendency to believe that these urban problems existed primarily as the result of the failure to solve the agrarian crisis. The material already presented will sufficiently modify this view. A reinterpretation of the literary evidence with consideration of the negative evidence and with assistance from some new numismatic information, will serve to bring into clearer focus the conditions which the younger Gracchus faced.

The end of the Numantine War (133 B.C.) and the Sicilian Slave War (shortly after) ended the drain on the treasury from these unprofitable conflicts, and it may be assumed that normal income was restored from mines and tribute. The rich kingdom of Pergamum came to Rome by the will of Attalus III in 133 B.C., and although some years of military operations were required to establish firm Roman control, the full treasury appears immediately to have come to Rome; when in 132 the royal personal property was sold at public auction there, frenzied bidding was reported.[53] Regardless of the depressed situation of the wage earners, there were those whose purses permitted them to buy these evidences of having arrived in society. If the Attalid treasury was actually used, as Tiberius Gracchus proposed,[54] to stock the new small farms, this outlay may have had some effect on the city's economy. The numismatic study indicates at least some rise in public spending,[55] but there is exceptional difficulty in establishing chronology of coin issues in these years.

The continued absence of public construction, which was not resumed until Gaius Gracchus' program demanded it, does not indicate a very complete recovery of an economy so dependent on state spending in the area. It has already been pointed out that the only major item of

---

[52] Appian *Civil Wars* 1.11.

[53] Pliny *Natural History* 33.149.
[54] Plutarch *Tiberius Gracchus* 14.
[55] "Numismatic Light," table A, p. 144, pp. 149 ff.

public building in the 120's before the tribunate of Gaius Gracchus was a relatively small aqueduct built in 125. The need for another aqueduct so soon after the construction of the huge Aqua Marcia in the 140's implies that neither Tiberius Gracchus' land distribution scheme nor the depression did much to reduce the population of the city.

A reform of the coinage, which probably took place in the late 120's, appears to have been a deliberately inflationary measure and was perhaps designed to relieve the load of the debtor class. Outstanding numismatists of this period have assigned this reform—revaluation of the *denarius* from ten to sixteen *asses*—to the interval between 133 and 122 and have usually connected it with the programs of one of the Gracchi.[56] The present writer has shown conclusively that the early issues of the revalued *denarii* were quite small and consequently not connected with any large spending program.[57] Since the *as* was the money of account or of reckoning, the measure was certainly inflationary.[58] Later issues of the revalued *denarius* were much larger and are perhaps those which reflect the heavy spending of Gaius Gracchus. The implication, then, is that sometime during the 120's, most likely just before the election of Gaius, this revaluation was carried through because of the deflated state of the monetary system, with the intention of giving relief to debtor groups. This move may have aided the poorer citizens somewhat, but it would have helped most the aristocrats who had been trying to keep up with the "Joneses"—the moneyed equestrians—

and had run their estates into debt. This was probably the answer of the senatorial aristocrats to the continued economic difficulties of the 120's. But it was not enough.

Perhaps, as in the year when Tiberius Gracchus was elected to office, there was a particularly acute crisis in 123, again involving the grain supply and hence the price of bread, still abnormally high.[59] If Orosius may be trusted, a locust plague devoured the grain crops of Africa in 125 B.C.[60] This would naturally have affected grain prices all over the Mediterranean. A little later, a Roman commander, Fabius, confiscated grain in Spain and sent it to Rome.[61] Since it was normally unprofitable as well as unnecessary to ship grain that distance to Rome, there must have been great need for it. On the motion of Gaius Gracchus, Fabius was censured by the Senate—presumably for mistreating allies—and payment was ordered.[62] Certain of Gaius' own measures to ensure a stable grain supply through the building of granaries and to supply grain to the Roman poor at reduced prices certainly reflect fluctuations both in supplies and prices of grain and may also bear testimony to a particularly acute crisis, which brought about his election to office.

The heavy government outlays of 123 and 122 B.C. may have "pump primed" the economy of the city of Rome back to a semblance of prosperity. Besides the building of granaries and the subsidization of a grain supply for the poor, Gracchus also furnished clothing free to citizens in the army, constructed many miles of graded, expensive roads, and established colonies. Plutarch describes him as continually surrounded by numerous con-

56 Sydenham, pp. xxviii f.; also Mattingly, in Appendix H of Sydenham, and in "Some New Studies of the Roman Republican Coinage," *Proceedings of the British Academy*, XVIII (London, 1933), 3–58.
57 "Numismatic Light," pp. 152 ff.
58 *Ibid.*, p. 153. For an opposing view, see Theodore V. Buttrey, Jr., "On the Retariffing of the Roman Denarius," American Numismatic Society *Museum Notes*, VII (1957), 57–65.

59 Heichelheim estimates that grain prices in 127 were twelve times those of 140. See fn. 45. His research shows a lowering of prices after 127 but indicates a continuing high level for many years. See *Finanzarchiv*, XV, 508.
60 5.11.2.
61 Plutarch *Gaius Gracchus* 6.
62 *Ibid.*

tractors and builders.[63] Gracchus' opponent in the tribunate in 122 B.C., Livius Drusus, with the backing of the Senate, also carried out a program to establish colonies, and some money would have been required for those which were actually established.[64] Ordinary public construction resumed in Rome in 121 B.C. when the consul, Opimius, built a basilica and refurbished the temple of Concord, and Q. Fabius Allobrogicus constructed the first of the great arches so typical of Roman *fora* in later times.[65]

This enormous increase in spending in and about the city of Rome after 122 B.C.—corroborated in the author's numismatic statistical study[66]—no doubt put an end, at least temporarily, to the long-drawn economic depression. The supply of grain may, for a time, have been sufficient to prevent a continuation of the especially onerous hardship of high-priced bread in a time of deflation and unemployment. Prices seem to have declined, but not to the level of mid-century.[67] The problem

of an adequate grain supply was not permanently solved and continued to plague the Roman authorities for centuries. Shortages of grain seem always to have given rise to an outcry of indignation demanding immediate action, as in the days of the Gracchi.

The conclusions reached in this paper can be summarized as follows. It appears that both of the Gracchi were faced with approximately the same problems: an overcrowded city, unemployment, unrest, and economic depression, plus an acute crisis due to grain shortage and consequent high prices of bread. Tiberius tried to solve the dilemma by reestablishing a class of "sturdy yeomen" (to use a term Englishmen have applied to about the same sort of program); Gaius, recognizing the failure of his brother's agrarian law, adopted other methods. The depression, which was tied in closely with the reduced level of state spending in the immediate vicinity of Rome, seems to have endured almost continuously for about fifteen years. The measures of the younger Gracchus, plus other stabilizing factors, appear to have ended the worst of the depression by 122 B.C.

---

63 *Ibid.*, 6, 7.
64 See my article "Livius Drusus," p. 31.
65 Platner and Ashby, p. 590.
66 "Numismatic Light," pp. 150 f.; cf. table A, p. 144.
67 See fn. 59.

Southern Illinois University

5. The Political Background of Tiberius Gracchus[*]

In 145 B.C., a portion of the senatorial oligarchy had seemed inclined to undertake reform, at least in a limited way. At first the circle of Scipio Aemilianus seemed to favor reform, but soon they abandoned it.

I. THE ORIGINS OF THE AGRARIAN REFORM (140–135 B.C.)

If Laelius and the majority of the *Patres*

* Jérôme Carcopino, "La République de 133 à 44 avant J.C.," *Histoire Romaine*, translated by Donald Kagan (Paris: Presses Universitaires de France, 1935), Vol. 2, pp. 171–174; 179–181; 189. Reprinted by permission of the publisher.

who followed Aemilianus finally declared against the rearrangement of the *ager publicus* in 140, a significant number of the nobles would not resign themselves to the abandonment of a project whose necessity safety would sooner or later impose. Some of them, shut out of the Scipionic circle or hostile to it, even counted on its coming due, which they considered inevitable, to drive out the dominant faction and seize the reins of government. At the head of this group of aristocrats, in opposition to the oligarchy of the moment, Cicero named Appius Claudius Pulcher, Q. Caecilius Metellus Macedonicus, P. Licinius Crassus, P. Mucius Scaevola. These were important names, indeed strong personalities who, united among themselves by family ties, associated the diversity of their temperaments and inclinations in the service of a just cause. In the case of Scaevola, a learned and scrupulous jurisconsult, it was oppressed right that protested. With Metellus and Crassus, who carried the title *Dives* among his surnames, the solidarity of the *nobilitas* and of the rich equestrians was affirmed. Pulcher, finally, perpetuated the ideal of the conservative demagogue that had inspired the Claudii, his ancestors. Having decided to depend upon the people, in favor of the distribution of the public domain, these nobles supported the tribunician initiatives which could bring it about while enlarging the role of the *comitia* and favoring their own candidacies.

Laelius had barely left office when, in 139, the tribune Gabinius, grandson of a slave, in connivance with the same group brought to a vote a proposal instituting the secret ballot in elections.... For the moment, at least, the law gave the people confidence in themselves, reawakened their activity, and assured the senatorial group, which did not at all rule in the Curia, of prevailing henceforth in the plebeian assemblies.

From 138 the ruling oligarchy began to be driven from its positions. It had seized all the key offices: the censorship in 142 for its great man, Aemilianus; the pontificate in 141 for Nasica, the cousin of Aemilianus; the consulship in 141 and 140 for C. Servilius Caepio and Q. Pompeius, then for Q. Servilius Caepio and C. Laelius, faithful supporters of Aemilianus. On the other hand, in 138, it could not prevent the consuls, D. Junius Brutus and

P. Scipio Nasica, from being sent to prison on the order of two plebeian tribunes, nor from being replaced by the incapable C. Hostilius Mancinus and by M. Aemilius Lepidus, a relative of Appius Claudius Pulcher. To be sure, it succeeded in recovering the highest magistracy for 136, awarded to two of Aemilianus' men, Sextus Atilius Serranus and L. Furius Philus. But this was paid for with two capitulations: Mancinus was handed over to the Celtiberians, and Aemilianus himself had to remain silent when a tribune who was hostile to him, L. Cassius Longinus, proposed the extension to popular jurisdiction of the secret vote by ballots. The oligarchy now contested the game by outbidding its opponents, and with this deadly game it "undermined the ground beneath it."

Then the dissident *Patres* pushed their advantage. First they allowed the Senate to invest Aemilianus with the splendid mission of inspecting the allied realms. Then, while he was visiting Egypt, Syria, and the kingdom of Pergamum in great pomp during 136 and part of 135, they profited by his absence to accentuate their propaganda. It was among them that the centuries chose the censors of 136: Appius Claudius Pulcher and M. Fulvius Nobilior. The latter hastened to designate his colleague *princeps senatus....*

[Carcopino goes on to describe the census of 136, carried out by these new censors, which showed a decrease in the number of citizens. He concludes that it was natural to attribute the depopulation to the distress of the citizens, driven from the *ager publicus* by the selfishness of the nobles. At the same time, Rome was experiencing serious military reverses in Spain and a great slave rebellion that broke out in Sicily but soon spread all over the Mediterranean, even to Italy and Rome itself.]

* * *

This last source of trouble was quickly extinguished, but those who ruled the Republic asked themselves, not unreasonably, whether it would not be rekindled some day. Rome at some future time would be forced to fight for her existence against an invisible conspiracy of slaves. These slaves, exalted by the egalitarian protection of their universal divinities, along with the overthrow of sacred institutions, would prepare the double revenge of the Orient over the hegemony of Italy and of the oppressed over the possessors. Among the nobles and the *equites*, the idea grew that the most solid rampart that could be built against rebellion consisted of the number and devotion of the free peasants, interested in preserving a civilization and an empire whose benefits they were at last invited to share. Thus the events of 134 opened many eyes, and many who were refractory were converted to the reform of the *ager publicus*.

It was then that the *Patres*, who favored reform, decided that the moment had come to run the risk of beginning the job at once. They did not linger to elaborate an entire new legislation. They were satisfied to take up again what was almost the *rogatio* of 145, amending it on several points whose defectiveness had weakened the bill. Then, since they counted on the tribes rather than on the centuries, they concerned themselves with winning the goodwill of the tribunes-elect and with gaining from among them a champion who would consent to use his right of initiative to serve as patron for their bill before the assembly, and to put it in the form of a *plebiscitum*. Now the tribunician college, which had been elected in the summer of 134, did not appear to contain opponents to their wishes; the most illustrious of its members, Tiberius Sempronius Gracchus, the son-in-law of the *princeps senatus*, who directed the reforming party, had adopted his program with the secret impetuousness of his nature.

He was ambitious for the honor of attaching his name to the bill. With the ascendancy that the glory of his family conferred on him, the integrity of his character, and above all with the eloquence with which he was endowed and which he had cultivated by meditation and study, he would try to carry the vote for what must be, for posterity, the *lex Sempronis*. Moreover, the difficulties disappeared before him. When he took possession of his plebeian magistracy on December 10, 134, the two consuls who might have thwarted him before long left the city: Aemilianus for Numantia, C. Fulvius for Sicily. Of their successors designated since autumn, one, L. Calpurnius Piso, was destined to inherit that warlike province; the other, who would remain at Rome, P. Mucius Scaevola, was ranked among the promoters of the agrarian law and would support it with his power. Truly, those who had backed Tiberius Gracchus had involved him in a fine game. But they had not counted on the inexorable spirit of a young man, disdainful of restraint and deceit, burning with pride and faith, who would have to hurry their pace, alter their object, and finally compromise their issue in the tragedy in which he perished.

[An account of the background and training of Tiberius follows. He was educated by Blossius of Cumae, a Stoic, and by Diophanes of Mitylene. Carcopino sees the former as a socialist and the latter as a proponent of a Periclean democracy. "All for the people was the maxim of the theorist of Cumae. All by the people seems to have been the last word of the orator of Mitylene."]

* * *

Pericles had governed the people and the empire of Athens by means of his rhetoric, which blew over the assembly the wisdom with which he was animated. Tiberius was encouraged by this grandiosity to try, in his turn in the forum, the only chance that circumstances had left to his ambition. The examples of Diophanes verified the precepts of Blossius, and, just as in the time of Anaxagor, as the eloquence of Pericles had manifested the sovereignty of mind through the sovereignty of the people, Tiberius tried to make an appeal from the Rostra to the *plebs*, who would undertake in Rome the rule of reason announced by the Stoa.

Here we touch on the misunderstanding that separated Tiberius from the *Patres*, and which lacerated his own conscience in spite of himself. His allies in the Senate were opportunists, who, in the interests of their preferments, believed that the time had come for reform imposed by conquest and destined to modify the apportionment of its profits in order to assure its growth. By means of an expedient habitual to the Roman aristocracy, they once again made use of the tribunate to bend their colleagues to their will, sanctioned by popular suffrage. Tiberius, on the contrary, was a doctrinaire who derived the proposed law from a moral obligation whose demands surpassed the bill and did not permit

temporizing or delays. Because of the lessons on which his youth had been nourished, more than because of the cruel disillusionment in which he had recently been steeped, he felt himself led to consider the tribunate, sustained by the vote of the citizens, as the supreme power of a rational state. This latent contradiction would tragically weigh upon his destiny. It explains unforseen changes that operated in him, in the increasing bitterness of his actions. It explains the divorce which, isolating him from the entire nobility, soon would deliver him without weapons or troops into the arms of his enemies. But the contradiction was only declared when it came into contact with obstacles. It was softened at first by the basic sincerity of Tiberius, who entered office to carry out loyally the mandate that Pulcher, Metellus, Crassus, and Scaevola had given him. It did not prevent him from producing an agrarian *rogatio*, which on all points conformed to the plans of his noble patrons, uniquely inspired in its arrangement by their enlightened patriotism and their conservative prudence.

6. Judgement on the Senate and the Roman People*

[His enemies] . . . razed the house of Gaius before selling his land and, by an unaccustomed refinement of cruel rigor, his wife's dowry was confiscated. The hatred of Opimius dishonored the victory of the nobles.

The cruelty by no means made the victory more durable. The Senate carried it off, but at what a price. Jealous of the *equites*, and exposed to their envious rivalry, the nobles were forced to enter into a compact with them, left to pay them the ransom for their complicity later

* Jérôme Carcopino, "La République de 133 à 44 avant J.C.," *Histoire Romaine*, translated by Donald Kagan (Paris: Presses Universitaires de France, 1935), Vol. 2, pp. 264–265. Reprinted by permission of the publisher.

on. Guardian of the constitution and of the *mos maiorum*, the nobility had sounded the revolutionary call to action. By means of the *senatus consultum ultimum*, that caricature of law, which raised up force as the arbiter of political conflicts, it had in advance made legitimate its defeat. The day would come when force, passed into the hands of generals in seditions or against seditions, would no longer belong to it. Charged with a venerable tradition of interests superior to those of the fatherland, the nobles identified them, sacrificed them to momentary interests, and treated as public enemies the only republicans who could still save the Republic. The government of Gaius has been defined as the first draft of Caesarism. In reality the regime of which the last and greatest of the Gracchi dreamed, and where the sword remained in its sheath, would have guaranteed the prosperity and greatness of Rome while avoiding Caesar. If Gaius had fulfilled his destiny, he would have rendered to Rome, in domestic peace and in the more flexible play of her free institutions, the services which historical evolution required. These services would come, after terrible convulsions and under the oppression of despotism, from the dictatorship of the empire: the reconstitution of the peasant class by the redistribution of public lands, the collaboration of senators and *equites*, the unification of Italy in the Roman state, the expansion of Italian civilization beyond the mountains and the seas. The misfortune is not only that Gaius failed in his vocation,

but that his vocation carried in itself contradictions by which he was forced to wear out his spirit. In the hard-hearted society that issued from conquest, persuasion alone was powerless to suppress indefinitely the antagonisms that he had to diminish. To suppose that it would arise in the bosom of the reconciled Roman state as by a miracle would have been as impossible a wager as to rely again on a people spoiled by fortune to restrain its share of the advantages spontaneously and to invite all Italy to the banquet. Gaius did not, like his brother, bear the burden of his imprudence and his faults. But, like him, he made the mistake of acting at a time when, equally insensible of everything that was not an immediate profit, the *plebs* could no longer, the nobles could not yet, understand him.

7. THE GRACCHAN INTERVENTION*

It is Smith's thesis that before Tiberius Gracchus, Rome was a compact, integrated society which was capable of achieving the reforms she needed if undisturbed. Rome, he thinks, had reached a point at which she needed to move slowly and carefully, "but a catastrophic chance" brought the Gracchi to power.

To understand the disaster of the Gracchi we must consider briefly the facts and theory of Rome's government at this time; for the tragedy lay in the means they adopted rather than in the ends they sought. Tiberius' aims were unoriginal; had his means but shared this quality, Rome's history might have been happier. The same may be said of Caius' aims in so far as they were those of his brother; but he went further, and the unintended results of his brother's means became with him a further end consciously pursued; to this extent he is the more guilty of the pair.

Rome was still governed by the machinery of the city-state from which she had

evolved. Annual magistrates elected by the people exercised for a year supreme power; they were appointed equally for civil and administrative duties and to command Rome's armies, though war was rapidly becoming highly professional. There were only the rudiments of a civil service to provide the routine administrative experience necessary to control an empire; while the junior magistrates attached to consuls and praetors were themselves learning their duties during their year of office. It was difficult for a magistrate to initiate a policy of reform during one year of office, and men tended therefore to carry out the normal work of their magistracy without attempting positive and possibly controversial reforms. But in spite of the inadequacy of such an organization to run an empire, Rome had not been unsuccessful; and this was due to the

* R. E. Smith, *The Failure of the Roman Republic* (Cambridge, England: Cambridge University Press, 1955), pp. 80–85. Reprinted by permission of the publisher.

Senate, where alone experience and ideas could be blended into policy. By origin a consultative body, it had over the centuries acquired great powers, which had been conceded not only because of the social predominance of the *nobiles*, but because of the success of the Senate's leadership in the great wars. The Senate was the only permanent body at Rome, continuously sitting, not unwieldy, and well-informed; and in governing an Empire something less fluid than an annual magistracy is necessary if there is to be continuity of policy, if, in fact, there is to be a *ratio imperii*. Within the Senate was gathered the accumulated wisdom of the State, for most ex-magistrates became members; and by hearing its debates as they climbed the ladder of promotion, they acquired an appreciation and understanding of the problems which they would later have to handle.

It had become the custom for the magistrates to consult the Senate on all important matters; and while they could act against the Senate's advice, they very seldom did. For this there were two reasons: first, the practical wisdom and administrative experience contained within the Senate was such as to command respect, and the acceptance of its advice gave strength to the magistrate if difficulties followed. And secondly, the higher magistrates, who came from the comparatively few families that constituted the governing class, felt a sense of loyalty to their class; to flout the Senate would have seemed tantamount to flouting their own class. Even more important, these dominant groups of nobles fashioned the policy which the members of their families, whose election to office they procured, were expected in their magistracy to carry out. There was a solidarity among themselves, not because they set their own interests above those of Rome, but because they identified the two; in their minds their good was Rome's good.

In this way a permanent and responsible form of government had evolved, which had shown itself capable of dealing with the domestic and political problems of the State. The aristocracy was at this time conservative but, except for a few, not reactionary; with their power and responsibility went privilege, and this fruit of government they would not lightly surrender. True, since 146 B.C. many of them had been enjoying the fruit without exercising the responsibility; but this, as we have pointed out, need only have been a passing phase. Until the Gracchi they had not been called upon to consider the surrender; they had assumed that they were the natural and proper heirs both to the responsibility and the fruit of government.

Yet their power rested on a very uncertain foundation. The Senate enjoyed its constitutional powers by precedent and usage; if seriously challenged, it could show no writ other than the successful history of the last century to authorize or justify its present powers; it could lose all in an hour. It was just this challenge that Tib. Gracchus posed; he initiated legislation to which the Senate was in the circumstances bitterly opposed; yet his laws were passed. He handled the legacy of Attalus, though it involved important considerations of foreign policy; and the Senate could only look on in impotent rage. When challenged, they had not the direct power. Caius did the same; for two years he was Rome's uncrowned king, and, in whatever sphere he wanted, he revealed the Senate's impotence.

The Gracchi behaved, for whatever laudable motive, in a way that was fundamentally irresponsible. By using the tribunate as an independent means of initiating legislation they revived latent powers which had in the process · of evolution long remained dormant, and which in the increased complexity of imperial administration should have continued dormant. Only by adapting the facts if not the theory of government to suit the changing needs had responsible government been possible; by their behaviour the

Gracchi undid the evolution of centuries. It was impossible to guarantee orderly government if one tribune after another, with all the personal differences of policy, could initiate legislation and deal with the highest affairs of State by bringing the business before a chance gathering of the Roman mob. There could be no necessary continuity of policy, and such a lack was fatal to imperial rule. Yet that was exactly what the Gracchi did, and with constitutional justification; and once done the precedent stood for all to imitate.

The effect on the governing class was disastrous. Conservative they were, and concerned, if directly challenged, to maintain a balance of society which gave them a dominating position. Any necessary reforms therefore must be gradual, and each step would be taken as its necessity became clear to a majority of the Senate. But each step would by that very fact be surely won and established, as having been granted by mutual agreement, or at least by a solid and accepted majority, not sullenly acquiesced in because it was impossible to interpose any constitutional opposition. Only indirect opposition was possible, and this could serve only to degrade 'constitutionality'. There were important men who supported Tib. Gracchus; with time more would have been persuaded to their ideas or to the need for resolving the problems those ideas were designed to solve. Reformers who try to do too much too quickly succeed only in doing harm; had the Gracchi but had the patience to submit to failure, they would eventually have succeeded, as did the Reformers in England.

The Gracchi came forward impatiently with their schemes, as though alternatives did not exist, and by their methods they directly challenged the position of the governing class; and with that position went the accompanying privilege and power. Hitherto they had taken it all for granted; but once they saw the dangerous threat, the defence of what they held

became their first concern. The problems of the State and the Empire began to recede into the background, to come to the front only to serve the interests of rival factions. The Gracchi put them on the defensive; their successors kept them in that posture. At once there grew up an antagonism, soon to become hostility, between the governing class and those ambitious persons who used the instrument the Gracchi had forged to serve their own purpose. They had shown the way to independence and irresponsibility, for tribunician legislation could not be a substitute for systematic government; while the Senate could only hope to succeed by developing a policy that would win 'popular' support, which in the circumstances of Rome could only mean to pander to the mob.

Caius had gone further; by organizing the Equites as a political power in opposition to the Senate, as he himself boasted, he had further divided Rome. No one would dispute that the Equites should be taken into partnership in government; but to have set them up in opposition to the only permanent body, and to have given them power which enabled them to forward their own interests without carrying part of the responsibility of government, this was a piece of ignorance or petty politics, damnable either way. The Senate reacted as was to be expected; and while we cannot praise the Senate for its part in the events which led to the deaths of the Gracchi, we must remember that, as the Gracchi themselves had shown, the Senate was without direct constitutional power. All they could do was to invoke emergency powers, which had been developed for the co-ordination of Italy, for domestic purposes, and thus create in the *senatus consultum ultimum* a further cause of strife between the Senate and its enemies. Their handling of the troubles served only to embitter the Gracchan followers, and sow seeds of resentment in the minds of men who had done no wrong.

SECTION VIII

The Roman Revolution—Phase Two: *Sulla*

In the years following the death of Gaius Gracchus the Senatorial aristocracy reasserted its dominance and retained it with little challenge until the emergence of a new kind of popular leader, Marius. His career demonstrated that a military leader, backed by a volunteer army owing allegiance to its general rather than to the state, could wreak havoc with the state and its constitution when allied with revolutionary political forces. The career of Sulla would show that even when allied with conservative forces, the politician on horseback was a menace not only to the old order but to the safety and property of all Roman citizens.

Sulla's life and activities were interesting from his first entry into public affairs, but the most significant part of his career begins with his return to Italy after the war with Mithridates. His victory in the civil war which ensued made possible his attempt to place the Roman republic on a firm foundation. His retirement from public life at the height of his power led Caesar to say that in politics Sulla did not even know his ABC's and has presented a puzzle to historians ever since. The latter part of Sulla's career is described in the selections from Appian and Plutarch. Various assessments of the man and his career are offered by Hugh Last, Theodor Mommsen, and Guglielmo Ferrero. The last two selections, by Carcopino and Stockton, address themselves to the vexed question of Sulla's retirement.

1. Sulla's Career from the Defeat of Mithridates to the Death of the Dictator (85-78 b.c.)*

Sulla now hastened his return to meet his enemies, having quickly finished all his business with Mithridates, as I have already related. Within less than three years he had killed 160,000 men, recovered Greece, Macedonia, Ionia, Asia, and many other countries that Mithridates had previously occupied, taken the king's fleet away from him, and from such vast possessions restricted him to his paternal kingdom alone. He returned with a large

---

* Appian, *The Civil Wars*, 1. 76–84; 95–106, translated by Horace White, pp. 52–57; 65–75.

and well-disciplined army, devoted to him and elated by its exploits. He had abundance of ships, money, and apparatus suitable for all emergencies, and was an object of terror to his enemies. Carbo and Cinna were in such fear of him that they despatched emissaries to all parts of Italy to collect money, soldiers, and supplies. They took their leading citizens into friendly intercourse and appealed especially to the newly created citizens of the towns, pretending that it was on their account that they were threatened with the present danger. They hastily repaired the ships, and recalled those that were in Sicily, guarded the coast, and, with fear and trembling, made rapid preparations in every way.

Sulla wrote to the Senate in a tone of superiority concerning himself. He recounted what he had done in Africa in the Jugurthine war while he was still quæstor, what he had done as lieutenant in the Cimbric war, as prætor in Cilicia and in the Social war, and as consul. Most of all he dwelt upon his recent victories in the Mithridatic war, enumerating to them the many nations that had been under Mithridates and that he had recovered for the Romans. Of nothing did he make more account than that those who had been banished from Rome by Cinna had fled to him, and that he had received the helpless ones and supported them in their affliction. In return for which he said that he had been declared a public enemy by his foes, his house had been destroyed, his friends put to death, and his wife and children had with difficulty made their escape to him. He would be there presently to take vengeance, for them and for the entire city, upon the guilty ones. He assured the other citizens, and the new citizens, that he made no complaint against them. When the contents of the letters became known fear fell upon all, and they began sending messengers to reconcile him with his enemies and to tell him in advance that if he wanted any security he should write to the Senate at

once. They ordered Cinna and Carbo to cease recruiting soldiers until Sulla's answer should be received. They promised to do so, but as soon as the messengers had gone they proclaimed themselves consuls for the ensuing year so that they need not come back to the city directly to hold the election. They traversed Italy, collecting soldiers whom they carried across by detachments on shipboard to Liburnia, as they expected to meet Sulla there.

The first detachment had a prosperous voyage. The next one encountered a storm and those who reached land went home immediately, as they did not relish the prospect of fighting their fellow-citizens. When the rest learned this they refused to cross to Liburnia. Cinna was angry and called them to an assembly in order to coerce them. They, angry also and ready to defend themselves, assembled. One of the lictors, who was clearing the road for Cinna, struck somebody who was in the way and one of the soldiers struck the lictor. Cinna ordered the arrest of the offender, whereupon a clamor rose on all sides, stones were thrown at him, and those who were near him drew their swords and stabbed him. So Cinna also perished during his consulship. Carbo recalled those who had been sent over by ship to Liburnia. As he was solicitous about the present state of things, he did not go back to the city, although the tribunes summoned him with urgency to hold an election for the choice of a colleague. When they threatened to reduce him to the rank of a private citizen he came back and ordered the holding of the consular election, but as the omens were unfavorable he postponed it to another day. When that day came lightning struck the temples of Luna and of Ceres; so the augurs prorogued the comitia beyond the summer solstice, and Carbo remained the sole consul.

Sulla answered those who came to him from the Senate, saying that he would never be on friendly terms with the men who had committed such crimes. Still he would not prevent the city from extending clemency to them. As for security he said that, as he had a devoted army, he could better furnish lasting security to them, and to those who had fled to his camp, than they to him; whereby it was made plain in a single sentence that he would not disband his army, but was contemplating the exercise of supreme power. He demanded of them his former dignity, his property, and the sacerdotal office, and that they should restore to him in full measure whatever other honors he had previously held. He sent some of his own men with the Senate's messengers to confer about these matters. As soon as they learned from the Brundusians that Cinna was dead and that Rome was in an unsettled state, they went back to Sulla without transacting their business. He started with five legions of Italian troops and 6000 horse, to whom he added some other forces from the Peloponnesus and Macedonia, in all about 40,000 men. He led them from the Piræus to Patræ, and then sailed from Patræ to Brundusium in 1600 ships. The Brundusians received him without a fight, for which favor he afterward gave them exemption from customs-duties, which they enjoy to this day. Then he put his army in motion and went forward.

He was met on the road by Cæcilius Metellus Pius, who had been chosen some time before to finish up the Social War, but who did not return to the city for fear of Cinna and Marius. He had been awaiting the turn of events in Liguria, and now offered himself as a volunteer ally with the force under his command, as he was still a proconsul; for those who have been chosen to this office retain it till they come back to Rome. After Metellus, came Pompey, who not long afterward was surnamed the Great, son of the Pompeius who was killed by lightning and who was supposed to be unfriendly to Sulla. The son removed this suspicion by coming with a legion which he had collected from the territory of Picenum on the reputation of his father, who had

been very influential there. A little later he recruited two more legions and became Sulla's most useful right-hand man in these affairs. So Sulla held him in honor, though still very young; and they say he rose at the entrance of none other than this youth. After the war was finished Sulla sent him to Africa to drive out the part of Carbo and to restore Hiempsal (who had been expelled by the Numidians) to his kingdom. For this service Sulla allowed him a triumph over the Numidians, although he was under age, and was still in the equestrian order. He took his start to greatness from this beginning, and was sent against Sertorius in Spain and later against Mithridates in Pontus. Cethegus also joined Sulla, although with Cinna and Marius he had been violently hostile to him and had been driven out of the city with them. He was now a suppliant, and offered his services to Sulla in any capacity he might desire.

Sulla now had plenty of soldiers and a sufficient number of friends of the higher orders, whom he used as lieutenants. He and Metellus, who were both proconsuls, marched in advance, for it seems that Sulla, who had been appointed proconsul against Mithridates, had at no time laid down his command, although he had been voted a public enemy at the instance of Cinna. Now Sulla moved against his enemies with a most intense yet concealed hatred. The people in the city, who had formed a pretty fair judgment of the character of the man, and who remembered his former attack and capture of the city, and who took into account the decrees they had proclaimed against him, and who had witnessed the destruction of his house, the confiscation of his property, the killing of his friends, and the narrow escape of his family, were in a state of terror. Conceiving that there was no middle ground between victory and utter destruction, they united with the consuls to resist Sulla, but with trepidation. They despatched messengers throughout Italy to collect soldiers, provisions, and money, and, as in cases of extreme peril, they omitted nothing that zeal and earnestness could suggest.

Gaius Norbanus and Lucius Scipio, who were then the consuls, and with them Carbo, who had been consul the previous year (all of them moved by equal hatred of Sulla and more fearful than others because they knew that they were more to blame for what had been done), levied the best possible army from the city, obtained an additional one from Italy, and marched against Sulla in detachments. They had 200 cohorts of 500 men each at first, and their forces were considerably augmented afterward. The sympathies of the people were much in favor of the consuls, because the action of Sulla, who was marching against his country, seemed to be that of an enemy, while that of the consuls, even if they were working for themselves, was ostensibly the cause of the republic. Many persons, too, who knew that they had shared the guilt of the consuls, and who were believed to share their fears, coöperated with them. They knew very well that Sulla was not meditating merely prevention, correction, and alarm for them, but destruction, death, confiscation, and complete extermination. In this they were not mistaken, for the war ruined everything. From 10,000 to 20,000 men were slain in a single battle more than once. Fifty thousand on both sides lost their lives around the city, and to the survivors Sulla was unsparing in severity, both to individuals and to communities, until, finally, he made himself the undisputed master of the whole Roman government, so far as he wished or cared to be.

It seems, too, that divine Providence foretold to them the results of this war. Sights terrible and unexpected were observed by many, both in public and in private, throughout all Italy. Ancient, awe-inspiring oracles were remembered. Many monstrous things happened. A mule gave birth to a colt. A pregnant woman was delivered of a viper instead of a baby.

There was a severe earthquake divinely sent and some of the temples in Rome were thrown down (the Romans gave altogether too much attention to such things). The Capitol, that had been built by the kings 400 years before, burned down, and nobody could discover the cause of the fire. All things seemed to point to a succession of slaughters, to the conquest of Italy and of the Romans themselves, to the capture of the city, and a change in the form of government.

This war began as soon as Sulla arrived at Brundusium, which was in the 174th Olympiad. Considering the magnitude of the work accomplished, its length was not great, compared with such wars in general, since the combatants rushed upon each other with the fury of private enemies. For this reason greater and more distressing calamities than usual befell the eager participants in a short space of time. Nevertheless the war lasted three years in Italy alone, until Sulla had secured the supreme power, but in Spain it continued even after Sulla's death.

[Appian then describes the details of the civil war, concluding with an account of Sulla's victory at the Colline Gate and the massacre of his opponents that followed.]

* * *

After accomplishing these deeds throughout Italy by war, fire, and murder, Sulla's generals visited the several cities and established garrisons at the suspected places. Pompey was despatched to Africa against Carbo and to Sicily against Carbo's friends who had taken refuge there. Sulla himself called the Roman people together in an assembly and made them a speech vaunting his own exploits and making other menacing statements in order to inspire terror. He finished by saying that he would bring about a change which would be beneficial to the public if they would obey him. He would not spare one of his enemies, but would visit them with the utmost severity. He would take vengeance by every means in his power on all prætors, quæstors, military tribunes, and everybody else who had committed any hostile act after the day when the consul Scipio violated the agreement made with him. After saying this he forthwith proscribed about forty senators and 1600 knights. He seems to have been the first one to punish by proscription, to offer prizes to assassins and rewards to informers, and to threaten with punishment those who should conceal the proscribed. Shortly afterward he added the names of other senators to the proscription. Some of these, taken unawares, were killed where they were caught, in their houses, in the streets, or in the temples. Others were picked up, carried to Sulla, and thrown down at his feet. Others were dragged through the city and trampled on, none of the spectators daring to utter a word of remonstrance against these horrors. Banishment was inflicted upon some and confiscation upon others. Spies were searching everywhere for those who had fled from the city, and those whom they caught they killed.

There was much killing, banishment, and confiscation also among those Italians who had obeyed Carbo, or Marius, or Norbanus, or their lieutenants. Severe judgments of the courts were rendered against them throughout all Italy on various charges—for exercising military command, for serving in the army, for contributing money, for rendering other service, or even giving counsel against Sulla. Hospitality, private friendship, the borrowing or lending of money, were alike accounted crimes. Now and then one would be arrested for doing a kindness to a suspect, or merely for being his companion on a journey. These accusations abounded mostly against the rich. When charges against individuals failed Sulla took vengeance on whole communities. He punished some of them by demolishing their citadels, or destroying their walls, or by imposing heavy fines and contributions on them. Among most of them he placed colonies of his troops in order to hold Italy under garrisons, sequestrating their lands and houses and dividing them among his soldiers, whom he thus made true to him during his life and even after his death. As they could not be secure in their own holdings unless all of Sulla's affairs were on a firm foundation, they were his stoutest champions even after he was deceased. While the affairs of Italy were in this state, Pompey sent a force and captured Carbo, who had fled with many persons of distinction from Africa to Sicily and thence to the island of Cossyra. He ordered his officers to kill all of the others without bringing them into his presence; but Carbo, who had been thrice consul, he caused to be brought before his feet in chains, and after making a public harangue at him, killed him and sent his head to Sulla.

When everything had been accomplished against his enemies as he desired, and there was no longer any hostile force except that of Sertorius, who was far distant, Sulla sent Metellus into Spain against him and managed everything in the city to suit himself. There was no longer any occasion for laws, or elections, or for casting lots, because everybody was shivering with fear and in hiding, or dumb. Everything that Sulla had done as consul, or as proconsul, was confirmed and ratified, and his gilded equestrian statue was erected in front of the rostra with the inscription, "Cornelius Sulla, a fortunate commander," for so his flatterers called him on account of his unbroken success against his enemies. And this flattering title still attaches to him. I have come across a history which relates that Sulla was styled Epaphroditus by a decree of the Senate itself. This does not seem to me to be inappropriate for he was also called Faustus (lucky), which name seems to have very nearly the same signification as Epaphroditus. There was also an oracle given to him somewhere which, in response to his question concerning the future, assured his prosperous career as follows:

"Believe me, Roman, the Cyprian goddess cares for the race of Æneas and has given it great power. Render yearly gifts to all the immortals, and do not forget them. Convey gifts to Delphi. There is also a place where men go up under snowy Taurus, a wide-reaching city of the Carians, whose inhabitants have named it for Aphrodite. Give the goddess an axe and you shall gain sovereign power."

Whichever decree the Romans voted when they erected the statue, they seem to me to have made the inscription by way of jest or cajolery. However, Sulla sent a golden crown and an axe to Venus with this inscription:

"The dictator Sulla dedicates this to thee, Venus, because in a dream he saw thee in panoply setting the army in order of battle and fighting with the weapons of Mars."

Thus Sulla became king, or tyrant, *de facto*, not elected, but holding power by force and violence. As, however, he needed some pretence of being elected it was managed in this way. The kings of the Romans in the olden time were chosen for their bravery, and when one of them died the senators held the royal power in succession for five days each, until the people could decide who should be the new king. This five-day ruler was called the Interrex, which means king for the time being. The retiring consuls always presided over the election of their successors in office, and if there chanced to be no consul at such a time an Interrex was appointed for the purpose of holding the consular comitia. Sulla took advantage of this custom. There were no consuls at this time, Carbo having lost his life in Sicily and Marius in Præneste. So Sulla went out of the city for a time and ordered the Senate to choose an Interrex. They chose Valerius Flaccus, expecting that he would soon hold the consular comitia. But Sulla wrote to Flaccus to bring before the people the proposition that he (Sulla) considered it advisable,

under present circumstances, that the city should be governed by a dictator according to a custom that had been abandoned 400 years. He told them not to appoint the dictator for any definite time, but until the city and Italy and the whole government, so shaken by factions and wars, should be put upon a firm foundation. That this proposal referred to Sulla himself was not at all doubtful. Sulla made no concealment of it. At the conclusion of the letter he declared openly that, in his judgment, he could be serviceable to the city in that capacity.

Such was Sulla's letter. The Romans were unwilling, but they had no more opportunities for elections according to law, and they considered that this matter was not altogether in their own power. So, in the absence of everything else, they welcomed this pretence of an election as an image and semblance of freedom and chose Sulla their absolute master for as long a time as he pleased. There had been autocratic rule of the dictators before, but it was limited to short periods. But in Sulla's time it first became unlimited and so an absolute tyranny; yet they added, for propriety's sake, that they chose him dictator for the enactment of such laws as he might deem best and for the regulation of the commonwealth. Thus the Romans, after having government by kings for sixty Olympiads, and a democracy, under consuls chosen yearly, for 100 Olympiads, resorted to kingly government again. This was in the 175th Olympiad according to the Greek calendar, but there were no Olympic games then except races in the stadium, since Sulla had carried away the athletes and all the sights and shows to Rome to celebrate his victories in the Mithridatic and Italian wars, under the pretext that the masses needed a breathing-spell and recreation after their toils.

Nevertheless, as the form of the republic remained he allowed them to appoint consuls. Marcus Tullius and Cornelius Dolabella were chosen. But Sulla, like a reigning sovereign, was dictator over the consuls. Twenty-four axes were borne in front of him, as was customary with dictators, the same number that were borne before the ancient kings, and he had a large body-guard also. He repealed laws and he enacted others. He forbade anybody to hold the office of prætor until after he had held that of quæstor, or to be consul before he had been prætor, and he prohibited any man from holding the same office a second time till after the lapse of ten years. He reduced the tribunician power to such an extent that it seemed to be destroyed. He curtailed it by a law which provided that one holding the office of tribune should never afterward hold any other office; for which reason all men of reputation or family, who formerly contended for this office, shunned it thereafter. I am not able to say positively whether Sulla transferred this office from the people to the Senate, where it is now lodged, or not. To the Senate itself, which had been much thinned by the seditions and wars, he added about 300 members from the best of the knights, taking the vote of the tribes for each one. To the plebeians he added more than 10,000 slaves of proscribed persons, choos-ing the youngest and strongest, to whom he gave freedom and Roman citizenship, and he called them Cornelii after himself. In this way he made sure of having 10,000 men among the plebeians always ready to obey his commands. In order to provide the same kind of safeguard throughout Italy he distributed to the twenty-three legions that had served under him a great deal of land among the communities, as I have already related, some of which was public property and some taken from the communities by way of fine.

So terrible was he and so uncontrollable in anger that he slew in the middle of the forum Q. Lucretius Ofella, the one who had besieged and captured Præneste and the consul Marius, and had won the final victory for him. He did this because, in spite of the new law, Lucretius persisted,

though Sulla opposed and forbade, in being a candidate for the consulship while he was still in the equestrian order and before he had been quæstor and prætor, presuming on the greatness of his services, according to the former custom, and cap-tivating the populace. Then Sulla assem-bled the people and said to them, "Know, citizens, and learn from me, that I caused the death of Lucretius because he dis-obeyed me." And then he told the follow-ing story: "A husbandman was bitten by fleas while ploughing. He stopped his ploughing twice in order to clear them out of his shirt. When they bit him again he burned his shirt, so that he might not be so often interrupted in his work. And I tell you, who have felt my hand twice, to take warning lest the third time fire be brought in requisition." With these words he terri-fied them and thereafter ruled as he pleased. He had a triumph on account of the Mithridatic war, during which some of the scoffers called his government "the royalty disavowed" because only the name of king was concealed. Others took the con-trary view, judging from his acts, and called it "the tyranny confessed."

Into such evils were the Romans and all the Italians plunged by this war; and so likewise were all the countries beyond Italy by the recent piracies, or by the Mithridatic war, or by the many exhausting taxes levied to meet the deficit in the public treasury due to the seditions. All the allied nations and kings, and not only the tributary cities, but those which had delivered themselves to the Romans voluntarily under sworn agreements, and those which by virtue of their furnishing aid in war or for some other merit were autonomous and not subject to tribute, all were now required to pay and to obey. Some that had surrendered themselves under treaty arrangements were deprived of their territory and their harbors. Sulla decreed that Alexander (the son of Alexander the former sovereign of Egypt), who had been reared in Cos and given to

Mithridates by the inhabitants of that island, and had fled to Sulla and become intimate with him, should be king of Alexandria. He did this because the government of Alexandria was destitute of a sovereign in the male line, and the women of the royal house wanted a man of the same lineage, and because he (Sulla) expected to reap a large reward from the rich kingdom. As Alexander behaved himself in a very offensive manner toward them, relying upon Sulla, the Alexandrians, on the nineteenth day of his reign, dragged him from the palace to the gymnasium and put him to death; so little fear had they of foreigners, either by reason of the magnitude of their own government or their inexperience as yet of external dangers.

The following year Sulla, although he was dictator, undertook the consulship a second time, with Metellus Pius for his colleague, in order to preserve the pretence and form of democratic government. It is perhaps from this example that the Roman emperors now make a showing of consuls to the country and even exhibit themselves in that capacity, considering it not unbecoming to hold the office of consul in connection with the supreme power. The next year the people, in order to pay court to Sulla, chose him consul again, but he refused the office and nominated Servilius Isauricus and Claudius Pulcher for their suffrages, and voluntarily laid down the supreme power, although nobody was troubling him. This act seems wonderful to me—that Sulla should have been the first, and till then the only one, to abdicate such vast power without compulsion, not to sons (like Ptolemy in Egypt, or Ariobarzanes in Cappadocia, or Seleucus in Syria), but to the very people over whom he had tyrannized. Almost incredible is it that after incurring so many dangers in forcing his way to this power he should have laid it down of his own free will after he had acquired it. Paradoxical beyond anything is the fact that he was afraid of nothing,

although more than 100,000 young men had perished in this war, and he had destroyed of his enemies ninety senators, fifteen consulars, and 2600 of the so-called knights, including the banished. The property of these men had been confiscated and many of their bodies cast out unburied. Undaunted by the relatives of these persons at home, or by the banished abroad, or by the cities whose towers and walls he had thrown down and whose lands, money, and privileges he had swept away, Sulla now returned to private life.

So great was this man's boldness and good fortune. It is said that he made a speech in the forum when he laid down his power in which he offered to give the reasons for what he had done to anybody who should ask them. He dismissed the lictors with their axes and discontinued his body-guard, and for a long time walked to the forum with only a few friends, the multitude looking upon him with awe even then. Once only when he was going home he was reproached by a boy. As nobody restrained this boy he made bold to follow Sulla to his house, railing at him, and Sulla, who had opposed the greatest men and states with towering rage, endured his reproaches with calmness and as he went into the house said, divining the future either by his intelligence or by chance, "This young man will prevent any other holder of such power from laying it down." This saying was shortly confirmed to the Romans, for Gaius Cæsar never laid down his power. Sulla seems to me to have been the same masterful and able man in all respects, whether striving to reach supreme power from private life, or changing back to private life from supreme power, or later when passing his time in rural solitude; for he retired to his own estate at Cumæ in Italy and there occupied his leisure in hunting and fishing. He did this not because he was afraid to live a private life in the city, nor because he had not sufficient bodily strength for whatever he might try to do. He was still of virile age and sound constitution, and there were 120,000 men throughout Italy who had recently served under him in war and had received large gifts of money and land from him, and there were the 10,000 Cornelii ready in the city, besides other people of his party devoted to him and still formidable to his opponents, all of whom rested upon Sulla's safety their hopes of impunity for what they had done in coöperation with him. But I think that he was satiated with war, with power, with city affairs, and that he took to rural life finally because he loved it.

Directly after his retirement the Romans, although delivered from slaughter and tyranny, began gradually to fan the flames of new seditions. Quintus Catulus and Æmilius Lepidus were chosen consuls, the former of the Sullan faction and the latter of the opposite party. They hated each other bitterly and began to quarrel immediately, from which it was plain that fresh troubles were brewing. While he was living in the country Sulla had a dream in which he thought he saw his Genius already calling him. Early in the morning he told the dream to his friends and in haste began writing his will, which he finished that day. After sealing it he was taken with a fever towards evening and died the same night. He was sixty years of age and had been the most fortunate of men even to the very last, and realized in all respects the title he bore; that is, if one can be considered fortunate who obtains all that he desires. Immediately a dissension sprang up in the city over his remains, some proposing to bring them in a procession through Italy and exhibit them in the forum and give him a public funeral. Lepidus and his faction opposed this, but Catulus and the Sullan party prevailed. Sulla's corpse was borne through Italy on a golden litter with royal splendor. Musicians and horsemen in great numbers went in advance and a great multitude of armed men followed on foot. His fellow-soldiers flocked from all directions under arms to join the procession, and each one was assigned his place in due order as he came. The crowd of other people that came together was unprecedented. The standards and the fasces that he had used while living and ruling were borne in the procession.

When the remains reached the city they were borne through the streets with an enormous procession. More than 2000 golden crowns which had been made in haste were carried in it, the gifts of cities and of the legions that he had commanded and of individual friends. It would be impossible to describe all the splendid things contributed to this funeral. From fear of the assembled soldiery all the priests and priestesses escorted the remains, each in proper costume. The entire Senate and the whole body of magistrates attended with their insignia of office. A multitude of the Roman knights followed with their peculiar decorations, and, in their turn, all the legions that had fought under him. They came together with eagerness, all hastening to join in the task, carrying gilded standards and silver-plated shields, such as are still used on such occasions. There was a countless number of trumpeters who by turns played the most mournful dirges. Loud cries were raised, first by the Senate, then by the knights, then by the soldiers, and finally by the plebeians. For some really longed for Sulla, but others were afraid of his army and his dead body, as they had been of himself when living. As they looked at the present spectacle and remembered what this man had accomplished they were amazed, and agreed with their opponents that he had been most beneficial to his own party and most formidable to themselves even in death. The corpse was shown in the forum on the rostra, where public speeches were usually made, and the most eloquent of the Romans then living delivered the funeral oration, as Sulla's son, Faustus, was still very young. Then strong men of the senators took up the litter and carried it to the Campus Martius, where only kings were buried, and the knights and the army coursed around the funeral pile. And this was the last of Sulla.

2. Plutarch on Sulla's Later Career*

This selection begins with Plutarch's description of Sulla's behavior immediately after his victory at the Colline Gate.

Sylla gathered together in the circus, as well these as other survivors of the party, to the number of six thousand, and just as he commenced speaking to the senate, in the temple of Bellona, proceeded to cut them down, by men appointed for that service. The cry of so vast a multitude put to the sword, in so narrow a space, was naturally heard some distance, and startled the senators. He, however, continuing his speech with a calm and unconcerned countenance, bade them listen to what he had to say, and not busy themselves with what was doing out of doors; he had given directions for the chastisement of some offenders. This gave the most stupid of the Romans to understand that they had merely exchanged, not escaped, tyranny. And Marius, being of a naturally harsh temper, had not altered, but merely continued what he had been, in authority; whereas Sylla, using his fortune moderately and unambitiously at first, and giving good hopes of a true patriot, firm to the interests both of the nobility and commonalty, being, moreover, of a gay and cheerful temper from his youth, and so easily moved to pity as to shed tears readily, has, perhaps deservedly, cast a blemish upon offices of great authority, as if they deranged men's former habits and character, and gave rise to violence, pride, and inhumanity. Whether this be a real change and revolution in the mind, caused by fortune, or rather a lurking viciousness of nature, discovering itself in authority, it

were matter of another sort of disquisition to decide.

Sylla being thus wholly bent upon slaughter, and filling the city with executions without number or limit, many wholly uninterested persons falling a sacrifice to private enmity, through his permission and indulgence to his friends, Caius Metellus, one of the younger men, made bold in the senate to ask him what end there was of these evils, and at what point he might be expected to stop? "We do not ask you," said he, "to pardon any whom you have resolved to destroy, but to free from doubt those whom you are pleased to save." Sylla answering, that he knew not as yet whom to spare, "Why, then," said he, "tell us whom you will punish." This Sylla said he would do. These last words, some authors say, were spoken not by Metellus, but by Afidius, one of Sylla's fawning companions. Immediately upon this, without communicating with any of the magistrates, Sylla proscribed eighty persons, and notwithstanding the general indignation, after one day's respite, he posted two hundred and twenty more, and on the third again, as many. In an address to the people on this occasion, he told them he had put up as many names as he could think of; those which had escaped his memory, he would publish at a future time. He issued an edict likewise, making death the punishment of humanity, proscribing any who should dare to receive and cherish a proscribed person without exception to brother, son, or parents. And to him who should slay any one proscribed person, he ordained two talents reward, even were it a slave

* Plutarch, "Sylla," *Plutarch's Lives*, 30–38, translated by John Dryden, pp. 569–573.

who had killed his master, or a son his father. And what was thought most unjust of all, he caused the attainder to pass upon their sons, and sons' sons, and made open sale of all their property. Nor did the proscription prevail only at Rome, but throughout all the cities of Italy the effusion of blood was such, that neither sanctuary of the gods, nor hearth of hospitality, nor ancestral home escaped. Men were butchered in the embraces of their wives, children in the arms of their mothers. Those who perished through public animosity or private enmity were nothing in comparison of the numbers of those who suffered for their riches. Even the murderers began to say, that "his fine house killed this man, a garden that, a third, his hot baths." Quintus Aurelius, a quiet, peaceable man, and one who thought all his part in the common calamity consisted in condoling with the misfortunes of others, coming into the forum to read the list, and finding himself among the proscribed, cried out, "Woe is me, my Alban farm has informed against me." He had not gone far before he was despatched by a ruffian, sent on that errand.

In the meantime, Marius, on the point of being taken, killed himself; and Sylla, coming to Præneste, at first proceeded judicially against each particular person, till at last, finding it a work of too much time, he cooped them up together in one place, to the number of twelve thousand men, and gave order for the execution of them all, his own host alone excepted. But he, brave man, telling him he could not accept the obligation of life from the hands of one who had been the ruin of his country, went in among the rest, and submitted willingly to the stroke. What Lucius Catilina did was thought to exceed all other acts. For having, before matters came to an issue, made away with his brother, he besought Sylla to place him in the list of proscription, as though he had been alive, which was done; and Catiline, to return the kind office, assassinated a certain Marcus Marius, one of the adverse party, and brought the head to Sylla, as he was sitting in the forum, and then going to the holy water of Apollo, which was nigh, washed his hands.

There were other things, besides this bloodshed, which gave offence. For Sylla had declared himself dictator, an office which had then been laid aside for the space of one hundred and twenty years. There was, likewise, an act of grace passed on his behalf, granting indemnity for what was passed, and for the future intrusting him with the power of life and death, confiscation, division of lands, erecting and demolishing of cities, taking away of kingdoms, and bestowing them at pleasure. He conducted the sale of confiscated property after such an arbitrary, imperious way, from the tribunal, that his gifts excited greater odium even than his usurpations; women, mimes, and musicians, and the lowest of the freed slaves had presents made them of the territories of nations and the revenues of cities: and women of rank were married against their will to some of them. Wishing to insure the fidelity of Pompey the Great by a nearer tie of blood, he bade him divorce his present wife, and forcing Æmilia, the daughter of Scaurus and Metella, his own wife, to leave her husband, Manius Glabrio, he bestowed her, though then with child, on Pompey, and she died in childbirth at his house.

When Lucretius Ofella, the same who reduced Marius by siege, offered himself for the consulship, he first forbade him; then, seeing he could not restrain him, on his coming down into the forum with a numerous train of followers, he sent one of the centurions who were immediately about him, and slew him, himself sitting on the tribunal in the temple of Castor, and beholding the murder from above. The citizens apprehending the centurion, and dragging him to the tribunal, he bade them cease their clamouring and let the centurion go, for he had commanded it.

His triumph was, in itself, exceedingly

splendid, and distinguished by the rarity and magnificence of the royal spoils; but its yet greatest glory was the noble spectacle of the exiles. For in the rear followed the most eminent and most potent of the citizens, crowned with garlands, and calling Sylla saviour and father, by whose means they were restored to their own country, and again enjoyed their wives and children. When the solemnity was over, and the time come to render an account of his actions, addressing the public assembly, he was as profuse in enumerating the lucky chances of war as any of his own military merits. And, finally, from this felicity he requested to receive the surname of Felix. In writing and transacting business with the Greeks, he styled himself Epaphroditus, and on his trophies which are still extant with us the name is given Lucius Cornelius Sylla Epaphroditus. Moreover, when his wife had brought him forth twins, he named the male Faustus and the female Fausta, the Roman words for what is auspicious and of happy omen. The confidence which he reposed in his good genius, rather than in any abilities of his own, emboldened him, though deeply involved in bloodshed, and though he had been the author of such great changes and revolutions of state, to lay down his authority, and place the right of consular elections once more in the hands of the people. And when they were held, he not only declined to seek that office, but in the forum exposed his person publicly to the people, walking up and down as a private man. And contrary to his will, a certain bold man and his enemy, Marcus Lepidus, was expected to become consul, not so much by his own interest, as by the power and solicitation of Pompey, whom the people were willing to oblige. When the business was over, seeing Pompey going home overjoyed with the success, he called him to him and said, "What a polite act, young man, to pass by Catulus, the best of men, and choose Lepidus, the worst! It will be well for you to be vigilant, now that you have strength-

ened your opponent against yourself." Sylla spoke this, it may seem, by a prophetic instinct, for, not long after, Lepidus grew insolent and broke into open hostility to Pompey and his friends.

Sylla, consecrating the tenth of his whole substance to Hercules, entertained the people with sumptuous feastings. The provision was so much above what was necessary, that they were forced daily to throw great quantities of meat into the river, and they drank wine forty years old and upwards. In the midst of the banqueting, which lasted many days, Metella died of a disease. And because that the priest forbade him to visit the sick, or suffer his house to be polluted with mourning, he drew up an act of divorce and caused her to be removed into another house whilst alive. Thus far, out of religious apprehension, he observed the strict rule to the very letter, but in the funeral expenses he transgressed the law he himself had made, limiting the amount, and spared no cost. He transgressed, likewise, his own sumptuary laws respecting expenditure in banquets, thinking to allay his grief by luxurious drinking parties and revellings with common buffoons.

Some few months after, at a show of gladiators, when men and women sat promiscuously in the theatre, no distinct places being as yet appointed, there sat down by Sylla a beautiful woman of high birth, by name Valeria, daughter of Messala, and sister to Hortensius the orator. Now it happened that she had been lately divorced from her husband. Passing along behind Sylla, she leaned on him with her hand, and plucking a bit of wool from his garment, so proceeded to her seat. And on Sylla looking up and wondering what it meant, "What harm, mighty sir," said she, "if I also was desirous to partake a little in your felicity?" It appeared at once that Sylla was not displeased, but even tickled in his fancy, for he sent out to inquire her name, her birth, and past life. From this time there passed between them many side glances, each continually turning round to look at the other, and frequently interchanging smiles. In the end, overtures were made, and a marriage concluded on. All which was innocent, perhaps, on the lady's side, but, though she had been never so modest and virtuous, it was scarcely a temperate and worthy occasion of marriage on the part of Sylla, to take fire, as a boy might, at a face and a bold look, incentives not seldom to the most disorderly and shameless passions.

Notwithstanding this marriage, he kept company with actresses, musicians, and dancers, drinking with them on couches night and day. His chief favourites were Roscius the comedian, Sorex the arch mime, and Metrobius the player, for whom, though past his prime, he still professed a passionate fondness. By these courses he encouraged a disease which had begun from unimportant cause; and for a long time he failed to observe that his bowels were ulcerated, till at length the corrupted flesh broke out into lice. Many were employed day and night in destroying them, but the work so multiplied under their hands, that not only his clothes, baths, basins, but his very meat was polluted with that flux and contagion, they came swarming out in such numbers. He went frequently by day into the bath to scour and cleanse his body, but all in vain; the evil generated too rapidly and too abundantly for any ablutions to overcome it. There died of this disease, amongst those of the most ancient times, Acastus, the son of Pelias; of later date, Alcman the poet, Pherecydes the theologian, Callisthenes the Olynthian, in the time of his imprisonment, as also Mucius the lawyer; and if we may mention ignoble, but notorious names, Eunus the fugitive, who stirred up the slaves of Sicily to rebel against their masters, after he was brought captive to Rome, died of this creeping sickness.

Sylla not only foresaw his end, but may be also said to have written of it. For in the two-and-twentieth book of his Memoirs, which he finished two days before his death, he writes that the Chaldeans foretold him, that after he had led a life of honour, he should conclude it in fulness of prosperity. He declares, moreover, that in a vision he had seen his son, who had died not long before Metella, stand by in mourning attire, and beseech his father to cast off further care, and come along with him to his mother Metella, there to live at ease and quietness with her. However, he could not refrain from intermeddling in public affairs. For, ten days before his decease, he composed the differences of the people of Dicæarchia, and prescribed laws for their better government. And the very day before his end, it being told him that the magistrate Granius deferred the payment of a public debt, in expectation of his death, he sent for him to his house, and placing his attendants about him, caused him to be strangled; but through the straining of his voice and body, the imposthume breaking, he lost a great quantity of blood. Upon this, his strength failing him, after spending a troublesome night, he died, leaving behind him two young children by Metella. Valeria was afterwards delivered of a daughter, named Posthuma; for so the Romans call those who are born after the father's death.

Many ran tumultuously together, and joined with Lepidus to deprive the corpse of the accustomed solemnities; but Pompey, though offended at Sylla (for he alone of all his friends was not mentioned in his will), having kept off some by his interest and entreaty, others by menaces, conveyed the body to Rome, and gave it a secure and honourable burial. It is said that the Roman ladies contributed such vast heaps of spices, that besides what was carried on two hundred and ten litters, there was sufficient to form a large figure of Sylla himself, and another representing a lictor, out of the costly frankincense and cinnamon. The day being cloudy in the morning, they deferred carrying forth the corpse till about three in the afternoon, expecting it would rain. But a strong wind blowing full upon the funeral pile, and setting it all in a bright flame, the body was consumed so exactly in good time, that the pyre had begun to smoulder, and the fire was upon the point of expiring, when a violent rain came down, which continued till night. So that his good fortune was firm even to the last, and did as it were officiate at his funeral. His monument stands in the Campus Martius, with an epitaph of his own writing; the substance of it being, that he had not been outdone by any of his friends in doing good turns, nor by any of his foes in doing bad.

3. JUDGMENT ON THE LIFE AND WORK OF SULLA*

Sulla's achievement demands no complicated judgment. For all their interest to a moralist like Plutarch, his private life and character are of slight concern to the historian. That he was a hard liver and a man ruthless in his ways with opposition are facts beyond dispute; but they have no bearing on the central issue—the question of his place in the constitutional development of Rome. Nor, again, is there any need to dwell on his capacity for organization. The arrangements which he made in Asia and his enduring development of the *iudicia publica* are enough to show that, when it was a matter of constructing machinery to perform the work of daily administration, Sulla was not inferior to Augustus himself. But it is on his conception of the constitution most suitable for Rome that his reputation depends. As has been said above, the problem was not of his own creation. First, the enfranchisement of Italy made it essential to curb the powers of the urban *plebs* which, masquerading as a typical selection of the Populus Romanus, had lately been claiming with a new insistence to exercise untrammelled the tremendous powers of a sovran *demos*. And, secondly, the Marian system of military recruitment had brought with it armies capable of such dangerous devotion to their leaders that measures were urgently needed to strengthen the control of the central government over its executive in the provinces. But the means which Sulla took to secure these ends were of his own choosing, and it is by the adequacy of these means that the value of his reform must be assessed. Sulla's attempt to increase the authority of the Senate, both by enlarging its numbers and the field on which it drew and by providing that indirect popular election, without the possibility of interference by the censors, should be the only mode of access to a seat, was an attempt on the most promising lines. Though the censorship was revived in 70 B.C. for a time, the constitution of the Sullan Senate differs from that of Augustus only in the lack of some minor regulations necessitated by the advent of a Princeps. Again, the *lex annalis*, likewise adopted by the Empire without essential change, served within its limits to curb the independence of the consuls. Save in 70 and 59 B.C., curule magistrates caused little trouble after Sulla's time, and on both these occasions it was an army which made them dangerous.

The tribunate, however, presented a more difficult problem. In fairness to Sulla it must be admitted that the positive powers which he allowed the tribunes to enjoy were peculiarly like those which they retained under the Augustan arrangements; but there was one essential difference—that Sulla left the Concilium Plebis alive, whereas under Augustus it was dead. So long as the plebeian assembly and the tribunate both survived, there was a danger: legislation might strive to keep them apart, but, if the legislation failed, the

* Hugh Last, "Sulla," *Cambridge Ancient History* (Cambridge, England: Cambridge University Press, 1932), Vol. 9, pp. 309–312. Reprinted by permission of the publisher.

way for a new Gracchus was clear. It has been seen that, in this situation, Sulla's hope was to kill the tribunate by depriving it of serious candidates for the office; but the blow he delivered was not mortal, and the tribunate recovered. In the end, his attack did no more than supply his enemies with a battle-cry in the demand for a restoration of the tribunes' pristine powers. But the attack itself was justified, and the misfortune of Sulla lay rather in his inability to destroy the office outright and—what was still more necessary—to end the activities of the Concilium Plebis for ever. He must not, indeed, be blamed for sparing the assemblies—the time was not ripe for their suppression: but it cannot be denied that the Julio-Claudians found a better way when they silently removed the People from the Roman Constitution. One point, however, must be added. Though Sulla did not permanently stop the demagogic agitation of the tribunes, he left the office so completely fettered that its holders were powerless for evil until their bonds were loosed. The sequel will reveal one fact of great importance—that in their struggle for freedom the tribunes could win no tangible success by their own efforts alone, and that it was only the championing of their cause by other men—men who had armies at their backs—which finally enabled the tribunate to throw off the shackles imposed by Sulla.

And so at length we reach the rock on which the Sullan system foundered. The divorce of the magistracy from the promagistracy was a development—hastened, indeed, by Sulla but started long before his time—which had the most beneficent effects when it was completed in 52 B.C., and subsequently accepted by Augustus. The arrangements to make possible an annual tenure of provincial commands were salutary so far as they might render it more difficult for governors to establish a personal claim on the loyalty of their troops. But all this went for nothing when politicians were generals and the armies depended on their generals for pensions at discharge. Even if commands had never run for more than a single year—a system most dangerous to the effective conduct of war—sooner or later, with the army as it was, a general and his troops were bound to discover that each could serve the other. To cope with such a threat no oligarchy could be competent: at best it could start a civil war by arming one of its members to meet the menace, and even that might mean no more than changing one master for another. Until the time should come when the armies would be the armies of the State, assured that the State itself had a system to reward faithful service with adequate provision for old age, and convinced that intervention in political affairs would be visited by punishment inevitable and condign, there was one way alone to provide security against recurrent military tyrannies. A monarch must be found to command all the Roman forces, and he must be allowed to choose his own subordinates, looking as much for loyalty to himself as for competence in the performance of their duties. For such a rôle Sulla was not cast. The age was not ready for a principate. The peril from the proconsuls had yet to be appreciated in all its gravity, and Rome had to pass through the fire of the Civil Wars before she would reluctantly accept even the veiled monarchy of Augustus.

For his day Sulla did well. The Senate could not be deposed; and so long as the Senate remained supreme it is hard to see what greater powers it could have been given or what stronger defences could have been erected against its enemies. The weakness of Sulla's work is to be ascribed partly to his failure to have done for good with the travesty of popular sovranty exercised by the urban mob, and still more to his own great refusal of the crown. Yet the fault was venial. Caesar might say that by surrendering the dictatorship Sulla showed ignorance of the political ABC, but it was largely from Caesar's own career that men grappling with the problem of the Roman government learnt the essence of their task. To blame Sulla for his ignorance is to blame him for having lived thirty years too soon.

But Sulla's work was not wasted. In administrative organization he served Rome well, and there is not one of his enactments under this head, which, if it did not survive intact, failed to bear fruit of value. Even in the sphere of politics Sulla taught his successors a lesson which none was so foolish as to ignore. His ideal of senatorial supremacy might be impossible, but his methods of seeking it were instructive. Once and for all he showed that an elaborate programme of legislation, of the sort which the Gracchi had lamentably failed to carry through with the support of the Concilium Plebis, could be enacted in all its parts by one who relied upon the army.

Of the two legs which carried the Augustan principate the Gracchi had rested on the *tribunicia potestas*. It was Sulla who showed the political value of the *imperium*: and of these two the *imperium* was incomparably the more valuable. If the Sullan system collapsed, as it shortly did, its collapse would be due to the action of the army, and the task of the next reformer would be to bring the army under control. Sulla had shown the means to be employed —the army itself. And so it emerged from Sulla's work that the business of Roman statesmanship was with military support to create a government able to command unbroken allegiance from the army. Though he did not supply the answer, Sulla set the problem in a form which minds less acute than those of Julius and Augustus could scarcely fail to grasp.

4. Judgment on the Life and Work of Sulla*

Nothing lay farther from Sulla than systematic ambition. He had too much sense to regard, like the average aristocrats of his time, the inscription of his name in the roll of the consuls as the aim of his life; he was too indifferent and too little of an ideologue to be disposed voluntarily to engage in the reform of the rotten structure of the state. He remained—where birth and culture placed him—in the circle of genteel society, and passed through the usual routine of offices; he had no occasion to exert himself, and left such exertion to the political working bees, of whom there was in truth no lack. Thus in 647[119 B.C.], on the allotment of the quaestorial places, accident brought him to Africa to the headquarters of Gaius Marius. The untried man-of-fashion from the capital was not very well received by the rough boorish general and his experienced staff. Provoked by this reception Sulla, fearless and skilful as he was,

rapidly made himself master of the profession of arms, and in his daring expedition to Mauretania first displayed that peculiar combination of audacity and cunning with reference to which his contemporaries said of him that he was half lion half fox, and that the fox in him was more dangerous than the lion. To the young, highborn, brilliant officer, who was confessedly the real means of ending the vexatious Numidian war, the most splendid career now lay open; he took part also in the Cimbrian war, and manifested his singular talent for organization in the management of the difficult task of providing supplies; yet even now the pleasures of life in the capital had far more attraction for him than war or even politics. During his praetorship, which office he held in 661 [92] after having failed in a previous candidature, it once more chanced that in his province, the least important of all, the first victory over king Mithradates and the first treaty with the mighty Arsacids, as well as their first humiliation, occurred.

* Theodor Mommsen, *The History of Rome*, translated by W. P. Dickson (New York: Charles Scribner's Sons, 1911), Vol. 4, pp. 142–150.

The Civil war followed. It was Sulla mainly, who decided the first act of it—the Italian insurrection—in favour of Rome, and thus won for himself the consulship by his sword; it was he, moreover, who when consul suppressed with energetic rapidity the Sulpician revolt. Fortune seemed to make it her business to eclipse the old hero Marius by means of this younger officer. The capture of Jugurtha, the vanquishing of Mithradates, both of which Marius had striven for in vain, were accomplished in subordinate positions by Sulla: in the Social war, in which Marius lost his renown as a general and was deposed, Sulla established his military repute and rose to the consulship; the revolution of 666 [87], which was at the same time and above all a personal conflict between the two generals, ended with the outlawry and flight of Marius. Almost without desiring it, Sulla had become the most famous general of his time and the shield of the oligarchy. New and more formidable crises ensued—the Mithradatic war, the Cinnan revolution; the star of Sulla continued always in the ascendant. Like the captain who seeks not to quench the flames of his burning ship but continues to fire on the enemy, Sulla, while the revolution was raging in Italy, persevered unshaken in Asia till the public foe was subdued. So soon as he had done with that foe, he crushed anarchy and saved the capital from the firebrands of the desperate Samnites and revolutionists. The moment of his return home was for Sulla an overpowering one in joy and in pain: he himself relates in his memoirs that during his first night in Rome he had not been able to close an eye, and we may well believe it. But still his task was not at an end; his star was destined to rise still higher. Absolute autocrat as was ever any king, and yet constantly abiding on the ground of formal right, he bridled the ultra-reactionary party, annihilated the Gracchan constitution which had for forty years limited the oligarchy, and compelled first the powers of the capitalists and of the urban proletariate which had entered into rivalry with the oligarchy, and ultimately the arrogance of the sword which had grown up in the bosom of his own staff, to yield once more to the law which he strengthened afresh. He established the oligarchy on a more independent footing than ever, placed the magisterial power as a ministering instrument in its hands, committed to it the legislation, the courts, the supreme military and financial power, and furnished it with a sort of bodyguard in the liberated slaves and with a sort of army in the settled military colonists. Lastly, when the work was finished, the creator gave way to his own creation; the absolute autocrat became of his own accord once more a simple senator. In all this long military and political career Sulla never lost a battle, was never compelled to retrace a single step, and, led astray neither by friends nor by foes, brought his work to the goal which he had himself proposed. He had reason, indeed, to thank his star. The capricious goddess of fortune seemed in his case for once to have exchanged caprice for steadfastness, and to have taken a pleasure in loading her favourite with successes and honours—whether he desired them or not. But history must be more just towards him than he was towards himself, and must place him in a higher rank than that of the mere favourites of fortune.

We do not mean that the Sullan constitution was a work of political genius, such as those of Gracchus and Caesar. There does not occur in it—as is, indeed, implied in its very nature as a restoration —a single new idea in statesmanship. All its most essential features—admission to the senate by the holding of the quaestorship, the abolition of the censorial right to eject a senator from the senate, the initiative of the senate in legislation, the conversion of the tribunician office into an instrument of the senate for fettering the *imperium*, the prolonging of the duration of the supreme office to two years, the transference of the command from the popularly-elected magistrate to the senatorial proconsul or propraetor, and even the new criminal and municipal arrangements—were not created by Sulla, but were institutions which had previously grown out of the oligarchic government, and which he merely regulated and fixed. And even as to the horrors attaching to his restoration, the proscriptions and confiscations—are they, compared with the doings of Nasica, Popillius, Opimius, Caepio and so on, anything else than the legal embodiment of the customary oligarchic mode of getting rid of opponents? On the Roman oligarchy of this period no judgment can be passed save one of inexorable and remorseless condemnation; and, like everything else connected with it, the Sullan constitution is completely involved in that condemnation. To accord praise which the genius of a bad man bribes us into bestowing is to sin against the sacred character of history; but we may be allowed to bear in mind that Sulla was far less answerable for the Sullan restoration than the body of the Roman aristocracy, which had ruled as a clique for centuries and had every year become more enervated and embittered by age, and that all that was hollow and all that was nefarious therein is ultimately traceable to that aristocracy. Sulla reorganized the state—not, however, as the master of the house who puts his shattered estate and household in order according to his own discretion, but as the temporary business-manager who faithfully complies with his instructions; it is superficial and false in such a case to devolve the final and essential responsibility from the master upon the manager. We estimate the importance of Sulla much too highly, or rather we dispose of those terrible proscriptions, ejections, and restorations—for which there never could be and never was any reparation— on far too easy terms, when we regard them as the work of a bloodthirsty tyrant whom accident had placed at the head of the state. These and the terrorism of the restoration

were the deeds of the aristocracy, and Sulla was nothing more in the matter than, to use the poet's expression, the executioner's axe following the conscious thought as its unconscious instrument. Sulla carried out that part with rare, in fact superhuman, perfection; but within the limits which it laid down for him, his working was not only grand but even useful. Never has any aristocracy deeply decayed and decaying still farther from day to day, such as was the Roman aristocracy of that time, found a guardian so willing and able as Sulla to wield for it the sword of the general and the pen of the legislator without any regard to the gain of power for himself. There is no doubt a difference between the case of an officer who refuses the sceptre from public spirit and that of one who throws it away from a cloyed appetite; but, so far as concerns the total absence of political selfishness—although, it is true, in this one respect only—Sulla deserves to be named side by side with Washington.

But the whole country—and not the aristocracy merely—was more indebted to him than posterity was willing to confess. Sulla definitely terminated the Italian revolution, in so far as it was based on the disabilities of individual less privileged districts as compared with others of better rights, and, by compelling himself and his party to recognize the equality of the rights of all Italians in presence of the law, he became the real and final author of the full political unity of Italy—a gain which was not too dearly purchased by ever so many troubles and streams of blood. Sulla however did more. For more than half a century the power of Rome had been declining, and anarchy had been her permanent condition: for the government of the senate with the Gracchan constitution was anarchy, and the government of Cinna and Carbo was a yet far worse illustration of the absence of a master-hand (the sad image of which is most clearly reflected in that equally confused and unnatural league with the Samnites), the most uncertain, most intolerable, and most mischievous of all conceivable political conditions—in fact the beginning of the end. We do not go too far when we assert that the long-undermined Roman commonwealth must have necessarily fallen to pieces, had not Sulla by his intervention in Asia and Italy saved its existence. It is true that the constitution of Sulla had as little endurance as that of Cromwell, and it was not difficult to see that this structure was no solid one; but it is arrant thoughtlessness to overlook the fact that without Sulla most probably the very site of the building would have been swept away by the waves; and even the blame of its want of stability does not fall primarily on Sulla. The statesman builds only so much as in the sphere assigned to him he can build. What a man of conservative views could do to save the old constitution, Sulla did; and he himself had a foreboding that, while he might doubtless erect a fortress, he would be unable to create a garrison, and that the utter worthlessness of the oligarchs would render any attempt to save the oligarchy vain. His constitution resembled a temporary dike thrown into the raging breakers; it was no reproach to the builder, if some ten years afterwards the waves swallowed up a structure at variance with nature and not defended even by those whom it sheltered. The statesman has no need to be referred to highly commendable isolated reforms, such as those of the Asiatic revenue-system and of criminal justice, that he may not summarily dismiss Sulla's ephemeral restoration: he will admire it as a reorganization of the Roman commonwealth judiciously planned and on the whole consistently carried out under infinite difficulties, and he will place the deliverer of Rome and the accomplisher of Italian unity below, but yet by the side of, Cromwell.

It is not, however, the statesman alone who has a voice in judging the dead; and with justice outraged human feeling will never reconcile itself to what Sulla did or suffered others to do. Sulla not only established his despotic power by unscrupulous violence, but in doing so called things by their right name with a certain cynical frankness, through which he has irreparably offended the great mass of the weakhearted who are more revolted at the name than at the thing, but through which, from the cool and dispassionate character of his crimes, he certainly appears to the moral judgment more revolting than the criminal acting from passion. Outlawries, rewards to executioners, confiscations of goods, summary procedure with insubordinate officers had occurred a hundred times, and the obtuse political morality of ancient civilization had for such things only lukewarm censure; but it was unexampled that the names of the outlaws should be publicly posted up and their heads publicly exposed, that a set sum should be fixed for the bandits who slew them and that it should be duly entered in the public account-books, that the confiscated property should be brought to the hammer like the spoil of an enemy in the public market, that the general should order a refractory officer to be at once cut down and acknowledge the deed before all the people. This public mockery of humanity was also a political error; it contributed not a little to envenom later revolutionary crises beforehand, and on that account even now a dark shadow deservedly rests on the memory of the author of the proscriptions.

Sulla may moreover be justly blamed that, while in all important matters he acted with remorseless vigour, in subordinate and more especially in personal questions he very frequently yielded to his sanguine temperament and dealt according to his likings or dislikings. Wherever he really felt hatred, as for instance against the Marians, he allowed it to take its course without restraint even against the innocent, and boasted of himself that no one had better requited friends and foes. He did not disdain on occasion of his plenitude of power to accumulate a colossal fortune. The first absolute monarch of the Roman state, he verified the maxim of absolutism —that the laws do not bind the prince— forthwith in the case of those laws which he himself issued as to adultery and extravagance. But his lenity towards his own party and his own circle was more pernicious for the state than his indulgence towards himself. The laxity of his military discipline, although it was partly enjoined by his political exigencies, may be reckoned as coming under this category; but far more pernicious was his indulgence towards his political adherents. The extent of his occasional forbearance is hardly credible: for instance Lucius Murena was not only released from punishment for defeats which he sustained through arrant perversity and insubordination, but was even allowed a triumph; Gnaeus Pompeius, who had behaved still worse, was still more extravagantly honoured by Sulla. The extensive range and the worst enormities of the proscriptions and confiscations probably arose not so much from Sulla's own wish as from this spirit of

indifference, which in his position indeed was hardly more pardonable. That Sulla with his intrinsically energetic and yet withal indifferent temperament should conduct himself very variously, sometimes with incredible indulgence, sometimes with inexorable severity, may readily be conceived. The saying repeated a thousand times, that he was before his regency a good-natured, mild man, but when regent a bloodthirsty tyrant, carries in it its own refutation; if he as regent displayed the reverse of his earlier gentleness, it must rather be said that he punished with the same careless nonchalance with which he pardoned. This half-ironical frivolity pervades his whole political action. It is always as if the victor, just as it pleased him to call his merit in gaining victory good fortune, esteemed the victory itself of no value; as if he had a partial presentiment of the vanity and perishableness of his own work; as if after the manner of a steward he preferred making repairs to pulling down and rebuilding, and allowed himself in the end to be content with a sorry plastering to conceal the flaws.

5. JUDGMENT ON THE LIFE AND WORK OF SULLA*

It is unnecessary to deal in detail with the history of the Civil War that followed; it must suffice merely to emphasise its one most important result. Sulla, hitherto the representative of neither party in the State, ended by becoming, against his own wish, the leader of the extreme reactionaries. On his arrival in Italy, the survivors of the Conservative party flocked from all sides to his standard, and hailed him as the deliverer they had so long expected. Attempts were at once made to use him as

* Guglielmo Ferrero, *The Greatness and Decline of Rome*, translated by A. E. Zimmern (New York: Putnam's & Coward-McCann, 1909), Vol. 2, pp. 110–117. Copyright 1909 by Putnam's & Coward-McCann. Reprinted by permission of the publisher.

the instrument of their partisan interest, and before long some of the younger men of the party found courage to take action. One of their number, Cnæus Pompeius, son of the Consul of the year 89, and a member of a noble but wealthy family, recruited a small force in Picenum. Another young noble, Marcus Licinius Crassus, who had lost a brother in the revolution, followed his example; so did Metellus Pius, son of the general who had fought against Jugurtha. Sulla, however, was not yet willing to become the tool of a party clique. He reassured the Italians by declaring that he would not go back upon the great measure of Italian emancipation, and consented further to treat with the popular party through the mediation of the

Senate. But it was all in vain. The chiefs of the popular party, who do not seem, with the exception of Sertorius, to have been men of any mark, were too distrustful of his intentions. With the whole of Italy at their back, they were not disposed to be frightened by the few legions of Sulla, and met all his advances with polite but determined evasion. Thus Sulla was at last driven to accept the offers of the Conservatives. He entrusted important commands to Pompey, Crassus and Metellus, and took up arms as the champion of the counter-revolution. His operations were marked by his customary rapidity and decision. Before long, by a skilful admixture of force and conciliation, he had restored some semblance of order to a society in which a long period of unrest and revolution had broken down all the ordinary restraints of morality. By the adroit use of his money he detached from the Democratic party a large number of its civil and military supporters, and those who resisted his temptations were discouraged by his decisive victories over all the leaders of the Democratic forces. One after the other they fell before his sword; Sertorius alone succeeded in escaping to Spain. Within a few months Sulla had overturned the revolutionary government and become supreme master of Italy, with an armed force at his back, while the popular party lay crushed beneath his heel, and the Senate sat by, an interested but impotent spectator.

From this time forward Sulla seems a changed man. The proud, lofty and cynical aristocrat had always kept concealed in his nature a strain of sensual brutality, which at last burst out in full force. His imperious disdain for his fellow men and the resentment inspired by his perils in the Civil War now turned him, whether by instinct or calculation, into a butcher. He was not to be deceived by the flattery men paid him after his victory. He realised that those very Conservatives to whom his victories had been so useful, and for whom he

entertained as sincere a contempt as for their opponents, would be the first to bring against him all the old party reproaches, the Treaty of Dardanus, the death of Fimbria, the Civil War, and the first to abandon him to the tender mercies of the Democrats unless order were re-established upon so secure a basis that his arrangements remained unassailable either in Italy or in the east. For the restoration of order he needed no party allegiance. He resolved to do his work thoroughly, and to do it alone.

His first step was to claim from the Senate the office of Dictator, which brought with it the right of life and death over every citizen for an indefinite period, and plenary powers for the reform of the Constitution. The Senate was not in a position to resist, and the *Lex Valeria* granting him the office was passed without opposition. Armed with these powers, he put to death an enormous number—according to one account 5000—of those who had in the present or previous generation supported the Democratic movement; he persecuted their families, reduced them to poverty by confiscations, annulled all their marriages with aristocratic houses, and decreed that the sons of the proscribed should be excluded for ever from every office in the State. Whole cities were punished by the infliction of fines, the demolition of fortifications, and the confiscation of public and private lands. He distributed these wholesale amongst his veterans, whom he settled upon the country, like colonists in a conquered province. Two thousand seven hundred knights and about 100 senators were put to death, and any one who had sinned in the least against the interests or the prejudices of the Conservative party went in danger of his life.

Unfortunately in a country already suffering from the effects of a whole generation of social disorder, a political reaction soon degenerated into an organised pillage. Sulla could hardly avoid collecting round him a heterogeneous crowd of adventurers as shameless and unscrupulous as himself —slaves and freed-men, plebeians and patricians, bankrupt nobles like Lucius Domitius Ahenobarbus and aristocratic financiers like Marcus Crassus. These men succeeded in piling up enormous riches by the simple process of buying up cheap the goods of the proscribed. Sulla could do nothing to interfere: perhaps he would not have wished to had he been able. Cold and merciless in the hour of victory as in the hour of danger, he was untouched by that desire for adulation so characteristic of usurping greatness; he seems to have felt an exquisite satisfaction in showing his comprehensive contempt at once for Conservatives and Democrats, rich and poor, Romans and Italians, nobles, financiers and plebeians. All equally trembled in his presence, as he sat enthroned and indifferent, in his palatial home, to receive the homage of all the greatest personages in Rome, when with hatred in their hearts they came to pay their humble respects to the supreme arbiter of life and death. He derived a cynical enjoyment from the spectacle of all that was noble or illustrious or aristocratic in Roman society, and young and old representatives of historic families and the fashionable ladies of the nobility, squabbling and elbowing for admission to the sumptuous dinners at which he sat, surrounded by his favourite singers, thinking only of his meat and drink, and not taking even the trouble to ask the names of his innumerable and illustrious guests. With the same sublime indifference he allowed his relatives and the friends of his youth to wrangle with the crowd of ambitious and greedy parasites in his vestibule and to trifle with his complaisance to secure the lands, the houses or the slaves of the proscribed; to extract a pardon for some less conspicuous victim or the condemnation of some innocent citizen whose wealth or character had exposed him to the hatred of his accusers. Nothing was too insignificant to escape the cupidity of these detestable informers; a chance friendship or relationship, or an inference drawn from some utterly innocent action were sufficient to provide material for a capital charge. The number of persons ruined in this way was very considerable. A great many took refuge with the barbarians in Spain and Mauretania, or at the Court of Mithridates. All who failed to secure the protection of some friend at Court spent their days in continual apprehension of arrest. The young son of that Caius Julius Cæsar, whose sister Marius had married, and who had died at Pisa of apoplexy a few years before, was one of those whose life was in especial danger; for he was not only the nephew of Marius, but had committed the additional offence of marrying Cornelia, the daughter of Cinna. The Dictator commanded him to divorce her; but Cæsar, who was of passionate temper, and was moreover very fond of his young wife, in whose favour he had refused a rich heiress, Cossutia, refused to obey. He preferred to see the confiscation of his own patrimony and of the dowry of his wife, and to leave the city at the imminent risk of proscription. Soon afterwards, however, Sulla was induced by the intervention of some of his relatives to extend him a free pardon.

The popular party was crushed for the moment; but it was necessary to provide against its possible revival. It was with this object that Sulla, who had now developed into a true representative of the Conservative cause, attempted to effect a great reform of the constitution on the lines foreshadowed by Rutilius Rufus and his small group of aristocratic followers, who now suddenly saw almost the whole of their programme put into execution. Sulla abolished the Censorship and the public distributions of corn; he increased the number of the Prætors to eight, and of the Quæstors to twenty; he took away from the Assembly the power of discussing laws without authorisation from the Senate; he transferred to the Assembly of the Centuries the powers which had belonged to the Assembly of the tribes; he deprived the tribunes of the people of the right of proposing laws, and of standing for the higher magistracies, leaving them only the right of hearing appeals. He decreed that no one should be elected to an office except in the normal order of promotion, and that re-election should only be possible after the lapse of ten years; he attempted to check the increase of crime by sharpening the penalties for offences of violence and fraud. He freed no less than 10,000 slaves and gave them full citizen rights, selecting the youngest and bravest of those who had belonged to the proscribed, added 300 equestrian members to the Senate, and restored to that body its old judicial prerogatives.

His main object, in short, was to break down the influence of the two new powers in the State, the middle class and the equestrian order, by a re-establishment, with slight modifications, of the old aristocratic constitution which had existed at the time of the first Punic War, when Italian society, then predominantly agricultural, aristocratic and military, had been composed of a perfectly rigid stratification of classes. At the top had been an aristocracy which, if not particularly enlightened, was at any rate both disciplined and powerful; next came the middle classes of the country districts, who were respectful, contented, and prosperous enough for their needs; beneath them again were the slaves, docile and as yet not very numerous, who were treated with strictness, but not with brutality. By the time when Sulla attempted to restore this old order, all these separate layers had become folded and broken and inextricably confused, at first by the gradual weakening of the aristocracy, then by the steady pressure of the middle class from below, and finally by the violent earthquake of the Revolution. He selected for the change the very moment when slaves had been incited to betray their proscribed masters, and when his own parasites were banding together in associations in which slave and freedman, aristocrat and *bourgeois* joined hands to do violence to law and custom, and to involve the whole of Italy in bloodshed and devastation. His settlement can hardly be classed as an aristocratic restoration, for the Roman aristocracy had already ceased to exist. Rather it was a wild and sanguinary carnival, in Italy and Asia and throughout the Roman dominions, of a small oligarchy of slaves and assassins, of needy aristocrats and unscrupulous adventurers, remorseless usurers and professional *condottieri*, triumphing over a vast Empire of oppressed millions who in one passionate and impotent access of fury had risen against their oppressors. Impassive amidst the carousals of the actors, singers, and dancers who nightly flocked to his halls, Sulla looked complacently on at a victory which he had not sought, but for which nevertheless he was alone responsible. The moment he felt secure of his life as a private individual in the Empire which he governed as Dictator, he abdicated his office to devote himself more completely to a life of pleasure. It did not spare him long. At the beginning of 78 he died.

It would be unjust to credit Sulla with the worst sort of ambition; he was a sincere Republican who hastened to give up his power the moment it was possible for him to do so without danger to his own life and that of his friends. But the force of circumstances and the peculiar limitations of his own nature caused him to play a less conspicuous part in history than might have been expected from a man of his activity and intelligence. He was far from being a model of the true Republican; to compare him with a man like Washington, for instance, would be ludicrous. Remarkable as he was for the clearness with which he conceived his ideas, and the infinite energy and resource which he displayed in their execution, he was incapable of any great depth of passion or of any really creative intellectual conception; he lacked just that spark of divine madness, that almost mystical power of inspiration which is reserved for the greatest spirits and seems somehow to embody, in confused and unconscious form, the vital instinct of our race as it presses onwards towards the future. Thinking only of self-indulgence, and indifferent to all that was outside this narrow range, nothing seized his attention in the life of his time but the confusion introduced into the structure of its society —a confusion due apparently to the perverseness and folly of mankind, and needing only, he thought, to be set right with the sword. Thus he succeeded in creating, not a Constitution or an Empire, but simply a gigantic system of police—conceived with unerring clearness, and executed with superhuman energy. These police measures were perhaps necessary at that moment to save the Empire and the whole of ancient civilisation from the destruction with which they were threatened by the desperate revolt of the oppressed thousands in Italy and Asia. But its value in history does not exceed that of all similar systems. Order, even in the best organised State, is only a smooth and specious fiction in the place of justice and wisdom. An ordered society is like a field which has periodically to be touched and torn by the plough before the soil receives the virtue to renew its creative power. The terrible upheaval in Italian society may perhaps be compared to a ploughshare penetrating into the very depths of the old order, turning and returning the soil of which it was com-

posed, bringing to light much that had been hidden, breaking up into powder much that for many months had been hardened in the sun, opening new pores for the showers of heaven, waking into activity all the living seeds within as a preparation for a new and abundant harvest. Marius had contributed his part to this great revival, in spite of the criminal ambitions of his later years, by tracing the large outlines of the new military organisation of Rome, and by helping to solve the question of Italian emancipation. Sulla contributed nothing at all. His work was even more self-contradictory than that of the Gracchi. He climbed into power by wielding the chief weapon of the new plutocracy, by the lavish use of money among friends and opponents. He used it to restore the political institutions of the age of agriculture. No wonder that his work and his influence were short-lived. The imposing edifice of his constitution was like a cabin of reeds put together on the sea-shore, that is carried away with one burst of rough sea wind. Nothing survived of his work but the fear inspired by a type of statesman new to the history of Rome, a type which contemporaries regarded as the personal creation of Sulla, but which was in reality simply the inevitable offspring of the commercial era and of democracy as it was understood in the ancient world—the type of the military chief at the head of a devoted army which he controls by his money and by the sword.

6. SULLA, *LA MONARCHIE MANQUÉE**

Sulla was neither one of those politicians who love power to do nothing with it, nor one of those masters who tolerate in order to be tolerated. He had been thrown

* Jérôme Carcopino, *Sylla ou la monarchie manquée*, translated by Donald Kagan (Paris: L'Artisan du Livre, 1931), pp. 240–243. Reprinted by permission of the publisher.

into action by the pride of his race, the ardor of his temperament, a burning thirst for freedom and command. But as happens with strong men, action revealed him to himself; and to the degree that his ambition mounted, his reflection and his patriotism sought in the satisfaction of these dominating instincts the satisfaction of the needs that agitated Italy and the provinces, the solution of what might, from this time forward, be called the world problem of Roman unity. Then, when he calculated that to realize his work new hecatombs were indispensable, and perhaps would not even be sufficient, he proceeded with a firm step and a bold countenance, because in politics the essential is to be right, and because he was sure of the reward that the future would sooner or later bring to this thought. And if the capacity of the statesman is measured by his faculty of foresight, who will deserve that title more than he? The work that he had undertaken did not mark a step toward the past; it tended toward the adaptation of Rome to the immensity of her territories and the diversity of her popular masses. Others after him will make the Empire, but it is he who first conceived it. He did not even leave to his successors the choice of means: step by step Augustus will walk in his footsteps and will establish the new government on foundations which Sulla had given his own regime. It would be equally wrong, then, to consider him as an obtuse, rough soldier who was not at all interested in public affairs, or as a hardened reactionary who rushes headlong to turn back the course of events. He was not an impotent and myopic opportunist who sees no further than the present moment and drags himself along day by day, or an incompetent or dishonest worker who tries to build anew with rubbish for his material. This military man was endowed with the most subtle intelligence, nourished with the vastest culture. This dissipate had profoundly pondered the gravest questions. This solitary man, whom no one seems ever to have influenced, had amassed treasures of experience. And it was in this way that, taking in the world with a divining glance, he was the precursor of the

revolution to which the conquests, pursued for one hundred and fifty years, would lead the Roman state a half-century later.

But with the same clarity of vision, Sulla had recognized the conditions of success: monarchy, whose hour he was convinced would one day come and which he would have liked to create immediately, required at the same time the collaboration of the aristocracy, the devotion of the army, and the enthusiasm of a popular mystique. If it were unable to obtain these all at once, it could only disappear or fall into ruin. Now, Sulla did not fall into that disorder of the mind which consists of believing that things are as one would like them to be, and he was forced to recognize quickly that the senatorial nobility, of whom he was compelled to ask assistance, shunned his invitation and, impatient with his hegemony, nibbled away at his authority while it disparaged it, an authority which it ought to have propagated, respected, and served. He sought to appease the nobility. It only hardened further. It riddled his entourage; it negotiated with his enemies; it secretly armed itself to circumvent him and bring him down. His relations with it reached the point in 78 B.C., when he had either to constrain it by the use of force, to undergo a humiliating compromise with it, or to leave it to its own responsibilities and immediately renounce everything. It is then that, at the crossroads, and free to make his own choice, Sulla chose an immediate retirement which, in safeguarding his dignity, preserved the principle and the future.

Whatever his intimate feelings were in this case, one can only bow before the decision that expressed them. Can it be that Sulla drew back before the risk of defeat rather than before the shedding of blood?

7. SULLA, *LE MONARQUE MALGRÉ LUI**

SULLA FELIX

It remains to say something about the great figure who closes this period of history, Lucius Cornelius Sulla Felix— "Lucky Jim" Sulla. We shall not have time to discuss the details of his legislation. What I propose to do now is to try to see Sulla's career in its broad setting, and to combat the startling and ingenious interpretation put forward by Carcopino in his book, *Sylla, ou la monarchie manquée*.

The intriguing question about Sulla is: why did he retire into private life at a moment when, to all outward seeming, he might have anticipated Julius Caesar and retained permanent control of the affairs of state? In trying to answer this question, I shall begin with a brief survey of his actions and legislation, interpreting them in line with the traditional view of his character and aims insofar as this view assumes that Sulla always meant to lay down his supreme power and retire to lead the life of a gentleman of leisure, with wealth and security enough to indulge what some scornfully and others enviously would call the apolaustic life. Further, I shall contend that Sulla never wanted supreme power in the first place, that it was thrust on him by circumstances, and that here lies the key to understanding Sulla. Sulla was no *monarque manqué*, but a *monarque malgré lui*.

When, on his return from the East and the defeat of the Cinnan faction, Sulla decided to re-organize the government of Rome, he naturally wanted a free hand, unhampered by the prejudice or scruples of others. Sulla had been a soldier all his life. Like the centurion in the gospel, he was used to saying to a man go and he goeth, and come and he cometh. Not for

him the cabals and compromises of the politician, the conversations in the corridors, the quiet decision to ignore issues until they had ceased to be awkward. Like Caesar a generation later, Sulla moved his general headquarters to Rome. Here then is nothing to surprise us or arouse suspicions. The type is well known; Cromwell, Napoleon, de Gaulle exemplify it. The qualities that make a great general— attention to detail, quick appreciation, authoritative decision—are carried over into political life. Sulla, confident in a judgment so often attended by success, habituated to the authority of command, approached the situation at Rome as he might approach any complex military problem, made an appreciation, and acted on it. True to his character and his experience, his action implies nothing about his long-range political ambitions.

The disturbed condition of the times furnished an excuse to revive in an entirely novel and unforseen form the obsolete office of dictator. Sulla commanded a great and victorious army, opposition to his known will was unthinkable. The Senate fell into line, and a law was passed appointing him *dictator rei publicae constituendae causa*. This new dictatorship had little in common with the office in its traditional form. It was to be of indefinite duration, terminable only by Sulla's death or resignation. While it endured, Sulla was to be free of all constitutional checks, invested with an *imperium* supreme over all other officers of state. All his earlier *acta* were ratified retrospectively. He had, as Plutarch (*Sulla* 33) puts it, "the power of life and death, the power to confiscate, to found colonies, to create cities and to plunder them, to make and break kings, to bestow his favours on whomsoever he wished." It is hard to see how he could do anything illegal, even if he tried.

Sulla now set out to find a way, not only to restore the Senate to power, but in

---

* From the unpublished lectures of David Stockton (Oxford, England: Brasenose College). Printed by permission of the author.

addition so to strengthen its hand that it would be able to govern unchallenged. Then he might himself retire, with a peaceful mind and the satisfaction of a job well done, to live out his remaining years unmolested.

The political influence of the knights was something that must be dealt with. They were badly hit by the proscriptions, but they would before long recover from this shock. Rome was a capitalist society, and capitalists must always exist there and seek to impose their wishes on the government, as in the past, playing their game of supporting whichever faction bid highest for their support. Sulla could hardly expect to effect a radical change in the economic structure of Rome: his task was to build up a governing machine powerful enough to resist capitalist pressure.

A new factor which Sulla had to face was the enfranchisement of Italy. This mass of new voters, spread through all the voting tribes, would obviously be an important factor in legislative and electoral assemblies. If they had bothered and afforded to come to Rome to register, they could also do so to vote. It was not easy to say which way they would lean. Judging by what happened later, it was toward the landowning, rather than the commercial, capitalists; but they by no means shared all the prejudices of the nobility, and they could give their support to men who were distasteful to the nobility, like Pompey and Cicero, whose influence seems to have been greater outside Rome than within. In the event, Sulla made no move either to encourage or to discourage the new voters. He took no chances, and decided to rob the popular assemblies altogether of their nuisance value (although he did abolish the corn distributions, probably hoping to rid the city of some of the *faex Romuli* and to discourage new additions).

Sulla's main device for strengthening the governing machine was a reconstruction of the Senate. The carnage of the last decade had reduced their numbers to about 150.

Sulla adopted the plan of electing into the Senate some new members of equestrian rank—who probably included a good proportion of members of senatorial families and small country magnates (we should not assume that any considerable number were drawn from the rich commercial class). At the same time, the number of quaestors was raised to twenty, and with entry into the Senate now automatic for these magistrates, the numbers of the Senate would eventually settle down at about six hundred.

By proscribing all his enemies within the Senate, and swamping it with his own nominees, Sulla created a body which he and his partisans might expect to dominate for a number of years to come. The power of the surviving noble families was greatly increased. Not only could they expect to lord it over the newcomers, *pedarii* mostly (so called because they took no active part in debates but simply used their feet, *pedes*, to go into the lobbies to vote); but further, like the first plebeian senators before them, these new senators would soon forget their origins and come to identify their interests with the interests of the Senate. Hence their *clientelae* would be at the Senate's disposal. Thus Sulla, by increasing the size of the Senate, at the same time increased its influence at elections.

The most important object of this enlargement of the Senate was, however, in my opinion, other than this. Sulla had to deal with the problem of the courts. Not only did he carry through a consolidation of the *quaestio* system, he also transferred the right to sit as *judices* outright to members of the Senate. This was a measure of vital importance, since the courts were very much a part, and not the least important part, of the political machinery of Rome; and control of the courts, as manifested in the composition of the panels of *judices*, had been a source of bitter political struggles for half a century. If the *quaestio* system was to be so consolidated as to rule out as far as possible the opportunity for *ad hoc* inquisitions of the type of the *quaestiones Mamilia* and *Variana*, and if the *judices* were to be drawn exclusively from the Senate, then the Senate must necessarily be enlarged to a size which would suffice to man the numerous and large panels.

Sulla also moved to set the traditional *auctoritas* of the Senate on a firm basis. This was required because, most evidently since the tribunates of the Gracchi, it had become clear that the customary authority of the Senate was an insufficient barrier against the assault of a coalition of knights and *populus* in the assemblies. Such alliances were, however, notoriously short-lived. By reshaping the constitution, Sulla ensured that such an alliance could only, if ever, accomplish anything after years of concerted effort.

The popular assemblies were allowed to retain their old electoral rights; and, in theory, there was nothing to stop them electing magistrates opposed to the senatorial oligarchy if enough votes were cast for such candidates. Sulla made it impossible for them to alter the policy of the Senate and the State until, with the lapse of years, such elections should have affected a majority in the Senate. So the tribunes were robbed of their initiative in presenting legislation by a law forbidding any proposal to go before an assembly before it had received the prior approval of the Senate. Alive to their great political danger, Sulla went a step further in crippling the tribunes, whose veto might still be a powerful weapon (and one sufficiently valuable to the *optimates* to make it undesirable to deprive them of it); he enacted that any man who had held office as tribune should thereby be rendered ineligible to hold any further magistracy. Thus Sulla might hope to restrict the tenure of the tribunate to the pliable and the unambitious.

The main criticism levelled against Sulla's reconstruction is that, despite the re-enactment of the *lex annalis*, with some

amendments, and the tightening up of the *maiestas* law as it affected provincial government, he failed to grapple seriously with the very danger which was in the end to bring the Republic down in ruins, a danger that recent history had advertised widely in (amongst others) Sulla's own career—the danger of the ambitious army commander.

The normal provincial armies were too small to be dangerous. The risk lay in the man who must be called on in an emergency to command large armies, and who might be tempted to exploit his power against political opponents. "Sulla potuit. Ego non potero?" It is hard to see what Sulla could have done about this. The solution was, as Augustus saw, to concentrate the overwhelming bulk of the armed forces of Rome under the command of one man, working through carefully screened and selected subordinate commanders, and focussing the loyalty of the troops relentlessly on the person of the *princeps*. It is not to be believed that such a solution would have been possible in Sulla's day: the Roman world had a long road to tread through blood and destruction before it was ready for that solution, before it was realized that, in Tacitus' words, *omnem potentiam ad unum conferri pacis interfuit* (*Hist.* I. 1). Such emergency great commands as that of Marius against the Germans and Sulla himself against Mithridates were bound to be needed from time to time. It was up to the Senate, invested by Sulla with so great power, to select the right man for the job, a man who could be relied on. In the end, it was the repeal in 70 B.C. of Sulla's legislation about the tribunes that opened the door to the grant of the great and destructive commands of Pompey and Caesar in the teeth of senatorial opposition.

Sulla's arrangements broke down, not because they were themselves weak, but because the body upon which they depended, the Senate, was weak. Riven by factional disputes, unready to sacrifice personal ambitions for the wider interests of their class, they opened the gates of their own citadel. The Senate was a poor tool, but it was the only one that Sulla had to hand. He had to make the best of it.

In 80 B.C., Sulla became consul again. His colleague was his old ally, Metellus Pius. His laws were duly ratified. Then in the middle of 79 B.C. he laid down his office of dictator, left Rome, and settled down to enjoy life. In 78 B.C. he died suddenly. He was sixty years old.

The natural interpretation of Sulla's career, as it appears in the ancient sources and most particularly in Plutarch's *Life*, is as that of a poor aristocrat of great ability, a member of a family which had been going downhill for a long time, who was determined to achieve wealth and distinction for the sake of personal pride and the pleasures and luxuries which wealth would buy; a man without strong political convictions, ready to follow any course which would bring him to his goal. The easiest and most obvious way lay via a military career to a provincial command, best of all a profitable war. This road Sulla chose, as men like Murena and Afranius were to choose it later, and along it he travelled to the point at which, his goal in sight, he was robbed of the Mithridatic command by Sulpicius who gave it to Marius. Sulla had to fight to recover his command, he had to fight to return to Italy, he had to crush opposition in Italy. Thus he was able to attain his goal only by first gaining supreme power. Such a reading of his career is perhaps too simple, and men are generally complex characters. Sulla was a proud man, and a good hater. He was a bit of a mystic. Like others, he was dependent on his supporters and had to accommodate their hopes and ambitions. Nonetheless, there is much truth in the picture.

It is, surely, quite incontestable that he resigned his supreme power of his own choice, as Appian emphasizes (*BC* I. 103). Julius Caesar himself, not a man likely to be ill-informed in such a matter, declared that "Sulla was a dunce to lay down his dictatorship" (Suetonius *DJ* 77), a statement which necessarily implies that Caesar believed that Sulla had a choice in the matter. (It shows, moreover, that the true dunce was Caesar, who paid with his own blood the price of not following Sulla's example. Sulla perhaps had a truer insight into the nature of Roman nobles than Caesar displayed when he trampled rough-shod on their pride and independence.) Juvenal in his first Satire shows that in his own day it was still a stock exercise at Roman schools to compose set speeches, urging on Sulla the arguments in favour of his laying down his dictatorship (*Sat.* I. 15–17: "Et nos consilium dedimus Sullae privatus ut altum dormiret"). Nowhere in all our ancient evidence is there any suggestion that Sulla, in resigning his autocratic power, was giving way to external pressures. And who could have applied such pressures? He was master of the largest and most seasoned army in the world; his veterans were settled in accessible locations in Italy. He was not the man to run at the threat of a handful of Pompey's legions. During his term of power, so far from gathering the reins of government into his own hands, he had heaped power on the Senate—with what reason, if he was a would-be Caesar? Caesars do not retire, nor are they allowed to.

Yet it is precisely this, that Sulla was a would-be Caesar, that he aimed at consolidating a position of supreme and autocratic power, that Carcopino has argued with all the dexterity and ingenuity (and they are considerable) at his command. His case may be briefly summarized as follows: (1) ancient tradition represents Sulla as a mere usurper; (2) Sulla, although by birth a noble and a patrician, did not belong to the governing clique of families (what Syme has called "the ruling oligarchy") but to the *noblesse déclinée*; (3) his nomination as dictator came as a shock to the Senate; (4) in his legislation, Sulla was building up a machine through which he could rule as a king; (5) his intimacy with *Fortuna*, his *cognomen* of *Felix*, were anticipations of the later deification of Caesar (here Carcopino's arguments have been carefully scrutinized and discredited by Balsdon in *JRS* 1952, pp. 1 ff.); (6) to the obvious question, why then did Sulla abdicate?, Carcopino replies that he had no choice, since he was outmanoeuvred by the Metelli and their supporters who compelled his abdication.

It is on this last argument that everything hinges. The others are largely reached by arguing back from the last, and cannot stand by themselves. In this case the proof of the pudding must be in the eating: Sulla's intentions must be judged by what he did. The vital question must be, did Sulla go of his own choosing or did he not? Yet for this last argument, Carcopino can produce hardly a scrap of ancient evidence to set against the overwhelming verdict that Sulla went voluntarily. He is reduced to pulling to pieces a speech of Cicero's, and then re-assembling it to his own pattern.

The speech in question is the *pro Roscio Amerino*, delivered almost at the beginning of Cicero's forensic career. (Carcopino dates the delivery of this speech to the beginning of 79 B.C., as against the traditional dating of 80 B.C. [his arguments are set out in an Appendix]; this re-dating is vital for Carcopino, because it enables him to link the case of Roscius closely with Sulla's resignation of his dictatorship shortly afterwards, but it is difficult to see how the evidence of Aulus Gellius and Quintilian, which places the speech in 80 B.C., is rebutted by Carcopino's arguments.) Carcopino sees the facts of the Roscius case more or less as follows (ch. 10).

The nobility, led by the Metelli, unable to attack Sulla openly, joyfully accepted the chance of getting at him through his henchman Chrysogonus, who had done Roscius down. Carcopino parades an impressive list of names, headed by the Metelli whom Cicero lists on the side of the injured Roscius: "sa cause était si limpide, son innocence si éclatante, ses spoliateurs avaient fait preuve de tant de perfidie et de méchanceté que les nobles auxquels il s'était addressé, et à qui pesait la domination de Sylla, accoururent à sa défense" (p. 155). ["his cause was so clear, his innocence so striking, his despoilers had proved so much perfidy and wickedness, that the nobles to whom the attack was addressed, and on whom Sulla's domination weighed, ran to his defense."] But, while it is true that in section 16 of the speech Cicero parades the Metelli, Servilii, and Scipiones as families with ties of friendship with Roscius *père*, they cannot be said to bulk large in the affair, and one gets the distinct impression that, *pâce* Cicero, they were sitting on the sidelines. Moreover, in section 30, Cicero admits that none of these nobles was actually taking an active part in the case on Roscius' behalf: "patronos huic [Roscio] defuturos putaverunt; desunt; qui libere dicat, qui cum fide defendat . . . non deest profecto".["They thought that he would be without defenders; he is. But a man who will speak freely, who will loyally defend him, is certainly not lacking."]. It is hard to see how Cicero could have made so little of the Metelli etc. in this speech if they were as vigorously behind young Roscius as Carcopino makes out.

For the rest, Carcopino is reduced to seeking nuances in the speech. Of course, there are nuances in all Cicero's speeches, plenty of them; and usually they tell us more, when we can detect them, than the direct statements. The trouble with nuances is that they are very elusive; in looking for them, Carcopino assumes as already proved what the nuances are themselves required to prove—he argues in a circle. Carcopino is trying to show that the Metelli etc., through Cicero, were getting in an attack on Sulla and his regime. But if we decline to accept this premiss, we may quite cheerfully refuse to draw the conclusions. Where Cicero is deferential to Sulla, Carcopino sees sarcasm, we see deference; and Carcopino can only establish that Cicero *is* being sarcastic by assuming that which the detection of the nuance of sarcasm is itself needed to prove. Which really gets us nowhere fast.

In fact, we are told that Chrysogonus took great care to see that Sulla did not know what he (Chrysogonus) was up to, and that Sulla was unaware of what was going on (section 22). Further, we may wonder whether Sulla cared if Chrysogonus failed to get away with it; or whether Cicero wanted the Metelli etc. on his side as friends of Sulla rather than as enemies in so delicate a matter. Certainly it is true that on any unprejudiced reading Cicero in this speech is at very great pains to be tactful to Sulla, and to dissociate him from any crimes committed by his henchmen.

Had Sulla wanted to save Chrysogonus, who could have stopped him? There is no evidence that he sought to intervene. Yet, even had he wished to, who was in a position to give him pause? To this, Carcopino's answer is: the Metelli, in alliance with young Pompey. But, leaving aside the absence of any evidence for such a concert, Pompey cannot have been a real threat to Sulla. Of the three army commanders, Sulla had by far the greatest experience, the greatest prestige, the largest number of men at his call. Metellus Pius even Carcopino allows to have been a staunch supporter of Sulla. Pompey might call on perhaps 30,000 men—but could he call on them to march against the legions of Sulla? And why should the nobles change one military despot for another, younger and more ambitious? And why could not Sulla easily have outbid the nobles for Pompey's support? The truth is that, at this time, Pompey was never a threat: he was a nuisance, and not too expensive to placate.

Carcopino further suggests that it was at this point that the Senate voted Cisalpine Gaul to Sulla as his province in much the same spirit as they were later to offer Caesar "silvae callesque"—to neutralize him. The argument for the date is unconvincing. But, even were he right about the date, it is odd that for Sulla, in whom Carcopino sees a would-be Caesar, Cisalpine Gaul should be poison, while for Caesar it was good red meat.

In short, we need not chase after Carcopino's hares once he has split them. When Cicero says of Sulla: "pacis constituendae rationem et belli gerendi potestatem solus habeat, cum omnes in unum spectent, unus omnia gubernet" ["one man alone has the means of establishing peace and of waging war; when all men look to one, one man governs all."], why not take him at his word? Sulla *was* all-powerful.

The overwhelming argument against Carcopino's interpretation of the *pro Roscio Amerino*, more powerful even than the silence or contrary implication of our ancient sources, comes from Cicero himself. Cicero, whom Carcopino assigns a key role in this *putsch* against Sulla, never evinced any love for Sulla. Cicero was nothing if not vain: he is not the man to allow his audiences to forget his past triumphs. Yet never do we find Cicero, on even one of the many occasions when such a claim would have been timely and apt, declaring: "Conscript fathers, once before, by the Grace of Heaven and with my help, you intimidated a would-be Caesar (or Catiline, or Antony) when that monster Sulla was forced to abandon his plans for a tyranny and resign his power." Anyone who knows anything about Cicero knows that Cicero could never have resisted such an opportunity—had it been available to him. But, on the contrary, we find Cicero assuming as a matter of common knowledge, not only in the *pro Roscio* (e.g., sections 22, 149), but also ten years later in the *Verrines*, that Sulla was working for the restoration of the nobility and not for personal supremacy. Verres, he points out (in *Verr.* II. i. 37), wanted to be able to cook his accounts, and this was why he joined

the Sullan faction, "non ut honos et dignitas nobilitati restiteuretur". This last
was the accepted aim of the Sullan faction
(cf. *pro Rab.* 16: "victoria nobilitatis").
Once Sulla had secured his own position,
paid his own debts, and fulfilled his obligations to his supporters, he withdrew
from the stage. He abdicated position,
however, not power. His power no one
could take from him. But he had better
things to do than found a dynasty and rule
an empire—like most sensible men.

There is, as Carcopino has said, no
enigma about Sulla. But Carcopino's
reasons are not the right reasons: he failed to
allow sufficient weight to the intervention
of circumstances. Carcopino's destructive
criticism of the views of his predecessors is remorseless and unanswerable.
We ought to hear no more of them. Sulla
had no reason to work loyally and self-
sacrificingly for the nobility: a change of
this kind in late middle-life is unthinkable
and quite out of character. But Sulla had
never *sought* supreme power: that is why
he was so ready to surrender it. To imagine
an Augustus or a Napoleon resigning
supreme power is fantastic: if they did, we
should be sure they were forced to it. But
if Sulla gave up what he had never wanted,
no surprise is called for. Here is no enigma:
only another example of the odd way
things have sometimes of working out.

When Sulla at last reached the consulship in 88 B.C., he was fifty years old. That
a Cornelius of such obvious ability should
have had to wait so long underlines the
fact that he had no strong political connec-
tions with the *optimates* or anyone else. He
was a noble, a patrician: but he belonged,
not to the ruling oligarchy, but to the
noblesse déclinée. Just such a man had been
Aemilius Scaurus, the great *princeps
senatus*; but Scaurus was taken up by the
ruling oligarchs and quickly advanced to
the heights. Not so Sulla. In all the
political hubbubs of the period of twenty
years before his consulship, the years of
Sulla's maturity, we never find his name

mentioned in any truly political connection. His slow advance up the ladder of
office is a purely military one. In 89 B.C.
his great successes in the Social War
marked him as Rome's ablest and most
tenacious commander, and brought the
soldier his long-earned reward—the consulship and a great military command
against Mithridates. As Appian's narrative
makes plain, in 88 B.C. other men's struggles brought Sulla perforce into politics.
Although prepared in the end, after a
formal display of consular authority, to
leave the political struggle at Rome to sort
itself out while he went off to deal with
Mithridates, he was brought up short by
Sulpicius' action in transferring his command to Marius. Sulla, understandably
indignant, was not prepared to acquiesce
in this. That Sulpicius and Marius were so
ill-prepared to meet Sulla's march on
Rome only emphasizes how little importance they had attached to Sulla in the
political game. They misjudged their man:
Sulla knew his army, and Sulla was tough-
minded. Abandoned by all his officers save
one, he set out for Rome meaning to "get
there firstest with the mostest." He did
(Appian, *BC*, I. 55–58).

Thus was Sulla drawn, willy-nilly, into
the vortex of politics to defend his own
interests, and drawn in as an opponent of
the *populares*. (Will anyone doubt that, had
it been an *optimate* magistrate who robbed
him of his command, Sulla would have
become a *popularis*?) Sulla's reaction was
a general's reaction, with no time for
political niceties. Patching up a settlement,
he left for the East. While he was away, a
counter-coup of the *populares* seized power.
To return to Italy, he had to fight again.
Toward the end of the Cinnan regime,
more and more *optimates* and moderates
went over to him: alongside enemies to
pay out, he acquired many friends to help.
That his final settlement took the form it
did is no surprise. Events, a change in circumstances and not a change in character,
had made Sulla a pro-noble *optimate*. Italy

was made safe for Sulla; Sulla's enemies were made to rue the day they had incurred his enmity, his friends reaped their due reward. Circumstance and the actions of others had charted his course: an imperious character, reinforced by long habit of military command, determined that he would approach his task in a brusque and authoritarian manner. The operation completed, he withdrew from the dust of an arena which he had never shown any willingness to enter.

SECTION IX

The Roman Revolution—Phase Three:
Caesar or Rex?

AFTER THE retirement and death of Sulla, his constitution was quickly destroyed, his attempt to restore the rule of the Senate proven a failure. The remaining years of the Roman Republic were occupied with a struggle among dynasts and senatorial factions to achieve dominance. From 49 to 46 B.C. Caesar and Pompey fought a great civil war that ended in total defeat for Pompey and the senatorial forces. Caesar was unchallenged master of the Roman world. His problem was to invent a system of government that would avoid the pitfalls of divided rule and yet rest upon widespread popular support. From antiquity to the present time, men have argued that his solution was nothing less than monarchy pure and simple. Others have denied that this was his goal. The question cannot be settled, for Caesar was assassinated before he could put his plans into practice, yet it is important to consider the problem both because of its intrinsic interest and because it represents a significant stage in the transition from republic to empire.

1. THE ACCOUNT OF DIO CASSIUS*

This Cæsar did as a preliminary step to making a campaign against the Parthians, but a baleful frenzy which fell upon certain men through jealousy of his onward progress and hatred of his being esteemed above others caused the death of the leader by unlawful means, while it added a new name to the annals of infamy; it scattered decrees to the winds and brought upon the Romans seditions again and civil wars after a state of harmony. They declared that they had proved themselves both destroyers of Cæsar and liberators of the people, but in fact their plot against him was one of fiendish malice, and they threw the city into disorder when at last it possessed a stable government. Democracy has a fair appearing name which conveys the impression of bringing equal rights to all from equal laws, but its results are seen not to agree at all with its title. Monarchy, on the contrary, strikes the ear unpleasantly, but is a very excellent government to live under. It is easier to find one single excellent man than many,

---

* Dio Cassius, 44. 1–11, translated by H. B. Foster, pp. 409–417.

267

and if even this seems to some a difficult feat, it is quite inevitable that the other proposition be acknowledged to be impossible; for the acquirement of virtue is not a characteristic of the majority of men. And again, even though one reprobate should obtain supreme power, yet he is preferable to a multitude of such persons, as the history of the Greeks and barbarians and of the Romans themselves proves. For successes have always been greater and more in number in the case both of cities and of individuals under kings than under popular rule, and disasters do not happen so easily in monarchies as in ochlocracies. In cases where a democracy has flourished anywhere, it has nevertheless reached its prime during a short period when the people had neither size nor strength that abuses should spring up among them from good fortune or jealousies from ambition. For a city so large as this, ruling the finest and the greatest part of the known world, containing men of many and diverse natures, holding many huge fortunes, occupied with every imaginable pursuit, enjoying every imaginable fortune, both individually and collectively,—for such a city to practice moderation under a democracy is impossible, and still more is it impossible for the people, unless moderation prevails, to be harmonius. If Marcus Brutus and Gaius Cassius had stopped to think this over they would never have killed the city's head and protector nor have made themselves the cause of countless ills both to their own persons and to all the rest of mankind then existing.

It happened as follows, and his death was due to the cause I shall presently describe. He had not aroused dislike without any definite justification, except in so far as it was the senators themselves who had by the novelty and excess of their honors sent his mind soaring; and then, after filling him with conceit, they found fault with his prerogatives and spread injurious reports to the effect that he was glad to accept them and behaved more haughtily as a result of them. It is true that sometimes Cæsar erred by accepting some of the honors voted him and believing that he really deserved them, yet most blameworthy are those who, after beginning to reward him as he deserved, led him on and made him liable to censure by the measures that they voted. He neither dared to thrust them all aside, for fear of being thought contemptuous, nor could he be safe when he accepted them. Excess in honors and praises renders conceited even the most modest, especially if such rewards appear to have been given with sincerity. The privileges that were granted him (in addition to all those mentioned) were of the following number and kinds. They will be stated all together, even if they were not all moved or ratified at one time. First, then, they voted that he should always appear even in the city itself wearing the triumphal garb and should sit in his chair of state everywhere except at festivals. At that time he got the right to be seen on the tribune's benches and in company with those who were successively tribunes. And they gave him the right to offer the so-called *spolia opima* at the temple of Jupiter Feretrius, as if he had slain some hostile general with his own hand, and to have lictors that always carried laurel, and after the Feriæ Latinæ to ride from Albanum to the city mounted on a charger. In addition to these remarkable privileges they named him father of his country, stamped his image on the coinage, voted to celebrate his birthday by public sacrifice, ordered that there be some statue of him in the cities and all the temples of Rome, and they set on the rostra two, one representing him as the savior of the citizens and the other as the rescuer of the city from siege, along with the crowns customary for such achievements. They also passed a resolution to build a temple of Concordia Nova, on the ground that through his efforts they enjoyed peace, and to celebrate an annual festival in her honor. When he had accepted these, they assigned to him the charge of filling the Pontine marshes, cutting a canal through the Peloponnesian isthmus, and constructing a new senate-house, since that of Hostilius although repaired had been demolished. The reason given for that action was that a temple of Good Fortune might be built there, which Lepidus, indeed, while master of the horse had completed: but the real intention was that the name of Sulla should not be preserved in it and that another senate-house, newly constructed, might be named the Julian, just as they had called the month in which he was born July, and one of the tribes (selected by lot) the Julian. And Cæsar himself, they voted, should be sole censor for life and enjoy the immunities bestowed upon the tribunes, so that if any one should outrage him by deed or word, that man should be an outlaw and involved in the curse, and further that his son, should he beget or adopt one, was to be appointed high priest. As he seemed to like this, a gilded chair was granted him, and a garb that once the kings had used and a body-guard of knights and senators: furthermore they decided that prayers should be made for him publicly every year, that they would swear by his Fortune and that all the deeds he was yet to do should receive confirmation. Next they bestowed upon him a quinquennial festival, as to a hero, and managers of sacred rites for the festival of naked boys in Pan's honor, constituting a third priestly college which they called the Julian, and on the occasion of all combats in armor one special day of his own each time both in Rome and the rest of Italy. When he showed himself pleased at this, too, then they voted that his gilded chair and crown set with precious gems and overlaid with gold should be carried into the theatre on an equal footing with those of the gods, and that on the occasion of the horse-races his chariot should be brought in. And finally they addressed him outright as Julian

Jupiter and ordered a temple to be consecrated to him and to his Clemency, electing Antony as their priest like some Dialis.

At the same time with these measures they passed another which well indicated their disposition. It gave him the right to place his tomb within the pomerium; and the decrees regarding this matter they inscribed with gold letters on silver tablets and deposited beneath the feet of the Capitoline Jupiter, thus pointing out to him very clearly that he was a man. When they began to honor him it was with the idea that he would be reasonably modest; but as they went on and saw that he was delighted at what they voted,—he accepted all but a very few of their gifts,— various men kept at different times proposing various greater marks of esteem, all in excess, some as an act of extreme flattery toward him, and others as one of sarcastic ridicule. Actually some dared to suggest permitting him to have intercourse with as many women as he liked, because even at this time, though fifty years old, he still had numerous mistresses. Others, and the majority, followed the course mentioned because they wished to make him envied and disliked as quickly as possible, that he might the sooner perish. Of course precisely that happened, though Cæsar took courage on account of these very measures to believe that he would never be plotted against by the men who had voted him such honors, nor by any one else, because they would prevent it; and in consequence from this time he dispensed with a body-guard. Nominally he accepted the privilege of being watched over by the senators and knights and thus did away with his previous guardians. Once on a single day they had passed in his honor an unusually large number of decrees of especially important character, that had been voted unanimously by all the rest except Cassius and a few others, who became notorious for this action: yet they suffered no harm, a fact which conspicuously displayed their ruler's clemency.

So, then, they approached him as he was sitting in the forepart of the temple of Venus with the intention of announcing to him in a body their decisions;—such business they transacted in his absence, in order to have the appearance of doing it not under compulsion but voluntarily. And either by some Heaven-sent fatuity or through excess of joy he received them sitting, an act which aroused so great indignation among them all, not only senators but all the rest, that it afforded his slayers one of their chief excuses for their plot against him. Some who subsequently tried to defend him said that owing to diarrhœa he could not control the movement of his bowels and had remained where he was in order to avoid a flux.

They were not able, however, to persuade the majority, since not long after this he arose and walked home without assistance; hence most men suspected him of being inflated with pride and hated him for his supercilious behavior, when it was they themselves who had made him disdainful by the extreme nature of their honors. After this occurrence suspicion was increased by the fact that somewhat later he submitted to being made dictator for life.

When he had reached this point, the conduct of the men plotting against him became no longer doubtful, and in order to embitter even his best friends against him they did their best to traduce the man and finally called him "king,"—a name which was often heard in their consultations. When he refused the title and rebuked in a way those that so saluted him, yet did nothing by which he could be thought to be really displeased at it, they secretly adorned his statue, which stood on the rostra, with a diadem. And when Gaius Epidius Marullus and Lucius Cæsetius Flavus, tribunes, took it down, he became thoroughly angry, although they uttered no insulting word and furthermore spoke well of him before the people as not

desiring anything of the sort. At this time, though vexed, he remained quiet; subsequently, however, when he was riding in from Albanum, some men again called him king, and he said that his name was not king but Cæsar: then when those tribunes brought suit against the first man that termed him king, he no longer restrained his wrath but showed evident irritation, as if these officials were actually aiming at the stability of his government. For the moment he took no revenge upon them: later, when they issued public notice to the effect that they found themselves not at liberty to speak freely and without molestation for the public good, he appeared exceedingly angry and brought them into the senate-house, where he accused them and put their conduct to the vote. He did not put them to death, though some declared them worthy of that penalty, but first having removed them from the tribuneship through the motion of Helvius Cinna, their colleague, he erased their names from the senate. Some were pleased at this, or pretended to be, on the ground that they would have no need to incur danger by free speech, and keeping out of politics they viewed events as from a watch tower. Cæsar, however, received an ill name from this fact, too, that whereas he should have hated those that applied to him the name of king, he let them go and found fault instead with the tribunes.

Something else that happened not long after these events proved still more clearly that while pretendedly he shunned the title, in reality he desired to assume it. When he had entered the Forum at the festival of the Lupercalia, at which naked boys competed, and was sitting on the rostra in his golden chair adorned with the royal apparel and conspicuous by his crown wrought of gold, Antony with his fellow priests saluted him as king and surrounding his brows with a diadem said: "The people gives this to you through my hands." He answered that

Jupiter alone was king of the Romans and sent the diadem to him to the Capitol, yet he was not angry and caused it to be inscribed in the records that the royalty presented to him by the people through the consul he had refused to receive. It was accordingly suspected that this had been done by some prearranged plan and that he was anxious for the name but wished to be somehow compelled to take it, and the consequent hatred against him was intense.

2. NICOLAUS OF DAMASCUS*

NICOLAUS WAS BORN to a distinguished Greek family in the first century B.C. He served as adviser and court historian to Herod the Great of Judea. In addition to the biography of the young Augustus, from which the following selection is taken, he wrote dramas, philosophical works, and a multi-volume history of the world.

From this point my narrative will investigate the manner in which the assassins formed their conspiracy against Caesar and how they worked out the whole affair, and what happened afterward when the whole state was shaken. Accordingly, I shall in the first place rehearse the circumstances of the plot itself, its reasons, and its final momentous outcome. In the next place I shall speak of Octavian on whose account this narrative was undertaken; how he came into power, and how, after he had taken his predecessor's place, he employed himself in deeds of peace and war.

At first a few men started the conspiracy, but afterwards many took part, more than are remembered to have taken part in any earlier plot against a commander. They say that there were more than eighty who had a share in it. Among those who had the most influence were: Decimus Brutus, a particular friend of Caesar, Gaius Cassius, and Marcus Brutus, second to none in the estimation of the Romans at that time. All these were formerly members of the opposite faction, and had tried to further Pompeius' interests, but when he was defeated, they came under Caesar's jurisdiction and lived quietly for the time being; but although Caesar tried to win them over individually by kindly treatment, they never abandoned their hope of doing him harm. He on his part was naturally without grudge against the beaten party, because of a certain leniency of disposition, but they, using to their own advantage his lack of suspicion, by seductive words and pretence of deeds treated him in such a way as to more readily escape detection in their plot. There were various reasons which affected each and all of them and impelled them to lay hands on the man. Some of them had hopes of becoming leaders themselves in his place if he were put out of the way; others were angered over what had happened to them in the war, embittered over the loss of their relatives, property, or offices of state. They concealed the fact that they were angry, and made the pretense of something more seemly, saying that they were displeased at the rule of a single man and that they were striving for a republican form of government. Different people had different reasons, all brought together by whatever pretext they happened upon.

At first the ringleaders conspired; then many more joined, some of their own accord because of personal grievances, some because they had been associated with the others and wished to show plainly

* Nicolaus of Damascus, *Life of Augustus*, 19–22, translated by Clayton M. Hall (Menascha, Wisconsin: George Banta, 1923), pp. 29, 31, 33, 35, 37, 39, 41. Reprinted by permission of Clayton M. Hall.

the good faith in their long-standing friendship, and accordingly became their associates. There were some who were of neither of these types, but who had agreed because of the worth of the others, and who resented the power of one man after the long-standing republican constitution. They were very glad not to start the affair themselves, but were willing to join such company when someone else had initiated proceedings, not even hesitating to pay the penalty if need be. The reputation which had long been attached to the Brutus family was very influential in causing the uprising, for Brutus' ancestors had overthrown the kings who ruled from the time of Romulus, and they had first established republican government in Rome. Moreover, men who had been friends of Caesar were no longer similarly well disposed toward him when they saw people who were previously his enemies saved by him and given honors equal to their own. In fact, even these others were not particularly well disposed toward him, for their ancient grudges took precedence over gratitude and made them forgetful of their good fortune in being saved, while, when they remembered the good things they had lost in being defeated, they were provoked. Many also hated him because they had been saved by him although he had been irreproachable in his behavior toward them in every respect; but nevertheless, the very thought of receiving as a favor the benefits which as victors they would readily have enjoyed, annoyed them very much.

Then there was another class of men, namely those who had served with him, whether as officers or privates, and who did not get a share of glory. They asserted that prisoners of war were enrolled among the veteran forces and that they received identical pay. Accordingly, his friends were incensed at being rated as equal to those whom they themselves had taken prisoners, and indeed they were even outranked by some of them. To many, also, the fact that they benefited at his hands, both by gifts of property and by appointments to offices, was a special source of grievance, since he alone was able to bestow such benefits, and everyone else was ignored as of no importance. When he became exalted through many notable victories (which was fair enough) and began to think himself superhuman the common people worshipped him, but he began to be obnoxious to the optimates and to those who were trying to obtain a share in the government. And so, every kind of man combined against him: great and small, friend and foe, military and political, every one of whom put forward his own particular pretext for the matter in hand, and as a result of his own complaints each lent a ready ear to the accusations of the others. They all confirmed each other in their conspiracy and they furnished as surety to one another the grievances which they held severally in private against him. Hence, though the number of conspirators became so great, no one dared to give information of the fact. Some say, however, that a little before his death, Caesar received a note in which warning of the plot was given, and that he was murdered with it in his hands before he had a chance to read it, and that it was found among other notes after his death.

However, all this became known subsequently. At that time some wished to gratify him by voting him one honor after another, while others treacherously included extravagant honors, and published them, so that he might become an object of envy and suspicion to all. Cæsar was of guileless disposition and was unskilled in political practices by reason of his foreign campaigns, so that he was easily taken in by these people, supposing, naturally enough, that their commendations came rather from men who admired him than from men who were plotting against him.

To those who were in authority this measure was especially displeasing: that the people were now rendered powerless to make appointments to office, and that Caesar was given the right of investure to bestow upon whomsoever he pleased. An ordinance voted not long before provided this. Furthermore, all sorts of rumors were being bandied about in the crowd, some telling one story, others another. Some said that he had decided to establish a capital of the whole empire in Egypt, and that Queen Cleopatra had lain with him and borne him a son, named Cyrus, there. This he himself refuted in his will as false. Others said that he was going to do the same thing at Troy, on account of his ancient connection with the Trojan race.

Something else, such as it was, took place which especially stirred the conspirators against him. There was a golden statue of him which had been erected on the Rostra by vote of the people. A diadem appeared on it, encircling the head, whereupon the Romans became very suspicious, supposing that it was a symbol of servitude. Two of the tribunes, Lucius and Gaius, came up and ordered one of their subordinates to climb up, take it down, and throw it away. When Caesar discovered what had happened, he convened the senate in the temple of Concordia and arraigned the tribunes, asserting that they themselves had secretly placed the diadem on the statue, so that they might have a chance to insult him openly and thus get credit for doing a brave deed by dishonoring the statue, caring nothing either for him or for the senate. He continued that their action was one which indicated a more serious resolution and plot: if somehow they might slander him to the people as a seeker after unconstitutional power, and thus (themselves stirring up an insurrection) to slay him. After this address, with the concurrence of the senate he banished them. Accordingly, they went off into exile and other tribunes were appointed in their place. Then the people clamored that he become king and they shouted that there should be no longer any

delay in crowning him as such, for Fortune had already crowned him. But Caesar declared that although he would grant the people everything because of their good will toward him, he would never allow this step; and he asked their indulgence for contradicting their wishes in preserving the old form of government, saying that he preferred to hold the office of consul in accordance with the law to being king illegally.

Such was the people's talk at that time. Later, in the course of the winter, a festival was held in Rome, called Lupercalia, in which old and young men together take part in a procession, naked except for a girdle, and anointed, railing at those whom they meet and striking them with pieces of goat's hide. When this festival came on Marcus Antonius was chosen director. He proceeded through the Forum, as was the custom, and the rest of the throng followed him. Caesar was sitting in a golden chair on the Rostra, wearing a purple toga. At first Licinius advanced toward him carrying a laurel wreath, though inside it a diadem was plainly visible. He mounted up, pushed up by his colleagues (for the place from which Caesar was accustomed to address the assembly was high), and set the diadem down before Caesar's feet. Amid the cheers of the crowd he placed it on Caesar's head. Thereupon Caesar called Lepidus, the master of horse, to ward him off, but Lepidus hesitated. In the meanwhile Cassius Longinus, one of the conspirators, pretending to be really well disposed toward Caesar so that he might the more readily escape suspicion, hurriedly removed the diadem and placed it in Caesar's lap. Publius Casca was also with him. While Caesar kept rejecting it, and among the shouts of the people, Antonius suddenly rushed up, naked and anointed, just as he was in the procession, and placed it on his head. But Caesar snatched it off, and threw it into the crowd. Those who were standing at some distance applauded this action, but those who were near at hand clamored that he should accept it and not repel the people's favor. Various individuals held different views of the matter. Some were angry, thinking it an indication of power out of place in a democracy; others, thinking to court favor, approved; still others spread the report that Antonius had acted as he did not without Caesar's connivance. There were many who were quite willing that Caesar be made king openly. All sorts of talk began to go through the crowd. When Antonius crowned Caesar a second time, the people shouted in chorus, 'Hail, King', but Caesar still refusing the crown, ordered it to be taken to the temple of Capitoline Jupiter, saying that it was more appropriate there. Again the same people applauded as before. There is told another story, that Antonius acted thus wishing to ingratiate himself with Caesar, and at the same time was cherishing the hope of being adopted as his son. Finally, he embraced Caesar and gave the crown to some of the men standing near to place it on the head of the statue of Caesar which was near by. This they did. Of all the occurrences of that time this was not the least influential in hastening the action of the conspirators, for it proved to their very eyes the truth of the suspicions they entertained.

Not long after this, the praetor Cinna propitiated Caesar to the extent of securing a decree which allowed the exiled tribunes to return; though in accordance with the wish of the people they were not to resume their office, but to remain private citizens, yet not excluded from public affairs. Caesar did not prevent their recall, so they returned. Caesar called the annual comitia

(for he had the authority of a decree to do so) and appointed Vibius Pansa and Aulus Hirtius as consuls for the ensuing year; for the year after that, Decimus Brutus, one of the conspirators, and Munatius Plancus. Directly after this, another thing happened that greatly aroused the conspirators. Caesar was having a large handsome forum laid out in Rome, and he had called together the artisans and was letting the contracts for its construction. In the meanwhile up came a procession of Roman nobles, to confer the honors which had just been voted him by common consent. In the lead was the consul (the one who was Caesar's colleague at that time), and he carried the decree with him. In front of him were lictors, keeping the crowd back on either side. With the consul came the praetors, tribunes, quaestors, and all the other officials. Next came the senate in orderly formation, and then a multitude of enormous size—never so large. The dignity of the nobles was awe-inspiring— they were entrusted with the rule of the whole empire, and yet looked with admiration on another as if he were still greater. Caesar was seated while they advanced and because he was conversing with men standing to one side, he did not turn his head toward the approaching procession or pay any attention to it, but continued to prosecute the business which he had on hand, until one of his friends, near by, said, 'Look at these people coming up in front of you.' Then Caesar laid down his papers and turned around and listened to what they had come to say. Now among their number were the conspirators, who filled the others with ill-will toward him, though the others were already offended at him because of this incident.

3. SUETONIUS*

Gaius Suetonius Tranquillus (ca. A.D. 69–150) was a wealthy Roman and secretary to the Emperor Trajan. He was a biographer and not a historian, collecting anecdotes, gossip, and all kinds of information in the form of a catalogue. We may be sure that any hostile tradition has found its way into the *Lives* of Suetonius.

His other words and actions, however, so far outweigh all his good qualities, that it is thought he abused his power, and was justly cut off. For he not only obtained excessive honours, such as the consulship every year, the dictatorship for life, and the censorship, but also the title of emperor, and the surname of FATHER OF HIS COUNTRY, besides having his statue amongst the kings, and a lofty couch in the theatre. He even suffered some honours to be decreed to him, which were unbefitting the most exalted of mankind; such as a gilded chair of state in the senate-house and on his tribunal, a consecrated chariot, and banners in the Circensian procession, temples, altars, statues among the gods, a bed of state in the temples, a priest, and a college of priests dedicated to himself, like those of Pan; and that one of the months should be called by his name. There were, indeed, no honours which he did not either assume himself, or grant to others, at his will and pleasure. In his third and fourth consulship, he used only the title of the office, being content with the power of dictator, which was conferred upon him with the consulship; and in both years he substituted other consuls in his room, during the three last months; so that in the intervals he held no assemblies of the people, for the election of magistrates, excepting only tribunes and ediles of the people; and appointed officers, under the name of præfects, instead of the prætors, to administer the affairs of the city during his absence. The office of consul having become vacant, by the sudden death of one of the consuls the day before the calends of

* Suetonius, *Julius Caesar*, 76–79, translated by Alexander Thomson, revised by T. Forester (London: Bell and Sons, 1816, 1896, 1917).

January [the 1st Jan.], he conferred it on a person who requested it of him, for a few hours. Assuming the same licence, and regardless of the customs of his country, he appointed magistrates to hold their offices for terms of years. He granted the insignia of the consular dignity to ten persons of prætorian rank. He admitted into the senate some men who had been made free of the city, and even natives of Gaul, who were semi-barbarians. He likewise appointed to the management of the mint, and the public revenue of the state, some servants of his own household; and entrusted the command of three legions, which he left at Alexandria, to an old catamite of his, the son of his freed-man Rufinus.

He was guilty of the same extravagance in the language he publicly used, as Titus Ampius informs us; according to whom he said, "The republic is nothing but a name, without substance or reality. Sylla was an ignorant fellow to abdicate the dictatorship. Men ought to consider what is becoming when they talk with me, and look upon what I say as a law." To such a pitch of arrogance did he proceed, that when a soothsayer announced to him the unfavourable omen, that the entrails of a victim offered for sacrifice were without a heart, he said, "The entrails will be more favourable when I please; and it ought not to be regarded as a prodigy that a beast should be found wanting a heart."

But what brought upon him the greatest odium, and was thought an unpardonable insult, was his receiving the whole body of the conscript fathers sitting, before the temple of Venus Genitrix, when they waited upon him with a number of decrees, conferring on him the highest dignities.

Some say that, on his attempting to rise, he was held down by Cornelius Balbus; others, that he did not attempt to rise at all, but frowned on Caius Trebatius, who suggested to him that he should stand up to receive the senate. This behaviour appeared the more intolerable in him, because, when one of the tribunes of the people, Pontius Aquila, would not rise up to him, as he passed by the tribunes' seat during his triumph, he was so much offended, that he cried out, "Well then, you tribune, Aquila, oust me from the government." And for some days afterwards, he never promised a favour to any person without this proviso, "if Pontius Aquila will give me leave."

To this extraordinary mark of contempt for the senate he added another affront still more outrageous. For when, after the sacred rites of the Latin festival, he was returning home, amidst the immoderate and unusual acclamations of the people, a man in the crowd put a laurel crown, encircled with a white fillet, on one of his statues; upon which, the tribunes of the people, Epidius Marullus, and Cæsetius Flavus, ordered the fillet to be removed from the crown, and the man to be taken to prison. Cæsar, being much concerned either that the idea of royalty had been sug-

gested to so little purpose, or, as was said, that he was thus deprived of the merit of refusing it, reprimanded the tribunes very severely, and dismissed them from their office. From that day forward, he was never able to wipe off the scandal of affecting the name of king, although he replied to the populace, when they saluted him by that title, "I am Cæsar, and no king." And at the feast of the Lupercalia, when the consul Antony placed a crown upon his head in the rostra several times, he as often put it away, and sent it to the Capitol for Jupiter, the Best and the Greatest. A report was very current, that he had a design of withdrawing to Alexandria or Ilium, whither he proposed to transfer the imperial power, to drain Italy by new levies, and to leave the government of the city to be administered by his friends. To this report it was added, that in the next meeting of the senate, Lucius Cotta, one of the fifteen, would make a motion, that as there was in the Sibylline books a prophecy, that the Parthians would never be subdued but by a king, Cæsar should have that title conferred upon him.

For this reason the conspirators precipitated the execution of their design, that they might not be obliged to give their assent to the proposal.

4. BRUTUS' VIEW OF CAESAR'S ASSASSINATION*

After the assassination of Caesar, the conspirators were surprised to find that much popular feeling was aroused against them and that the removal of the dictator did not automatically restore the Republic. A new civil war threatened and Cicero tried to employ the services of Octavian, Caesar's heir, in the senatorial cause. In this letter Brutus objects vigorously and provides an insight into the thinking of the conspirators.

M. IUNIUS BRUTUS TO CICERO (AT ROME)

MACEDONIA (MAY). I have read an extract from your letter to Octavius which

---

* Cicero, *Letters to Brutus*, 1. 16, translated by E. S. Shuckburgh (London: G. Bell and Sons, 1917), Vol. 4.

was sent me by Atticus. Your zeal and care for my safety gave me no novel pleasure; for it is not merely a matter of habit, but of daily habit, to be told of you that you have said or done something in defence of my position which displayed your fidelity and complimentary opinion of me. But that same extract of your letter to Octavius about us caused me a distress as great as my heart is capable of feeling. For you thank him in the name of the Republic in such terms! With such abject and whispering humbleness—why must I write the word? I blush to think of my position and high estate, yet I must write it—you commend *our* safety to *him*! Could any death be a worse disaster? You, in fact, avow that the slavery is not abolished, only the master changed! Recall your words and dare to say that those prayers are not the prayers of an enslaved subject to a tyrant. The one and only thing —you say—that is demanded and expected of him is that he consent to the safety of those citizens, of whom the loyalists and the people have a good opinion. What? If he doesn't consent, shall we not be safe? And yet it is better not to be than to be by his favour. Upon my honour I do not think that all the gods are so hostile to the safety of the Roman people, that we need entreat Octavius for the safety of any citizen, not to say for "the liberators of the world"—for there is a certain advantage in using strong language, and at any rate there is a propriety in doing so to people who do not know what every man ought to fear or to aim at.

Do you confess, Cicero, that Octavius has this power, and are you his friend? Or, if you regard me with affection, do you wish me to appear at Rome, when in order to do so safely I have had to be recommended to that boy? Why do you thank him, if you think he has to be asked to allow and suffer us to keep our lives? Is it to be regarded as a favour that he has preferred to be himself rather than a second Antony, to whom we had to make petitions like that? Does anyone address to the destroyer of another's tyranny, and not rather to its successor, a prayer that those who have done the most splendid services to their country may be allowed their lives? This is mere weakness and a counsel of despair. And the fault is not

yours more than everyone else's. It was this that egged on Cæsar to desire royalty, and induced Antony after his death to aim at occupying the place of the dead man, and has at the present moment put that boy of yours on such a pedestal, as to make you think that he must be absolutely entreated to grant life to such men as us, and that we shall even now be able to enjoy a bare safety from the pity of one man, and by nothing else whatever. But if we had remembered that we were Romans, these dregs of mankind would not have conceived the ambition of playing the tyrant with more boldness than we should have forbidden it: nor would Antony have had his ambition more roused by Cæsar's royalty, than his fears excited by Cæsar's death. For yourself, a consular and the avenger of such abominable crimes—and I fear that by their suppression the mischief was only postponed by you for a short time—how can you contemplate your own achievements, and at the same time countenance, or at any rate endure these things with such abject humbleness as to have the air of countenancing them? Again, what was your private and personal quarrel with Antony? Why, it was just because he made this very claim—that our safety should be asked as a favour from him; that we should hold our civil rights on sufferance—we from whom he had himself received his freedom; that he should be absolute in the Republic—it was for these reasons that you thought we must take up arms to prevent his playing the tyrant. Was the object of doing so that, when he had been prevented, we should have to petition another man to allow himself to be put in his place? Or was it that the Republic should be its own master and at its own disposal? Surely: unless we are to suppose that our objection was not to slavery but to the terms of our slavery! And yet, not only had we the opportunity of supporting our high estate with Antony as a liberal master, but even of enjoying rewards and honours as his partners to the top of our ambition: for what would he have refused to men, whose submissiveness he saw would be the greatest bulwark of his tyranny? But nothing seemed sufficient to make us barter our honour and freedom.

This very boy, whom the name of Cæsar appears to instigate against the slayers of Cæsar, what would he give, if there were a chance of such traffic, to be as powerful with our support, as he certainly will be when we choose life for its own sake, and the possession of money, and the title of consulars! But Cæsar will have perished in vain: for why did we rejoice at his death, if we were to become none the less slaves when he is dead? No one else cares about these things, but may the gods and goddesses take from me everything sooner than the resolution of never conceding what I would not endure in Cæsar—I won't say to the heir of the man I killed, but even to my father himself if he were to come to life again—namely, that he should, without a protest from me, be more powerful than the laws and the senate. Are you so deluded as to think that the rest of the world will be free from one without whose consent there is no footing for us in Rome? Moreover, how can you possibly get what you ask? For you ask that he would consent to our safety: do we therefore appear likely to accept safety, since we have accepted life? But how can we accept it, if we previously give up position and liberty? Do you count the fact of living at Rome as complete citizenship? It is circumstance, not the particular place of residence, that must secure me that. I was neither properly a full citizen while Cæsar was alive, except when I had resolved upon doing that deed; nor can I ever be anywhere an exile so long as I abhor servitude and submission to insult worse than every other evil. To ask a man who has adopted a tyrant's name as his own for the safety of the avengers and destroyers of the tyranny—is not this to fall back into the very dungeon from which you have just escaped? Why, in Greek states when tyrants are put down their sons are included under the same punishment. Am I to desire to see a state, or to regard it as a state at all, which is incapable of recovering even a freedom handed down by its ancestors and rooted in its very being, and which is more afraid of the name of a slain tyrant in the person of a mere boy, than confident in itself, though seeing the very man who possessed the most over-weening power removed by the valour of a few? For myself—do not henceforth recommend me to your Cæsar, nor yourself either, if you will listen to me. You must have a great value for the few years that your time of life allows you, if for their sake you are going to be a suppliant to that boy of yours. Again, take care that those very splendid attacks which you have made and are still making upon Antony, instead of getting you credit for courage, are not misinterpreted into a belief that you are afraid. For if you think Octavius the sort of person from whom to make petitions for our safety, you will be thought not to have fled from a master, but to have looked out for a more agreeable master. Of your praising him for his conduct up to this time I quite approve, for it deserves to be praised, provided that he adopted these measures against the tyrannical power of another and not in support of his own. But when you shew your opinion that he is not only to be allowed so much power, but is even to have so much tendered to him by yourself, as to be petitioned not to refuse us our lives, you are making a very bad bargain with him, for you are giving away to him the very thing of which the Republic seemed to be in possession through him. And it does not occur to you that, if Octavius deserves those honours for waging war on Antony, to those who have cut up that mischief by the roots—of which the present position is but the last trace—the Roman people will never give what is an adequate reward of their service, though it should heap everything it had to give upon them at once. See too how much more awake people are to actual fear than to the memory of past terrors. Because Antony is still alive and in arms, while in regard to Cæsar what could and was bound to be done is all over and cannot be undone, Octavius is the man whose decision as to us is awaited by the Roman people; we are in such a position that one man has to be petitioned to enable us to live. I however— to return to your policy—so far from being the sort of man to supplicate, am one forcibly to coerce those who demand that supplications should be addressed to them. If I can't do that, I will withdraw far from the servile herd and will for myself regard as Rome wherever I am able to be free. I shall feel only pity for men like yourself, if neither age nor honours nor the example of other men's courage has been able to lessen your clinging to life. For my part I shall only think myself happy if I abide with firmness and persistency in the idea that my patriotism has had its reward: for what is there better than the memory of good actions, and for a man—wanting nothing except liberty— to disregard the vicissitudes of human life? But at any rate I will not yield to the yielders, nor be conquered by those who are willing to be conquered themselves. I will try every expedient, every plan: and I will never desist from the attempt to rescue our country from slavery. If the luck follows which ought to follow, I shall rejoice: if not, I shall rejoice all the same, for on what better deeds or thoughts can my life be spent than on those which are directed to the liberation of my fellow citizens? For you, Cicero, I beg and entreat you not to give in to fatigue or despair. In warding off actually existing evils ever seek to discover those that will occur if they are not prevented, and so prevent their creeping in upon us. Consider that the brave and independent spirit, with which as consul and now as a consular you have vindicated the freedom of the state, ceases to exist if a consistent and even tenor of conduct is not preserved. For I confess that tried virtue is in a harder position than virtue that is unknown. We exact good deeds as a debt: we assail the reverse with anger in our hearts, as though we were cheated by such men. So, for instance, though it is a most laudable thing that Cicero should resist Antony, yet because the consul of that time is thought naturally to guarantee the consular of to-day, no one admires him. And if this same Cicero when dealing with others has distorted his judgment, which he kept unshaken with such steadiness and high spirit in routing Antony, he will not only snatch the glory of future action from his own grasp, but will even force his past career to fade from sight (for there is nothing which is truly great in itself, unless it is deliberate and systematic), because no one is under a greater obligation to love the Republic and to be the champion of liberty, whether we regard his ability or his great past or the eager demands upon him from all the world. Wherefore Octavius ought not to be petitioned to consent to our safety. Rather do you rouse yourself to the fixed belief that the state in which you have performed the most splendid services will be free and honoured, if only the people have leaders in their resistance to the plots of traitors.

5. THE FOUNDATION OF CAESAR'S DIVINE MONARCHY*

Before Cæsar could begin his campaign against the Getae and the Parthians, it remained to crown the structure, to introduce officially what was already factual, a monarchy established according to all proprieties as a lasting, legally recognized constitution of the Roman empire. It belongs among those scarcely conceivable things which we frequently come across in historical judgments that Napoleon—who knew very well why the lifelong consulship could not be sufficient and why he allowed himself to be crowned emperor—explained that Caesar had not sought the royal title since the reality of power would be enough for him and that the title would get him nothing. In reality, precisely in the case of monarchy, the title belongs altogether indivisibly to the essence of power. For it first puts an end to the transitional stage, and sets forth as definitive the new organization of the state. Caesar's purposes and the steps he had taken toward the final goal lay as clearly before one's eyes as something in his History.

The kingship that he sought was not, as Mommsen believes, the Roman elective monarchy as it was set forth in the city's chronicles, even if he allowed his statue to be placed next to the kings'. He emphasized more sharply, with an appeal to his descent from Iulus, the son of Aeneas, the hereditary monarchy of Alba, glittering in the haze of myth on account of which he took to wearing a loose purple robe and red boots, whether this had already been established by tradition or the dress was constructed for this purpose. But his empire did not embrace the small circuit of a city but rather the entire unified

civilized world, and his predecessor and model is the divine kingship of the Hellenistic world-monarchy as Alexander created it and as it was fully developed then in the great Asiatic empires of Antigonus and the Seleucids.

How the idea of divine kingship grew out of the political theory of the Greek world, and the task of adapting the free law-state of the Republic to a totalitarian state of the world empire, led by the centralized will of the ruler was, by inner necessity, driven ever forward toward this solution, we may not pursue here. It was carried over by the Hellenistic states for the new rulers of the world, the Romans; games for the Roman state were established in the Greek states, a temple was occasionally built, and divine honors were frequently obtained for the governors in the Asiatic provinces. Thus it is only natural that Caesar, "the scion of Mars and Venus," immediately after his victory in 48 was celebrated by a joint decree of the "cities, municipalities, and tribes of Asia," as, "the god manifest and the common savior of the human race," just as Augustus was later on. But while he regularly refused these divine honors within the Roman-Italian world—and his successor, as far as he maintained the constitution of the Principate upright, followed him in this— Caesar wanted this position precisely in Rome itself and within the ruling people, as Alexander exacted it from the Greek republics.

[Meyer proceeds to recount the steps Caesar took to elevate himself to full divinity and monarchy by emphasizing his relationship with Mars and Venus through every possible device.]

* * *

In fact, for Caesar all that was granted him was insufficient. As for Napoleon the lifelong consulship, so for him the lifelong

* Eduard Meyer, *Cäsars Monarchie und das Principat des Pompejus*, 2nd ed., translated by Donald Kagan (Stuttgart: J. G. Cotta'sche Buchhandlung Nachfolger, 1919), pp. 508–510; 518–519; 526–530. Reprinted by permission of the publisher.

dictatorship was only a preliminary stage of the openly recognized monarchy. How he conceived his position was clear to the whole world when the Senate in ceremonial procession, led by the consul Antony and the rest of the magistrates with their lictors, sought him out to deliver to him the honorary decrees which then were to be engraved on silver tablets with gold letters and laid at the feet of the Capitoline Jupiter. He himself sat on his golden seat near the temple of Venus Genetrix, and when the Senate appeared, he did not stand but received the honors, among them the dictatorship for life, while seated. This caused a tremendous sensation and created a deeply held bitterness, and in his excuse it was maintained that he was unwell, or that, occupied with his affairs, he did not notice the approach of the Senate. These absurdities require no refutation; but even so it is perverse to see an attack of the whim of a sultan in his attitude. Rather, Caesar had used the occasion to make his position quite clear to the Senate: the divine monarch receives his council of state in a public ceremony of state while sitting when it offers him homage. Much more believable is the account that he would have stood, but the minister Balbus, who knew his thoughts best, held him back, or that Trebatius, the affable jurist, reminded him to stand, but that he looked at him in an unfriendly manner. In any case, here, too, Caesar knew exactly what he was doing. But it is natural that the Senate could view his attitude only as a serious insult.

* * *

In carrying out the senatorial decree, Caesar, probably on February 14, resigned his annual dictatorship and assumed the dictatorship for life. After this the title *dict. perpetuo* appears most often on his coins, and occasionally in its place *parens patriae*. But even earlier he had taken the first steps toward the attainment of the royal title. In this matter there was nothing

to be done with the Senate and so he had to elevate the claims of the popular assembly. For, like Pompey and later Augustus, Caesar would have liked to be forced to take upon himself the burden which his heart desired. On January 26, when he rode in the ceremonial procession of the Latin festival, his statue on the Rostra was decorated with a laurel-crowned diadem, and he was hailed as king (*Rex*) by the crowd. Apparently unwilling and misunderstanding the address, he answered with an unfortunate pun, which indeed escaped him only with difficulty, "My name is not Rex but Caesar." The diadem was removed from the statue by the tribunes C. Epidius Marcellus and L. Caesetius Flavus, and they proceeded against the authors of the scandal, and the prisoners shared in the general approval. For Caesar no longer held back his true thoughts. He next tried to compel the father of Caesetius, a Roman knight, to induce his son to resign the tribuneship. When he refused, Caesar charged both tribunes in a session of the Senate in the temple of Concordia with stirring the people to hatred of him by means of the accusation that he aspired to kingship and so deserved the death penalty. Of course he did not want to go so far, but he did induce their colleague Helvius Cinna to propose their exile—naturally the Comitia had to obey—and thereby thrust the power of his moral authority from the Senate.

A little later, on February 15 at the Lupercalia, the same incident was repeated, this time in a more formal manner. The Consul Antony who, as Lupercus Julianus, celebrated the ancient traditional naked footrace, approached Caesar who, dressed in his ostentatious royal dress, sat on a previously granted golden throne. With a ceremonial speech, Antony presented to Caesar a diadem with the words, "The Roman people send you this through me." The naive interpretation that Antony acted on his own responsibility requires no refutation here. But the expected approval from the multitude was not forthcoming and Caesar refused the often repeated offer; indeed, he bared his throat and said he was ready to receive a thrust if anyone cared to give it. He ordered the diadem to be brought to Jupiter on the Capitol since he alone was king of the Romans and that it be entered in the *Acta* immediately that Caesar would not accept the royal title requested by the consul from the people.

It was clear that in this manner it would not be possible to reach this goal without open violence. So he seized upon another means: the Quindecemvir Lucius Cotta (consul for 65) discovered in the Sibylline books the saying that the Parthians could only be defeated by a king. This divine instruction the pious Senate must obey, just as it did twelve years earlier for the intervention in Egypt. For that, Caesar was ready on his part to meet them halfway and at the same time to hold fast formally to his declaration that he had made at the festival: Rome and Italy would remain exempt from the kingdom, the royal title would only be valid in the subject lands. Even this declaration has become

disputed. It has not been noticed that it accords completely with the organization that Alexander and then Antigonus and the Seleucids after Antiochus II had given their world empire. Here, too, the Greek states remained free under their own administration and their own laws; they were separated from the area of power of the king, and his officials could not give them commands. But instead of that they acknowledged him as a god and were therefore obliged to receive the declarations of his wishes as divine commands and to obey him as an oracle. Just as in these ways the free law-states of the Greek world were adapted to the universal monarchy, henceforth Rome and Italy would stand as a free state within the monarchy of Caesar, with this exception only; that Caesar could still intervene immediately since he was not only god, but also a magistrate of Rome. Thus the organization of the world had transformed itself into its opposite as in Alexander's empire. From the people who ruled the world while their armies conquered the world, they had become one rank in the universal imperial order of the world-monarchy.

6. Caesar and Hellenistic Monarchy*

Many men in Rome, especially those who inherited Hellenistic traditions, were no doubt very ready to treat Caesar as more than human. To them deification meant little more than the expression of gratitude and admiration. When they had seen Caesar's triumph move up to the Capitol, it was a small thing for them to continue the procession to Olympus or wherever else gods might dwell. But

* F. E. Adcock, "Caesar's Dictatorship," *Cambridge Ancient History* (Cambridge, England: Cambridge University Press, 1932), Vol. 9, pp. 721–724; 727. Reprinted by permission of the publisher.

it remains true that the evidence falls short of attesting the official admission of Caesar in his lifetime to a place among the gods of the Roman State. Almost all the honours paid to him can be explained as due to an extravagant form of recognition of what he had done. It is therefore hazardous to attribute them to any deliberate religious policy of his own. Amid the honours paid to him he presumably remained coolly detached. He might none the less have used the confused thinking of others to promote his plans. But if that theory is not forced upon us it may be rejected as little suited to what we know of Caesar's own acts and of his attitude of mind. As Pontifex Maximus he undoubtedly cared for the State religion of which he was the head. It was to him, we may assume, as to other cultivated Roman aristocrats of the day, at least the symbol of the Republic's greatness. When his head appears on the coins of the State it bears either the laurel wreath of a *triumphator* or the veil of the Pontifex Maximus. He was careful to secure the ancient rights of the Vestals, *rex sacrorum* and *flamines* in the city, and in his charter for the colony of Genetiva Julia he provides for the establishment and performance of public worship on the Roman model. It may be imagined that his own instinct would be against innovations in the State religion, but though he declined some honours, he could not be always refusing distinctions which he valued at their true worth, even if he suspected that they were prompted by malice as well as by enthusiasm.

We may, then, attribute to Caesar at Rome no more than a policy of *laissez-faire* in religious matters. The same is even more true of Caesar in the provinces. Hellenistic States had hailed him as a god after Pharsalus, as they would have hailed Pompey if the day had gone for him. Since the time of Flamininus they had shown gratitude for favours, respect for power or fear of punishment by this language of compliment, and their readiness to offer to Caesar divine honours does not mean that he claimed them. It is true that these honours would have smoothed Caesar's path if he sought to make himself a monarch of the Hellenistic type; but they are equally consistent with the absence of any such intention.

It is not, in fact, easy to attribute to Caesar any such serious design. The philosophical justification of the Hellenistic monarchy, with its insistence on the duty of promoting common goodwill and its conception of the responsibility of the monarch towards his subjects, might well appeal to the best sides of Caesar's character. Yet the great days of those monarchies were over: the last of them was a precarious survival in which the divinity that hedged a king was slight protection against an Alexandrian riot or an insurrection of fellahin. Despite real services to civilization and to the economic development of their subjects the Hellenistic monarchies had proved in the end a political failure. It is true that the Roman Republican constitution was ill adapted to govern the Mediterranean world. The task was too great to be left to the interplay of Senatorial coteries, to the rivalries of ambitious nobles who used their short reign in the provinces to secure power or wealth, to improvised armies, to irresponsible taxation bringing profits to Roman capitalists. None the less, when compared with the Hellenistic monarchies, the Roman system of the radiation of power from a city-state had proved a great success.

Caesar himself had led the armies of the West to victory in the Hellenistic East. In a military sense the centre of gravity of the Mediterranean world still lay in Italy, as the Civil War had proved, and the potential sea-power and the specialist troops of the Greek East cannot have counted for much with a soldier who had always put his faith in the legions. Hellenistic monarchy had become a shadow, and a realist, such as Caesar's writings and whole past career show him to have been, was not likely to sacrifice the substance of power for the shadow. That by the last year of his life Caesar had determined to enjoy autocratic power for the remainder of his days is plain. But to suppose that this autocratic power would be fortified by abandoning the traditions of the West in favour of those of the Greek East would have argued political blindness almost unthinkable of Caesar. Italy and the West might endure autocracy for the sake of a beneficent autocrat or to be secured from civil war. But to break autocracy loose from the sentiment of what was still the strongest political and military complex in the world was to root it up. The care which Caesar had taken to be sure of the West during his Parthian campaign shows, if it needs to be shown, that this almost self-evident fact had not escaped him.

The cure for the weaknesses that beset Rome's government of the Mediterranean world was, beyond doubt, some kind of autocracy or, if not precisely that, the entrusting to one man of the solution of its recurrent problems. For a generation Roman political thought had been inclining towards such a constitutional change in theory at least, though the memory of the time when the Senate embodied a steady control presented a constant rival. Augustus sought to reconcile the two ideas in an apparent compromise. Caesar was not the man for compromises, but he may have believed that in what remained of his life he might work out a permanent form of autocracy which would reconcile the traditions of East and West. But into what his autocracy might have been transformed we cannot say. He was killed because of what he was, not because of what he might be; and even the assertion that he had formed any clear plan for the future of the Roman State goes beyond the evidence and is not made necessary by his character. We have seen that as a general he trusted his genius to find a triumphant way out of the problems which war presented. He may well have postponed the problem of a final constitutional settlement until after his return from Parthia. One thing he did not do, he did not mark out anyone to be a successor to his power.

* * *

We may now return to Caesar's own position in Rome. It was no more royal than it was divine. It is true that Caesar claimed descent from kings as well as gods, and sometimes wore high red boots which tradition associated with the kings of Alba from which the Julian *gens* claimed to have

sprung. But much more than that was needed to make him king in Rome. Caesar's right to wear a laurel wreath and a purple robe and to sit upon a gilded chair, marked him out as *triumphator*, not as king. Pompey, too, had worn his robe after his last triumph. That these insignia were complimentary and not the evidence of a constitutional position is shown by the fact that the occasions on which Caesar was invited to make use of them were first few, then many, then unlimited. One piece of evidence which cannot be lightly dismissed is the decree to place Caesar's head on the coins of the State during the last year of his life. This was an innovation which might be regarded as admitting a claim to kingship. It might be thought that Rome had become a monarchy like those States which issued coins bearing the heads of their rulers. Yet if the Senate had decreed the issue of coins that meant to the Romans that Caesar was their king, it is hard to see why the imputation that he aimed at monarchy remained to be made. Faustus Sulla had issued coins bearing the head of the dictator Sulla within a generation of his death; the quaestor of Cn. Pompeius in Spain had struck coins with the head of Pompey the Great. The difference lay in the fact that Caesar was still living, but adulation might bridge that gap. It may fairly be supposed that the Senate were adding simply one compliment more to those paid to the dictator. Nor is it easy to suppose that the appearance of Caesar's head was thought to mark the end of the Republic. Within two years of Caesar's death Brutus allowed his head to be placed on coins which, though struck in the provinces, purported to be coins of the Roman State and bore, in one issue, the daggers and cap of liberty of the Ides of March. The autocracy of Caesar, like that of Sulla, might be described as a *regnum* by those who felt that it curtailed their freedom or went beyond the normal practice of the Republic, but the word has not the force of a legal or constitutional definition. It is intended to convey the reproach of tyranny: so far as it looked back in Roman history, it looked back to the last Tarquin and that is all.

7. CAESAR THE DICTATOR*

About Caesar's ultimate designs there can be opinion, but no certainty. The acts and projects of his Dictatorship do not reveal them. For the rest, the evidence is partisan—or posthumous. No statement of unrealized intentions is a safe guide to history, for it is unverifiable and therefore the most attractive form of misrepresentation. The enemies of Caesar spread rumours to discredit the living Dictator: Caesar dead became a god and a myth, passing from the realm of history into literature and legend, declamation and propaganda. By Augustus he was exploited in two ways. The avenging of Caesar fell to his adopted son who assumed the title of *Divi filius* as consecration for the ruler of Rome. That was all he affected to inherit from Caesar, the halo. The god was useful, but not the Dictator: Augustus was careful sharply to discriminate between *Dictator* and *Princeps*. Under his rule Caesar the Dictator was either suppressed outright or called up from time to time to enhance the contrast between the unscrupulous adventurer who destroyed the Free State in his ambition and the modest magistrate who restored the Republic. In its treatment of Caesar the inspired literature of the Augustan Principate is consistent and instructive. Though in different words, Virgil, Horace and Livy tell the same tale and point the same moral.

Yet speculation cannot be debarred from playing round the high and momentous theme of the last designs of Caesar the Dictator. It has been supposed and contended that Caesar either desired to establish or had actually inaugurated an institution unheard of in Rome and un-

imagined there—monarchic rule, despotic and absolute, based upon worship of the ruler, after the pattern of the monarchies of the Hellenistic East. Thus may Caesar be represented as the heir in all things of Alexander the Macedonian and as the anticipator of Caracalla, a king and a god incarnate, levelling class and nation, ruling a subject, united and uniform world by right divine.

This extreme simplification of long and diverse ages of history seems to suggest that Caesar alone of contemporary Roman statesmen possessed either a wide vision of the future or a singular and elementary blindness to the present. But this is only a Caesar of myth or rational construction, a lay-figure set up to point a contrast with Pompeius or Augustus—as though Augustus did not assume a more than human name and found a monarchy, complete with court and hereditary succession; as though Pompeius, the conqueror of the East and of every continent, did not exploit for his own vanity the resemblance to Alexander in warlike fame and even in bodily form. Caesar was a truer Roman than either of them.

The complete synthesis in the person of Caesar of hereditary monarchy and divine worship is difficult to establish on the best of contemporary evidence, the voluminous correspondence of Cicero. Moreover, the whole theme of divine honours is fertile in misunderstandings. After death Caesar was enrolled among the gods of the Roman State by the interested device of the leaders of the Caesarian party. It might appear that subsequent accounts have been guilty of attributing a part at least of the cult of *Divus Julius* to that very different person, Caesar the Dictator.

The rule of Caesar could well be branded

* Ronald Syme, *The Roman Revolution* (Clarendon, 1939), pp. 53–59. Reprinted by permission of The Clarendon Press, Oxford.

as monarchy on a partisan or conventional estimate. The terms 'rex' and 'regnum' belong to the vocabulary of Roman political invective, applicable alike to the domination of Sulla and the arbitrary power exercised by Cicero during his consulate—for the new man from Arpinum was derided as 'the first foreign king at Rome since the Tarquinii'. It was to silence rumour that Caesar made an ostentatious refusal of the diadem at a public ceremony. 'Caesarem se, non regem esse.' Beyond doubt the Dictator's powers were as considerable as those of a monarch. Caesar would have been the first to admit it: he needed neither the name nor the diadem. But monarchy presupposes hereditary succession, for which no provision was made by Caesar. The heir to Caesar's name, his grand-nephew, attracted little attention at the time of his first appearance in Rome. The young man had to build up a faction for himself and make his own way along the road to power, beginning as a military demagogue.

If Caesar must be judged, it is by facts and not by alleged intentions. As his acts and his writings reveal him, Caesar stands out as a realist and an opportunist. In the short time at his disposal he can hardly have made plans for a long future or laid the foundation of a consistent government. Whatever it might be, it would owe more to the needs of the moment than to alien or theoretical models. More important the business in hand: it was expedited in swift and arbitrary fashion. Caesar made plans and decisions in the company of his intimates and secretaries: the Senate voted but did not deliberate. As the Dictator was on the point of departing in the spring of 44 B.C. for several years of campaigning in the Balkans and the East, he tied up magistracies and provincial commands in advance by placing them, according to the traditional Roman way, in the hands of loyal partisans, or of reconciled Pompeians whose good sense should guarantee peace. For that period,

at least, a salutary pause from political activity: with the lapse of time the situation might become clearer in one way or another.

At the moment it was intolerable: the autocrat became impatient, annoyed by covert opposition, petty criticism and laudations of dead Cato. That he was unpopular he well knew. 'For all his genius, Caesar could not see a way out', as one of his friends was subsequently to remark. And there was no going back. To Caesar's clear mind and love of rapid decision, this brought a tragic sense of impotence and frustration—he had been all things and it was no good. He had surpassed the good fortune of Sulla Felix and the glory of Pompeius Magnus. In vain—reckless ambition had ruined the Roman State and baffled itself in the end. Of the melancholy that descended upon Caesar there stands the best of testimony— 'my life has been long enough, whether reckoned in years or in renown.' The words were remembered. The most eloquent of his contemporaries did not disdain to plagiarize them.

The question of ultimate intentions becomes irrelevant. Caesar was slain for what he was, not for what he might become. The assumption of a Dictatorship for life seemed to mock and dispel all hope of a return to normal and constitutional government. His rule was far worse than the violent and illegal domination of Pompeius. The present was unbearable, the future hopeless. It was necessary to strike at once—absence, the passage of time and the solid benefits of peace and order might abate men's resentment against Caesar, insensibly disposing their minds to servitude and monarchy. A faction recruited from the most diverse elements planned and carried out the assassination of the Dictator.

That his removal would be no remedy but a source of greater ills to the Commonwealth, the Dictator himself observed. His judgement was vindicated in blood and suffering; and posterity has seen fit to condemn the act of the Liberators, for so they were styled, as worse than a crime—a folly. The verdict is hasty and judges by results. It is all too easy to label the assassins as fanatic adepts of Greek theories about the supreme virtue of tyrannicide, blind to the true nature of political catch-words and the urgent needs of the Roman State. The character and pursuits of Marcus Brutus, the representative figure in the conspiracy, might lend plausible colouring to such a theory. Yet it is in no way evident that the nature of Brutus would have been very different had he never opened a book of Stoic or Academic philosophy. Moreover, the originator of the plot, the dour and military Cassius, was of the Epicurean persuasion and by no means a fanatic. As for the tenets of the Stoics, they could support doctrines quite distasteful to Roman Republicans, namely monarchy or the brotherhood of man. The Stoic teaching, indeed, was nothing more than a corroboration and theoretical defence of certain traditional virtues of the governing class in an aristocratic and republican state. Hellenic culture does not explain Cato; and the *virtus* about which Brutus composed a volume was a Roman quality, not an alien importation.

The word means courage, the ultimate virtue of a free man. With *virtus* go *libertas* and *fides*, blending in a proud ideal of character and conduct—constancy in purpose and act, independence of habit, temper and speech, honesty and loyalty. Privilege and station imposed duties, to family, class and equals in the first place, but also towards clients and dependents. No oligarchy could survive if its members refused to abide by the rules, to respect 'liberty and the laws'.

To his contemporaries, Marcus Brutus, firm in spirit, upright and loyal, in manner grave and aloof, seemed to embody that ideal of character, admired by those who did not care to imitate. His was not a simple personality—but passionate, intense and repressed. Nor was his political conduct wholly to be predicted. Brutus might well have been a Caesarian—neither he nor Caesar were predestined partisans of Pompeius. Servilia reared her son to hate Pompeius, schemed for the Caesarian alliance and designed that Brutus should marry Caesar's daughter. Her plan was annulled by the turn of events in the fatal consulate of Metellus. Caesar was captured by Pompeius: Julia, the bride intended for Brutus, pledged the alliance.

After this the paths of Brutus and of Caesar diverged sharply for eleven years. But Brutus, after Pharsalus, at once gave up a lost cause, receiving pardon from Caesar, high favour, a provincial command and finally the praetorship in 44 B.C. Yet Cato, no sooner dead, asserted the old domination over his nephew more powerfully than ever in life. Brutus came to feel shame for his own disloyalty: he composed a pamphlet in honour of the Republican who died true to his principles and to his class. Then he strengthened the family tie and obligation of vengeance yet further by divorcing his Claudia and marrying his cousin Porcia, Bibulus' widow. No mistake about the meaning of that act; and Servilia disapproved. There were deeper causes still in Brutus' resolve to slay the tyrant— envy of Caesar and the memory of Caesar's amours with Servilia, public and notorious. Above all, to Brutus as to Cato, who stood by the ancient ideals, it seemed that Caesar, avid for splendour, glory and power, ready to use his birth and station to subvert his own class, was an ominous type, the monarchic aristocrat, recalling the kings of Rome and fatal to any Republic.

Brutus and his allies might invoke philosophy or an ancestor who had liberated Rome from the Tarquinii, the first consul of the Republic and founder of *Libertas*. Dubious history—and irrelevant. The Liberators knew what they were about. Honourable men grasped the assassin's dagger to slay a Roman aristocrat, a friend and a benefactor, for better reasons than that. They stood, not merely for the traditions and the institutions of the Free State, but very precisely for the dignity and the interests of their own order. Liberty and the laws are high-sounding words. They will often be rendered, on a cool estimate, as privilege and vested interests.

It is not necessary to believe that Caesar planned to establish at Rome a 'Hellenistic Monarchy', whatever meaning may attach to that phrase. The Dictatorship was enough. The rule of the *nobiles*, he could see, was an anachronism in a world-empire; and so was the power of the Roman plebs when all Italy enjoyed the franchise. Caesar in truth was more conservative and Roman than many have fancied; and no Roman conceived of government save through an oligarchy. But Caesar was being forced into an autocratic position. It meant the lasting domination of one man instead of the rule of the law, the constitution and the Senate; it announced the triumph soon or late of new forces and new ideas, the elevation of the army and the provinces, the depression of the traditional governing class. Caesar's autocracy appeared to be much more than a temporary expedient to liquidate the heritage of the Civil War and reinvigorate the organs of the Roman State. It was going to last—and the Roman aristocracy was not to be permitted to govern and exploit the Empire in its own fashion. The tragedies of history do not arise from the conflict of conventional right and wrong. They are more august and more complex. Caesar and Brutus each had right on his side.

8. CATONISM AND CAESARISM*

My subject in this chapter is the ideal of the republic which became associated with Cato's name, the conflict between that ideal and Caesarism, and the manner in which Augustus resolved that conflict by laying claim to the republicanism of Cato. To understand that conflict it will be necessary to consider the attempt of Caesar, later successfully carried through by Augustus, to break the old combinations of nobles and clients and organize all the citizens of Rome into a single "party," or, more correctly, into a group of clients, united in loyalty to the ruler. Throughout the discussion I am under constant obligation to Anton von Premerstein and Ronald Syme, a German and a British scholar who in the 'thirties independently interpreted the political struggles of the period in the light of the rise of National Socialism.

Party divisions in the Civil War and the persistence of the divisions into the Augustan Age have been fully discussed by Syme. They will be touched on briefly here. It should be stated at the outset that, except for a brief flare-up after the death of Caesar, the old political intrigues, the heated and often violent struggles in public meetings, assemblies, and law courts were practically ended at Rome after Caesar crossed the Rubicon. Henceforth party conflict was mainly in the hands of trained soldiers, men who had taken an oath of allegiance to their commander and were fighting to bring about his victory and the bonus he had promised them. Although the Civil War was technically a war between Caesar and the senate, actually it was fought by the personal armies of Pompey and Caesar.

It had been expected that the good men, combining their influence with Pompey's

*L. R. Taylor, *Party Politics in the Age of Caesar* (Berkeley, California: University of California Press, 1949), pp. 162–175. Reprinted by permission of the publisher.

in the Italian towns, would be able to recruit a considerable army, but they were slow about the business of recruiting, they lost to Caesar many of the troops they had gathered, and they were soon barred by Caesar's swift march down the Adriatic from access to their supporters. Most of the men who fought on the senatorial side in the final contest were in Pompey's service. After he was cut off from Italy and had lost most of his army in Spain, the troops consisted in large part of foreign soldiers supplied by client princes under obligation to Pompey. The party of Pompey, pictured by Caesar as a barbarian horde, was fighting against the party of Caesar.

Ideologies, which hardly affected the armies, were emphasized by the leaders of both sides at the beginning of the war. The senatorials, with Cato once more taking a prominent part in the discussions, declared that they were saving the state from the tyranny of Caesar, and Caesar asserted that he was freeing the state from the domination of an oligarchy. Both sides claimed thus to be preserving the *res publica*. From Cicero's letters it is clear that at first he was conscious of Caesar's defiance of the senate. When Pompey and the consuls ordered all senators and knights to leave Rome with them and declared that they would consider as enemies any who failed to do so, public opinion among the senators was strong enough to make most of them not actually committed to Caesar go along. Even Caesar's father-in-law went with the others.

Caesar in his constant communications to the senate stressed particularly his *dignitas*, a word that Syme renders "rank, prestige and honor," but he managed to relate his *dignitas* to the cause of the people that he was championing. Caesar's position had been guaranteed by the law of the ten tribunes passed in 52, the law that granted Caesar the privilege of standing for the consulship *in absentia*. This privilege,

this *beneficium populi*, the oligarchs had, according to Caesar, taken from him. Caesar and the people were one, and, as he quotes his conversation with Lentulus, he was liberating both, *se et populum Romanum*, from the *factio paucorum*, the tyranny of an oligarchy. Caesarism meant the identification of the Roman people with Caesar.

But in spite of the emphasis on ideologies at the beginning of the war, personal considerations that were always paramount in Roman politics proved for most men to be the decisive factor. Caesar's father-in-law and other prominent senators eventually adopted the course of neutrality that Caesar was ready to approve. Among them was even Gaius Marcellus, the consul of the previous year who had commissioned Pompey to defend the state against Caesar. He was married to Caesar's great-niece, and Caesar brought pressure. It was almost certainly a personal tie with Pompey that led Caesar's best general, Titus Labienus, to desert Caesar for Pompey. It was the debt to Pompey, who had brought him back from exile, that decided Cicero, after long months of considering a neutral course, to depart for Pompey's camp. Cicero had no illusions about the republicanism of Pompey. Both Pompey and Caesar were seeking a tyranny, he declares, and rings the changes over and over again on that idea. Although perhaps a majority of the senators not too old to travel decided in the end to follow Pompey to the East, most of the knights and the landowners of Italy stayed out of the conflict. They were interested mainly in peace and the protection of their possessions and were reassured when Caesar showed an unexpectedly high regard for private property.

As time went on, the rival propaganda stressed personal interests rather than ideologies. The senatorials talked about low morale among Caesar's troops, spreading abroad reports that came before the war broke out and that were apparently confirmed by Labienus after he left Caesar. The leading men of the senate, notably Pompey, also dealt in threats, hints of proscription for the men who failed to align themselves with the senatorials. Pompey, according to Cicero, was turning into a Sulla.

Caesar's propaganda was far more effective because he had success to back it up and also because he had experienced agents to carry it out. The speed of Caesar's movements down the Adriatic, the success of his maneuvers as contrasted with the inefficiency of Pompey, and the favor shown Caesar by the municipalities were all stressed.

But the great stock in trade of the Caesarians was Caesar's policy of mercy, what Cicero calls his *insidiosa clementia* as contrasted with the *iracundia* of the senatorials. As Caesar captured one detachment of enemy troops after another, he consistently followed the same course. He enrolled the troops under military oath in his own army and let the leaders go free. The policy may have originated from a natural abhorrence of cruelty in civil strife, an abhorrence born of the terrible examples he remembered in Marian and Sullan days. But the great publicity Caesar gave to the policy shows that he was trying to gain adherents, especially to add members of the upper class to his party. This is from a letter sent to his agents Oppius and Balbus, dutifully circulated by these gentlemen: "Let this be the new thing in our victory that we fortify ourselves by mercy and generosity." And later Caesar writes to Cicero: "I am not moved by the fact that those whom I have let off free are said to have gone away to make war on me anew, I like nothing better than to be like myself and to let them be like themselves." It was shrewd propaganda, based on the personal traditions of Roman politics, for Caesar had conferred a favor on the men he set free, and he could arouse sympathy by convicting them of ingratitude.

In the rival camps during the war, Caesar on the one side had complete control, but Pompey on the other was hampered by his eminent associates who considered themselves his equals. It was not Pompey's party, Pompey was a member of the party; *non Magni partes sed Magnum in partibus esse*, Lucan says. Pompey could not command; he had to beg Domitius not to make a stand against Caesar at Corfinium, and he begged in vain and was helpless while Domitius lost an army.

Cato, according to the legend that grew up about his activity in the war, was in favor of giving Pompey at once the supreme command that was eventually conferred. But for the early weeks of the conflict we can check Cato's course from Cicero's letters, and it is clear that at that time Cato was one of the troublemakers. Appointed to take charge of Sicily and the levies there and in southern Italy, Cato was slow in leaving to assume his task. He wanted to have a share in the exchange of communications with Caesar. Perhaps too he was afraid, as others were, that Caesar would succeed in his efforts to detach Pompey from the good men. Cicero wished Cato would go, for Caesar would have been easier to deal with if Cato had been eliminated from senatorial councils. Cato was willing to make some concessions, but the negotiations broke down on his unalterable condition that Caesar should first withdraw to his province. Cato then went off to Sicily, but too late to save the army from Caesar's forces; to avert needless bloodshed among the inhabitants he abandoned the island without a struggle.

In the senatorial camp in Macedonia, Cato seems to have stayed aside from the quarrels that were going on according to the regular traditions of the Roman senate. Marcus Marcellus and Cicero became disgusted and withdrew into inactivity. Domitius, Lentulus, and Scipio vied with one another for Caesar's office of *pontifex maximus*. Cato, meanwhile, was concerned with the good name of the senate. In the senatorial council he sponsored a decree that no allied city should be plundered, thus emphasizing, as he had done all his life, Rome's responsibility to subject peoples. By another decree, that no Roman citizen should be put to death except on the field of battle, he tried to introduce to the senatorial side something of Caesar's clemency. Both decrees were needed to check the cupidity and cruelty of his senatorial colleagues.

In military affairs Cato claimed no prominent position, insisting that as a man of praetorian rank he was inferior to his consular associates. Pompey, according to Plutarch, was afraid to give him an important command for fear that, in the event of victory, he himself might be eliminated by Cato. In the end Pompey placed Cato in charge of the port and lines of communication at Dyrrachium.

It was at Dyrrachium that Cato and Cicero received from Labienus the news of the disaster, of the death of Domitius and the flight of Pompey. There was a heated meeting soon afterward in Corcyra, in which Cato is said to have urged Cicero to take the supreme command, and, when Cicero declared his intention of withdrawing from the war, Pompey's son was, according to Plutarch, kept by Cato from murdering Cicero. The survivors of the senatorial army split up. Cicero, Cato's nephew Brutus, the able soldier Cassius, and eventually Favonius returned to Italy to enjoy the mercy of the dictator. Brutus and Cassius actually took service under Caesar. Cato managed to salvage fifteen cohorts, and he, Scipio, and Labienus, after learning of the death of Pompey, made their way to Africa.

The struggle that took place in Africa was the final contest of the Roman republicans against Caesar. The subsequent war with Pompey's sons and Labienus in Spain was simply a contest with the party of Pompey. In Africa the great dependence was upon the alliance with King Juba of Numidia. It was thus, as the Caesarians pointed out, another alliance of Romans with a barbarian.

Cato, while yielding the supreme command to his old enemy Scipio, who outranked him, seems to have had a major part in the effective preparations for the war. Once more in the final contest he was not on the field of battle. He was in charge of the port city of Utica when the news came of Caesar's decisive victory at Thapsus. Cato's first aim was to hold Utica, but Caesarian sympathies, long evident in the inhabitants, were now openly expressed. He strove, as we know not only from his panegyrists but from the Caesarian who wrote a history of this war, to save the lives of the Uticenses, threatened by the cruelty of the fugitives from battle. He concerned himself too for his comrades in arms, both those who wished to continue the fight in Spain and those who were ready to return to make peace with the victor.

But for Cato there was no place with the party of Pompey, and no return. When his arrangements were all completed, he dined and retired to his chamber. After reading the great discourse of the condemned Socrates on the immortality of the soul, Cato stabbed himself. The scene of his death is described in one of the finest passages Plutarch wrote. As Pope put it in the prologue to the rather frigid tragedy that Addison wrote on Cato, he is in that scene

A great man struggling in the storms of fate
And greatly falling with a falling state.

The hostile population of Utica appreciated Cato's greatness and honored him with a public funeral.

Cato had chosen to die with the republic. Henceforth the men who revered his memory were republicans rather than *optimates*. Let us pause for a moment to consider Cato's conception of the republic whose personification he became. *Res Publica* meant *res populi*, public possession of and public responsibility for Roman government. The public that counted was Cato's own class, the hereditary nobility who as magistrates and senators represented the people. Cato committed suicide because Roman government had now become the responsibility of one man. The state was *res unius, res ad unum redacta*; it was the private possession of a monarch.

Cato had set forth his views on public responsibility in countless speeches: short, pithy speeches, or, if he needed to upbraid the senate and people or to use up time in a filibuster, endless harangues. The speeches are lost; most of them he did not leave in written form. The only one known in antiquity was the speech on the Catilinarians of which Sallust has given us an eloquent version. Fortunately, besides Sallust, Cicero, directly or indirectly, tells us a good deal about Cato's speeches.

Cato's cure for the ills of his day was apparently much like Cicero's in the *Republic* and the *Laws*, a return to the constitution of pre-Gracchan days when men like his great-grandfather had guided the state with a virtue that, in Cato's nostalgic view, accorded with the Stoic ideal set forth by his Greek teachers. He spoke constantly of abstractions such as *virtus, constantia, severitas, innocentia, continentia*. He was not unaware of the great problems of his time. Better than any of his optimate colleagues except Lucullus he understood the responsibilities of empire, and better than Lucullus he knew the corroding effects of empire on the body politic. It was, as Cato saw it, Rome's destiny to pacify and dominate the world, but he insisted on a rule of justice and of self-restraint in dealing with allies and conquered people. He was unwilling to vote on a triumph until he had looked at the record and found out whether the victorious general had conducted himself with fairness toward his foes.

Cato's attitude on imperial rule comes out in the correspondence between him and Cicero in the year 50. Cicero had heard Cato declaim on the subject in the senate, and when he wanted a thanksgiving for minor successes in Cilicia he wrote to Cato to stress with justifiable pride the uprightness of his rule. Cato answered in a priceless letter, the only thing we have from his pen, explaining why he had not voted with the majority for the thanksgiving but instead had proposed a congratulatory endorsement of Cicero. The letter is crammed with Cato's abstractions. "I did what I could conscientiously do in my speech and vote," Cato writes. "I praised your upright and wise defense of the province, the preservation of King Ariobarzanes and his kingdom, the restoration of the allies to a ready acceptance of our rule. As for the thanksgiving that was decreed, I am glad of it if, in a matter that was in no wise left to chance but was secured for the republic by your remarkable prudence and self-control, you prefer to have us thank the gods rather than give the credit to you. But if you think a thanksgiving is a forerunner of a triumph and that is why you prefer to have thanks given to chance rather than to you, [I remind you that] a triumph does not always follow a thanksgiving and that it is a much more splendid thing than a triumph to have the senate decide that a province was held and preserved rather by the mercy and incorruptibility of the commander than by the strength of a military force or the favor of the gods. That was what I expressed in my motion."

Cicero paid tribute to Cato when he replied, "If I don't say all men but many men were Catos in our state, where the marvel is that one Cato has arisen, what triumphal chariot or what laurel could I compare with praise from you?" Immediately afterward, as Caesar took pains to point out to Cicero, Cato proved that he was not the figure of perfection his admirers made him out to be. Cato voted for a thanksgiving for the hardly more important successes of his son-in-law Bibulus. For members of his family Cato could relax his sternness. Nor was he as completely uncompromising as he was later made out to be. Years before, he had yielded to Caesar and Clodius and involved himself in their unconstitutionality, and he was ready to make some concessions to Caesar even in 49.

Yet he was a great man and a patriot in an age of corruption and decay. He was not a great statesman. He failed in life to achieve the identification with the state that his admirers accorded him after his death. He was a resourceful obstructionist, but he lacked constructive ideas. When he compromised, it was too late. He saw the problems of his day but he did not know how to meet them. Like so many good men of our own time, he was almost without hope. He knew the selfishness and greed of his optimate colleagues, and he was fully alive to the perils of the alliance with Pompey. Seneca says he looked forward to death if Caesar won and voluntary exile if Pompey were victorious. The story goes that after the Civil War began he refused as a sign of mourning to shave his beard or cut his hair, and would not put on a garland at banquets. The story, like many other details of his conduct during the Civil War, may be apocryphal, but there can be no doubt that Cato consciously went into the war as a doomed man in a doomed state.

We return to the events immediately following the death of Cato. At Rome, among the old nobles who had been pardoned and were living under Caesar's dictatorship, the story of Cato's death made far more impression than the news of Caesar's victory in Africa. The nobles were still permitted under Caesar's mild rule to talk and write with relative freedom, and some of them were talking and writing of the republic, of the old days of public responsibility for the body politic. And Cato's unconquered soul speedily became identical with the republic and liberty.

Cicero felt frankly envious of Cato's fame and wished that he had had the courage to die in like manner. At Brutus'

request he wrote a laudation of Cato, a book that was the foundation of the Cato legend that went down into the empire. It is an irreparable loss that the book was not preserved. Cicero approached the problem with some trepidation, for he knew that if he gave Cato the praise he deserved, the Caesarians, with whom Cicero was then associating, would not like it, since, he tells Atticus, Cato "foresaw that everything that has happened would take place, and he fought to prevent it from happening and died to keep from witnessing its accomplishment." One cannot doubt that in his *Cato* Cicero was as outspoken about the conditions under which he was living as he was in his history of oratory written a few months earlier. In that work he praised the good fortune of Hortensius, who died without seeing the Forum denuded of the law courts, and spoke of the night that had fallen on the republic. Brutus and other men in Rome also wrote laudations of Cato.

It was Cicero's *Cato* that prompted Caesar, while he was still absent on the Spanish campaign, to compose a pamphlet in reply, an *Anticato*. Perhaps because he was conscious of the justice of Cato's indictments, Caesar had hated Cato for years and had been unable to view Cato's acts with the generosity that he showed to other foes in civil life. Caesar's *Anticato* is lost, but we can see his attitude in the commentaries on the Civil War where he explains Cato's opposition on the ground of long-standing personal enmity and indignation over his defeat for the consulship.

The *Anticato* was couched in oratorical form, divided into two parts. I believe that it was presented, as Roman political pamphlets often were, as a speech for the prosecution, divided, as such speeches regularly were, into two acts. Thus Caesar, whom the living Cato had vowed to bring to trial, was himself accusing his dead enemy. We do not know what was the charge under which Cato was arraigned. Perhaps it was *maiestas*, treason against the state, a crime with which Cato may have threatened to charge Caesar. The work was designed to conciliate Cicero, whose literary art received the most extravagant praise, and to prove the falsity of the ideal of Catonism that was now taking form in the minds of the republicans. Caesar's work apparently followed the worst traditions of Roman invective oratory as we know it from some of Cicero's coarsest speeches. It dealt with Cato's private life and particularly with his fondness for wine. Cato's friends, who had enjoyed with him long evenings of philosophical conversation, conceded that he did like wine, but Caesar made him out a sot. Caesar also accused Cato of avarice. That was given as the motive for his divorce of his wife so that she could marry Hortensius and his subsequent remarriage with her when Hortensius left her a rich widow. There may even have been charges of gross immorality. In treating Cato's public life, Caesar, as Cicero tells us, either denied the facts set forth by Cicero or objected to the motives assigned or tried to show that the acts which were extolled were not praiseworthy. Caesar's vicious and unjust attack served only to build up Cato's reputation. It contributed to the revival of republicanism at Rome.

To that revival Caesar also contributed by the policy he followed when, six months before his death, he came home from his victory over the Pompeians in Spain. Men had been hoping that, after the Civil War had ended, Caesar would restore the constitution and make the laws and the courts function again. When, before Caesar left for Spain, he had pardoned Marcus Marcellus, the bitterest of his enemies still alive after Cato died, Cicero took Caesar's *clementia*, now turned into kingly munificence, as a promise of republicanism, and exhorted him in a warmly laudatory speech to reestablish the constitution.

Sallust, a partisan of Caesar, understood the situation better than Cicero did, and in another pamphlet, addressed to Caesar a few months before the speech for Marcellus, he has not a word to say about the old popular program or about the reorganization of the constitution that he had recommended a few years before. Instead he counsels an absolute ruler on certain social reforms that would improve the condition of the state.

As time went on, Cicero became less and less hopeful. He saw for instance the statue set up to Caesar, "the unconquered god," in the temple of Quirinus, perhaps a subtle piece of rival propaganda against the image of Cato's unconquered soul forming in the minds of the nobles. But Brutus apparently went on hoping. Just before Caesar's return from Spain, Brutus wrote to Cicero that Caesar was becoming converted to the good men, that is, was becoming an optimate. Cicero was very skeptical by this time.

There proved to be reason for the skepticism, for Caesar on his return did not settle down to put the state in order. In view of the brief time he spent in the city (not more than sixteen months between 49 and his death in 44), he accomplished wonders in the reforms he carried out in Rome and Italy, and in provincial organization. He demonstrated, as already he had done in Gaul, that he was a great administrator and that he had the welfare of the state at heart. But he had neither time for republican government nor interest in it. He was embarking on further wars, planning for a great Parthian expedition, and his idea was to leave behind him, not the old disorders of courts and assemblies and of senatorial wrangling, but a stable government responsible to him alone.

Caesar was completely disillusioned about old forms. As early as 49 he had had his difficulties with a tribune (a Caecilius Metellus, the last free representative of that old family) who had barred the way to the treasury and had, to the wrath of the people, been pushed away from the door so that Caesar could take possession of state funds. After that, Caesar, when he was in Rome, functioned only as a dictator, an office which the tribunes could not touch. Even so, tribunes continued to have a nuisance value.

Caesar was showing a constantly increasing scorn for republican institutions. The republic, he was quoted as saying, was but a name without substance or form. It seemed at times that it was only to make a mockery of the constitution that Caesar maintained the assemblies and the senate. He called the assemblies only to have them vote in the affirmative on laws constructed in his offices and to elect the candidates he had commended. He nominated the consuls and half the other offices, leaving the people free to choose the others—that is the way the annoying tribunes got in. His scorn of the constitution was shown by an event of the last day of 45, two and a half months before his death. Word came that a consul in office had suddenly died, and Caesar hastily called the centuriate assembly and had it elect on his commendation a man to serve part of a day. "This may seem amusing to you," Cicero writes to a friend. "You weren't here. If you had seen it you couldn't have kept back the tears."

In the senate, too, Caesar was showing the same contempt toward republican institutions. Cicero, now one of the elder *consulares*, got letters from foreign princes he had never heard of, thanking him for voting them honors of which he knew nothing. The senate, controlled by Caesar's henchmen, whom he had added to it in large numbers, was as subservient as the assemblies. Only in plumbing the depths of servile flattery did the senators take the initiative, as they voted Caesar every distinction that Rome had ever devised for her great men and invented new and un-Roman honors that placed him among the gods in heaven.

Caesar was a monarch, and, while making sport of the old constitution, he was concerned, as every monarch must be,

to establish a firm basis in popular support. Before setting out for the Parthian War he took steps to reward his adherents, increase their numbers, and unite them in loyalty to him. He depended first of all on his soldiers, and he rewarded them generously with cash bonuses and sent out in colonies, with ample grants of land, those who had served him longest. He settled them in units according to their old formations, sometimes with their centurions as magistrates of the colony. Thus they could easily be called out at need to serve him again. He had already enfranchised the populous Transpadane region, thus increasing by perhaps as much as fifty per cent the citizen rolls and making the new citizens his personal clients. He restored the old Marian families to office and recalled the men exiled by the courts and disgraced by the censors. He enlarged the senate from about 600 to 900 members, bringing new men into the ranks of office holders. Many of them came from sections of Italy enfranchised in the Social War but since then debarred from any share in office. He was thus uniting Rome and Italy; by taking in also men from across the Po and even from across the Alps he brought the provinces closer to the central regime. All these men were under personal obligation to Caesar for their advancement.

And Caesar took a further step, the significance of which was first understood by Premerstein. Caesar attempted to bind to himself in a kind of superclientele all the senators and citizens alike. The step was not taken until the last months, perhaps the last weeks, of Caesar's life. The servile senate made the proposals. It voted that Caesar should be dictator for life, that his person should be sacrosanct like that of a tribune, that he should be called the father of his country, and (this is the detail that concerns us particularly) that all citizens should take oath by his Genius, his attendant spirit. Suetonius and Appian are specific about the oath, and they indicate that everyone, and not merely the senators, as has been generally assumed, took it. There probably was not time before Caesar's death to administer the oath universally, but the senators had certainly taken it.

The oath, according to Appian, pledged men to guard Caesar and Caesar's body with all their strength and invoked a curse on any man who did not offer Caesar such protection. It was thus much like the oath the Italians took to Livius Drusus, and also like the oaths of allegiance later taken to the emperors. The senators who had sworn the oath were a bodyguard for Caesar, who refused in the city to have his person protected by a military guard. Even the conspirators took the oath, if we can credit Appian's version (very different from Shakespeare's) of the speech Brutus made just after Caesar's murder. In it Brutus defended himself and his associates against the charge of perjury. That charge was also made against them in Antony's funeral oration; according to Appian (here again Shakespeare's version is different), he read the text of the oath. By this oath, actually taken or to be taken by all the Romans, Caesar was accepted as the patron or rather the *pater* of the whole state and the old relationship of *fides*, the tie that bound patron and client or father and son, united him with all the citizens.

Caesar, I believe, wished to cement the union by having himself declared king. The divine honors that he accepted, the temple, the priest, the name Divus Julius, and the festivals that marked the rule of the Hellenistic monarchs, all point in that direction. But Caesar was still sensitive enough to public opinion to refuse the crown offered him by Mark Antony a month before the assassination. The title was relatively unimportant. Already, as dictator for life, he was all-powerful.

It was in his acceptance of that title that Caesar particularly outraged Roman sentiment. When the senators brought him the decree, as he was seated in his golden chair before the new temple of Venus, the mother of his house, Caesar failed to rise to thank the fathers. He was, as Premerstein points out, the patron, the master, receiving his clients. The incident is given by some ancient writers as the motive of Caesar's murder.

9. THE ACHIEVEMENT AND FAILURE OF CAESAR*

Alexander alone in antiquity rivals Caesar in the range and speed of his exploits:

> *fu di tal volo*
> *che nol seguiteria lingua nè penna.*

It was inevitable that he should be compared with Alexander because of his victories and because of his death, cut off as he was in the plenitude of his power as was Alexander in the midst of his days. Yet the likeness between them belongs to rhetoric rather than to history. The story went that as praetor in Spain Caesar had lamented that he had achieved so little by the age at which Alexander had died. Beyond that, there is no evidence that Caesar set Alexander before himself as his model. There are no good grounds for supposing that his project to march against Parthia was in imitation of Alexander's conquering invasion of the Persian Empire. Gossip that Caesar dreamed of returning from Parthia past the Caspian to Scythia and then through Germany back to Gaul may be evidence that the Alexander-legend was strong, but it is evidence of nothing else. In judging Alexander it must not be forgotten that he was not the heir to Greek

* F. E. Adcock, "Caesar's Dictatorship," *Cambridge Ancient History* (Cambridge, England: Cambridge University Press, 1932), Vol. 9, pp. 739–740. Reprinted by permission of the publisher.

tradition. The old Greek advice of Aristotle to be a leader to the Greeks, a master to the barbarians, fell on deaf ears. The Greek ideas of Alexander were new ideas, the ideas of the unity of mankind. Caesar was a Roman aristocrat, steeped in the Roman tradition of reasonable, calculated, but inflexible domination, the belief in power rather than in conquest, in the extension of Rome to the Romanized, in steady progress but in continuity of policy.

His ambition was compounded of the Roman desire to achieve the distinction which his birth and genius claimed for him and of an unresting zeal for good administration and the greatness of Rome. In his clemency there may have been a touch of contempt, a masterful challenge of the future. The cold prudence of the maxim 'Stone-dead hath no fellow' would have belittled him. For men of his own aristocratic stamp or for men who followed the trade of arms, which was nearest to his heart, he had a generous sympathy. But he did not hesitate to requite craft with deeper craft or to strike terror by cruelty if barbarians crossed him. There can be no doubt that in his *Commentaries* he was an advocate for Caesar. But he deceived others as little as might be, and deceived himself not at all. The politicians of his day found him hard to trust, because they could not but see that his appetite for power grew with eating, and they judged him by themselves. To the end he remained to them incalculable. Yet his genius was the hard practical genius of Rome raised to the highest power: he was a keen edge on the old blade.

But he reached power late, too late for patience. The impulses of fifteen years of tremendous activity still spurred him, but he was tiring; 'satis diu vel naturae vixi vel gloriae.' His health was breaking, he had few friends and no one whom he would trust to help him bear the burden as Octavian was to trust Agrippa. For this reason he could not admit Time to his counsels, nor share them with others. Thus he became, in a sense, un-Roman in the last year of his life. There came the clash between his genius and the Roman steady tradition, and in the clash he was broken, with plans unachieved and plans unmade.

He had shown the world the greatest of the Romans, but he was not the creator of a new epoch. Whatever he might have done, he had as yet neither destroyed the Republic nor made the Principate. His life had set an example of autocracy which his death converted into a warning. The civil wars that followed the Ides of March prepared the way for a statesman who was the heir to Caesar's name, the avenger of Caesar's death—but no Caesar. The aristocracy was almost destroyed, the legions became the servants of a man who was not a soldier first. The Roman world became ready to welcome the Empire that was peace. Caesar had done much for the State in his reforms, but he did Rome no greater service than by his death. The cruel years during which Octavian fought his way to undivided power were the last blood-letting of the body politic. A spark of Caesar glowed smokily in Antony and was extinguished: there remained Octavian.

SECTION X

The Augustan Principate

THE ASSASSINATION of Caesar, far from restoring republican government, merely prolonged the period of civil war for more than a decade. From the struggle arose one man as undisputed master of the world, Caesar's adopted son and heir, Octavian, or, as he preferred to be called, Caesar. Like his adoptive father, the young Caesar was faced with the problem of constructing a state and a government, of converting his position from leader of a faction to ruler of an empire. The question of the means he employed and their significance is of great importance. On the one hand, the system he established served, with some modifications, as the constitution of Rome for hundreds of years. On the other hand, by studying the gradual evolution of the Augustan Principate, we may learn what forces operated in Rome and forced the decisions that produced neither Republic nor Oriental despotism but something unprecedented, a middle way.

1. THE OFFICIAL VERSION OF THE AUGUSTAN SETTLEMENT*

THE ACCOMPLISHMENTS OF AUGUSTUS (RES GESTAE DIVI AUGUSTI)

The following document, from the hand of Augustus, is perhaps the most famous ancient inscription—"the queen of Latin inscriptions" Mommsen called it. A vast literature has grown up around it—numerous editions, commentaries, and discussions of its nature and purpose. Shortly before he died, Augustus deposited with the Vestal Virgins a number of state papers in one of which he set forth "an

account of his accomplishments, which he desired to be inscribed in two bronze pillars to be set up before his mausoleum" (Suetonius *Life of Augustus* ci. 4). The *Res Gestae* is preserved in an almost complete copy, together with a Greek translation, inscribed on the walls of the temple of Rome and Augustus at Ancyra (modern Ankara), in the province of Galatia (hence it is commonly called the *Monumentum Ancyranum*); portions of the Greek and Latin texts have also been found in Apollonia and Antioch in Pisidia. Intended primarily for the people of the city of Rome, Augustus' account of his stewardship summarizes his career under three headings: the offices and honors conferred upon him; his expenditures out of his own funds for public purposes; his deeds in war and peace. Though largely factual, it is not an historical chronicle

* Naphtali Lewis and Meyer Reinhold, *Roman Civilization, Vol. 2: The Empire* (New York: Columbia University Press, 1955), pp. 9–19 (abridged). Reprinted by permission of the publisher.

but a subjective political document. It is in the tradition of the inscriptions commemorating the achievements of distinguished Romans of the Republic and is similar in content to the well-known inscriptions set up by Oriental kings. Despite Augustus' profession of "restoring the Republic," a monarchical tone pervades the *Res Gestae*.

Below is a copy of the accomplishments of the deified Augustus by which he brought the whole world under the empire of the Roman people, and of the moneys expended by him on the state and the Roman people, as inscribed on two bronze pillars set up in Rome.

1. At the age of nineteen, on my own initiative and at my own expense, I raised an army by means of which I liberated the Republic, which was oppressed by the tyranny of a faction. For which reason the senate, with honorific decrees, made me a member of its order in the consulship of Gaius Pansa and Aulus Hirtius, giving me at the same time consular rank in voting, and granted me the *imperium*. It ordered me as propraetor, together with the consuls, to see to it that the state suffered no harm. Moreover, in the same year, when both consuls had fallen in the war, the people elected me consul and a triumvir for the settlement of the commonwealth.

2. Those who assassinated my father I drove into exile, avenging their crime by due process of law; and afterwards when they waged war against the state, I conquered them twice on the battlefield.

3. I waged many wars throughout the whole world by land and by sea, both civil and foreign, and when victorious I spared all citizens who sought pardon. Foreign peoples who could safely be pardoned I preferred to spare rather than to extirpate. About 500,000 Roman citizens were under military oath to me. Of these, when their terms of service were ended, I settled in colonies or sent back to their own municipalities a little more than 300,000, and to all of these I allotted lands or granted money as rewards for military service. I captured 600 ships, exclusive of those which were of smaller class than triremes.

4. Twice I celebrated ovations, three times curule triumphs, and I was acclaimed *imperator* twenty-one times. When the senate decreed additional triumphs to me, I declined them on four occasions. I deposited in the Capitol laurel wreaths adorning my *fasces*, after fulfilling the vows which I had made in each war. For successes achieved on land and on sea by me or through my legates under my auspices the senate decreed fifty-five times that thanksgiving be offered to the immortal gods. Moreover, the number of days on which, by decree of the senate, such thanksgiving was offered, was 890. In my triumphs there were led before my chariot nine kings or children of kings. At the time I wrote this document, I had been consul thirteen times, and I was in the thirty-seventh year of my tribunician power.

5. The dictatorship offered to me in the consulship of Marcus Marcellus and Lucius Arruntius by the people and by the senate, both in my absence and in my presence, I refused to accept. In the midst of a critical scarcity of grain I did not decline the supervision of the grain supply, which I so administered that within a few days I freed the whole people from imminent panic and danger by my expenditures and efforts. The consulship, too, which was offered to me at that time as an annual office for life, I refused to accept.

6. In the consulship of Marcus Vinicius and Quintus Lucretius, and again in that of Publius Lentulus and Gnaeus Lentulus, and a third time in that of Paullus Fabius Maximus and Quintus Tubero, though the Roman senate and people unitedly agreed that I should be elected sole guardian of the laws and morals with supreme authority, I refused to accept any office offered me which was contrary to the traditions of our ancestors. The measures

which the senate desired at that time to be taken by me I carried out by virtue of the tribunician power. In this power I five times voluntarily requested and was given a colleague by the senate.

7. I was a member of the triumvirate for the settlement of the commonwealth for ten consecutive years. I have been ranking senator for forty years, up to the day on which I wrote this document. I have been *pontifex maximus*, augur, member of the college of fifteen for performing sacrifices, member of the college of seven for conducting religious banquets, member of the Arval Brotherhood, one of the Titii sodales, and a fetial.

8. In my fifth consulship I increased the number of patricians, by order of the people and the senate. Three times I revised the roll of senators. And in my sixth consulship, with Marcus Agrippa as my colleague, I conducted a census of the people. I performed the *lustrum* after an interval of forty-two years. At this *lustrum* 4,063,000 Roman citizens were recorded. Then a second time, acting alone, by virtue of the consular power, I completed the taking of the census in the consulship of Gaius Censorinus and Gaius Asinius. At this *lustrum* 4,233,000 Roman citizens were recorded. And a third time I completed the taking of the census in the consulship of Sextus Pompeius and Sextus Appuleius, by virtue of the consular power and with my son Tiberius Caesar as my colleague. At this *lustrum* 4,937,000 Roman citizens were recorded. By new legislation which I sponsored I restored many traditions of our ancestors which were falling into desuetude in our generation; and I myself handed down precedents in many spheres for posterity to imitate.

* * *

13. The temple of Janus Quirinus, which our ancestors desired to be closed whenever peace with victory was secured by sea and by land throughout the entire empire of the Roman people, and which before I was born is recorded to have been closed only twice since the founding of the city, was during my principate three times ordered by the senate to be closed.

14. My sons Gaius and Lucius Caesar, whom fortune took from me in their youth, were, in my honor, made consuls designate by the Roman senate and people when they were fifteen years old, with permission to enter that magistracy after a period of five years. The senate further decreed that from the day on which they were introduced into the Forum they should attend its debates. Moreover, the whole body of Roman *equites* presented each of them with silver shields and spears and saluted each as *princeps iuventutis*.

* * *

34. In my sixth and seventh consulships, after I had put an end to the civil wars, having attained supreme power by universal consent, I transferred the state from my own power to the control of the Roman senate and people. For this service of mine I received the title of Augustus by decree of the senate, and the doorposts of my house were publicly decked with laurels, the civic crown was affixed over my doorway, and a golden shield was set up in the Julian senate house, which, as the inscription on this shield testifies, the Roman senate and people gave me in recognition of my valor, clemency, justice, and devotion. After that time I excelled all in authority, but I possessed no more power than the others who were my colleagues in each magistracy.

35. When I held my thirteenth consulship, the senate, the equestrian order, and the entire Roman people gave me the title of "father of the country" and decreed that this title should be inscribed in the vestibule of my house, in the Julian senate house, and in the Augustan Forum on the pedestal of the chariot which was set up in my honor by decree of the senate. At the time I wrote this document I was in my seventy-sixth year.

2. Dio Cassius on the Augustan Settlement*

Dio's is the most complete account we have of the Principate of Augustus. Its reliability may, however, be affected by his well-known imperial bias. In any case, Dio reports that in 27 B.C. Augustus came before the Senate and made a speech in which he appeared to surrender all his power and to restore the Republic. Dio then reports the response to this speech.

While Cæsar was engaged in setting his decision before them, a varied feeling took possession of the senators. A few of them knew his real intention and as a result they kept applauding him enthusiastically. Of the rest some were suspicious of what was said and others believed in it, and therefore both marveled equally, the one class at his great artifice and the other at the determination that he had reached. One side was displeased at his involved scheming and the other at his change of mind. For already there were some who detested the democratic constitution as a breeder of factional difficulties, were pleased at the change of government, and took delight in Cæsar. Consequently, though the announcement affected different persons differently, their views in regard to it were in each case the same. As for those who believed his sentiments to be genuine, any who wished it could not rejoice because of fear, nor the others lament because of hopes. And as many as disbelieved it did not venture to accuse him and confute him, some because they were afraid and others because they did not care to do so. Hence they all either were compelled or pretended to believe him. As for praising him, some did not have the courage and others were unwilling. Even in the midst of his reading there were frequent shouts and afterward many more. The senators begged that a monarchy be established, and directed all their remarks to that end until (naturally) they forced him to assume the reins of government. At once they saw to it that twice as much pay was voted to the

men who were to compose his body-guard as to the rest of the soldiers, that this might incite the men to keep a careful watch of him. Then he began to show a real interest in setting up a monarchy.

In this way he had his headship ratified by the senate and the people. As he wished even so to appear to be democratic in principle, he accepted all the care and superintendence of public business on the ground that it required expert attention, but said that he should not personally govern all the provinces and those that he did govern he should not keep in his charge perpetually. The weaker ones, because (as he said) they were peaceful and free from war, he gave over to the senate. But the more powerful he held in possession because they were slippery and dangerous and either had enemies in adjoining territory or on their own account were able to cause a great uprising. His pretext was that the senate should fearlessly gather the fruits of the finest portion of the empire, while he himself had the labors and dangers: his real purpose was that by this plan the senators be unarmed and unprepared for battle, while he alone had arms and kept soldiers. Africa and Numidia, Asia and Greece with Epirus, the Dalmatian and Macedonian territories, Sicily, Crete, and Libya adjacent to Cyrene, Bithynia with the adjoining Pontus, Sardinia and Bætica, were consequently held to belong to the people and the senate. Cæsar's were—the remainder of Spain, the neighborhood of Tarraco and Lusitania, all Gauls (the Narbonensian and the Lugdunensian, the Aquitani and the Belgæ), both themselves and the aliens among them. Some of the Celtæ whom we

---

* Dio Cassius, 53. 11–12, 16–22, 30–32 (abridged), translated by H. B. Foster.

call Germani had occupied all the Belgic territory near the Rhine and caused it to be called Germania, the upper part extending to the sources of the river and the lower part reaching to the Ocean of Britain. These provinces, then, and the so-called Hollow Syria, Phœnicia and Cilicia, Cyprus and the Egyptians, fell at that time to Cæsar's share. Later he gave Cyprus and Gaul adjacent to Narbo back to the people, and he himself took Dalmatia instead.

* * *

These matters were so ordained at that time,—or, at least, one might say so. In reality Cæsar himself was destined to hold absolute control of all of them for all time, because he commanded the soldiers and was master of the money; nominally the public funds had been separated from his own, but in fact he spent the former also as he saw fit.

* * *

Cæsar had received many honors previously, when the matter of declining the sovereignty and that regarding the division of the provinces were under discussion. For the right to fasten the laurel in front of his royal residence and to hang the oak-leaf crown above the doors was then voted him to symbolize the fact that he was always victorious over enemies and preserved the citizens. The royal building is called Palatium, not because it was ever decreed that that should be its name, but because Cæsar dwelt on the Palatine and had his headquarters there; and his house secured some renown from the mount as a whole by reason of the former habitation of Romulus there. Hence, even if the emperor resides somewhere else, his dwelling retains the name of Palatium.

When he had really completed the details of administration, the name Augustus was finally applied to him by the senate and by the people. They wanted to call him by some name of their own and some proposed this, while others chose

that. Cæsar was exceedingly anxious to be called Romulus, but when he perceived that this caused him to be suspected of desiring the kingship, he no longer insisted on it but took the title of Augustus, signifying that he was more than human. All most precious and sacred objects are termed *augusta*. Therefore they saluted him also in Greek as *sebastó*, meaning an *august* person, from the verb *sebazesthai*.

In this way all the power of the people and that of the senate reverted to Augustus, and from his time there was a genuine monarchy. Monarchy would be the truest name for it, no matter how much two and three hold the power together. This name of monarch the Romans so detested that they called their emperors neither dictators nor kings nor anything of the sort. Yet since the management of the government devolves upon them, it can not but be that they are kings. The offices that commonly enjoy some legal sanction are even now maintained, except that of censor. Still, everything is directed and carried out precisely as the emperor at the time may wish. In order that they may appear to hold this power not through force, but according to law, the rulers have taken possession,—names and all,—of every position (save the dictatorship) which under the democracy was of mighty influence among the citizens who bestowed the power. They very frequently become consuls and are always called proconsuls whenever they are outside the pomerium. The title of imperator is invariably given not only to such as win victories but to all the rest, to indicate the complete independence of their authority, instead of the name "king" or "dictator." These particular names they have never assumed since the terms first fell out of use in the State, but they are confirmed in the prerogatives of these positions by the appellation of imperator. By virtue of the titles mentioned they get the right to make enrollments, to collect moneys, declare wars, make peace, rule foreign and native territory alike everywhere and always, even to the extent of putting to death both knights and senators within the pomerium, and all the other privileges once granted to the consuls and other officials with full powers. By virtue of the office of censor they investigate our lives and characters and take the census. Some they list in the equestrian and senatorial class and others they erase from the roll, as pleases them. By virtue of being consecrated in all the priesthoods and furthermore having the right to give the majority of them to others and from the fact that *one* of the high priests (if there be two or three holding office at once) is chosen from their number, they are themselves also masters of holy and sacred things. The so-called tribunician authority which the men of very greatest attainment used to hold gives them the right to stop any measure brought up by some one else, in case they do not join in approving it, and to be free from personal abuse. Moreover if they are thought to be wronged in even the slightest degree not merely by action but even by conversation they may destroy the guilty party without a trial as one polluted. They do not think it lawful to be tribune, because they belong altogether to the patrician class, but they assume all the power of the tribuneship undiminished from the period of its greatest extent; and thereby the enumeration of the years they have held the office in question goes forward on the assumption that they receive it year by year along with the others who are successively tribunes. Thus by these names they have secured these privileges in accordance with all the various usages of the democracy, in order that they may appear to possess nothing that has not been given them.

They have gained also another prerogative which was given to none of the ancient Romans outright to apply to all cases, and it is through this alone that it would be possible for them to hold the above offices and any others besides. They are freed from the action of the laws, as the very words in Latin indicate. That is, they are liberated from every consideration of compulsion and are subjected to none of the written ordinances. So by virtue of these democratic names they are clothed in all the strength of the government and have all that appertains to kings except the vulgar title. "Cæsar" or "Augustus" as a mode of address confers upon them no distinct privilege of its own but shows in the one case the continuance of their family and in the other the brilliance and dignity of their position. The salutation "father" perhaps gives them a certain authority over us which fathers once had over their children. It was not used, however, for this purpose in the beginning, but for their honor, and to admonish them to love their subjects as they would their children, while the subjects were to respect them as they respect their fathers.

Such is the number and quality of the titles to which those in power are accustomed according to the laws and according to what has now become tradition. At present all of them are, as a rule, bestowed upon the rulers at once, except the title of censor: to the earlier emperors they were voted separately and from time to time. Some of the emperors took the censorship in accordance with ancient custom and Domitian took it for life. This is, however, no longer done at the present day. They possess its powers and are not chosen for it and do not employ its name except in the censuses.

Thus was the constitution made over at that time for the better and in a way to provide greater security. It was doubtless absolutely impossible for the people to be preserved under a democracy.

* * *

Augustus attended with considerable zeal to all the business of the empire to make it appear that he had received it in accordance with the wishes of all, and he also enacted many laws. (I need not go into each one of them in detail except those which have a bearing upon my history. This same course I shall follow in the case of later events, in order not to become wearisome by introducing all such matters as not even those who specialize on them most narrowly know with accuracy.) Not all of these laws were enacted on his sole responsibility: some of them he brought before the public in advance, in order that, if any features caused displeasure, he might learn it in time and correct them. He urged that any one at all give him advice, if any one could think of anything better. He accorded them full liberty of speech and some provisions he actually did alter. Most important of all, he took as advisers for six months the consuls or the consul (when he himself also held the office), one of each of the other kinds of officials, and fifteen men chosen by lot from the remainder of the senatorial body. Through them he was accustomed to a certain extent to communicate to all the rest the provisions of his laws. Some features he brought before the entire senate. He deemed it better, however, to consider most of the laws and the greater ones in company with a few persons at leisure, and acted accordingly. Sometimes he tried cases with their assistance. The entire senate by itself sat in judgment as formerly and transacted business with occasional groups of envoys and heralds from both peoples and kings. Furthermore the people and the plebs came together for the elections, but nothing was done that would not please Cæsar. Some of those who were to hold office he himself chose out and nominated and others he put, according to ancient custom, in the power of the people and the plebs, yet taking care that no unfit persons should be appointed, nor by factious cliques nor by bribery. In this way he controlled the entire empire.

I shall relate also in detail all his acts that need mentioning, together with the names of the consuls under whom they were performed. In the year previously named, seeing that the roads outside the wall had become through neglect hard to traverse, he ordered different senators to repair different ones at their own expense. He himself attended to the Flaminian Way.

* * *

Augustus was for the eleventh time consul with Calpurnius Piso, when he fell so sick once more as to have no hope of saving his life. He accordingly arranged everything in the idea that he was about to die, and gathering about him the officials and the other foremost senators and knights he appointed no successor, though they were expecting that Marcellus would be preferred before all for the position. After conversing briefly with them about public matters he gave Piso the list of the forces and the public revenues written in a book, and handed his ring to Agrippa. The emperor became unable to do even the very simplest things, yet a certain Antonius Musas managed to restore him to health by means of cold baths and cold drinks. For this he received a great deal of money from both Augustus and the senate, as well as the right to wear gold rings,—he was a freedman,—and secured exemption from taxes for both himself and the members of his profession, not only those then living but also those of coming generations. But he who assumed the powers of Fortune and Fate was destined soon after to be well worsted. Augustus had been saved in this manner: but Marcelus, falling sick not much later, was treated in the same way by Musas and died. Augustus gave him a public burial with the usual eulogies, placed him in the monument which was being built, and honored his memory by calling the theatre, the foundations of which had already been laid by the former Cæsar, the Theatre of Marcellus. He ordered also that a gold image of the deceased, a golden crown, and his chair of office be carried into the theatre at the Ludi Romani and be placed in the midst of the officials having charge of the function. This he did later.

After being restored to health on this occasion he brought his will into the senate and wished to read it, by way of showing people that he had left no successor to his position. He did not, however, read it, for no one would permit that. Quite every one, however, was astonished at him in that since he loved Marcellus as son-in-law and nephew yet he failed to trust him with the monarchy but preferred Agrippa before him. His regard for Marcellus had been shown by many honors, among them his lending aid in carrying out the festival which the young man gave as ædile; the brilliance of this occasion is shown by the fact that in midsummer he sheltered the Forum by curtains overhead and introduced a knight and a woman of note as dancers in the orchestra. But his final attitude seemed to show that he was not yet confident of the youth's judgment and that he either wanted the people to get back their liberty or Agrippa to receive the leadership from them. He understood well that Agrippa and the people were on the best of terms and he was unwilling to appear to be delivering the supreme power with his own hands. When he recovered, therefore, and learned that Marcellus on this account was not friendly toward Agrippa, he immediately despatched the latter to Syria, so that no delay and desultory dispute might arise by their being in the same place. Agrippa forthwith started from the City but did not make his way to Syria, but, proceeding even more moderately than usual, he sent his lieutenants there and himself lingered in Lesbos.

Besides doing this Augustus appointed ten prætors, feeling that he did not require any more. This number remained constant for several years. Some of them were intended to fulfill the same duties as of yore and two of them to have charge of the administration of the finances each year. Having settled these details he resigned the consulship and went to Albanum. He himself ever since the constitution had been arranged had held office for the entire year, as had most of his colleagues, and he wished now to interrupt this custom again, in order that as many as possible might be consuls. His resignation took place outside the city, to prevent his being hindered in his purpose.

For this act he received praise, as also because he chose to take his place Lucius Sestius, who had always been an enthusiastic follower of Brutus, had campaigned with the latter in all his wars, and even at this time made mention of him, had his images, and delivered eulogies. So far from disliking the friendly and faithful qualities of the man, the emperor even honored him.

The senate consequently voted that Augustus be tribune for life and that he might bring forward at each meeting of the senate any business he liked concerning any one matter, even if he should not be consul at the time, and allowed him to hold the office of proconsul once for all perpetually, so that he had neither to lay it down on entering the pomerium nor to take it up again outside. The body also granted him more power in subject territory than the several governors possessed. As a result both he and subsequent emperors gained a certain legal right to the use of the tribunican authority, in addition to their other powers. But the actual name of tribune neither Augustus nor any other emperor has held.

3. The Account of Suetonius*

He twice entertained thoughts of restoring the republic; first, immediately after he had crushed Antony, remembering that he had often charged him with being the obstacle to its restoration. The second time was in consequence of a long illness, when he sent for the magistrates and the senate to his own house, and delivered them a particular account of the the empire. But reflecting at the same time that it would be both hazardous to himself to return to the condition of a private person, and might be dangerous to the public to have the government placed again under the control of the people, he resolved to keep it in his own hands, whether with the better event or intention, is hard to say. His good intentions he often affirmed in private discourse, and also published an edict, in which it was declared in the following terms: "May it be permitted me to have the happiness of establishing the commonwealth on a safe and sound basis, and thus enjoy the reward of which I am ambitious, that of being celebrated for moulding it into the form best adapted to present circumstances; so that, on my leaving the world, I may carry with me the hope that the foundations which I have laid for its future government, will stand firm and stable."

* * *

The more important provinces, which could not with ease or safety be entrusted to the government of annual magistrates, he reserved for his own administration: the rest he distributed by lot amongst the proconsuls; but sometimes he made exchanges, and frequently visited most of both kinds in person. Some cities in alliance with Rome, but which by their great licentiousness were hastening to ruin, he deprived of their independence. Others, which were much in debt, he relieved, and rebuilt such as had been destroyed by earthquakes. To those that could produce any instance of their having deserved well of the Roman people, he presented the freedom of Latium, or even that of the City. There is not, I believe, a province, except Africa and Sardinia, which he did not visit. After forcing Sextus Pompeius to take refuge in those provinces, he was indeed preparing to cross over from Sicily to them, but was prevented by continual and violent storms, and afterwards there was no occasion or call for such a voyage.

* * *

With respect to the army, he distributed the legions and auxiliary troops throughout the several provinces. He stationed a fleet at Misenum, and another at Ravenna, for the protection of the Upper and Lower Seas. A certain number of the forces were selected, to occupy the posts in the city, and partly for his own body-guard; but he dismissed the Spanish guard, which he retained about him till the fall of Antony; and also the Germans, whom he had amongst his guards, until the defeat of Varus. Yet he never permitted a greater force than three cohorts in the city, and had no (prætorian) camps. The rest he quartered in the neighbourhood of the nearest towns, in winter and summer camps. All the troops throughout the empire he reduced to one fixed model with regard to their pay and their pensions; determining these according to their rank in the army, the time they had served, and their private means; so that after their discharge, they might not be tempted by age or necessities to join the agitators for a revolution. For the purpose of providing a fund always ready to meet their pay and pensions, he instituted a military ex-

---

* Suetonius, *Augustus*, 28, 47, 49, 52–58, translated by Alexander Thomson, revised by T. Forester.

chequer, and appropriated new taxes to that object. In order to obtain the earliest intelligence of what was passing in the provinces, he established posts, consisting at first of young men stationed at moderate distances along the military roads, and afterwards of regular couriers with fast vehicles; which appeared to him the most commodious, because the persons who were the bearers of dispatches, written on the spot, might then be questioned about the business, as occasion occurred.

* * *

Although he knew that it had been customary to decree temples in honour of the proconsuls, yet he would not permit them to be erected in any of the provinces, unless in the joint names of himself and Rome. Within the limits of the city, he positively refused any honour of that kind. He melted down all the silver statues which had been erected to him, and converted the whole into tripods, which he consecrated to the Palatine Apollo. And when the people importuned him to accept the dictatorship, he bent down on one knee, with his toga thrown over his shoulders, and his breast exposed to view, begging to be excused.

He always abhorred the title of *Lord*, as ill-omened and offensive. And when, in a play, performed at the theatre, at which he was present, these words were introduced, "O just and gracious lord," and the whole company, with joyful acclamations, testified their approbation of them, as applied to him, he instantly put a stop to their indecent flattery, by waving his hand, and frowning sternly, and next day publicly declared his displeasure, in a proclamation. He never afterwards would suffer himself to be addressed in that manner, even by his own children or grand-children, either in jest or earnest, and forbad them the use of all such complimentary expressions to one another. He rarely entered any city or town, or departed from it, except in the

evening or the night, to avoid giving any person the trouble of complimenting him. During his consulships, he commonly walked the streets on foot; but at other times, rode in a close carriage. He admitted to court even plebeians, in common with people of the higher ranks; receiving the petitions of those who approached him with so much affability, that he once jocosely rebuked a man, by telling him, "You present your memorial with as much hesitation as if you were offering money to an elephant." On senate days, he used to pay his respects to the Conscript Fathers only in the house, addressing them each by name as they sat, without any prompter; and on his departure, he bade each of them farewell, while they retained their seats. In the same manner, he maintained with many of them a constant intercourse of mutual civilities, giving them his company upon occasions of any particular festivity in their families; until he became advanced in years, and was incommoded by the crowd at a wedding. Being informed that Gallus Terrinius, a senator, with whom he had only a slight acquaintance, had suddenly lost his sight, and under that privation had resolved to starve himself to death, he paid him a visit, and by his consolatory admonitions diverted him from his purpose.

On his speaking in the senate, he has been told by one of the members, "I did not understand you," and by another, "I would contradict you, could I do it with safety." And sometimes, upon his being so much offended at the heat with which the debates were conducted in the senate, as to quit the house in anger, some of the members have repeatedly exclaimed: "Surely, the senators ought to have liberty of speech on matters of government." Antistius Labeo, in the election of a new senate, when each, as he was named, chose another, nominated Marcus Lepidus, who had formerly been Augustus's enemy, and was then in banishment; and being asked by the latter, "Is there no other person more deserving?" he replied, "Every man has his own opinion." Nor was any one ever molested for his freedom of speech, although it was carried to the extent of insolence.

Even when some infamous libels against him were dispersed in the senate-house, he was neither disturbed, nor did he give himself much trouble to refute them. He would not so much as order an enquiry to be made after the authors; but only proposed, that, for the future, those who published libels or lampoons, in a borrowed name, against any person, should be called to account.

Being provoked by some petulant jests, which were designed to render him odious, he answered them by a proclamation; and yet he prevented the senate from passing an act, to restrain the liberties which were taken with others in people's wills. Whenever he attended at the election of magistrates, he went round the tribes, with the candidates of his nomination, and begged the votes of the people in the usual manner. He likewise gave his own vote in his tribe, as one of the people. He suffered himself to be summoned as a witness upon trials, and not only to be questioned, but to be cross-examined, with the utmost patience. In building his Forum, he restricted himself in the site, not presuming to compel the owners of the neighbouring houses to give up their property. He never recommended his sons to the people, without adding these words, "If they deserve it." And upon the audience rising on their entering the theatre while they were yet minors, and giving them applause in a standing position, he made it a matter of serious complaint.

He was desirous that his friends should be great and powerful in the state, but have no exclusive privileges, or be exempt from the laws which governed others. When Asprenas Nonius, an intimate friend of his, was tried upon a charge of administering poison at the instance of Cassius Severus, he consulted the senate for their opinion what was his duty under the circumstances: "For," said he, "I am afraid, lest, if I should stand by him in the cause, I may be supposed to screen a guilty man; and if I do not, to desert and prejudge a friend." With the unanimous concurrence, therefore, of the senate, he took his seat amongst his advocates for several hours, but without giving him the benefit of speaking to character, as was usual. He likewise appeared for his clients; as on behalf of Scutarius, an old soldier of his, who brought an action for slander. He never relieved any one from prosecution but in a single instance, in the case of a man who had given information of the conspiracy of Muræna; and that he did only by prevailing upon the accuser, in open court, to drop his prosecution.

How much he was beloved for his worthy conduct in all these respects, it is easy to imagine. I say nothing of the decrees of the senate in his honour, which may seem to have resulted from compulsion or deference. The Roman knights voluntarily, and with one accord, always celebrated his birth for two days together; and all ranks of the people, yearly, in performance of a vow they had made, threw a piece of money into the Curtain lake, as an offering for his welfare. They likewise, on the calends [first] of January, presented for his acceptance new-year's gifts in the capitol, though he was not present: with which donations he purchased some costly images of the Gods, which he erected in several streets of the city; as that of Apollo Sandaliarius, Jupiter Tragœdus, and others. When his house on the Palatine hill was accidentally destroyed by fire, the veteran soldiers, the judges, the tribes, and even the people, individually, contributed, according to the ability of each, for rebuilding it; but he would accept only of some small portion out of the several sums collected, and refused to take from any one person more than a single denarius. Upon his return home from any of the provinces, they attended him not only with joyful acclamations, but with songs. It is also remarked, that as often as he entered the city, the infliction of punishment was suspended for the time.

The whole body of the people, upon a sudden impulse, and with unanimous consent, offered him the title of FATHER OF HIS COUNTRY. It was announced to him first at Antium, by a deputation from the people, and upon his declining the honour, they repeated their offer on his return to Rome, in a full theatre, when they were crowned with laurel. The senate soon afterwards adopted the proposal, not in the way of acclamation of decree, but by commissioning M. Messala, in an unani-mous vote, to compliment him with it in the following terms: "With hearty wishes for the happiness and prosperity of your-self and your family, Cæsar Augustus, (for we think we thus most effectually pray for the lasting welfare of the state), the senate, in agreement with the Roman people, salute you by the title of FATHER OF YOUR COUNTRY." To this compliment Augustus replied, with tears in his eyes, in these words (for I give them exactly as I have done those of Messala): "Having now arrived at the summit of my wishes, O Conscript Fathers, what else have I to beg of the Immortal Gods, but the con-tinuance of this your affection for me to the last moments of my life?"

4. TACITUS ON AUGUSTUS*

Publius Cornelius Tacitus (A.D. *ca.* 55–120) was a Roman aristocrat who had a distin-guished career as orator, lawyer, and administrator in addition to his accomplishments as the greatest historian of imperial Rome. The attitude which appears in his historical works is that of a man who yearns for the Republic which, he recognizes, is no longer possible. His bias against the emperors is most noteworthy when he writes of Domitian and Tiberius, but is by no means absent from his account of Augustus.

Rome at the beginning was ruled by kings. Freedom and the consulship were established by Lucius Brutus. Dictator-ships were held for a temporary crisis. The power of the decemvirs did not last beyond two years, nor was the consular jurisdiction of the military tribunes of long duration. The despotisms of Cinna and Sulla were brief; the rule of Pompeius and of Crassus soon yielded before Cæsar; the arms of Lepidus and Antonius before Augustus; who, when the world was wearied by civil strife, subjected it to empire under the title of "Prince." But the successes and reverses of the old Roman people have been recorded by famous historians; and fine intellects were not wanting to describe the times of Augustus, till growing sycophancy scared them away. This histories of Tiberius, Caius, Claudius, and Nero, while they were in power, were falsified through terror, and after their death were written under the irritation of a recent hatred. Hence my purpose is to relate a few facts about Augustus—more particularly his last acts, then the reign of Tiberius, and all which follows, without either bitterness or partiality, from any motives to which I am far removed.

When after the destruction of Brutus and Cassius there was no longer any army of the Commonwealth, when Pompeius was crushed in Sicily, and when, with Lepidus pushed aside and Antonius slain, even the Julian faction had only Cæsar left to lead it, then, dropping the title of triumvir, and giving out that he was a

* Tacitus, *Annals*, 1. 1–4, translated by A. J. Church and W. J. Brodribb.

Consul, and was satisfied with a tribune's authority for the protection of the people, Augustus won over the soldiers with gifts, the populace with cheap corn, and all men with the sweets of repose, and so grew greater by degrees, while he concentrated in himself the functions of the Senate, the magistrates, and the laws. He was wholly unopposed, for the boldest spirits had fallen in battle, or in the proscription, while the remaining nobles, the readier they were to be slaves, were raised the higher by wealth and promotion, so that, aggrandised by revolution, they preferred the safety of the present to the dangerous past. Nor did the provinces dislike that condition of affairs, for they distrusted the government of the Senate and the people, because of the rivalries between the leading men and the rapacity of the officials, while the protection of the laws was unavailing, as they were continually deranged by violence, intrigue, and finally by corruption.

Augustus meanwhile, as supports to his despotism, raised to the pontificate and curile ædileship Claudius Marcellus, his sister's son, while a mere stripling, and Marcus Agrippa, of humble birth, a good soldier, and one who had shared his victory, to two consecutive consulships, and as Marcellus soon afterwards died, he also accepted him as his son-in-law. Tiberius Nero and Claudius Drusus, his stepsons, he honoured with imperial titles, although his own family was as yet undiminished. For he had admitted the children of Agrippa, Caius and Lucius, into the house of the Cæsars; and before they had yet laid aside the dress of boyhood he had most fervently desired, with an outward show of reluctance, that they should be entitled "princes of the youth," and be consuls-elect. When Agrippa died, and Lucius Cæsar as he was on his way to our armies in Spain, and Caius while returning from Armenia, still suffering from a wound, were prematurely cut off by destiny, or by their step-mother Livia's treachery, Drusus too having long been dead, Nero remained alone of the stepsons, and in him everything tended to centre. He was adopted as a son, as a colleague in empire and a partner in the tribunitian power, and paraded through all the armies, no longer through his mother's secret intrigues, but at her open suggestion. For she had gained such a hold on the aged Augustus that he drove out as an exile into the island of Planasia, his only grandson, Agrippa Postumus, who, though devoid of worthy qualities, and having only the brute courage of physical strength, had not been convicted of any gross offence. And yet Augustus had appointed Germanicus, Drusus's offspring, to the command of eight legions on the Rhine, and required Tiberius to adopt him, although Tiberius had a son, now a young man, in his house; but he did it that he might have several safeguards to rest on. He had no war at the time on his hands except against the Germans, which was rather to wipe out the disgrace of the loss of Quintilius Varus and his army than out of an ambition to extend the empire, or for any adequate recompense. At home all was tranquil, and there were magistrates with the same titles; there was a younger generation, sprung up since the victory of Actium, and even many of the older men had been born during the civil wars. How few were left who had seen the republic!

Thus the State had been revolutionised, and there was not a vestige left of the old sound morality. Stript of equality, all looked up to the commands of a sovereign without the least apprehension for the present, while Augustus in the vigour of life, could maintain his own position, that of his house, and the general tranquillity. When in advanced old age, he was worn out by a sickly frame, and the end was near and new prospects opened, a few spoke in vain of the blessings of freedom, but most people dreaded and some longed for war.

5. THE CONSTITUTIONAL BASIS OF THE PRINCIPATE*

Scholars of the nineteenth century were most interested in the purely legal question of the constitutional basis for the rule of Augustus. Mommsen, the most influential of all, believed that the Principate was in fact a "dyarchy" in which princeps and Senate shared power. Although Bury does not accept this theory, he does accept the constitutional bases proposed by Mommsen and widely accepted as the only real sources of Augustan power at that time.

The task which devolved upon Cæsar when he had resigned the triumvirate and the proconsular power which had been conferred on him in 43 B.C., was to restore the republic and yet place its administration in the hands of one man, to disguise the monarchy, which he already possessed, under a constitutional form, to be a second Romulus without being a king. He still held the tribunician power which had been given him for life in 36 B.C.

On January 16, in the year of the city 727, three days after Cæsar had laid down his extraordinary powers, the Roman Empire formally began. Munatius Plancus on that day proposed in the senate that the surname *Augustus* should be conferred on Cæsar in recognition of his services to the state. This name did not bestow any political power, but it became perhaps the most distinctive and significant name of the Emperor. It suggested religious sanctity and surrounded the son of the deified Julius with a halo of consecration. The actual power on which the Empire rested, the *imperium proconsulare*, was conferred upon, or rather renewed for, Augustus (so we may now call him) for a period of ten years, but renewable after that period. This imperium was of the same kind as that which had been given to Pompeius by the Gabinian and Manilian laws. The Imperator had an exclusive command over the armies and fleet of the republic,

and his "province" included all the most important frontier provinces. But this imperium was essentially military; and Rome and Italy were excluded from its sphere. It was therefore insufficient by itself to establish a sovranty, which was to be practically a restoration of royalty, while it pretended to preserve the republican constitution. The idea of Augustus, from which his new constitution derived its special character, was to supplement and reinforce the imperium by one of the higher magistracies.

His first plan was to combine the proconsular imperium with the consulship. He was consul in 27 B.C., and he caused himself to be re-elected to that magistracy each year for the four following years. The consular imperium, which he thus possessed, gave him not only a *locus standi* in Rome and Italy, but also affected his position in the provinces. For if he only held the proconsular imperium he was merely on a level legally with other proconsular governors, although his "province" was far larger than theirs. But as consul, his imperium ranked as superior (*maius*) over that of the proconsuls. He found, however, that there were drawbacks to this plan. As consul he had a colleague, whose power was legally equal; and this position was clearly awkward for the head of the state. Moreover, if one consul was perpetual, the number of persons elected to the consulship must be smaller; and consequently there would be fewer men available for those offices which were only filled by men of consular rank. The consuls too were regarded as in a certain way representative of the senate;

* J. B. Bury, *A History of the Roman Empire from Its Foundation to the Death of Marcus Aurelius, 27 B.C.–180 A.D.* (London: John Murray, 1900), pp. 12–15. Reprinted by permission of the publisher.

and the Emperor, the child of the democracy, might prefer to be regarded as representative of the people. His thoughts therefore turned to the tribunate, which was specially the magistracy of the people. But it would have been more awkward to found supremacy in civil affairs on the authority of one of ten tribunes than on the powers of one of two consuls. Accordingly Augustus fell back on the *tribunicia potestas*, which he had retained, but so far seems to have made little use of.

In 23 B.C. he gave up his first tentative plan and made the *tribunicia potestas*, instead of the consulship, which he resigned on June 27, the second pillar of his power. The tribunician power was his for life, but he now made it annual as well as perpetual, and dated from this year the years of his reign. Thus in a very narrow sense the Empire might be said to have begun in 23 B.C.; in that year at least the constitution of Augustus received its final form. After this year, his eleventh consulship, Augustus held that office only twice (5 and 2 B.C.). Subsequent Emperors generally assumed it more than once; but it was rather a distinction for the colleague than an advantage for the Emperor.

But the *tribunicia potestas* alone was not a sufficient substitute for the *consulare imperium* which Augustus had surrendered by resigning the consulate. Accordingly a series of privileges and rights were conferred upon him by special acts in 23 B.C. and the following years. He received the right of convening the senate when he chose, and of proposing the first motion at its meetings (*ius primae relationis*). His proconsular imperium was defined as "superior" (*maius*) to that of other proconsuls. He received the right of the twelve fasces in Rome, and of sitting between the consuls, and thus he was equalised with the consuls in external dignity (19 B.C.). He probably received too the *ius edicendi*, that is, the power of issuing magisterial edicts. These rights, conferred upon Augustus by separate acts,

were afterwards drawn up in a single form of law, by which the senate and people conferred them on each succeeding Emperor. Thus the constitutional position of the Emperor rested on three bases: the proconsular imperium, the tribunician potestas, and a special law of investiture with certain other prerogatives.

The title *imperator* expressed only the proconsular and military power of the Emperor. The one word which could have expressed the sum of all his functions as head of the state,—*rex*—was just the title which Augustus would on no account have assumed; for by doing so he would have thrown off the republican disguise which was essential to his position. The key to the Empire, as Augustus constituted it, is that the Emperor was a magistrate, not a monarch. But a word was wanted, which without emphasizing any special side of the Emperor's power should indicate his supreme authority in the republic. Augustus chose the name *princeps* to do this informal duty. The name meant "the first citizen in the state"—*princeps civitatis*—and thus implied at once supremacy and equality, quite in accordance with the spirit of Augustus' constitution; but did not suggest any definite functions. It was purely a name of courtesy. It must be carefully distinguished from the title *princeps senatus*. The senator who was first on the list of the conscript fathers, and had a right to be asked his opinion first, was called *princeps senatus*; and that position had been assigned to Augustus in 28 B.C. But when he or others spoke or wrote of the *princeps*, they did not mean "prince of the senate," but "prince of the Roman citizens." The Empire as constituted by Augustus is often called the Principate, as opposed to the absolute monarchy into which it developed at a later stage. The Principate is in fact a stage of the Empire; and it might be said that while Augustus founded the Principate, Julius was the true founder of the Empire.

According to constitutional theory, the

state was still governed under the Principate by the senate and the people. The people delegated most of its functions to one man, so that the government was divided between the senate and the man who represented the people. In the course of time the republican forms of the constitution and the magisterial character of the Emperor gradually disappeared; but at first they were clearly marked and strictly maintained. The senate possessed some real power; assemblies of the people were held; consuls, prætors, tribunes, and the other magistrates were elected as usual. The Principate was not formally a monarchy, but rather a "dyarchy," as German writers have called it; the Princeps and the senate together ruled the state. But the fellowship was an unequal one, for the Emperor, as supreme commander of the armies, had the actual power. The dyarchy is a transparent fiction. The chief feature of the constitutional history of the first three centuries of the Empire is the decline of the authority of the senate and the corresponding growth of the powers of the Princeps, until finally he becomes an absolute monarch. When this comes to pass, the Empire can no longer be described as the Principate.

6. The Nature of Augustan Power*

Ronald Syme is one of the leaders in a movement which has turned the attention of scholars away from the purely constitutional questions toward what some consider the more basic realities of political power and propaganda. He has emphasized Augustus' position as the leader of a faction, a *Dux* who was compelled by success to seek a broader base of power. Syme's enlightening summation that barely touches on purely constitutional matters stands in sharp contrast to the older approach.

That the power of Caesar Augustus was absolute, no contemporary could doubt. But his rule was justified by merit, founded upon consent and tempered by duty. Augustus stood like a soldier, 'in statione'—for the metaphor, though it may have parallels in the language of the Stoics, is Roman and military. He would not desert his post until a higher command relieved him, his duty done and a successor left on guard. Augustus used the word 'statio': so did contemporaries.

Augustus' rule was dominion over all the world. To the Roman People his relationship was that of Father, Founder and Guardian. Sulla had striven to repair the shattered Republic; and Cicero, for saving Rome in his consulate, had been hailed as *pater patriae*. But Sulla, with well-grounded hate, was styled 'the sinister Romulus'; Cicero, in derision of his pretensions, the 'Romulus from Arpinum'. Augustus, however, had a real claim to be known and honoured as the Founder, 'augusto augurio', in the phrase of Ennius. The Roman could feel it in his blood and in his traditions.

* * *

Augustus' relation to the Roman Commonwealth might also be described as organic rather than arbitrary or formal. It was said that he arrogated to himself all the functions of Senate, magistrates and laws. Truly—but more penetrating the remark that he entwined himself about the body of the Commonwealth. The new member reinvigorated the whole and could not have been severed without damage.

His rule was personal, if ever rule was, and his position became ever more monarchic. Yet with all this, Augustus was

* Ronald Syme, *The Roman Revolution* (Clarendon, 1939), pp. 520–524. Reprinted by permission of The Clarendon Press, Oxford.

not indispensable—that was the greatest triumph of all. Had he died in the early years of the Principate, his party would have survived, led by Agrippa, or by a group of the marshals. But Augustus lived on, a progressive miracle of duration. As the years passed, he emancipated himself more and more from the control of his earlier partisans; the *nobiles* returned to prominence, and the Caesarian party itself was transformed and transcended. A government was created.

'Legiones classes provincias, cuncta inter se conexa.' So Tacitus described the Empire and its armed forces. The phrase might fittingly be applied to the whole fabric of the Roman State. It was firm, well-articulated and flexible. By appeal to the old, Augustus justified the new; by emphasizing continuity with the past, he encouraged the hope of development in the future. The New State established as the consolidation of the Revolution was neither exclusive nor immobile. While each class in society had its peculiar functions, there was no sharp division between classes. Service to Rome won recognition and promotion for senator, for knight or for soldier, for Roman or for provincial. The rewards were not so splendid as in the wars of the Revolution; but the rhythm, though abated, was steady and continuous.

It had been Augustus' most fervent prayer that he might lay the foundations of the new order deep and secure. He had done more than that. The Roman State, based firmly on a united Italy and a coherent Empire, was completely renovated, with new institutions, new ideas and even a new literature that was already classical. The doom of Empire had borne heavily on Rome, with threatened ruin. But now the reinvigorated Roman People, robust and cheerful, could bear the burden with pride as well as with security.

Augustus had also prayed for a successor in the post of honour and duty. His dearest hopes, his most pertinacious designs, had been thwarted. But peace and the Principate endured. A successor had been found, trained in his own school, a Roman aristocrat from among the *principes*, by general consent capable of Empire. It might have been better for Tiberius and for Rome if Augustus had died earlier: the duration of his life, by accustoming men's minds to the Principate as something permanent and enhancing his own prestige beyond that of a mortal man, while it consolidated his own régime and the new system of government, none the less made the task of his successor more delicate and more arduous.

The last decade of Augustus' life was clouded by domestic scandals and by disasters on the frontiers of empire. Yet for all that, when the end came it found him serene and cheerful. On his death-bed he was not plagued by remorse for his sins or by anxiety for the Empire. He quietly asked his friends whether he had played well his part in the comedy of life. There could be one answer or none. Whatever his deserts, his fame was secure and he had made provision for his own immortality.

During the Spanish wars, when stricken by an illness that might easily have been the end of a frail life, Augustus composed his *Autobiography*. Other generals before him, like Sulla and Caesar, had published the narrative of their *res gestae* or recounted their life, deeds and destiny for glory or for politics: none can have fabricated history with such calm audacity. Others generals had their memorial in the trophies, temples or theatres they had erected; their mailed statues and the brief inscribed record of their public services adorned Augustus' Forum of Mars Ultor. This was the recompense due to 'boni duces' after death. Sulla had been 'Felix', Pompeius had seized the title of 'Magnus'. Augustus, in glory and fortune the greatest of *duces* and *principes*, intended to outshine them all. At the very moment when he was engaged upon the ostensible restoration of the Republic, he constructed in the Campus Martius a huge and dynastic monument, his own Mausoleum. He may already, in the ambition to perpetuate his glory, have composed the first draft of the inscription that was to stand outside his monument, the *Res Gestae*; or at the least, it may be conjectured that some such document was included in the state papers which the Princeps, near to death, handed over to the consul Piso in 23 B.C. But earlier versions may more easily be surmised than detected. The *Res Gestae* in their final form were composed early in A.D. 13, along with the last will and testament, to be edited and published by Tiberius.

This precious document, surviving in provincial copies, bears the hall-mark of official truth: it reveals the way in which Augustus wished posterity to interpret the incidents of his career, the achievements and character of his rule. The record is no less instructive for what it omits than for what it says. The adversaries of the Princeps in war and the victims of his public or private treacheries are not mentioned by name but are consigned to contemptuous oblivion. Antonius is masked and traduced as a faction, the Liberators as enemies of the Fatherland, Sex. Pompeius as a pirate. Perusia and the proscriptions are forgotten, the *coup d'état* of 32 B.C. appears as a spontaneous uprising of all Italy, Philippi is transformed into the victory of Caesar's heir and avenger alone. Agrippa indeed occurs twice, but much more as a date than as an agent. Other allies of the Princeps are omitted, save for Tiberius, whose conquest of Illyricum under the auspices of Augustus is suitably commemorated.

Most masterly of all is the formulation of the chapter that describes the constitutional position of the Princeps—and most misleading. His powers are defined as legal and magisterial; and he excels any colleague he might have, not in *potestas*, but only in *auctoritas*. Which is true as far as it goes—not very far. *Auctoritas*,

however, does betray the truth, for *auctoritas* is also *potentia*. There is no word in this passage of the *tribunicia potestas* which, though elsewhere modestly referred to as a means of passing legislation, nowhere betrays its formidable nature and cardinal role in the imperial system— 'summi fastigii vocabulum'. Again, there is nowhere in the whole document even a hint of the *imperium proconsular* in virtue of which Augustus controlled, directly or indirectly, all provinces and all armies. Yet these powers were the twin pillars of his rule, firm and erect behind the flimsy and fraudulent Republic. In the employment of the tribunes' powers and of *imperium* the Princeps acknowledges his ancestry, recalling the dynasts Pompeius and Caesar. People and Army were the source and basis of his domination.

Such were the *Res Gestae Divi Augusti*. It would be imprudent to use the document as a sure guide for history, petulant and pointless to complain of omission and misrepresentation. No less vain the attempt to discover ultimate derivation and exact definition as a literary form. While the Princeps lived, he might, like other rulers, be openly worshipped as a deity in the provinces or receive in Rome and Italy honours like those accorded to gods by grateful humanity: to Romans he was no more than the head of the Roman State. Yet one thing was certain. When he was dead, Augustus would receive the honours of the Founder who was also Aeneas and Romulus, and, like *Divus Julius*, he would be enrolled by vote of the Roman Senate among the gods of Rome for his great merits—and for reasons of high politics. None the less, it will not help to describe the *Res Gestae* as the title-deeds of his divinity. If explained they must be, it is not with reference to the religions and kings of the Hellenistic East but from Rome and Roman practice, as a combination between the *elogium* of a Roman general and the statement of accounts of a Roman magistrate.

Like Augustus, his *Res Gestae* are unique, defying verbal definition and explaining themselves. From the beginning, from his youthful emergence as a revolutionary leader in public sedition and armed violence, the heir of Caesar had endured to the end. He died on the anniversary of the day when he assumed his first consulate after the march on Rome. Since then, fifty-six years had elapsed.

Throughout, in act and policy, he remained true to himself and to the career that began when he raised a private army and 'liberated the State from the domination of a faction'. Dux had become Princeps and had converted a party into a government. For power he had sacrificed everything; he had achieved the height of all mortal ambition and in his ambition he had saved and regenerated the Roman People.

7. THE *IMPERIUM* OF AUGUSTUS*

Recent scholarship has reasserted the importance of the constitutional base of the Principate. In the following two selections, A. H. M. Jones and E. T. Salmon take it very seriously and offer new hypotheses for the ultimate nature of the Augustan constitution.

There has been a tendency among some modern scholars to regard the constitutional position of Augustus as of negligible importance. This is a natural reaction from the excessive legalism of Mommsen and his school, and has had valuable results in elucidating extra-constitutional elements in the position of the first Princeps, such as his outstanding *autoritas* and his huge *clientela*. I do not think however that we can lightly brush aside the constitutional basis of his power. I do not wish to suggest that the restored Republic was intended to be genuine, or even that Augustus meant to share his power with the Senate and People: never for one moment did he part with his control over the great bulk of the legions. But I would suggest he would not have created the elaborate façade of Republican legitimacy, and moreover have subjected his original scheme to at least one radical revision, unless there had been some important element in the State to which the constitution mattered, and mattered so

profoundly that its dissatisfaction would endanger the stability of the régime.

This element was not, I think, primarily the nobility. They were too hard boiled to be put off by Augustus' sham Republic, and it was not the Republic that they so much lamented as their lost power. Moreover they had been decimated in the Civil Wars, and Augustus never trusted what was left of them: they do not hold high military commands as his *legati*. Nor do I think that it was the Roman People, if by this is meant the *plebs urbana*: the events of Augustus' reign prove that they wanted a popular dictatorship like Caesar's, and from time to time they broke out, demanding that Augustus accept a life-long consulship or dictatorship. Nor was it the rank and file of the army, who followed him because he was Caesar's son, and were to continue for generations to give blind allegiance to any Caesar, even a Nero. Who then were the republicans? The greatest republican constitutionalist of the last days of the Republic was Cicero, a new man from an Italian town. Velleius Paterculus, the enthusiastic panegyrist of the restored Republic, came from an Italian family enfranchised in the Social War. Livy, the Pompeian historian, who

* A. H. M. Jones, "The *Imperium* of Augustus," *Journal of Roman Studies*, 41 (London: Society for the Promotion of Roman Studies, 1951), pp. 112–119. Reprinted by permission of the publisher.

glorified the stern fathers of the Republic, came from Padua. Looking a little later, Thrasea Paetus and his fellow admirers of Brutus and Cassius were worthy bourgeois from the *municipia et coloniae*, and Tacitus himself came from the same milieu. It was, I think, the great Italian middle class, most of whom were Roman citizens of the third generation only, who venerated the republican traditions of Rome. And they were important politically; for from them were drawn the centurions and equestrian officers of the army, and picked men from among them were promoted to the Senate and held the higher army commands, in so far as these were not monopolized by the imperial family. Finally they were quite content with the form of the Republic, for their republicanism was sentimental and antiquarian: they had never tasted power under the old régime and had rarely even aspired to do so.

To turn to the events. In 27 B.C., having purged the Senate, Imperator Caesar restored the Republic with a great flourish of trumpets and was rewarded with the *cognomen* of Augustus by the grateful Senate. The legal powers enjoyed by the Princeps at this moment were somewhat limited. He possessed the sacrosanctity of a tribune, granted in 36 B.C. He was moreover one of the consuls of the year. Of what happened next we have only Dio's account, and according to him Augustus was voted a number of provinces for ten years. These provinces Dio enumerates according to their later boundaries: in 27 B.C. they could have been summed up as Hither Spain, Transalpine Gaul, Syria, and Egypt.

It has been argued *ad nauseam* whether Augustus' *imperium* at this stage was consular or proconsular. I do not believe that the question arose. Augustus was consul, and the Senate assigned him a *provincia*: no grant of *imperium* was required, for, to quote Appius Claudius Pulcher, speaking as consul, about to depart for his province at the end of 54 B.C., 'se quoniam ex senatus consulto provinciam habaret lege Cornelia imperium habiturum quoad in urbem introisset.' It is true that the Lex Pompeia de provinciis had since then modified the position by inserting a five years' interval between magistracy and promagistracy, but this law had evidently either been abrogated or fallen in abeyance before 27 B.C., since Augustus either re-enacted or revived it in that year. The revival of the Lex Pompeia would naturally have come after the assignment of Augustus' province, which, as an extraordinary command, would in any case have been (and of course was) exempted from its provisions. The grant of the provinces must have included the right to appoint numerous *legati*, which Pompey and Caesar had received before. It was probably at this date also that Augustus was given the right to declare war and make treaties which is mentioned by Strabo and by the Lex de imperio Vespasiani. There were Republican precedents for this in the Lex Manilia and the Lex Trebonia and it was a not unnatural privilege for the magistrate who was to control most of the frontiers for the next ten years; it also incidentally gave Augustus control over the numerous and powerful kings of the Empire. Though this right proved to be life long as Strabo describes it, I think that it was probably originally linked with the *provincia*, as in the cases of Pompey and of Crassus.

We tend, I think, knowing what did happen next, to assume too readily that it was an open secret at the time that Augustus was going to be consul year after year. Dio, for what he is worth, represents the majority of the Senate as being in the dark, and if this is true many of them may have hoped and expected that Augustus would, like Caesar in 59, go and govern his provinces, or at the worst, like Pompey in 55, hang about in Italy as proconsul, governing his provinces through his legats. But if so they were disappointed; for Augustus stood for, and was naturally elected to, the consulship in 26, and again in 25, and in 24, and in 23.

He thus placed himself in a position which could hardly be called republican. The only recent precedent for a continuous series of consulships was Marius, hardly a reputable figure. Moreover, in addition to ruling the great *provincia* which the Senate had assigned to him, he possessed the vast and undefined powers of a consul, which he could stretch to include an ultimate control over all proconsuls; for according to that excellent republican jurist, Cicero, 'omnes in consulis iure et imperio debent esse provinciae' and to the consuls 'more maiorum concessum est vel omnes adire provincias'. It is doubtful whether Augustus used this prerogative; for he spent these years within his provinces of Spain or Gaul, or in Italy. But the incident of Primus, proconsul of Macedonia, charged with making war on the Odrysae without authorization, proves that Augustus was suspected of ordering proconsuls about; for Primus claimed in defence that he had acted on Augustus' orders, and when Augustus, questioned by the praetor, denied this, Primus' counsel Murena asked him what he was doing in court in that case, implying that he doubted his word. And even if Augustus did not interfere with other proconsuls, he was from time to time in Rome, where as consul he could dominate the Senate. Matters were made worse by the too obvious parade of Marcellus as heir apparent, which suggested a hereditary tyranny: Primus at his trial exploited this suspicion by claiming that Marcellus had given him instructions, and Augustus after Marcellus' death thought it prudent to offer to publish his will to prove that he had no intention of founding a hereditary monarchy.

That this state of affairs caused bitter dissatisfaction is proved by the conspiracy of Caepio and Murena, misplaced by Dio in 22, really belonging to the previous year: this conspiracy was all the more serious in that Murena was what Velleius calls a good man, that is a Caesarian, and it must have been a sharp reminder to Augustus that, if he was to avoid his adoptive father's fate, something must be done. This, I think, is the true explanation of Augustus' abrupt resignation from his consulship in 23. He had, it is true, been very ill, and had even made arrangements envisaging the possibility of his death, handing his seal to Agrippa, and the accounts of the Empire to his colleague Piso. But his weakened health was no more than a convenient excuse for the constitutional change which he now made, a change which did not effectively reduce the amount of work or responsibility which he had to undertake.

For what happened in 23 we are again dependent on Dio. Augustus resigned his consulship, and to prove his good republican principles, filled its remaining term by L. Sestius, an open admirer of Brutus, who had fought on his side in the Civil Wars. To compensate for the abandonment of the consulate the Senate voted him τὴν ἀρχὴν τὴν ἀνθύπατον ἐσαεὶ καθάπαξ ἔχειν, ὥστε μήτε ἐν τῇ εἰσόδῳ τῇ εἴσω τοῦ πωμηρίου κατατίθεσθαι αὐτὴν μήτ' αὖθις ἀνανεοῦσθαι, καὶ ἐν τῷ ὑπηκόῳ τὸ πλεῖον τῶν ἑκασταχόθι ἀρχόντων ἰσχύειν [(the power) to hold the office of proconsul once for all perpetually, so that he had neither to lay it down on entering the pomerium nor to take it up again outside. The body also granted him more power in subject territory than the several governors possessed].* Dio is wrong if he meant that the Senate gave Augustus an *imperium*: he had already had it as proconsul of his province. That there was no break in his provincial command is proved by the fact that it was renewed at the end of the original ten years. What the Senate did was to modify that *imperium* in two

---

* Translated by H. B. Foster.

ways; by enacting that it should not lapse when Augustus re-entered the *pomerium* as did an ordinary proconsul's *imperium*, so that Augustus could when he wished attend to affairs in the capital, leaving his provinces to his legates, without having to have his *imperium* renewed each time; and secondly by making his *imperium maius* in relation to that of other proconsuls. This latter point has been the subject of infinite debate, and I have nothing new to say on it. I can only say that I do not rate Dio so low as to think he made up this clause, and that in my view some of the Cyrene edicts, and also an edict to Asia preserved by Josephus, display Augustus exercising a *maius imperium*. The opponents of the idea seem to me to be tilting against windmills. They transform a *maius imperium* whereby one proconsul's wish prevails over the wills of other proconsuls in case of a clash into the revolutionary *imperium* whereby the triumvirs claimed to appoint all magistrates and promagistrates and treat them as their delegates, and then quite truly assert that Augustus claimed no such power. The *maius imperium* was perhaps intended as some compensation for the loss of the vague overriding powers which Augustus may have been deemed to hold as consul, or may have been initially voted to enable Augustus to undertake the tour of the provinces upon which he did in fact next year embark.

Dio's statement that the *imperium* was granted once for all seems to conflict with his later statements that the provincial command was renewed for terms of five or ten years. Technically I think that Dio is correct. According to the Lex Cornelia de provinciis a proconsul held his *imperium* not for any fixed time, but 'quoad in urbem introisset'. The Senate had removed this limitation and Augustus' *imperium* became thereby perpetual. But the *imperium* without any *provincia* in which to exercise it was a tenuous conception—it was in fact merely the capacity to assume a *provincia* when assigned without waiting for a law conferring *imperium*. It could only be actualized by the grant of a *provincia*, and this was done from time to time so as to make Augustus perpetual proconsul. In my view from 23 Augustus was a proconsul exercising his *imperium* in the province assigned to him, but with power to exercise it in other provinces if he disagreed with their proconsuls.

As far as the provinces were concerned Augustus was thus placed by formal grant in the position which he had occupied hitherto in virtue of his undefined powers as consul. In Rome and Italy he had no *locus standi*. As this point is important, I had better elaborate it. A proconsul possessed *imperium* from the passing of his *lex curiata* (whether as consul, or, if he were a *privatus*, when his province was assigned to him) till he re-entered the city; but he could exercise his *imperium*, except by special authorization, only in his province. The later imperial lawyers are explicit on this point. As Ulpian says 'proconsul ubique quidem proconsularia insignia habet, statim atque urbem egressus est: potestatem autem non exercet nisi in ea provincia sola quae ei decreta est'. That this rule goes back to Sulla at any rate is indicated by Cicero's remark in the *in Pisonem*: 'mitto exire de provincia, educere exercitum, bellum sua sponte gerere, in regnum iniussu populi Romani aut senatus accedere, quam cum plurimae leges veteres, tum lex Cornelia maiestatis, Iulia de pecuniis repetundis planissime vetat.' There are two exceptions to this rule. A proconsul might exercise a jurisdiction 'non contentiosam sed voluntariam', e.g. manumit slaves, outside his province. Secondly, a proconsul on his way to or from his province might be authorized by the Senate to perform some particular task, as it was proposed that Verres should round up some insurgent slaves at Tempsa, and that Cicero should take charge of Sicily: it was sometimes more convenient to revive the dormant *imperium* of a passing proconsul than send someone with *imperium* from Rome. But such an exercise of *imperium* could, it would seem, be undertaken only 'iussu populi Romani aut senatus'.

To provide Augustus with a modest position in Rome the Senate, and no doubt the People, voted that he should possess *tribunicia potestas* for life. I believe this to have been the first occasion that the *tribunicia potestas* was granted to him, for the good reason that Augustus numbers his tenure of it from this year. It may also be noted that Augustus distinguishes a perpetual grant of *sacrosanctitas* from a grant of *tribunicia potestas* for life. Appian and Orosius must therefore be wrong in speaking of a grant of *tribunicia potestas* in 36, when Dio speaks only of *sacrosanctitas*. The additional rights which Augustus acquired with the full power of a tribune would have been those of *auxilium* and *intercessio*, the *ius agendi cum plebe*, and the *ius consulendi senatus*.

These powers were useful but neither very essential nor very adequate. The power of *intercessio* was very occasionally used by Tiberius and Nero to quash sentences by the Senate, but it was scarcely essential: on the rare occasion when a defiant magistrate flouted him he could surely have relied on one of the ten tribunes exercising his veto on his behalf. The *ius agendi cum plebe* Augustus himself used to put through some of his social legislation. But it was hardly necessary for him to be the formal mover: for the rare occasion when a law was called for he could always find an obliging consul, and in fact for several of his major social laws—the Lex Junia, the Lex Fufia Caninia, the Lex Aelia Sentia, the Lex Papia Poppaea—not to speak of the Lex Valeria Cornelia which remodelled the electoral procedure, and such minor measures as the Lex Quinctia de aquaeductibus, he did use the consuls. The *ius consulendi senatus* was more practically useful, but here also it was always possible to use the consuls,

and in point of fact it so happens that all the surviving *senatus consulta* of the reign were moved by the consuls. Moreover a tribune enjoyed a very low priority in summoning or consulting the Senate, which was hardly consonant with the dignity of Augustus, and from the very start he was accorded the special right of putting one question in each session even if not consul, and in the following year the special right of summoning the Senate when he wished: these rights are recorded in the Lex de imperio with others of a similar kind. It is to my mind suggestive that, when Tiberius on Augustus' death summoned the Senate by virtue of his *tribunicia potestas* (not yet possessing the special prerogatives), he explicitly stated, in a somewhat apologetic fashion, that he was using this power. This surely implies that Augustus had not normally so used it. Augustus in fact hardly needed to use his *tribunicia potestas* at all, since he could achieve the same ends by his *auctoritas* A formal veto was not needed when a hint would suffice: it was not necessary to make proposals to the Senate or the People when others acting on his advice would carry through his measures.

Yet Augustus made the tribunician power, as Tacitus puts it, 'summi fastigi vocabulum,' numbering the year of his reign by it and granting it most sparingly to his colleagues to mark them out as his potential successors. One reason why he did so was, no doubt, the very fact that it did convey so little power; by making it appear that his position rested on so harmless a prerogative he could conceal the real constitutional basis of his power. Another reason was, I suspect, that the tribunate was popular. We do not, I think, sufficiently appreciate the sentimental associations of the tribunate in the minds of the common people. In the optimate tradition, which we mainly hear, the tribunate was a baneful institution and the great tribunes were villains. But contrast Cicero writing for an upper class audience, and Cicero addressing the people: in his public speeches the Gracchi are heroes; and Caesar could find no better *casus belli* to inflame his troops with wrath than the violation of the tribunes. By posing as tribune of the *plebs* Augustus hoped to rally this popular sentiment for himself, and to represent that he occupied his high position 'ad tuendam plebem'. The assumption of the tribunician power was in short a gesture, and a gesture to two parties in the State. To the *plebs*, it was a guarantee—which as subsequent events proved they did not consider adequate—that Augustus was not abandoning them to the optimates, to the optimates a threat that Augustus might revive the popular tradition of his adoptive father if they would not play ball with him.

The text books usually represent the settlement of 23 B.C. as the final step, after which they all lived happily ever after. It was in fact the signal for a prolonged and violent agitation. In the following year there were riots, and Augustus was pressed to accept a dictatorship or a perpetual and annual consulship, and according to Dio a perpetual censorship and a *cura annonae* with sweeping powers like that given to Pompey in 57 B.C.; Augustus admits that he accepted a *cura annonae* as a temporary measure, and he had censors elected, which suggests that Dio is right in saying that the censorship was pressed upon him. After Augustus had left for the East, the people insisted on electing him consul for 21 B.C. and for long refused to fill the vacancy when he would not accept office. In 21 B.C. Agrippa was sent to Italy, and succeeded in getting a second consul elected for that year, and in arranging the consular elections for the next year. But after his departure, when the elections for 19 B.C. came on, the people again insisted on reserving one consulship for Augustus. The situation grew so serious that in the summer of 19 B.C. the Senate passed the SC *ultimum*, and the one consul begged Augustus to return, which he did on 12th

October: the Senate's relief was revealed by its sending a special delegation to meet him in Campania and voting an altar of Fortuna Redux.

These disturbances are of course susceptible of two explanations, and I think that there may be some truth in both. They would hardly have been so sustained unless there had been some popular feeling behind them, and it looks as if the populace took Augustus' resignation of the consulship very seriously, and feared that its champion was going to abandon his dominating position and that the anarchy of the Republic would begin again: the people, it seems, cared little for the constitution but wanted a strong man to rule. On the other hand Augustus was probably not ill pleased to prove to the constitutionalists that if he withdrew to his provinces and abandoned control of Rome to them, ruin would follow. In his nervousness in 23 he had jumped back further than he wanted; now he could step forward once more, and the Senate would be only too thankful to give him the necessary powers.

Dio says that these were consular powers for life—τὴν δὲ τῶν ὑπάτων (sc. ἐξουσίαν) διὰ βίου ἔλαβεν, ὥστε καὶ ταῖς δώδεκα ῥάβδοις ἀεὶ καὶ πανταχοῦ χρῆσθαι καὶ ἐν μέσῳ τῶν ἐὰι ὑπατευόντων ἐπὶ τοῦ ἀρχικοῦ δίφρου καθίζεσθαι [and he took the consular power for life so that he might use the twelve lictors always and everywhere and sit on the curule chair in the midst of the consuls of any year]. These words of Dio have been interpreted so that the consecutive clause defines and qualifies the opening sentence; that is, Augustus received so much of the consular *imperium* as consisted in the twelve lictors and the seat between the consuls. Dio's words will bear this interpretation, but other facts seem to me to indicate that he is right in assigning to Augustus from this date a consular *imperium* which was valid in Rome and Italy. The chief objection brought against this view is that Augustus never mentions such an *imperium* in his *Res Gestae* or his titulature. But this is rather naïve. Augustus may have told nothing but the truth, but he certainly did not feel it necessary to tell the whole truth. I challenge any impartial reader to find in the *Res Gestae* any allusion to the main basis of his power, his *imperium* in his own *provincia*. From the *Res Gestae* one would infer that Augustus had held many consulates and other honours and waged many wars, but never that for forty-one years continuously he had been proconsul of half the empire: that would not have looked well. And in his imperial titles similarly Augustus blazoned the number of his consulates and imperial salutations, the years of his tribunician power, and harmless offices and titles such as *pontifex maximus* and *pater patriae*, but never mentioned his proconsular *imperium*.

On the other hand there are many powers which Augustus exercised in Italy and even in Rome which could only be based on the *imperium*. And here I think that I must pause to draw a distinction between what could be done by *auctoritas* and what by *imperium*. By *auctoritas* Augustus could get many important things done: he could get a *senatus consultum* passed in the sense which he wished or he could get A and B elected consuls instead of C and D. But to give commands to soldiers and to exercise jurisdiction he required *imperium*; one could not say 'C. Seium gladio animadverti placet' in virtue of *auctoritas*. Now Augustus did command troops, the Praetorian cohorts, stationed in Italian towns, and the three Urban cohorts and the *vigiles* actually in the city. He exercised a civil and criminal jurisdiction within the city which Dio at any rate derives from the *imperium*. He exercised magisterial *coercitio* not only against actors, but also against a Roman knight, Ovid, whom he relegated to Tomi. He also apparently levied troops by conscription both in Italy and Rome. What is most significant he appointed a

praefectus urbi, a specifically consular prerogative, and delegated *imperium* within the city to him.

The chronology of the urban prefects is particularly interesting. Augustus first appointed a *praefectus urbi*, Messalla Corvinus, in 26 or 25 B.C. when he was consul, but had to be absent to look after his province. Between 22 and 19 he was again away but he appointed no *praefectus* and there seem to have been no troops available to keep order in Rome. All that Augustus did was to send Agrippa to Rome in 21, apparently without any official position. It is perhaps noteworthy that the attempt of the consuls to appoint a *praefectus urbi* for the Latin festival occasioned riots and had to be abandoned: the populace perhaps resented what looked like an attempt by the consuls to arrogate to themselves an appointment which the people wished Augustus to exercise. But when Augustus next left Rome in 16 B.C. he appointed a *praefectus urbi*, Statilius Taurus. By what power unless he now held a consular *imperium*? Another less striking but specifically consular prerogative which Augustus exercised in the latter part of his reign was that of receiving *professiones* (or making *nominationes*) for the consular and praetorian elections, concurrently with the consuls. Finally Augustus himself explicitly states that on two occasions he used a *consulare imperium* in Italy, to conduct the censuses of 8 B.C. and A.D. 14. This is generally explained away as an *ad hoc* grant, but such an explanation is most implausible. If special powers had to be voted to him, it would have been more economical and more modest to ask for a *censoria potestas*: a *consulare imperium* was a very heavy tool for the conduct of a census, which needed no *imperium* at all. If on the other hand Augustus possessed a consular *imperium* already, it was natural that he should use it for conducting his censuses, instead of applying for special powers.

What precise form the enactment of

19 B.C. took it is scarcely possible to say. I find it rather difficult to believe what Dio appears to say, that Augustus received a consular *imperium* in addition to his existing *imperium* in provinces. It would seem more plausible that the Senate declared Augustus' *imperium* to be equal to that of the consuls, thus releasing it from its territorial limitations. The titles given to the *imperium* are not very helpful in solving this question. The *imperium* in Italy was in Augustus' day called consular, as Augustus himself testifies; but so, no doubt, as Pelham has argued, was the *imperium* which Augustus held *pro consule* in the provinces. By Claudius' day terminology seems to have changed, if Tacitus is accurate in saying that the young Nero was in 51 granted 'proconsulare imperium extra urbem'. This phrase implies that Claudius' *imperium* (which presumably would have been valid *intra urbem* also) was deemed to be proconsular not only in the provinces, but in Italy. And indeed Claudius seems to have thought that his position was not quite that of a consul when he asked for ὑπάτου τινὰ ἐξουσίαν [consular power] to celebrate his triumphal games. For what it is worth I think that this evidence suggests that the emperors possessed one *imperium* only which was earlier called consular, later proconsular. But whatever the technicalities it seems to me clear that from 19 B.C. Augustus exercised his *imperium* not only in his own provinces, and when occasion arose in the public provinces, but also in Italy and Rome itself.

Augustus shared his *imperium* with various colleagues from time to time, but not, it would appear, his *imperium* over Italy. Agrippa's position in 23–13 B.C. is a well-known tangle; it is perhaps sufficient for my purpose to note that he exercised his *imperium* in Gaul and Spain, and in the eastern provinces, but that in Italy, where he was in 21, his position seems to have been unofficial. In 13 B.C. his *imperium* was renewed and is explicitly stated to

have been *maius* outside Italy (μεῖζον αὐτῷ τῶν ἑκασταχόθι ἔξω τῆς Ἰταλίας ἀρχόντων ἰσχῦσα: ἐπιτρέψας) [greater powers than officials outside of Italy exercised]. For Augustus' later colleagues no very clear evidence exists until we come to the renewal of Tiberius' powers in A.D. 13. On this occasion our authorities imply that Tiberius was granted a position more nearly equal to Augustus than any colleague had hitherto enjoyed, 'ut aequum ei ius in omnibus provinciis exercitibusque esset quam erat ipsi' [that he should have in all provinces and armies a power equal to his own] according to Velleius; according to Suetonius, 'ut provincias cum Augusto communiter administraret, simulque censum ageret' [that he should govern the provinces jointly with Augustus and hold the census with him]. But even now nothing is said of Italy, and it is indeed implicitly excluded by the special powers granted to Tiberius to hold the census concurrently with Augustus.

This circumstance may explain the awkward situation which arose on Augustus' death. I find Tacitus' narrative very confusing, and I doubt whether he grasped the niceties of the constitutional position. He seems for instance to regard Tiberius' action in continuing to issue orders to the provincial armies as illegal. On the generally accepted view, on the other hand, no problem would have presented itself at all. Except for a few ornamental offices and titles, like *pontifex maximus*, *Augustus* and *pater patriae*, and a few minor powers, like the special right to convoke and consult the Senate, Tiberius would have stood in precisely the same position as Augustus without any further ado. If my view is correct, however, Tiberius was back where Augustus had been in 23 B.C.; he had command over his provinces and their armies and a *maius imperium* over other proconsuls, but in Italy he had only the tribunician power, which he used to summon the Senate. His assumption of command over the

Praetorian and Urban cohorts was probably *ultra vires*, but what else could he do? And it would seem that the office of prae-fect of the city temporarily lapsed, since the magistracy which had delegated the *imperium* to it had disappeared. This would explain the well-known puzzle of Lucius Piso, who is stated to have served as prefect of the city for twenty years down to his death in A.D. 32, but in A.D. 14 is conspicuously absent from the group of high officials who take the oath.

The general picture that I would draw of the reign is then that after the restoration of the Republic it falls into three phases. In the first Augustus attempted too blatant an exhibition of power; checked by the fear of assassination he next made a sharp retreat, and let the Senate realize that they could not do without his guiding hand in Rome; in the third he recovered, but in a less obtrusive form, much of the same power that he had possessed before 23 B.C.

8. THE EVOLUTION OF AUGUSTUS' PRINCIPATE*

It is now some thirty years or so since the publication by Ramsay and von Premerstein of the fragments of the *Res Gestae* from Pisidian Antioch touched off a fresh and somewhat feverish reappraisal of the constitutional position of Augustus in which a wide variety of opinions, some sound, some subtle, some silly, were advanced. All scholars continued to agree, of course, that his was a position of supremacy; but they were certainly far from being unanimous about the way that his position of supremacy was maintained. Today, one generation of scholars and one bimillenary celebration later, it is perhaps possible to discern what has emerged from the flurry of speculation.

One thing appears to have become clear. Most scholars today are of the opinion that, even though there may have been extra-legal aspects to Augustus' authority, that does not mean he therefore lacked a solid juristic basis for his power. This is a development to be welcomed. The rejection of Mommsen's legalistic approach has at times been carried to luxuriant and even ludicrous lengths during the past quarter of a century, and it is not surprising if a reaction should

now have set in. Nor is this all. It is likewise usually conceded today that the juristic basis for Augustus' power was built up gradually. More than one so-called settle-ment proved necessary. There was, in fact, an evolution, and it is with that evolution that this paper deals.

We need not go further back than 28 B.C. Augustus' career before that date would appear to be largely irrelevant to this inquiry, since we have the Princeps' own implied admission that until that year his behaviour had not been "constitu-tional". We shall begin then with the "settlement" of 27 B.C. It was in 28/27 B.C., whether because of the memory of the Ides of March, or because of his need of senatorial cooperation, or (more probably) because of his distaste for the role of arbitrary despot, that Augustus made his first serious effort to regularize his position in the State. As he himself puts it: *in consulatu sexto et septimo ... rem publican ex mea potestate in senatus populique Romani arbitrium transtuli* [in my sixth and seventh consulships ... I transferred the state from my own power to the control of the senate and Roman people].

This was the famous occasion when, in the words of documents that are more or less official and more or less contemporary, *rem publicam restituit*. Now this expression can hardly mean: "He restored the

* E. T. Salmon, "The Evolution of Augustus' Principate," *Historia* 6 (Wiesbaden: Franz Steiner Verlag, 1956), pp. 456–459; 470–478. Reprinted by permission of the publisher.

Republic", a thing which he most certainly did not do. The expression *res publica*, of course, does not necessarily mean what we mean by the word "republic": Béranger has recently reminded us that a monarchy could be described as a *res publica*. Augustus' view would appear to be that, during the days of revolution, the *res publica* had to all intents and purposes become the *res privata* of military adventurers, a condition of affairs which he had proceeded to cure by applying a homoeopathic remedy. Augustus makes this clear at the very beginning of the *Res Gestae*: *exercitum* privato *consilio et* privata *impensa comparavi per quem rem publicam a dominatione factionis oppressam in libertatem vindicavi* [on my own initiative and at my own expense, I raised an army by means of which I liberated the Republic, which was oppressed by the tyranny of a faction]. In other words, it was thanks to his private exertion and his private expense that the State had ceased to be virtually a *res privata* and had become a *res publica* again. This must be what is meant by *rem publicam restituit*, a much better translation for which would be: "He restored constitutional government". Now, constitutional government is not necessarily republican government, and the Senate and People did not revive a republican constitution for the *res publica* which Augustus had reestablished. They permitted him, the People with enthusiasm, the Senate much more grudgingly, to fashion a new, monarchical form of government.

The evidence for Augustus' determination to be the monarch is clear and it is contemporary. Nicolaus Damascenus, who was personally acquainted with the Princeps, implies in the surviving fragments of his *Life of Caesar* that well before 31 B.C. Augustus had already made up his mind to be master of the State. Strabo, like Nicolaus, an exact contemporary, also has no doubts about Augustus' fixed monarchical intentions. The appeals, which

the exiled Ovid addresses to Augustus *ad nauseam*, are the appeals of a subject to his monarch. Above all, there are the recorded words of Augustus himself. The *Res Gestae*, as Westermann pointed out years ago, reveal Augustus' monarchical outlook: it is significant that the only persons actually mentioned by name in that document as achieving memorable exploits are either the monarch himself or his intended successors in the position: viz. Augustus himself, Agrippa, Marcellus, Gaius, Lucius, Tiberius. No less revealing is the letter written by Augustus to his grandson Gaius in A.D. 1, in which he calls his position in the State his *statio*: this military expression was commonly used to describe the position of Plato's philosopher-king. Then, too, one can adduce the famous edict which Augustus issued, possibly in 23 B.C. although the year is uncertain: *ita mihi salvam ac sospitem rem publicam sitere in sua sede liceat atque eius rei fructum percipere quem peto ut optimi status auctor dicar et moriens ut feram mecum spem mansura in vestigio suo fundamenta rei publicae quae iecero* [may it be my privilege to establish the State in a firm and secure position, and reap from that act the fruit that I desire; but only if I may be called the author of the best possible government, and bear with me the hope that when I die the foundations which I have laid for the State will remain unshaken]. Surely, if these words mean anything, they mean that Augustus, so far from claiming to have restored the old Republic, is insisting that he has devised a completely new and (he hopes) lasting type of government.

But even though Augustus' aim from the very outset was simply to remain master of the State and never surrender his firm control of it, we must not therefore assume that he also from the very outset had a precise and clearcut programme, complete in all its details, for achieving that aim. It is much more probable that his policy, in the immemorial tradition of his countrymen, was one of opportunism. His object being simply not to lose power, he just took whatever measures seemed necessary to that end from time to time. As problems arose he devised solutions for them; and his own final resulting position in the State was much more the result of piecemeal construction than of doctrinaire planning.

[Analyses of the settlements of 27 and 23 B.C. follow.]

* * *

So long as he was out of Italy it mattered little to Augustus that his Tribunician Power did not fully compensate for his relinquished consulship. But once he got back to Rome, another "settlement" would be required. He returned in 19 B.C., and by then he was, of course, no longer consul and, in addition, his proconsular *imperium* was not supposed to be wielded in Italy. True, when this *imperium* had been made *maius* in 23 B.C. the stipulation had been added that it was not to lapse in Italy or even inside the *pomerium*; but that does not mean that Augustus took the "unconstitutional" step of actually making it the legal basis for his authority there; it merely means that he was relieved of the tiresome formality of getting his *imperium* renewed each time he moved out of the city.

The Tribunician Power, although it evidently provided some constitutional sanction for his position in Italy, or more accurately perhaps in Rome itself, was, as we have seen, not a complete or exact substitute for the consulship. The powers of a tribune were largely negative, those of a consul largely positive. Occasions and circumstances might conceivably arise in Rome and Italy which were outside the scope of his Tribunician Power. This had, in fact, been drastically demonstrated from the moment Augustus vacated the consulship. The year 22 B.C., the first

year since 32 B.C. that he had been without the office, had happened to coincide with a food shortage in Rome and the urban mob promptly rioted, demanding that he be named dictator. He declined to accept so dangerous a distinction but quietened the uproar for the time being by reluctantly consenting to become commissioner of the grain supply. When, however, after his departure from Rome in that same year the consular elections were staged and he was not a candidate, riots broke out again. The senatorial nobility might resent his monopolization of the consulship, the *plebs urbana* evidently held other views: they wanted him to accept a consulship that, like his Tribunician Power, would be both perpetual and annual. Augustus sent Agrippa to restore order in the city, but Agrippa found his task no easy one: he had the greatest difficulty, in Dio's phraseology, in checking the ailments that were still festering, possibly because the legal and constitutional basis of his authority in Rome was not clear. Exactly what status Agrippa enjoyed during Augustus' absence from the capital, other than that of son-in-law to the Princeps, cannot be determined. Gardthausen's suggestion that he was Prefect of the City seems to be refuted by Dio; and it might also be pointed out incidentally that Augustus, being no longer consul, could not legally have appointed Agrippa as such, although no doubt he could have "induced" one of the consuls to name Agrippa to the post.

Actually Augustus' return in 19 B.C. was somewhat hastened by the urban disturbances, which in itself would be enough to induce him, once back, to think about ways and means for preventing a repetition of such incidents. The Tribunician Power by itself clearly was not enough. It did not empower him to appoint a Prefect of the City to keep order while he was away; it did not enable him to preside in person at the consular elections, which is precisely where the worst rioting had occurred; and it did not permit him, strictly speaking, to exercise jurisdictional functions, a restriction which he had evidently found irksome in 22 B.C. It is therefore not surprising to learn that in 19 B.C. Augustus acquired what Dio calls "the power of the consuls". Dio's statement has, of course, been challenged, and it is in fact rather carelessly worded. It is not, however, the vagueness of its verbiage but rather the fact that (like so much else in Dio) it is entirely unsupported by any other ancient writer that has rendered it suspect. Yet what Dio says on this occasion is surely, in view of the circumstances existing at the time, by no means incredible. Even the vagueness of his language, so far from telling against him, might be regarded as corroborative. For it seems likely that in 19 B.C. what Augustus obtained was not the *consulare imperium*, much less a lifetime consulship, but merely some of the consul's prerogatives, just as he had already done in 23 B.C. A lifetime consulship is ruled out by Augustus' own explicit denial. As for an authentic *consulare imperium*, it surely would have left more abundant traces in the literary tradition; it would have been bound to excite comment; the spectacle of a Princeps with consular *imperium* alongside the two regular consuls almost inevitably would have been productive of sardonic remarks about the third consul, the consuls' colleague and the like, and these would have found some reflection in the literature of the period. If Augustus in 19 B.C. merely supplemented those prerogatives of a consul which he already had with some additional ones, viz. with those that he felt he needed, then not only would he be behaving like his usual self, but Dio's lack of preciseness would also receive some explanation. Hence I suggest that in 19 B.C. Augustus was authorized to discharge some of the functions and to enjoy certain of the privileges that normally belonged to the consuls. We cannot say definitely which they were: Dio mentions the right to have twelve *fasces* permanently

and to occupy a curule chair between the two consuls; but to these we can confidently add the right to appoint the Prefect of the City and possibly other rights as well.

It is commonly thought that as a result of the "settlements" of 27, 23 and 19 B.C. the Augustan Principate had virtually reached its final form; and some colour is lent to this view by the fact that the Secular Games were staged shortly afterwards, in 17 B.C., as if in celebration of a firmly consolidated New Age. Yet, in fact, the evolutionary process had not yet reached its end. Augustus would indeed by now appear to have provided for most, if not all, contingencies; and yet circumstances could still arise, even after 19 B.C., calling for special measures and possibly for the granting of special powers.

Something of the sort occurred in 8 B.C. In that year, so Augustus tells us, he conducted a census of the Roman People *consulari cum imperio*. Now, throughout his regime Augustus refused to accept the actual office of censor, either temporarily or permanently, although it was pressed upon him: possibly he remembered that traditionally the censors were regarded as holding a whiphand over the Senate and he wished to avoid the imputation that he was dragooning that select body. One result of this was that he had difficulty in discovering the most suitable method for performing the functions which under the Republic had been carried out by the censors: the experiments he conducted in connection with *lectiones senatus* will be remembered. This, however, hardly explains why he found it necessary to assume a *consulare imperium* in order to conduct a census of the People in 8 B.C. Jones is certainly right in insisting that "a *consulare imperium* was a very heavy tool for the conduct of a census, which needed no *imperium* at all". The explanation should probably be sought, as usual, in the necessities of the moment. We ought to look at the contemporary military situation. In 8 B.C. Roman armies had been heavily engaged for a number of years along the northern frontier under the command of Augustus' stepsons, Tiberius and Drusus. Drusus indeed had died on active service in the area in 9 B.C., and Augustus felt it necessary to be present there in person in the very year that we are discussing, 8 B.C. These Rhineland operations must have imposed demands on Rome's military manpower. Accordingly one may suspect that the census of 8 B.C. had more in view than a mere counting of heads. If it was accompanied by the levying of troops, then the use of the *imperium* by Augustus is adequately accounted for, since one who enrolled troops had to be a holder of *imperium*. A similar explanation suggests itself even more spontaneously for the other occasion when Augustus conducted a census with *consulare imperium*. This was in A.D. 14 in the difficult years immediately following the Pannonian revolt and the loss of Varus' three legions in the Teutoburg Forest, when we know that strenuous efforts were being made to bring the army up to strength.

There were also other occasions after 19 B.C. when Augustus pursued his customary opportunist policy of adopting such measures as seemed necessary. I would direct attention to the years 5 and 2 B.C. in each of which he briefly held the consulship. One purpose of these, respectively his twelfth and thirteenth, consulships was no doubt to launch his grandsons, Gaius and Lucius, into public life with fitting dignity and ceremony. But he may also have had another motive. Pelham almost three quarters of a century ago directed attention to Augustus' penchant for synchronizing certain of his activities. In particular, his discharge of duties which had been performed by the censors in the days of the Republic regularly occurred in the years when his proconsular *imperium* came up for renewal. The years 5 and 2 B.C. appear to provide examples of similar behaviour on Augustus' part. In those years the introduction of the young Caesars to public life did indeed take place. But simultaneously something happened to the consulship.

It will be remembered that in Augustus' later years the duration of the consulship was first shortened and then ultimately stabilized at six months. The reason for this, I suggest, is made clear by a development which has been recently emphasized by Birley. He has demonstrated that the number of senators in the service of the Princeps was always comparatively small: at no time apparently were as many as fifty percent of the Senate able or willing to accept appointments. Now, Augustus could increase the supply of qualified men by shortening the consulship, and he could increase the supply of willing men by tightening his control over the elections; and it looks as if he took both steps in 5 B.C., the year of his twelfth consulship. The evidence collated by Degrassi indicates that it was in that year that a consulship of less than twelve months became the regular rule. And the Tabula Hebana found in Etruria in 1947 reveals that, in addition, a method was devised for ensuring that those appointed to the office should include men, *novi homines* if necessary, who were willing to serve the Princeps. This famous inscription discloses that, well before the death of Augustus, elections in the Centuriate Assembly itself had become a formality to a large extent: consuls, and praetors also, were regularly "designated' by ten special centuries composed of senators and judiciary *equites* taken from thirty-three of the thirty-five tribes. This was the procedure known as *destinatio*. When it was first introduced the Tabula Hebana does not say, and the literary sources, apart from such hints as those in Pliny's Panegyricus, are completely silent about it. The Tabula does reveal that the ten designating centuries were named after Gaius and Lucius Caesar in A.D. 5, but that does not prove that it was then that they were first used as an electoral college. Tibiletti is inclined to date *destinatio* from 27 B.C., but this is implicitly denied by Suetonius and, as Last points out, the year of the "restoration of the Republic" is hardly indicated as the year for so momentous a change. Moreover the necessity to take measures against electoral bribery in 18 B.C. and even as late as 8 B.C. makes it improbable that *destinatio* was being used then, since candidates presumably would not waste money on bribes for a foregone conclusion. Augustus himself, however, tells us that the Senate played a part in "designating" Gaius Caesar as consul in 5 B.C., and unless Jones, like Mommsen before him, is right in thinking that the Senate's role was merely to grant the youthful Gaius dispensation from the regulation concerning the age of candidates, this will be an instance, in fact the earliest recorded instance, of *destinatio*.

And it may well be the earliest actual instance. Shortly before 13 B.C. the vigintivirate had been made a regular step in the senatorial *cursus honorum*. Now it was from the ranks of the vigintiviri that the Princeps recruited the bright young men for his service. By 5 B.C. a crop of them would be ready for the praetorship; yet, in view of the domination which the *nobiles* appear to have exercised over elections in the Comitia Centuriata in Augustus' middle years, their chances of election to the higher magistracies if they were *novi homines* would be small. *Destinatio*, therefore, may have been introduced for their benefit. It may have been first used in 5 B.C. in order to ensure the election to the praetorship of *novi homines* who as vigintiviri some eight years earlier had demonstrated their eagerness as well as their fitness to serve the Princeps. If that were the case we might expect *novi homines* to make their appearance in the

consular *fasti* some eight or nine years later. And in fact they do: *novi homines* becomes common, beginning with A.D. 4. Moreover if *destinatio* was used in the first instance to "designate" no less a person than Gaius, the grandson of the Princeps, then the practice would automatically acquire some respectability. In addition it might explain why it was only after the death of Gaius in A.D. 4, and not after the death of his brother Lucius, two years earlier, that the device of naming the nominating centuries after the young Caesars was adopted. Thus it looks as if Augustus became consul in 5 B.C. in order to confer dignity on the curtailed consulship and in order simultaneously to emphasize his personal interest in a notable electoral reform.

The year of Augustus' thirteenth consulship, 2 B.C., was also a significant year; indeed from the constitutional standpoint it was an exceptionally significant year. If we once again pay heed to the evidence collated by Degrassi, it would appear that it was in 2 B.C. that the shortened consulship was made of specifically six months duration, with *consules ordinarii* assuming office on 1 January and *consules suffecti* on 1 July. It was likewise in 2 B.C. that Augustus was officially named Pater Patriae. This title, of course, is always regarded as purely honorific; and as a matter of fact it did not make any very precise or specific addition to the positive powers of the Princeps. Yet Augustus himself evidently attached the highest importance to it: he brings the *Res Gestae* to an end with his citation as Pater Patriae. Readers of that document are thus left with the impression that Augustus reached the culminating point, the peak and pinnacle of his career when the Senate, the Equestrian Order and the Roman People named him Pater Patriae in 2 B.C. It seems to me that, if scholars are determined to find some basis other than the *imperium* for Augustus' authority, they would do better to scrutinize the last chapter of the *Res Gestae* than the penultimate one. At any rate Augustus himself seems inclined to stress his title of Pater Patriae more than his *auctoritas*. The implications of the title suggest the reason why. Just as a family is in the *potestas* of the *pater familias*, so is the State in the *potestas* of the *pater patriae*. If any title or honour divulges Augustus' monarchical status it is this one. And if it was in 2 B.C. that his *patria potestas* was openly recognized as embracing the whole State, then that year ought perhaps to be regarded as the one when Augustus' Principate had evolved into its final form. Nor is it difficult to guess why Augustus chose that particular year to announce that his position of absolute authority in the State, resembling that of a father in his household, could now be regarded as finally settled. It was because he wished to have everything regularized and in order before the beginning of the year that he regarded as his "grand climacteric". Suetonius insists at some length that Augustus was a superstitious man, and Augustus himself has recorded his belief that his sixty-third year, in other words the year 1 B.C., would be the critical one for him, the one which might witness his passing. Hence his determination to have the position of the Princeps fully fashioned by 2 B.C.

Augustus had not indeed fashioned it suddenly or overnight. He had preferred the evolutionary method, largely because as a *circumspectissimus et prudentissimus princeps* he was disposed to take steps only when they were needed. In part, too, he may have avoided haste out of a desire to accommodate to his new system the

practices and traditions of the old for which he had so genuine a regard: not for nothing does he insist that he acted *maiorum nostrorum exemplo*. And yet another factor making for gradualness was possibly his habit of consultation with others; for, as Crook has recently remarked, "the Romans had an immemorial tradition that men in positions of responsibility should not take decisions alone", and we may be sure that in his scrupulous respect for other traditions, Augustus did not ride roughshod over this one. Dio's famous picture of him seeking the advice of Agrippa and Maecenas is no doubt fictitious, but the state of affairs which it implies surely must be accepted as fact. We know, indeed, that Augustus consulted with Agrippa on matters military, and there are good grounds for believing that he sought his counsel, and that of others as well, on other matters too. The summit, however, is a lonely place. In the last analysis the responsibility for fashioning the new form of government must have rested with him and not with his aides. As he proudly remarks, he surpassed all in *auctoritas*; surely he then was the *auctor* of the *optimi status*, of the system we call the Principate.

Like Augustus himself, I suggest that it was in 2 B.C. rather than in 19 B.C. that that system achieved its true and authentic form. From that year onwards Augustus was not only the monarch in fact but owing to his title of Pater Patriae could almost be described as to all intents and purposes the monarch in name. And so it is with that year that we can appropriately draw this study of the evolution of Augustus' Principate to a close.

SECTION XI

The Character of Domitian and the Judgment of Tacitus

To a remarkable degree, our picture of the Roman Principate in the first century is shaped by Tacitus. Although we have other accounts, we are most impressed by the literary genius and the powerful convictions of this historian. Recent scholarship has called his judgment and reliability into question. His scope of interest has been called too narrow, his concern for detailed accuracy insufficient, his prejudice against the emperors obsessive. The reign of Tiberius is the one most thoroughly treated by Tacitus. It would take more space than is available to deal with it properly here but another interesting test case is available. Tacitus' treatment of Domitian is every bit as hostile as his account of Tiberius. Better still, Tacitus knew and served under Domitian as did his father-in-law, Agricola. We can form the best opinion of the reliability of Tacitus as a historian from his account of the relationship of Agricola to Domitian. The evidence was directly available to the historian and we are able to check his picture of the emperor against two other versions. What sort of a man was Domitian? Did he treat Agricola properly? Does Tacitus distort the truth? What is the nature and source of his bias?

1. Domitian and Agricola*

Agricola was governor of Britain under Domitian. In the passages preceding the following selection, Tacitus has described Agricola's spectacularly successful efforts at the pacification of that province.

Of this series of events, though not exaggerated in the despatches of Agricola

---

* Tacitus, *Agricola*, 39–46, translated by A. J. Church and W. J. Brodribb.

by any boastfulness of language, Domitian heard, as was his wont, with joy in his face but anxiety in his heart. He felt conscious that all men laughed at his late mock triumph over Germany, for which there had been purchased from traders people whose dress and hair might be made to resemble those of captives, whereas now a real and splendid victory, with the destruction of thousands of the enemy, was being celebrated with just applause. It was, he thought, a very alarming thing for him that the name of a subject should be raised above that of the Emperor; it was to no purpose that he had driven into obscurity the pursuit of forensic eloquence and the graceful accomplishments of civil life, if another were to forestall the distinctions of war. To other glories he could more easily shut his eyes, but the greatness of a good general was a truly imperial quality. Harassed by these anxieties, and absorbed in an incommunicable trouble, a sure prognostic of some cruel purpose, he decided that it was best for the present to suspend his hatred until the freshness of Agricola's renown and his popularity with the army should begin to pass away.

For Agricola was still the governor of Britain. Accordingly the Emperor ordered that the usual triumphal decorations, the honour of a laurelled statue, and all that is commonly given in place of the triumphal procession, with the addition of many laudatory expressions, should be decreed in the senate, together with a hint to the effect that Agricola was to have the province of Syria, then vacant by the death of Atilius Rufus, a man of consular rank, and generally reserved for men of distinction. It was believed by many persons that one of the freedmen employed on confidential services was sent to Agricola, bearing a despatch in which Syria was offered him, and with instructions to deliver it should he be in Britain; that this freedman in crossing the straits met Agricola, and without even saluting him made his way back to Domitian; though I cannot say whether the story is true, or is only a fiction invented to suit the Emperor's character.

Meanwhile Agricola had handed over his province in peace and safety to his successor. And not to make his entrance into Rome conspicuous by the concourse of welcoming throngs, he avoided the attentions of his friends by entering the city at night, and at night too, according to orders, proceeded to the palace, where, having been received with a hurried embrace and without a word being spoken, he mingled in the crowd of courtiers. Anxious henceforth to temper the military renown, which annoys men of peace, with other merits, he studiously cultivated retirement and leisure, simple in dress, courteous in conversation, and never accompanied but by one or two friends, so that the many who commonly judge of great men by their external grandeur, after having seen and attentively surveyed him, asked the secret of a greatness which but few could explain.

During this time he was frequently accused before Domitian in his absence, and in his absence acquitted. The cause of his danger lay not in any crime, nor in any complaint of injury, but in a ruler who was the foe of virtue, in his own renown, and in that worst class of enemies—the men who praise. And then followed such days for the commonwealth as would not suffer Agricola to be forgotten; days when so many of our armies were lost in Mœsia, Dacia, Germany, and Pannonia, through the rashness or cowardice of our generals, when so many of our officers were besieged and captured with so many of our auxiliaries, when it was no longer the boundaries of empire and the banks of rivers which were imperilled, but the winter-quarters of our legions and the possession of our territories. And so when disaster followed upon disaster, and the entire year was marked by destruction and slaughter, the voice of the people called Agricola to the command; for they all contrasted his vigour, firmness, and experience in war, with the inertness and timidity of other generals. This talk, it is quite certain, assailed the ears of the Emperor himself, while affection and loyalty in the best of his freedmen, malice and envy in the worst, kindled the anger of a prince ever inclined to evil. And so at once, by his own excellences and by the faults of others, Agricola was hurried headlong to a perilous elevation.

The year had now arrived in which the pro-consulate of Asia or Africa was to fall to him by lot, and, as Civica had been lately murdered, Agricola did not want a warning, or Domitian a precedent. Persons well acquainted with the Emperor's feelings came to ask Agricola, as if on their own account, whether he would go. First they hinted their purpose by praises of tranquillity and leisure; then offered their services in procuring acceptance for his excuses; and at last, throwing off all disguise, brought him by entreaties and threats to Domitian. The Emperor, armed beforehand with hypocrisy, and assuming a haughty demeanour, listened to his prayer that he might be excused, and having granted his request allowed himself to be formally thanked, nor blushed to grant so sinister a favour. But the salary usually granted to a pro-consul, and which he had himself given to some governors, he did not bestow on Agricola, either because he was offended at its not having been asked, or was warned by his conscience that he might be thought to have purchased the refusal which he had commanded. It is, indeed, human nature to hate the man whom you have injured; yet the Emperor, notwithstanding his irascible temper and an implacability proportioned to his reserve, was softened by the moderation and prudence of Agricola, who neither by a perverse obstinacy nor an idle parade of freedom challenged fame or provoked his fate. Let it be known to those whose habit it is to admire the disregard of authority, that there may be great men even under bad emperors, and that obedience and submission, when joined to activity and vigour, may attain a glory which most men reach only by a perilous career, utterly useless to the state, and closed by an ostentatious death.

The end of his life, a deplorable calamity to us and a grief to his friends, was regarded with concern even by strangers and those who knew him not. The common people and this busy population continually inquired at his house, and talked of him in public places and in private gatherings. No man when he heard of Agricola's death could either be glad or at once forget it. Men's sympathy was increased by a prevalent rumour that he was destroyed by poison. For myself, I have nothing which I should venture to state for fact. Certainly during the whole of his illness the Emperor's chief freedmen and confidential physicians came more frequently than is usual with a court which pays its visits by means of messengers. This was, perhaps, solicitude, perhaps espionage. Certain it is, that on the last day the very agonies of his dying moments were reported by a succession of couriers, and no one believed that there would be such haste about tidings which would be heard with regret. Yet in his manner and countenance the Emperor displayed some signs of sorrow, for he could now forget his enmity, and it was easier to conceal his joy than his fear. It was well known that on reading the will, in which he was named co-heir with Agricola's excellent wife and most dutiful daughter, he expressed delight, as if it had been a complimentary choice. So blinded and perverted was his mind by incessant flattery, that he did not know that it was only a bad Emperor whom a good father would make his heir.

Agricola was born on the 13th of June, in the third consulate of Caius Cæsar; he died on the 23rd of August, during the consulate of Collega and Priscus, being in the fifty-sixth year of his age. Should posterity wish to know something of his appearance, it was graceful rather than commanding. There was nothing formidable in his appearance; a gracious look predominated. One would easily believe him a good man, and willingly believe him to be great. As for himself, though taken from us in the prime of a vigorous manhood, yet, as far as glory is concerned, his life was of the longest. Those true blessings, indeed, which consist in virtue, he had fully attained; and on one who had reached the honours of a consulate and a triumph, what more had fortune to bestow? Immense wealth had no attractions for him, and wealth he had, even to splendour. As his daughter and his wife survived him, it may be thought that he was even fortunate—fortunate, in that while his honours had suffered no eclipse, while his fame was at its height, while his kindred and his friends still prospered, he escaped from the evil to come. For, though to survive until the dawn of this most happy age and to see a Trajan on the throne was what he would speculate upon in previsions and wishes confided to my ears, yet he had this mighty compensation for his premature death, that he was spared those later years during which Domitian, leaving now no interval or breathing space of time, but, as it were, with one continuous blow, drained the life-blood of the Commonwealth.

Agricola did not see the senate-house besieged, or the senate hemmed in by armed men, or so many of our consulars falling at one single massacre, or so many of Rome's noblest ladies exiles and fugitives. Carus Metius had as yet the distinction of but one victory, and the noisy counsels of Messalinus were not heard beyond the walls of Alba, and Massa Bæbius was then answering for his life. It was not long before our hands dragged Helvidius to prison, before we gazed on the dying looks of Manricus and Rusticus, before we were steeped in Senecio's innocent blood. Even Nero turned his eyes away, and did not gaze upon the atrocities which he ordered;

with Domitian it was the chief part of our miseries to see and to be seen, to know that our sighs were being recorded, to have, ever ready to note the pallid looks of so many faces, that savage countenance reddened with the hue with which he defied shame.

Thou wast indeed fortunate, Agricola, not only in the splendour of thy life, but in the opportune moment of thy death. Thou submittedst to thy fate, so they tell us who were present to hear thy last words, with courage and cheerfulness, seeming to be doing all thou couldst to give thine Emperor full acquittal. As for me and thy daughter, besides all the bitterness of a father's loss, it increases our sorrow that it was not permitted to watch over thy failing health, to comfort thy weakness, to satisfy ourselves with those looks, those embraces. Assuredly we should have received some precepts, some utterances to fix in our inmost hearts. This is the bitterness of our sorrow, this the smart of our wound, that from the circumstance of so long an absence thou wast lost to us four years before. Doubtless, best of fathers, with that most loving wife at thy side, all the dues of affection were abundantly paid thee, yet with too few tears thou wast laid to thy rest, and in the light of thy last day there was something for which thine eyes longed in vain.

If there is any dwelling-place for the spirits of the just; if, as the wise believe, noble souls do not perish with the body, rest thou in peace; and call us, thy family, from weak regrets and womanish laments to the contemplation of thy virtues, for which we must not weep nor beat the breast. Let us honour thee not so much with transitory praises as with our reverence, and, if our powers permit us, with our emulation. That will be true respect, that the true affection of thy nearest kin. This, too, is what I would enjoin on daughter and wife, to honour the memory of that father, that husband, by pondering in their hearts all his words and acts, by cherishing the features and lineaments of his character rather than those of his person. It is not that I would forbid the likenesses which are wrought in marble or in bronze; but as the faces of men, so all similitudes of the face are weak and perishable things, while the fashion of the soul is everlasting, such as may be expressed not in some foreign substance, or by the help of art, but in our own lives. Whatever we loved, whatever we admired in Agricola, survives, and will survive in the hearts of men, in the succession of the ages, in the fame that waits on noble deeds. Over many indeed, of those who have gone before, as over the inglorious and ignoble, the waves of oblivion will roll; Agricola, made known to posterity by history and tradition, will live for ever.

2. Dio's Domitian*

Domitian was both bold and passionate, both treacherous and given to dissembling. Hence, from these two characteristics, rashness on the one hand and craftiness on the other, he did much harm, falling upon some persons with the swiftness of a thunderbolt and damaging others by carefully prepared plots. The divinity that he chiefly revered was Minerva, so that he was wont to celebrate the Panathenæa on a magnificent scale: on this occasion he had contests of poets and chroniclers and gladiators almost every year at Albanum. This district, situated below the Alban Mount, from which it was named, he had set apart as a kind of acropolis. He had no genuine affection for any human being save a few women, but he always pretended to love the person whom at any time he was most determined to slay. He could not be relied upon even by those who did him some favor or helped him in his most revolting crimes, for whenever any persons furnished him with large sums of money or lodged information against numbers of men, he was sure to destroy these benefactors, being especially careful to do so in the case of slaves who had given information against their masters. [Accordingly, such individuals, though they received money and honors and offices all at once from him, lived in no greater honor and security than other men. The very offences to which they had been urged by Domitian commonly were made pretexts for their destruction, the emperor's object being to have the actual perpetrators appear solely responsible for their wrongdoing. It was the same intention which led him once to issue a public notice to the effect that, when an emperor does not punish informers, he is the cause of the existence of such a class.]

Though this was his behavior to all throughout the course of his reign, still he quite outdid himself in dealing dishonor and ruin to his father's and brother's friends. [To be sure, he himself posted a notice that he would ratify all the gifts made to any persons by them and by other emperors. But this was mere show.] He hated them because they did not supply all his demands, many of which were unreasonable, as also because they had been held in some honor. [Whatever had enjoyed their affection and the benefit of their influence beyond the ordinary he regarded as hostile to him.] Therefore, although he himself had a passion for a eunuch named Earinus, nevertheless, because Titus had also shown great liking for castrated persons, he carried his desire to cast reflections on his brother's character to the extent of forbidding any one thereafter in the Roman empire to be castrated. In

* Dio Cassius, *History of Rome*, 67. 1–18, translated by H. B. Foster.

general, he was accustomed to say that those emperors who failed to punish large numbers of men were not good, but merely fortunate. [Personally, he paid no attention to those who praised Titus for not causing a single senator's death, nor did he care that the senate frequently saw fit to pass decrees that the emperor should not be permitted to put to death any of his peers. The emperor, as he believed, was far and away superior to them and might put any one of them out of the way either on his own responsibility or with the consent of the rest; it was ridiculous to suppose that they could offer any opposition or refuse to condemn a man. Some would praise Titus, only not in Domitian's hearing; for such effrontery would be deemed as grave an offence as if they were to revile the emperor in his presence and within hearing: but . . . because he understood that they were doing this secretly. . . . Then there was another thing] that resembled play-acting. Domitian pretended that he too loved his brother and mourned him. He read, with tears, the eulogies upon him [and hastened to have him enrolled among the heroes], pretending just the opposite of what he really wished. (Indeed he abolished the horse-race on Titus's birthday.) People in general were not safe whether they sympathized with his indignation or with his joy. In one case they were sure to offend his feelings and in the other to let their lack of genuineness appear.

His wife, Domitia, he planned to put to death on the ground of adultery, but, having been dissuaded by Ursus, he sent her away and midway on the road murdered Paris, the dancer, because of her. And when many people paid honor to that spot with flowers and perfumes, he gave orders that they, too, should be slain. After this he took into his house, quite undisguisedly, his own niece,—Julia, that is to say. [Then on petition of the people he became reconciled, to be sure, with Domitia,

but continued none the less his relations with Julia.]

He was removing many of the foremost men on many pretexts and by means of murders and banishments. [He also conveyed many to some out-of-the-way place, where he got rid of them; and not a few he caused to die in some way or other by their own acts that they might seem to have suffered death by their own wish and not through outside force.] He did not spare even the vestal virgins, but punished them on charges of their having had intercourse with men. It is further reported that since their examination was conducted in a harsh and unfeeling manner, and many of them were accused and constantly being punished, one of the pontifices, Helvius Agrippa, could not endure it, but, horror-stricken, expired there in the senate where he sat. [Domitian also took pride in the fact that he did not bury alive, as was the custom, the virgins he found guilty of debauchery, but ordered them to be killed by some different way.]

After this he set out for Gaul and plundered some of the tribes across the Rhine enjoying treaty rights,—a performance which filled him with conceit as if he had achieved some great success. Presumably on account of the victory he increased the soldiers' wages, so that whereas each had been receiving seventy-five denarii he commanded that a hundred be given them. Later he thought better of it, but instead of diminishing the amount he curtailed the number of men-at-arms. Both of these steps entailed great injury to the public weal: he had made the defenders of the State too few, while rendering their support an item of great expense.

Next he made a campaign into Germany and returned without having seen a trace of war anywhere. And what need is there of mentioning the honors bestowed upon him at this juncture for his exploit or from time to time upon the other emperors who were like him? For the object in any case was simply not to arouse the rage of those despots by letting them suspect, in consequence of the small number and insignificance of the rewards, that the people saw through them. Yet Domitian had this worst quality of all, that he desired to be flattered, and was equally displeased with both sorts of men, those who paid court to him and those who did not. He disliked the former because their attitude seemed one of cajolery and the latter because it seemed one of contempt. Notwithstanding [he affected to take pleasure in the honorary decrees voted him by the senate. Ursus he came near killing because he was not pleased with this sovereign's exploits, and then, at the request of Julia, he appointed him consul.] Subsequently, being still more puffed up by his folly, he was elected consul for ten years in succession, and first and only censor for life of all private citizens and emperors: and he obtained the right to employ twenty-four lictors and the triumphal garb whenever he entered the senate-house. He gave October a new name, Domitianum, because he had been born in that month. Among the charioteers he instituted two more parties, calling one the Golden and the other the Purple. To the spectators he gave many objects by means of balls thrown among them; and once he gave them a banquet while they remained in their seats and at night provided for them wine that flowed out in several different places. All this caused pleasure seemingly to the populace, but was a source of ruin to the powerful. For, as he had no resources for his expenditures, he murdered numbers of men, bringing some of them before the senate and accusing others in their absence. Lastly, he put some out of the way by concocting a plot and administering to them secret drugs.

Many of the peoples tributary to the Romans revolted when contributions of money were forcibly extorted from them. The Nasamones are an instance in point. They massacred all the collectors of the money and so thoroughly

defeated Flaccus, governor of Numidia, who attacked them, that they were able to plunder his camp. Having gorged themselves on the provisions and the wine that they found there they fell into a slumber, and Flaccus becoming aware of this fact assailed and annihilated them all and destroyed the non-combatants. Domitian experienced a thrill of delight at the news and remarked to the senate: "Well, I have put a ban on the existence of the Nasamones."

Even as early as this he was insisting upon being regarded as a god and took a huge pleasure in being called "master" and "god." These titles were used not merely orally but also in documents.

The greatest war that the Romans had on their hands at this time was one against the Dacians. Decebalus was now king of the latter [since Douras, to whom the sovereignty belonged, had voluntarily withdrawn from it in favor of Decebalus, because]. He had a good comprehension of the rules of warefare and was good at putting them in practice, displayed sagacity in advancing, took the right moment for retreating, was an expert in ambuscades, a professional warrior, knew how to make good use of a victory and how to turn a defeat to advantage. Hence he showed himself for a long time a worthy antagonist of the Romans.

I call the people Dacians, just as they name themselves and as the Romans do; but I am not ignorant that some of the Greeks refer to them as Getæ, whether that is the right term or not. I myself know Getæ that live along the Ister, beyond the Hæmu range.

Domitian made an expedition against them, to be sure, but did not enter into real conflict. [Instead, he remained in a city of Mœsia, rioting, as was his wont.] (Not only was he averse to physical labor and timorous in spirit, but also most profligate and lewd toward women and boys alike.) But he sent others to officer the war and for the most part he got the worst of it.

Decebalus, king of the Dacians, carried on negotiations with Domitian, promising him peace. Domitian sent against him Fuscus with a large force. On learning of it Decebalus sent an embassy to him anew, sarcastically proposing to make peace with the emperor in case each of the Romans should choose to pay two asses as tribute to Decebalus each year; if they should not choose to do so, he affirmed that he should make war and afflict them with great ills.

Dio ... 67th Book ... "When the soldiers making the campaign with Fuscus asked him to lead them."

Meantime he conceived a wish to take measures against the Quadi and the Marcomani because they had not assisted him against the Dacians. So he entered Pannonia to make war upon them, and the second set of envoys that they sent in regard to peace he killed.

The same man laid the blame for his defeat, however, upon his commanders. All the superior plans he claimed for himself, though he executed none of them, but for the inferior management he blamed others, even though it was through his orders that some accident had taken place. Those who succeeded incurred his hatred and those who failed his censure.

Domitian, being defeated by the Marcomani, took to flight and by hastily sending messages to Decebalus, king of the Dacians, induced him to make a truce with him. The monarch's frequent previous requests had always met with refusal. Decebalus now accepted the arrangement, for he was indeed hard pressed, yet he did not wish personally to hold a conference with Domitian, but sent Diegis with other men to give him the arms and a few captives, whom he pretended were the only ones he had. When this had been accomplished, Domitian set a diadem on the head of Diegis, just as if he had in very truth conquered and could make some one king over the Dacians. To the soldiers he granted honors and money. Like a

victor, again, he sent on ahead to Rome, besides many other things, envoys from Decebalus, and something which he affirmed was a letter of his, though rumor declared it had been forged. He graced the festival that followed with many articles pertaining to a triumph, though they did not belong to any booty he had taken;—quite the reverse: and besides allowing the truce he made an outlay of a great deal of money immediately and also presented to Decebalus artisans of every imaginable profession, peaceful and warlike, and promised that he would give him a great deal more. [These exhibits came from the imperial furniture which he at all times treated as captive goods, because he had enslaved the empire itself.]

So many rewards were voted him that almost the whole world (so far as under his dominion) was filled with his images and statues of both silver and gold. He also gave an extremely costly spectacle in regard to which we have noted nothing that was striking for historical record, save that virgins contended in the foot-race. After this, in the course of holding what seem to have been triumphal celebrations, he arranged numerous contests. First of all, in the hippodrome he had battles of infantry against infantry, and again battles of cavalry, and next he gave a naval battle in a new place. And there perished in it practically all the naval combatants and numbers of the spectators. A great rain and violent storm had suddenly come up, yet he allowed no one to leave the spectacle; indeed, though he himself changed his clothing to a thick woolen cloak, he would not permit the people to alter their attire. As a result, not a few fell sick and died. By way of consoling them for this, he provided them at public expense a dinner lasting all night. Often, too, he would conduct games at night, and sometimes he would pit dwarfs and women against each other.

So at this time he feasted the populace

as described, but on another occasion he entertained the foremost men of the senate and the knights in the following fashion. He prepared a room that was pitch black on every side, ceiling, walls and floor, and had ready bare couches, all alike, resting on the uncovered ground; then he invited in his guests alone, at night, without their attendants. And first he set beside each of them a slab shaped like a gravestone, bearing a person's name, and also a small lamp, such as hangs in tombs. Next, well-shaped, naked boys, likewise painted black, entered after the manner of phantoms, and, after passing around the guests in a kind of terrifying dance, took up their stations at their feet. After that, whatever is commonly dedicated in the course of offerings to departed spirits was set before them also, all black, and in dishes of a similar hue. Consequently, every single one of the guests feared and trembled and every moment felt certain that he was to be slain, especially as on the part of everybody save Domitian there was dead silence, as if they were already in the realms of the dead, and the emperor himself limited his conversation to matters pertaining to death and slaughter. Finally he dismissed them. But he had previously removed their servants, who stood at the doorway, and gave them in charge of other, unknown slaves, to convey either to carriages or litters, and by this act he filled them with far greater fear. Scarcely had each one reached home and was beginning to a certain extent to recover his spirits, when a message was brought him that some one was there from the Augustus. While they were expecting, as a result of this, that now at last they should surely perish, one person brought in the slab, which was of silver, then another something else, and another one of the dishes set before them at the dinner, which proved to be made of some costly material. Finally came that particular boy who had been each one's familiar spirit, now washed and decked

out. Thus, while in terror all night long, they received their gifts.

Such was the triumph or, as the crowd said, such was the expiatory service that Domitian celebrated for those who had died in Dacia and in Rome. Even at this time, too, he killed off some of the foremost men. And he took away the property of whoever buried the body of any one of them, because the victim had died on ground belonging to the sovereign.

Here are some more events worth recording, that took place in the Dacian War. Julianus, assigned by the emperor to take charge of the war, made many excellent regulations, one being his command that the soldiers should inscribe their own names and those of the centurions upon their shields, in order that those of them who committed any particular good or bad action might be more readily observed by him. Encountering the enemy at Tapai, he killed a very great number of them. Among them Vezinas, who ranked next to Decebalus, since he could not get away alive, fell down purposely as if dead. In this way he escaped notice and fled during the night. Decebalus, fearing that the Romans now they had conquered would proceed against his residence, cut down the trees that were on the site and attached weapons to the trunks, to the end that his foes might think them soldiers, and so be frightened and withdraw. This actually took place.

Chariomerus, king of the Cherusci, had been driven out of his kingdom by the Chatti on account of his friendship for the Romans. At first he gathered some companions and was successful in his attempt to return. Later he was deserted by these men for having sent hostages to the Romans and so became the suppliant of Domitian. He was not accorded an alliance but received money.

Antonius, a certain commander of this period in Germany, revolted against Domitian: him Lucius Maximus overcame and overthrew. For his victory he does not deserve any remarkable praise; [for many others have unexpectedly won victories, and his soldiers contributed largely to his success:] but for his burning all the documents that were found in the chests of Antonius, thus esteeming his own safety as of slight importance in comparison with having no blackmail result from them, I do not see how I may celebrate his memory as it deserves. But Domitian, as he had got a pretext from that source, proceeded to a series of slaughters even without the documents, and no one could well say how many he killed. [Indeed, he condemned himself so for this act that, to prevent any remembrance of the dead surviving, he prohibited the inscribing of their names in the records. Furthermore, he did not even make any communication to the senate regarding those put out of the way, although he sent their heads as well as that of Antonius to Rome and exposed them in the Forum.] But one young man, Julius Calvaster, who had served as military tribune in the hope of getting into the senate, was saved in a most unexpected fashion. Inasmuch as it was being proved that he had frequent meetings with Antonius alone and he had no other way to free himself from the charge of conspiracy, he declared that he had met him for amorous intercourse. The fact that he was of an appearance to inspire passion lent color to his statement. In this way he was acquitted.

After just one more remark about the events of that time, I will cease. Lusianus Proculus, an aged senator, who spent most of his time in the country, had come out with Domitian from Rome under compulsion so as to avoid the appearance of deserting him when in danger and the death that might very likely be the result of such conduct. When the news came, he said: "You have conquered, emperor, as I ever prayed. Therefore restore me to the country." Thereupon he left him without

more ado and retired to his farm. And after this, although he survived for a long time, he never came near him.

During this period some had become accustomed to smear needles with poison and then to prick with them whomsoever they would. Many persons thus attacked died without even knowing the cause, and many of the murderers were informed against and punished. And this went on not only in Rome but over practically the entire civilized world.

To Ulpius Trajan and to Acilius Glabrio, who were consuls then, the same signs are said to have appeared. They foretold to Glabrio destruction, but to Trajan the imperial office. [Numerous wealthy men and women both were punished for adultery, and some of the women had been debauched by *him*. Many more were fined or executed on other charges.] A woman was tried and lost her life because she had stripped in front of an image of Domitian [and another for having had dealings with astrologers]. Among the many who perished at this time was also Mettius Pompusianus, whom Vespasian had refused to harm in any way after learning from some report that he would one day be sole ruler, but rather honoured, saying: "You will certainly remember me and will certainly honor me in return." But Domitian first exiled him to Corsica and later put him to death, one of the complaints being that he had the inhabited world painted on the walls of his bedchamber and another that he had excerpted and was wont to read the speeches of kings and other eminent men that are written in Livy. Also Maternus, a sophist, met his death because in a practice speech he had said something against tyrants. The emperor himself used to visit both those who were to accuse and those who were to give evidence for condemnation, and he would frame and compose everything that required to be said. Often, too, he would talk to the prisoners alone, keeping tight hold of their chains with his hands. In the former case he would not entrust to others what was to be said, and in the latter he feared the men even in their bonds.

In Mœsia, the Lygians, who had been at war with some of the Suebi, sent envoys, asking Domitian for an alliance. They obtained one that was strong, not in numbers, but in dignity: in other words, they were granted only a hundred knights. The Suebi, indignant at this, added to their contingent the Iazygæ and began to prepare well in advance to cross the Ister.

Masyus, king of the Semnones, and Ganna, a virgin (she was priestess in Celtica after Veleda), came to Domitian and having been honored by him returned.

As censor, likewise, his behavior was noteworthy. He expelled Cæcilius Rufinus from the senate because he danced, and restored Claudius Pacatus, though an ex-centurion, to his master because he was proved to be a slave. What came after, to be sure, can not be described in similar terms,—his deeds, that is to say, as emperor. *Then* he killed Arulenus Rusticus for being a philosopher and for calling Thrasea sacred, and Herennius Senecio because in his long career he had stood for no office after the quæstorship and because he had compiled the life of Helvidius Priscus. Many others also perished as a result of this same charge of philosophizing, and all remaining members of that profession were again driven from Rome. One Juventius Celsus, however, who had been conspicuous in conspiring with certain persons against Domitian and had been accused of it, saved his life in a remarkable way. When he was on the point of being condemned, he begged that he might speak a few words with the emperor in private. Having gained the opportunity he did obeisance before him and after repeatedly calling him "master," and "god" (terms that were already being applied to him by others), he said: "I have done nothing of the sort. And if I obtain a

respite, I will pry into everything and both inform against and convict many persons for you." He was released on these conditions, but did not report any one; instead, by advancing different excuses at different times, he lived until Domitian was killed.

During this period the road leading from Sinuessa to Puteoli was paved with stones. And the same year Domitian slew among many others Flavius Clemens the consul, though he was a cousin and had to wife Flavia Domitilla, who was also a relative of the emperor's. The complaint brought against them both was that of atheism, under which many others who drifted into Jewish ways were condemned. Some of these were killed and the remainder were at least deprived of their property. Domitilla was merely banished to Pandateria; but Glabrio, colleague of Trajan in the consulship, after being accused on various regular stock charges, and also of fighting with wild beasts, suffered death. This ability in the arena was the chief cause of the emperor's anger against him,— an anger prompted by jealousy. In the victim's consulship Domitian had summoned him to Albanum to attend the so-called Juvenalia and had imposed on him the task of killing a large lion. Glabrio not only had escaped all injury but had despatched the creature with most accurate aim.

As a consequence of his cruelty the emperor was suspicious of all mankind and ceased now to put hopes of safety in either the freedmen or the prefects, whom he usually caused to be tried during their very term of office. Moreover, Epaphroditus, who belonged to Nero, he first drove out and then slew, censuring him for not having defended Nero; his object was by the vengeance that he took in this person's case to terrify his own freedmen long enough in advance to prevent their ever attempting a similar deed. It did him no good, however, for he became the object of a conspiracy in the following year and perished in the consulship of Gaius Valens (who died after holding the consular office in his ninetieth year) and of Gaius Antistius. Those who attacked him and prepared the undertaking were Parthenius his cubicularius (though he was the recipient of such marks of imperial favor as to be allowed to wear a sword) and Sigerus, who was also a member of the excubiæ, as well as Entellus, the person entrusted with the care of the state documents, and Stephanus, a freedman. The plot was not unknown to Domitia, the emperor's wife, nor to the prefect Norbanus, nor to the latter's partner in office, Petronius Secundus: at least, this is the tradition. Domitia was ever an object of the imperial hatred and consequently stood in terror of her life; the rest no longer loved their sovereign, some of them because complaints had been lodged against them and others because they were expecting them to be lodged. For my part, I have heard also the following account,—that Domitian, having become suspicious of all these persons, conceived a desire to kill them, and wrote their names on a two-leaved tablet of linden wood, and put it under his pillow on the couch where he was wont to repose; and one of the naked prattling boys, while the emperor was asleep in the daytime, filched it away and kept it without knowing what it contained. Domitia then chanced upon it and reading what was written gave information of the matter to those involved. As a result, they changed their plans somewhat and hastened the plot; yet they did not proceed to action until they had determined who was to succeed to the office. Having conversed with various persons, when they found that no one would accept it (everybody was afraid of them, thinking that they were simply testing people's loyalty) they betook themselves to Nerva. He was of most noble birth and most suitable character and had, besides, encountered danger through being

slandered by astrologers [who declared that he should be sovereign]. Thus they the more easily persuaded him to be the next to receive the power. In truth, Domitian, who conducted an investigation of the days and the hours when the foremost men had been born, had consequently ere this despatched not a few even of those who entertained no hopes of gaining any power. And he would have slain Nerva, had not one of the astrologers who favored the latter declared that he would die within a few days. [Believing that this would really prove true, he did not desire to be guilty of this additional murder, inasmuch as Nerva in any event was to meet death so very soon.]

Since no occurrence of such magnitude is without previous indications, various unfavorable tokens appeared in his case, too. In a vision he himself beheld Rusticus approaching him with a sword; and he thought that Minerva, whose statue he kept in his bedchamber, had thrown away her weapons and, mounted upon a chariot drawn by black horses, was being swallowed up in an abyss. But the feature which of all claims our wonder is connected with the name of Larginus Proculus. He had publicly foretold in Germany that the emperor should die on the day when he actually did die, and was, therefore, sent on to Rome by the governor. brought before Domitian he declared once more that this should be so. A death sentence was postponed in order that he might be put to death after the emperor had escaped the danger. Meanwhile Domitian was slain, his life was saved, and he received a hundred thousand denarii from Nerva. Some one else had on a previous occasion told the ruler both when and how he should perish, and then being asked what manner of death he, the prophet, should meet, he answered that he would be despatched by dogs. Thereupon command was given that the fellow should be burned alive, and the fire was applied to him. But just then there was a great downpour of rain, the pyre was extinguished, and later dogs found him lying upon it with his hands bound behind him and tore him to pieces.

I have one more astonishing fact to record, which I shall touch on after I have given the account of Domitian's end. As soon as he rose to leave the court-house and was ready to take his afternoon nap, as was his custom, first Parthenius took the blade out of the sword, which always lay under his pillow, so that he should not have the use of that. Next he sent in Stephanus, who was stronger then the rest. The latter smote Domitian, and though it was not an opportune blow the emperor was knocked to the ground, where he lay. Then, fearing an escape, Parthenius leaped in, or, as some believe, he sent in Maximus, a freedman. Thus both Domitian was murdered, and Stephanus perished like-wise in a rush that those who had not shared in the conspiracy made upon him.

The matter of which I spoke, saying that it surprises me more than anything else, is this. A certain Apollonius of Tyana on the very day and at that very hour when Domitian was being murdered (this was later confirmed by other events that happened in both places) climbed a lofty stone at Ephesus (or possibly some other town) and having gathered the populace, uttered these words: "Bravo, Stephanus! Good, Stephanus! Smite the wretch! You have struck, you have wounded, you have killed him!!" This is what really took place, though there should be ten thousand doubters. Domitian had lived forty-four years, ten months, and twenty-six days. His reign had lasted fifteen years and five days. His body was stolen away and buried by his nurse, Phyllis.

3. SUETONIUS ON THE LIFE OF DOMITIAN*

Domitian was born on the ninth day before the Kalends of November of the year when his father was Consul-elect and was about to enter on the office in the following month, in a street of the sixth region called "the Pomegranate," in a house which he afterwards converted into a temple of the Flavian family. He is said to have passed the period of his boyhood and his early youth in great poverty and infamy. For he did not possess a single piece of plate and it is a well known fact that Claudius Pollio, a man of praetorian rank, against whom Nero's poem entitled "The One-eyed Man" is directed, pre-served a letter in Domitian's handwriting and sometimes exhibited it, in which the future Emperor promised him an assigna-tion; and there have not been wanting those who declared that Domitian was also debauched by Nerva, who succeeded him. In the war with Vitellius he took refuge in the Capitol with his paternal uncle Sabinus and a part of the forces under him. When the enemy forced an entrance and the temple was fired, he hid during the night with the guardian of the shrine, and in the morning, disguised in the garb of a follower of Isis and mingling with the priests of that fickle superstition, he went across the Tiber with a single companion to the mother of one of his school-fellows. There he was so effectually concealed, that though he was closely followed, he could not be found, in spite of a thorough search. It was only after the victory that he ventured forth and after being hailed as Caesar, he assumed the office of City Praetor with consular powers, but only in

* Suetonius, "Domitian," *The Lives of the Twelve Caesars*, translated by Joseph Gavorse (New York: Random House, 1931), pp. 344–361. Reprinted by permission of Random House, Afred A. Knopf.

name, turning over all the judicial business to his next colleague. But he exercised all the tyranny of his high position so lawlessly, that it was even then apparent what sort of a man he was going to be. Not to mention all details, after making free with the wives of many men, he went so far as to marry Domitia Longina, who was the wife of Aelius Lamia, and in a single day he assigned more than twenty positions in the city and abroad, which led Vespasian to say more than once that he was surprised that he did not appoint the Emperor's successors with the rest.

He began an expedition against Gaul and the Germanies, which was uncalled for and from which his father's friends dissuaded him, merely that he might make himself equal to his brother in power and rank. For this he was reprimanded, and to give him a better realization of his youth and position, he had to live with his father, and when they appeared in public he followed the Emperor's chair and that of his brother in a litter, while he also attended their triumph over Judaea riding on a white horse. Moreover, of his six consulships only one was a regular one, and he obtained that only because his brother gave place to him and recommended his appointment.

He himself too made a remarkable pretense of modesty and especially of an interest in poetry, an art which had previously been as unfamiliar to him as it was later despised and rejected, and he even gave readings in public. Yet in spite of all this, when Vologaesus, King of the Parthians, had asked for auxiliaries against the Alani and for one of Vespasian's sons as their leader, Domitian used every effort to have himself sent rather than Titus. And because the affair came to nothing, he tried by gifts and promises to induce other eastern kings to make the same request.

On the death of his father he hesitated for some time whether to offer a double largess to the soldiers, and he never had any compunction about saying that he had been left a partner in the imperial power, but that the will had been tampered with. And from that time on he never ceased to plot against his brother secretly and openly, until Titus was seized with a dangerous illness, when Domitian ordered that he be left for dead, before he had actually drawn his last breath. And after his death he bestowed no honor upon him, save that of deification, and he often assailed his memory in ambiguous phrases, both in his speeches and in his edicts.

At the beginning of his reign he used to spend hours in seclusion every day, doing nothing but catch flies and stab them with a keenly-sharpened stylus. Consequently when some one once asked whether any one was in there with Caesar, Vibius Crispus made the witty reply: "Not even a fly."

Soon after his advancement he bestowed the name of Augusta on his wife Domitia. He had had a son by her in his second consulship, and in the following year a daughter. He divorced her because of her love for the actor Paris, but could not bear the separation and soon took her back, alleging that the people demanded it.

In his administration of the government he for some time showed himself inconsistent, with about an equal number of virtues and vices, but finally he turned the virtues also into vices. For, so far as one may guess, it was contrary to his natural disposition that he was made rapacious through need and cruel through fear.

He constantly gave grand and costly entertainments, both in the amphitheater and in the Circus, where in addition to the usual races between two-horse and four-horse chariots, he also exhibited two battles, one between forces of infantry and the other by horsemen. And he even gave a naval battle in the amphitheater. Besides he gave hunts of wild beasts, gladiatorial shows at night by the light of torches, and not only combats between men but between women as well. He was always present too at the games given by the Quaestors, which he revived after they had been abandoned for some time, and invariably granted the people the privilege of calling for two pairs of gladiators from his own school, and brought them in last in all the splendor of the court. During the whole of every gladiatorial show there always stood at his feet a small boy clad in scarlet, with an abnormally small head, with whom he used to talk a great deal, and sometimes seriously. At any rate, he was overheard to ask him if he knew why he had decided at the last appointment day to make Mettius Rufus Prefect of Egypt. He often gave sea-fights almost with regular fleets, having dug a pool near the Tiber and surrounded it with seats; and he continued to witness the contests amid heavy rains.

He also celebrated Secular games, reckoning the time, not according to the year when Claudius had last given them, but by the previous calculation of Augustus. In the course of these, to make it possible to finish a hundred races on the day of the contests in the Circus, he diminished the number of laps from seven to five.

He also established a quinquennial contest in honor of Jupiter Capitolinus of a threefold character, comprising music, riding, and gymnastics, and with considerably more prizes than are awarded nowadays. For there were competitions in prose declamation both in Greek and in Latin. And in addition to contests of the lyre-players, there were others of several playing together as well as singly but without singing, while in the stadium there were races even between maidens. He presided at the competitions in half-boots, clad in a purple toga in the Greek fashion, and wearing upon his head a golden crown with figures of Jupiter, Juno, and Minerva, while by his side sat the Priest of Jupiter and the college of the Flaviales,

similarly dressed, except that their crowns bore his image as well. He celebrated the Quinquatria too every year in honor of Minerva at his Alban villa, and established for her a college of priests, from which men were chosen by lot to act as officers and give splendid shows of wild beasts and stage plays, besides holding contests in oratory and poetry.

He made a present to the people of three hundred sesterces each on three occasions, and in the course of one of his shows in celebration of the feast of the Seven Hills gave a plentiful banquet, distributing large baskets of victuals to the Senate and Knights, and smaller ones to the Commons. And he himself was the first to begin to eat. On the following day he scattered gifts of all sorts of things to be scrambled for, and since the greater part of these fell where the people sat, he had five hundred tickets thrown into each section occupied by the senatorial and equestrian orders.

He restored many splendid buildings which had been destroyed by fire, among them the Capitolium, which had again been burned, but in all cases with the inscription of his own name only, and with no mention of the original builder. Furthermore, he built a new temple on the Capitoline hill in honor of Jupiter Custos and the Forum which now bears the name of Nerva; likewise a temple to the Flavian family, a stadium, an Odeum, and a pool for sea-fights. From the stone used in this last the Circus Maximus was afterwards rebuilt, when both sides of it had been destroyed by fire.

His campaigns he undertook partly without provocation and partly of necessity. That against the Chatti was uncalled for, while the one against the Sarmatians was justified by the destruction of a legion with its commander. He made two against the Dacians, the first when Oppius Sabinus an ex-consul was defeated, and the second on the overthrow of Cornelius Fuscus,

Prefect of the praetorian guard, to whom he had entrusted the conduct of the war. After several battles of varying success he celebrated a double triumph over the Chatti and the Dacians. His victories over the Sarmatians he commemorated merely by the offering of a laurel crown to Jupiter of the Capitol.

A civil war which was set on foot by Lucius Antonius, Governor of Upper Germany, was put down in the Emperor's absence by a remarkable stroke of good fortune, for at the very hour of the battle the Rhine suddenly thawed and prevented his barbarian allies from crossing over to Antonius. Domitian learned of this victory through omens before he actually had news of it, for on the very day when the decisive battle was fought a magnificent eagle enfolded his statue at Rome with its wings, uttering exultant shrieks, and soon afterwards a report of the death of Antonius become so current, that several went so far as to assert positively that they had seen his head brought to Rome.

He made may innovations also in common customs. He did away with the dole of food distributed in baskets to the people and revived the old custom of regular public dinners. He added two factions of drivers in the Circus, with gold and purple as their colors, to the four former ones. He forbade the appearance of actors on the stage, but allowed the practice of their art in private houses. He prohibited the castration of males, and kept down the price of the eunuchs that remained in the hands of the slave dealers. Once upon the occasion of a plentiful wine crop, attended with a scarcity of grain, thinking that the fields were neglected through too much attention to the vineyards, he made an edict forbidding any one to plant more vines in Italy and ordering that the vineyards in the provinces be cut down, or but half of them at most be left standing. But he did not persist in carrying out the measure. He divided some of the most

important offices of the court between the freedmen and Roman Knights. He prohibited the uniting of two legions in one camp and the deposit of more than a thousand sesterces by any one soldier at headquarters, because it was clear that Lucius Antonius had been especially led to attempt a revolution by the amount of such deposits in the combined winter quarters of two legions. He increased the pay of the soldiers one-fourth, by the addition of three gold pieces each year.

He administered justice scrupulously and conscientiously, frequently holding special sittings on the tribunal in the Forum. He rescinded such decisions of the Hundred Judges as had been made through favor or interest. He often warned the arbiters not to grant claims for freedom made under false pretenses. He degraded jurors who accepted bribes, together with all their associates. He also induced the Tribunes of the Commons to prosecute a corrupt Aedile for extortion, and to ask the Senate to appoint jurors in the case. He took such care to exercise restraint over the city officials and the Governors of the provinces, that at no time were they more honest or just, whereas after his time we have seen many of them charged with all manner of offenses.

Having undertaken the correction of public morals, he put an end to the license at the theaters, where the general public occupied the seats reserved for the Knights. He did away with the prevailing publication of scurrilous lampoons, in which distinguished men and women were attacked, and imposed ignominious penalties on their authors. He expelled an ex-quaestor from the Senate, because he was given to acting and dancing. He deprived notorious women of the use of litters, as well as of the right to receive inheritances and legacies. He struck the name of a Roman Knight from the list of jurors, because he had taken back his wife after divorcing her and charging her with adultery. He condemned several men of both orders, offenders against the Scantinian law. And the incest of Vestal Virgins, condoned even by his father and his brother, he punished severely in divers ways, at first by capital punishment, and afterwards in the ancient fashion. For while he allowed the sisters Oculata and also Varronilla free choice of the manner of their deaths, and banished their paramours, he later ordered that Cornelia, a chief-Vestal who had been acquitted once but after a long interval again arraigned and found guilty, be buried alive; and her lovers were beaten to death with rods in the Comitium, with the exception of an ex-praetor, whom he allowed to go into exile, because he admitted his guilt while the case was still unsettled and the examination and torture of the witnesses had led to no result. To protect the Gods from being dishonored with impunity by any sacrilege, he caused a tomb which one of his freedmen had built for his son from stones intended for the temple of Jupiter of the Capitol to be destroyed by the soldiers and the bones and ashes contained in it thrown into the sea.

In the earlier part of his reign he so shrank from any form of bloodshed, that while his father was still absent from the city, he planned to issue an edict that no oxen should be offered in sacrifice, recalling the line of Vergil,

"Ere godless men, restrained from blood in vain,
Began to feast on flesh of bullocks slain."

He was equally free from any suspicion of love of gain or of avarice, both in private life and and for some time after becoming Emperor. On the contrary, he often gave strong proofs not merely of integrity, but even of liberality. He treated all his intimates most generously, and there was nothing which he urged them more frequently, or with greater insistence, than that they should not be niggardly in any of their acts. He would not accept inheritances left him by those who had children. He even annulled a legacy in the will of Rustus Caepio, who had provided that his heir should yearly pay a specified sum to each of the Senators on his entrance into the House. He canceled the suits against those who had been posted as debtors to the public treasury for more than five years, and would not allow a renewal except within a year and on the condition that an accuser who did not win his suit should be punished with exile. Scribes of the Quaestors who carried on business, which had become usual although contrary to the Clodian law, he pardoned for past offenses. Parcels of land which were left unoccupied here and there after the assignment of lands to the veterans he granted to their old-time owners as by right of possession. He checked false accusations designed for the profit of the privy purse and inflicted severe penalties on offenders. And a saying of his was current, that an Emperor who does not punish informers hounds them on.

But he did not continue this course of mercy or integrity, although he turned to cruelty somewhat more speedily than to avarice. He put to death a pupil of the pantomimic actor Paris, who was still a beardless boy and ill at the time, because in his skill and his appearance he seemed not unlike his master; also Hermogenes of Tarsus because of some allusions in his History, besides crucifying even the slaves who had written it out. A householder who said that a Thracian gladiator was a match for the *murmillo*, but not for the giver of the games, he caused to be dragged from his seat and thrown into the arena to dogs, with this placard: "A favorer of the Thracians who spoke impiously."

He put to death many Senators, among them several ex-consuls, including Civica Cerealis, at the very time when he was Proconsul in Asia, Salvidienus Orfitus, and Acilius Glabrio while he was in exile, under the pretense they were plotting revolution.

For the rest, any charge served, no matter how trivial. He slew Aelius Lamia for joking remarks, which were reflections on him, it is true, but made long before and harmless. For when Domitian had taken away Lamia's wife, the latter replied to some one who praised his voice: "I practice continence"; and when Titus urged him to marry again, he replied: "Are you too looking for a wife?" He put to death Salvius Cocceianus, because he had kept the birthday of the Emperor Otho, his paternal uncle; Mettius Pompusianus, because it was commonly reported that he had an imperial nativity and carried about a map of the world on parchment and speeches of the Kings and Generals from Titus Livius, besides giving two of his slaves the names of Mago and Hannibal. He put Sallustius Lucullus, Governor of Britain, to death for allowing some lances of a new pattern to be called "Lucullean," after his own name; Junius Rusticus, because he had published eulogies of Paetus Thrasea and Helvidius Priscus and called them the most upright of men, banishing, on the occasion of this charge, all the philosophers from the city and from Italy. He executed the younger Helvidius, alleging that in a farce composed for the stage he had under the characters of Paris and Oenone censured Domitian's divorce from his wife; also Flavius Sabinus, one of his cousins, because on the day of the consular elections the crier had inadvertently announced him to the people as Emperor-elect, instead of Consul.

After his victory in the civil war he became even more cruel, and to discover any conspirators who were in hiding, tortured many of the opposite party by a new form of inquisition, inserting fire in their privates; and he cut off the hands of some of them. It is certain that of the more conspicuous only two were pardoned, a Tribune of senatorial rank and a Centurion, who the more clearly to prove their freedom from guilt, showed that they were of shameless unchastity and could therefore have had no influence with the general or with the soldiers.

His savage cruelty was not only excessive, but also cunning and sudden. He invited one of his stewards to his bedchamber the day before crucifying him, made him sit beside him on his couch, and dismissed him in a secure and gay frame of mind, even deigning to send him a share of his dinner. When he was on the point of condemning the ex-consul Arrecinius Clemens, one of his intimates and tools, he treated him with as great favor as before, if not greater, and finally, as he was taking a drive with him, catching sight of his accuser he said: "Pray, shall we hear this base slave tomorrow?"

To abuse men's patience the more insolently, he never pronounced an unusually dreadful sentence without a preliminary declaration of clemency, so that there came to be no more certain indication of a cruel death than the leniency of his preamble. He had brought some men charged with treason into the Senate, and when he had introduced the matter by saying that he would find out that day how dear he was to the members, he had no difficulty in causing them to be condemned to suffer the ancient method of punishment. Then appalled at the cruelty of the penalty, he interposed a veto, to lessen the odium, in these words (for it will be of interest to know his exact language): "Allow me, Fathers of the Senate, to prevail on you by your love for me to grant a favor which I know I shall obtain with difficulty, namely that you allow the condemned free choice of the manner of their death; for thus you will spare your own eyes and all men will know that I was present at the meeting of the Senate."

Reduced to financial straits by the cost of his buildings and shows, as well as by the additions which he had made to the pay of the soldiers, he tried to lighten the military expenses by diminishing the number of his troops. But perceiving that in this way he exposed himself to the attacks of the barbarians, and nevertheless had difficulty in easing his burdens, he had no hesitation in resorting to every sort of robbery. The property of the living and the dead was seized everywhere on any charge brought by an accuser. It was enough to allege any action or word derogatory to the majesty of the prince. Estates of those in no way connected with him were confiscated, if but one man came forward to declare that he had heard from the deceased during his lifetime that Caesar was his heir. Besides other taxes, that on the Jews was levied with the utmost rigor, and those were prosecuted who without publicly acknowledging that faith yet lived as Jews, as well as those who concealed their nationality and did not pay the tribute levied upon their people. I recall being present in my youth when the person of a man ninety years old was examined before the Procurator and a very crowded court, to see whether he was circumcised.

From his youth he was far from being of an affable disposition, but was on the contrary presumptuous and unbridled both in act and in word. When his father's concubine Caenis returned from Histria and offered to kiss him as usual, he held out his hand to her. He was vexed that his brother's son-in-law had attendants clad in white, as well as he, and uttered the words

"Not good is a number of rulers."

When he became Emperor, he did not hesitate to boast in the Senate that he had conferred their power on both his father and his brother, and that they had but returned him his own; nor on taking back his wife after their divorce, that he had "recalled her to his divine couch." He delighted to hear the people in the amphitheater shout on his feast day: "Good Fortune attend our Lord and Mistress." Even more, in the Capitoline competition when Palfurius Sura received the prize for oratory and all the people begged with concerted unanimity that he be restored to his place in the Senate from which he had been banished some time before, Domitian deigned no reply, but merely had a crier bid them be silent. With no less arrogance he began as follows in issuing a circular letter in the name of his procurators, "Our Master and our God bids that this be done." And so the custom arose of henceforth addressing him in no other way even in writing or in conversation. He suffered no statues to be set up in his honor in the Capitol, except of gold and silver and of a fixed weight. He erected so many and such huge vaulted passageways and arches in the various regions of the city, adorned with chariots and triumphal emblems, that on one of them some one wrote in Greek: "It is enough."

He held the consulship seventeen times, more often than any of his predecessors. Of these the seven middle ones were in successive years, but all of them he filled in name only, continuing none beyond the first of May and few after the Ides of January. Having assumed the surname Germanicus after his two triumphs, he renamed the months of September and October from his own names, calling them "Germanicus" and "Domitianus," because in the former he had come to the throne and was born in the latter.

In this way he became an object of terror and hatred to all, but he was overthrown at last by a conspiracy of his friends and favorite freedmen, to which his wife was also privy. He had long since had a premonition of the last year and day of his life, and even of the very hour and manner of his death. In his youth astrologers had predicted all this to him, and his father once even openly ridiculed him at dinner for refusing mushrooms, saying that he showed himself unaware of his destiny in not rather fearing the sword. Therefore he was at all times timorous and worried, and was disquieted beyond measure by even the slightest suspicions. It is thought that nothing had more effect in inducing him to ignore his proclamation about cutting down the vineyards than the circulation of notes containing the following lines:

"Gnaw me to my root, O goat, yet shall my juice suffice
To wet your head when you are led to sacrifice."

It was because of this same timorousness that although he was most eager for all such honors, he refused a new one which the Senate had devised and offered to him, a decree, namely, that whenever he held the consulship Roman Knights selected by lot should precede him among his Lictors and attendants, clad in the trabea and bearing lances.

As the time when he anticipated danger drew near, becoming still more anxious every day, he lined the walls of the colonnades in which he used to walk with phengite stone, to be able to see in its brilliant surface the reflection of all that went on behind his back. And he did not give a hearing to any prisoners except in private and alone, even holding their chains in his hands. Further, to convince his household that one must not venture to kill a patron even on good grounds, he condemned Epaphroditus, his confidential secretary, to death, because it was believed that after Nero was abandoned the freedmen's hand had aided him in taking his life.

Finally he put to death his own cousin Flavius Clemens, suddenly and on a very slight suspicion, almost before the end of his consulship. And yet Flavius was a man of most contemptible laziness and Domitian had besides openly named his sons, who were then very young, as his successors, changing their former names and calling the one Vespasian and the other Domitian. And it was by this deed

in particular that he hastened his own destruction.

For eight successive months so many strokes of lightning occurred and were reported, that at last he cried: "Well, let him now strike whom he will." The temple of Jupiter of the Capitol was struck and that of the Flavian family, as well as the palace and the Emperor's own bedroom. The inscription too on the base of a triumphal statue of his was torn off in a violent tempest and fell upon a neighboring tomb. The tree which had been overthrown when Vespasian was still a private citizen but had sprung up anew, then on a sudden fell down again. Fortune of Praeneste had throughout his whole reign, when he commended the new year to her protection, given him a favorable omen and always in the same words. Now at last she returned a most direful one, not without the mention of bloodshed.

He dreamed that Minerva, whom he worshipped with superstitious veneration, came forth from her shrine and declared that she could no longer protect him, since she had been disarmed by Jupiter. Yet there was nothing by which he was so much disturbed as a prediction of the astrologer Ascletarion and what befell him. When this man was accused before the Emperor and did not deny that he had spoken of certain things which he had foreseen through his art, he was asked what his own end would be. When he replied that he would shortly be rent by dogs, Domitian ordered him killed at once, but to prove the fallibility of his art, he ordered besides that his funeral be attended to with the greatest care. While this was being done, it chanced that the pyre was overset by a sudden storm and dogs mangled the corpse, which was only partly consumed, and that an actor of farces called Latinus, who happened to pass by and see the incident, told it to Domitian at the dinner table, with 'the rest of the day's gossip.

The day before he was killed he gave orders to have some apples which were offered him kept until the following day, and added: "If only I am spared to eat them." Then turning to his companions, he declared that on the following day the moon would be stained with blood in Aquarius, and that a deed would be done of which men would talk all over the world. At about midnight he was so terrified that he leaped from his bed. The next morning he conducted the trial of a soothsayer sent from Germany, who when consulted about the lightning strokes had foretold a change of rulers, and condemned him to death. While he was vigorously scratching a festered wart on his forehead, and had drawn blood, he said: "May this be all." Then he asked the time, and by prearrangement the sixth hour was announced to him, instead of the fifth, which he feared. Filled with joy at this, and believing all danger now past, he was hastening to the bath, when his head chamberlain Parthenius changed his purpose by announcing that some one had called about a matter of great moment and would not be put off. Then he dismissed all his attendants and went to his bedroom, where he was slain.

Concerning the nature of the plot and the manner of his death, this is about all that became known. As the conspirators were deliberating when and how to attack him, whether at the bath or at dinner, Stephanus, Domitilla's steward, at the time under accusation for embezzlement, offered his aid and counsel. To avoid suspicion, he wrapped up his left arm in woolen bandages for some days, pretending that he had injured it, and concealed in them a dagger. Then pretending to betray a conspiracy and for that reason being given an audience, he stabbed the Emperor in the groin as he was reading a paper which the assassin handed him, and stood in a state of amazement. As the wounded prince attempted to resist, he was slain with seven wounds by Clodianus, a subaltern, Maximus, a freedman of Parthenius, Satur, head chamberlain, and a gladiator from the imperial school. A boy who was engaged in his usual duty of attending to the images of the household Gods in the bedroom, and so was a witness of the murder, gave this additional information. He was bidden by Domitian, immediately after he was dealt the first blow, to hand him the dagger hidden under his pillow and to call the servants. But he found nothing at the head of the bed save the hilt, and besides all the doors were closed. Meanwhile the Emperor grappled with Stephanus and bore him to the ground, where they struggled for a long time, Domitian trying now to wrest the dagger from his assailant's hands and now to gouge out his eyes with his lacerated fingers.

He was slain on the fourteenth day before the Kalends of October in the forty-fifth year of his age and the fifteenth of his reign. His corpse was carried out on a common bier by those who bury the poor, and his nurse Phyllis cremated it at her suburban estate on the Via Latina. But his ashes she secretly carried to the temple of the Flavian family and mingled them with those of Julia, daughter of Titus, whom she had also reared.

He was tall of stature, with a modest expression and a high color. His eyes were large, but his sight was somewhat weak. He was handsome and graceful too, especially when a young man, and indeed in his whole body with the exception of his feet, the toes of which were somewhat cramped. In later life he had the further disfigurement of baldness, a protruding belly, and spindle legs, though the latter has become thin from a long illness. He was so conscious that the modesty of his expression was in his favor, that he once made this boast in the Senate: "So far, at any rate, you have approved my heart and my countenance." He was so sensitive about his baldness, that he regarded it as a personal insult if any one else was twitted with that defect in jest or in earnest, though in a book "On the Care of the Hair," which he published and dedicated to a friend, he wrote the following by way of consolation to the man and himself:

"'Do you not see that I am comely, too, and tall?'

And yet the same fate awaits my hair, and I bear with resignation the aging of my locks in youth. Be assured that nothing is more pleasing than beauty, but nothing shorter-lived."

He was incapable of exertion and seldom went about the city on foot, while on his campaigns and journeys he rarely rode on horseback, but was regularly carried in a litter. He took no interest in arms, but was particularly devoted to archery. There are many who have more than once seen him slay a hundred wild beasts of different kinds on his Alban estate, and purposely kill some of them with two successive shots in such a way that the arrows gave the effects of horns. Sometimes he would have a slave stand at a distance and hold out the palm of his right hand for a mark, with the fingers spread. Then he directed his arrows with such accuracy that they passed harmlessly between the fingers.

At the beginning of his rule he neglected liberal studies, although he provided for having the libraries, which were destroyed by fire, renewed at very great expense, seeking everywhere for copies of the lost works, and sending scribes to Alexandria to transcribe and correct them. Yet he never took any pains to become acquainted with history or poetry, or even to acquiring an ordinarily good style. He read nothing except the memoirs and transactions of Tiberius Caesar. For his letters, speeches and proclamations he relied on others' talents. Yet his conversation was not inelegant, and some of his sayings were even noteworthy. "How I wish," said he, "that I were as fine looking as Maecius

thinks he is." He declared too that the head of a certain man, whose hair had changed color in such a way that it was partly reddish and partly gray, was like "snow on which mead had been poured."

He used to say that the lot of princes was most unhappy, since when they discovered a conspiracy, no one believed them unless they had been killed.

Whenever he had leisure he amused himself with playing at dice, even on working days and in the morning hours. He went to the bath before the end of the forenoon and lunched to the point of satiety, so that at dinner he rarely took anything except a Matian apple and a moderate amount of wine from a jug. He gave numerous and generous banquets, but usually ended them early. In no case did he protract them beyond sunset, or follow them by a drinking bout. In fact, he did nothing until the hour for retiring except walk alone in a retired place.

He was excessively lustful. His constant sexual intercourse he called bed-wrestling, as if it were a kind of exercise. It was reported that he depilated his concubines with his own hand and swam with common prostitutes. After persistently refusing his niece, who was offered him in marriage when she was still a maid, because he was entangled in an intrigue with Domitia, he seduced her shortly afterwards when she became the wife of another, and that too during the lifetime of Titus. Later, when she was bereft of father and husband, he loved her ardently and without disguise, and even became the cause of her death by compelling her to get rid of a child of his by abortion.

The people received the news of his death with indifference, but the soldiers were greatly grieved and at once attempted to call him the Deified Domitian, while they were prepared also to avenge him, had they not lacked leaders. This, however, they did accomplish a little later by most insistently demanding the execution of his murderers. The Senators on the contrary were so overjoyed, that they raced to fill the House, where they did not refrain from assailing the dead Emperor with the most insulting and stinging kind of outcries. They even had ladders brought and his shields and images torn down before their eyes and dashed upon the ground. Finally they passed a decree that his inscriptions should everywhere be erased, and all record of him obliterated.

A few months before he was killed, a raven perched on the Capitolium and cried "All will be well," an omen which some interpreted as follows:

"Late croaked a raven from Tarpeia's height,
'All is not yet, but shortly will be, right.'"

Domitian himself, it is said, dreamed that a golden hump grew out of his back, and he regarded this as an infallible sign that the condition of the empire would be happier and more prosperous after his time. And this was shortly shown to be true through the uprightness and moderate rule of the succeeding Emperors.

4. TACITUS, AGRICOLA, DOMITIAN, AND THE PROBLEM OF THE PRINCIPATE*

At the end of that long section of the twelfth book of his *Histories* in which he inveighs against the faults and deficiencies of Timaeus' method of writing history Polybius comes to the conclusion that things will never go well with the writing of history unless and until either those men who are or have been engaged in political affairs will make it their business to write history not as a *parergon* or as personal memoirs but *ex professo* and to the fullest extent, or those who set out to write history will first seek to acquire that ἕξις which can only come from a knowledge of public affairs.

Since Polybius wrote these words it has become amply clear that we should have but little history of the kind that Polybius demands if the job of writing it had been left exclusively to active or retired statesmen. But since by necessity scholars have had to take up the job if it was to be done at all, the demand which Polybius makes on those "who set out to write history" would still appear to be justified. At least, in making historical investigations, scholars

should try to avoid using a logic that is completely dissociated from the realities of human life, whether public or otherwise. Or more concretely: if someone, whether or not he was ever personally engaged in public affairs, has been lucky enough never to have come in contact with an absolutistic regime and nevertheless wishes to write about certain problems of the Roman Empire, he might do well first to read some books such as, for instance, the *Mémoires du duc de Saint-Simon*, in order to acquire a feeling for the atmosphere of such a regime and the personal problems arising in it—though it fact the problems of the Roman Principate are somewhat more complicated still, since under Louis XIV it was clear that his subjects were his subjects, while during the early phases of the Empire it was not clear whether the Roman citizens were the subjects of the Emperor or his fellow citizens.

I do not like to engage in personal polemics. If therefore in what follows I shall use as an example of what appears to me a defective method of historical reasoning a little article or note that has recently been published in this journal I wish to state right at the beginning that it would be easy to make quite a collection

* Kurt von Fritz, "Tacitus, Agricola, Domitian, and the Problem of the Principate," reprinted from *Classical Philology*, 52 (1957), pp. 73–77; 93–96. Copyright 1957 by the University of Chicago.

of similar examples from recently published scholarly literature on both sides of the Atlantic, and that I have chosen this particular example only because it touches incidentally on a problem that appears to me of fundamental importance for a full understanding of the Roman Principate, a problem, however, which cannot be seen, much less solved, as long as such methods of historical reasoning are applied.

On pages 255–57 of Volume XLIX of *Classical Philology* (1954), H. W. Traub discusses a story told by Tacitus in his little pamphlet on the life and virtues of his father-in-law Agricola. In 91 B.C., so Tacitus tells us, there was to be a *sortitio* of the two senatorial provinces Asia and Africa and Agricola was to draw lots for them. He was, however, approached by some people *cogitationum principis periti* who asked him whether he would accept the office and then first began to praise the leisure and tranquillity of private life, but finally ended by threatening him with dire consequences if he would not forthwith ask to be excused from the governorship. Consequently Agricola proceeded to ask the Emperor to be excused, and Domitian, according to Tacitus,

"armed beforehand with hypocrisy, and assuming a haughty demeanor, listened to his prayer that he might be excused, and having granted his request allowed himself to be formally thanked, nor blushed to grant so sinister a favor. But the salary usually granted to a proconsul, and which he had himself given to some governors, he did not bestow upon Agricola, either because he was offended at its not having been asked, or was warned by his conscience that he might be thought to have purchased the refusal which he had commanded."*

According to Traub this passage implies "that Agricola's refusal of the governorship was unnatural" and that "it was the

---

* Translated by A. J. Church and W. J. Brodribb.

fault of Domitian that Agricola did not receive the *salarium* regularly offered on such occasions." He then tries to show that both implications are in all likelihood not justified.

In order to prove his point Traub collects a number of passages from Fronto, from an inscription of A.D. 281, and even from Tacitus himself to show that, in other periods of the Empire also, persons occasionally begged to be excused from a governorship for reasons of health or age or what not, and that the granting of such a request was considered a *beneficium*. Now it is certainly in the best tradition of accurate scholarship to collect and present all the evidence, brought together, as in this case, from the most distant sources. But though in our mechanistically minded age this point is somewhat less often stressed by contemporary critics, it would appear at least as important to consider carefully the relevance of the evidence to the problem at hand. In the present case in fact I should think that, even if we had no concrete evidence whatever, we should be entitled to assume, on general grounds, that in an age in which people did not or not always compete for offices but were designated for them by the Senate or the Emperor occasions must inevitably have arisen in which someone asked to be excused from such office for reasons of health, for family reasons, or the like. If then the granting of such a request had not been called a *beneficium* it would probably have been designated by some other word of approximately the same meaning. But what in the world has all this to do with the implications of Tacitus' story?

I cannot find in Tacitus' story the slightest indication of the implication that a request to be excused from an office was something in itself "unnatural." If Tacitus implies anything it is the opposite. What he says in the clearest possible way is that in the particular case of Agricola the request and its acceptance were a comedy—

a comedy because Agricola had to act as if his request was caused by natural reasons of the usual kind, while in actual fact it was induced by the threats of Domitian's agents—and he does imply indeed that for a serious man like Agricola it was not particularly pleasant to have to play a part in such a comedy. Assuming that the facts as told by Tacitus are correct, I cannot even see why in this particular case we should quarrel with his judgment.

Traub, it is true, also questions the veracity of Tacitus' statement of the facts. "It appears," he says, "inconsistent with Agricola's stated policy (*Agricolae consilium*) of not taking part in affairs of state that he had to be first terrified . . . to make his excuses. The whole passage seems all the more strange because these so-called 'agents of the emperor' encouraged Agricola to pursue *quietem et otium*, almost the very words that Tacitus had used earlier to describe the retiring policy of Agricola: *tranquillitatem atque otium penitus hausit.*"

Now the passage last quoted occurs in a description of Agricola's life and attitude *in Rome* after his return from his governorship of Britain. The whole passage runs as follows: "Anxious henceforth to temper the military renown, which annoys men of peace, with other merits, he studiously cultivated retirement and leisure, simple in dress, courteous in conversation, and never accompanied but by one or two friends, so that the many who commonly judge great men by their external grandeur, after having seen and attentively surveyed him, asked the secret of the greatness which but few could explain,"* and it has clearly nothing whatsoever to do with the question of accepting or rejecting another governorship. The other passage quoted (*Agricolae consilium*) does indeed have something to do with this latter question though it

---

* Translated by A. J. Church and W. J. Brodribb.

certainly does not say anything about a "stated policy." The expression occurs in a sentence that immediately precedes the passage about the agents of Domitian who approached Agricola with their warning. This sentence is as follows: "As Civica had lately been murdered, Agricola did not want a warning, or Domitian a precedent." It refers to the fact that Civica had been executed on the order of Domitian during his governorship. It obviously means that consequently Agricola had had a warning (*consilium*) as to what could happen to him if he should accept another governorship and Domitian had a precedent (of having a proconsul executed during his term of office). The following sentences then mean clearly that not content with the warning that Agricola might have found in Civica's death (after all Domitian could not know how strong its effect on Agricola would be) Domitian in addition sent his agents to Agricola to deter him from accepting the governorship, though, as Tacitus had stated a little earlier, the Emperor not long before had hinted that he wished Agricola to have another governorship soon after his expected return from Britain.

Traub does not say in so many words that he accuses Tacitus of a barefaced lie in regard to an event of which the latter claims that it happened to his own father-in-law at a time when he, Tacitus, was a grown-up man and of which, therefore, if it did happen, he must have had rather firsthand knowledge. But this appears to be implied by Traub's phrase, "certainly it is more reasonable to believe that Agricola of his own free will refused the governorship," following directly on the statement that the whole passage in which Tacitus tells of Domitian's agents is "strange." If he did not mean to imply that much he should have been more explicit. For this is after all the salient point. If we reject the story of the agents we accuse Tacitus of deliberately falsifying the facts.

If we do not, we merely question his judgment. This certainly makes a fundamental difference in our evaluation of the historian. Also, as shown above, if the facts as told by Tacitus are accepted, the whole question of whether others had refused governorships before for natural reasons becomes totally irrelevant.

But let us assume that Traub meant merely to say that in all likelihood Agricola would have rejected the governorship anyway and that, though the affair of the agents did occur, Tacitus misled the judgment of his readers by suggesting that Agricola would have accepted the governorship if he had not been approached by Domitian's agents and by thus making the story look more important than it actually was.

If we wish to arrive at a full understanding of the problem on this basis we shall have to make an attempt to dot some *i*'s and to cross some *t*'s where both Tacitus and Traub have neglected to do so. I think it can be said without reservation that nobody who reads Tacitus' *Agricola* from beginning to end will receive the impression that a man of Agricola's capability and sense of responsibility would not have been willing to serve the state again and again in important positions under normal conditions, though Tacitus tries to represent him as a man rather free from personal ambition. Tacitus, on the other hand, does make it very clear that, knowing Domitian's suspicions and jealousies, Agricola after his return from Britain was very retiring and careful to avoid giving the impression that he was striving for new powers and distinctions. These are the passages quoted by Traub, and certainly there is no contradiction thus far in what Tacitus says and what he implies.

Following his description of Agricola's general attitude after his return from Britain, Tacitus goes on to say that the execution of Civica could serve Agricola as a warning with regard to the possible acceptance of a new governorship. Then he tells the story about the agents of. Domitian. Here Tacitus does not say what answer Agricola gave to the agents when they first asked him whether he was going to accept a new governorship. But the fact that, according to the story, they finally proceeded to threaten him, clearly implies that his answer was not right from the beginning firmly in the negative. At this point one might find a certain inconsistency in Tacitus' account, since he had said that Agricola had had a general warning before, and one might therefore suspect that, though the facts of the story are in general true, Tacitus distorted it slightly in order to give it a slant still more unfavorable to the Emperor. But is there a real inconsistency even here? Tacitus does not give the reasons for Agricola's initial noncommittal attitude toward the agents of Domitian, and it is not possible for us to know them with any degree of certainty. But Traub himself expresses the opinion that Domitian may have been (according to Traub even justifiedly) offended by Agricola's not asking for the *salarium*. So long as Agricola did not know for sure whether Domitian wanted him to accept or to refuse the governorship he may very well have considered it wiser not to commit himself, quite apart from any other reasons that he may possibly have had to desire another governorship in spite of the warning provided by the death of Civica—which after all did not deter everybody from accepting governorships: otherwise there would have been no provincial governors in the last years of Domitian. For a refusal against the wishes of the Emperor, who had publicly announced that Agricola was designated for a new governorship, and this while Agricola was obviously in good health, might also have been considered an offense against the *princeps*.

Agricola's noncommittal attitude, however, caused the Emperor's agents to make the latter's wishes very clear and to insist on an immediate settlement of the matter. Thus Agricola had to go through with the comedy of acting as if he declined for personal reasons what the Emperor offered him so graciously, while he actually acted under the influence of the indirect and direct threats of the same emperor. It may then be left to the personal feeling of the reader to decide whether he feels that the comedy was not humiliating for Agricola, because the death of Civica might have caused him to decline the governorship anyway, and whether he thinks that Agricola should have asked for the *salarium* and so have risked the additional humiliation of a refusal, or whether he agrees with Tacitus who seems to think that it would have been at least a slightly redeeming grace on the part of Domitian if in the circumstances he had given Agricola the *salarium* without having been asked for it. But I do hope to have proved that there is not one shred of evidence that would entitle us to accuse Tacitus of a bare-faced lie in regard to the incident as a whole and that the apparent inconsistency of what he says about Agricola's attitude which Traub has pointed out is not even sufficient to prove that he gave a distorted picture of the incident.

All this does, of course, not mean that everything that Tacitus says either in his *Agricola* or in his two large historical works must be taken at its face value. Probably no one who reads Tacitus' historical works, and especially his *Annals*, with close attention will escape the impression that some of the facts narrated there, especially in the first books about Tiberius, admit of an interpretation somewhat less unfavorable to this emperor. It has often been noted that Tacitus when he tells of rumors that were current at a certain time is frequently careful to characterize them as rumors and yet appears deliberately to give his readers the impression that they may have contained some truth, or, when he does try to prove

that the rumor was untrue in regard to the facts, nevertheless suggests that the depravity of character of a certain emperor was so great that such rumors were bound to arise so that, though factually untrue, the rumors did not do great injustice to the character of the emperor concerned. Finally, it also appears significant that none of the three other historians who wrote on the period or part of it and whose works are either partly or wholly preserved, Velleius Paterculus, Cassius Dio, and Suetonius, gives quite as gloomy a picture of the rule of the early emperors as Tacitus does, though Dio cannot be said to be favorably biased toward them and Suetonius has certain characteristics of a scandalmongering sensationalist. But even if all this is admitted and taken into account to the fullest extent, it does not suggest that Tacitus would lightly tell an untruth in regard to facts, especially when he had firsthand knowledge of them, but rather the opposite, so that there is no reason on this count either to question the truth of the story he tells about Agricola and Domitian.

[Here follows a lengthy analysis of Tacitus' portrayal of Tiberius and its significance for the nature of the early Principate and for our understanding of Tacitus.]

* * *

The overwhelming majority of the ancient authors who wrote about the period of the early Principate or about parts of it agreed that all through this period there was something fundamentally wrong, though some sections of the period were better than others. Tacitus had convinced himself that there was no fundamental difference between the different periods or subperiods, that the evil was always there, only sometimes a little more concealed through dissimulation and hypocrisy, and consequently he drew a picture of continued human depravity.

What then is Tacitus' fault as a historian, since there appears to be general agreement that, however great he may be as a literary artist, there is something fundamentally wrong with him from the historian's point of view? Certainly not that he was in the habit of telling deliberate lies. There is not, so far as I can see, the slightest evidence to warrant such an assumption. Nor can he be severely blamed for his uncritical attitude toward the tradition. For though indubitably in this respect he does not come up to the most exacting modern standards he certainly was more critical than Dio Cassius and Suetonius and also than his great predecessor Livy, who wrote about an earlier period of Roman history. The fault of which he has been accused most often in recent times is that, not so much by outright lies or distortions of facts or even by uncritical acceptance of slanderous gossip as by a most subtle art of influencing his reader by all sorts of innuendo and indirect hints, he managed to blacken the character of the early emperors and has given an entirely distorted picture of the whole period. But it has been shown that in a way Tacitus, by using this subtle art of innuendo, merely has tried to give a consistent explanation of the events where his predecessors were baffled by apparent contradictions. In other words he has tried to attend to the historian's task, which is to explain what on the surface appears strange and inexplicable. Thus he found the explanation of the apparent discrepancy between the good and the bad features of Tiberius' Principate in the Emperor's profound dissimulation and hypocrisy which he practiced with great skill during the first part of his rule when he was not yet sure of his power, but gradually dropped when he found them no longer necessary. Even in this respect, however, Tacitus was not entirely wrong, since it has been shown that a certain, though greatly varying, degree of dissimulation and hypocrisy was inevitably inherent in the relations between the Emperors and the Senate from the time of Tiberius down even to that of Trajan.

Yet it is exactly at this point that we find the real and essential deficiency of Tacitus as a historian. His only explanation of the evils of his time and of the preceding periods is the depravity of character of the actors on the political scene, the lust for power on the part of the emperors and the servility on the part of the majority of their prominent contemporaries. Both Klingner and Miss Walker have laid great stress on the fact that Tacitus, in contrast to most of his predecessors and to the common opinion of his time, extended the prevailing unfavorable judgment of the early emperors to Octavianus Augustus, to the founder of the Principate himself. Miss Walker interprets this as a sign of Tactitus' dissatisfaction with his description of the Principate of Tiberius and as a token of his desire to find the causes of the disease farther back in history. And indeed, there is a great deal of truth in the second part of this interpretation, though hardly in its first part. For the evidence of such a search for causes farther back in history is found not only in the first chapters of the *Annals*, which possibly could be a late insertion, but in Tacitus' much earlier writings, the *Dialogue* and the *Agricola*. But in all those chapters and passages in which Tacitus tries to find the origins of later evils in Pre-Tiberian times the only principle of explanation is still the depravity of character of the actors on the political scene. Augustus' dominating character trait in Tacitus' opinion was his *cupido dominandi*. He was able to establish his power because of the general exhaustion after the civil wars. He later retained this power through violence and deception, just like his successor Tiberius, but also like Gaius, Claudius, Nero, and, of course, Domitian.

If we go still farther back, it is the quarrels of the powerful among themselves, the avarice of those in high positions, the lack of respect for the law, the greed for money, and the ruthlessness of individuals in striving for the aims of their ambition that destroyed the Republic and led to the creation of the Principate. There is, of course, a good deal of truth in this diagnosis. But it is not a historical explanation. The Romans after all had lived under a republican order for several centuries. The Greek historian Polybius had contended that their constitution was an excellent example of what he considered the best form of a political constitution: a mixed constitution and a system of checks and balances. Polybius had further contended that a constitution of this kind was more stable than any other political order and that it provided a guaranty of liberty. Why then was this constitution destroyed and replaced by the poorly concealed despotism of the Principate, since the Romans after all had proved to be capable of liberty? And if the reason of the downfall of this constitution is to be found in the gradual decline of the *prisca virtus* of the Romans, as Tacitus appears to believe, what was the cause of this decline?

It is the great difference between Tacitus and the great Greek historians Thucydides, Polybius, and Posidonius that he has no eye for what may be called the impersonal forces in history. There is no word anywhere in his works about the enormous changes in the social composition of the population of the city of Rome and of Italy in the century and a half that preceded the downfall of the Roman Republic, about the no less important changes in the composition of the popular assemblies, or about the fact that certain constitutional devices originally created for the protection of the lower classes had become tools in the hands of the ruling aristocracy enabling it to prevent necessary reforms, and that the citizen armies of the early Republic had gradually become replaced by professional armies more and more dissociated from the rest of the popu-

lation and filled with distrust of the civilian government.

This is, of course, not a deficiency of Tacitus alone, but of all the historians of his period, and also obviously of his fellow aristocrats. None of them appears to have realized what after all should have been none too difficult to see: that the indispensable precondition for the restoration of political liberty and of a republican order would have been the reintegration of the army with the civilian population and the restoration of its confidence in a civilian government, and that, as long as this tremendous problem was not solved, the fundamental lie on which the Principate rested and which had such a poisonous effect on the characters of men could be eliminated only by the establishment of an openly professed absolute monarchy, an end toward which the Roman Empire, though slowly and with many detours, was actually proceeding.

If Tacitus had been aware of this and similar no less important factors in the historical development of the Roman Empire he would certainly have arrived at a juster evaluation of the characters of some of the early emperors and of those of many of their subjects, and he would not always have attributed to personal depravity and viciousness what often was the result of circumstances against which the individual had been struggling with all his power, but in vain. But in spite of these very serious deficiencies Tacitus is not only a great writer and a great artist, but also a great historian, who has given a description of the poisonous atmosphere of dissimulation and tyranny, of suppressed rebelliousness and servility prevailing under the early emperors that is to a large extent true, and indeed unsurpassed, if one disregards the lack of any investigation into its underlying causes. At any rate, there cannot be the slightest doubt that those modern attempts to correct Tacitus which start consciously or unconsciously from such utterly naive considerations as these, that things cannot have been so bad because that would be a slight on human nature or that a certain emperor, as for instance Nero (!), must have been an excellent monarch because the provinces were in a comparatively flourishing state at his time, will inevitably lead to a much more superficial and historically inaccurate view of the period than that of Tacitus which they try to correct.

In conclusion we may return to Polybius, from whose observations we started, and say that in order to criticize the contents of a great historian of antiquity it is not sufficient to apply more or less, in fact sometimes less, correctly some methods that one can learn in a philological seminar but that one has first also to have acquired some knowledge of the facts of political life. Perhaps it is permissible to make even a somewhat larger application of the principle. It is simply not true, though in wide circles it appears to be considered an incontestable fact, that it is a precondition of good scholarship and conducive to accurate results never to look beyond the narrow confines of one's special field. In order to interpret a philosophical text correctly it is not sufficient to be a philosopher and not sufficient to be a philologist; one has to be both. And the same is true, *mutatis mutandis*, of a mathematical text—though in this case the philologists, who consider themselves self-sufficient in most other fields, usually for good reasons leave the business to the mathematicians—of a historical text, and of course also of poetry. If philological interpretation is not, on the pretense of being truly scholarly and scientific, to become entirely sterile, these artificial boundaries have to be taken down, and if an individual is not able to manage both sides of his subject he should ask the advice of or collaborate with others.

5. AGRICOLA AND DOMITIAN*

It is now generally acknowledged that in the concluding chapters of the *Agricola* Tacitus is on several occasions guilty of distortion of the truth. The story told in 40. 2, for example, of the secret mission of one of Domitian's confidential freedmen with an offer of the governorship of Syria as a bribe to Agricola in case he should appear reluctant to obey the orders for his recall is obviously sheer fabrication, designed solely to intensify the picture of suspicion and distrust on the part of the Emperor that Tacitus is endeavouring to create. Again, though in 43. 2 Tacitus records the rumour that Agricola had been poisoned by Domitian (the rumour is repeated by Dio Cassius, lxvi. 20, as sober truth), he does so in such a way as to indicate that he himself did not believe this charge, though he hoped his readers would. There are, however, three points that have never been satisfactorily explained: the relations between Agricola and Domitian between A.D. 85 and 93, Agricola's refusal of the proconsulship of Asia, and the reason for his non-employment in the Danubian wars.

The discrepancy between the factual and the non-factual elements in Tacitus, which is fully discussed by Miss B. Walker in her recent book *The Annals of Tacitus*, is particularly noticeable in the last eight chapters of the *Agricola*, where the non-factual material is used not to heighten, but to obscure, the general narration of the facts. The resultant picture is that of a man whose great natural abilities only made him incur the jealousy, hatred, and

* T. A. Dorey, "Agricola and Domitian," *Greece and Rome*, second series 7 (Clarendon, 1960), pp. 66–71. Reprinted by permission of The Clarendon Press, Oxford.

mistrust of his Emperor; his modest and upright behaviour did to some extent mitigate the hostility of the Princeps, but, it is implied, only his comparatively early death saved him from falling a victim to tyranny in the end. An examination of the facts, however, presents an entirely different picture. According to the facts that Tacitus records, Agricola was superseded after seven years in Britain, he was given the honours normally granted to a successful general, with a statue as an additional mark of distinction, and there was a belief current at Rome that he would be appointed to the vacant province of Syria; however, after a formal audience with the Princeps, he retired into private life and lived very quietly until his death eight years later; during this period his name was considered for a military appointment on the Danube, but he was in the end not employed, while c. A.D. 90, when he was due to hold a proconsulship, friends of his who were in Domitian's confidence urged him to ask the Emperor to be excused this office, advice which in the end he took, though with some reluctance; finally, in his last illness Domitian showed great concern and anxiety for his health, sent him his own personal physicians, and expressed considerable grief at the news of his death, while, on learning that Agricola had appointed him co-heir, the Emperor manifested a delight that even Tacitus admits as being sincere.

The evidence of these facts points to the conclusion that there did exist a genuine friendly relationship between Domitian and Agricola, a relationship marked by loyal and conscientious service on the one side and sympathetic consideration on the other. On the other hand, Tacitus' attempt to prove Domitian's jealousy and hostility and Agricola's mortal peril rests on very insecure foundations. Its primary hypothesis is the contrast between Agricola's victories and the bogus and ignominious military record of Domitian. But this con-

trast arises from a complete misunderstanding, if not deliberate distortion, of the military considerations involved. While allowing all possible credit to Agricola, it must be admitted that his task in Britain had not been a difficult one. He had succeeded two capable and energetic governors, Petilius Cerialis and Julius Frontinus, who had built up the morale and efficiency of their troops and had already begun to break the back of the British resistance. With a strong force of four legions and their quota of auxiliaries, he had been able to press forward on a conveniently narrow front against an enemy that was undisciplined, disorganized, and comparatively few in numbers. His successes had been well earned, but their contribution to the general welfare and military security of the Empire had not been particularly important.

Domitian's military operations were of far more vital importance than those of Agricola. His campaign against the Chatti, involving the annexation of the Mount Taunus region, the driving of a salient into Germany, the construction of the *limes*, and the shortening of the frontier, had results that were of great permanent value; while the fact that the operations were so skilfully planned and carried out that heavy fighting was avoided enhances rather than diminishes Domitian's credit, though this would not be appreciated by the more blimpish Roman historians who measured the success of an expedition solely by the number of enemy casualties. On the Danube he was not completely successful, but the difficulties that he had to face were considerable. The frontier was long and difficult to guard, it had been grossly neglected for generations, and the tribes that lay beyond it, the Sarmatians, the Suevi, and the Dacians, were numerous, powerful, and well organized. The dangerous irruption of Decebalus into Moesia was speedily beaten back, and the subsequent defeat of Fuscus was fully avenged at Tapae. In granting peace to Decebalus, Domitian showed a wise appreciation of the situation; he knew that Rome was in no position to afford a prolonged war along the whole of the Danube. The basis of the peace was the nominal recognition of Roman suzerainty over Dacia; the gifts of money and the loan of engineers constituted a practical concession that made the Dacians' dependent status more acceptable to them. Although these terms seemed discreditable to the more old-fashioned Romans, who believed that the unconditional surrender of the enemy was a necessary part of any honourable peace, it cannot be denied that Decebalus gave Rome no further trouble until Trajan was ready to embark on his policy of conquest. Of the fighting against the Sarmatians and the Suevi, insufficient details have survived to show whether the successes obtained outweighed the losses that were undoubtedly suffered. However, taking the picture as a whole, there is no doubt that Domitian's military credit must stand high.

The second assumption on which Tacitus bases the alleged hostility of Domitian is that human nature makes it inevitable for a man to hate those whom he has wronged (Tac. *Agr*. 42. 4): 'proprium humani ingenii est odisse quem laeseris.' But the minor premiss of this syllogism is defective, for it is difficult to find any act of injustice towards Agricola of which Domitian could feel guilty. Tacitus seems to be referring to the Emperor's failure to give Agricola the *salarium proconsulare* in lieu of office, but it is very doubtful whether such a grant was the normal practice at that date, and it may have been confined to cases where financial hardship would otherwise have been caused. (The whole of this episode is very involved, and Domitian's attitude, as portrayed by Tacitus, is almost inexplicable. If, as Tacitus alleges, the Emperor hoped to use the proconsulship as an excuse for getting Agricola put to death on some charge of treason, it is difficult to see why he should have gone to such lengths to prevent Agricola's accepting the post.) Nor, again, had Domitian committed any injustice in recalling Agricola from Britain; the latter had held his command longer than usual, he had been allowed to bring the Caledonians to battle, and after his decisive victory the only logical alternatives were that Agricola should be recalled and a policy of withdrawal and consolidation pursued, or that he should be retained and an attempt made to include in the Roman province the wild and desolate parts of Scotland, a task that would be not only unprofitable but also, in view of the lengthened lines of communication, difficult and dangerous. For the same reasons Domitian was perfectly justified in refusing to countenance the invasion of Ireland.

The third assumption that Tacitus makes to support his case is that any successful general was regarded by Domitian as a danger to his position. This assumption is completely unwarranted. It is significant that the great majority of Domitian's victims fall into one of two classes, either leaders of the Stoic opposition in the Senate and the noble families connected with them, or members of the Emperor's own family and household. There are, in fact, only three generals whose deaths are recorded during this reign. Of these, one was Antonius Saturninus, who was killed after an unsuccessful revolt; the others were Vettulenus Civica Cerealis (Tac. *Agr*. 42. 1, Suet. *Dom*. 10. 2), who was put to death on a charge of attempted revolution while proconsul of Asia, and Sallustius Lucullus, the governor of Britain, condemned for giving his own name to a new type of lance (Suet. *Dom*. 10. 2). It is uncertain exactly when Civica and Sallustius were executed, but there is sufficient evidence to fix an approximate date. Civica, who had governed Moesia Inferior in A.D.

82, was put to death shortly before Agricola was due to hold his proconsulship (Tac. *Agr*. 42. 1: 'occiso Ciuica nuper'), and it may well be that the province was still vacant. As a proconsulship became due about twelve or thirteen years after the holding of the consulship, Agricola's turn would have come in A.D. 89 or 90. This gives rise to the possibility that Civica was put to death early in 89 for complicity in the revolt of Saturninus. Sallustius Lucullus, the date of whose command in Britain is unknown, may similarly have been implicated, as it is reasonable to suppose that Saturninus would have tried to enlist the help of the governor of Britain. On the other hand, besides Domitian's general popularity with the troops, of which the insistence of the Praetorian Guard on the punishment of his murderers is a striking example, he seems to have had complete confidence in his generals. Julius Frontinus served with distinction against the Chatti after winning great glory in Britain through the successful completion of a difficult campaign against the Silures; Tettius Julianus does not seem to have incurred the imperial displeasure for his decisive victory over the Dacians at Tapae; Verginius Rufus, who in addition to his long-standing military reputation had twice been offered imperial power, enjoyed greater security under Domitian than he had under Galba and Vitellius; while Trajan's exceptional energy and ability marked him out not for hostility and suspicion, but for special distinction in the grant of the *consulatus ordinarius* and the important command of Germania Superior.

A final and almost conclusive argument against the existence of any hostility on Domitian's part towards Agricola is provided by Tacitus' own career. He himself admits that he owed promotion to Domitian (Tac. *Hist*. i. 1: 'dignitatem nostram . . . a Domitiano longius prouectam non abnuerim'). He must have held the tribunate or aedileship soon after Domitian's accession; in A.D. 88 he was praetor and *quindecimuir sacris faciundis*, in which capacities he assisted in the celebration of the Ludi Saeculares (Tac. *Ann*. xi. 11); and from A.D. 89 to 93 he was away from Rome, an absence that can only be explained by the supposition that during this period he was *legatus pro praetore* of one of the imperial provinces. No man could have held these important appointments at a time when his father-in-law was *persona non grata* with the Emperor.

However, if it is accepted that a friendly relationship did exist between Agricola and Domitian, it will be necessary to find an alternative explanation for Agricola's inactivity during the last eight years of his life and his failure to accept a proconsulship. Now an open-minded review of Agricola's career will bring out the following facts: an energetic and ambitious man, after a crowded and active life of twenty-five years' public service, of which the last fifteen years had involved the almost uninterrupted holding of onerous, responsible positions and had included ten active soldiering years in a turbulent and warlike province, suddenly goes into complete retirement, in spite of the fact that there were several obvious opportunities for the employment of his well-proved military gifts, refuses a comparatively easy civilian appointment, and finally, after eight years of inactivity, dies at the early age of fifty-three. These facts are prima facie evidence that Agricola's retirement and early death were due to a breakdown in health occasioned by continuous overwork. This theory is further supported by what is known of Agricola's personality. He was a man of dynamic energy who drove himself hard; he used to carry out reconnaissances in person, and would himself select the sites for encampments and forts; he took particular care in the selection of his subordinates, and it appears that he was reluctant to delegate responsibility; at a time of personal sorrow he sought relief in hard work. The general picture that emerges is that of a highly conscientious man who paid meticulous attention to detail and regarded no trouble as too great in the interests of efficiency. It is significant that at times he gave way to outbursts of violent anger (Tac. *Agr*. 22. 4: 'apud quosdam acerbior in conuiciis narrabatur'), something that is often a symptom of excessive strain. It seems possible, then, that Agricola belonged to that type of man who has worn himself out by early middle-age.

The acceptance of this hypothesis will provide a satisfactory explanation for Agricola's strange inactivity after his return from Britain. He was not offered further military employment because of his ill health. The very quiet style of life that he adopted was due to the same cause. When his turn came to draw lots for a proconsulship, his high sense of duty made him reluctant to refuse what he no doubt considered a necessary public service. But his friends, with the consent and possibly on the suggestion of Domitian, who seems to have been genuinely well disposed towards Agricola, persuaded him to ask to be excused the post, acceptance of which might prove too much for his poor state of health.

It may be objected to this theory that nowhere does Tacitus make any suggestion of Agricola's ill health. In the face of this objection it is necessary to consider, very briefly, the nature of the *Agricola*. It is not a piece of sober historical writing, having as its object the recording of facts and the explanation of their connexion with each other; it is, without question, a highly rhetorical composition. Being of a rhetorical nature, it is designed to persuade its readers to adopt a certain point of view, namely that Agricola, though he served Domitian loyally and did not fall a victim to his judicial massacres, deserved to be enshrined alongside the Stoic 'martyrs', or even to be ranked higher. It seems that Tacitus wrote and published this work at a time when feeling against Domitian was still very violent, and the historian wished to exculpate his father-in-law from any suspicion of having enjoyed the tyrant's favour. To make good his case he would naturally ignore anything that might interfere with his chosen interpretation of the facts.

07/29/66

Christianity and the Roman Empire

THE RISE OF Christianity and its spread throughout the Mediterranean presented a serious problem to the magistrates of the Roman Empire. Like most pagans, the Romans were tolerant of most religious beliefs. Persecution on religious grounds was unusual among the Romans. The Christians, however, were very different from votaries of Isis, Mithra, Magna Mater, even from the Jews. One of the questions treated in this section is the nature of this difference. The Romans did, in fact, persecute the Christians with varying degrees of severity. What was the cause of this persecution? What was its legal and juridical basis? How severe was it? What was its meaning for the future of Rome and for the future of Christianity?

1. ST. PAUL AND THE ROMAN EMPIRE*

11 Setting sail therefore from Tro'as, we made a direct voyage to Sam'othrace, and the following day to Ne-ap'olis, 12 and from there to Philippi, which is the leading city of the district of Macedo'nia, and a Roman colony. We remained in this city some days; 13 and on the sabbath day we went outside the gate to the riverside, where we supposed there was a place of prayer; and we sat down and spoke to the women who had come together. 14 One who heard us was a woman named Lydia, from the city of Thyati'ra, a seller of purple goods, who was a worshipper of God. The Lord opened her heart to give heed to what was said by Paul. 15 And when she was baptized, with her household, she besought us, saying, "If you have judged me to be faithful to the Lord, come to my house and stay." And she prevailed upon us.

16 As we were going to the place of prayer, we were met by a slave girl who had a spirit of divination and brought her owners much gain by soothsaying. 17 She followed Paul and us, crying, "These men are servants of the Most High God, who proclaim to you the way of salvation." 18 And this she did for many days. But Paul was annoyed, and turned and said to the spirit, "I charge you in the name of Jesus Christ to come out of her." And it came out that very hour.

---

* The Acts of the Apostles 16.11–18.17; 19.21–41; 21.27–26.32. The Scripture quotations in this publication are from the *Revised Standard Version of the Bible*, copyrighted 1946 and 1952 by the Division of Christian Education, National Council of Churches, and used by permission.

Justice

19 But when her owners saw that their hope of gain was gone, they seized Paul and Silas and dragged them into the market place before the rulers; 20 and when they had brought them to the magistrates they said, "These men are Jews and they are disturbing our city. 21 They advocate customs which it is not lawful for us Romans to accept or practice." 22 The crowd joined in attacking them; and the magistrates tore the garments off them and gave orders to beat them with rods. 23 And when they had inflicted many blows upon them, they threw them into prison, charging the jailer to keep them safely. 24 Having received this charge, he put them into the inner prison and fastened their feet in the stocks.

25 But about midnight Paul and Silas were praying and singing hymns to God, and the prisoners were listening to them, 26 and suddenly there was a great earthquake, so that the foundations of the prison were shaken; and immediately all the doors were opened and every one's fetters were unfastened. 27 When the jailer woke and saw that the prison doors were open, he drew his sword and was about to kill himself, supposing that the prisoners had escaped. 28 But Paul cried with a loud voice, "Do not harm yourself, for we are all here." 29 And he called for lights and rushed in, and trembling with fear he fell down before Paul and Silas, 30 and brought them out and said, "Men, what must I do to be saved?" 31 And they said, "Believe in the Lord Jesus, and you will be saved, you and your household." 32 And they spoke the word of the Lord to him and to all that were in his house. 33 And he took them the same hour of the night, and washed their wounds, and he was baptized at once, with all his family. 34 Then he brought them up into his house, and set food before them; and he rejoiced with all his household that he had believed in God.

35 But when it was day, the magistrates sent the police, saying, "Let those men go." 36 And the jailer reported the words to Paul, saying, "The magistrates have sent to let you go; now therefore come out and go in peace." 37 But Paul said to them, "They have beaten us publicly, uncondemned, men who are Roman citizens, and have thrown us into prison; and do they now cast us out secretly? No! let them come themselves and take us out." 38 The police reported these words to the magistrates, and they were afraid when they heard that they were Roman citizens; 39 so they came and apologized to them. And they took them out and asked them to leave the city. 40 So they went out of the prison, and visited Lydia; and when they had seen the brethren, they exhorted them and departed.

17

Now when they had passed through Amphip'olis and Apollo'nia, they came to Thessaloni'ca, where there was a synagogue of the Jews. 2 And Paul went in, as was his custom, and for three weeks he argued with them from the scriptures, 3 explaining and proving that it was necessary for the Christ to suffer and to rise from the dead, and saying, "This Jesus, whom I proclaim to you, is the Christ." 4 And some of them were persuaded, and joined Paul and Silas; as did a great many of the devout Greeks and not a few of the leading women. 5 But the Jews were jealous, and taking some wicked fellows of the rabble, they gathered a crowd, set the city in an uproar, and attacked the house of Jason, seeking to bring them out to the people. 6 And when they could not find them, they dragged Jason and some of the brethren before the city authorities, crying, "These men who have turned the world upside down have come here also, 7 and Jason has received them; and they are all acting against the decrees of Caesar, saying that there is another king, Jesus." 8 And the people and the city authorities were disturbed when they heard this. 9 And when they had taken security from Jason and the rest, they let them go.

10 The brethren immediately sent Paul and Silas away by night to Beroe'a; and when they arrived they went into the Jewish synagogue. 11 Now these Jews were more noble than those in Thessaloni'ca, for they received the word with all eagerness, examining the scriptures daily to see if these things were so. 12 Many of them therefore believed, with not a few Greek women of high standing as well as men. 13 But when the Jews of Thessaloni'ca learned that the word of God was proclaimed by Paul at Beroe'a also, they came there too, stirring up and inciting the crowds. 14 Then the brethren immediately sent Paul off on his way to the sea, but Silas and Timothy remained there. 15 Those who conducted Paul brought him as far as Athens; and receiving a command for Silas and Timothy to come to him as soon as possible, they departed.

16 Now while Paul was waiting for them at Athens, his spirit was provoked within him as he saw that the city was full of idols. 17 So he argued in the synagogue with the Jews and the devout persons, and in the market place every day with those who chanced to be there. 18 Some also of the Epicurean and Stoic philosophers met him. And some said, "What would this babbler say?" Others said, "He seems to be a preacher of foreign divinities"—because he preached Jesus and the resurrection. 19 And they took hold of him and brought him to the Are-op'agus, saying, "May we know what this new teaching is which you present? 20 For you bring some strange things to our ears; we wish to know therefore what these things mean." 21 Now all the Athenians and the foreigners who lived there spent their time in nothing except telling or hearing something new.

22 So Paul, standing in the middle of the Are-op'agus, said: "Men of Athens, I perceive that in every way you are very religious. 23 For as I passed along, and observed the objects of your worship, I found also an altar with this inscription, 'To an unknown god.' What therefore you worship as unknown, this I proclaim to you. 24 The God who made the world and everything in it, being Lord of heaven and earth, does not live in shrines made by man, 25 nor is he served by human hands, as though he needed anything, since he himself gives to all men life and breath and everything. 26 And he made from one every nation of men to live on all the face of the earth, having determined allotted periods and the boundaries of their habitation, 27 that they should seek God, in the hope that they might feel after him and find him. Yet he is not far from each one of us, 28 for

'In him we live and move and have our being';

as even some of your poets have said,

'For we are indeed his offspring.'

29 Being then God's offspring, we ought not to think that the Deity is like gold, or ✗✗✓ silver, or stone, a representation by the art and imagination of man. 30 The times of ignorance God overlooked, but now he commands all men everywhere to repent, 31 because he has fixed a day on which he will judge the world in righteousness by a man whom he has appointed, and of this he has given assurance to all men by raising ✗✗✓ him from the dead."

32 Now when they heard of the resurrection of the dead, some mocked; but others said, "We will hear you again about this." 33 So Paul went out from among them. 34 But some men joined him and believed, among them Dionys'ius the ⒉+ Are-op'agite and a woman named Dam'-aris and others with them.

18

After this he left Athens and went to Corinth. 2 And he found a Jew named Aquila, a native of Pontus, lately come from Italy with his wife Priscilla, because

Claudius had commanded all the Jews to leave Rome. And he went to see them; 3 and because he was of the same trade he stayed with them, and they worked, for by trade they were tentmakers. 4 And he argued in the synagogue every sabbath, and persuaded Jews and Greeks.

5 When Silas and Timothy arrived from Macedo'nia, Paul was occupied with preaching, testifying to the Jews that the Christ was Jesus. 6 And when they opposed and reviled him, he shook out his garments and said to them, "Your blood be upon your heads! I am innocent. From now on I will go to the Gentiles." 7 And he left there and went to the house of a man named Titius Justus, a worshiper of God; his house was next door to the synagogue. 8 Crispus, the ruler of the synagogue, believed in the Lord, together with all his household; and many of the Corinthians hearing Paul believed and were baptized. 9 And the Lord said to Paul one night in a vision, "Do not be afraid, but speak and do not be silent; 10 for I am with you, and no man shall attack you to harm you; for I have many people in this city." 11 And he stayed a year and six months, teaching the word of God among them.

12 But when Gallio was proconsul of Acha'ia, the Jews made a united attack upon Paul and brought him before the tribunal, 13 saying, "This man is persuading men to worship God contrary to the law." 14 But when Paul was about to open his mouth, Gallio said to the Jews, "If it were a matter of wrongdoing or vicious crime, I should have reason to bear with you, O Jews; 15 but since it is a matter of questions about words and names and your own law, see to it yourselves; I refuse to be a judge of these things." 16 And he drove them from the tribunal. 17 And they all seized Sos'thenes, the ruler of the synagogue, and beat him in front of the tribunal. But Gallio paid no attention to this.

* * *

21 Now after these events Paul resolved in the Spirit to pass through Macedo'nia and Acha'ia and go to Jerusalem, saying, "After I have been there, I must also see Rome." 22 And having sent into Macedonia two of his helpers, Timothy and Eras'tus, he himself stayed in Asia for a while.

23 About that time there arose no little stir concerning the Way. 24 For a man named Deme'trius, a silversmith, who made silver shrines of Ar'temis, brought no little business to the craftsmen. 25 These he gathered together, with the workmen of like occupation, and said, "Men, you know that from this business we have our wealth. 26 And you see and hear that not only at Ephesus but almost throughout all Asia this Paul has persuaded and turned away a considerable company of people, saying that gods made with hands are not gods. 27 And there is danger not only that this trade of ours may come into disrepute but also that the temple of the great goddess Ar'temis may count for nothing, and that she may even be deposed from her magnificence, she whom all Asia and the world worship."

28 When they heard this they were enraged, and cried out, "Great is Ar'temis of the Ephesians!" 29 So the city was filled with the confusion; and they rushed together into the theater, dragging with them Ga'ius and Aristar'chus, Macedo'nians who were Paul's companions in travel. 30 Paul wished to go in among the crowd, but the disciples would not let him; 31 some of the A'si-archs also, who were friends of his, sent to him and begged him not to venture into the theater. 32 Now some cried one thing, some another; for the assembly was in confusion, and most of them did not know why they had come together. 33 Some of the crowd prompted Alexander, whom the Jews had put forward. And Alexander motioned with his hand, wishing to make a defense to the people. 34 But when they recognized that he was a Jew, for about two hours they all

with one voice cried out, "Great is Ar'-temis of the Ephesians!" 35 And when the town clerk had quieted the crowd, he said, "Men of Ephesus, what man is there who does not know that the city of the Ephesians is temple keeper of the great Ar'temis, and of the sacred stone that fell from the sky? 36 Seeing then that these things cannot be contradicted, you ought to be quiet and do nothing rash. 37 For you have brought these men here who are neither sacrilegious nor blasphemers of our goddess. 38 If therefore Deme'trius and the craftsmen with him have a complaint against any one, the courts are open, and there are proconsuls; let them bring charges against one another. 39 But if you seek anything further, it shall be settled in the regular assembly. 40 For we are in danger of being charged with rioting today, there being no cause that we can give to justify this commotion." 41 And when he had said this, he dismissed the assembly.

* * *

27 When the seven days were almost completed, the Jews from Asia, who had seen him in the temple, stirred up all the crowd, and laid hands on him, 28 crying out, "Men of Israel, help! This is the man who is teaching men everywhere against the people and the law and this place; moreover he also brought Greeks into the temple, and he has defiled this holy place." 29 For they had previously seen Troph'-imus the Ephesian with him in the city, and they supposed that Paul had brought him into the temple. 30 Then all the city was aroused, and the people ran together; they seized Paul and dragged him out of the temple, and at once the gates were shut. 31 And as they were trying to kill him, word came to the tribune of the cohort that all Jerusalem was in confusion. 32 He at once took soldiers and centurions, and ran down to them; and when they saw the tribune and the soldiers, they stopped

beating Paul. 33 Then the tribune came up and arrested him, and ordered him to be bound with two chains. He inquired who he was and what he had done. 34 Some in the crowd shouted one thing, some another; and as he could not learn the facts because of the uproar, he ordered him to be brought into the barracks. 35 And when he came to the steps, he was actually carried by the soldiers because of the violence of the crowd; 36 for the mob of people followed, crying, "Away with him!"

37 As Paul was about to be brought into the barracks, he said to the tribune, "May I say something to you?" And he said, "Do you know Greek? 38 Are you not the Egyptian, then, who recently stirred up a revolt and led the four thousand men of the Assassins out into the wilderness?" 39 Paul replied, "I am a Jew, from Tarsus in Cili'cia, a citizen of no mean city; I beg you, let me speak to the people." 40 And when he had given him leave, Paul, standing on the steps, motioned with his hand to the people; and when there was a great hush, he spoke to them in the Hebrew language, saying:

22   Heb.

"Brethren and fathers, hear the defense which I now make before you."
2 And when they heard that he addressed them in the Hebrew language, they were the more quiet. And he said:
3 "I am a Jew, born at Tarsus in Cili'cia, but brought up in this city at the feet of Gama'li-el, educated according to the strict manner of the law of our fathers, being zealous for God as you all are this day. 4 I persecuted this Way to the death,   Way binding and delivering to prison both men and women, 5 as the high priest and the whole council of elders bear me witness. From them I received letters to the brethren, and I journeyed to Damascus to take those also who were there and bring them in bonds to Jerusalem to be punished.

6 "As I made my journey and drew near to Damascus, about noon a great light from heaven suddenly shone about me. 7 And I fell to the ground and heard a voice saying to me, 'Saul, Saul, why do you persecute me?' 8 And I answered, 'Who are you, Lord?' And he said to me, 'I am Jesus of Nazareth whom you are persecuting.' 9 Now those who were with me saw the light but did not hear the voice of the one who was speaking to me. 10 And I said, 'What shall I do, Lord?' And the Lord said to me, 'Rise, and go into Damascus, and there you will be told all that is appointed for you to do.' 11 And when I could not see because of the brightness of that light, I was led by the hand by those who were with me, and came into Damascus.

12 "And one Anani'as, a devout man according to the law, well spoken of by all the Jews who lived there, 13 came to me, and standing by me said to me, 'Brother Saul, receive your sight.' And in that very hour I received my sight and saw him. 14 And he said, 'The God of our fathers appointed you to know his will, to see the Just One and to hear a voice from his mouth; 15 for you will be a witness for him to all men of what you have seen and heard. 16 And now why do you wait? Rise and be baptized, and wash away your sins, calling on his name.'

17 "When I had returned to Jerusalem and was praying in the temple, I fell into a trance 18 and saw him saying to me, 'Make haste and get quickly out of Jerusalem, because they will not accept your testimony about me.' 19 And I said, 'Lord, they themselves know that in every synagogue I imprisoned and beat those who believed in thee. 20 And when the blood of Stephen thy witness was shed, I also was standing by and approving, and keeping the garments of those who killed him.' 21 And he said to me, 'Depart; for I will send you far away to the Gentiles.'"

22 Up to this word they listened to him; then they lifted up their voices and said, "Away with such a fellow from the earth! For he ought not to live." 23 And as they cried out and waved their garments and threw dust into the air, 24 the tribune commanded him to be brought into the barracks, and ordered him to be examined by scourging, to find out why they shouted thus against him. 25 But when they had tied him up with the thongs, Paul said to the centurion who was standing by, "Is it lawful for you to scourge a man who is a Roman citizen, and uncondemned?" 26 When the centurion heard that, he went to the tribune and said to him, "What are you about to do? For this man is a Roman citizen." 27 So the tribune came and said to him, "Tell me, are you a Roman citizen?" And he said, "Yes." 28 The tribune answered, "I bought this citizenship for a large sum." Paul said, "But I was born a citizen." 29 So those who were about to examine him withdrew from him instantly; and the tribune also was afraid, for he realized that Paul was a Roman citizen and that he had bound him.

30 But on the morrow, desiring to know the real reason why the Jews accused him, he unbound him, and commanded the chief priests and all the council to meet, and he brought Paul down and set him before them.

23

And Paul, looking intently at the council, said, "Brethren, I have lived before God in all good conscience up to this day." 2 And the high priest Anani'as commanded those who stood by him to strike him on the mouth. 3 Then Paul said to him, "God shall strike you, you whitewashed wall! Are you sitting to judge me according to the law, and yet contrary to the law you order me to be struck?" 4 Those who stood by said, "Would you revile God's high priest?" 5 And Paul said, "I did not know, brethren, that he was the high priest; for it is written, 'You shall not speak evil of a ruler of your people.'"

6 But when Paul perceived that one part were Sad'ducees and the other Pharisees, he cried out in the council, "Brethren, I am a Pharisee, a son of Pharisees; with respect to the hope and the resurrection of the dead I am on trial." 7 And when he had said this, a dissension arose between the Pharisees and the Sad'ducees; and the assembly was divided. 8 For the Sad'ducees say that there is no resurrection, nor angel, nor spirit; but the Pharisees acknowledge them all. 9 Then a great clamor arose; and some of the scribes of the Pharisees' party stood up and contended, "We find nothing wrong in this man. What if a spirit or an angel spoke to him?" 10 And when the dissension became violent, the tribune, afraid that Paul would be torn in pieces by them, commanded the soldiers to go down and take him by force from among them and bring him into the barracks. *God in the story*

11 The following night the Lord stood by him and said, "Take courage, for as you have testified about me at Jerusalem, so you must bear witness also at Rome."

12 When it was day, the Jews made a plot and bound themselves by an oath neither to eat nor drink till they had killed Paul. 13 There were more than *40* forty who made this conspiracy. 14 And they went to the chief priests and elders, and said, "We have strictly bound ourselves by an oath to taste no food till we have killed Paul. 15 You therefore, along with the council, give notice now to the tribune to bring him down to you, as though you were going to determine his case more exactly. And we are ready to kill him before he comes near."

16 Now the son of Paul's sister heard of their ambush; so he went and entered the barracks and told Paul. 17 And Paul called one of the centurions and said, "Bring this young man to the tribune; for he has something to tell him." 18 So he

took him and brought him to the tribune and said, "Paul the prisoner called me and asked me to bring this young man to you, as he has something to say to you." 19 The tribune took him by the hand, and going aside asked him privately, "What is it that you have to tell me?" 20 And he said, "The Jews have agreed to ask you to bring Paul down to the council tomorrow, as though they were going to inquire somewhat more closely about him. 21 But do not yield to them; for more than forty of their men lie in ambush for him, having bound themselves by an oath neither to eat nor drink till they have killed him; and now they are ready, waiting for the promise from you." 22 So the tribune dismissed the young man, charging him, "Tell no one that you have informed me of this."

23 Then he called two of the centurions *9 P.M?* and said, "At the third hour of the night get ready two hundred soldiers with seventy horsemen and two hundred spear- *70 +* men to go as far as Caesarea. 24 Also pro- *200* vide mounts for Paul to ride, and bring him safely to Felix the governor." 25 And he wrote a letter to this effect:

26 "Claudius Lys'ias to his Excellency *letter* the governor Felix, greeting. 27 This man was seized by the Jews, and was about to be killed by them, when I came upon them with the soldiers and rescued him, having learned that he was a Roman citizen. 28 And desiring to know the charge on which they accused him, I brought him down to their council. 29 I found that he was accused about questions of their law, but charged with nothing deserving death or imprisonment. 30 And when it was disclosed to me that there would be a plot against the man, I sent him to you at once, ordering his accusers also to state before you what they have against him."

31 So the soldiers, according to their instructions, took Paul and brought him by night to Antip'atris. 32 And on the morrow they returned to the barracks,

leaving the horsemen to go on with him. 33 When they came to Caesare'a and delivered the letter to the governor, they presented Paul also before him. 34 On reading the letter, he asked to what province he belonged. When he learned that he was from Cili'cia 35 he said, "I will hear you when your accusers arrive." And he commanded him to be guarded in Herod's praetorium.

24

5 days

And after five days the high priest Anani'as came down with some elders and a spokesman, one Tertul'lus. They laid before the governor their case against Paul; 2 and when he was called, Tertul'lus began to accuse him, saying:

"Since through you we enjoy much peace, and since by your provision, most excellent Felix, reforms are introduced on behalf of this nation, 3 in every way and everywhere we accept this with all gratitude. 4 But, to detain you no further, I beg you in your kindness to hear us briefly. 5 For we have found this man a pestilent fellow, an agitator among all the Jews throughout the world, and a ringleader of the sect of the Nazarenes. 6 He even tried to profane the temple, but we seized him. 8 By examining him yourself you will be able to learn from him about everything of which we accuse him."

9 The Jews also joined in the charge, affirming that all this was so.

10 And when the governor had motioned to him to speak, Paul replied:

"Realizing that for many years you have been judge over this nation, I cheerfully make my defense. 11 As you may ascertain, it is not more than twelve days since I went up to worship at Jerusalem; 12 and they did not find me disputing with any one or stirring up a crowd, either in the temple or in the synagogues, or in the city. 13 Neither can they prove to you what they now bring up against me. 14 But this I admit to you, that according to the Way, which they call a sect, I worship the God of our fathers, believing everything laid down by the law or written in the prophets, 15 having a hope in God which these themselves accept, that there will be a resurrection of both the just and the unjust. 16 So I always take pains to have a clear conscience toward God and toward men. 17 Now after some years I came to bring to my nation alms and offerings. 18 As I was doing this, they found me purified in the temple, without any crowd or tumult. But some Jews from Asia—19 they ought to be here before you and to make an accusation, if they have anything against me. 20 Or else let these men themselves say what wrongdoing they found when I stood before the council, 21 except this one thing which I cried out while standing among them, "With respect to the resurrection of the dead I am on trial before you this day.'" *Why?*

22 But Felix, having a rather accurate knowledge of the Way, put them off, saying, "When Lys'ias the tribune comes down, I will decide your case." 23 Then he gave orders to the centurion that he should be kept in custody but should have some liberty, and that none of his friends should be prevented from attending to his needs.

24 After some days Felix came with his wife Drusil'la, who was a Jewess; and he sent for Paul and heard him speak upon faith in Christ Jesus. 25 And as he argued about justice and self-control and future judgment, Felix was alarmed and said, "Go away for the present; when I have an opportunity I will summon you." 26 At the same time he hoped that money would be given him by Paul. So he sent for him often and conversed with him. 27 But when two years had elapsed, Felix was succeeded by Porcius Festus; and desiring to do the Jews a favor, Felix left Paul in prison.

25

Now when Festus had come into his province, after three days he went up to Jerusalem from Caesare'a. ² And the chief priests and the principal men of the Jews informed him against Paul; and they urged him, ³ asking as a favor to have the man sent to Jerusalem, planning an ambush to kill him on the way. ⁴ Festus replied that Paul was being kept at Caesare'a, and that he himself intended to go there shortly. ⁵ "So," said he, "let the men of authority among you go down with me, and if there is anything wrong about the man, let them accuse him."

6 When he had stayed among them not more than eight or ten days, he went down to Caesare'a; and the next day he took his seat on the tribunal and ordered Paul to be brought. ⁷ And when he had come, the Jews who had gone down from Jerusalem stood about him, bringing against him many serious charges which they could not prove. ⁸ Paul said in his defense, "Neither against the law of the Jews, nor against the temple, nor against Caesar have I offended at all." ⁹ But Festus, wishing to do the Jews a favor, said to Paul, "Do you wish to go up to Jerusalem, and there be tried on these charges before me?" ¹⁰ But Paul said, "I am standing before Caesar's tribunal, where I ought to be tried; to the Jews I have done no wrong, as you know very well. ¹¹ If then I am a wrongdoer, and have committed anything for which I deserve to die, I do not seek to escape death; but if there is nothing in their charges against me, no one can give me up to them. I appeal to Caesar." ¹² Then Festus, when he had conferred with his council, answered, "You have appealed to Caesar; to Caesar you shall go."

13 Now when some days had passed, Agrippa the king and Berni'ce arrived at Caesare'a to welcome Festus. ¹⁴ And as they stayed there many days, Festus laid Paul's case before the king, saying, "There is a man left prisoner by Felix; ¹⁵ and when I was at Jerusalem, the chief priests and the elders of the Jews gave information about him, asking for sentence against him. ¹⁶ I answered them that it was not the custom of the Romans to give up any one before the accused met the accusers face to face, and had opportunity to make his defense concerning the charge laid against him. ¹⁷ When therefore they came together here, I made no delay, but on the next day took my seat on the tribunal and ordered the man to be brought in. ¹⁸ When the accusers stood up, they brought no charge in his case of such evils as I supposed; ¹⁹ but they had certain points of dispute with him about their own superstition and about one Jesus, who was dead, but whom Paul asserted to be alive. ²⁰ Being at a loss how to investigate these questions, I asked whether he wished to go to Jerusalem and be tried there regarding them. ²¹ But when Paul had appealed to be kept in custody for the decision of the emperor, I commanded him to be held until I could send him to Caesar." ²² And Agrippa said to Festus, "I should like to hear the man myself." "Tomorrow," said he, "you shall hear him."

23 So on the morrow Agrippa and Berni'ce came with great pomp, and they entered the audience hall with the military tribunes and the prominent men of the city. Then by command of Festus Paul was brought in. ²⁴ And Festus said, "King Agrippa and all who are present with us, you see this man about whom the whole Jewish people petitioned me, both at Jerusalem and here, shouting that he ought not to live any longer. ²⁵ But I found that he had done nothing deserving death; and as he himself appealed to the emperor, I decided to send him. ²⁶ But I have nothing definite to write to my lord about him. Therefore I have brought him before you, and, especially before you, King Agrippa, that, after we have examined him, I may

have something to write. 27 For it seems to me unreasonable, in sending a prisoner, not to indicate the charges against him.''

26

Agrippa said to Paul, "You have permission to speak for yourself." Then Paul stretched out his hand and made his defense:

2 "I think myself fortunate that it is before you, King Agrippa, I am to make my defense today against all the accusations of the Jews, 3 because you are especially familiar with all customs and controversies of the Jews; therefore I beg you to listen to me patiently.

4 "My manner of life from my youth, spent from the beginning among my own nation and at Jerusalem, is known by all the Jews. 5 They have known for a long time, if they are willing to testify, that according to the strictest party of our religion I have lived as a Pharisee. 6 And now I stand here on trial for hope in the promise made by God to our fathers, 7 to which our twelve tribes hope to attain, as they earnestly worship night and day. And for this hope I am accused by Jews, O king! 8 Why is it thought incredible by any of you that God raises the dead?

9 "I myself was convinced that I ought to do many things in opposing the name of Jesus of Nazareth. 10 And I did so in Jerusalem; I not only shut up many of the saints in prison, by authority from the chief priests, but when they were put to death I cast my vote against them. 11 And I punished them often in all the synagogues and tried to make them blaspheme; and in raging fury against them, I persecuted them even to foreign cities.

12 "Thus I journeyed to Damascus with the authority and commission of the chief priests. 13 At midday, O king, I saw on the way a light from heaven, brighter than the sun, shining round me and those who journeyed with me. 14 And when we had

all fallen to the ground, I heard a voice saying to me in the Hebrew language, 'Saul, Saul, why do you persecute me? It hurts you to kick against the goads.' 15 And I said, 'Who are you, Lord?' And the Lord said, 'I am Jesus whom you are persecuting. 16 But rise and stand upon your feet; for I have appeared to you for this purpose, to appoint you to serve and bear witness to the things in which you have seen me and to those in which I will appear to you, 17 delivering you from the people and from the Gentiles—to whom I send you 18 to open their eyes, that they may turn from darkness to light and from the power of Satan to God, that they may receive forgiveness of sins and a place among those who are sanctified by faith in me.'

19 "Wherefore, O King Agrippa, I was not disobedient to the heavenly vision, 20 but declared first to those at Damascus, then at Jerusalem and throughout all the country of Judea, and also to the Gentiles, that they should repent and turn to God and perform deeds worthy of their repentance. 21 For this reason the Jews seized me in the temple and tried to kill me. 22 To this day I have had the help that comes from God, and so I stand here testifying both to small and great, saying nothing but what the prophets and Moses said would come to pass: 23 that the Christ must suffer, and that, by being the first to rise from the dead, he would proclaim light both to the people and to the Gentiles.''

24 And as he thus made his defense, Festus said with a loud voice, "Paul, you are mad; your great learning is turning you mad." 25 But Paul said, "I am not mad, most excellent Festus, but I am speaking the sober truth. 26 For the king knows about these things, and to him I speak freely; for I am persuaded that none of these things has escaped his notice, for this was not done in a corner. 27 King Agrippa, do you believe the prophets? I know that you believe." 28 And Agrippa

said to Paul, "In a short time you think to make me a Christian!" 29 And Paul said, "Whether short or long, I would to God that not only you but also all who hear me this day might become such as I am—except for these chains."

30 Then the king rose, and the governor and Berni'ce and those who were sitting with them; 31 and when they had withdrawn, they said to one another, "This man is doing nothing to deserve death or imprisonment." 32 And Agrippa said to Festus, "This man could have been set free if he had not appealed to Caesar."

2. THE PERSECUTION BY NERO*

Such indeed were the precautions of human wisdom. The next thing was to seek means of propitiating the gods, and recourse was had to the Sibylline books, by the direction of which prayers were offered to Vulcanus, Ceres, and Proserpina. Juno, too, was entreated by the matrons, first, in the Capitol, then on the nearest part of the coast, whence water was procured to sprinkle the fane and image of the goddess. And there were sacred banquets and nightly vigils celebrated by married women. But all human efforts, all the lavish gifts of the emperor, and the propitiations of the gods, did not banish the sinister belief that the conflagration was the result of an order. Consequently, to get rid of the report, Nero fastened the guilt and inflicted the most exquisite tortures on a class hated for their abominations, called Christians by the populace. Christus, from whom the name had its origin, suffered the extreme penalty during the reign of Tiberius at the hands of one of our procurators, Pontius Pilatus, and a most mischievous superstition, thus checked for the moment, again broke out not only in Judæa, the first source of the evil, but even in Rome, where all things hideous and shameful from every part of the world find their centre and become popular. Accordingly, an arrest was first made of all who pleaded guilty; then, upon their information, an immense multitude was convicted, not so much of the crime of firing the city, as of hatred against mankind. Mockery of every sort was added to their deaths. Covered with the skins of beasts, they were torn by dogs and perished, or were nailed to crosses, or were doomed to the flames and burnt, to serve as a nightly illumination, when daylight had expired.

Nero offered his gardens for the spectacle, and was exhibiting a show in the circus, while he mingled with the people in the dress of a charioteer or stood aloft on a car. Hence, even for criminals who deserved extreme and exemplary punishment, there arose a feeling of compassion; for it was not, as it seemed, for the public good, but to glut one man's cruelty, that they were being destroyed.

* Tacitus, *Annals*, 15. 44, translated by A. J. Church and W. J. Brodribb.

3. TRAJAN AND THE CHRISTIANS*

Gaius Plinius Caecilius Secundus (A.D. 61 or 62– before 114) was a lawyer, orator, and administrator. He was the imperial governor of Bithynia under Trajan, and the following correspondence comes from Book Ten of his collected *Letters*.

* Pliny, *Letters*, 10. 96 and 97, translated by William Melmoth.

To the Emperor Trajan

It is a rule, Sir, which I inviolably observe, to refer myself to you in all my doubts; for who is more capable of guiding my uncertainty or informing my ignorance? Having never been present at any trials of the Christians, I am unacquainted with the method and limits to be observed either in examining or punishing them. Whether any difference is to be made on account of age, or no distinction allowed between the youngest and the adult; whether repentance admits to a pardon, or if a man has been once a Christian it avails him nothing to recant; whether the mere profession of Christianity, albeit without crimes, or only the crimes associated therewith are punishable—in all these points I am greatly doubtful.

In the meanwhile, the method I have observed towards those who have been denounced to me as Christians is this: I interrogated them whether they were Christians; if they confessed it, I repeated the question twice again, adding the threat of capital punishment; if they still persevered, I ordered them to be executed. For whatever the nature of their creed might be, I could at least feel no doubt that contumacy and inflexible obstinacy deserved chastisement. There were others also possessed with the same infatuation, but being citizens of Rome, I directed them to be carried thither.

These accusations spread (as is usually the case) from the mere fact of the matter being investigated and several forms of the mischief came to light. A placard was put up, without any signature, accusing a large number of persons by name. Those who denied they were, or had ever been, Christians, who repeated after me an invocation to the Gods, and offered adoration, with wine and frankincense, to your image, which I had ordered to be brought for that purpose, together with those of the Gods, and who finally cursed Christ—

none of which acts, it is said, those who are really Christians can be forced into performing—these I thought it proper to discharge. Others who were named by that informer at first confessed themselves Christians, and then denied it; true, they had been of that persuasion but they had quitted it, some three years, others many years, and a few as much as twenty-five years ago. They all worshipped your statue and the images of the Gods, and cursed Christ.

They affirmed, however, the whole of their guilt, or their error, was, that they were in the habit of meeting on a certain fixed day before it was light, when they sang in alternate verses a hymn to Christ, as to a god, and bound themselves by a solemn oath, not to any wicked deeds, but never to commit any fraud, theft or adultery, never to falsify their word, nor deny a trust when they should be called upon to deliver it up; after which it was their custom to separate, and then reassemble to partake of food—but food of an ordinary and innocent kind. Even this practice, however, they had abandoned after the publication of my edict, by which, according to your orders, I had forbidden political associations. I judged it so much the more necessary to extract the real truth, with the assistance of torture, from two female slaves, who were styled *deaconesses*: but I could discover nothing more than depraved and excessive superstition.

I therefore adjourned the proceedings, and betook myself at once to your counsel. For the matter seemed to me well worth referring to you,—especially considering the numbers endangered. Persons of all ranks and ages, and of both sexes are, and will be, involved in the prosecution. For this contagious superstition is not confined to the cities only, but has spread through the villages and rural districts; it seems possible, however, to check and cure it. 'Tis certain at least that the temples, which had been almost deserted, begin now to be frequented; and the sacred festivals, after

Economic reasons for Rome, persecution

a long intermission, are again revived; while there is a general demand for sacrificial animals, which for some time past have met with but few purchasers. From hence it is easy to imagine what multitudes may be reclaimed from this error, if a door be left open to repentance.

TRAJAN TO PLINY

The method you have pursued, my dear Pliny, in sifting the cases of those denounced to you as Christians is extremely proper. It is not possible to lay down any general rule which can be applied as the fixed standard in all cases of this nature. No search should be made for these people; when they are denounced and found guilty they must be punished; with the restriction, however, that when the party denies himself to be a Christian, and shall give proof that he is not (that is, by adoring our Gods) he shall be pardoned on the ground of repentance, even though he may have formerly incurred suspicion. Informations without the accuser's name subscribed must not be admitted in evidence against anyone, as it is introducing a very dangerous precedent, and by no means agreeable to the spirit of the age.

4. IN DEFENSE OF THE CHRISTIANS*

Quintus Septimius Florens Tertullianus (A.D. 160–225) was born a pagan in the Roman province of Africa. After his conversion he became an able defender of Christianity against pagan attack. The *Apology*, written in A.D. 197, is addressed to Roman governors and presents the Christian view of the place of Christianity within the Roman Empire.

But now, if it is really certain that we are of all men the most criminal, why do you yourselves treat us otherwise than those like us, the rest of the criminal classes, when the same treatment belongs to the same fault? Whatever you charge against us, when you so charge others, they use their own eloquence, they hire the advocacy of others, to prove their innocence. There is freedom to answer, to cross-question, since in fact it is against the law for men to be condemned, undefended and unheard. But to Christians alone it is forbidden to say anything to clear their case, to defend Truth, to save the judge from being unjust. No! one thing is looked for, one alone, the one thing needful for popular hatred—the confession of the name. Not investigation of the charge! Yet, if you are trying any other criminal, it does not follow at once from his confessing to the name of murderer, or temple-robber, or adulterer, or enemy of the state (to touch on *our* indictments!), that you are satisfied to pronounce sentence, unless you pursue all the consequent investigation, such as the character of the act, how often, where, how, when, he did it, his accessories, his confederates. In our case nothing of the kind! Yet it ought just as much to be wrung out of us (whenever that false charge is made) how many murdered babies each of us had tasted, how many acts of incest he had done in the dark, what cooks were there—yes, and what dogs. Oh! the glory of that magistrate who had brought to light some Christian who had eaten up to date a hundred babies!

And yet we find it is forbidden even to hunt us down. For when Plinius Secundus

* Reprinted by permission of the publishers from Loeb Classical Library, Tertullian, *Apologeticus*, 2. 1–12, translated by T. R. Glover (Cambridge, Mass.: Harvard University Press, 1953).

was governing his province and had condemned some Christians and driven others from their steadfastness, and still the sheer numbers concerned worried him as to what he ought to do thereafter, he consulted the Emperor Trajan. He asserted that, apart from an obstinacy that refused to sacrifice, he had learnt nothing about the Christian mysteries—nothing beyond meetings before dawn to sing to Christ and to God, and to band themselves together in discipline, forbidding murder, adultery, dishonesty, treachery, and the other crimes. Trajan replied in a rescript that men of this kind were not to be sought out, but if they were brought before Pliny they must be punished. What a decision, how inevitably entangled! He says they must not be sought out, implying they are innocent; and he orders them to be punished, implying they are guilty. He spares them and rages against them, he pretends not to see and punishes. Why cheat yourself with your judgement? If you condemn them, why not hunt them down? If you do not hunt them down, why not also acquit them? To track down bandits through all the provinces is a duty assigned by lot to the garrisons. Against those guilty of treason, against public enemies, every man is a soldier; inquiry is extended to confederates, to accessories. The Christian alone may not be hunted down; but he may be haled before the magistrate; as if hunting down led to anything but haling to the court. So you condemn a man when haled to court—a man whom nobody wished to be sought out, who (I suppose) really has not deserved punishment because he is guilty, but because, forbidden to be looked for, he was found!

Then, again, in that matter, you do not deal with us in accordance with your procedure in judging criminals. If the other criminals plead Not guilty, you torture them to make them confess; the Christians alone you torture to make them deny. Yet if it were something evil, we should deny our guilt, and you would use torture to force us to confess it. For you would not hold judicial investigation of our crimes needless, on the ground that you were certain of their commission from the confession of the name; for to this day, though the murderer confesses, and though you know what murder is, none the less you rack out of him the story of his crime. So much the more upside down is your procedure with us, when you presume our crimes from our confession of the name and then try by torture to force us to cancel our confession, in order that, by denying the name, we may really deny the crimes too, which you had presumed from our confession of the name. But, of course, I suppose you do not want us to be done to death—though you believe us the worst of men. For that is your way—to say to the murderer, "Deny!" and to order the temple-thief to be mangled, if he will insist on confession! If that is not your procedure with regard to us in our guilt, then it is clear you count us the most innocent of men, when you will not have us (as being the most innocent of men) persist with a confession which you know you will have to condemn, not because justice requires it, but of necessity.

5. The Conduct of the Roman Empire Toward the Christians*

If we seriously consider the purity of the Christian religion, the sanctity of its moral precepts, and the innocent as well as austere lives of the greater number of those who, during the first ages, embraced the faith of the gospel, we should naturally suppose that so benevolent a doctrine would have been received with due reverence, even by the unbelieving world; that the learned and the polite, however they might deride the miracles, would have esteemed the virtues of the new sect; and that the magistrates, instead of persecuting, would have protected an order of men who yielded the most passive obedience to the laws, though they declined the active cares of war and government. If, on the other hand, we recollect the universal toleration of Polytheism, as it was invariably maintained by the faith of the people, the incredulity of philosophers, and the policy of the Roman senate and emperors, we are at a loss to discover what new offence the Christians had committed, what new provocation could exasperate the mild indifference of antiquity, and what new motives could urge the Roman princes, who beheld, without concern, a thousand forms of religion subsisting in peace under their gentle sway, to inflict a severe punishment on any part of their subjects, who had chosen for themselves a singular, but an inoffensive, mode of faith and worship.

The religious policy of the ancient world seems to have assumed a more stern and intolerant character, to oppose the progress of Christianity. About fourscore years after the death of Christ, his innocent disciples were punished with death, by the sentence of a proconsul of the most amiable and philosophic character, and,

according to the laws of an emperor, distinguished by the wisdom and justice of his general administration. The apologies which were repeatedly addressed to the successors of Trajan, are filled with the most pathetic complaints, that the Christians, who obeyed the dictates, and solicited the liberty, of conscience, were alone, among all the subjects of the Roman empire, excluded from the common benefits of their auspicious government. The deaths of a few eminent martyrs have been recorded with care; and from the time that Christianity was invested with the supreme power, the governors of the church have been no less diligently employed in displaying the cruelty, than in imitating the conduct, of their Pagan adversaries. To separate (if it be possible) a few authentic, as well as interesting, facts, from an undigested mass of fiction and error, and to relate, in a clear and rational manner, the causes, the extent, the duration, and the most important circumstances of the persecutions to which the first Christians were exposed, is the design of the present Chapter.

The sectaries of a persecuted religion, depressed by fear, animated with resentment, and perhaps heated by enthusiasm, are seldom in a proper temper of mind calmly to investigate, or candidly to appreciate, the motives of their enemies, which often escape the impartial and discerning view even of those who are placed at a secure distance from the flames of persecution. A reason has been assigned for the conduct of the emperors towards the primitive Christians, which may appear the more specious and probable as it is drawn from the acknowledged genius of Polytheism. It has already been observed that the religious concord of the world was principally supported by the implicit

---

* Edward Gibbon, *The Decline and Fall of the Roman Empire*, J. B. Bury, ed. (London: Macmillan, 1896), pp. 71–82; 95–98; 138–139.

assent and reverence which the nations of antiquity expressed for their respective traditions and ceremonies. It might therefore be expected that they would unite with indignation against any set of people which should separate itself from the communion of mankind, and, claiming the exclusive possession of divine knowledge, should disdain every form of worship, except its own, as impious and idolatrous. The rights of toleration were held by mutual indulgence; they were justly forfeited by a refusal of the accustomed tribute. As the payment of this tribute was inflexibly refused by the Jews, and by them alone, the consideration of the treatment which they experienced from the Roman magistrates will serve to explain how far these speculations are justified by facts, and will lead us to discover the true causes of the persecution of Christianity.

Without repeating what has been already mentioned of the reverence of the Roman princes and governors for the temple of Jerusalem, we shall only observe that the destruction of the temple and city was accompanied and followed by every circumstance that could exasperate the minds of the conquerors, and authorize religious persecution by the most specious arguments of political justice and the public safety. From the reign of Nero to that of Antoninus Pius, the Jews discovered a fierce impatience of the dominion of Rome, which repeatedly broke out in the most furious massacres and insurrections. Humanity is shocked at the recital of the horrid cruelties which they committed in the cities of Egypt, of Cyprus, and of Cyrene, where they dwelt in treacherous friendship with the unsuspecting natives; and we are tempted to applaud the severe retaliation which was exercised by the arms of the legions against a race of fanatics, whose dire and credulous superstition seemed to render them the implacable enemies not only of the Roman government, but of human kind. The enthusiasm of the Jews was supported by the opinion that it was unlawful for them to pay taxes to an idolatrous master; and by the flattering promise which they derived from their ancient oracles, that a conquering Messiah would soon arise, destined to break their fetters and to invest the favourites of heaven with the empire of the earth. It was by announcing himself as their long-expected deliverer, and by calling on all the descendants of Abraham to assert the hope of Israel, that the famous Barchochebas collected a formidable army, with which he resisted, during two years, the power of the emperor Hadrian.

Notwithstanding these repeated provocations, the resentment of the Roman princes expired after the victory; nor were their apprehensions continued beyond the period of war and danger. By the general indulgence of polytheism, and by the mild temper of Antoninus Pius, the Jews were restored to their ancient privileges, and once more obtained the permission of circumcising their children, with the easy restraint that they should never confer on any foreign proselyte that distinguishing mark of the Hebrew race. The numerous remains of that people, though they were still excluded from the precincts of Jerusalem, were permitted to form and to maintain considerable establishments both in Italy and in the provinces, to acquire the freedom of Rome, to enjoy municipal honours, and to obtain, at the same time, an exemption from the burdensome and expensive offices of society. The moderation or the contempt of the Romans gave a legal sanction to the form of ecclesiastical police which was instituted by the vanquished sect. The patriarch, who had fixed his residence at Tiberias, was empowered to appoint his subordinate ministers and apostles, to exercise a domestic jurisdiction, and to receive from his dispersed brethren an annual contribution. New synagogues were frequently erected in the principal cities of the empire; and the sabbaths, the fasts, and the festivals, which were either commanded by the Mosaic law or enjoined by the traditions of the Rabbis, were celebrated in the most solemn and public manner. Such gentle treatment insensibly assuaged the stern temper of the Jews. Awakened from their dream of prophecy and conquest, they assumed the behaviour of peaceable and industrious subjects. Their irreconcileable hatred of mankind, instead of flaming out in acts of blood and violence, evaporated in less dangerous gratifications. They embraced every opportunity of over-reaching the idolaters in trade; and they pronounced secret and ambiguous imprecations against the haughty kingdom of Edom.

Since the Jews, who rejected with abhorrence the deities adored by their sovereign and by their fellow-subjects, enjoyed, however, the free exercise of their unsocial religion; there must have existed some other cause, which exposed the disciples of Christ to those severities from which the posterity of Abraham was exempt. The difference between them is simple and obvious; but, according to the sentiments of antiquity, it was of the highest importance. The Jews were a *nation*; the Christians were a *sect*; and, if it was natural for every community to respect the sacred institutions of their neighbours, it was incumbent on them to persevere in those of their ancestors. The voice of oracles, the precepts of philosophers and the authority of the laws unanimously enforced this national obligation. By their lofty claim of superior sanctity, the Jews might provoke the Polytheists to consider them as an odious and impure race. By disdaining the intercourse of other nations they might deserve their contempt. The laws of Moses might be for the most part frivolous or absurd; yet, since they had been received during many ages by a large society, his followers were justified by the example of mankind; and

it was universally acknowledged that they had a right to practise what it would have been criminal in them to neglect. But this principle which protected the Jewish synagogue afforded not any favour or security to the primitive church. By embracing the faith of the Gospel, the Christians incurred the supposed guilt of an unnatural and unpardonable offence. They dissolved the sacred ties of custom and education, violated the religious institutions of their country, and presumptuously despised whatever their fathers had believed as true, or had reverenced as sacred. Nor was this apostacy (if we may use the expression) merely of a partial or local kind; since the pious deserter who withdrew himself from the temples of Egypt or Syria would equally disdain to seek an asylum in those of Athens or Carthage. Every Christian rejected with contempt the superstitions of his family, his city, and his province. The whole body of Christians unanimously refused to hold any communion with the gods of Rome, of the empire, and of mankind. It was in vain that the oppressed believer asserted the inalienable rights of conscience and private judgment. Though his situation might excite the pity, his arguments could never reach the understanding, either of the philosophic or of the believing part of the Pagan world. To their apprehensions, it was no less a matter of surprise that any individuals should entertain scruples against complying with the established mode of worship, than if they had conceived a sudden abhorrence to the manners, the dress, or the language of their native country.

The suprise of the Pagans was soon succeeded by resentment; and the most pious of men were exposed to the unjust but dangerous imputation of impiety. Malice and prejudice concurred in representing the Christians as a society of atheists, who, by the most daring attack on the religious constitution of the empire, had merited the severest animadversion of the civil magistrate. They had separated themselves (they gloried in the confession) from every mode of superstition which was received in any part of the globe by the various temper of polytheism; but it was not altogether so evident what deity or what form of worship they had substituted to the gods and temples of antiquity. The pure and sublime idea which they entertained of the Supreme Being escaped the gross conception of the Pagan multitude, who were at a loss to discover a spiritual and solitary God, that was neither represented under any corporeal figure or visible symbol, nor was adored with the accustomed pomp of libations and festivals, of altars and sacrifices. The sages of Greece and Rome, who had elevated their minds to the contemplation of the existence and attributes of the First Cause, were induced, by reason or by vanity, to reserve for themselves and their chosen disciples the privilege of this philosophical devotion. They were far from admitting the prejudices of mankind as the standard of truth; but they considered them as flowing from the original disposition of human nature; and they supposed that any popular mode of faith and worship which presumed to disclaim the assistance of the senses would, in proportion as it receded from superstition, find itself incapable of restraining the wanderings of the fancy and the visions of fanaticism. The careless glance which men of wit and learning condescended to cast on the Christian revelation served only to confirm their hasty opinion, and to persuade them that the principle, which they might have revered, of the divine unity was defaced by the wild enthusiasm, and annihilated by the airy speculations, of the new sectaries. The author of a celebrated dialogue which has been attributed to Lucian, whilst he affects to treat the mysterious subject of the Trinity in a style of ridicule and contempt, betrays his own ignorance of the weakness of human reason, and of the inscrutable nature of the divine perfections.

It might appear less surprising that the founder of Christianity should not only be revered by his disciples as a sage and a prophet, but that he should be adored as a God. The Polytheists were disposed to adopt every article of faith which seemed to offer any resemblance, however distant or imperfect, with the popular mythology; and the legends of Bacchus, of Hercules, and of Æsculapius had, in some measure, prepared their imagination for the appearance of the Son of God under a human form. But they were astonished that the Christians should abandon the temples of those ancient heroes who, in the infancy of the world, had invented arts, instituted laws, and vanquished the tyrants or monsters who infested the earth; in order to choose, for the exclusive object of their religious worship, an obscure teacher who, in a recent age, and among a barbarous people, had fallen a sacrifice either to the malice of his own countrymen or to the jealousy of the Roman government. The Pagan multitude, reserving their gratitude for temporal benefits alone, rejected the inestimable present of life and immortality which was offered to mankind by Jesus of Nazareth. His mild constancy in the midst of cruel and voluntary sufferings, his universal benevolence, and the sublime simplicity of his actions and character were insufficient, in the opinion of those carnal men, to compensate for the want of fame, of empire, and of success; and, whilst they refused to acknowledge his stupendous triumph over the powers of darkness and of the grave, they misrepresented, or they insulted, the equivocal birth, wandering life, and ignominious death of the divine Author of Christianity.

The personal guilt which every Christian had contracted, in thus preferring his private sentiment to the national religion, was aggravated, in a very high degree, by the number and union of the criminals. It is well known, and has been already observed, that Roman policy viewed with the utmost jealousy and distrust any association among its subjects; and that the privileges of private corporations, though formed for the most harmless or beneficial purposes, were bestowed with a very sparing hand. The religious assemblies of the Christians, who had separated themselves from the public worship, appeared of a much less innocent nature: they were illegal in their principle and in their consequences might become dangerous; nor were the emperors conscious that they violated the laws of justice, when, for the peace of society, they prohibited those secret and sometimes nocturnal meetings. The pious disobedience of the Christians made their conduct, or perhaps their designs, appear in a much more serious and criminal light; and the Roman princes, who might perhaps have suffered themselves to be disarmed by a ready submission, deeming their honour concerned in the execution of their commands, sometimes attempted by rigorous punishments to subdue this independent spirit, which boldly acknowledged an authority superior to that of the magistrate. The extent and duration of this spiritual conspiracy seemed to render it every day more deserving of his animadversion. We have already seen that the active and successful zeal of the Christians had insensibly diffused them through every province and almost every city of the empire. The new converts seemed to renounce their family and country, that they might connect themselves in an indissoluble band of union with a peculiar society, which everywhere assumed a different character from the rest of mankind. Their gloomy and austere aspect, their abhorrence of the common business and pleasures of life, and their frequent predictions of impending calamities, inspired the Pagans with the apprehension of some danger which would arise from the new sect, the more alarming as it

was the more obscure. "Whatever," says Pliny, "may be the principle of their conduct, their inflexible obstinacy appeared deserving of punishment."

The precautions with which the disciples of Christ performed the offices of religion were at first dictated by fear and necessity; but they were continued from choice. By imitating the awful secrecy which reigned in the Eleusinian mysteries, the Christians had flattered themselves that they should render their sacred institutions more respectable in the eyes of the Pagan world. But the event, as it often happens to the operations of subtile policy, deceived their wishes and their expectations. It was concluded that they only concealed what they would have blushed to disclose. Their mistaken prudence afforded an opportunity for malice to invent, and for suspicious credulity to believe, the horrid tales which described the Christians as the most wicked of human kind, who practised in their dark recesses every abomination that a depraved fancy could suggest, and who solicited the favour of their unknown God by the sacrifice of every moral virtue. There were many who pretended to confess or to relate the ceremonies of this abhorred society. It was asserted, "that a new-born infant, entirely covered over with flour, was presented, like some mystic symbol of initiation, to the knife of the proselyte, who unknowingly inflicted many a secret and mortal wound on the innocent victim of his error; that, as soon as the cruel deed was perpetrated, the sectaries drank up the blood, greedily tore asunder the quivering members, and pledged themselves to eternal secrecy, by a mutual consciousness of guilt. It was as confidently affirmed that this inhuman sacrifice was succeeded by a suitable entertainment, in which intemperance served as a provocative to brutal lust; till, at the appointed moment, the lights were suddenly extinguished, shame was banished, nature was forgotten; and, as accident might direct, the darkness of the night was polluted by the incestuous commerce of sisters and brothers, of sons and of mothers."

But the perusal of the ancient apologies was sufficient to remove even the slightest suspicion from the mind of a candid adversary. The Christians, with the intrepid security of innocence, appeal from the voice of rumour to the equity of the magistrates. They acknowledge that, if any proof can be produced of the crimes which calumny has imputed to them, they are worthy of the most severe punishment. They provoke the punishment, and they challenge the proof. At the same time they urge, with equal truth and propriety, that the charge is not less devoid of probability than it is destitute of evidence; they ask whether any one can seriously believe that the pure and holy precepts of the Gospel, which so frequently restrain the use of the most lawful enjoyments, should inculcate the practice of the most abominable crimes; that a large society should resolve to dishonour itself in the eyes of its own members; and that a great number of persons of either sex, and every age and character, insensible to the fear of death or infamy, should consent to violate those principles which nature and education had imprinted most deeply in their minds. Nothing, it should seem, could weaken the force or destroy the effect of so unanswerable a justification, unless it were the injudicious conduct of the apologists themselves, who betrayed the common cause of religion, to gratify their devout hatred to the domestic enemies of the church. It was sometimes faintly insinuated, and sometimes boldly asserted, that the same bloody sacrifices, and the same incestuous festivals, which were so falsely ascribed to the orthodox believers, were in reality celebrated by the Marcionites, by the Carpocratians, and by several other sects of the Gnostics, who, notwithstanding they might deviate into the paths of heresy, were still actuated by the sentiments of men, and still governed by the precepts of Christianity. Accusations of a similar kind were retorted upon the church by the schismatics who had departed from its communion; and it was confessed on all sides that the most scandalous licentiousness of manners prevailed among great numbers of those who affected the name of Christians. A Pagan magistrate, who possessed neither leisure nor abilities to discern the almost imperceptible line which divides the orthodox faith from heretical pravity, might easily have imagined that their mutual animosity had extorted the discovery of their common guilt. It was fortunate for the repose, or at least for the reputation, of the first Christians, that the magistrates sometimes proceeded with more temper and moderation than is usually consistent with religious zeal, and that they reported, as the impartial result of their judicial inquiry, that the sectaries who had deserted the established worship appeared to them sincere in their professions and blameless in their manners; however they might incur, by their absurd and excessive superstition, the censure of the laws.

History, which undertakes to record the transactions of the past, for the instruction of future, ages, would ill deserve that honourable office, if she condescended to plead the cause of tyrants, or to justify the maxims of persecution. It must, however, be acknowledged that the conduct of the emperors who appeared the least favourable to the primitive church is by no means so criminal as that of modern sovereigns who have employed the arm of violence and terror against the religious opinions of any part of their subjects. From their reflections, or even from their own feelings, a Charles V. or a Louis XIV. might have acquired a just knowledge of the rights of conscience, of the obligation of faith, and of the innocence of error. But the princes and magistrates of ancient Rome were strangers to those principles which inspired and authorized the inflexible obstinacy of the Christians in the cause of truth, nor could they themselves discover in their own breasts any motive which would have prompted them to refuse a legal, and as it were a natural, submission to the sacred institutions of their country. The same reason which contributes to alleviate the guilt, must have tended to abate the rigour, of their persecutions. As they were actuated, not by the furious zeal of bigots, but by the temperate policy of legislators, contempt must often have relaxed, and humanity must frequently have suspended, the execution of those laws which they enacted against the humble and obscure followers of Christ. From the general view of their character and motives we might naturally conclude: I. That a considerable time elapsed before they considered the new sectaries as an object deserving of the attention of government. II. That, in the conviction of any of their subjects who were accused of so very singular a crime, they proceeded with caution and reluctance. III. That they were moderate in the use of punishments; and IV. That the afflicted church enjoyed many intervals of peace and tranquillity. Notwithstanding the careless indifference which the most copious and the most minute of the Pagan writers have shewn to the affairs of the Christians, it may still be in our power to confirm each of these probable suppositions by the evidence of authentic facts.

* * *

Punishment was not the inevitable consequence of conviction, and the Christians, whose guilt was the most clearly proved by the testimony of witnesses, or even by their voluntary confession, still retained in their own power the alternative of life or death. It was not so much the past offence, as the actual resistance, which excited the indignation of the magistrate. He was persuaded that he offered them an easy pardon, since, if they consented to cast a few grains of incense upon the altar, they were dismissed from the tribunal in safety and with applause. It was esteemed the duty of a humane judge to endeavour to reclaim, rather than to punish, those deluded enthusiasts. Varying his tone according to the age, the sex, or the situation of the prisoners, he frequently condescended to set before their eyes every circumstance which could render life more pleasing, or death more terrible; and to solicit, nay, to intreat them, that they would show some compassion to themselves, to their families, and to their friends. If threats and persuasions proved ineffectual, he had often recourse to violence; the scourge and the rack were called in to supply the deficiency of argument, and every art of cruelty was employed to subdue such inflexible and, as it appeared to the Pagans, such criminal obstinacy. The ancient apologists of Christianity have censured, with equal truth and severity, the irregular conduct of their persecutors, who, contrary to every principle of judicial proceeding, admitted the use of torture, in order to obtain not a confession but a denial of the crime which was the object of their inquiry. The monks of succeeding ages, who, in their peaceful solitudes, entertained themselves with diversifying the death and sufferings of the primitive martyrs, have frequently invented torments of a much more refined and ingenious nature. In particular, it has pleased them to suppose that the zeal of the Roman magistrates, disdaining every consideration of moral virtue or public decency, endeavoured to seduce those whom they were unable to vanquish, and that, by their orders, the most brutal violence was offered to those whom they found it impossible to seduce. It is related that pious females, who were prepared to despise death, were sometimes condemned to a more severe trial, and called upon to determine whether they set a higher value on their religion or on their chastity. The youths to whose licentious embraces they were abandoned received a solemn exhortation from the judge to exert their most strenuous efforts to maintain the honour of Venus against the impious virgin who refused to burn incense on her altars. Their violence, however, was commonly disappointed; and the seasonable interposition of some miraculous power preserved the chaste spouses of Christ from the dishonour even of an involuntary defeat. We should not, indeed, neglect to remark that the more ancient, as well as authentic, memorials of the church are seldom polluted with these extravagant and indecent fictions.

The total disregard of truth and probability in the representation of these primitive martyrdoms was occasioned by a very natural mistake. The ecclesiastical writers of the fourth or fifth centuries ascribed to the magistrates of Rome the same degree of implacable and unrelenting zeal which filled their own breasts against the heretics or the idolaters of their own times. It is not improbable that some of those persons who were raised to the dignities of the empire might have imbibed the prejudices of the populace, and that the cruel disposition of others might occasionally be stimulated by motives of avarice or of personal resentment. But it is certain, and we may appeal to the grateful confessions of the first Christians, that the greatest part of those magistrates who exercised in the provinces the authority of the emperor, or of the senate, and to whose hands alone the jurisdiction of life and death was intrusted, behaved like men of polished manners and liberal educations, who respected the rules of justice, and who were conversant with the precepts of philosophy. They frequently declined the odious task of persecution, dismissed the charge with contempt, or suggested to the accused Christian some legal evasion by which he might elude the severity of the laws. Whenever they were invested with a discretionary power, they used it much less for the oppression than for the relief and benefit of the afflicted church. They were far from condemning all the Christians who were accused before their tribunal, and very far from punishing with death all those who were convicted of an obstinate adherence to the new superstition. Contenting themselves, for the most part, with the milder chastisements of imprisonment, exile, or slavery in the mines, they left the unhappy victims of their justice some reason to hope that a prosperous event, the accession, the marriage, or the triumph of an emperor might speedily restore them, by a general pardon, to their former state. The martyrs, devoted to immediate execution by the Roman magistrates, appear to have been selected from the most opposite extremes. They were either bishops and presbyters, the persons the most distinguished among the Christians by their rank and influence, and whose example might strike terror into the whole sect; or else they were the meanest and most abject among them, particularly those of the servile condition, whose lives were esteemed of little value, and whose sufferings were viewed by the ancients with too careless an indifference. The learned Origen, who, from his experience as well as reading, was intimately acquainted with the history of the Christians, declares, in the most express terms, that the number of martyrs was very inconsiderable. His authority would alone be sufficient to annihilate that formidable army of martyrs whose relics, drawn for the most part from the catacombs of Rome, have replenished so many churches, and whose marvellous achievements have been the subject of so many volumes of holy romance. But the general assertion of Origen may be explained and confirmed by the particular testimony of his friend Dionysius, who, in the immense city of Alexandria, and under the rigorous persecution of Decius, reckons only ten men and seven women who suffered for the profession of the Christian name.

* * *

We shall conclude this chapter by a melancholy truth which obtrudes itself on the reluctant mind; that even admitting, without hesitation or inquiry, all that history has recorded, or devotion has feigned, on the subject of martyrdoms, it must still be acknowledged that the Christians, in the course of their intestine dissensions, have inflicted far greater severities on each other than they had experienced from the zeal of infidels. During the ages of ignorance which followed the subversion of the Roman empire in the West, the bishops of the Imperial city extended their dominion over the laity as well as clergy of the Latin church. The fabric of superstition which they had erected, and which might long have defied the feeble efforts of reason, was at length assaulted by a crowd of daring fanatics, who, from the twelfth to the sixteenth century, assumed the popular character of reformers. The church of Rome defended by violence the empire which she had acquired by fraud; a system of peace and benevolence was soon disgraced by proscriptions, wars, massacres, and the institution of the holy office. And, as the reformers were animated by the love of civil, as well as of religious, freedom, the Catholic princes connected their own interest with that of the clergy, and enforced by fire and the sword the terrors of spiritual censures. In the Netherlands alone, more than one hundred thousand of the subjects of Charles the Fifth are said to have suffered by the hand of the executioner; and this extraordinary number is attested by Grotius, a man of genius and learning, who preserved his moderation amidst the fury of contending sects, and who composed the annals of his own age and country, at a time when the invention of printing had facilitated the means of intelligence and increased the danger of detection. If we are obliged to submit our belief to the authority of Grotius, it must be allowed that the number of Protestants who were executed in a single province and a single reign far exceeded that of the primitive martyrs in the space of three centuries and of the Roman empire. But, if the improbability of the fact itself should prevail over the weight of evidence; if Grotius should be convicted of exaggerating the merit and sufferings of the Reformers; we shall be naturally led to inquire what confidence can be placed in the doubtful and imperfect monuments of ancient credulity; what degree of credit can be assigned to a courtly bishop, and a passionate declaimer, who, under the protection of Constantine, enjoyed the exclusive privilege of recording the persecutions inflicted on the Christians by the vanquished rivals, or disregarded predecessors of their gracious sovereign.

6. POLITICAL PERSECUTION*

CAUSE AND EXTENT OF PERSECUTION

We have now determined the main facts in regard to the action of the State towards the Christians before A.D. 170. We have next to inquire into the reason why the Empire proscribed this sect. The question is presented to us as a paradox: the Empire being remarkably tolerant, as a general rule, in religious matters, what reason was there for the persecution of this religion?

[Ramsay first discusses popular dislike of the Christians and dismisses it as a basic cause of the persecutions.]

* * *

REAL CAUSES OF STATE PERSECUTION

The success of the Imperial Government in the provinces rested greatly on its power of accommodating itself to the ways and manners and religion of the subjects; it accepted and found a place in its system for all gods and all cults. Religious intolerance was opposed to the fundamental principles of the Imperial rule, and few traces of it can be discerned. It proscribed the Christians, and it proscribed the Druids. In these two cases there must have seemed to the Imperial Government to be some characteristic which required exceptional treatment. In both cases there was present the same dangerous principle: both maintained an extra-Imperial unity, and were proscribed on political, not on religious, grounds.

On the other hand, the Jews must have appeared to the Government to resemble the Christians very closely. Almost every trait in the picture drawn by Aristides

---

* W. M. Ramsay, The Church in the Roman Empire Before A.D. 170., 2nd ed. (London: Hodder and Stoughton, 1893), pp. 346; 354–360; 371–374. Reprinted by permission of the publisher.

applies to them, and they also were the object of general hatred. But so far from yielding to the popular feeling in this case, the Imperial policy protected the Jews on many occasions from the popular dislike.

If the Jews appeared to the Empire to resemble the Christians so much, and yet were treated so differently, the reason for the difference in treatment must have lain in those points in which the Christians differed from the Jews in the estimate of the Imperial Government. In so far the Jews were merely a body professing a different religion; the Emperors allowed them the completest toleration. But so long as the Jews maintained an articulated organisation, centred in the Temple at Jerusalem, they maintained a unity distinct from that of the Empire; and this fact was brought home to the Emperors by the great rebellion of 65–70. The Flavian policy made a distinction between the Jewish religion and the Jewish organised unity; the former was protected, but the latter was proscribed. Titus conceived that the destruction of the temple would destroy the unity centred in it; and he substituted the temple of Jupiter for the temple at Jerusalem, collecting for the former the tax hitherto contributed by the Jews for the latter.

With the Jews it was found possible to separate their religion from their organisation. The destruction of the temple, indeed, had to be completed under Hadrian by the destruction of Jerusalem, and the foundation of a new Roman city there. But, to a great extent after 70, and completely after 134, the Jews accepted the situation assigned them by the State—religious toleration on condition of acquiescence in the unity of the Empire.

Titus at first entertained the belief that the Christians also had their centre in the temple, and that their unity would perish with it. But soon the Flavian Government recognised that their united organisation was no whit weakened by the destruction of the temple. The Christians still continued, no less than before, to maintain a unity independent of, and contrary to, the Imperial unity, and to consolidate steadily a wide-reaching organisation. Such an organisation was contrary to the fundamental principle of Roman government. Rome had throughout its career made it a fixed principle to rule by dividing; all subjects must look to Rome alone; none might look towards their neighbours, or enter into any agreement or connection with them. But the Christians looked to a non-Roman unity; they decided on common action independent of Rome; they looked on themselves as Christians first, and Roman subjects afterwards; and, when Rome refused to accept this secondary allegiance, they ceased to feel themselves Roman subjects at all. When this was the case, it seems idle to look about for reasons why Rome should proscribe the Christians. If it was true to itself, it must compel obedience; and to do so meant death to all firm Christians. In the past the success of the Roman Government had been greatly due to the rigour with which it suppressed all organisations; and the Church was a living embodiment of the tendency which hitherto Rome had succeeded in crushing. Either Rome must now compel obedience, or it must acknowledge that the Christian unity was stronger than the Empire.

This disobedience to the principles of Roman administration is only one form of that spirit of insubordination and obstinacy, which is so often attributed to the Christians by the ancient writers, and which seemed to Pliny to justify their condemnation. In his note on the passage (Pliny, *ad Traj.*, 96), Mr. Hardy rightly remarks that "the feature of Christianity which Pliny here points out as a sufficient reason for punishing them, was exactly the point which, as Christianity grew, made it seem politically dangerous to the authority of the Empire, and which, more than religious intolerance, was at the root of later persecutions." We ask why it should be left for Pliny to make the discovery that the Christian principles were dangerous. He was not the first governor of a province in which Christians were numerous. He was not the character to display special insight into the probable political outcome of new principles, or to be specially jealous of the authority of the Empire. He was not a practised administrator. He had never before held a province. He had been a skilful financier and good lawyer, whose entire official life had been spent in Rome with the single exception of the necessary months of military service as a tribune, and even this term he had spent in managing the accounts of the legion. He had been selected for this government because the finances of the cities were in a bad state, and a trustworthy and hardworking officer and good financier was needed to administer the province. It is not too much to say that, if Pliny perceived forthwith the disobedience that was inherent in the new religion, every governor of any Asiatic province, every Emperor of Rome, and every prefect of the city, must have made the same discovery for himself long before 112.

The cause here suggested, obvious as it appears, has been ridiculed as impossible by Aubé, who thinks it inconceivable that Nero should already have begun to suspect that the growth of the organised Christian religion might prove dangerous to the Empire. It is difficult to reply to such an argument. For my own part, I can see nothing improbable even in this supposition, and still less in the theory that the Flavian Emperors considered Christianity to involve a dangerous principle. I should only be surprised if the watchful Roman administration had failed to recognise at a very early moment that the principles of the new sect were opposed to its policy. Trajan refused to permit an organisation of 150 firemen in Nicomedeia, or to allow a few poor people to improve their fare by dining in company, on the express ground that such organisations involved political danger. The Christians so managed their organisation as to elude the law prohibiting *sodalitates*; but they could not elude the notice of the Emperors.

How can we understand the marvellous power which the Empire showed of Romanising the provinces, except on the supposition that it showed great practical ability in dealing with the various views and principles of different peoples? and how is such practical ability to be explained, except on the supposition that the Imperial Government was keenly alive to the character and probable effect of any such system? The Emperors were aiming at a great end; they pursued it with all the experience and wisdom of Roman law and Roman organisation; and they punished rigorously those who impeded their action.

The principle of government just described is connected with, but still must be distinguished from, the restrictions imposed on the formation of *collegia* and *sodalitates*. The same jealousy on the part of the Government and the same distrust of the loyalty of the people underlies both. While Rome was a republic, all citizens had the right of forming associations at will; but as soon as the Empire began, it distrusted such associations, and Julius restricted them within the narrowest limits; for the Roman Government now considered the Roman people as a danger to be guarded against. The old rule of prohibiting all attempts at union among the subject populations, appears under the Empire mainly under the form of prohibiting *collegia* and *sodalitates*; but it was really of much wider scope, and this prohibition was only one special application of a general principle.

This jealous principle of Roman administration was fatal to all vigorous life and political education among the subject peoples. It was an inheritance from the old narrow Roman system, which regarded the subject peoples merely as conducive to the benefit of Rome. The true interest of the Empire lay in abandoning this narrow and jealous spirit, and training the provincials to higher conceptions of political duty than mere obedience to the laws and the magistrates. Only in this way could it carry out its mission of creating a great unified state, characterised by universal citizenship and patriotism. Here, as in many other cases, the Church carried out the ideas and forms towards which the Empire was tending, but which it could not realise without the aid of Christianity.

Political and religious facts were in ancient time far more closely connected than they are now. It was under the protection of religion that law, social rules, and politics, gradually developed. Before they had strength to exist apart, they maintained themselves as religious principles, enforced by religious sanctions and terrors. Thus the right of free general intercourse and free union among all subjects of the Empire, had for a long time no existence except as a religious fact.

The strength of the Imperial Government lay in its recognising, more fully than any administration before or since has done, the duty of maintaining a tolerable standard of comfort among the poorer classes of citizens. But while it showed great zeal as regards their physical comfort, it was less attentive to the other duty of educating them. The education imparted on a definite plan by the State did not go beyond a regular series of amusements, some of a rather brutalising tendency. Christianity came in to the help of the Imperial Government, urging the duty of educating, as well as feeding and amusing, the mass of the population. The theory of universal education for the people has never been more boldly and thoroughly stated than by Tatian. The weak side of the Empire—the cause of the ruin of the first Empire—was the moral deterioration of the lower classes: Christianity, if adopted in time, might have prevented this result.

[After discussing the organization of the early church, Ramsay emphasizes the importance of the episcopal office, and the role played by Ignatius in its development.]

* * *

The really striking development implied by Ignatius is, that a much clearer distinction between bishop and presbyter had now become generally recognised. This distinction was ready to become a difference of rank and order; and he first recognised that this was so. Others looked at the bishops under prepossessions derived from the past: he estimated them in view of what they might become in the future.

For our purpose, the important point is the aspect which the institution would wear in the estimation of the Emperors. It was illegal; it was a device for doing more efficiently what the State forbade to be done at all. How far its character was known to the Government, we cannot tell; but that the Emperors studied this political phenomenon—the Christian organisation —I cannot, in the nature of the Roman administration, doubt. That they must condemn an organisation such as we have described, judging it by the fundamental principle of Roman government, is certain. That the policy of the Flavian Emperors is inexplicable in any other way seems equally certain. An organisation, strong, even if only rudimentary, is required to explain the Imperial history; and such an organisation is attested by the Christian documents. Trajan found himself unable to resist the evidence that this organisation was dangerous and illegal; yet his instinctive perception of wider issues prevented him from logically carrying out the principle. All sides of the evidence work in

with one another, and all are derived from the simplest and fullest interpretation of the documents as they lie before us. Christianity was proscribed, not as a religion, but as interfering with that organisation of society which the Empire inculcated and protected.

The question whether the Christian sect was treasonable was not first raised under the Flavian Emperors. It had been agitated from an early period, and was naturally revived on every occasion when the character of the sect formed a subject of consideration to the Government.

The earliest charge against Christians was that of setting up a king of their own in opposition to the Emperor. Jesus was condemned on this ground; and it reappears in Acts vxii. 7. Eusebius mentions that a similar charge against the grandchildren of Judas, the Lord's brother, was investigated· by Domitian, and dismissed.

Again, according to the old Roman view, it was justifiable, and even required, that the magistrates should proceed actively against Romans who had deserted the national religion, and also against those who had been concerned in converting them. But, in fact, it would appear that this was not a frequent ground on which to found proceedings against the Christians. The feeling of pride in Roman citizenship and the exclusiveness against non-Roman rites, became much weaker as the citizenship was widened. Moreover, religious feeling in the Empire was very weak during the first century. The attempted revival of the national religion under Augustus was not lasting. Tiberius preserved the tradition of Augustus' policy; but the mad sacrilege of Caligula must have weakened it fatally. Under Domitian, however, the revival of the national worship was a marked feature of the Imperial policy.

While the sect was condemned, it did not appear sufficiently important to require any special measures to put it down. The Government was content to lay down the principle that Christians should be dealt with by all governors under the general instructions. But the Roman administration maintained a very small staff of officials, and the public safety was very insufficiently attended to. Brigandage was rife, and brigands were followed in a very spiritless and variable way. Christians, who were classed along with brigands, profited by the remissness of the Government. In practice the execution of the general principle would greatly depend on popular co-operation; and though popular feeling was strongly against the Christians, popular action was of a very uncertain character. The proscription exercised a strong influence on the Church, causing it to unite still more closely through mutual sympathy and the tendency among the persecuted to help one another; but it was unable to diminish seriously the numbers of the Christians. It merely made the Church stronger, more self-reliant, and more spirited.

7. Religious Persecution*

JURIDICAL CHARACTER OF THE PERSECUTIONS

The persecutions were not the effect merely of the application of laws previously existing.

The existence of a special legislative act explicitly prohibiting Christianity has nevertheless been much discussed. It has been said that it was sufficient to apply to Christians existing laws specifying penalties for the crime of sacrilege or of *lèse majesté*, as this would involve them in punishments. But sacrilege properly so called supposes a positive criminal act, which could not be found in the case of Christians; as for the crime of *lèse majesté*, closely connected, in point of fact, with that of sacrilege, committed in refusing to take part in the cult of the Emperor's divinity, we do not see Christians explicitly accused of this in the first two centuries: it is only in the third that the magistrates tried regularly to force Christians to sacrifice to the divinity of the emperor in consequence of new edicts of persecution, and condemned them if they refused to do so.

Doubtless one may say that the crime existed implicitly from the beginning, inasmuch as Christians did not recognise the Emperor as a god, and hence adopted an attitude which was bound to lead to their being regarded as defective citizens or subjects. But before the third century no text proves that the proper motive of the persecution of the Christians was a refusal which made them guilty of *lèse majesté*. They were accused rather, at first, of failing to reverence the gods of the Empire in general, and even this did not make them officially atheists, as they were judged to be by popular ignorance.

The same is true of the accusation of other especially serious crimes against common law, such as magic, incest, or infanticide: it was never more than popular rumour which imputed these to the Christians, and official justice did not take up these accusations. Hence we shall not find in previous penal law the precise juridical basis of the persecutions.

Nor were they due merely to the coercive power of the magistrates.

Others have sought for this basis in the power of *coercitio*, i.e., police powers which belonged to all the Roman magistrates. In order to maintain public order, these had a very extensive authority which went as far as putting to death anyone who disturbed

---

* Jules Lebreton and Jacques Zeiller, *The History of the Primitive Church*, translated by Ernest C. Messenger (New York: The Macmillan Company, 1942), Vol. 1, pp. 376–381.

the peace. Hence it is suggested that it was as public disturbers that the Christians, disobeying the injunction to abandon a profession of faith which was in itself a public disorder, were condemned by the decision of the magistrates, without any need of applying to them a more express law.

But if the magistrates merely had to exercise towards the Christians their power of *coercitio*, why did they more than once think it necessary to consult the prince as to the way to treat them, as we see Pliny the Younger writing to Trajan, and other governors under Antoninus or Marcus Aurelius? Moreover, Pliny speaks formally of the steps taken against the Christians as resulting from the exercise of criminal jurisdiction, *cognitio*, and accordingly, not as a result of *coercitio*. Lastly, the *coercitio* extending to the capital penalty could not be exercised in the case of a Roman citizen.

SPECIAL LEGISLATION AGAINST THE CHRISTIANS

Thus we are compelled to accept the reality of special legislative measures against the Christians, of which the Emperor Nero was the author, as in fact affirmed by Tertullian. From his reign to that of Septimius Severus, who introduced a new regime, the juridical situation of Christians in the Roman Empire remained the same: they were proscribed, not as guilty of crimes against the common law such as incest, cannibalism or magic, as imputed to them so often by popular hostility, itself caused by difference of beliefs and customs, nor of the crimes of sacrilege or *lèse majesté*, but as guilty of professing a religion which had been forbidden: *christianos esse non licet*. Thus it is the very name of Christian, the *nomen christianum*, that was forbidden and condemned, as Christian apologists more than once contended.

THE CLARIFICATIONS IN TRAJAN'S RESCRIPT

The rescript of Trajan added to the principle of Nero about half a century later some necessary clarifications, the need of which had been shown in practice. This imperial reply to the questions from a governor consisted of three points. The first two were modifications of a rule which the progress of a propaganda that could in no wise be stopped made it difficult to apply in all strictness, as is shown well by Pliny's hesitation before the prospect of too numerous condemnations.

The Emperor accordingly declared in substance: 1. Governmental authority is not to take the initiative in the processes: it is not to seek out Christians, *christiani conquirendi non sunt*. 2. Those who are accused and who declare that they are not Christians, or are such no longer, that is to say, those who have committed the legal crime of being Christians but have effaced it by apostasy, manifested by an external act of adhesion to paganism, are to be dismissed. 3. Those who confess to being Christians are to be condemned.

The letter of Pliny, and the sequence of events, show that his condemnation could only be the capital penalty, i.e., death, or one of the penalties which, like exile or forced labour in the mines, involved civil death. But on the other hand, and in virtue of the second point in the rescript, we shall no more see governors before whom Christians are taken doing their utmost to obtain from them a word, or sometimes just a simple act, such as offering a few grains of incense to the statue of the Emperor, which could be interpreted as a disavowal, even if only a temporary one, of the Christian faith.

Tortures were in many instances less a punishment than a means attempted in order to extract this denial from the accused. As for the Emperors themselves, the best of them, as we shall see in detail in the case of Hadrian and Antoninus, if not Marcus Aurelius, who regarded Christians with contempt rather than pity, added new precautions which mitigated the application of a legal system the principle of which they were nevertheless careful to maintain in all its strictness.

Main Idea of the Legislation against the Christians

What, then, was the underlying idea which alone explains the transformation of an expedient of the frightened Nero into a rule of the State? It was that Christianity, a strictly monotheistic religion, whose God would not divide his honour with other divinities or with the world, could not be reconciled with the fundamental conceptions upon which the Roman State rested. For this was closely associated with a number of religious traditions, if not also of habits of life, which were incompatible with the new faith; the mere fact that the Christians did not worship the gods of Rome made them rebels, or at least suspect, even before the time when the worship or refusal of worship of the Emperor's statue became the touchstone of their Roman conformity.

The religious position of the Jews was similar; but they had before the year 70 formed a national body which had received privileges and retained them after their final dispersion. Even when the obligation to sacrifice to the Emperor could be imposed upon every citizen, they obtained legal dispensations which safeguarded them from persecution. Doubtless the Roman authority only gradually learnt to make a distinction between Christians and Jews. But the day came when all confusion ceased. Christians did not, like the Jews, form a compact national body, but a religious society scattered abroad from its origin, the members of which were all equally subjects who could not claim any

special favour. This explains the imperial legislation against Christianity.

Juridical Origin and Form of this Legislation

The juridical origin was probably an ancient law of the republican epoch which forbade *superstitio illicita*, and its form an imperial edict. Like the edicts of the prætors of the Republic, this particular edict was theoretically in force only during the reign of the Emperor who had published it. Thus it had to be renewed, and adopted, so to speak, by his successor.

This gives us, perhaps, a first reason for the intermittent character the persecutions at first displayed. Trajan decided at the beginning of the second century that there were to be no measures against Christians without previous accusation. But in the first place, these measures had to be in conformity with the imperial will. This was expressed for the first time by Nero. But then there was no severity towards Christians under the two first Flavians. The anti-Christian laws were renewed, in circumstances which we shall explain later, under Domitian; and this commencement of persecuting legislation by the two first century rulers who had left the worst reputations enabled the Christian apologists of the second century to set forth the idea that hostility towards Christianity emanated from bad emperors, and those whom every Roman had cause to hate.

But Trajan, the *optimus princeps* as he was called in his own lifetime, and whose reputation for goodness survived the Middle Ages, when faced with the question put to him by Pliny, who was worried by the prospect of the great number of capital sentences which would have to be pronounced against people who did not seem to be great criminals—Trajan could not avoid the issue, and it is by his reply that we know the principle of the laws directed against the Christians. True, the precise instructions emanating from him constitute already a modification, since he forbids the authorities to take the initiative—an interdiction so radical that the emperors themselves, when Christians boldly declared themselves by addressing to them their apologies for their faith, never answered what might seem to us to be challenges— if they ever know of these—by juridical measures. Nothing shows better the singular and exceptional character of this legislation against the Christians than this disposition, by which the State seemed to take no cognisance of a legal crime so long as the guilty were not specifically pointed out, though it nevertheless punished with death those denounced in the appointed way. It is like a tacit confession of regret at having to punish in virtue of old ordinances, which nevertheless the State did not wish to revoke.

SECTION XIII

Diocletian, Constantine, and the Great Effort to Save the Roman Empire

THE THIRD CENTURY produced a fateful crisis in the Roman Empire. The "good emperors" were gone, the Roman peace was shattered, the imperial borders penetrated, the army and the populace at each other's throats, the economy in chaos; domestically and in foreign affairs the Roman Empire faced ruin. Into the breach stepped Emperor Diocletian, and on the basis of his work Constantine could go further in shoring up the edifice of imperial Rome. Together, their reforms saved the whole empire for a time and the eastern half for more than a millennium. What were the problems they faced? How suitable were their solutions? Did they save Rome or help to transform her beyond recognition? Did they check the forces of decline or intensify them?

1. THE ORIENTAL DESPOTISM*

At the end of the third century, after a bloody and cruel civil and social war which had lasted for scores of years, the general situation was very similar to what it had been at the end of the civil war of the first century B.C. The people, including a large part of the soldiers, were wearied and disgusted and craved for peace and order; the fighting temper of large groups of the population had passed away and everyone was ready to accept, or to submit to, any conditions that should guarantee the security of life and the possibility of resuming daily work without the daily apprehension of a new convulsion, a new wave of war and destruction. But the Roman Empire of the third century A.D. was very different from the Roman Empire of the first century B.C. The civil war of the first century was ultimately a fight against the domination of a small group of families, and an attempt to remodel the structure of the state in accordance with the changed conditions of its life, to adapt the constitution of the city-state of Rome to the needs of the Roman

---

* M. Rostovtzeff, *The Social and Economic History of the Roman Empire*, 2nd ed., revised by P. M. Fraser (Clarendon, 1957), Vol. 1, pp. 502–532. Reprinted by permission of The Clarendon Press, Oxford.

Empire. After a period of transition, in-augurated by the reforms of Augustus—a period when the struggle against the old senatorial class, representing the ancient ruling families of Rome, was brought to a close and the new structure of the state was gradually consolidated and accepted by the population (as was shown in the crisis of 69)—the constitutional Empire of Rome, based on the cities and on the city *bourgeoisie*, enjoyed a period of calm and of peaceful development. The civil war and its sequel, the military tyranny, did not affect the most vital forces of the Empire and of the ancient world in general. It left intact the most important institution of the ancient world, with which ancient civilization stood and fell—the city-state. It seemed as if, after long efforts, a constitutional arrangement had been found by which the city-state was made the basis of a world-empire. That arrangement was the enlightened constitutional monarchy, assisted by an influential and well-trained body of experts, the Roman senate and the Roman knights, and by thousands of similar bodies all over the Empire, the municipal councils.

So long as the Empire was not faced by grave external dangers, so long as the awe which Roman arms, Roman organization, and ancient civilization inspired in the neighbours of the Empire endured, the fabric of the new Roman state remained firm. When, however, the feeling of awe gradually vanished and Rome's neighbours renewed their attacks, the structure of the state began to show dangerous signs of yielding. It became clear that the Empire, based on the propertied classes alone, could not stand the strain of foreign wars, and that an enlargement of the basis was necessary to keep the structure erect and firm. The city *bourgeoisie*, whose economic life had for centuries rested on the work and toil of the lower classes, and especially of the class that tilled the soil, appeared unwilling and unable to shoulder the burden of defending the Empire against foreign enemies. The attempts to revive the *bourgeoisie*, to increase its numbers, and to restore its military spirit, which were made over and over again by all the emperors of the dynasty of the Antonines and of the Severi, proved futile. For the defence of the state the emperors were forced to resort to the tillers of the soil, on whom the economic prosperity of the Empire rested and whose toil and travail never brought them any share either in the civilized life of the cities or in the management of local affairs. The Roman army gradually became an army of peasants, led and commanded by members of the ruling classes, and indeed an army of the poorer peasants, of peasant-proletarians, since they were the only men who would volunteer or would be sent by a village community when a compulsory levy was ordered. As regards its social (though not its racial and political) composition, the army of the second half of the second century was thus no different from the armies of Marius and Sulla, Pompey and Caesar, Antony and Octavian.

It was natural, then, that this army should in the end seek to realize the ambitions of the lower classes of the Empire, just as the armies of the first century B.C. had expressed the desires of the poorer Roman citizens of Italy. The instruments through which it tried to realize them were, of course, its leaders, the emperors, whom it appointed and supported. As its aspirations were never clearly formulated and its programme—if the vague desires of the soldiers can be so described—was more negative than positive, the process assumed very chaotic forms. Moreover, the *bourgeoisie* gradually became aware of the danger which threatened it and strove repeatedly through the same military leaders, the emperors, to save its privileged position and to prevent the overthrow of the structure of the state as it was in the second century. Hence the renewed outbreaks of civil war which raged all over the Empire and brought it to the verge of utter destruction. What the army wanted was an equal share in the management of the Empire, a thorough levelling. As far as this negative side of its programme was concerned, the struggle was crowned with success. The *bourgeoisie* was terrified and decimated; the cities were brought to the verge of ruin; the new rulers, both emperors and officials, sprang mostly from the peasant class.

Gradually, however, as in the first century B.C., it became evident that the civil war was disastrous to the state as a whole, and that its main result was the political and economic ruin of the Empire. On the other hand, as we have said, the masses of the people became weary of the strife and longed for peace at any price. It became evident, too, that the chief task of the moment was the restoration of the fabric of the state, the preservation of the Empire. As soon as this task was achieved by the strenuous efforts of the army itself and of its great leaders, a reorganization of the state in accordance with the changed conditions, stabilizing and systematizing them, became imperative and did not brook delay. It was the same situation as in the time of Augustus. Here again the main lines of reconstruction were dictated by the social and economic conditions, and were laid down by the practice of the leaders in the civil war and the partial reforms which they carried out. To the activity of Marius, Sulla, Pompey, and Caesar corresponded that of Septimius, Gallienus, and Aurelian; and the great work of Augustus, Vespasian, and the Antonines was paralleled by the reorganization of the state effected by Diocletian and Constantine and their successors. The chief reform needed was one which would, above all, stabilize the state and organize it in a manner that would accord with the changed conditions, economic, social, political, and psychological. Levelling and equalization were dictated as the basis of the reform by the imperative desire of the people, and it was evident that in the new state there was no place for the leading role which the cities and the city *bourgeoisie* had played in the state of Augustus and of the Antonines. The state had now to be based on the country and the peasants. On the other hand, a simplification of its structure was a necessary consequence of the changed economic and cultural conditions.

Thus arose the state of Diocletian and Constantine. In organizing it the emperors did not have a free hand. They took over a heavy heritage from the third century, to which they had to conform. In this heritage there was almost nothing positive except the fact of the existence of the Empire with all its natural resources. The men who inhabited it had utterly lost their balance. Hatred and envy reigned everywhere: the peasants hated the landowners and the officials, the city proletariate hated the city *bourgeoisie*, the army was hated by everybody, even by the peasants. The Christians were abhorred and persecuted by the heathens, who regarded them as a gang of criminals bent on undermining the state. Work was disorganized and productivity was declining; commerce was ruined by the insecurity of the sea and the roads; industry could not prosper, since the market for industrial products was steadily contracting and the purchasing power of the population diminishing; agriculture passed through a terrible crisis, for the decay of commerce and industry deprived it of the capital which it needed, and the heavy demands of the state robbed it of labour and of the largest part of its products. Prices constantly rose, and the value of the currency depreciated at an unprecedented rate. The ancient system of taxation had been shattered and no new system was devised. The relations between the state and the taxpayer were based on more or less organized robbery: forced work, forced deliveries, forced loans or gifts were the order of the day. The administration was corrupt and demoralized. A chaotic mass of new government officials was growing up, superimposed on and superseding the former administrative personnel. The old officials still existed but, foreseeing their doom, strove to avail themselves to the full of their last opportunities. The city *bourgeoisie* was tracked out and persecuted, cheated, and maltreated. The municipal aristocracy was decimated by systematic persecution and ruined by repeated confiscations and by the responsibility imposed on it of ensuring the success of the organized raids of the government on the people. The most terrible chaos thus reigned throughout the ruined Empire. In such circumstances the task of any reformer would be to reduce the chaos to some sort of stable order, and the simpler and more primitive the methods, the better. The more refined system of the past was utterly destroyed and beyond restoration. What existed was the brutal practice of the third century, rude and violent as it was. That practice was to a certain extent created by the situation, and the simplest way out of the chaos was to fix and stabilize it, reducing it to a system and making the system as simple and as primitive as possible. The reform of Diocletian and Constantine was the legitimate offspring of the social revolution of the third century, and was bound to follow in the main the same lines. In their task those emperors had as little freedom as Augustus. For both of them the goal was the restoration of the state. By his genius Augustus succeeded in restoring not only the state but also the prosperity of the people. Diocletian and Constantine sacrificed, certainly against their will, the interests of the people to the preservation and the salvation of the state.

The chief object of this volume has been to investigate the social and economic conditions of the early Roman Empire, to trace the evolution which gradually resulted in the suppression of the leading part played by the cities in the history of the ancient world. The new state based on the peasants and the country was a new phenomenon in history, and its progressive development requires as careful an examination as we have endeavoured to make of the history of its genesis. The reader will, therefore, not expect a detailed analysis of its growth in this book. Another volume of the same size, and written from the same point of view, would be necessary for a study of the social and economic conditions of the late Roman Empire. No such book has yet been written. Nevertheless a short sketch of the main lines which the reforms of Diocletian and Constantine followed, as well as a general picture of the social and economic conditions, may be desirable here to convey some idea of the new régime and its relation to the world of the early Roman Empire.

The problems which Diocletian and his successors had to face were manifold. One of the most important was that relating to the central power, the *power of the emperor*. There was no question of eliminating that power. If there was one thing that held together the fabric of the Empire and guaranteed its existence, if there was any institution popular among the masses, it was the imperial power and the personality of the reigning emperor. Everything else was discredited. Despite the convulsions through which the Empire had passed, the idea of the imperial power stood intact. If there was any salvation for the Roman Empire—such was the general belief of the people—it must come from above. There was a deeply rooted feeling among all its inhabitants that without an emperor Rome could not and would not exist. And the bitter facts of the third century showed the truth of this belief. The only question was how to stabilize and organize the supreme power so that the emperor would no longer be a puppet in the hands of the soldiery. The conception of the imperial power formed in the first two centuries was too subtle, too complicated and refined, to be understood by the masses of the peasants on whom it was based. It was a creation of the high culture of the privileged classes. These classes were decimated and demoralized, and even their standard had become degraded and simplified. The idea of the ruler as first magistrate of the Roman citizens, whose authority was based on the conception of duty and on consecration by the great Divine Power ruling the universe, was one which did not reach, and was not comprehensible to, the mass of semi-barbarians and barbarians who now formed the staff of officials, the army, and the class which supplied both—the peasant population of the Empire. A simpler conception was urgently needed, a broader and plainer idea which would be intelligible to every one. Diocletian himself still adhered to the old idea of the ruler as the supreme magistrate, of the imperial power as vested in the best man or the best men, the *princeps* or *principes*. He emphasized, however, the supernatural and sacred character of his power, which was expressed in the identification of the emperor with God and in the Oriental ceremonial introduced at court. The cult of the emperor, which had been impersonal in the second century, became attached to the person of the emperor. The doctrine thus introduced was not new. Many attempts had been made to establish it— by Caligula and Nero, by Domitian and Commodus, by Elagabal and Aurelian. They had failed because the doctrine had adhered too much to the special religions of particular sections of the population. Apollo and Hercules were vague conceptions which made no general appeal; the Syrian Sol, Mithra, the amalgamation of Jupiter and Donar, appealed to a minority but did not satisfy the masses. The prominent feature of the spiritual life of the Empire was the increase of religiosity. Religion was gradually becoming paramount for almost everybody. The more religious society grew, the sharper became the divisions between the various groups. A believer in Mithra would not accept an emperor who was the incarnation of the German Donar, an adherent of the Egyptian cults would not devote his soul to the incarnation of such a vague deity as the Stoic Hercules, and so forth. Moreover, the Christians would resolutely reject them all and refuse to accept a living incarnation of God in a mortal man. It was futile to persecute them: every persecution made their cohesion closer and the organization of the church more solid. In the third century the Christian church acquired enormous strength. As a state within the state, its organization steadily improved in proportion as that of the state deteriorated. Oppression, compulsion, persecution were the mottoes of the state; love, compassion, consolation were the maxims of the church. The church, unique in this respect among the other religious communities, not only administered spiritual relief but promised and gave practical help in the miseries of actual life, while the state oppressed and persecuted the helper.

But the Christians, increasing in numbers and in strength, grew tired of being outcasts and of fighting the state. The time was ripe for a reconciliation of state and church, each of which needed the other. In the opinion of some scholars it was a stroke of genius in Constantine to realize this and act upon it. Others believe this was a major error, to which he was led by his superstitious tendencies. For my own part, I believe that both factors combined, and that the final impulse came from reasons of state. In any case, he offered peace to the church, provided that she would recognize the state and support the imperial power. The church—to her detriment, as many scholars believe—accepted the offer. For the first time the imperial power became firmly established on a solid basis, but it lost almost completely, save for some irrelevant formulae, the last remnants of its constitutional character as the supreme magistrate of the people of the Empire. It now resembled the Persian monarchy of the Sassanidae and its predecessors in the East, the monarchies of Babylonia, Assyria, Egypt, and the rest. It was based at once on force and compulsion and on religion. Individual emperors might fall victims to military conspiracies and court-plots. The imperial power was eternal like the church, which supported it, and it was a world-power as the church was a world-church. The work of simplification was thus accomplished and the new supreme power was acceptable at least to that part of the population which was prepared resolutely to reject any other solution. Gradually the Christian minority became, with the help of the state, a strong majority and imposed itself on those who never were able nor prepared to fight and to make sacrifices for their religious creed. Even to them Christianity brought in the main a satisfactory solution of their religious aspirations.

Second in importance to the question of the imperial power, and intimately connected with it, was the problem of the reorganization of the *imperial army*. Our last chapter showed how critical this problem was for the Empire. In view of the grave foreign wars and the repeated inroads of the tribes bordering on the Empire, the army had to be increased in numbers and its discipline and technique maintained at the level reached under Trajan, Hadrian, and M. Aurelius. On the other hand, an army levied, as the existing army was, by conscription from the ranks of the peasants—a militia composed of the poorer peasants with a long term of service —was an instrument both inefficient and dangerous. The only way out of this difficulty was to return to the more primitive and simpler military system of the Hellenistic and the Oriental monarchies.

The first steps towards a reorganization of the army were taken by Diocletian. Realizing, as no emperor before him had done, the necessity of permanent reserves for the frontier armies of the provinces, he increased the military forces on a large scale; but, while augmenting the number of effectives, he introduced no new methods of recruiting nor did he change the military system. These reforms were reserved for Constantine. The main military force of the Empire, as Constantine saw, could only be an enlarged praetorian guard, a strong army of horse and foot, stationed near the residence of the emperor, or the residences of the co-emperors, and always ready to march against the enemy. This field army, like the armies of the Hellenistic kings (with the exception of the Antigonids of Macedonia), had to be a mercenary one, consisting mostly of barbarians, recruited among the allied and vassal German and Sarmatian tribes and among those of the same stock who lived within the Empire. It was composed of different corps, some of them strictly belonging to the emperor's bodyguard, but the most important were the *comitatenses*, one part of which was called the *palatini*, and which formed a ready well-trained and well-organized field army. The armies which garrisoned the provinces, and whose duty it was to suppress revolts within their borders and to meet the first onslaughts of external foes, were organized on the pattern of the reserve of the Hellenistic kings. The soldiers of the provincial armies were conscripted from among the men who were settled on the frontiers with the obligation of hereditary military service. These military settlers were largely barbarians, Germans and Sarmatians, while some were descendants of the active soldiers and veterans who had received land from the emperors of the third century in the border districts. If more troops were needed, they were obtained by the enrolment of volunteers and by compulsory enlistment among the population of the Empire, mostly the rural population of the more warlike provinces, Thrace, Syria, Britain, and the two Mauretanias. The emphasis was laid on the *auxilia*, the barbarian units, while the legions, the regiments of Roman citizens, played but a subsidiary part. The leading idea of the Roman Republic and of the early Empire, obligatory military service for all the inhabitants of the Empire, was not dropped. But in practice the obligation of service was transformed into a tax, the *aurum tironicum*, levied from the landowners and expended in meeting part of the cost of the mercenary army and in finding sufficient recruits among men who were not attached to a special profession or to a plot of land within the Empire (*vagi*). In no case was the staff of officers for these types of troops drawn from any special class. The senatorial class was barred from military service, the equestrian class disappeared. Every one who showed military capacity could hope to rise gradually from the position of non-commissioned officer to that of an officer (*tribunus*), commanding a detachment or a legion or an auxiliary regiment, and then to the post of commander of an army (*dux*) or even commander-in-chief of the cavalry or infantry (*magister equitum* or *peditum*). Such at least was the theory and sometimes the practice. Naturally the families of higher officers became in course of time the main source of supply of officers in general, and thus a new military aristocracy was formed, which, however, never became a closed caste.

In remodelling the *administration* of the Empire, the policy of the emperors of the fourth and fifth centuries was to increase the number of officials, to simplify and standardize their duties, and to a certain extent to give the hierarchy a quasi-military character. While the governing bodies of the cities, the municipal councils, lost one after another almost all their rights of self-government, and were reduced to the position of unpaid agents of the state, responsible for the repartition and the collection of taxes, as well as for the apportionment of compulsory work and other burdens lying on the population of the city and the territory attached to the city, the staff of state officials, alike in the capital and in the provinces, grew in numbers and importance. In the early Empire the bureaucratic system was slowly replacing the system of city government in the capital, but was more or less adjusted to, and co-ordinated with, the principle of local self-government in the provinces and in Italy. Now it was systematically developed and extended to every field of administration. We cannot trace here the gradual growth of the organization of the all-powerful bureaucracy of the late Roman Empire, and its successive modifications. It was a sphere in which almost all the emperors endeavoured to introduce some changes and some improvements—a feature which is common to all bureaucratic governments, reforms being here both easy and in appearance efficient. Suffice it to say that from the time of Diocletian and Constantine the aim of the central government was to build up a well-organized bureaucratic machinery which, under central direction, would be equal to the task of managing all the affairs of an immense state. Compared with the delicate and complicated system of the early Empire, in which stress was laid on the self-government of the cities, while the bureaucracy was a subsidiary organ and an organ of control, the system of the late Empire, despite its apparent complexity, was much simpler, much more primitive and infinitely more brutal. Being supreme and omnipotent, and not subject to any control exercised in one way or another by those who were the life-blood of the state, the bureaucracy gradually became utterly corrupt and dishonest and at the same time comparatively inefficient, in spite of the high professional training of its members. Bribes and illicit gains were the order of the day, and it was idle to seek to put an end to them by means of a vast system of espionage and of mutual control exercised by officials over each other. Every addition to the army of officials, every addition to the host of supervisors, served to increase the number of those who lived on bribery and corruption. The worst were the thousands of secret police agents, the *agentes in rebus*, who were the successors of the *frumentarii* and whose duty it was to keep an eye on the population and on the host of imperial officials. Corruption and inefficiency is the fate of all bureaucracies which are not checked by wide powers of self-government vested in the people, whether they are created in the name of autocracy or of communism. Manifestly a highly elaborate system of bureaucratic government was incompatible with the fusion of military and civil government in the hands of the higher officials; and the two departments, which there had always been a tendency to manage separately, were now sharply divided and highly specialized. Manifestly, also, the host of officials must be recruited not from a special class but from the ranks of those who seemed to be the most suitable. Yet, in view of the privileges attaching to the position of a government officer, official posts naturally tended to become the hereditary privilege of a special caste. The higher posts were distributed among the candidates by the emperors personally, and many new men obtained them in this way. But by force of circumstances a new aristocracy of higher bureaucrats arose, and this aristocracy had practically a monopoly of all the higher offices of the Empire.

It is easy to understand why the emperors replaced the old system of administration by the new. The social revolution of the third century had been directed against the cities and the self-government of the

cities, which had practically been concentrated in the hands of the city *bourgeoisie*. It was much easier and much safer for the central government, instead of remodelling municipal self-government on new and more democratic lines—which required a great deal of creative initiative—to accept existing conditions and to kill the whole idea of self-government by making all the members of the city community responsible to the state, and by piling up duties on them without any corresponding rights. The self-government of the cities being thus destroyed, the functions of control had to be performed by somebody else, and supervisors had to be appointed to watch and coerce the municipal councils; the natural candidates for this office were the officials of the central government, who had hitherto played a modest part in the life of the provinces. It is futile to maintain that this reform was gradually and systematically built up by the early Empire because of the bankruptcy of the cities, which had demonstrated their utter incapacity to manage properly municipal affairs. The bureaucracy of the early Empire was different in principle from that of the late Empire. It managed, as was natural, the affairs of the state and interfered very little with the affairs of the cities. If it did interfere, it was to help the cities to develop a more efficient management of their own affairs. The change was brought about by the revolution of the third century. The self-government of the cities was destroyed by the long period of anarchy. Instead of restoring it on new lines, the late Empire left things as they were, and put the cities, not under the control, but under the command, of the agents of the central government, made them the servants and the slaves of the state, and reduced their role to that which they had played in the Oriental monarchies, save for their responsibility for the payment of taxes. The reform was carried out not for the sake of the people but for the sake of simplifying the government's task. The interests of the people were sacrificed to what seemed to be the interests of the state. The germs of self-government, which had developed in the village communities in the second century and even in the third, were involved in the common ruin and disappeared.

Closely connected with the reform of the administration was the momentous and pernicious reform of *taxation*. We have often insisted on the fact that the taxation of the early Empire, highly differentiated as it was and based on the traditions prevailing in the various parts of the Empire, was not very oppressive. The stress was laid on the indirect taxes and on the income derived by the state and the emperor from the land and other real estate owned by them. The direct taxes—the land-tax and the poll-tax—were paid in the various provinces in accordance with their traditions. Of their amount we have no knowledge except for the province of Egypt. But we know that many parts of the Empire were partly or completely (as in the case of Italy) exempt from these taxes, and that this exemption was rather extended than limited. If the provinces complained of their burdens, it was not because of the taxes. What bore heavily on them was the extraordinary payments, the provisioning of the armies and of the officials by means of compulsory deliveries, the war requisitions, the spasmodic confiscations, and the forced work. The responsibility for the assessment and the collection of the taxes was not resented as a very heavy burden by the municipal aristocracy. What they complained of was the responsiblity for the extraordinary burdens imposed on the population, and compulsory payments like the crown gold. It was the chaotic manner in which the extraordinary payments were exacted that ruined the city *bourgeoisie* and the working classes alike. In the troubled times of the third century these extraordinary payments became the main revenue of the state.

The state was living not on its normal income but on a system of more or less organized robbery.

The Roman state had never had a regular budget, and when it was faced with financial difficulties, it had no fixed and stable reserve to draw upon. From time to time thrifty emperors had accumulated some money, but it was easily squandered by spendthrifts who happened to occupy the throne, and it never represented capital well managed and invested in good securities. In case of emergency, therefore, the emperors had no reserve to resort to, nor did they ever seek to increase the regular income by a gradual increase in taxation; the usual way of getting the money, according to the principles of the city-state, was to demand it from the population either by means of extraordinary taxation or by means of requisitions and confiscations. It is not surprising that in the difficult times of the third century the ordinary taxes were rather neglected, and that greater store was set by the extraordinary taxes (especially the crown gold) and by extraordinary deliveries of foodstuffs, raw material, and manufactured goods. This and the general insecurity of the times led to the disorganization of trade and industry, and therefore to an enormous decrease in the yield of indirect taxes. The foolish policy of the emperors in systematically depreciating the currency, and the general economic conditions, as well as the system of organized pillage (the liturgies), produced violent and spasmodic fluctuations of prices which did not keep pace with the steady depreciation of the currency. Such were the conditions inherited by the emperors of the fourth century from their predecessors. So long as they lasted, there was no hope of restoring economic stability and of placing the currency on a sound basis. All attempts in this direction failed. The most notorious failure was that of Diocletian, both in respect of the currency and in regard to stabilization of prices. His well-known edict of 301, by which fixed prices were established for the various products, was no novelty. The same expedient had often been tried before him and was often tried after him. As a temporary measure in a critical time, it might be of some use. As a general measure intended to last, it was certain to do great harm and to cause terrible bloodshed, without bringing any relief. Diocletian shared the pernicious belief of the ancient world in the omnipotence of the state, a belief which many modern theorists continue to share with him and with it.

After the civil war had quieted down a little, it became evident to every one that the time had come to settle the mode of taxation. Two courses were open to Diocletian. He might go back to the traditions of the Antonines, cancel the emergency measures which had accumulated like a deposit over the system of the early Empire, and, in doing so, take account of the pecularities of economic life in the various provinces. This, of course, was the more difficult and the more painful path. To restore the prosperity of the Empire years of quiet development were required—as many years of peace and of orderly government as were granted to the Roman Empire by Augustus, who had faced almost the same difficulties after the end of the civil wars. Diocletian was unwilling, and probably unable, to wait. Circumstances were not such as to allow him patiently to lead the Empire back to normal conditions. On the frontiers enemies were ready to attack, the internal situation was far from quiet, and the increased and reorganized army absorbed enormous sums of money. Thus, Diocletian and his successors never thought of restoring the ancient complicated and individual system of taxation. They followed the other course which was open to them: to take for granted the practice of the third century, to transform the emergency measures into a system,

and to simplify and generalize that system as far as possible by applying it to all the provinces without taking into consideration the peculiarities of their economic life and social structure. As the currency was debased and unstable, the system of taxation could not be a monetary one. In place of money-taxes the emperors of the third century had invented or revived the primitive system of taxes in kind, under the form of repeated emergency collections of foodstuffs for the use of the army, the city of Rome, and the agents of the state; in addition thereto, raw material and manufactured goods were collected in the same way. This was the famous *annona*. What was easier than to transform these emergency deliveries into a regular tax? The needs of the army, the capitals, the court, and the officials would be covered, and the other expenditure of the state might be met as before from the old taxes, which were not abolished, and from the systemized extraordinary payments of the third century. It was not, however, easy to foresee what the needs of the state would be in the future: they might increase or decrease according to circumstances. That was the reason why the *annona* retained its aspect of an emergency delivery. Every year the emperor fixed the amount of payments required for the current year. The *annona* was thus stabilized, but stabilized in the worst possible form. In the third century men still hoped that the day might dawn when taxation would become regular and fixed. By the organization of Diocletian that hope was turned into a dream. Nobody could know in advance what he would have to pay in the next year; no calculations were possible until the state had announced the amount of its demands for that year.

Yet by the establishment of the *annona* as a permanent institution the problem of taxation was far from settled. The most important question was that of a fair and just assessment. In the third century this question had been settled differently for the different provinces. In Egypt it was based on the elaborate register of cultivated land, in the urbanized provinces on the data of the census and on the paying capacity of the various cities and other large units of taxation (the imperial and senatorial estates, and the land belonging to the temples and to vassal princes). This system was too complicated and elaborate for Diocletian. It depended in most of the provinces on the activity of the cities, and it was not easy to grasp at once in all its details. It was much simpler to leave aside the work of centuries and to introduce the most rough and primitive system of assessment which had ever existed. Every soldier could understand it, although any fool could see that in this case what was simple was not fair and just. The cultivated land, whether arable or planted, was divided into *iuga* or teams of oxen. The size of the *iugum* varied according as the land was situated in a plain or on a mountain slope, and according as it produced grain or wine or olive-oil. No further differentiation was attempted. No local conditions were taken into account. It may be that our idea of the reform of Diocletian, incompletely known as it is, exaggerates its simplicity. Perhaps the system was less rigid than it appears, and varied in different places. However, its main lines are beyond doubt and they show a tendency to simplify the problem of taxation, even if it be to the detriment of the taxpayer. It may be also that the intention was to establish a system adapted to the intelligence of the peasants, on which it depended, and to distribute the burdens equally on the population. The emperors of the period of the military monarchy were anxious to appear just and benevolent to the *humiliores*; this policy was never abandoned, at least in theory, and Diocletian often emphasized it. The *iugum* may have been familiar to Diocletian from his own experience, and

may have been used as a unit of taxation among the Illyrians and Thracians who still lived under the conditions of tribal economy.

The division into *iuga*—the *iugatio*—was, however, only one side of Diocletian's system. A plot of land without labour is a lifeless thing: a *iugum* presupposes a *caput* —a head, a man who cultivates it. The question of labour had grown acute in the third century. The population of the Empire became more and more shifting. Oppressed in one place, the tillers of the soil would try another. We have quoted many documents in which the final argument of the peasants is a firm threat to take to flight and seek another home if their desires are not granted. The ancient world grew up in the fixed belief that a man belonged to a particular place, his *origo* or ἰδαί. But only the serfs of the old Oriental monarchies were bound to their place of residence. Ever since the Roman Empire had united the civilized world, all others had been free to move as they liked. Such freedom was prejudicial to the success of the primitive *iugatio* of Diocletian. A piece of land might be cultivated one year and left waste the next: the peasant might migrate and settle somewhere else, or he might drop his profession altogether and become a proletarian in one of the cities. The yield of the large estates was proportionate not only to the number of *iuga* which it contained but, above all, to the number of *capita*. The gradual depopulation of the Empire, and especially the decrease in the number of peasant cultivators, made the unit of taxation not so much the *iugum* as the *caput*. Hence the taxable unit after Diocletian was a combination of both. Every one who cultivated a piece of land was supposed to make a declaration of the land which he cultivated and of the number of *capita* employed on it, including the animals. This declaration made the man responsible for his land and his *capita*: wherever he was, he was bound to pay the tax assessed upon it. As he formed with the land a single unit, he lost his liberty of movement, he became bound to his land and to his work, exactly like his predecessors the 'royal peasants' of the Oriental and Hellenistic kings. There was nothing new in this system for Egypt and some parts of Asia Minor, nor perhaps for some Celtic lands; the novelty lay in the revival and general application of a system which in the time of Hadrian seemed to have been doomed to disappear for ever.

The same primitive system of assessment was applied to other taxes, none of which was new. While in respect of foodstuffs and certain raw materials the needs of the state were met by the landowners, the money and manufactured goods required had to be found chiefly by the cities and their inhabitants. The artisans and the shopowners were expected to pay a uniform tax. How it was assessed, we do not know. They were also expected to deliver a certain amount of manufactured goods to the state or to the city at a special price. The large landed proprietors, the senators, paid a special tax in money for their estates (*collatio glebalis*). Finally, the artisans, the cities, and the senators had to pay the traditional crown gold (under different names) once every five years, and additional money when a new emperor came to the throne. The reorganization of taxation brought no improvement in the matter of compulsory exactions in cases of emergency. In time of war, requisitions and robbery reigned as before, and in the long list of the obligations of the people there still figured compulsory work and deliveries of draught cattle for transport (ἀγγαρεῖαι). How heavy the latter burden was, is shown by the 'constitutions' of the Codex Theodosianus and by the speech of Libanius Περὶ τῶν ἀγγαρειῶν. Everywhere, then, we meet with the same policy of simplification coupled with a policy of brutal compulsion, to which the ancient world

had become accustomed in the dark days of the third century.

The mode of collecting the taxes has already been spoken of. The system of the city-state, which used the services of tax-farmers, was to a large extent gradually superseded under the early Empire, and in those branches of taxation where it was retained (the customs and the collection of the payments in kind and money-taxes assessed on the imperial estates) it was very effectively improved. A highly specialized army of state-officials was created to check the attempts of the tax-farmers to cheat both the treasury and the taxpayers. Most of the taxes, however, apart from a few which were managed directly by the state (the inheritance tax, the taxes on manumission and auctions, and the customs-duties), were collected by the cities and paid by their representatives into the treasury of a given province. How they were collected inside the city was a matter of indifference to the state. The co-operation of the agents of the state—the governors of the provinces and their staffs and the imperial procurators—with the city magistrates was limited to a joint settlement of the amount of the taxes to be paid by the city, which was based on the municipal census and on a similar census carried out for the whole province by the central government. In giving a free hand to the cities, the emperors insisted upon two main points, that the assessment must be fair and just, and that the taxes must be paid in full without arrears. For this the municipal administration was responsible. In actual fact arrears accumulated in difficult times, and the emperors very often cancelled them completely or partially. To make the collection of the taxes more methodical and to guarantee themselves against arrears, the emperors appointed (in addition to the governors and the procurators) special agents of high standing to assist the cities in managing their financial affairs. From the time of Hadrian they tried to check the accumulation of arrears by making the richest members of the community responsible for them, especially for those connected with the departments of emergency-deliveries and supplementary taxation. In the third century, when the burdens of collecting the taxes, securing transport for the state, and provisioning the armies became excessively heavy, imperial pressure on the municipal *bourgeoisie* steadily increased and its responsibility to the state was more and more minutely regulated. Compulsion was freely used as the *bourgeoisie* became more impoverished and reduced in numbers, and as the paying capacity of the taxpayers decreased. Some of the essential rights of free men and citizens of Rome, as the municipal *bourgeois* were from the legal point of view, were curtailed. The government became harsh and sometimes violent. And yet the *bourgeoisie* remained the privileged class of the provincial population and still enjoyed some of its old privileges.

Diocletian made no effort to change the conditions which he inherited from the military anarchy of the third century. He never thought either of reducing the city *bourgeoisie* to the level of the rest of the population of the city territory by making every member of it a mere taxable unit, or of restoring the past glory of the cities. He took over the legislation of his predecessors, which tended to transform the *bourgeoisie* into a group of unpaid hereditary servants of the state, and developed it in the same spirit. The *curiales* (those who were eligible for the municipal council and the magistracies) formed a group of richer citizens responsible to the state through the magistrates and the council both for the welfare, peace, and order of the city and for the fufilment by the population of all its obligations towards the state. Like the tillers of the soil, each of the *curiales* personally formed a single unit for purposes of taxation, and the whole of the *curiales* formed one large unit, representing

the amount of tax and of compulsory work demanded from the population of the city. It was natural that every *curialis* and the group as a whole should be treated in the same way as the individual tillers of the soil. Their responsibility was not only material but personal. Thus they had strictly to observe the rule of *origo*, to remain in their city and not seek to escape to another place of residence, and in dying they had to substitute for themselves another taxable and responsible unit in the person of their children. An army of officials was on the spot to keep close watch on them, and to use compulsion and violence if any of them tried to break away from the iron circle in which he was included. Have we not here the plainest proof of Diocletian's utter incapacity to invent anything new or so to adapt existing institutions to the conditions of his time as to safeguard as far as possible the rights and the prosperity of the people? Like the rest of his reforms, his reorganization of municipal life appears to me to be a striking *testimonium paupertatis*, typical of an age devoid of all creative power and helplessly submitting to current practice, which owed its origin to a period of revolution and anarchy. Augustus had faced the same difficulties, for the time of the civil wars had been a time of oppression and of legalized robbery; but he never dreamt of legalizing robbery and oppression in his turn and making them permanent. In the mind of Diocletian the state meant compulsion, and organization meant organized violence. We cannot say that his hand was forced by the will of the army. Diocletian never thought of eliminating the antagonism between city and country by transferring the responsibility for taxation and compulsory work from the city councils to state officials. He kept the antagonism alive, with the result that in the fourth and fifth centuries the country hated the city as cordially as it had done in the third: witness Salvian and his attacks on the tyrants from the cities. We cannot say, then, that Diocletian had no other course open to him. Many were open to him, but he took the old beaten track which led directly to ruin and slavery.

The return of stable conditions and the restoration of a certain peace and order could not fail to have some effect. The terrors of the second civil war were not followed by an Augustian Golden Age; but it cannot be denied that some improvement in economic conditions occurred after the reforms of Diocletian and Constantine. For example, Egypt enjoyed a certain revival in the fourth century and the same is true also of various cities of the Roman Empire. It is no less significant that Constantine succeeded in a field where Diocletian had failed: namely in stabilizing the currency and in restoring, to some extent, the prestige of money in public and private life. But this restoration was of brief duration, not because of the external conditions or of the incompetence of the successors of Diocletian and Constantine, but mainly because of the system, which had been responsible for the decay and contained in itself the seeds of a further decline. Oppressive and unjust taxation based on the enslavement alike of the tillers of the soil and of the city-artisans; the immobilization of economic life, which was hampered in its free development by the chains which bound every individual; the cruel annihilation, consciously pursued and gradually effected, of the most active and the most educated class of the Roman Empire, the city *bourgeoisie*; the steady growth of dishonesty and of violence among the members of the imperial administration, both high and low; the impotence of the emperors, despite the best intentions, to check lawlessness and corruption, and their boundless conservatism as regards the fundamental principles of the reforms of Diocletian and Constantine—all these factors did not fail to produce their natural effect. The spirit of the population remained as crushed as

it had been in the times of the civil war. The only difference was that a wave of resignation spread over the Roman Empire. It was useless to fight, better to submit and bear silently the burden of life with the hope of finding a better life—after death. The feeling was natural, for the best efforts of honest men were bound to fail, and the more one produced, the more would be taken by the state. If a peasant succeeded in improving his land and adding to it, he knew that his fate was to be promoted to the position of a *curialis*, which meant slavery, oppression, and, in the last resort, ruin. Better to produce enough to support his family and not make useless efforts to better his position. A soldier knew very well that, so long as he was a soldier and so long as he condemned his children to the same life, he might be comparatively prosperous. As soon as he tried to break the spell, he knew that his fate, too, or at least the fate of his children, would be to join the *curia* and exchange bad for worse. The tenant of a large landowner was content to perform his duties and to enjoy the protection, and the oppression, of his master. The fate of his neighbour, the free peasant, was not attractive enough to induce him to strive to become one. The same was true of the artisans of the cities and the unfortunate *curiales*. In moments of despair the individual might try by desperate means to ameliorate his lot: the *colonus* and the peasant might seek to enter the army or to turn to robbery, the soldier to desert the army, the *curialis* to become anything—an official, a soldier, a *colonus*, or a peasant. It was all in vain. If they succeeded, their situation was every whit as bad. Thus the reigning mood was resignation, and resignation never leads to prosperity.

The salient trait of the economic life of the late Roman Empire was gradual impoverishment. The poorer the people became, the more primitive grew the economic life of the Empire. Commerce decayed, not only because of piracy and barbarian inroads, but mainly because customers disappeared. The best clients, the city *bourgeoisie*, decreased constantly in numbers and in purchasing power. The peasants lived in extreme poverty and reverted to an almost pure 'house economy', each home producing for itself what it needed. The only customers left were the members of the privileged classes, the officials, the soldiers, and the large landed proprietors, and they were provided for, as far as the necessities of life were concerned, either by the state (their salary being paid in kind) or by the produce of their own estates. Thus the first branch of commerce to suffer decay was the most important one, commerce in articles of prime necessity within a province and between provinces. Local retail-trade still lingered on, and trade in luxuries even prospered. This accounts, for instance, for the revival of the commerce with the East. The commercial class as such, however, remained unprogressive and despised. There was no chance to develop any large commercial enterprise. As soon as a man tried to do so, as soon as he bought ships or established commercial relations, he was made a member of one of the corporations, the *navicularii* or *mercatores*, and was forced to work for the state, to transport goods on its behalf, and for a miserable remuneration, or to give the state the first offer of what he had to sell. Thus the situation of the merchants and shipowners was as bad as that of the *curiales*, and compulsion was employed to keep the members of these groups bound to their profession and to keep the number of the groups complete by enrolment of fresh members. Like the ownership of land, commerce and transportation became a hereditary burden from which there was no escape. The same held good of industry. Customers were few, the market became more and more restricted, and the state more and more oppressive. Apart from the produc-

tion of some standardized articles for the masses and some luxuries for the few rich, industry lived on the orders of the state. But the state was a selfish and a brutal customer: it fixed the prices and, if we take into consideration the profits of the officials, fixed them ruinously low for the artisans. Naturally the large industrial concerns gradually disappeared. As the state needed them, especially for the army, for the court, and for the officials, many industrial establishments were transformed into state factories, which were managed on Egyptian and Oriental patterns, with a staff of workmen bound to their profession and bearing a hereditary burden.

In the preceding chapters we have endeavoured to show that the social crisis of the third century had been, to a large extent, brought about by a revolutionary movement of the masses of the population which aimed at a general levelling. Was this aim achieved by the reforms of Diocletian and Constantine? Can we say that the late Roman Empire was more democratic than the Empire of the Julio-Claudians, the Flavians, and the Antonines? It is true that one privileged class of the past, the equestrian, disappeared. It is true that for a time advancement in the army and in the civil service was open to everybody, especially in the third century. But in actual fact the late Roman Empire, though it was a democracy of slaves, was less democratic than the early Empire. There were no castes in the early Empire. An active and clever man could easily, by increasing his fortune, rise from the position of peasant to that of land-owner, and as such he could join the ranks of the municipal aristocracy, receive the Roman citizenship, become a knight, and finally a member of the senatorial aristocracy. We have seen that such an advance was easily accomplished in two or three generations. Even in the army promotion from the rank of private to the high post of first centurion was normal, although the advance of a common soldier to the equestrian or senatorial posts in the army was rare and exceptional. So it was in the civil service. Even slaves were no exception to the general rule. Emancipated slaves had brilliant opportunities of becoming procurators of high standing, and there was nothing to prevent them or their children from entering the ranks of the municipal aristocracy.

The situation was different after the reforms of Diocletian and Constantine. There was no legal way of advancing from the position of a *colonus* even to that of a free peasant or a city proletarian, not to speak of other classes. A *colonus* might exceptionally become a soldier, but it was a very rare exception. The reform of taxation by Diocletian and the edicts of later emperors made the *colonus* a serf, so that, already in fact bound by heredity to his plot of earth, he became bound to his domicile and to his master; he became a member of a close hereditary caste. The same was true of the free small landowner, who was a member of a village community: he was tied to his land, to his village, to his profession. The only possible advance was to the position of a *curialis*, which in fact was a move downwards. Some might serve in the army, particularly if they happened to live in military provinces; but, as the legislation against deserters shows, this was not regarded as an enviable privilege. The municipal landowners, the *curiales*, were in the same position. They were less free than even the small landowners, and they formed a close and very select class, select because everybody dreaded the very idea of entering it. The rest of the city population—the shipowners, the merchants, the artisans, the workmen—were all gradually bound to their profession and to their place of residence. One privileged class was that of the workless proletarians and beggars in the city and in the country, for whom the Christian church was supposed to care. They at least

were free—to starve and to riot. Another free and privileged class was the robbers, who steadily increased in numbers on sea and land. The class of officials was not indeed hereditary, at any rate not legally. It was a privilege to be an official, and the emperor was free to recruit his officials from the best men in the country. But his freedom was limited. A *curialis* could not become an official, and if one of them succeeded in evading the rule, he might expect every moment to be sent back to his *curia*. Nor were merchants and shipowners eligible. The peasants and the city proletariate do not come into consideration. The military career was sharply separated from the civil, and a soldier was not eligible for a civil office. Thus by force of circumstances officials were recruited from the families of officials, and the official class became practically, though not legally, a close caste. The same description applies to the new senatorial aristocracy. It was an aristocracy of service, admission to which was granted by the emperors to the higher civil and military officers, and membership was hereditary. Gradually it became also an aristocracy of birth and education, for the intellectual traditions of the class were jealously guarded.

From the social point of view, then, there was no levelling and no equalization. In the late Roman Empire society was subdivided not into classes, but into real castes, each as close as possible, in some cases because of the privileges connected with the caste, in others because of the burdens and hardships, which prevented anybody from desiring to be admitted, and made membership hereditary and compulsory. Nor was there even equality in the common slavery to the state. There was indeed equality of a negative kind, for no political freedom was tolerated, no remnant of self-government was left, no freedom of speech, thought, or conscience was permitted, especially after the victory of Christianity; but even this equality of slavery was superficial and relative. The great landed proprietors were slaves of the emperor but masters of the tenant-serfs who lived on their estates. The *curiales* were slaves of the administration and were treated by it as such, but they were masters not only of the tenants of their estates, but also of the population of the city and the city territory, inasmuch as they apportioned and collected the taxes and supervised the compulsory work; and by these they were regarded and hated as masters who were themselves unfree and could not protect but only cheat their own slaves. Little wonder if these slaves appealed for protection to senators, officials, and soldiers, and were ready to pay any price for it and to deprive themselves of the little money and the little liberty which they still had. The working class of the cities stood in the same relation to the members of the various corporations, the owners of ships, shops, and factories. The last were in truth much more like minor supervisors of their own concerns on behalf of the state than their owners; they were themselves in bondage to the officials of the various departments and of the commanders of the various military units. Lastly, the officials and the soldiers of various ranks, though wielding an enormous power over thousands of men, were subjected to an iron discipline of a servile type and were practically slaves of each other and of the agents of the secret police. General servitude was, indeed, the distinctive feature of the age, but while there were different grades and shades of bondage, there was no equality. Slavery and equality are incompatible, a fact which should not be forgotten by the many modern defenders of the principle of equality.

Above all, there was no equality whatsoever in the distribution of property. The senators, the knights, the municipal aristocracy, the petty *bourgeoisie* of the early Empire were, of course, ruined and degraded. Their patient and creative work, by which they had accumulated their fortunes and built up the civilized life of the cities, had disappeared for ever. But the old propertied classes were replaced by new ones, which even from the economic point of view were much worse than their predecessors. The fortunes of the early Empire were the result of the growing prosperity of the Empire in general. They were derived from commerce and industry, and the capital acquired was invested in land, improving its cultivation and the types of crop produced. The wars of the second century undermined these fortunes and retarded or even arrested economic development. Yet they did not work ruin, and a recovery under more normal conditions was possible. The catastrophe of the third century dealt a severe blow to the prosperity of the Empire and weakened the creative energies of the better part of the population. The reforms of Diocletian and Constantine, by giving permanence to the policy of organized robbery on the part of the state, made all productive economic activity impossible. But it did not stop the formation of large fortunes, rather it contributed to their formation, while altering their character. The foundation of the new fortunes was no longer the creative energy of men, nor the discovery and exploitation of new sources of wealth, nor the improvement and development of commercial, industrial, and agricultural enterprises; it was in the main the skilful use of a privileged position in the state to cheat and exploit the state and the people alike. Public officials, both high and low, grew rich on bribery and corruption. The senatorial class, being free from municipal burdens, invested their spoil in land and used their influence, the influence of their caste—which in this respect was more powerful than the emperors and nullified all their good intentions—to divert the burdens of taxation on to the other classes, to cheat the treasury directly, and to enslave ever larger numbers of workmen. We cannot here discuss how and under what title they grabbed large tracts of fertile land, both private and crown property. We have seen them at work in Egypt in the third century. In the fourth they proceeded farther on the same path. Purchase, lease, patronage, lease without term, hereditary lease with the obligation to cultivate (*emphyteusis*) were all used to make the senatorial class the class of large landed proprietors *par excellence*, and to form vast estates scattered all over the provinces and resembling small principalities. Few of the members of the senatorial class lived in the capital or in the cities. The majority of them built large and beautiful fortified villas in the country and dwelt there, surrounded by their family, their slaves, a real retinue of armed clients, and thousands of rural serfs and dependants. We are well acquainted with their mode of life from the descriptions of Ausonius, Paulinus of Pella, Sidonius Apollinaris, and Salvian, from the numerous ruins of their villas, and from some mosaics which portrayed on their floors the beauty of their châteaux in town and country. The class was large and influential. Every successful 'new' man tried hard to become a member of it, and many succeeded. They were good patriots, they possessed a genuine love of Rome and the Empire, they were faithful servants of the emperors, and they appreciated civilization and culture very highly. Their political outlook was narrow, their servility was unbounded. But their external appearance was majestic, and their grand air impressed even the barbarians who gradually became masters of the Empire. For the other classes they had sympathy and understanding in theory only, expressing their commiseration in literature, without practical results. They regarded them as far inferior beings, in this respect resembling the aristocracy of Rome in the first century B.C. and the first century A.D. The senators of the second century were not nearly so exclusive or so self-confident. There were, of course, exceptions, but they were few. Thus, more than ever before, society was divided into two classes: those who became steadily poorer and more destitute, and those who built up their prosperity on the spoils of the ruined Empire—real drones, who never made any contribution to economic life but lived on the toil and travail of other classes.

The social revolution of the third century, which destroyed the foundations of the economic, social, and intellectual life of the ancient world, could not produce any positive achievement. On the ruins of a prosperous and well-organized state, based on the age-old classical civilization and on the self-government of the cities, it built up a state which was based on general ignorance, on compulsion and violence, on slavery and servility, on bribery and dishonesty. Have we the right to accuse the emperors of the fourth century of having deliberately and of their own choice built up such a state, while they might have taken another path and have constructed, not the slave-state of the late Roman Empire, but one free from the mistakes of the early Empire and yet not enshrining the brutal practice of the revolutionary period? It is idle to ask such a question. The emperors of the fourth century, and above all Diocletian, grew up in the atmosphere of violence and compulsion. They never saw anything else, they never came across any other method. Their education was moderate, and their training exclusively military. They took their duties seriously, and they were animated by the sincerest love of their country. Their aim was to save the Roman Empire, and they achieved it. To this end they used, with the best intentions, the means which were familiar to them, violence and compulsion. They never asked whether it was worth while to save the Roman Empire in order to make it a vast prison for scores of millions of men.

2. THE REFORMS OF DIOCLETIAN AND CONSTANTINE*

DIOCLETIAN AND THE TETRARCHY

To divide the administrative responsibilities of the vast Empire, prevent a recurrence of the military anarchy of the preceding half century, and guarantee orderly succession to the throne, Diocletian in A.D. 293 established a four-man rule, the tetrarchy. In 305 Diocletian and Maximian, the two senior members, abdicated, but their provisions for the continuation of the system by a new tetrarchy proved short-lived.

Aurelius Victor *Lives of the Emperors* xxix. 17–48 (abridged)

Forthwith he proclaimed as coemperor Maximian, a faithful friend, a semi-rustic with, however, great military talent and native ability. Afterward he acquired the surname Herculius, from the cult of Hercules, his favorite divinity, while Valerius [Diocletian] took the surname of Jovius; and these surnames were assigned to those military units which excelled the rest of the army. . . . [The rise of usurpers and foreign attacks decided the two emperors] to select as Caesars Julius Constantius and Galerius Maximianus, surnamed Armentarius, and to associate them with themselves in marriage. The former received Herculius' stepdaughter, the latter Diocletian's daughter, the previous marriage of each being dissolved, just as Augustus had once done in the case of Tiberius Nero and his daughter Julia. All these men were, indeed, natives of Illyria; but although little cultured, they were of great service to the state, because they were inured to the hardships of rural life and of war. . . . The harmony which prevailed among them proved above all that their native ability and their skill in military science, which

they had acquired from Aurelian and Probus, almost sufficed to compensate for lack of high character. Finally, they looked up to Valerius [Diocletian] as to a father or as one would to a mighty god. . . .

As the burden of the wars mentioned above became heavier, a sort of division of the Empire was made: all the countries beyond the Gallic Alps were entrusted to Constantius; Herculius had Africa and Italy; Galerius, Illyria as far as the Black Sea; and Diocletian retained all the rest. After this, part of Italy was subjected to the heavy burden of paying tribute. . . . A new law for regular tax payments was introduced. At that time it was still endurable, because not excessive, but it has grown in our age into a scourge. . . .

With no less zeal [than in their military exploits] did the emperors take up the administration of civil affairs, in which connection their laws were eminently just. They suppressed the *frumentarii*, a group that was a veritable scourge and whom now the *agentes in rebus* closely resemble. These men, who appear to have been established to investigate and report possible seditious movements that might exist in the provinces, trumped up false accusations, and under the universal terror they inspired, especially in persons in very remote areas, they practiced shameful rapine everywhere. The emperors showed no less concern and solicitude for the provisioning of the city and the welfare of those who paid tribute. . . . The ancient cults were maintained in all their purity. Rome and other cities, especially Carthage, Milan, and Nicomedia, were extraordinarily embellished with new structures of great splendor. . . .

Diocletian kept his eyes on threatening dangers, and when he saw that the Roman state, in the course of destiny, was going to become a prey to civil wars and was

* Naphtali Lewis and Meyer Reinhold, *Roman Civilization, Vol. 2: The Empire* (New York: Columbia University Press, 1955), pp. 457–460; 464–466; 475–487. Reprinted by permission of the publisher.

approaching its breakup, so to speak, he celebrated the twentieth anniversary of his reign and abdicated the government of the state, although he was in good health. Herculius, who had held power one year less, he induced to follow his example, though he did so with great reluctance. Although there exists a variety of explanations [for Diocletian's abdication], and the truth has been perverted, it is my view that it was out of the excellence of his character that, scorning ambition for power, he descended to the life of an ordinary citizen.

DIOCLETIAN'S ADMINISTRATIVE REORGANIZATION

Diocletian, the reorganizer of the Empire after the military anarchy, completed and systematized the political, social, and economic changes brought about by the revolution of the third century. The pattern of society he established, brought to completion by Constantine, remained the basis of the regimented life of the people in the Roman Empire for centuries to come. The following evaluation by a Christian writer of Diocletian's reorganization is colored by the severe persecution of the Christian during his reign.

Lactantius *On the Deaths of the Persecutors* vii

While Diocletian, who was the inventor of wicked deeds and the contriver of evils, was ruining everything, he could not keep his hands even from God. This man, through both avarice and cowardice, overturned the whole world. For he made three men sharers of his rule; the world was divided into four parts, and armies were multiplied, each of the rulers striving to have a far larger numbers of soldiers than former emperors had had when the state was ruled by single emperors. The number of those receiving [pay from the state] was so much larger than the number of those paying [taxes] that, because of the enormous size of the assessments, the resources

of the tenant farmers were exhausted, fields were abandoned, and cultivated areas were transformed into wilderness. And to fill everything with fear, the provinces also were cut into bits; many governors and more minor offices lay like incubi over each region and almost on every municipality, likewise many procurators of revenues, administrators, and deputy prefects. Very few civil cases came before all of these, but only condemnations and frequent confiscations, and there were not merely frequent but perpetual exactions of innumerable things, and in the process of exaction intolerable wrongs.

Whatever was imposed with a view to the maintenance of the soldiery might have been endured; but Diocletian, with insatiable avarice, would never permit the treasury to be diminished. He was constantly accumulating extraordinary resources and funds so as to preserve what he had stored away untouched and inviolate. Likewise, when by various iniquities he brought about enormously high prices, he attempted to legislate the prices of commodities. Then much blood was spilled . . . nothing appeared on the market because of fear, and prices soared much higher. In the end, after many people had lost their lives, it became absolutely necessary to repeal the law.

In addition, he had a certain endless passion for building, and made no small exactions from the provinces for maintaining laborers and artisans and for supplying wagons and whatever else was necessary for the construction of public works. Here basilicas, there a circus, here a mint, there a shop for making weapons here a house for his wife, there one for his daughter. Suddenly a great part of the city [of Nicomedia] was demolished. All went elsewhere with their wives and children, as from a city taken by enemies. And when those structures were completed, to the ruin of the provinces, he said, "They are not properly made; let them be done on another plan." Then they had to be pulled down, and remodeled, to undergo perhaps another demolition. By such constant folly did he endeavour to make Nicomedia the equal of Rome.

I omit mentioning, indeed, how many perished on account of their possessions or wealth; for this was a common thing and became almost lawful as people grew accustomed to these evils. But this was peculiar to him, that wherever he saw a rather well-cultivated field, or an uncommonly elegant house, a false accusation and capital punishment were ready against the owner, so that it seemed as if he could not seize someone else's property without bloodshed.

THE EDICT ON MAXIMUM PRICES

Adapted in part from the translation of E. Graser

The Emperor Caesar Gaius Aurelius Valerius DIOCLETIAN Pius Felix Invictus Augustus, *pontifex maximus*, Germanicus Maximus for the sixth time, Sarmaticus Maximus for the fourth time, Persicus Maximus for the second time, Brittannicus Maximus, Carpicus Maximus, Armenicus Maximus, Medicus Maximus, Adiabenicus Maximus, holding the tribunician power for the eighteenth year, seven times consul, acclaimed *imperator* for the eighteenth time, father of his country, proconsul; and the Emperor Caesar Marcus Aurelius Valerius MAXIMIAN [corresponding titles]; and Flavius Valerius CONSTANTIUS [corresponding titles], most noble Caesar; and GALERIUS Valerius Maximian [corresponding titles], most noble Caesar, declare:

As we recall the wars which we have successfully fought, we must be grateful to the fortune of our state, second only to the immortal gods, for a tranquil world that reclines in the embrace of the most profound calm, and for the blessings of a peace that was won with great effort. That this fortune of our state be stabilized and suitably adorned is demanded by the law-abiding public and by the dignity and majesty of Rome. Therefore we, who by the gracious favor of the gods previously stemmed the tide of the ravages of barbarian nations by destroying them, must surround the peace which we established for eternity with the necessary defences of justice.

If the excesses perpetrated by persons of unlimited and frenzied avarice could be checked by some self-restraint—this avarice which rushes for gain and profit with no thought for mankind . . .; or if the general welfare could endure without harm this riotous license by which, in its unfortunate state, it is being very seriously injured every day, the situation could perhaps be faced with dissembling and silence, with the hope that human forbearance might alleviate the cruel and pitiable situation. But the only desire of these uncontrolled madmen is to have no thought for the common need. Among the unscrupulous, the immoderate, and the avaricious it is considered almost a creed . . . to desist from plundering the wealth of all only when necessity compels them. Through their extreme need, moreover, some persons have become acutely aware of their most unfortunate situation, and can no longer close their eyes to it. Therefore we, who are the protectors of the human race, are agreed, as we view the situation, that decisive legislation is necessary, so that the long-hoped-for solutions which mankind itself could not provide may, by the remedies provided by our foresight, be vouchsafed for the general betterment of all. . . .

We hasten, therefore, to apply the remedies long demanded by the situation, satisfied that no one can complain that our intervention with regulations is untimely or unnecessary, trivial or unimportant. These measures are directed against the unscrupulous, who have perceived in our silence of so many years a lesson in restraint but have been unwilling to imitate it. For who is so insensitive and so devoid of human feeling that he can be unaware or has not perceived that uncontrolled prices are widespread in the sales taking place in the markets and in the daily life of the cities? Nor is the uncurbed passion for profiteering lessened either by abundant supplies or by fruitful years. . . .

But now we must set forth in detail the causes which have pressed and driven us to cease our long-enduring forbearance and to take steps. . . . Who does not know that wherever the common safety requires our armies to be sent, the profiteers insolently and covertly attack the public welfare, not only in villages and towns, but on every road? They charge extortionate prices for merchandise, not just fourfold or eightfold, but on such a scale that human speech cannot find words to characterize their profit and their practices. Indeed, sometimes in a single retail sale a soldier is stripped of his donative and pay. Moreover, the contributions of the whole world for the support of the armies fall as profits into the hands of these plunderers, and our soldiers appear to bestow with their own hands the rewards of their military service and their veterans' bonuses upon the profiteers. The result is that the pillagers of the state itself seize day by day more than they know how to hold.

Aroused justly and rightfully by all the facts set forth above, and in response to the needs of mankind itself, which appears to be praying for release, we have decided that maximum prices of articles for sale must be established. We have not set down fixed prices, for we do not deem it just to do this, since many provinces occasionally enjoy the good fortune of welcome low prices and the privilege, as it were, of prosperity. Thus, when the pressure of high prices appears anywhere—may the

gods avert such a calamity!—avarice . . . will be checked by the limits fixed in our statute and by the restraining curbs of the law.

It is our pleasure, therefore, that the prices listed in the subjoined schedule be held in observance in the whole of our Empire. And every person shall take note that the liberty to exceed them at will has been ended, but that the blessing of low prices has in no way been impaired in those places where supplies actually abound. . . . Moreover, this universal edict will serve as a necessary check upon buyers and sellers whose practice it is to visit ports and other provinces. For when they too know that in the pinch of scarcity there is no possibility of exceeding the prices fixed for commodities, they will take into account in their calculations at the time of sale the localities, the transportation costs, and all other factors. In this way they will make apparent the justice of our decision that those who transport merchandise may not sell at higher prices anywhere.

It is agreed that even in the time of our ancestors it was the practice in passing laws to restrain offences by prescribing a penalty. For rarely is a situation beneficial to humanity accepted spontaneously; experience teaches that fear is the most effective regulator and guide for the performance of duty. Therefore it is our pleasure that anyone who resists the measures of this statute shall be subject to a capital penalty for daring to do so. And let no one consider the statute harsh, since there is at hand a ready protection from danger in the observance of moderation. . . . We therefore exhort the loyalty of all, so that a regulation instituted for the public good may be observed with willing obedience and due scruple, especially as it is seen that by a statute of this kind provision has been made, not for single municipalities and peoples and provinces but for the whole world. . . .

Constantine's Administrative and Military Reorganization

The system of the tetrarchy established by Diocletian did not long survive his abdication in A.D. 305. Out of the rivalries among his successors there emerged in 313 two joint emperors, Licinius and Constantine, and in 324 the latter, after defeating his colleague, became sole ruler. Constantine brought to completion the imperial reorganization initiated by Diocletian. The essence of his administrative reforms was the fractioning of the power of his chief functionaries and the almost universal separation of civil and military functions. These remained the fundamental principles of the imperial administration for the next three centuries, during which the size and power of the Byzantine bureaucracy increased steadily. Constantine also transformed the Roman military system. Reducing the importance and strength of the frontier garrisons, which become local border militias (*limitanei*, *riparienses*) commanded by *duces* (dukes) and *comites* (counts), he based the imperial defenses primarily on mobile field armies (*comitatenses*), under the direct command of himself and his deputies. In a further break with tradition, Constantine made the cavalry, instead of the infantry, his basic military arm, thus introducing the type of military organization which prevailed throughout the Middle Ages.

Zosimus *Recent History* II. xxxii–xxxv (abridged)

Constantine drastically reorganized the long-established offices. There had been two Praetorian prefects, who administered the office jointly and controlled by their supervision and power not only the Praetorian cohorts but also those which were entrusted with the guarding of the city and those which were stationed in the outskirts. The office of Praetorian prefect had been considered second to that of the emperor; he made the distributions of grain and redressed all offenses against military discipline by appropriate punishments. Constantine, altering this good institution, divided the single office into four. To one prefect he assigned all Egypt, together with the Pentapolis in Libya, and the East as far as Mesopotamia, and, in addition, Cilicia, Cappadocia, Armenia, the entire coast from Pamphylia to Trapezus, and the forts along the Phasis river; to the same person were entrusted Thrace, and Moesia as far as the Haemus and Rhodope mountains, and the territory of the town of Doberus, and likewise Cyprus and the Cyclades Islands except Lemnos, Imbros, and Samothrace. To another he assigned Macedonia, Thessaly, Crete, Greece together with the nearby islands, both Epiruses, and in addition the Illyrians, the Dacians, the Triballians, the Pannonians as far as Valeria, and Upper Moesia besides. To the third prefect he entrusted all Italy and Sicily with the neighboring islands, and also Sardinia and Corsica, and Africa from the Syrtes to Cyrene; to the fourth, the Transalpine Gauls and Iberia, and in addition the island of Britain. Having thus divided the office of these prefects, he strove to reduce their power in other ways. For though there were not only centurions and tribunes in command of the soldiers everywhere but also those called *duces*, who in each district held the rank of commanders, he established masters of the soldiers, some for the cavalry, some for the infantry, and by transferring to these the power of marshaling the soldiers and punishing offenders, he diminished in this respect the authority of the prefects. . . .

Constantine likewise took another measure, which gave the barbarians unhindered access into the lands subject to the Romans. For the Roman Empire was, by the foresight of Diocletian, everywhere protected on its frontiers . . . by towns and fortresses and towers, in which the entire army was stationed; it was thus impossible for the barbarians to cross over, there being everywhere a sufficient opposing force to repel their inroads. But Constantine destroyed that security by removing the greater part of the soldiers from the frontiers and stationing them in cities that did not require protection; thus he stripped those of protection who were harassed by the barbarians and brought ruin to peaceful cities at the hands of the soldiers, with the result that most have become deserted. He likewise softened the soldiers by exposing them to shows and luxuries. To speak plainly, he was the first to sow the seeds of the ruinous state of affairs that has lasted up to the present time.

LEGISLATION ON TAXATION

Theodosian Code XI. vii. 3; A.D. 320

In connection with the payment of taxes due, no person shall fear that he will suffer, at the hands of perverse and enraged judges, imprisonment, lashes of leaded whips, weights, or any other tortures devised by the arrogance of judges. Prisons are for criminals. . . . In accordance with this law, taxpayers shall proceed in security; or indeed, if a man is so alien to human feeling that he contumaciously abuses this indulgence, he shall be detained in the free and open military custody established for ordinary use. If he persists in his stubborn wickedness, his fellow citizens shall be given access to his property and all his substance, and with the ownership of his substance they shall undertake the performance of his obligations [to the state]. Since we grant such an opportunity, we believe that all men will be the more inclined to pay that which is demanded for the use of our army in behalf of the common safety.

Theodosian Code XI. xvi. 3; A.D. 324/25

Whenever it is necessary for a tax assessment to be made, the assessment of each municipality shall be made in accordance with the plans and direction of the governor so that the mass of the lower classes may not be subjected to the wantonness and subordinated to the interests of the more powerful and thus suffer the infliction of grave and iniquitous outrages.

Theodosian Code XI. iii. 2; A.D. 327

Slaves assessed in the census rolls shall be sold within the boundaries of the province, and any persons who obtain ownership by purchase shall know that they must look into this. It is reasonable that the same rule should be observed also in the case of landholding . . . [where] the burdens and public payments shall pertain to the duty of those to whose ownership the said holdings have passed.

ECONOMIC DISTRESS: REMISSION OF TAXES

Latin Panegyrics V. v–xiv (abridged)

I have told, O Emperor [Constantine], how much the Aeduans deserved the aid you brought them; it follows that I should tell how serious was their distress. . . . Our community lay prostrate, not so much because of the destruction of our walls as from exhaustion of resources, ever since the severity of the new tax assessment had drained our very life. We could not, however, rightly complain, since we had the lands which had been assigned to us, and we were comprised in the common formula of the Gallic assessment, we who can be compared to none in our good fortune. Wherefore, O Emperor, all the more do we give thanks to your clemency for granting remedies of your own accord and making us appear to have obtained justly what we could not rightfully request. . . .

And yet anyone would deservedly forgive these tillers of the soil, who are grieved by labor that brings no return. Indeed a field which never meets expenses is of necessity deserted; likewise the poor country folk, staggering beneath debts, were not permitted to bring in water or cut down forests, so that whatever usable soil there was has been ruined by swamps and choked with briers. . . . Why should I speak of other districts of that community, over which you admitted that you yourself wept? For whereas throughout the fields or other cities you saw almost all parts under cultivation, cleared and flowering, and accessible roads, and rivers under navigation washing the very gates of the towns, here directly from the bend which leads the highway back toward Belgica, you saw everything waste, uncultivated, neglected, silent, shadowy—even military roads so broken . . . that scarcely half-filled, sometimes empty wagons cross them. As a result it often happens that our taxes are late, since our little produce is more difficult for us to transport than a great abundance for others. . . .

You gave us our whole life. . . . To relieve the tax assessment you restricted the total; to remit our arrears you asked how much we owed. . . . You remitted 7,000 *capita*, more than a fifth of our assessment, and yet you inquired often whether this would be enough for us. . . . By your remission of 7,000 *capita* you gave strength to 25,000 [persons]. . . . You remitted our arrears for five years. . . . Therefore the immortal gods created you emperor for us especially; for each of us this felicity was born when you began to rule. . . . How many, Emperor Augustus, whom poverty had compelled to lie in hiding on the estates, or even to go into exile, are coming forth to the light, returning to their native land, as a result of this remission of arrears!

Compulsory Public Services

Under the fiscal system of the Dominate, compulsory public services became an all-pervading institution of rigidly controlled, hereditary classes. Those who suffered the heaviest economic burdens were the town decurions, who were liable with their own property for imperial taxes due from the local population. They constantly sought to evade their burdensome responsibilities by flight into the army, bureaucracy, or clergy.

Theodosian Code XI. xvi. 4; A.D. 328

The assessment of extraordinary public services shall not be entrusted to chief decurions, and therefore governors of the provinces shall be admonished to perform this assessment themselves and with their own hand write out and in ink annex the names. The following general rule shall be observed, namely, that the services to be given shall be rendered first by the more powerful and then by those of middle and lowest station. A farmer urgently occupied in planting or in gathering his harvest shall never be dragged off to extraordinary burdens, since it is a matter of prudence to satisfy such necessities at the opportune season. The neglect of these regulations affects the honorable status of your vicars, and shall entail capital punishment for the office staffs of governors. Moreover, governors must write with their own hand what is needed and in what obligation for each *caput*—how much public post service or how much personal service or what and in what measure it must be furnished. Thus they shall write that they have certified it, and the aforesaid order of exaction among the richer, the middling, and the lowest shall be observed.

Theodosian Code XV. ii. 1; A.D. 330

It is our will that the landholders over whose lands the courses of aqueducts pass shall be exempt from extraordinary burdens, so that by their work the aqueducts may be cleansed when they are choked with dirt. The said landholders shall not be subject to any other burden of a super-indiction, lest they be occupied in other matters and not be present to clean the aqueducts. If they neglect this duty, they shall be punished by the forfeiture of their landholdings; for the fisc will take possession of the landed estate of any man whose negligence contributes to the damage of the aqueducts. Furthermore, persons through whose landed estates the aqueducts pass should know that they may have trees to the right and left at a distance of fifteen feet from the aqueducts, and your office shall see to it that these trees are cut out if they grow too luxuriantly at any time, so that their roots may not injure the structure of the aqueduct.

BURDENS OF DECURIONS

Theodosian Code XII. i. 1; A.D. 313/26

No judge shall attempt to grant exemption from compulsory municipal services to any decurion, nor shall he free anyone from the municipal council at his own discretion. For if anyone is impoverished by a misfortune of such kind that he needs to be relieved, his name should be referred to our wisdom, so that an exemption from compulsory municipal services may be extended to him for a limited space of time.

Theodosian Code XII. i. 10; A.D. 325

Since we have granted to different persons the privilege of being assigned to the legions or cohorts or of being restored to the military service, if any person should produce a grant of this kind, inquiry shall be made as to whether he is of a family of decurions or whether he had been previously nominated to the municipal council, so that, if any such thing is proved, he may be returned to his own municipal council and municipality. It will be appropriate to observe this general rule with reference to all who have already been approved and are serving in military offices, or who have already been restored and are protected by the oath of military service, or who shall be approved hereafter by official decisions.

Theodosian Code XII, i. 11; A.D. 325

Since some men desert the municipal councils and flee for refuge to the protection of the military service, we command that all persons who are found to be not yet under the authority of the chief centurion shall be discharged from the military service and shall be returned to the same municipal council. Only those persons shall remain in the military service who, in accordance with their position and rank, are already in the commissary service.

Theodosian Code XII. i. 12; A.D. 325

If anyone derives his origin from a greater or lesser municipality, and if in an effort to avoid [the duties of] the said origin he betakes himself to another municipality for the purpose of establishing residence there and attempts to submit a plea [to the emperor] about this or to depend on any fraud whatsoever in order to escape the origin of his own municipality, he shall sustain the burdens of the decurionate of both municipalities, in the one because of his personal desire, in the other because of his origin.

Theodosian Code XII. i. 13; A.D. 326

Since we have learned that the municipal councils are being left deserted by persons who, though subject to them through origin, are requesting military service for themselves through supplications [to the emperor] and are running away to the legions and the various government offices, we order all municipal councils to be advised that if they catch any persons in government service less than twenty years who have either fled from [the duties of] their origin or, rejecting nomination [to municipal office], have enrolled themselves in the military service, they shall drag such persons back to the municipal councils. . . .

Theodosian Code XVI. ii. 3; A.D. 320 or 329

An enactment was issued which directs that henceforth no decurion or descendant of a decurion or even any person provided with adequate resources and suitable for undertaking compulsory public services shall take refuge in the name and service of the clergy, but that in the future only such persons shall be chosen in place of deceased clerics as have slender fortunes and are not held bound to such compulsory municipal services. But we have learned that those persons are also being disturbed who joined in the fellowship of the clergy before the promulgation of the law. We therefore command that such persons be freed from all annoyance, but that those who after the issuance of the law took refuge in the number of the clergy in evasion of public duties shall be completely separated from that body, shall be restored to their municipal councils and [social] orders, and shall perform their municipal duties.

OCCUPATIONS BECOME HEREDITARY

The crisis of the third century had led to steadily tighter imperial control over the numerous trade associations or "guilds" (*collegia, corpora, consortia*) of the Empire, especially those engaged in activities essential to the provisioning of urban centers and of the military or to the protection of life and property (cf. § 122). With the increase in taxes collected in kind under the Dominate, regimentation of persons concerned with the shipment, storage, and processing of such revenues was deemed essential by the state. Like the decurions, persons bound to such services sought to escape their obligations by entry into the army or civil service, or by becoming tenant farmers. By the time of Constantine many occupations (including military service: cf. Note 44 above) had been transformed into compulsory hereditary obligations to the state.

Theodosian Code VII. xxii. 1; A.D. 313 or 319

Of the veterans' sons who are fit for military service, some indolently object to the performance of their compulsory military duties and others are so cowardly that they desire to evade the necessity of military service by mutilation of their bodies. If they should be judged useless for

military service because of amputated fingers, we order them to be assigned to the compulsory services and duties of decurions with no ambiguity.

Theodosian Code XIII. v. 1; A.D. 314

If any shipmaster by birth becomes captain of a lighter, he shall nonetheless continue right along to remain in the same group in which his parents appear to have been.

Theodosian Code XIII. v. 2; A.D. 314/15

Shipmasters nominated to the guild of city breadmakers but not subject to these breadmakers by any succession of inheritance must be released from this compulsory public service. But if they should chance to be bound to the breadmakers by hereditary right, they shall have the opportunity, if they perchance prefer, to relinquish the adventitious inheritance of breadmakers to the said guild or yield it to any next of kin of the deceased, in order to free themselves from the guild of breadmakers. But if they embrace the inheritance, it is necessary for them to undertake association in the compulsory public service of breadmaking by reason of the inheritance, and to sustain from their own resources the burdens of shipmasters. Evidently the prefect of the city, *vir clarissimus*, will make decisions concerning such matter.

THE COLONATE: TENANT FARMERS BOUND TO THE SOIL

The crisis in Roman agriculture during the third and early fourth centuries was partly due to the decline in the rural population and to flight from the land because of heavy fiscal burdens. For some time, barbarians had been settled inside the Empire as state tenants bound to their tenancies (cf. § 116), and the *coloni* of imperial and private estates had tended all through the Principate to become hereditary tenants (see § 123). Now, in keeping with the tendency toward making all occupations hereditary, a long series of laws formally transformed the *coloni* into hereditary serfs permanently bound to the soil of the estates they tilled. The earliest datable enactment of this series is the following rescript of Constantine.

Theodosian Code V. xvii. 1; A.D. 332

Any person whatsoever in whose possession a *colonus* belonging to another is found not only shall restore the said *colonus* to his place of origin but shall also assume the capitation tax on him for the time [that he had him]. And as for *coloni* themselves, it will be proper for such as contemplate flight to be bound with chains to a servile status, so that by virtue of such condemnation to servitude they may be compelled to fulfill the duties that befit free men.

CHILD ASSISTANCE

Theodosian Code XI. xxvii. 1; A.D. 315 or 329

A law shall be written on bronze or waxed tablets or on linen cloth, and posted throughout all the municipalities of Italy, to restrain the hands of parents from infanticide and turn their hopes to the better. Your office shall administer this regulation, so that, if any parent should report that he has offspring which on account of poverty he is unable to rear, there shall be no delay in issuing food and clothing, since the rearing of a new-born infant can not tolerate delay. For this matter we order that both our fisc and our privy purse shall furnish their services without distinction.

Theodosian Code XI. xxvii. 2; A.D. 322

We have learned that provincials suffering from scarcity of food and lack of sustenance are selling or pledging their children. Therefore, if any such person is found who is sustained by no substance of family possessions and is supporting

his children with hardship and difficulty, he shall be assisted through our fisc before he becomes a prey to calamity. The proconsuls, governors, and procurators of accounts throughout all Africa shall have the power and shall distribute the necessary support to all persons whom they observe to be placed in dire need, and they shall immediately assign adequate substance from the [state] storehouses. For it is repugnant to our customs to allow any person to be destroyed by hunger or rush forth to the commission of a shameful deed.

EFFORTS TO SUPPRESS OFFICIAL CORRUPTION

The ever present corruption practiced by the huge bureaucracy of the Empire during earlier centuries reached unprecedented proportions in the enlarged officialdom of the autocratic state. Constantine's fulminations against official corruption were followed by a long series of similar enactments by the emperors of succeeding centuries in a continuing but largely futile attempt to control the rapacity of their functionaries (cf. also § 132).

Theodosian Code I. xii. 2; A.D. 319

It is to the interest of public discipline, and it likewise befits the proconsular dignity, that you should bring under your power the administration and cognizance of public-revenue collection and all other matters. You shall not be content with the prepared reports and fraudulent statements of the functionaries, but you shall study the administration of the very judges and the statement of the prefect of the grain supply and of the procurators of accounts [to determine] whether the aforesaid prepared reports are trustworthy. For thus it will be possible to afford relief to the provincials against unjust exactions.

Theodosian Code I. xvi. 7; A.D. 331

The rapacious hands of the functionaries shall immediately stop, they shall stop, I say; for, if after due warning they do not stop, they shall be cut off with the sword. The curtain of the judge['s chamber] shall not be venal; entrance shall not be purchased; his private chamber shall not be notorious for its bids; the very sight of the governor shall not be at a price. The ears of the judge shall be open equally to the poorest as well as to the rich. The introduction of persons inside shall be free from depredation by the one who is called the office head; the assistants of the said office heads shall employ no extortion on litigants; the intolerable onslaught of the centurions and other officials who demand small and large sums shall be crushed; and the unsated greed of those who deliver records to litigants shall be restrained. The ever-watchful diligence of the governor shall see that nothing is taken from a litigant by the aforesaid classes of men. And if they imagine they have to demand something in connection with civil cases, armed punishment will be at hand to cut off the heads and necks of the scoundrels, for all persons who have suffered extortion will be given an opportunity to provide information for an investiga.:on by the governors. And if they dissemble, we open to all persons the right of complaint thereon before the *comites* of the provinces—or before the Praetorian prefects, if they are closer at hand—so that we may be informed by their referrals and may produce punishments for such villainy.

Theodosian Code I. xxxii. 1; A.D. 333

Through the fault of the procurators of the privy purse, of dye-works, and of weaving establishments, our private substance is being diminished, the products manufactured in the weaving establishments are being ruined, and in the dye-works the fraudulent admixture of impure dye produces blemishes. Such procurators shall abstain from the patronage whereby they obtain the aforementioned administrative positions, or, if they contravene

this order, they shall be removed from the number of Roman citizens and beheaded.

Theodosian Code X. iv. 1; A.D. 313 or 326

If any person is harassed by an agent or procurator of our privy purse, he shall not hesitate to lodge a complaint concerning his chicanery and depredations. When such charge is proved, we sanction that such person as dares to contrive anything against a provincial shall be publicly burned, since graver punishment should be fixed against those who are under our jurisdiction and ought to observe our mandates.

RESTRICTIONS ON INFORMERS

CIL, Vol. III, No. 12,043, lines 1–45 (=*FIRA*, Vol. I, No. 94); A.D. 314/23

Copy of Sacred Edict

. . . It has been proved that many men are punished not only by loss of their property . . . and that in cases of this kind accused as well as witnesses experience very serious troubles. Wherefore, taking counsel for the security of our provinces, we have provided the following remedies.

An accuser shall not be completely denied access to court, but anyone who is confident that he can adduce proofs for his charges shall have ready opportunity of access to a judge and shall expose a defendant by clear evidence of the offense, so that suitable punishment in proportion to the nature of the acts may be inflicted upon the person convicted. But if he cannot at all prove his charges, he must know that he himself is to be subjected to a severe sentence. Indeed, if someone brings a charge of treason against another, since an accusation of this kind affords no one the slightest protection against rigorous examination through privilege of rank, he must know that he, too, is to be subjected to torture if he is unable to prove his accusation by other clear evidence and proofs, since in the case of a person who is discovered to be of such temerity this also ought to be extracted by torture, namely, upon whose advice and instigation he appears to have resorted to the accusation, so that punishment can be meted out to all the accomplices of so great an offense.

In regard to [professional] informers, however, it is known to all to what extent opportunity of access to a judge has been denied by the statutes of our parents as well as by our own enactments, since a hearing must not be afforded to persons of this kind, inasmuch as it is fitting that they be subjected to punishment for daring so great a crime.

In the case also of slaves or freedmen who attempt to accuse or inform against their masters or patrons, we decree that the following regulation—according to a statute of the ancient law, too—is to be observed, namely, that the expression of such outrageous impudence shall be forthwith suppressed at the very beginning of the offense by sentence of the court, and [the accuser] denied a hearing and crucified for resorting to such villainy, thus providing an example to others, so that no one may display like impudence in the future.

Furthermore, that counsel may be taken in every direction for the security of innocent people, it is our pleasure also that libelous statements shall not be admitted. If anyone finds any such posted anonymously, he must at once pull them down and tear them up or destroy them by fire. In such cases, too, judges ought to observe the following practice: if perchance such a statement is brought to them, they shall instruct that it be consumed by fire, since writings of this kind ought to be entirely removed from the cognizance of judges; and an investigation shall continue against those daring to offer statements of this kind, so that when found they may be subjected to the punishments their temerity deserves.

LEGISLATION ON SLAVES

The institution of slavery survived for centuries after the triumph of Christianity. Under Christian influence, however, the growing tendency of the preceding centuries toward more humane treatment of slaves (cf. § 68) received fresh impetus. The following is a directive of Constantine on the subject.

Theodosian Code II. xxv. 1; A.D. 325 or 334

When ... estates in Sardinia were recently distributed among the various present proprietors, the division of holdings ought to have been made in such a way that a whole family of slaves would remain with one individual landholder. For who could tolerate that children should be separated from parents, sisters from brothers, and wives from husbands? Therefore, any persons who have separated slaves and dragged them off to serve under different ownerships shall be forced to restore such to single ownership; and anyone who loses slaves through the reuniting of families shall be given slaves in exchange by the person who receives the aforesaid. And take pains that throughout the province no complaint shall hereafter persist over the separation of the loved ones of slaves.

3. Diocletian the Reformer*

During the years that Constantine was at court, Diocletian was steadily remodelling administration, defence and finance. On the administrative side the chief weakness lay in the lowest stratum of the structure, where it was becoming more and more difficult to goad town councils into performing their functions. Diocletian did much to keep the councils up to strength, and it was probably in his reign that the doctrine became established that sons of decurions were legally bound to enter the council. Even so, every election of a magistrate or collector on the council produced a crop of appeals to the provincial governor, and arrears in requisitions had frequently to be exacted by his officials. In the larger provinces it became impossible for the governor to keep pace with the work. Moreover, the relations between civil administration and military command were very anomalous: in some frontier provinces the provincial governor still, according to the old tradition, commanded the local army, in some there was an independent army commander.

To Diocletian's tidy mind this muddle was intolerable. He uniformly relieved the governor of the military command. He reduced provinces to a manageable and more or less uniform size—some huge old provinces were subdivided into four or five—and carved Italy, hitherto officially under the senate, into provinces. Finally, in order to relieve the central government from the increasing burden of routine administrative work, Diocletian created a new unit, the diocese, between the province and the centre. The diocese was controlled by a deputy prætorian prefect, responsible for the same services as his chief, and also had an accountant, and an intendent of imperial domains, who answered to the Masters for their respective departments. The twelve dioceses were substantial areas —Britain, Gaul (northern France with the Rhineland and Low Countries), Viennensis (southern France), Spain (including Portugal and Morocco), Italy (including Sicily, Sardinia and Corsica), Africa (Algeria, Tunisia and Tripolitania), Pannonia, Moesia and Thrace (the western, central and eastern Balkans), Asiana and Pontica (south-western and north-eastern Asia Minor) and the Orient (Cilicia, Syria, Palestine and Egypt with Cyrenaica).

In military affairs Diocletian's chief work was to raise the strength of the army. The Roman soldier had never been in armament substantially superior to his barbarian opponent: his superiority had lain in discipline and training. He had now in large measure lost that advantage, and there was no alternative but to increase numbers if the frontier was to be held. According to his bitter critic Lactantius, Diocletian more than quadrupled the armed forces. This is an obvious exaggeration, but a study of the later army list of the Roman empire shows that Diocletian raised many new units, and it is significant that voluntary recruitment ceased to provide a sufficient intake. Diocletian had to make the military service of the sons of veterans compulsory, and to introduce a new system of conscription from the rural population of all the provinces. To ensure regular supplies of arms and uniforms, Diocletian established in numerous towns armament factories and wool and linen-weaving establishments, the former manned by soldier artificers, the latter by slaves and convicts.

In strategy Diocletian was conservative. He held to the old system of a continuous line of defence strung out along the frontiers, reinforcing it with fresh units, building new forts and linking them with additional new roads: in the deserts of

---

* A. H. M. Jones, *Constantine and the Conversion of Europe* (London: The English Universities Press Limited, 1948), pp. 22–28. Reprinted by permission of the publisher.

Syria and North Africa his roads can still be traced and his forts still stand. For emergencies the regiments of the retinue provided a nucleus of a field army, but they had to be supplemented by drafts from the frontiers for any serious war. The command of the armies, now separated from the civil government of the frontier provinces, was entrusted to area commanders, each responsible for a given length of frontier.

Diocletian attempted a reform of the currency, issuing gold coins weighing $\frac{1}{60}$ lb. and genuine silver coins of $\frac{1}{90}$ lb.; as well as the old denarius, by now a copper coin weighing about four grammes. But he failed to stabilise it, and his famous edict of 301, in which he fixed prices and wages in the minutest detail, though enforced at first with ruthless severity, merely drove goods off the market, and had to be allowed to lapse. But in finance in the wider sense, including requisitions in kind, Diocletian carried out a reform of capital importance. The fault of the old assessment system had been its complication and rigidity; the new requisitions were levied haphazard without regard to capacity to pay. Diocletian invented a new unit of assessment (*iugum*), an area of land the tax on which should be equal to the poll tax on an individual (*caput*): the actual area naturally varied according to the quality of the land and the type of cultivation, olives and vineyards being for instance rated much higher than arable, and cattle entered into the assessment. The scheme was completed by a vast census, or series of censuses extending over many years, whereby the population was numbered and the land of every proprietor, city and province was assessed in the new unit.

Henceforth it was possible, by an extremely simple multiplication sum, to calculate the yield from a given city, province or diocese, or from the whole empire, of a levy at any given rate on every *caput* and *iugum* it contained, and the Ro-

man empire for the first time could have an annual budget, the indiction, calculated to meet estimated expenditure. The system was applied to levies of all kinds, not only money and food crops, but textiles for uniforms and horses for the postal system and recruits for the army.

Diocletian was gradually bringing order out of chaos, but the price was heavy. "He made three partners of his realm, dividing the empire into four parts and multiplying the armies, while each of them aspired to have a far larger number of troops than earlier emperors had had when they governed alone. The numbers of those who received began to be larger than the number of those who gave, so much so that the resources of the peasants were exhausted by outrageous levies. The fields were deserted and arable turned into forest. And to fill every place with terror, the provinces were chopped into fragments. There were more governors and more officials to watch over individual districts and almost individual cities, not to speak of hosts of accountants and controllers and deputies of the prefects, all of whom were little occupied with civil actions, but with constant condemnations and confiscations, frequent, or I should rather say continual, exactions of innumerable kinds, and intolerable brutalities in these exactions. Equally intolerable were the methods used in levying recruits. With insatiable avarice he never allowed his treasuries to be depleted, but always piled up extraordinary resources for his expenditure, so that he could keep what he hoarded complete and untouched. When by his various iniquities he caused a huge rise in prices, he tried to enact a law fixing the prices of goods offered for sale. Then much blood was shed on paltry and trifling charges, and nothing appeared on the market for fear, until inevitably, after many had died, the law was relaxed. To this was added an insatiable passion for building, and a corresponding exaction from the provinces, in producing labourers, craftsmen, wagons and everything needed for building works. Here he built a law court, there a race-course, here a mint, there an armament factory, here a palace for his wife, there one for his daughter."

Lactantius' prejudice is obvious, but there is more than a grain of truth in his criticisms. Diocletian could find no way to secure the defence of the frontiers save to increase the number of troops, and his efforts to make the creaking wheels of the administration revolve only resulted in more and more officials. There were coming to be more idle mouths than the primitive economic system of the Roman empire could feed. It is hard to remember that, despite its great achievements in law and administration, the splendid architecture of its cities and the luxurious standard of living of its aristocracy, the Roman empire was, in its methods of production, in some ways more primitive than the early Middle Ages. Agriculture followed a wasteful two-field system and alternate crop and fallow. Yarn was spun by hand with a spindle, and textiles laboriously woven on clumsy hand looms. Even corn was ground in hand querns or at best in mills turned by oxen: windmills had not been invented and watermills were a scientific curiosity. In these circumstances the feeding and cloth-ing of an individual demanded a vast expenditure of human labour, and the maintenance of any substantial number of economically unproductive persons laid a heavy burden on the rest.

The result of the government's increas-ing demands for supplies, coming on top of his landlord's rent, was that a peasant cultivating land of marginal value could not make ends meet, and deserted his holding. Even on good land he could not feed his children, and the population could not expand to meet the increased demand for soldiers and for workmen in the mills which supplied them. A chronic shortage of manpower ensued, and to safeguard essential industries, the government froze the labour employed in them, compelling the workers to remain in their jobs and their children after them. It is difficult to trace the stages whereby labour in all industries essential to the state was gradually frozen, but in the key industry, agriculture, the peasant was probably already tied to his plot by Diocletian, by the ruling that where he was entered on the census registers there he must stay.

Diocletian was by tradition and tempera-ment a conservative. Like all the emperors of the later third century, he claimed to be the restorer of the Roman world: he was not trying to shape a new order of society, but to press the rebellious forces of the age back into the old moulds. To make the old order work, he was obliged to introduce revolutionary changes, but his conserva-tive, even reactionary, instincts are shown in such details as his insistence on dating by the Roman consuls. In religion, too, he was a conservative: he went back to the Roman gods, choosing Jupiter Optimus Maximus as his patron rather than new deities, such as the Unconquered Sun to whom Aurelian had accorded the highest honour. On one religious problem, the treatment of Christians, there were two series of precedents which he might follow, and here he was to change his mind.

4. The Meaning and Effect of the Reforms*

The Roman Empire nearly perished in the great crisis which covers the period from 235 to 268. At last, the barbarians were repelled by the Illyrian Emperors, Claudius II, Aurelian and Probus, and political unity was restored. Nevertheless the situation remained precarious. The necessary changes were effected by two personalities of the highest calibre, Diocletian and Constantine. Some would have them idealists, visionaries and dreamers. This is an amazing misconception; they were practical minds, the former especially. They began by jettisoning what was necessary to save the ship. It was obvious that one man alone could not govern from the Euphrates to the Atlantic, and from the Sahara to Caledonia, two worlds, the Greek and the Latin, incapable of being welded together. To prevent any revolt on the part of a rival, Diocletian chose one and tried to turn him into both a colleague and a friend. The unity of the Empire, at least in theory, was thus maintained. Constantine made the separation of the two worlds final by changing aggrandized Byzantium into a new Rome (330). Thanks to its position, Byzantium could be saved from invasion; but for this inspiration of genius, Greek civilization would have disappeared, and like that of Chaldæa, it would be known to us only by some shapeless fragments.

A religious malady, Christianity, was threatening Roman society. Diocletian had not advanced beyond the old idea that the sect could be destroyed by force. Constantine in an apparent or real fit of madness saw in it a power to be utilized in the service of the Roman State. In the East, the Orthodox Church, Greek civilization

and the State came to be so well fused that to be received into the bosom of the Church was *eo ipso* to become a Greek-speaking "Roman", at least for several centuries.

After capturing Christianity, the emperors next turned to the fiscal machinery which they strained to its utmost. To fight the barbarians and also to buy them off, and to keep the magnificent edifice of the Empire standing, great resources were needed.

But the Mediterranean world had suffered from a very serious economic upheaval. It was ruined and completely retrograde at the moment when the needs of the State were more pressing than ever. Fiscal ruthlessness ended by setting up a real caste system. The peasant was henceforth bound to the soil; this was not the only cause of the serfdom of the soil, the origins of which go back to a remote past, but the extension of this system to free labourers is one of the features of the Later Empire. Obliged to become a member of a *collegium*, the artisan was bound to his craft and the merchant to his calling. What shall we say of the workers in the mines and in the imperial factories who were branded with red-hot iron? They could not run away and their condition was hereditary. The middle classes were no less "regulated". The *curiales* formed a *consortium* responsible for the taxes and the putting of the land under cultivation; every avenue by which they might escape from the *curia* was closed.

The following was the result: the government broke all resistance, but also all independence; it completely changed the people into a herd of "rayahs", in the Turkish fashion.

Nevertheless we have not before us a purely selfish despotism, nor a long-matured, scientific and planned system. It was not with any deliberate purpose that

---

* Ferdinand Lot, *The End of the Ancient World and the Beginning of the Middle Ages* (London: Routledge & Kegan Paul, 1961), pp. 183–186. Reprinted by permission of the publisher.

the Emperors achieved centralization, unification and uniformity. A blind, unavoidable, irresistible necessity forced them to grind down everything so that the Empire might be able to exist.

These Emperors were busy with humanitarian schemes to which their legislation bears ample and frequent evidence, too frequent indeed for their decisions to have been effective. They wished to protect the lower and middle classes of the towns and they set up *defensores civitatis*. The *collegia* of tradesmen and artisans enjoyed privileges; they were allowed to make their own regulations and they were not harassed in their internal arrangements.

The Emperors wished to allow the complaints of their subjects to reach their own ears. They wished to put a check on the absolutism of their functionaries. Hence significant though at bottom fruitless institions, such as the provincial councils, one of which, that of the Gauls, was to last until the end of the Western Empire. Lastly, individual measures, such as remissions of taxes, and the punishment of men in high places guilty of the betrayal of truth or of oppression, were not rare.

In spite of all, the State failed in its rôle of protector. It was ill served and betrayed by its own agents. The latter, the high functionaries, or, to speak more accurately, the "magistrates" and "judges", belonged to the class of large landowners. They shared its ideas, customs and interests. This aristocracy was disloyal in its service to the government, while cowering before it. It secretly thwarted it, not so much from hatred as from a spirit of opposition and from selfishness. Debarred from the army, confined to honorary functions, suspected and watched, the ruling class lost all spontaneity and initiative, and in its case also character fell very low.

The fundamental cause of the decay and later of the breaking up of the Roman Empire appears to us to have been the following:

The Empire had become too vast, too cunning and too complicated a mechanism; the Mediterranean world, economically retrograde since the third century, could no longer support its weight. It split in two, the *pars Orientis* and *pars Occidentis*, from the end of this century. Even for the exercise of its authority, the State was under the necessity of narrowing its field of action. The same necessity was soon to force the West to break up into half-Roman, half-barbarian States. The latter in their turn would become subdivided, and the territorial splitting up was to go on increasingly without a stop for long centuries, until the twelfth century. This narrowing of political action was accompanied by a narrowing of public spirit, which was destined to go as far as the annihilation of the conception of public interest, and the disappearance of the notion of a State in the period of the barbarians.

Thus, under a still majestic appearance, the Roman Empire, at the end of the fourth century, was no longer anything but a hollow husk. It was powerless to withstand a violent shaking and soon it was to suffer a new and terrible attack from the barbarians. The East was destined to emerge from it as best it could, but the West was to be shivered in pieces.

There is something deeper and more stable than political forms, which are always ephemeral, and that is what is called civilization. In its highest reaches, literature, the arts, philosophy and religion, the changes are no less striking than in the political sphere. The old naïve nature deities, Greek or Latin, gave place to the Oriental "superstitions", Judaism, Christianity, Mithraism, Manicheism, etc., coming from Egypt, Syria and Persia. These foreign arrivals transformed the ethics and altered the psychology of the man of Antiquity. His art and literature felt the consequence of these great mutations. The blighting worship of the great models and certain defects inherent in the classical spirit, made an æsthetic renewal almost impossible. The triumph of Christianity and later of Islam were to detach men's souls from the ancient forms of beauty. Even before being condemned by religion, plastic art was to succumb, a victim to a revolution in taste originating in the East; line was sacrified to colour and nobility of style to the fantastic and chimerical. Ancient literature was condemned by the Church. Wholly pagan, it ceased to be understood and to be loved. Unfortunately the twofold Christian literature, Greek and Latin, which sought to replace it, thought it would succeed in this by pouring itself into the same mould. But new thoughts and feelings need a new form. Christian literature, from the point of view of art, was still-born. Science and philosophy succumbed under the competition of Oriental mysticism which brought about a real transformation of values.

This transformation is as phenomenal as if a sleeper on waking should see other stars shining above his head.